LINCOLN'S CITADEL

ALSO BY KENNETH J. WINKLE

Abraham and Mary Lincoln

Oxford Atlas of the Civil War
(with James McPherson and Steven Woodworth)

The Young Eagle: The Rise of Abraham Lincoln

The Politics of Community:
Migration and Politics in Antebellum Ohio

LINCOLN'S CITADEL

THE CIVIL WAR
IN
WASHINGTON, DC

Kenneth J. Winkle

W. W. Norton & Company NEW YORK • LONDON

For information about permission to reproduce selections from
this book, write to Permissions, W. W. Norton & Company, Inc.,
500 Fifth Avenue, New York, NY 10110

For information about special discounts for bulk purchases,
please contact W. W. Norton Special Sales
at specialsales@wwnorton.com or 800-233-4830

Manufacturing by RR Donnelley, Harrisonburg, VA
Book design by Brooke Koven
Production manager: Anna Oler

Library of Congress Cataloging-in-Publication Data

Winkle, Kenneth J.
Lincoln's citadel : the Civil War in
Washington, DC / Kenneth J. Winkle. — First edition.
pages cm
Includes bibliographical references and index.
ISBN 978-0-393-08155-8 (hardcover)
1. Washington (D.C.)—History—Civil War, 1861–1865.
2. Lincoln, Abraham, 1809–1865. I. Title.
E501.W76 2013
975.3'02—dc23
2013017206

W. W. Norton & Company, Inc.
500 Fifth Avenue, New York, N.Y. 10110
www.wwnorton.com

W. W. Norton & Company Ltd.
Castle House, 75/76 Wells Street, London W1T 3QT

1 2 3 4 5 6 7 8 9 0

For Ann

CONTENTS

Part III

"AN UNKNOWN SOMETHING CALLED FREEDOM"

Illustrations follow page 204

PREFACE

THE POET Walt Whitman arrived in Washington, DC, in December 1862 to locate his brother George, who had been wounded at the Battle of Fredericksburg. He stayed for the remainder of the Civil War, working for the government and, on his own time, visiting the city's military hospitals almost daily to comfort the sick and wounded. Here, in the national capital, he came face-to-face with the full spectrum of wartime humanity—suffering and sacrifice, enslavement and emancipation, defeat and determination. In the wake of the conflict, as military histories and generals' autobiographies proliferated, Whitman concluded pessimistically that "the real war will never get in the books." What he had in mind was an "interior history" of the Civil War that would probe behind the presidents and generals, the speeches and statutes, and the moldering monuments to bring to life the human story of the war as ordinary men and women experienced it.[1]

This study is dedicated to presenting the kind of "interior history" of the Civil War in Washington, DC, that Whitman envisioned. While considering the attitudes, actions, and motivations of Lincoln as well as his generals, cabinet members, family, private staff, allies, and enemies, I have striven to do the same for the ordinary and often anonymous Americans who found themselves living within a capital under siege. The soldiers and civilians, the slaves and the newly free, the wounded and their nurses, and a host of others suffered, strove, and sacrificed along with the great and powerful as they did their best to survive and shape the outcome of the war.

Beyond the people who lived and died there over the course of the war, Washington, DC, itself is one of the main characters within this book. Apart from its essential functions as the national capital, Washington's strategic location abreast the Civil War's most active and critical military front, the Eastern Theater, lent it pivotal strategic importance. Believing that the loss of Washington would lead to immediate Union defeat, many secessionists dreamed of capturing the city and making it the capital of the Confederacy, even before Lincoln could arrive to take his oath of office. General Robert E. Lee's thrusts into Maryland and Pennsylvania in 1862 and 1863, which culminated in the Battles of Antietam and Gettysburg, were primarily designed to threaten Washington, encourage southern sympathizers in the North, and challenge the Lincoln administration's authority to govern. To secure the capital, the Union Army constructed a thirty-seven-mile ring of fortifications that by the end of the war boasted sixty-eight forts and ninety-three artillery positions. In July 1864, when General Jubal Early's army attacked the city directly, the defenses held. Apart from its paramount offensive and defensive value, Washington was the Union's most important military depot, supplying the Army of the Potomac with a steady stream of troops, weaponry, and provisions throughout the war. The capital, of course, also represented the nerve center for the entire Union Army. Not only the War Department but also the Navy Department, the Union Army Headquarters, the headquarters of the Army of the Potomac, and the Headquarters Defenses of Washington all sat within walking distance of the White House. Lincoln frequented them personally, making the rounds as he sought to orchestrate a coordinated war effort.

At the same time, Washington's isolated and precarious location, sandwiched between Confederate Virginia to the west and secessionist Maryland to the east, continually tested Lincoln's ability to prosecute the war. The capital's three vital links to the North—the Baltimore and Ohio Railroad, the Chesapeake and Ohio Canal, and the Potomac River—were all cut or blockaded for extended periods. Five days after the surrender of Fort Sumter, a riot erupted in Baltimore as Union soldiers were rushing through the city to reach Washington. Maryland officials responded by destroying bridges along the Baltimore and Ohio Railroad and imploring Lincoln not to send additional troops through their state. Lincoln acted decisively, suspending the writ of habeas corpus along the military line connecting the capital with the North, restoring the railroad link, and adopting extraordinary measures to secure it for the remainder of the war. Even after Maryland's Unionists forestalled a campaign to join the Confederacy, secessionists in the southern half of the state continued to defy federal authority by creating a clandestine network that channeled mail, contraband goods, and spies between Washington and Richmond and helped deserters from the Union Army—and later John Wilkes Booth—to escape.

The city itself presented Lincoln and his administration with a multitude of challenges. When Lincoln assumed the presidency, he entered a capital that was not only a southern, slaveowning city but was openly hostile to his administration's twin goals of stopping the westward expansion of slavery and reuniting the nation. The city had a long tradition of both organized and spontaneous mob violence that targeted African Americans, abolitionists, immigrants, and later Republicans. As secession swept the South, Washington divided against itself, heightening the capital's traditional social and political tensions and threatening renewed violence. Even before Lincoln's inauguration, congressional Republicans mounted an investigation of subversive activities in Washington that continued and indeed escalated throughout the war. As president, Lincoln endorsed a campaign to suppress disloyalty in the capital by removing the Democratic mayor, supporting a Unionist city government, reforming the antiquated police department, and building an extensive provost guard with sweeping military authority to restore order, all of which he labeled "cleaning the devil out of Washington." As the war ended, however, the process remained regrettably incomplete, as his own assassination at Ford's Theatre five days after General Lee's surrender attests.[2]

The war flooded the capital with hundreds of thousands of sick

and wounded soldiers. Every campaign and major battle in the Eastern Theater poured thousands of casualties into Washington for
emergency medical treatment. At the beginning of the war, the city
had a single general hospital that admitted fewer than two hundred
patients a year, and the entire U.S. Army boasted only thirty surgeons. During the first year of the war alone, the army treated 56,000
sick and wounded soldiers in Washington. At the peak of the fighting in 1864, on a single day, the capital accommodated 18,000 sick
and wounded soldiers.[3] To accomplish that heroic feat, the government hastily created more than one hundred military hospitals and
recruited thousands of surgeons and nurses to staff them. A series of
medical crises prompted experimentation with new hospital designs,
novel approaches to transporting the wounded, and the recruitment
of female nurses, mostly volunteers, on a massive scale. The Lincolns
took a personal interest in the welfare and morale of the hospitalized
soldiers and the delivery of appropriate medical care.

During the war, Washington more than tripled in population,
from 65,000 in 1860 to 200,000 just one year later, presenting a critical threat to public health. Washington's already underdeveloped
infrastructure and inadequate sanitation deteriorated under the novel
burdens imposed by the war. Epidemic diseases, including smallpox
and typhoid fever, plagued the hundreds of thousands of soldiers who
passed through the city and the 40,000 fugitive slaves who arrived
over the course of the conflict. Congress, which governed the District of Columbia, neglected Washington under the press of seemingly more urgent wartime issues. The human toll was heartrending
and included the Lincolns' eleven-year-old son Willie, who succumbed to typhoid fever early in 1862. Lincoln himself nearly died
from smallpox in the weeks that followed his Gettysburg Address.

Washington's greatest transformation, which represented an
unforeseen opportunity for Lincoln and his administration, was its
gradual transformation from slavery to freedom. Since the 1830s,
abolitionists from across the North and abroad had called for emancipation in the District of Columbia as the beginning of a campaign to
eliminate slavery throughout the South. From the moment of secession, fugitive slaves fled the Confederacy to claim their freedom, and

more of them sought out Washington than any other destination. The immediate challenge was defining the legal status of the fugitives. Initially considered criminals under the Fugitive Slave Law of 1850, they were arrested, lodged in the Washington jail, and returned to their owners. After the Union Army innovated a policy of confiscating the slaves of disloyal owners as a way of denying them to the Confederacy and utilizing their labor, the Lincoln administration began welcoming the fugitives and sheltered them in military camps and within the city itself. In April 1862, Lincoln endorsed an act of Congress that freed the District of Columbia's three thousand slaves, under the first federal program of emancipation in the nation's history, eight months before he issued his Emancipation Proclamation. Failing to repeal the Fugitive Slave Law until June 1864, however, Congress left fugitives from the loyal slave states, including Maryland, at risk of arrest and reenslavement. The dual policy toward slavery engendered bitterness and created a conflict between the fugitives' claim to freedom and the enforcement of federal law. Meanwhile, Lincoln's Emancipation Proclamation called on African Americans to join the Union military. The District of Columbia raised a regiment that attained both real and symbolic significance as the 1st Regiment United States Colored Troops.

Washington was a microcosm of the Civil War. The national capital faced the same wartime challenges as the rest of the Union, but often sooner and more urgently. Many of the policies that Lincoln pursued on a national scale had their roots in the turmoil that afflicted Washington, beginning with his two years in Congress, during which he lived in a Capitol Hill boardinghouse dubbed "Abolition House." The wartime security measures that Lincoln improvised grew out of his imposition of martial law along the railroad to Baltimore, the loyalty oaths that he imposed on government workers in Washington, and the "arbitrary arrests" that he authorized to secure the city in the opening months of the war. His embrace of emancipation and movement toward equal rights reflected his personal immersion in the crucible of slavery and freedom that he encountered in Washington. His enthusiasm for African American enlistment arose in part from his personal role in creating and observing the 1st Regiment USCT and other military units in the Eastern Theater. A range of initiatives, including the recruitment and later conscription of Union soldiers, their medical treatment, their countless burials, and the public memorialization of their sacrifices, all unfolded before Lincoln's eyes from his vantage point in the White House. Washington afforded Lincoln his most personal and poignant "window on the war." *Lincoln's Citadel* invites readers to peer through that window along with Lincoln.

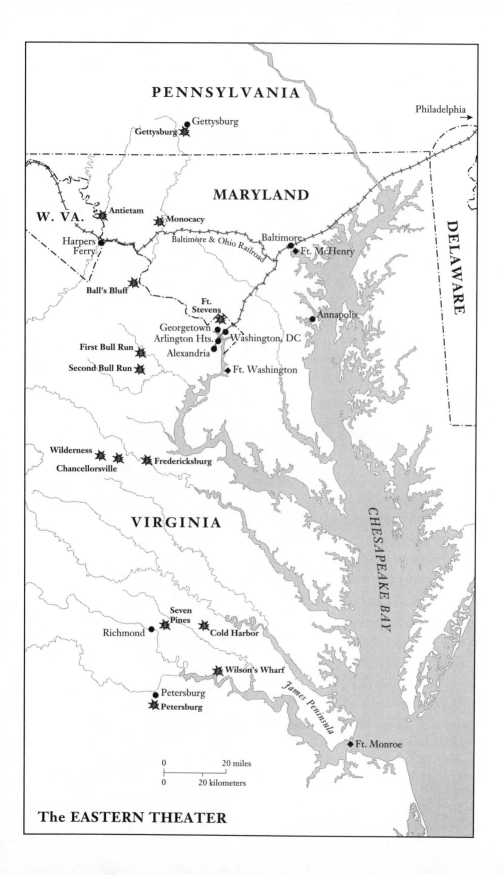

The **EASTERN THEATER**

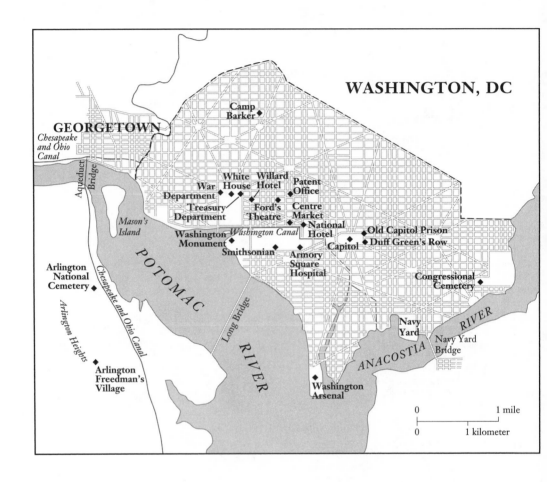

WASHINGTON, DC

GEORGETOWN

Camp
Barker

*Chesapeake
and Ohio
Canal*

*Aqueduct
Bridge*

*Mason's
Island*

White   Willard
House   Hotel   Patent
War   Office
Department
Treasury   Ford's   Centre
Department   Theatre   Market

Washington   *Washington Canal*   National
Monument   Hotel
           Smithsonian   Old Capitol Prison
                              Armory   Capitol   Duff Green's Row
                              Square
                              Hospital

Arlington
National
Cemetery   Congressional
                                                      Cemetery

P O T O M A C

Chesapeake and Ohio Canal

Arlington Heights

Long Bridge

Arlington
Freedman's
Village

R I V E R

Navy
Yard   Navy Yard
         Bridge

A N A C O S T I A   *R I V E R*

Washington
Arsenal

0   1 mile

0   1 kilometer

PART I

"Abolition House"

CHAPTER ONE

"Getting the Hang of the House"
Congressman Abraham Lincoln

A BRAHAM LINCOLN'S introduction to Washington City, as it
was then known, began in December 1847 when he arrived to
begin his single term in Congress, a disappointing venture that he
later lamented as an act of "political suicide." Washington City was
a decidedly artificial community, created as "simply a convenience
for the assembling of Congress," as one visitor put it. The national
capital was renowned for its dual character as the "federal city," conceived by the French architect Pierre L'Enfant, overlaid on top of
the "local city," the cluster of southern towns, villages, and farms
that had preceded it. "Like a great lubberly lout in clothes much too
large for its body and limbs," the improvised city had not yet grown
into the grandiose federal plan. The entire assemblage was loosely
knit together by L'Enfant's unnaturally wide avenues that converged
diagonally at its dozens of public squares and circles. Visiting the
capital in 1842, Charles Dickens judged it a "City of Magnificent
Intentions," boasting "spacious avenues that begin in nothing, and
lead nowhere; streets, mile-long, that only want houses, roads, and
inhabitants; public buildings that need but a public to be complete."[1]

The official city was seasonal, busiest while Congress was in session, when it awoke and grew more socially alive and culturally active.
Federal Washington was decidedly more northern in character than
the sedate, sleepier "permanent city" that languished in near neglect
most summers and falls while the government did its best to shut

down. In a community that suffered a perennial housing shortage, seasonal residents, including congressmen, generally rented their lodgings. In the 30th Congress, which included Lincoln, only nine senators and representatives occupied houses of their own. Accommodating the other three hundred or so congressmen who descended on the capital every December was one of the most lucrative economic enterprises in the city. "The greatest and most respectable business that is done in Washington," one observer wrote, "is keeping boarding houses." Congressmen preferred the boardinghouses that dotted Capitol Hill, which were more affordable and conveniently located than the more expensive hotels that lined Pennsylvania Avenue.[2]

Courting what they labeled "transient" lodgers, boardinghouse keepers, most of whom were widows, coveted this respectable and relatively stable congressional clientele. The greatest prize was landing one of the congressional "messes" that would settle into a location en masse and stay for two years or even longer. The messes formed at the start of each new Congress, when the members coalesced along regional and party lines to establish what they hoped would be congenial assemblages of like-minded colleagues. Boardinghouse keepers therefore promoted their rooms as "well adapted for the use of a mess of Members of Congress or other gentlemen," or "admirably suited for a mess of Congressmen or a large family," or simply "eligibly situated." These "congressional boardinghouses," as they were known, resembled nothing so much as college fraternities, providing basic accommodations, regular meals, and social camaraderie in a convenient locale, replete with the nineteenth-century equivalent of a house mother, allowing the boarders to focus on their work.[3]

Under the dictum that "only a man of independent means could afford to bring his wife to Washington," most congressmen deferred to necessity and left their families at home. Although hardly "a man of independent means" at this point in his career, Lincoln brought his family along from Springfield. When Judge David Davis, Lincoln's legal colleague and later campaign manager, heard about this exceptional nod to domesticity, he apprised his wife that "Mrs. L., I am told, accompanies her husband to Washington city next winter." Resenting Mary Lincoln's reputed influence on her husband's political career—like most of Lincoln's colleagues—he concluded, "She wishes to loom largely." Defying both custom and Judge Davis's censure, the Lincolns rented out their home in Springfield and traveled to Washington with their two sons, Robert Todd Lincoln, who was four years old, and Edward Baker Lincoln, who was not quite two. Lincoln may have had several motivations for bringing his family to Washington. Gregarious by nature, at age thirty-eight he had never before lived alone. Instinctively parsimonious, he may have bristled at the thought of keeping two separate households eight hundred miles apart. The family had already boarded briefly in Springfield, so they were familiar with the routine. Above all, Lincoln grew sullen when separated from his family, as experience would prove. At any rate, the Lincolns rented out their house at Eighth and Jackson streets and traveled as a family to Washington.[4]

On their first night in the city, they stayed in one of the oldest hotels on Pennsylvania Avenue, the fashionable Brown's, better known as the "Indian Queen" after the image of Pocahantas that graced its sign. There the family registered as "A. Lincoln & Lady 2 children, Illinois." Their final destination was more modest and better suited to a congressman's $8 per diem, a room in Mrs. Ann Sprigg's boardinghouse, which stood across the street directly east from the Capitol, on First Street. The three-story townhouse sat in the middle of Carroll's Row, a block of six large brick buildings already half a century old when the Lincolns arrived. This line of imposing Georgian structures owed its existence to Daniel Carroll, the substantial landowner who had donated the Capitol grounds to the federal government. Before Congress could move from Philadelphia and into the new capital, the members needed housing. Private investors were reluctant to put up houses because the capital's commissioners, in the name of both aesthetics and fire prevention, banned single-story and wooden structures. Anxious to make the city functional for the new government, George Washington himself built the first boardinghouse on Capitol Hill, by way of setting an example. Two years later, in 1800, Carroll, who had already erected twenty buildings in the neighborhood, converted some of them, including the row of substantial brick buildings that bore his name, into congressional boardinghouses. Carroll's Row enjoyed a long and colorful history. The rowhouses hosted the capital's first inaugural ball, held for President James Madison in 1809. During the War of 1812, the invading British army commandeered one of the buildings as its headquarters and another as its hospital—after scorching the Capitol across the street. During the Civil War, the row became Washington's first refuge for fugitive slaves and later, as the renamed Carroll Prison, housed suspected spies and other traitors. The whole structure met its end in 1887, demolished to make way for the Library of Congress's new Jefferson Building.[5]

When consummate Washington insider Duff Green bought the block of buildings during the 1830s, as both a home and an investment, they acquired their secondary sobriquet, "Duff Green's Row." Green, a native Kentuckian, was a political gadfly who had served in President Andrew Jackson's Kitchen Cabinet while editing the *United States Telegraph*, the administration newspaper in Washington. When Vice President John C. Calhoun fell out with Jackson, Green aligned with the South Carolinian and followed him into the Whig Party. (Calhoun eventually returned to the Democrats, but Green remained a Whig.) The two became in-laws when Calhoun's son married Green's daughter. Occupying his time as an investor, speculator, inventor, and part-time diplomat, Green lived with his family in the southernmost house in the row—at the corner of First and A streets—and rented out three of the other buildings to boardinghouse keepers, including Mrs. Sprigg. Perhaps not coincidentally, Mrs. Sprigg ran a decidedly Whig house, which comported with Green's political convictions. Beyond owning the boardinghouse, Green and his family were day boarders, meaning that they ate their meals at Mrs. Sprigg's, three doors up from their own home. Green, as it happened, was one of Mary Lincoln's numerous Todd relations, the uncle of her brother-in-law Ninian Edwards, one of the most prominent politicians in Springfield. As the family's only connection to Washington, Green must have recommended Mrs. Sprigg to the Lincolns—and vice versa. Boardinghouse keepers depended on references, mostly through word of mouth, to attract not only enough boarders to keep their rooms filled but above all the right kind of boarders, known by the catchall label "respectable." The Lincolns, of course, were respectable, but Mrs. Sprigg was in no position to reject even distant relatives of her landlord, in any event.[6]

MRS. SPRIGG, a widow from Virginia who was in her late forties, was by all accounts a gracious hostess who kept a comfortable house. Five years before the Lincolns arrived, a "transient" lodger, the Connecticut abolitionist Theodore Dwight Weld, described the accommodations that she provided. "I have a pleasant room on the second floor," he wrote home, "with a good bed, plenty of covering, a bureau, table, chairs, closets and cloathes press, a good fire place, and plenty of dry wood to burn in it." Beyond these expected amenities, Weld was a "Grahamite," a follower of Sylvester Graham's dietary reforms, an eccentricity that Mrs. Sprigg was willing to indulge. Describing his diet as "anti-meat, butter, tea and coffee, etc *ism*," Weld welcomed all of the bread and milk, mush, apples, potatoes, turnips, parsnips, almonds, raisins, figs, and spinach that Mrs. Sprigg could provide. The milk, Weld assured his wife, fellow abolitionist Angelina Grimké, was *"very good."* He also offered a glimpse of Mrs. Sprigg's customary table fare by emphasizing that "the puddings, pies, cakes, etc., etc., I have of course nothing to do with." Another lodger, Joshua Giddings, the renowned evangelical Whig who represented Ohio's Western Reserve in Congress, took a room at Mrs. Sprigg's when he first arrived in Washington in 1838. He liked it immediately and stayed there during every session of Congress for the next twelve years. "I am east of the Capitol 20 or 40 rods in a large brick house," he wrote to his family after moving in. "In the second story, in a fine large room with a bureau, table writing desk bed wash stand." From his window, looming over Capitol Hill, he reported "a fine view" of the Capitol dome, the Potomac, and even parts of Virginia and Maryland.[7]

The house was certainly "eligibly situated," indeed ideally located for a congressional mess. "Mrs. Spriggs is directly in front of the Capitol," Weld wrote to his wife. "The iron railing around the Capitol Park comes within fifty feet of our door. Our dining room overlooks the whole Capitol Park which is one mile around and filled with shade trees and shrubbery." (As a physical culture enthusiast, Weld walked, ran, and jumped in the thirty-five-acre Capitol Park for an hour every morning.) Lincoln could not have chosen a better location for an earnest, young politician to begin his congressional career. "Congressman Lincoln was always neatly but very plainly dressed, very simple and approachable in manner, and unpretentious," another boarder, physician Samuel Busey, recalled in his memoirs. "He attended to his business, going promptly to the House and remaining till the session adjourned, and appeared to be familiar with the progress of legislation." Inauspiciously, however, the congressional lottery that assigned seating awarded Lincoln a less favorable location in the Hall of Representatives, a desk in the last row, all too emblematic of his eventual historical reputation as a "backbencher" during his single term. As the only Whig representative from Illinois, Lincoln received appointment to two committees—Post Offices and Post Roads, and Expenditures in the War Department—that befitted his expertise in economic issues and his commitment to national development. The two committees commanded substantial respect, but they also demanded considerable labor and presented little opportunity for distinction.[8]

Beyond the Capitol building itself, Washington's boardinghouses represented the congressmen's primary workplace. When not in the House Chamber, the residents of Mrs. Sprigg's boardinghouse worked incessantly. Their committee assignments demanded endless rounds of paperwork, which they complained about continually. "The truth is they make me work too hard while here," Giddings, a member of the Committee on Indian Affairs, grumbled. "The way in which the letters are piled on to me every morning and evening is a caution to lasy folks." Busily writing speeches and preparing legislation, the boarders read voluminously, aided by their borrowing privileges at the Library of Congress across the street in the Capitol. Giddings wrote home that "the papers are down upon me like a duck upon a june-bug" and reported that his desk was "covered with papers and filled up under it with books and books piled up each side of it." After hours, the congressmen received a stream of callers—"evening visitations," another lodger, Congressman Seth Gates of New York, called them. Above all, they anxiously awaited—and sometimes dreaded—the twice-daily ring of the "mail bell." So enmeshed were the boardinghouses in the congressional routine that the Capitol post office delivered mail directly to the members in their boardinghouses. "When the mail arrives there," Theodore Dwight Weld explained, "the post master and his clerks seperate out the letters, papers, etc., of each member of Congress, enclose them in a wrapper and dispatch messengers to the lodgings *of every member* with whatever he may have." When the "house bell" announced the arrival of mail every morning, the boarders assembled in the sitting room to pick it up. Each evening, a messenger visited all of the rooms to collect outgoing letters. As a practical demonstration of this ever looming deadline, Weld abruptly ended a letter to his wife by lamenting, "The mail boy is about going and I must close."[9]

Within this fundamentally male workspace, Mary Lincoln had little opportunity to "loom large" and proved "so retiring that she was rarely seen except at the meals," according to Dr. Busey. Most social interactions at Mrs. Sprigg's, in fact, took place at mealtime. Nineteenth-century boarders shared what was known as "boarding-house fare" around a "common table" at fixed mealtimes—typically breakfast at six, dinner at noon, and supper at five, each announced by a bell or, in some of the more extravagant boardinghouses, a gong. During these regimented meals in Mrs. Sprigg's dining hall, Dr. Busey recalled "occupying a seat at the table nearly opposite Abraham Lincoln, whom I soon learned to know and admire for his simple and unostentatious manners, kind-heartedness, and amusing jokes, anecdotes, and witticisms." The gregarious Lincoln clearly savored these opportunities to amuse and educate his fellow boarders. "When about to tell an anecdote during a meal," Busey related, "he would lay down his knife and fork, place his elbows upon the table, rest his face between his hands, and begin with the words 'that reminds me,' and proceed. Everybody prepared for the explosions sure to follow."[10]

Not all explosions at mealtimes were lighthearted. All of the congressmen at Mrs. Sprigg's were Whigs, but they personified the same looming divisions over slavery that threatened to disrupt their party. "Conscience" Whigs were increasingly uneasy with southern slavery and hoped, if not to eliminate it, to keep it from spreading westward.

"Cotton" Whigs embraced or at least tolerated slavery as a lucrative labor system with economic benefits for not only southern slaveowners but the northern textile industry as well. During the Mexican-American War, David Wilmot, a congressman from Pennsylvania, proposed a proviso excluding slavery from any territory the United States might eventually acquire from Mexico. The Wilmot Proviso was never enacted but provoked a powerful "free soil" movement that focused on preventing the extension of slavery farther into the West. A growing number of Conscience Whigs were nonextensionists, or free soilers as they became known, hoping to contain the spread of slavery and even hasten its demise. As Dr. Busey reminisced, "The Wilmot Proviso was the topic of frequent conversation and the occasion of very many angry controversies." On occasions such as these Lincoln played the part of peacemaker. "When such conversation would threaten angry or even unpleasant contention," Busey recalled, "he would interrupt it by interposing some anecdote, thus diverting it into a hearty and general laugh, and so completely disarrange the tenor of the discussion that the parties engaged would either separate in good humor or continue conversation free from discord." Lincoln's highest priority was always to keep the discussion civil. Quite understandably, "This amicable disposition made him very popular with the household."[11]

Lincoln's first speech in the Capitol arose from his membership on the Committee on Post Offices and Post Roads, centering on a postal contract for the Great Southern Mail. Not surprisingly, he used humor to make points and enliven his delivery, which the *Congressional Globe* recorded through the interjection "[a laugh]," as when he referred to "the lawyers in this House (I suppose there are some) [a laugh]." This maiden speech occurred at the end of the day and dominated the evening's conversation across the street at Mrs. Sprigg's. "I recall with vivid pleasure the scene of merriment at the dinner after his first speech in the House of Representatives," Dr. Busey remembered, "occasioned by the descriptions, by himself and other of the Congressional mess, of the uproar in the House during its delivery." Afterward, Lincoln wrote home to his law partner in Springfield, William Herndon: "As to speech-making, by way of getting the hang of the House I made a little speech two or three days ago on a post-office question of no general interest." Lincoln reported with seeming self-confidence that "I find speaking here and elsewhere about the same thing. I was about as badly scared, and no worse, as I am when I speak in court."[12]

During the 30th Congress, the Whig Party enjoyed a rare opportunity to influence the course of government. Coming in the midst of the Mexican-American War, the election of 1846 gave them a slim and fleeting majority—by only one vote—in the House, and they were determined to make the most of it. By the time Lincoln's term began, the war with Mexico had all but ended. President James K. Polk's administration was negotiating a peace treaty, which would go to the Democratic-dominated Senate, but not the House, for ratification. Within three months, in fact, Lincoln was writing back to Illinois: "It now seems to be understood on all hands that the war is over—that the treaty sent in will be ratified." Whigs therefore had only the briefest opportunity to dispute the conduct of the war. Lincoln was one of the first to weigh in.[13]

Mere weeks after arriving, Lincoln introduced his famous "Spot Resolutions," a series of eight queries that focused on the origins of the war and particularly Polk's insistence that Mexico, as the aggressor, had "invaded our territory, and shed the blood of our fellow citizens on our own soil." The most pointed of the resolutions questioned the validity of American ownership of the disputed territory on which the first clash with Mexican troops had taken place. The implication was that the president had provoked an unnecessary and even unjust war with territorial acquisition—to make new slave states—as his primary goal. Lincoln asked Polk whether the "spot" on which the war began was truly American soil or legally the possession of Mexico. Hence, the designation "Spot Resolutions" and the even more unfortunate label for their author, "Spotty Abe." Lincoln's combative attack on Polk caught his friends and political allies by surprise. Springfield's Whig newspaper published the resolutions without endorsing them, emphasizing that "the whigs have not opposed the war measures of the administration. They have given all the men and money called for. They are for a vigorous prosecution of this war. They wish it ended." In fact, Lincoln's stand on the war reflected the conventional views of eastern Whigs, who insisted that they did not oppose the

Mexican-American War itself but only the suspicious circumstances under which it began. "Mr. Polk's War," as they labeled it, seemed an attempt to enhance southern political power by adding new slave territory to the Union. Ironically, in an effort to tie the entire Whig Party to the resolutions, Illinois Democrats pointed out that Lincoln's predecessor in Congress had taken exactly the same stand. (This was Edward Baker, after whom the Lincolns named their second son, Eddie.) Still, the Whigs of Lincoln's congressional district never endorsed nor repudiated his views, leaving him to stand alone.[14]

Underestimating the popularity of the war in his own western state of Illinois, Lincoln followed up his Spot Resolutions with a full-blown speech on the origins of the war, which he delivered in January 1848. Essentially a personal and partisan challenge to the president with thinly disguised political overtones, it ended by labeling Polk "a bewildered, confounded, and miserably perplexed man." When running for Congress, Lincoln had agreed to serve only one term, but soon after arriving in Washington he began to change his mind. Just one month into his term, he mused complacently that "if it should so happen that nobody else wishes to be elected, I could not refuse the people the right of sending me again." Now, his speech on the war doomed any hope of reelection. William Herndon began warning his law partner about "extensive defections" among Illinois Whigs and tried to dissuade him from committing "political suicide." In reply, Lincoln defended himself by pointing out that he opposed the commencement of the war but fully supported its prosecution once it had begun. He insisted that "the whigs have, from the beginning, made and kept the distinction between the two." Indeed, most Whigs, including Lincoln (but not his messmate Joshua Giddings), voted to supply American troops still in the field while condemning the president's motives for leading the country into war in the first place. As Lincoln assured Herndon, "I have always intended, and still intend to vote supplies." Fundamentally, however, he viewed Polk's motives for fighting the war as constitutionally unwarranted, even monarchical or, as he put it, "Kingly." The founders, he reasoned, "resolved to so frame the Constitution that *no one man* should hold the power of bringing this oppression upon us." Still, Lincoln conceded to Herndon that "if *you* misunderstand, I fear other good friends will also." In fact, Lincoln's position proved a tremendous liability during the next congressional election, when Illinois Whigs lost the Seventh District, their only reliable "safe seat," for the first time in a decade.[15]

Ever supportive of her husband's political career, Mary Lincoln sat in the gallery of the House to hear the Spot Resolutions and Lincoln's speech on the origins of the war. After little more than a month in Washington, however, she left Mrs. Sprigg's with the two boys and went to Lexington, Kentucky, to visit her family. This parting, which appears amicable, was undoubtedly a realistic concession to the demands of Lincoln's hectic congressional work schedule, which consumed most Saturdays. A few months after Mary left Mrs. Sprigg's, Lincoln wrote to her gloomily. "In this troublesome world, we are never quite satisfied. When you were here, I thought you hindered me some in attending to business; but now, having nothing but business—no variety—it has grown exceedingly tasteless to me." Sharing the lot of most of his colleagues, who labored in their congressional messes in stoic solitude, he admitted that "I hate to sit down and direct documents, and I hate to stay in this old room by myself." But his family's departure also suggests that some friction had arisen at Mrs. Sprigg's. In the same letter, Lincoln hinted that Mary had not gotten on with all of her fellow boarders, perhaps because of the presence in the house, which was essentially a male workplace, of their two boys. Years later, Dr. Busey praised young Bobby Lincoln as a "bright boy" but remembered that he "seemed to have his own way" at Mrs. Sprigg's. Ever the permissive parents, the Lincolns countenanced what they considered harmless play, but their "dear rascals" sometimes seemed more like "brats" to the less forgiving, including William Herndon. Lincoln himself conceded, "We never controlled our children much," while his wife avowed that "if *I* have erred, it has been, in being too indulgent." Lincoln therefore betrayed a palpable tension when he wrote to Mary, "All the house—or rather, all with whom you were on decided good terms—send their love to you. The others say nothing."[16]

CHAPTER TWO

"At War with Washington"
The Abolitionists

—————◆◆◆—————

THE NATION'S capital was a natural target for the rising antislavery movement. Under the Constitution, Congress controlled the District of Columbia through "exclusive legislation in all cases whatsoever" and could eliminate the slave trade and slavery itself within its borders at any time. The Residence Act of 1790, which located the capital between Maryland and Virginia, stipulated that the laws of those states would remain in force until the federal government moved in. When that happened, in 1800, Congress simply agreed to maintain Maryland law in the city of Washington, including both slavery and a "Black Code" that restricted the freedom of all African Americans, slave and free. Slavery took root in Washington immediately. Facing a scarcity of labor, the federal commissioners charged with creating the city soon turned to slaves to fell trees, fire bricks, quarry stone, and erect public buildings, including the Capitol. Washington's first slave auction took place in 1794, with the sale of a mother, son, and daughter, along with six other males and females ranging in age from ten to nineteen. In 1800, when the federal government arrived, 30 percent of the district's residents were African Americans, fewer than one-fifth of them free. Soon after Abigail Adams moved into the White House, she wrote contemptuously, "The effects of slavery are visible everywhere." From its very beginning, visitors and government officials from the North and abroad condemned the city for its open slave markets and its economic reliance on slavery. "Being under the supreme local government of Congress," observed Joseph Sturge, the English Quaker who founded the British and Foreign Anti-Slavery Society, "it presents almost the only tangible point for the political efforts of those hostile to slavery." Sturge considered the national capital "the grand point of attack" upon American slavery.[1]

The institution continued to take root in the capital until 1830, when the number of slaves in Washington reached its peak, representing 12 percent of the city's 19,000 people. At the same time, Washington began supplanting Baltimore as the center of Maryland and Virginia's slave trade. Plantation slavery entered a slow but permanent decline in the Chesapeake region as tobacco prices fell and planters shifted their land to wheat production, which was far less lucrative. Wheat farming was also more seasonal and less labor-intensive, so planters in Maryland and Virginia began selling many of their slaves westward to the fresh plantations opening up along the Gulf Coast, where an unprecedented cotton boom was under way. "The adjoining, and once fertile and beautiful States of Virginia, Maryland, and North Carolina," Joseph Sturge reported after touring the region, "are now blasted with sterility, and ever-encroaching desolation." Interregional slave dealers advertised for the planters' excess slaves and established slave pens in Washington to exploit this growing traffic. They sent thousands of slaves in a "coastwise" trade down the Potomac, into Chesapeake Bay, and on to New Orleans in a virtual fleet of slave ships.[2]

In the 1830s, Sturge found the District of Columbia "the chief seat of the American slave-trade" and observed that "Washington is one of the best supplied and most frequented slave marts in the world." Until Congress ended the slave trade in the District of Columbia as part of the Compromise of 1850, Washington's slave traders operated a half-dozen major "Georgia pens" or "slave jails" within the city. The most notorious slave market in Washington was William H. Williams's "Yellow House," which sat just south of the Smithsonian Institution along the National Mall. Named after the paint on its outer walls, Williams's private jail was disguised as an innocent-looking two-story brick house but conducted a massive trade with the New Orleans and Mississippi River markets by means of two slave ships, the *Tribune* and the *Uncas*, which the firm owned and operated. Possessing "a virtual monopoly on the private-jail business" in Washington, in 1836 Williams ran an advertisement offering "cash for Four Hundred Negroes" to be shipped southwestward. Solomon Northup was a free African American who was kidnapped in Washington in 1841 and held as a slave for the next twelve years. In the slave narrative that he published in 1853, he described Williams's slave pen, where he spent his first two weeks of captivity. "Its outside presented only the appearance of a quiet private residence," Northup wrote. "A stranger looking at it, would never have dreamed of its execrable uses. Strange as it may seem, within plain sight of this same house, looking down from its commanding height upon it, was the Capitol." A yard sat at the rear of the building, surrounded by a brick wall ten or twelve feet high, protected by an iron gate. "It was like a farmer's barnyard in most respects," he recalled, "save it was so constructed that the outside world could never see the human cattle that were herded there." Imprisoned in a dank cell with masonry walls and a barred window, Northup underwent a severe flogging before being marched by night through the streets, in a coffle with other handcuffed slaves, to a wharf on the Potomac. A steamboat took him to Virginia, where he spent the following night in yet another slave pen in Richmond. In the morning, he began his journey to his ultimate destination, New Orleans.[3]

Directly across the street from the Yellow House stood Robey's Tavern, a rendezvous for slave traders. Run by Washington Robey, the tavern boasted a pen where the substantial slave-trading firm of Joseph W. Neal and Company did its business. Other slave pens and private jails dotted Washington. Along Pennsylvania Avenue not far from the Capitol sat Center Market, the city's largest public marketplace, where slaves were bought and sold along with cattle. Nearby stood Lloyd's Tavern at the city's busiest intersection, Pennsylvania Avenue and Seventh Street. Two hotels, the St. Charles Hotel and the United States Hotel, where slaver James Burch, Solomon Northup's abductor, operated, kept slave pens. The St. Charles assured its guests that their slaves would be "well cared for" in its basement, which boasted six "holding" pens, each an arched cell thirty-six feet long, complete with grated iron doors, shackles, and "wall rings." The management guaranteed that "IN CASE OF ESCAPE, FULL VALUE OF THE NEGRO WILL BE PAID BY THE PROPRIETOR." Within sight of the Capitol, public auctions took place at the Pennsylvania Avenue Slave Stand. Only blocks from the White House, two more slave pens operated at Lafayette Tavern, just two blocks east, and in the courtyard of the Decatur House—onetime home of Commodore Stephen Decatur before he died in a duel—on the northwest corner of Lafayette Square. When these private slave pens filled up, slaveowners were welcome to lodge their slaves in the Washington County jail, labeled the "Blue Jug" in honor of its distinctive "dull blue walls." Traders paid thirty-four cents a day for the keep of their slaves and sometimes conducted private sales within its walls.[4]

As the slave trade drained laborers from the faltering tobacco plantations of the Chesapeake region, slavery began to decline in Washington itself. Between 1830 and 1860, the slave population fell from its peak of 12 percent to just 3 percent of the city's residents. Slaveowners with only seasonal demands for labor, including wheat farmers, found slavery increasingly less economical and developed an elaborate system of hiring out. Planters kept their slaves working in agriculture during the growing season and then hired or "rented" them out in Washington during the fall and winter, when Congress was in session and the urban economy flourished. Often, they hired out their female slaves as domestic servants for a year at a time. Such "term slaves," who worked as hirelings for a fixed period, had the opportunity to retain some of their wages and thus could contemplate the possibility, however remote, of eventually buying their freedom. Hiring out also benefited slaveowners by discouraging their slaves from escaping. A hireling who enjoyed a degree of autonomy and looked forward to achieving his freedom someday was much less likely to become a fugitive. Washington's free African American population continually absorbed these former slaves and grew threefold between 1830 and 1860. Baltimore was the only American city with more free African Americans on the eve of the Civil War. As slavery declined in Washington and the city moved increasingly toward a wage-labor model, however, southerners grew all the more aggressive in defending it. In 1842, a Washington abolitionist observed that the South made "a point of honor" of defending slavery in the capital, not so much for its own sake but as "a sort of symbol and proof of its control over the government of the country."[5]

The abolition movement first emerged as a political force in Washington when former president John Quincy Adams took his seat in the House of Representatives in 1831. Adams ran for Congress a year after leaving the presidency and represented a steadfast anti-slavery constituency in Massachusetts for the next seventeen years. As the most vocal and eloquent critic of slavery in the House, he spent his entire congressional career doing all he could to propel the antislavery movement to the top of the national political agenda. His initial strategy was simply introducing into the House the numerous petitions he received from constituents advocating the abolition of slavery in the capital. In 1835, the American Anti-Slavery Society, founded two years earlier in Philadelphia, aided this effort by mounting an aggressive "petition campaign" that sent a flood of antislavery petitions, resolutions, and memorials from every northern state pouring onto the floor of Congress, more than 400,000 of them during the first year alone. Southern congressmen from both parties closed ranks against this threat by imposing a "gag rule" on the House, under which antislavery petitions would be received (as required by the First Amendment) but immediately tabled, allowing "no further action whatever," effectively stifling congressional discussion of slavery. Adams and an expanding circle of antislavery Whigs fought the gag rule for the next eight years.[6]

The growing core of antislavery Whigs pointed to the gag rule to confirm the power of slavery to infringe freedom of speech, even on the floor of the House, diminishing the civil liberties of Americans of all races. Before 1840, Adams was joined in the House by a handful of disciples, William Slade of Vermont, Seth Gates of New York, and Joshua Giddings of Ohio. Giddings represented the Western Reserve's Ashtabula County, widely praised or scorned as the most abolitionist, indeed "abolitionized," county in America. Revering Adams as "Old Man Eloquent," Giddings became his second-in-command and soon gained a title of his own, "the Lion of Ashtabula." Born into a farming family with New England roots, Giddings, like Lincoln, grew up working on his father's farm and educated himself through voracious reading. While teaching school, he studied law and took on Benjamin F. Wade, who later served as a Republican radical in the Civil War Senate, as his partner. A Congregationalist, during the 1830s Giddings imbibed the evangelical fervor of the Western Reserve's revivalism and plunged into antislavery politics. In the process, he adopted a new philosophy of "political abolitionism," rejecting persuasion as the chief tool of antislavery advocacy and experimenting with strategies for using the federal government to undermine and eventually eliminate the institution. He worked with Adams in the fight against the gag rule, seized every opportunity to debate slavery as a violation of eternal, natural rights, and insisted that the federal government have nothing to do with it. Giddings venerated "Father Adams" for igniting "a great revolution" in Congress and exulted that "many members now wish themselves to be regarded as the advocates of the rights of man who would have been angry at being called an abolitionist six months since."[7]

With his typical audacity and flair for controversy, Giddings dubbed the growing cadre of antislavery advocates in Congress the "Select Committee on Slavery." Their goal was to break the congressional "conspiracy of silence" and preempt the nation's legislative agenda through an unrelenting assault on federal support for slavery. Southerners had long argued that slavery was a creation of the states and that the national government possessed no right to interfere with it. Adams, Giddings, and their allies cleverly subverted that argument, stigmatizing slavery as a purely local or "municipal" institution that the federal government had no constitutional power or moral right to support. Freedom was national in foundation, slavery only local. Outside the boundaries of a slave state—in a federal territory, in international waters, or in the District of Columbia—slavery had no legal foundation and must give way to the natural law of human freedom.[8]

The "Select Committee on Slavery" dissented from prominent abolitionists, including William Lloyd Garrison, who considered the Constitution a fatally flawed proslavery document. Calling the federal government itself a "covenant with death" because of its concessions to slave owning, the Garrisonians rejected political approaches to antislavery, especially those involving compromise, as sinful. Instead, Adams and Giddings enunciated an emerging antislavery interpretation of the Constitution that would turn the federal government into an ally of abolitionism and the most important tool in the fight against slavery. An apt example was the mutiny aboard the Spanish slave-trading ship, the *Amistad*, in 1839. When fifty-three African slaves seized the *Amistad* in international waters and claimed their freedom, Adams successfully represented them before the U.S. Supreme Court. He seized this opportunity to defend "those great & eternal principles of right, of liberty & of law that lie at the foundation of all genuine democratic and righteous government." The Supreme Court decision heartened abolitionists by ruling that where slavery was illegal and natural law prevailed, a "right of revolution" empowered slaves to free themselves.[9]

As one of the "permanent residents" of Washington, Adams owned a house in the city, one block north of Pennsylvania Avenue. His disciples, Giddings, Slade, and Gates, as "transient" members of Congress, boarded at Mrs. Sprigg's. During the winter of 1841–42, when Whigs secured their first majority in the House of Representatives, Giddings recruited Theodore Dwight Weld and Joshua Leavitt to help craft, implement, and defend a comprehensive antislavery agenda in the House. Weld and Leavitt were two of the country's most influential and experienced abolitionists. Both of them had edited the *Emancipator*, published by the American Anti-Slavery Society, and Weld had organized that society's highly successful petition campaign. Weld also co-wrote an incisive treatise, *American Slavery as It Is: Testimony of a Thousand Witnesses*, with his wife and his sister-in-law, Angelina and Sarah Grimké. Their book, an encyclopedic chronicle documenting the horrors of slavery, helped to inspire Harriet Beecher Stowe's immensely popular and persuasive novel *Uncle Tom's Cabin*. The "Select Committee" hired

Weld to conduct research in the Library of Congress, where Giddings secured him a desk. Leavitt, who was a Congregational minister and lawyer, had just published *The Financial Power of Slavery*, an authoritative critique of the institution as an economic system. He first came to Washington to help organize the defense of the *Amistad* mutineers. As congressional reporter for the *Emancipator*, he stayed on as both an observer and architect of the unfolding Whig antislavery campaign.[10]

Weld and Leavitt joined Giddings, Slade, and Gates as boarders at Mrs. Sprigg's, which the five of them rechristened "Abolition House" in recognition of the work that they hoped to accomplish there. "Mrs. Sprigg has now *twenty five boarders*," Weld boasted to his wife, Angelina, "and here is a singular fact, and one that speaks well for Abolition in Washington—it is that for the last two years this has been known as the 'Abolition house.' " Weld went on to characterize the boarders as "Giddings, Gates, and Leavitt, abolitionists, and all the other boarders favourably inclined." Giddings, too, wrote proudly to his wife, Mary, "Our house is now *filled*. Indeed Mr Weld whom you will recollect has been compelled to room and bed with Mr Leavitt in order to get a chance to stay at the *abolition* house." Giddings and Weld construed Mrs. Sprigg's success as a confirmation of the rising respectability of abolitionism in Congress. "I am highly pleased at Mrs Spriggs prosperity," Giddings reported. "When Slade and I first took lodging here many fears were entertained that it would injure her house to be called an abolition house. The result has fully proven otherwise. Hers is probably the only boarding house in the city that is filled." Weld agreed that "Mrs. Sprigg has always feared that the character of her house would be hurt by it and that members of Congress would shun her. We have feared so too." Giddings, in fact, took personal credit for the growing popularity of both abolitionism and Mrs. Sprigg's. "Well I am here with thirteen members of Congress all in one mess," he marveled. "A larger mess than any other in the City. All impute it to me as they wish to get along with an abolitionist. Most of the mess have come fully into my views concerning abolition."[11]

An opportunity for Giddings to indict the federal government's relationship with slavery appeared when a case similar to that of the *Amistad* arose in November 1841. An American vessel, the *Creole*, was bound from Hampton Roads, Virginia, for New Orleans as part of the coastwise slave trade when its cargo of 130 slaves rebelled, took control of the ship, and sailed it to Nassau in the Bahamas. Under British law, the slaves were free, but the U.S. State Department supported the *Creole*'s American owners in demanding their return. The gag rule prevented debate over antislavery petitions but not diplomatic questions that involved slavery, such as the rendition of the *Creole*. Building on Weld's research and rhetorical advice, Giddings prepared an incisive denial of federal responsibility for sustaining slavery, which he delivered in the House. His nine resolutions repudiating federal protection for slavery in international waters challenged, by implication, the same protection for slavery in the District of Columbia and the federal territories. At the height of the *Creole* episode, the southern reaction was violent enough to worry Giddings's and Weld's families and friends. "There were so many threats of assassination and so much said in the papers on those points, that I greatly feared that you may think some slaveholder might feel it an object to assail me as they call me an *abolitionist*," Giddings wrote to his daughter in February 1842. "But no one gave me a disrespectful word during the whole conflict, although weapons were drawn upon others and lives threatened." In the end, Giddings's fate was not assassination but censure. The Whigs, who held a slim majority in the House, considered Giddings's resolutions so disruptive to party unity that they supported a resolution of censure. Southern members, including most Whigs, were virtually unanimous, and almost one-half of northern Whigs voted for the resolution, which passed overwhelmingly. In March 1842, Giddings resigned his seat in the House, went back to Ohio, defiantly ran for reelection, and won. Soon he was back, with a justifiable sense of vindication, at "Abolition House."[12]

THAT EPITHET took on a new meaning when the slaves who worked for Mrs. Sprigg began escaping. The day after Theodore Weld arrived at the boardinghouse he wrote to his wife to explain that "Mrs. Sprigg, our landlady, is a Virginian, *not* a slaveholder, but hires slaves. She has eight servants all colored, 3 men, one boy and 4 women. All are free but 3 which she hires and these are buying themselves." Self-purchase through hiring out was the primary route to freedom for Washington's slave families. Hirelings who married could buy the freedom of family members one by one until they were all free. Self-purchases usually followed an installment plan, which entailed risk because a slave who was ultimately denied his freedom had no legal recourse to recover his payments. Often, a family member who was already free paid the installments and literally bought his or her husband, wife, mother, or father. Husbands usually preferred to free their wives first and then work toward their own freedom so that any children born in the interim would be free. In a remarkable elaboration of this process, Alethia Tanner, a Washington slave, purchased her own freedom in 1810 and then bought her sister and her five children sixteen years later. By the time she died in 1864, Tanner had purchased and freed twenty-two relatives and friends.[13]

Still other hirelings pursued a more direct and immediate route to freedom. Soon after arriving in Washington, Weld noted: "Slaves are running away from the District almost daily." After just a month in Washington, he wrote his wife with an apparent mixture of excitement and satisfaction that "*all* the table waiters that were here last year have *run away*. Mrs. Sprigg thinks it quite unsafe to have slaves in such close contact with Abolitionists, so she has taken care to get *free* colored servants in their places!" Soon Giddings himself was explaining with exaggerated amazement the procedure through which Mrs. Sprigg was losing the slaves in her boardinghouse. "*Poor Robert* who I believe was here when you visited us *has left* and his whereabouts is now regarded by his mistress as altogether *uncertain*," he wrote in a letter home. "He was owned by a Miss Harrington living east of us and Mrs Sprig paid her fifteen dollars per month." When his owner opened a boardinghouse of her own and tried to reclaim Poor Robert from Mrs. Sprigg, he disappeared. "He left on Friday evening some weeks since and the next he was heard from he was '*way up there in York State*,' full tilt," Giddings crowed. Indeed, an underground railroad had begun channeling fugitive slaves from Washington through

Philadelphia to Albany, Troy, and Buffalo, New York, and ultimately to Canada. "He left in company of some other very valuable *chattels*," Giddings reported. "Some swear that there is a *subterannean rail road* by which they travel *under ground*. Men women & children all go whole families disappear."[14]

Giddings had helped turn Washington from a center of the slave trade into a focus of abolitionism. Initial antislavery efforts in Washington, organized by Quakers based in Philadelphia, had pursued voluntary and gradual emancipation, depending heavily on legal suits for freedom, manumissions, and self-purchase. In 1830, Ohio Quaker Benjamin Lundy published the city's first antislavery newspaper, the *Genius of Universal Emancipation*, but when a proslavery reaction produced an indictment for libel, Lundy left Washington. The widespread religious revivalism of the 1830s emboldened evangelicals in New England, New York, and Ohio's Western Reserve to begin calling for immediate emancipation. Washington became one of the primary targets of the newly formed American Anti-Slavery Society, which sent a small army of organizers to press for abolition in the national capital. In 1841, Charles Torrey, an ordained minister from Massachusetts who was educated at Yale College and Andover Theological Seminary, arrived in Washington to put a practical plan for abolition into action. He began by helping a family of slaves escape when they were threatened with sale farther south. Soon he enlisted the aid of Thomas Smallwood, a former Maryland slave who had purchased his own freedom and became the Washington correspondent for an Albany newspaper, the *Tocsin of Liberty*. The team of Torrey and Smallwood developed a full-blown underground railroad that operated for the next twenty years, escorting large groups of slaves northward to Philadelphia, New York, and often Canada. Torrey was editor of a Liberty Party newspaper, the *Albany Patriot*, and the Washington correspondent for several other antislavery newspapers. In the process, he began working with Giddings and other members of the "Select Committee" in their efforts to challenge the gag rule, dissociate the federal government from slavery, and promote freedom in Washington. Writing under a pseudonym to protect his identity, Smallwood published letters in the *Patriot*, reporting that Torrey and he had abetted 150 slave escapes in a mere eight months. Torrey later claimed that he had helped a total of four hundred fugitives reach Canada. In 1846, while serving a six-year term for aiding runaways, he died of tuberculosis in the Maryland penitentiary. Paying the ultimate price for his defiance of slavery, he declared on his deathbed that "it is better to die in prison with the peace of God in our breasts than to live in freedom with a polluted conscience."[15]

In 1848, while Lincoln was living at Mrs. Sprigg's, former congressman Seth Gates wrote to Giddings from upstate New York to report that Poor Robert had indeed escaped to Canada six years earlier but had eventually returned to the United States. He now had a family in Buffalo and was working as a cook on a lake boat. Gates had heard from another former slave that Robert was "steady & doing well." He also told Giddings that a slave named Scott, who had also worked at "Abolition House," had fled with Robert. He, too, had "got safe off to Canada" and was now living in Buffalo. The most dramatic story that Gates related, however, involved a mass escape of eighteen slaves that included John Douglass, yet another waiter at Mrs. Sprigg's. According to Gates, Douglass and the other fugitives traveled on foot from Washington until they passed Philadelphia and could board a train. Like Robert and Scott, Douglass reached Canada, where he lived for eighteen months before returning to the United States, settling in Rochester, New York. Gates informed Giddings that Douglass "is married there has one child, is well clothed, has good recommendations & appears very well and very happy." In fact, Gates had just seen Douglass, who visited him in Warsaw, New York, and "stayed with me over the last sabbath." Gates's story ended on an even more hopeful note. Douglass's brother had fled from Washington with the help of Charles Torrey and Thomas Smallwood and joined him in Rochester. Now the Douglass brothers were raising funds to buy their mother and reunite with her in New York. Gates cautioned Giddings, "This should not be known in Washington however, as it might enhance the price."[16]

The conclusion is inescapable that the "Select Committee on Slavery," with Giddings at its head, had escalated its legislative assaults on slavery to the point of complicity in the flight of at least three of the slaves who worked at Mrs. Sprigg's. Long after their deaths, evidence emerged identifying both Giddings and Gates as underground railroad "operators" before the Civil War. Giddings's oldest son, Addison, revealed that his father "had an out-of-the-way bedroom in one wing of his house at Jefferson, Ohio, that was kept in readiness for fugitive slaves." Mrs. Sprigg herself must have condoned the escape process after the fact, if indeed she had no direct role in its operation. In his letter to Giddings chronicling the odyssey of John Douglass, for example, Gates disclosed that more than five years after leaving Congress he was still communicating with Mrs. Sprigg. "I have mentioned seeing him to Mrs Sprigg," he wrote Giddings, "but have not told her where either he or Robert are." Less than two weeks later, former congressman William Slade, another founding member of "Abolition House," wrote to Giddings from Troy to report that "Mrs Dodson the mother of the colored girl living with me, requests that letters directed to her may be enclosed to you, and the accompanying letter is therefore sent you." The implications are striking. Five years after boarding at Mrs. Sprigg's, Slade was harboring a former slave who had escaped from Washington. (If she were not a fugitive, she could have written to her mother directly. Instead, she was depending on Giddings to relay a letter to her mother, who was presumably still a slave.) Slade's letter went on to identify Mrs. Sprigg herself as another potential channel between the mother in Washington and the daughter in his home. "If Mrs Dodson does not call for it," Slade told Giddings, "perhaps Mrs Sprigg (with whom I suppose you still board) will know where she lives & send it to her." In short, while he served in Congress, Abraham Lincoln may well have been living in a literal, rather than merely figurative, "Abolition House."[17]

Giddings's rhetorical and practical strikes against slavery in the seat of national power clearly hit home and marked him, if not all the residents of "Abolition House," as a target for proslavery reprisal. During the 30th Congress, the Speaker of the House, conservative "Cotton" Whig Robert Winthrop, lamented that Giddings seemed to be "at war with Washington." Inside the House, his legislative strategy—"attacking every movement tending to make slavery a subject of national concern"—enraged southern members. His challenges to slavery and racism outside Congress—associating with African Americans, attending slave auctions, inviting some of the country's most visible abolitionists to Washington—offended the capital's permanent residents just as acutely. Above all, Washingtonians suspected that he was helping fugitive slaves escape from his self-proclaimed "Abolition House" across the street from the Capitol. Giddings fully expected Washington to strike back.[18]

CHAPTER THREE

"A Western Free State Man"
Lincoln and Slavery

———◆·◆·◆———

O N JANUARY 14, 1848, two days after Lincoln delivered his controversial critique of the war and just after Mary left Washington with their sons, three armed men burst into the boardinghouse and seized one of the waiters, Henry Wilson, a slave who had been hired out to Mrs. Sprigg. Wilson's wife, Sylvia, who was free, worked as a maid in the boardinghouse, where the couple lived with their ten-year-old son. Under an agreement with his owner, the Wilsons had spent three years buying Henry's freedom, making periodic payments toward his $300 purchase price. Around thirty years old, Sylvia Wilson had been born into freedom and was a servant at the White House during William Henry Harrison's presidency. A marriage between a free African American woman and a male slave was an efficient strategy for securing a family's freedom. Making joint payments, the couple could secure Henry Wilson's freedom all the sooner. In this fashion, the servants at Mrs. Sprigg's could hope to gain their freedom under her employ. The Wilsons had paid all but $15 and expected to make the final payment within a matter of days.[1]

With the conclusion of Henry's self-purchase imminent, his owner surreptitiously sold him to a slave dealer for the entire $300, a common practice among Washington's slaveowners. On a Friday evening, while Giddings and other congressmen were absent, the slave dealer and two assistants entered Mrs. Sprigg's without warning to retrieve Wilson. "One of them seized him by the throat to prevent his making a noise," Giddings discovered upon his return, "when the others placed hand-cuffs upon his wrists, and then drawing their pistols drove the servants and family back." Out in the street, they shoved Wilson into a hack and drove him to a nearby slave pen. "Poor Sylvia was overwhelmed with grief," Giddings recalled. "She at once looked to us for relief, with an apparent hope that we might bring back her 'affectionate husband,' as she called him. Our landlady, I think, would have suffered no greater grief if death had entered her family." If Lincoln did not know it already, he soon discovered that the seemingly innocuous boardinghouse kept by Mrs. Sprigg was Washington's most notorious enclave of abolitionism.[2]

After finding the boardinghouse in an uproar, Giddings and messmate Abraham McIlvaine, a Whig from Pennsylvania, rushed to Williams's slave pen, where a large dog was guarding the front door. They were told that Wilson had already been sent to Alexandria, Virginia, and was on a ship leaving for New Orleans that very night, "to drag out the remainder of his existence in the cotton-fields of the South," as Giddings presumed. Suspecting that Wilson was in reality still at the Yellow House, Giddings sought a writ of habeas corpus. On Monday morning, he informed the House of the events at Mrs. Sprigg's and declared that "outrages like the foregoing have been of common occurrence in this District, and are sanctioned by the laws of Congress, and are extremely painful to many members of this House, as well as in themselves inhuman." He then presented a resolution asking that a select committee of five investigate the abduction and "the propriety of repealing such acts of Congress as sustain or authorize the slave trade in this District, or to remove the seat of government to some free State." A southern member moved to table the resolution, but to everyone's surprise, the motion to table failed by one vote, 85–86, with two southern representatives voting against it. "At the announcement of the vote great sensation was visible among southern members," Giddings recalled. "They appeared astonished." Both sides hurriedly summoned absent members to the floor of the House for the vote on Giddings's resolution. Hoping to attract more Whig support, Giddings amended the resolution by deleting his rhetorical reference to removing the national capital. A Democratic representative from Georgia moved to table the amended resolution, and southerners used parliamentary maneuvers—a long series of trivial points of order—to delay the vote for an hour, while more members trickled into the chamber. In the end, the southerners prevailed. The vote to table the amended resolution passed 94–88, with Lincoln supporting Giddings's proposal.[3]

This predictable but disappointing legislative defeat left Giddings to pursue Wilson's freedom on his own. He appealed to the slave's former owner, a Washington widow whom he labeled an "old Jezebel," and to the slave dealer who had bought him, but both refused to reconsider the sale. Running out of options, the distraught Giddings received support from an unlikely ally. Duff Green, Mary Lincoln's in-law and the owner of Mrs. Sprigg's, was not only a slaveowner but a vocal defender of slavery, a southern expansionist, and a states' rights advocate who condemned abolitionism as an inflammatory threat to national unity. As Wilson languished in the ghastly Yellow House, however, Green stepped forward to help Giddings secure the slave's release. Green's motives are debatable. He may have viewed Wilson's sale southward as a counterproductive maneuver that would strengthen Giddings's congressional campaign against slavery. As a lawyer, he may have objected on principle to the violation of Wilson's self-purchase contract. As a boarder at Mrs. Sprigg's, he must have known the Wilson family and may have harbored a sincere concern for their welfare. He probably resented the brutal intrusion into Mrs. Sprigg's boardinghouse, which after all he owned and visited thrice daily with his family. Above all, Green had a private history of helping slaves attain their freedom that belied his public reputation as a "strident proslavery activist."[4]

At the very moment that the slave traders seized Henry Wilson, Green was in the midst of pursuing a "freedom suit" on behalf of an eight-year-old slave girl. This complex legal case, which held momentous implications for slavery in Washington, DC, had been brewing for a decade. It began when a slave couple, Mary and Daniel Bell, set out to free themselves and their nine children. Daniel Bell was an iron molder in the Washington Navy Yard, where his owner rented him out to work for the U.S. government. Like many slaves who hired out, he eventually accumulated enough money—$1,630—to buy his own freedom. Mary Bell's owner, Robert Armistead, was a master caulker at the Navy Yard. In 1835, Armistead freed her for the nominal sum of $1. He also set up a schedule under which her children would gain their freedom at various ages that ranged from thirty to forty, turning them into the kind of "term slaves" who proliferated in Washington as slavery in the region declined. When Armistead died, however, his widow Susannah contested the manumissions and, further, claimed ownership of the Bells' daughter Eleanora, who had been born after Mary Bell had achieved her freedom. Born of a free woman, Eleanora should have been automatically free. Instead, Susannah Armistead hired her out and kept her wages.[5]

In an effort to free her daughter, Mary Bell turned to Duff Green, who practiced law in Washington with his son, Benjamin. Fifteen years earlier, Green had bought a slave named Lewis Bell with the express purpose of hiring him out so he could purchase his own freedom. If Lewis Bell was a member of the same family, Green would have had a personal motive in helping Mary Bell pursue her daughter's freedom. In January 1848, Green and his son prepared a petition on behalf of Eleanora Bell, as well as a restraining order preventing Armistead's widow from removing the eight-year-old girl from Washington, selling any of the Bells' children, and separating the family. The Greens investigated the case and recorded the recollections of over twenty witnesses who had knowledge of the Bell and Armistead families and particularly Robert Armistead's determination that all of Mary Bell's children would ultimately be free. In January 1848, they filed a petition in the U.S. Circuit Court for the District of Columbia to secure Eleanora's freedom.[6]

While the Bells' suit was still pending, Giddings asked Green to help rescue Henry Wilson. According to the Cleveland *Daily True Democrat*, an antislavery newspaper in the Western Reserve, Giddings "laid the case in all its hideous enormity before Duff Green, (who owns the house from which Henry was taken) and he immediately investigated the matter and volunteered his assistance." Known as "General" Duff Green in recognition of his commission in the Missouri state militia, he instantly took command. His first step was to send an imperious letter to William H. Williams, the slave-dealing owner of the Yellow House who had purchased Wilson for $300 and then seized him at Mrs. Sprigg's. In reply, Williams coolly informed the Greens that he had sent Wilson to Richmond and might require a payment of $700, his value in the Richmond slave market, to set him free. Green responded forcefully, emphasizing that his inquiries had established that Wilson was entitled to his freedom, that the district attorney might consider it his duty to undertake an investigation, and that he had resolved to secure Wilson's freedom in any event. "If this be not done immediately," he assured Williams, "we will take efficient measures to compel his return and do all that is in our power to prevent the recurrence of a similar outrage."[7]

Offended and likely surprised by this aggressive response, Williams turned over the letter to Richard Wallach, an attorney and member of Washington's Common Council, himself a slaveowner from Virginia. Wallach told the Greens that Williams was "highly aroused" and would only communicate with them through him. The Greens agreed to work through Wallach and asked him to inform Williams, "We have examined into the facts & believe that the boy can recover his freedom in any court in any of the southern states." They then asked Wallach to advise Williams that "he owes it to himself and to those, whose opinions he must respect to prove by his conduct now that at the time he sent the boy out of the district he did not know that he was entitled to his freedom." Williams eventually buckled and agreed to return Wilson for no more than his purchase price. Wilson's original owner was willing to repay Williams but had already spent $180 of the purchase price, which she now demanded before authorizing the slave's release, return to Washington, and legal manumission. "Mr. Giddings and others being confident that the laws were insufficient to effect them in the least, (although *they* were not aware of it,) concluded to make the best of it," the Cleveland *Daily True Democrat* reported, "and give them the amount required." Giddings raised the $180 by collecting $5 donations from Whigs in

Congress, a task that reportedly took him "some twenty or thirty minutes." By the end of February, Wilson had rejoined his family at Mrs. Sprigg's. "The slave case brought to the notice of the House of Representatives a few weeks since, by Mr. Giddings, has terminated better than was anticipated," Washington's antislavery newspaper, the *National Era*, exulted. "By the well-timed efforts, we learn, of Mr. Duff Green, Henry was brought back to the city." For his part, Green signaled his disapproval of the slave dealer's tactics by labeling his own records of the negotiations with the annotation "In the case of Henry Wilson, colored, kidnapped—settled."[8]

Securing Wilson's freedom was a welcome victory for Giddings. His campaign to set the terms of debate and to recruit converts in the House seemed to be making headway. He had successfully defended the integrity of "Abolition House" with the aid of two southern slaveowners, Duff Green and Richard Wallach. Another potential ally at Mrs. Sprigg's, a Kentucky-born representative from Illinois, must have posed an irresistible challenge. In fact, Lincoln came to Congress with a long-standing interest in the abolition of slavery in Washington. A decade earlier, as a young state legislator in Illinois, his first public stand on slavery—indeed, his first recorded use of the word—had defended the power of Congress to abolish slavery in the District of Columbia. As abolitionism arose and became a force to be reckoned with during the 1830s, a conservative reaction swept the North and touched off a wave of anti-abolition violence. Mob activity peaked during the 1830s, with 115 major riots during the decade and about half that number during the 1840s. Northern mob actions against abolitionists and African American communities were most frequent between 1834 and 1837. As Lincoln himself recognized in his famous Lyceum Address, which he delivered in Springfield in 1838, "Accounts of outrages committed by mobs, form the every-day news of the times. They have pervaded the country, from New England to Louisiana."[9]

As part of this conservative reaction, in March 1837 the Illinois legislature adopted a set of resolutions supporting southern slavery and condemning the formation of northern abolition societies. The resolutions affirmed the following three principles:

Resolved by the General Assembly of the State of Illinois,
That we highly disapprove of the formation of abolition societies,
and of the doctrines promulgated by them.

Resolved, That the right of property in slaves, is sacred to the
slave-holding States by the Federal Constitution, and that they
cannot be deprived of that right without their consent.

Resolved, That the General Government cannot abolish slavery in the District of Columbia, against the consent of the citizens of said District without a manifest breach of good faith.

These conservative sentiments were virtually articles of faith in a state
that was dominated by transplanted southerners. Lincoln attempted
to amend the third resolution on abolition in the capital by moving the insertion of the qualifying phrase "unless the people of the
said District petition for the same." If adopted, his amendment would
have upheld the principle of majority rule in the nation's capital while
endorsing the right of the people to submit antislavery petitions to
Congress. With the congressional gag rule only a year old, Lincoln's
defiant use of the word "petition" was surely deliberate. His amendment failed on a voice vote.[10]

The resolutions received overwhelming support. Only six members of the legislature in both branches voted against them, including Lincoln and another Whig, Daniel Stone. Signaling their strong
opposition to the resolutions, Lincoln and Stone filed a protest.
While reiterating the majority's opposition to abolition societies,
they challenged the legislature's endorsement of slavery as a sacred
right. In fact, they went even further and labeled it an injustice,
declaring that "the institution of slavery is founded on both injustice
and bad policy." Lincoln and Stone also agreed with the legislature
that Congress had no power under the Constitution to "interfere
with the institution of slavery in the different States." Most Americans, north and south, including prominent abolitionists, agreed
with this constitutional interpretation. The protest's third clause
urged Congress not to abolish slavery in the nation's capital without the consent of the citizens of the District of Columbia. Their
subtle restatement of the legislature's resolution, however, empha-

sized what Congress could do rather than what it could not do. Their protest insisted that "the Congress of the United States has the power, under the constitution, to abolish slavery in the District of Columbia; but that that power ought not to be exercised unless at the request of the people of said District." In Lincoln's revision of the legislature's language, "cannot abolish slavery" became "ought not." Finally, the protest dropped Lincoln's earlier endorsement of the right of petition in favor of the broader "request of the people," which might include a referendum.[11]

In short, ten years before arriving in Congress, this twenty-eight-year-old Illinois legislator had issued a comprehensive public declaration of his beliefs about slavery. Above all, slavery was an "injustice." Abolitionism, however, was a counterproductive approach to undermining slavery, in light of the vicious and tenacious reactions it provoked in both the South and the North. In fact, just nine months later an anti-abolition mob killed Elijah Lovejoy, publisher of an anti-slavery newspaper in nearby Alton, Illinois. Along with most other Americans, Lincoln believed that Congress had no constitutional power to interfere with, let alone abolish, slavery in southern states. Finally, Congress did have the power to abolish slavery in the District of Columbia but should do so only at the request of its residents or, as he put it, "the people." Lincoln's first recorded use of the word "slavery" concluded by focusing on the nation's capital as a potential target for abolition. As the Republican nominee for president twenty-three years later, he emphasized that his protest "defined his position on the slavery question; and so far as it goes, it was then the same that it is now."[12]

DURING HIS first year in Congress, Lincoln's voting record on slavery adhered faithfully to the statement of principles that he had enunciated a decade earlier. He supported every antislavery measure that came before the House, most of which called for the abolition of slavery or the slave trade in the District of Columbia. All of them were tabled, however, with Lincoln voting in the negative. While doing everything possible to stifle debate over abolition in the national capital, the Whig-controlled House acted aggressively to prevent slavery from spreading westward. Lincoln was a consistent supporter of that effort. Shortly before running for Congress, Lincoln summed up the core of his nonextension philosophy in a letter to a supporter in Illinois. "I hold it to be a paramount duty of us in the free states, due to the Union of the states, and perhaps to liberty itself (paradox though it may seem) to let the slavery of the other states alone," he declared, "while, on the other hand, I hold it to be equally clear, that we should never knowingly lend ourselves directly or indirectly, to prevent that slavery from dying a natural death—to find new places for it to live in, when it can no longer exist in the old." In short, Lincoln supported the nonextension of slavery, and its gradual demise, but not its abolition in southern states.[13]

During the war with Mexico, Whigs had adopted the Wilmot Proviso as their basic tool for preventing the spread of slavery westward. First proposed in August 1846, the Wilmot Proviso endorsed the power of Congress to ban slavery in the western territories and sought to apply that prohibition to any new territory acquired from Mexico. The House consistently approved the Proviso, and the Senate just as consistently voted it down. In the 30th Congress, House Democrats tried to admit slavery into the western territories of California, New Mexico, and Oregon five different times, and the Whig members, with Lincoln's support, stopped every attempt. Lincoln went on record in Congress as a self-declared "Western free state man, with a constituency I believe to be, and with personal feelings I know to be, against the extension of slavery." In his famed Peoria Speech of October 1854, Lincoln boasted that while he was in Congress, "The 'Wilmot Proviso' or the principle of it, was constantly coming up in some shape or other, and I think I may venture to say I voted for it at least forty times." In fact, that number was five, but Lincoln faithfully did his part in helping to keep slavery from spreading westward.[14]

TWO MONTHS after Henry Wilson's return to Mrs. Sprigg's, a major escape attempt in Washington heightened opposition to abolitionism both inside and outside Congress. In April 1848, William Chaplin, who replaced Charles Torrey as editor of the *Albany Patriot*, organized a massive escape of slaves from Washington. After Torrey's death, Chaplin had begun purchasing the freedom of slaves, with support from New York philanthropist and Liberty Party organizer Gerrit Smith. When Daniel and Mary Bell's efforts to secure the freedom of their nine children through legal action faltered and they saw the children's owner preparing to separate the family, they turned to Chaplin for help. Chaplin boldly suggested that the entire Bell family flee from Washington to Philadelphia aboard a ship that he offered to rent just for that purpose. Chaplin sought the help of an experienced ship's captain, Daniel Drayton, who had carried seven slaves away from Washington a year earlier and now agreed to help the Bell family for a $100 fee. Drayton, in turn, recruited Edward Sayres, who was operating a 150-ton schooner, the *Pearl*, that he had leased to carry coal in the coastwise trade. The team of Drayton and Sayres sailed from Philadelphia to Washington with the intention of picking up the Bell family. When the *Pearl* docked along the Potomac at the foot of Seventh Street, a Washington contact, rumored to be Joshua Giddings, told Drayton that besides the Bells "quite a number of others" would join in the escape. Drayton replied that he was willing to carry any number of slaves to Philadelphia.[15]

On April 15, 1848, seventy-six slaves from Washington, including thirteen children, boarded the *Pearl* and sailed southward down the Potomac toward Chesapeake Bay. Unfortunately for the runaways, a storm rose up and forced them to anchor at the mouth of the Potomac. When their owners awoke and found them missing the following morning, they organized a search that led them ultimately downstream in a steamboat that belonged to the owner of three of the runaways. The posse of thirty-five armed men caught up with the *Pearl* the next day, arrested Drayton and Sayres, and towed the schooner, with its cargo of fugitive slaves, upriver back to Washington. "A large crowd met them at the wharf," Giddings recalled, claiming that it included members of the House, "and as the slave-catchers and their victims slowly wended their way towards the city prison, the mass of spectators became so dense that the police were called upon to aid the piratical slave-hunters in conveying their victims to the prison." When the crowd passed one of the slave pens on Seventh Street, the owner rushed out and tried to stab Drayton. A general desire to force him to identify the organizers of the escape likely saved Drayton from lynching.[16]

Washington slaveowners, as well as northern observers, believed that abolitionists both inside and outside Congress had helped to organize this and many other slave escapes in the capital. After the capture of the *Pearl*, the *New York Herald*'s Washington correspondent confirmed that "for some years, slave property has become very unsafe in this quarter, and the presence of several abolitionists in Congress, has encouraged the colored population of Washington to a systematic co-operation with the abolitionists of the North." The leading suspects included Giddings, Senator John P. Hale of New Hampshire, Representative Horace Mann of Massachusetts, and Gamaliel Bailey, editor of the *National Era*. Chaplin informed both Giddings and Bailey of the escape just after the *Pearl* sailed. To the end of his life, Giddings acknowledged that much but never admitted any foreknowledge. Even so, Giddings suffered numerous verbal attacks, including threatening notes left under the door of his room at Mrs. Sprigg's. In the midst of the crisis, he wrote guardedly to his daughter, "Well I suppose you and your mother by this time have become weary of looking to find an account of my being lynched."[17]

Bailey's *National Era*, founded by the American and Foreign Anti-Slavery Society, proved the more tempting target. Three days after the escape attempt, a mob estimated at up to four thousand members—the *National Intelligencer* called it an "assembled multitude"—surrounded the newspaper office, three blocks north of Pennsylvania Avenue, breaking its windows and threatening to destroy it. During the 1830s, Bailey had edited an antislavery newspaper in Cincinnati whose press had twice been demolished by anti-abolitionist mobs. His *National Era* had survived its first sixteen months in Washington only by forswearing overt attacks on slavery and acknowledging its constitutionality in southern states. Now Bailey tried to dispel the mob by printing a handbill denying any involvement in the escape attempt on the *Pearl*. Bailey reiterated that he had always "abstained from invective and denunciation, and addressed myself to the reason, the conscience, the patriotism and sense of honor of the slaveholders, many of them being near relatives and personal friends." The city councils issued their own plea for order and authorized the mayor to appoint special police constables. When informed of the potential violence, President Polk wrote in his diary, "The outrage committed by stealing or seducing the slaves from their owners, and the attempt of abolitionists to defend the white men who had perpetrated it, had produced the excitement and the threatened violence on the abolition press." Still, he issued an order forbidding government employees from participating in the riot and offered his aid to the city authorities. When the crowd reassembled on the following night, they found perhaps a hundred peace officers surrounding the *National Era* office. Bailey "behaved with great firmness, stepped out in front of his door, and addressed the excited mob," in Giddings's words, "and by his coolness, endeavored to prevent violence and bloodshed. And after a while, the police having made several arrests, the mob dispersed." The *National Era* survived, and Bailey continued to publish it until his death a decade later.[18]

Against Bailey's advice, Giddings himself went to the county jail to counsel Drayton and Sayres. He promised them that they would not be lynched, that they would receive a fair trial, and that he would secure them a lawyer. He also visited the cells where the fugitive slaves were being held and examined by slave dealers. While he was in the jail, a mob of thirty to forty obtained a key and broke in. Giddings believed that they were slave traders from Baltimore, Annapolis, Alexandria, and Richmond—"a miserable mass of moral putridity," he called them—looking for bargains. "The mass of beings before them was dense and highly enraged," Giddings wrote later, "uttering profane imprecations against the writer and all abolitionists." Drayton and Sayres were charged with stealing seventy-six slaves, with their bail set at $1,000 per slave.[19]

Most of the fugitives suffered precisely the fate that they had been attempting to avoid, separation from their families and sale at auction. Within ten days of their capture, most of the runaways on the *Pearl* had been sold to professional slave dealers for sale farther south.

A single slave trader from Baltimore marched fifty men, women, and children from the jail, along Pennsylvania Avenue, and onto a train, the men and boys chained together, with more than a hundred African Americans looking on. Giddings wrote home gloomily, "The poor wretches that started to get away from chains and bondage, have nearly all been sold and taken to Baltimore to be shipped south." Duff Green, who had tried in vain to secure eight-year-old Eleanora Bell's freedom, learned of her fate, ironically, from John C. Calhoun. The South Carolina senator sent Green a list of the nine Bell children—Andrew, Mary Ellen, Caroline, George Washington, Daniel, Harriet, Thomas, Laura, and Eleanora—followed by the notation "bought by Walter & John Campbell of Baltimore." Afterward, family members spent years trying to locate and contact *Pearl* fugitives in hopes of buying them back, succeeding in some instances. As late as 1855, fund-raising efforts, to collect what abolitionists considered "ransom," continued.[20]

The U.S. attorney for the District of Columbia, Philip Barton Key—Francis Scott Key's son—charged Drayton and Sayres with forty-one counts of larceny for stealing the slaves of forty-one different masters, and seventy-four counts of transporting slaves out of the District. Key hoped that their testimony would implicate leading abolitionists as conspirators in the *Pearl* escape. In fact, those very abolitionists helped Drayton and Sayres mount an effective defense, led by Massachusetts congressman Horace Mann, who argued that the defendants were innocent of larceny because they had never intended to steal the slaves, just set them free. After fighting off the larceny counts, Drayton and Sayres both pleaded guilty to transporting slaves out of the District and received fines of over $10,000. While Drayton and Sayres sat in Washington's county jail, New York philanthropist Gerrit Smith mounted a campaign to raise enough funds to pay this enormous sum. In August 1852, after they had endured four years in the notorious "Blue Jug," at the behest of Massachusetts senator Charles Sumner, President Millard Fillmore pardoned the pair.[21]

The *Pearl* episode provoked a tumultuous debate in Congress. In the House, a supporter of Giddings introduced a resolution that did not focus on slavery but instead called for the prevention of "riots and unlawful assemblages in the city of Washington." Under an intense onslaught from southern members, Giddings defended the right of slaves to flee, which he called their duty, and justified the killing of anyone who tried to stop them. In reply, a representative from Tennessee told him that he "ought to be hanged." In the Senate, John P. Hale of New Hampshire introduced a bill to prevent mobbing in Washington. Mississippi's Jefferson Davis labeled it a "bill to protect incendiaries and kidnappers." Davis's colleague from Mississippi, Henry Foote, told Hale that "he should be hanged by a mob to the first convenient tree." South Carolina's John C. Calhoun announced that he would "just as soon argue with a maniac from bedlam as with the Senator from New Hampshire." For three rancorous days, the House debated a resolution calling for an inquiry into the rioting occasioned by the *Pearl* escape attempt. Eventually, a member from Mississippi moved to table the resolution of inquiry, "believing that the excitement here ought to be allowed to pass away, as it had in the city of Washington, and that the debate on this subject ought not to be sent to the country to a greater extent than it had already gone out." The motion to table passed 130–42. Lincoln now ended his unbroken string of votes in support of antislavery resolutions when he sided with the majority and voted yea to close the debate. The next morning, the conservative *National Intelligencer* reported that "the House of Representatives yesterday relieved itself from the further annoyance of the worse than useless debate which has occupied the three days of its valuable time."[22]

The attempted escape on the *Pearl* proved profoundly counterproductive, both for slaves in Washington and abolitionists in Congress. The wide scope of the conspiracy, the careful execution of the plan, and the brazen boldness of the organizers, who may have included members of Congress, heightened the insecurity of slaveowners in the capital to unprecedented levels. They rushed to sell their slaves to the Southwest, and sales in the District surged over the next two years. Meanwhile, funding for Washington's underground railroad withered. Guessing that William Chaplin had masterminded the *Pearl* escape attempt, Washington police set a trap for him at the Maryland border and caught him helping two slaves escape. Their owners, Georgia congressmen Alexander Stephens and Robert Toombs, promptly sold them south as punishment. Northern abolitionists who had supported the underground railroad, including New York's Gerrit Smith, had to divert their funds to pay Chaplin's bail, set at an astounding $19,000. Once he was released, Chaplin refused to stand trial and fled to New York, so his supporters lost the bail. These same abolitionists assumed the simultaneous challenge of retrieving *Pearl* fugitives from slavery farther south. New York minister Henry Ward Beecher earned his abolitionist credentials by helping to raise the "exorbitantly large" sum of $2,250 demanded for the release of two of the *Pearl* slaves, sisters Emily and Mary Edmonson, from the Bruin and Hill Company's slave jail in Alexandria. Beecher's Plymouth Church congregation in Brooklyn spent years raising funds to buy back, one by one, a total of five members of the Edmonson family, who became the most celebrated fugitives aboard the *Pearl*. Their story helped to inspire Beecher's sister, Harriet, to write her fictional account of slavery, *Uncle Tom's Cabin*. Her moving portrayal of the resilience of African American families in the face of the horrors inflicted by slavery and the slave trade debuted, quite fittingly, in Gamaliel Bailey's Washington newspaper, the *National Era*. Still, many abolitionists, including Gerrit Smith, condemned Bailey's self-preservationist stance during the "*National Era* Riots" as heartless and cowardly, without understanding the hazards inherent in operating an antislavery newspaper in a southern, slaveowning city.[23]

Joshua Giddings called the 30th Congress "a President-making Congress," and indeed the looming election of 1848 overshadowed all other issues. Lincoln joined other moderate Whigs in embracing the military hero General Zachary Taylor. Although Taylor's political opinions were entirely unknown, Lincoln believed that no other Whig candidate could win the presidency in 1848, including his longtime favorite Henry Clay. "In my judgment," he wrote, "we can elect nobody but Gen; Taylor." Although Taylor was a southerner and a slaveowner, so was Clay himself. Undoubtedly influenced by the Whig support for free soil that he saw on the floor of Congress every day, Lincoln believed that any Whig president must endorse nonextension. "Our only chance is with Taylor," he insisted. "I go for him, not because I think he would make a better president than Clay, but because I think he would make a better one than Polk, or Cass, or Buchanan, or any such creatures, one of whom is sure to be elected, if he is not." Lincoln joined a group of moderate Whigs in the House, calling themselves the "Young Indians," to organize support for Taylor. One of their primary goals was helping to bridge the widening sectional gap that was threatening the Whig Party's unity and indeed its future. Five of the seven Young Indians were moderate southerners, including Georgia representatives Alexander Stephens and Robert Toombs. Lincoln described Stephens, who became his closest confidant in the 30th Congress, as "a little slim, pale-faced, consumptive man." When Stephens joined him in speaking out against the Mexican-American War, Lincoln called it "the very best speech, of an hour's length, I ever heard." A southern unionist, Stephens outdid even Lincoln in castigating Polk, labeling his policies "dishonorable," "disgraceful," "reckless," and "ruinous."[24]

Congressional Whigs devoted the summer of 1848 to kicking off their presidential campaign on the floor of the House. In June, Lincoln gave a speech on internal improvements that he told William Herndon "I suppose nobody will read," and then in July he delivered another on "the Presidential Question." In recommending Taylor for the presidency, Lincoln admitted that he wasn't certain that Taylor would support the Wilmot Proviso but pledged to vote for him anyway, because he knew with certainty that Lewis Cass, the Democratic nominee, would do his best to open the western territories to slavery. This speech contained the most memorable passage of Lincoln's entire congressional career. In contrasting Cass's military record against Taylor's, Lincoln disparaged his own, depicting himself as a "military hero" during the Black Hawk War. "I had a good many bloody struggles with the musquetoes," he recalled, "and, although I never fainted from loss of blood, I can truly say I was often very hungry." For his part, Giddings objected to Taylor as a slaveowner with no record of opposing the spread of slavery. He worked with other antislavery Whigs against the "Taylor movement" in favor of a more acceptable candidate. Overoptimistic, Giddings attended an "anti Taylor" meeting in January 1848 and concluded that "I do not think Taylor will be the next president." When antislavery Whigs and Democrats began to organize a new Free Soil Party, founded on the Wilmot Proviso's principle of nonextension, Giddings refused to support it, firm in his conviction that "the Whigs will nominate no man for President whose sentiments are not known to be opposed to extending slavery." When Taylor won the Whig nomination, however, Giddings bolted what he had once called the "Whig Church" and joined the new Free Soil Party, even vying for its vice presidential nomination. Lincoln opposed the new antislavery party simply because it had no chance of winning an election and would in fact help to elect a Democrat by dividing the Whigs.[25]

Toward the end of the first session, in July 1848, Mary Lincoln wanted to return to Washington with their two boys, and her husband readily agreed. "Come on just as soon as you can," he urged. "I want to see you, and our dear—*dear* boys very much." They joined him near the end of July. After Congress adjourned, the family stayed in Washington through August while Lincoln worked in the "Whig document room," mailing out thousands of pieces of campaign literature to support Taylor's election. He sent out 7,580 copies of his own speeches that he purchased for one cent apiece and mailed for free under his congressional franking privilege. A month later, Lincoln undertook a speaking tour of New England to support Taylor and, more specifically, to prevent antislavery Whigs from bolting to the new Free Soil Party. In effect, he campaigned against the Free Soil Party as well as for Taylor. He delivered eight speeches in two weeks, typically speaking for an hour and a half. Distilling his major congressional speeches, he argued that both Whigs and Free Soilers opposed the extension of slavery but that only the Whigs could defeat the Democrats and keep slavery out of the territories. As summarized in the press, his primary dispute with the Free Soilers was that "the whole probable result of their action would be an assistance in electing Gen. Cass." On his way back to Illinois, he met Mary and the boys at Albany. They took a train to Buffalo and then a steamer along the Great Lakes to Illinois. Serving as an assistant elector for Taylor, Lincoln made the same points in eight speeches before local audi-

ences to try to keep nonextensionists in the Whig fold. His overall
message was the importance of unity in conducting the antislavery
effort. "The abolition of slavery in the territory of the United States
can never be accomplished unless the North is united," he insisted.
"But the North cannot be united until old party lines are broken
down. But these lines cannot be broken down unless every man is
willing to sacrifice his attachment to minor questions and make
opposition to slavery the leading idea." In November, Taylor won the
presidency with a plurality of 47 percent but lost the state of Illinois.
The Free Soil Party's nominee, former president Martin Van Buren,
won an impressive 10 percent of the national vote.[26]

CHAPTER FOUR

"Is the Center Nothing?"
Lincoln's Middle Ground

———◆◆◆———

T HE VERY success of the Free Soil Party in 1848, in the unsettling wake of the *Pearl* disaster, produced a shift within the antislavery movement in Congress. The seemingly counterproductive focus on ending slavery in the District of Columbia now yielded to a broader northern campaign dedicated to stopping the spread of the institution into territories where it did not yet exist. The attempted escape on the *Pearl*, along with its bitter reverberations in Congress and its legacy of heightened discrimination against African Americans, may well have provoked a change in Lincoln's personal perspective on how best to undermine slavery. Before the mass escape attempt, Lincoln had voted against tabling every petition and resolution regarding abolition in the district that came to the floor of the House. During the rancorous exchange that engulfed the House for three days in April 1848 in the aftermath of the *Pearl* episode, however, he voted to end the debate. This was his first vote against his messmate Giddings and other antislavery Whigs. Then, for the rest of his term, he voted to table every subsequent effort to end slavery in the District of Columbia. Far from signaling a proslavery stance or even ambivalence on the part of Congressman Lincoln, as some critics have argued, his negative votes in the second session reflected a shift in his priorities away from ending slavery where it already existed, which increasingly appeared futile and counterproductive, and toward nonextension as a more effective method for undermining the institution.[1]

When the members reassembled in December 1848 for the second, "short" session of the 30th Congress, Mary, Robert, and Eddie stayed behind in Springfield. Lincoln arrived in Washington three days late, which may have signaled his reluctance to return without them. The previous session's breach between the "Taylor party" and the abolitionists now boiled over in both the House Chamber and Mrs. Sprigg's. Upon arriving, Giddings noticed immediately that many of his former friends in the House "exhibited evidence of personal dislike," and a few even "looked daggers at me." Undaunted, he immediately summoned half a dozen of the most vocal antislavery members, including David Wilmot, to Mrs. Sprigg's to coordinate an aggressive campaign against federal support for slavery. His target was not the Democratic Party at all but the incoming Whig administration. As he confided to one of his allies, his ultimate goal was to "blow the Taylor party sky high." This heightened antislavery presence in the boardinghouse annoyed some of Giddings's fellow boarders, particularly the Taylor men, who were formerly cordial but were now spoiling for a fight. "My messmates appeared very in ill humor," he reported, "and endeavored to provoke me into controversy with them on the subject of Free Soil."[2]

A personal turning point for Lincoln came about a week into the second session, when an antislavery Whig from Massachusetts sought to introduce a bill repealing all laws that supported slavery and the slave trade in the District of Columbia. Lincoln voted with the majority to table the resolution and was the only northern Whig to do so, as Giddings himself carefully noted in his *History of the Rebellion* in 1864. The next item on the agenda was a resolution instructing the Committee on Territories to report a bill excluding slavery from the territorial governments of California and New Mexico. Lincoln probably voted to table the district bill to clear the agenda for the territorial measure that upheld the Wilmot Proviso. (The House passed the territorial resolution 106–80 with Lincoln's vote.) Later that day, Lincoln and another messmate, James Pollock of

Pennsylvania, openly challenged Giddings's priorities. As Giddings noted glumly in his diary, "Mr. Pollock & Lincoln of our mess were very insulting after the adjournment." By the end of 1848, Lincoln, along with other antislavery Whigs, had made a strategic shift from abolition in the District of Columbia to the nonextension of slavery into the territories—free soil—as his top priority.[3]

A few days later, the acrimony spilled over from the floor of the House into Mrs. Sprigg's boardinghouse just across First Street. Giddings related the scene that erupted on that Saturday morning when he opposed the spread of slavery into the new territories acquired from Mexico. "I denounced it [at the] breakfast table this morning," he wrote home to his son, "and it kicked up a row such as we have never had at our boarding house. Pollock denounced me as an agitator, and that all I desired was to keep up an excitement. I replied that I was unwilling to have my motives impugned by a miserable Doughface who had not mind enough to form an opinion, nor courage enough to avow it." With this exchange of insults, the argument escalated. "He sprang from the table as he sat on the opposite side and marched around to where I was. I was however on my feet, and he cooled down." Several of the Taylor men, including Lincoln, tried to defuse this outburst of "ill-humor" with "some remarks conciliatory," which ironically convinced Giddings that the Illinoisan was too "timid" in his approach to dealing with the South. Lincoln, however, was not alone.[4]

Two days later, Giddings introduced a bill calling for a plebiscite to decide the fate of slavery in the District of Columbia, with all male inhabitants—including African Americans, both free and slave—voting for "Slavery" or "Liberty," which Giddings himself characterized as "giving the slaves a right to vote." Lincoln voted to table the bill, but David Wilmot went further and told Giddings directly that he was "alarmed" and considered African American suffrage unacceptable. The National Era's editor, Gamaliel Bailey, took Giddings to task for adding a provision enfranchising African Americans, including slaves, to an emancipation bill, which could only guarantee its defeat. The bill was therefore not only counterproductive but "calculated to arouse feelings of fierce hostility," in Bailey's opinion. "This

I regard as the unkindest cut of all," Giddings reflected after reading the editorial. Back home in the Western Reserve, the *Ohio Standard*, a Free Soil newspaper aligned with newly elected Ohio senator Salmon Chase, faulted Giddings's "misguided zeal" for African American rights at the expense of the territorial question. Feeling abandoned by both the Free Soil press and his former Whig friends, Giddings noted, "Most of the Taylor men now omit all exchange of salutations when we meet."[5]

On Christmas Day, Giddings sat sullenly in his room waiting for former Whig friends to pay him a complimentary visit. "None came," he wrote dejectedly. While making holiday calls of his own on Pennsylvania Avenue, he heard that "the northern Taylor men held a meeting last evening and resolved that they would not vote with me any more on the slave question." As if signaling the passing of the older era of petition campaigns, gag rules, and the personal involvement of its members in the struggle for freedom in the national capital, in the midst of the 30th Congress John Quincy Adams suffered a paralytic seizure at his desk and collapsed onto the floor of the House. He died two days later at the age of eighty. Lincoln was a member of the committee that made his funeral arrangements.[6]

But Lincoln was not yet done with the District. In the same *National Era* editorial that faulted Giddings's bill as counterproductive and confrontational, Gamaliel Bailey called for a more workable emancipation plan. "For our own part, we should like to see a bill prepared, submitting the question to the qualified voters of the District, with the distinct intimation that a liberal appropriation would be made to aid in the act of emancipation," Bailey suggested. "Such a bill, we doubt not, would pass Congress, and we have just as little doubt as to the decision of the citizens of this District under it." Bailey believed that any emancipation proposal that lacked a compensation provision would free virtually no one, because before it could take effect, "almost every slave in the District would be sold to the South." Lincoln may not have read the *National Era*, but within ten days, in January 1849, he had written just such a bill calling for compensated emancipation in the District of Columbia. Lincoln may have viewed this quixotic effort as the fulfillment of the idealistic "protest" that he had issued with colleague Daniel Stone in the Illinois legislature twelve years earlier. If so, it flew in the face of his constituents and the Illinois legislature itself. Not long after Lincoln issued his protest, the legislature approved a resolution that specifically opposed the abolition of slavery in the District of Columbia, calling it "unwise and unjust." (Ironically, this resolution was introduced by Mary Lincoln's in-law and Duff Green's nephew, Ninian Edwards.) More probably, Lincoln was seeking a pragmatic solution to a sectional issue that was vexing Congress and dividing the nation, not to mention the Whig Party itself, hoping to clear the way for the looming battle over slavery in the territories.[7]

While Lincoln was preparing and presenting his bill, a "conference" of all of the southern members of the 30th Congress, both Democrats and Whigs, was meeting at the behest of Senator John C. Calhoun and other proslavery leaders. The goal of this sectional caucus was the establishment of a unified response to what Calhoun considered an increasingly aggressive northern campaign against slavery. Calhoun served on a committee to produce a statement of principles, an "address" that he ended up writing single-handedly. In fact, African American abolitionist Frederick Douglass called it "an old speech of John C. Calhoun, newly vamped up." The resulting "Address of the Southern Delegates in Congress, to their Constituents," recited all of the constitutional protections for slavery that the South had come to depend upon, while decrying the recent "measures of aggression" perpetrated during the second session of the 30th Congress. "Although Congress has been in session but little more than one month," Calhoun wrote, "a greater number of measures of an aggressive character have been introduced, and they more aggravated and dangerous, than have been for years before." The "series of acts of aggression and encroachment" in Congress that Calhoun listed ended with a reference to "a member from Illinois," which historians consider an allusion to Lincoln's proposal. To Calhoun, the trend was unmistakable: "The great body of the North is united against our peculiar institution." The solution, "the first and indispensable step, without which nothing can be done," he exhorted southerners, "is to be united among yourselves, on this great and most vital question."

The final step, failing all else, would be a "resort to all means necessary" to repel the northern assault, a veiled reference to secession.
During its four acrimonious meetings, the caucus of southern members reflected anything but sectional unity. Just 40 percent of them
signed the "Address," including only one Whig.[8]

The possibility that Lincoln presented a District emancipation
plan in the midst of a southern flirtation with secession, with the
intention of fanning the sectional flames, as Giddings might have
done, contradicts everything historians believe about him—and certainly anything that the boarders at Mrs. Sprigg's had witnessed.
Instead, as an inveterate peacemaker, he quite probably hoped to
defuse a potentially ugly sectional rift that threatened to divide the
Whig Party, disrupt the incoming Taylor administration, and derail
free soil measures in the House. In devising his plan, Lincoln was
quite likely constructing what he considered a compromise, col-
laborating with a range of contending interests in Congress and the
Washington community and cobbling together enough preferences
from all quarters to allow representatives from both parties and both
sections to find something to like about it. While running for president, Lincoln told James Quay Howard, who interviewed him for a
campaign biography, "Before giving notice to introduce a bill to abolish slavery in the District of Columbia, I visited [the] Mayor, senators,
and others whom I thought best acquainted with the sentiment of the
people, to ascertain if a bill such as I proposed would be endorsed by
them according to its provisions." He said that he heard nothing but
"hearty approbation."[9]

Lincoln's convoluted, patchwork plan appears hopelessly conservative in contrast to some of the piously righteous proposals introduced
by the abolitionists in the 30th Congress, a triumph of parliamentary
pragmatism in the name of moderation. In fact, it technically couldn't
qualify as an "abolition" plan at all in the sense of envisioning immediate and universal emancipation. But he doubtlessly considered it
the kind of "compromise measure" that so many statesmen of the
period, including his *beau ideal* Henry Clay and his *bête noire* Stephen
Douglas, established their reputations by proposing. Five years later,
in his speech at Peoria, Lincoln summed up the rationale for his pro-

posal quite simply: "I heard no one express a doubt that a system of gradual emancipation, with compensation to owners, would meet the approbation of a large majority of the white people of the District."[10]

Under Lincoln's proposal, emancipation would be voluntary, compensated, and gradual. The plan would take effect only after approval in a referendum of legal voters in the district—white adult males. Once it took effect it would allow, but not require, slaveowners to free their slaves, in exchange for payment of their "full cash value" from the U.S. Treasury. The children of women who remained enslaved would become free on January 1, 1850, but would continue in a state of apprenticeship until an age that Lincoln never specified. Lincoln also stipulated that the constitutional provision for the rendition of fugitive slaves would remain in force and that officers of the federal government from slave states could bring "necessary servants" into the District while conducting public business. The referendum would be held the following April, and a board consisting of the president, the secretary of state, and the secretary of the treasury would assess the value of each slave to be emancipated.[11]

In crafting this complex plan, Lincoln worked closely with John Dickey, a Whig representative from Pennsylvania and a fellow boarder at Mrs. Sprigg's. On the morning of January 8, 1849, Lincoln and Dickey met with Giddings at the boardinghouse, and Lincoln paid him a second visit later that day. "Mr Dickey of Pa and Mr Lincoln of Illinois were busy preparing resolutions to abolish slavery in the DC. this morning," Giddings wrote in his diary. "I had a conversation with them and advised that they should draw up a bill for that purpose and push it through. They hesitated and finally adopted my proposition." By the end of the day, Lincoln had drafted a bill, which he showed to Giddings. "Mr Lincoln called on me this evening read his bill and asked my opinion which I freely gave." Giddings apparently suggested amending the bill, because the next day, according to his diary, "Mr. Lincoln called at my room and read to me his bill as he had amended it." Lincoln told him that he had met with the mayor of Washington, William Seaton, a Whig who edited the conservative *National Intelligencer*. Seaton believed that Giddings would oppose the bill. Many abolitionists objected on principle to paying for slaves, even in the process of freeing them. Giddings had amply demonstrated that he preferred freedom through escape rather than purchase. He had also proposed a referendum on abolition in the district that would have included free African American men. Lincoln's astuteness in trying to balance divergent perspectives in the name of compromise comes through in Giddings's diary entry reporting, "The Mayor thought I should be opposed to it and Mr Lincoln thinking that such an idea may be useful, did not undeceive him." In fact, as Giddings confided to his diary, "I believed it as good a bill as we could get at this time and was willing to pay for slaves in order to save them from the southern market as I suppose nearly every man in the District would sell his slaves if he saw that slavery was to be abolished."[12]

On the following day, Lincoln read his emancipation proposal into the record on the floor of the House, announcing that he had consulted with "about fifteen of the leading citizens of the District of Columbia," all of whom approved of it. That evening at Mrs. Sprigg's, according to Giddings, "our whole mess remained in the dining room after tea and conversed upon the subject of Mr Lincolns bill to abolish slavery. It was approved by all." Three days later, Lincoln notified the House that he intended to introduce the plan as a bill in its own right. In fact, he never did, and nothing came of Lincoln's attempt to abolish slavery in the District of Columbia. "Subsequently I learned that many leading southern members of Congress, had been to see the Mayor and the others who favored my bill and had drawn them over to their way of thinking," Lincoln explained to James Quay Howard in 1860. "Finding that I was abandoned by my former backers and having little personal influence, I dropped the matter, knowing that it was useless to prosecute the business at that time."[13]

Even Giddings never believed that his own resolutions calling for abolition in the District had any chance of succeeding. "The object of these movements was," he admitted, "to inform the people of the free States that they were involved in the crimes and disgrace of maintaining slavery and the slave trade." In other words, they were primarily rhetorical, designed to influence public opinion across the North rather than to enact legislation. In Lincoln's situation, Giddings would have pressed forward, expecting to lose the fight, in an effort to demonstrate that even so conservative a proposal had no hope of acceptance. (This may be why he had advised Lincoln to "push it through.") For Giddings, the fight itself was a victory. As he confided to his diary, "no bill could be drawn that would not be wrong in some shape." Giddings's private pessimism casts Lincoln's thrust against slavery in the District of Columbia as surprisingly intrepid, if ultimately quixotic. No less than the redoubtable John Quincy Adams, early in the contentious petition campaign, had given up on the prospect of ending slavery in the District, viewing the endeavor as unwinnable and counterproductive, a quixotic distraction from other, more sweeping initiatives, above all the threat of slavery's spread westward. Even a compromise plan, and perhaps especially a compromise plan with appeal to both sections, posed a genuine threat to slaveowners not only in Washington but across the South. As Virginia representative Jeremiah Morton observed, if slavery ended in the District, the national capital itself would become "a fort and arsenal, from which enemies and madmen may with impunity hurl the missiles of sedition" and "the grand center from which southern institutions may be assailed"—in other words, an entering wedge. If so, then Lincoln's stand comports with Samuel Busey's impression, formed in the dining room at Mrs. Sprigg's, that he was a stealthy "radical" who "was so discreet in giving expression to his convictions on the slavery question as to avoid giving offence to anybody."[14]

Probably unaware of Lincoln's decade-long interest in abolishing slavery in the District and his consultations with the dozen and more Washington denizens across the ideological spectrum, Giddings may have considered the emancipation proposal a sign of his own growing influence over the newcomer. His diary entries seem self-congratulatory, as if he had recruited another convert. Real or imagined, however, any such influence was decidedly short-lived. Sometime after withdrawing his bill, Lincoln discreetly left Mrs. Sprigg's, moving into other quarters in the city that to this day remain unknown. Four decades later, Dr. Busey wrote enigmatically, "During the short session of that Congress Mr. Lincoln lived down town, where I do not now remember." A few months after becoming president, Lincoln received a letter from Mrs. Sprigg that has since been lost but probably requested a government appointment of some kind. Lincoln endorsed the letter and sent it to Caleb Smith, his secretary of the interior. "When I was a member of Congress a dozen years ago, I boarded with the lady who writes the within letter," he wrote. "She is a most worthy and deserving lady; and if what she desires can be consistently done, I shall be much obliged[.] I say this sincerely and earnestly." At the bottom of the same page, beneath his notation, Mary Lincoln added, "We boarded some months, with Mrs. Sprigg, & found her a most estimable lady & would esteem it a personal favor, if her request, could be granted." Three years later, Lincoln wrote more urgently on Mrs. Sprigg's behalf to Secretary of the Treasury William Pitt Fessenden to tell him, "She now is very needy; & any employment suitable to a lady could not be bestowed on a more worthy person." During the Civil War, the government needed female clerks, and Mrs. Sprigg received an appointment in the loan branch of the Treasury Department. These recommendations appear heartfelt and suggest that neither of the Lincolns harbored any personal grievance toward Mrs. Sprigg herself. Lincoln and his landlady must have parted on amicable terms, given her presumption that she could call on him so many years later, in his new station as president, for a personal favor. Lincoln's reason for leaving lay elsewhere.[15]

Giddings's biographer James B. Stewart has faulted him for insulating himself in Washington, DC. Instead of using his time in Congress (he had twenty years) to solicit divergent perspectives, engage colleagues from other regions and different backgrounds, and consider new ideas, Giddings sought to reinforce and indeed to reproduce the political culture of his own district, the evangelical and antislavery Western Reserve. Beyond the House Chamber, he established a mess a stone's throw from the Capitol—literally across the street— and spent more than a decade filling it with fellow abolitionists and evangelicals who already shared his views. On the day he arrived at Mrs. Sprigg's, for example, Theodore Dwight Weld applauded the boarders' uniformly congenial openness to abolitionism. "Only Gates and Giddings [are] abolitionists, but *all* the others are *favorable*," he marveled. "They treat brother Leavitt and myself exactly as though we were not fan[a]tics, and we talk over with them at the table and elsewhere abolition just as we should at home." Beyond the walls of their boardinghouse, of course, Washington was not the Western Reserve or the Burned-Over District but a regional "middle ground," where values intermixed and conflicted, and absolutes melted away to became pliant gray areas of ambiguity and compromise. Despite his courageous stand against slavery in the District, Giddings's unwillingness or even inability to engage with the more complex and heterogeneous culture he found there precluded effective dialogue, let alone compromise, with his peers.[16]

Lincoln was undoubtedly far more at home in the national capital than were Giddings and his circle of northeastern Whigs. Born in a slave state, he grew up in the lower Midwest, in a similar "middle ground" where elements of both free and slave societies commingled. Central Illinois was a transitional zone between the early southern settlers moving slowly northward along the rivers and the latecoming Yankee evangelicals arriving via the Great Lakes from New York and New England. Lincoln's greatest political asset was his ability and willingness to negotiate the social and cultural divide between the nation's two dominant and increasingly conflicting cultures, a skill that he quickly cultivated and eventually mastered. By the time he came to Washington, negotiation, moderation, and compromise were his second nature. He developed a wide circle of acquaintances beyond Mrs. Sprigg's that bridged the sectional and ideological divides, ranging from southern slaveowner Alexander Stephens to Whig conservative Daniel Webster to northern antislavery reformer Horace Mann, elected to the House to serve out John Quincy Adams's term. Naturally gregarious, he attended the rounds of social events that encouraged mixing across partisan and sectional lines. For his part, Giddings shunned Washington's social swirl, in which he considered himself "allmost a stranger."[17]

Lincoln's compromise proposal on slavery in the District was a product of the kind of balancing of sectional interests that he had practiced in Illinois—and that he would later pursue as president. By the time he left Congress, Lincoln was keenly aware of his pivotal geographical situation on the dividing line between North and South—and the political value of his experience practicing politics on this ambiguous middle ground. After leaving Washington, he spent a tense summer contending for an appointment under the new Taylor administration. As the scramble for patronage wore on, he grew increasingly frustrated as he watched southern Illinois and northern Illinois wrangling what he considered the best offices. Tired of trusting party functionaries (including Duff Green) to present his own claims to an office, at last he wrote directly to President Taylor. As he pleaded his case for an appointment worthy of his political weight, he presented a geographical argument that acknowledged the interests of the competing northern and southern factions. He stated his quandary bluntly. "I am in the center," he told the president. Then he asked, "Is the center nothing?"[18]

ABRAHAM LINCOLN's experiences in Washington during his single term in Congress were richer than we have ever before imagined. His first foray against slavery as a young legislator in Illinois had focused on abolition in the nation's capital, which comported with the primary thrust of the antislavery movement during the 1830s. The American Anti-Slavery Society's petition campaign, the notorious gag rule, and the appearance of the first antislavery members in Congress, including John Quincy Adams and Joshua Giddings, all placed abolition in the District of Columbia at the heart of the emerging strategy of political abolitionism. Just before coming to Congress in the mid-1840s, Lincoln began articulating the nonextension philosophy that would form the centerpiece of his approach to undermining slavery for the next fifteen years. He could not have served at a more pivotal time for the future of slavery in Washington. His single term exposed him to the worst enormities of slavery as practiced in the nation's capital. It was not his first direct contact with the institution but undoubtedly enriched his understanding of it.

The impressions that he formed in Washington resurfaced in the more urgent, elaborate, and personal indictment of slavery that he issued in his speeches during the 1850s, as when he denounced slavery at Peoria in 1854. Picturing a slave pen in Washington, which was probably William H. Williams's Yellow House, he described "a peculiar species of slave trade in the District of Columbia, in connection with which, in view from the windows of the capitol, a sort of negro-livery stable, where droves of negroes were collected, temporarily kept, and finally taken to Southern markets, precisely like droves of horses." In the same speech, Lincoln's depiction of the slave trader himself exhibited a visceral repugnance reflective of intense personal experience. "Again, you have amongst you, a sneaking individual, of the class of native tyrants, known as the 'SLAVE-DEALER,' " he reminded his audience. "You despise him utterly. You do not recognize him as a friend, or even as an honest man. Your children must not play with his," he cautioned. "It is common with you to join hands with the men you meet," Lincoln admonished, "but with the slave dealer you avoid the ceremony—instinctively shrinking from the snaky contact." Lincoln's experience in Washington with the likes of Williams and his Yellow House, the seizure of Henry Wilson, and the agony surrounding the *Pearl* lent him insights into slavery, and the violence that its defenders were capable of inflicting, that the typical northern politician might never have acquired.[19]

During his first term in Congress, Lincoln supported the abolitionists in their efforts to attack the slave trade and slavery itself within the District of Columbia. Across the street, he shared both quarters and mealtimes with the most vocal and intractable opponent of slavery in either house of Congress, Joshua Giddings, at Mrs. Sprigg's fabled "Abolition House." Although not a single record survives—if indeed he left any—of Lincoln's thoughts or actions in response to the seizure of Henry Wilson and the fate of the *Pearl*, these dramatic episodes and others must have left him pondering the wisdom of attacking slavery directly, in its very den. Giddings was successful in helping or at least encouraging the slaves at Mrs. Sprigg's to achieve their freedom, but abetting the massive escape attempt on the *Pearl* proved immensely counterproductive. Even the smaller victories, as important as they were to their beneficiaries, were possible only when Congress was in session. As Thomas Smallwood observed, "in the recess of Congress, the coloured people suffer much more than when Congress is here." In the absence of the northern members, the city's permanent residents held sway and, quite possibly, exacted retribution. "God help the poor defenceless ones!" Smallwood concluded. Lincoln's vote to close the House discussion of the *Pearl* and the succeeding *National Era* Riots was, if nothing else, a prudent concession to reality.[20]

After he returned to Washington in the fall of 1848, Lincoln never again voted to support discussion of abolition in the District. In fact, he shifted his focus away from the District and the abolitionists in favor of nonextension into the territories, or free soil, as a more productive and promising albeit indirect approach to undermining slavery. He provided consistent support for the Wilmot Proviso, which he later exaggerated, and quite possibly misremembered, as voting for it "at least forty times." His own effort to end slavery in the capital, as a compromise of sorts between the intractable extremes of the abolition champion Giddings and the proslavery zealot Calhoun, unraveled when the Washington insiders, the city's permanent residents, rejected the mildest solution imaginable—voluntary, gradual, and compensated emancipation. Lincoln must have concluded what Adams and Giddings had already conceded, that "no bill could be drawn that would not be wrong in some shape." He may also have gained respect for the power of Washington's permanent residents to shape the outcome of any initiative that might threaten their absolute control over slavery. In rescuing Henry Wilson, even Duff Green, the consummate Washington insider, had to yield to Richard Wallach, the Virginia-born slaveowner who was apparently even more adept at speaking William H. Williams's language.[21]

Despite all of the controversy its members generated, both within the Capitol and beyond, the 30th Congress in the end resolved nothing. Defending the principle of the Wilmot Proviso, the House steadfastly rejected every attempt by the Senate to introduce slavery into the territories, leaving the next Congress to decide whether and how to organize California, New Mexico, and Oregon territories. Just as consistently, the House ultimately rejected every measure directed against slavery and the slave trade in the District of Columbia. The next Congress, the 31st, was left to struggle with those issues and resolve them through the patchwork of partisan and sectional concessions known as the Compromise of 1850. Engineered by Lincoln's idol, Henry Clay, and his rival, Stephen Douglas, the compromise addressed a range of sectional issues, admitting California as a free state, imposing popular sovereignty in the Southwest, and crafting a stringent Fugitive Slave Law. Washington's abolitionists could claim a victory, at last, in the final provision of the package, which prohibited the slave trade in the nation's capital. Despite Henry Clay's blunt insistence that the prohibition was, in practice, meaningless because Washington's slaveowners could continue to buy and sell their slaves outside the District, southerners in Congress still voted against it unanimously.[22]

The impact of the Compromise of 1850 on Washington's African Americans was at best ironic. The practical effect of the prohibition on slave sales in the District was to move all of the slave pens and auctions to Alexandria, Virginia, a mere seven miles away, where Washington's slaveowners could still sell their slaves southward at will. William Chaplin declared that through the spring of 1850, "scarcely a day passed that gangs of chained slaves did not pass through the city." The accompanying Fugitive Slave Law, which put Washington's community of longtime fugitives at risk of recapture, impelled them to flee northward. The national capital correspondingly declined as an arena of contention between slavery and abolitionism. After 1850, Washington was no longer "the grand point of attack." Two months after the Compromise of 1850, Giddings himself moved out of Mrs. Sprigg's after twelve tumultuous years. He seemed pleased to be in a new boardinghouse, writing to his wife, "I am now at Stevens! have a good room and am quite comfortable." He was never again able to assemble the critical mass of acolytes necessary to reproduce his erstwhile "Abolition House."[23]

The Compromise of 1850 was intended to settle the sectional issues that the 30th Congress had been unable to resolve. Historians have labeled the compromise the "Armistice of 1850," because it quelled but did not resolve sectional and partisan divisions over slavery. All of those divisions emerged anew four years later when

Stephen Douglas's Kansas-Nebraska Act allowed popular sovereignty to decide the question of slavery in the Kansas and Nebraska territories. The act, which northerners called the "Nebraska Outrage," repealed the Missouri Compromise, which had banned slavery above 36°30'. Under the guise of popular sovereignty, southerners regained the opportunity to add new slave states to the Union. The uneasy lull following the Compromise of 1850 is evident in Lincoln's recollection that "In 1854, his profession had almost superseded the thought of politics in his mind, when the repeal of the Missouri compromise aroused him as he had never been before." Lincoln felt a new sense of urgency, "took to the stump," as he put it, and soon earned his reputation as an eloquent opponent of slavery, advocating not its immediate abolition—in Washington or anywhere else—but its eventual demise throughout the nation. "I have always hated slavery, I think as much as any Abolitionist," Lincoln declared. "I have always hated it, but I have always been quiet about it until this new era of the introduction of the Nebraska Bill began." Until the repeal of the Missouri Compromise threatened to renew the extension of slavery westward, Lincoln had hoped and believed that the institution was already on the decline. His primary strategy for attacking slavery was, characteristically, gradual—"arrest the further spread of it, and place it where the public mind shall rest in the belief that it is in course of ultimate extinction"—but also moderate enough to win broad acceptance throughout the North. Lincoln promoted his free soil message eloquently and forcefully throughout the rest of the decade. He rarely raised the issue of abolition in the District of Columbia, and then only to disavow any interest in it. In his remarkable speech at Peoria, in which he first enunciated the themes that he would pursue and elaborate throughout the 1850s, he explicitly denied calling for the abolition of slavery in the nation's capital.[24]

Instead of attacking slavery where it already existed, Lincoln considered arresting its spread a far more promising strategy for ending it. He understood the principle, which his experiences in Washington undoubtedly reinforced, that once slavery entered any region, it became difficult if not impossible to legislate it out again. "At last, if ever the time for voting comes, on the question of slavery, the institution already in fact exists in the country, and cannot well be removed," he argued. "The first few may get slavery IN, and the subsequent many cannot easily get it OUT," he reasoned, in a blunt reference to the probable result of popular sovereignty. "The facts of its presence, and the difficulty of its removal will carry the vote in its favor." He therefore had no faith in popular sovereignty as an effective mechanism for containing the expansion of slavery, let alone eliminating it anywhere. During his debates with Douglas, the leading advocate of popular sovereignty, Lincoln consistently championed free soil as the ideal resolution to the slavery issue. Popular sovereignty, he argued, could only result in "the *perpetuity and nationalization of slavery*," while free soil would condemn it to "ultimate extinction." During the first of the Lincoln-Douglas debates of 1858, at Ottawa, Douglas—whose main strategy was to push his opponent "off message"—asked him if he was pledged to the abolition of slavery in the District of Columbia. Lincoln answered in the second debate, declaring that "I do not stand to-day pledged to the abolition of slavery in the District of Columbia." While denying a pledge, Lincoln went on to voice support for abolition in the District if it were gradual, voluntary (via a referendum), and compensated—the three basic components of his earlier emancipation plan. "With these three conditions," he insisted, "I confess I would be exceedingly glad to see Congress abolish slavery in the District of Columbia, and, in the language of Henry Clay, 'sweep from our Capital that foul blot upon our nation.'"[25]

In the sixth debate, at Quincy, Lincoln returned to the issue, this time in an effort to reinforce the moderation of Republican proposals to contain the spread of slavery. While proclaiming the institution "a moral, a social and a political wrong," Lincoln reiterated his long-standing belief that the federal government had no power to interfere with it in a southern state. "We go further than that," he continued, "we don't propose to disturb it where, in one instance, we think the Constitution would permit us." He then addressed the District of Columbia as a kind of gray area—a "middle ground," perhaps—in the struggle between freedom and slavery. While the federal government had the power to abolish slavery in the District, Republicans were willing for the moment to leave it alone. "We think the Constitution would permit us to disturb it in the District of Columbia," Lincoln reasoned. "Still we do not propose to do that, unless it should be in terms which I don't suppose the nation is very likely soon to agree to—the terms of making the emancipation gradual and compensating the unwilling owners. Where we suppose we have the constitutional right, we restrain ourselves in reference to the actual existence of the institution and the difficulties thrown about it." In short, while defending the power of the federal government to abolish slavery in the capital, Lincoln held up the Republicans' unwillingness to attack the institution there as an example of their moderation and, one might add, pragmatic patience. He considered every diversion from the "territorial question" counterproductive. To counter the radical tone of his oft-expressed commitment to achieving the "ultimate extinction" of slavery, Lincoln presented the free soil doctrine that he championed as fundamentally conservative. In his pivotal February 1860 speech at New York City's Cooper Union, he assured an eastern audience that the founders had written a Constitution that was intended to promote the eventual demise of the institution. Republicans, he argued, "stick to, contend for, the identical old policy" that the Constitution was designed to set in motion.[26]

The election of 1860 produced five nominees for president, each proposing a different solution to the slavery issue. In April, the Democratic Party convened in Charleston, South Carolina, and split into two wings. Delegates from the Lower South demanded a federal fugitive slave code in the territories and refused to support Douglas because of his commitment to popular sovereignty. Through fifty-seven contentious ballots, Douglas failed to achieve the necessary two-thirds vote to win the nomination. Delegates from eight states in the Lower South walked out of the convention, which then adjourned. Northern Democrats reassembled six weeks later in Baltimore and nominated Douglas for president, adopting a platform that advocated popular sovereignty in the western territories. Southern Democrats nominated John C. Breckinridge of Kentucky, who was James Buchanan's vice president and a defender of slavery expansion. The Constitutional Union Party, popular in the Upper South, supported the Union and advocated compromise on slavery, such as extending the Missouri

Compromise line to the Pacific Ocean. The Constitutional Unionists nominated John Bell of Tennessee. The Radical Abolition Party nominated New Yorker Gerrit Smith, the founder of the Liberty Party and the leading benefactor of the Washington, DC, abolition movement. Running for president, Smith advocated an immediate end to slavery throughout the nation.[27]

Within this fragmented electorate, the Republicans could win the presidency in 1860 without a single southern vote, but only if they swept the North solidly. They already commanded impressive majorities in the Upper North but needed to capture the Lower North, running from New Jersey to Illinois, requiring moderation on the slavery issue. Their platform pledged not to interfere with slavery where it already existed while proposing free soil as the only way to prevent its expansion. The moderate Republican platform called for a moderate nominee. Eastern Republican leaders, such as Salmon Chase, William Seward, and Charles Sumner, had radical reputations and represented states—Ohio, New York, and Massachusetts—that were "safe," already solidly within the Republican fold. Lincoln had many advantages as a nominee. He had worked hard to establish a reputation for moderation, supporting free soil while renouncing abolitionism as counterproductive. A native southerner, he hailed from an important "doubtful" state that he could virtually guarantee to the Republicans.[28]

The Republican convention, meeting in Chicago in May, initially leaned toward Seward. Lincoln's supporters argued that he was the only Republican who had a chance of winning the entire North. They won pledges from Seward, Sumner, and Chase delegates to make him their second choice. During the balloting, Lincoln sat nervously in the telegraph office in Springfield awaiting the result. As support for the leading contenders faded, Lincoln's friends sent him telegrams that grew increasingly confident in tone: "We are quiet but moving heaven & Earth"—"Prospects fair friends at work night & day"—"Dont be frightend keep cool things is working"— "Am hopeful dont be Excited." Finally, after the third ballot, the word arrived: "To Abe Lincoln We did it glory to God." In the general election, Lincoln captured all but three electoral votes in the free states. He won a resounding victory in the electoral college but less than 40 percent of the overall popular vote.[29]

Lincoln never doubted that free soil, the foundation of the Republican Party, could arrest the spread of slavery westward and gradually but inevitably produce its "ultimate extinction," throughout the South and in Washington, DC. He held true to this principle during the secession crisis, when he repeatedly denied any interest in undermining slavery in the District of Columbia. In December 1860, for example, he replied to a query from a southern conservative that "I have no thought of recommending the abolition of slavery in the District of Columbia, nor the slave trade among the slave states, even on the conditions indicated; and if I were to make such recommendation, it is quite clear Congress would not follow it." In February 1861, he wrote to Senator William Seward, his future secretary of state, to delineate exactly where he would and would not compromise. He reiterated his long-established principle that "on the territorial question—that is, the question of extending slavery under the national auspices, —I am inflexible. I am for no compromise which assists or permits the extension of the institution on soil owned by the nation." He then embedded abolition in the nation's capital into a list of questions on which he was indeed willing to be flexible. "As to fugitive slaves, District of Columbia, slave trade among the slave states, and whatever springs of necessity from the fact that the institution is amongst us, I care but little," he assured Seward, "so that what is done be comely, and not altogether outrageous." "Altogether outrageous" was likely a reference to immediate and uncompensated emancipation. Given his experiences during the 30th Congress, Lincoln undoubtedly viewed outright abolition in the capital as both impossible and counterproductive.[30]

By 1860, the nation's most committed abolitionists approved of Lincoln's strategy for undermining slavery. During the campaign, Gerrit Smith, the Radical Abolition candidate for president, wrote of Lincoln that "I feel confident that he is in his heart an abolitionist." Certain of Republican victory, Smith assured Joshua Giddings that "Lincoln will be President—& his victory will be regarded by the South as an Abolition victory—not less so than if you yourself were elected President." Joshua Leavitt, who had helped turn Mrs. Sprigg's into "Abolition House" nearly twenty years earlier, originally dismissed Lincoln as "a Southern Man" and supported Seward as the ideal Republican nominee. After the Chicago convention, Leavitt concluded that Lincoln embodied the "nature, object and spirit of the party" after all. Lincoln's election delighted him, and he wrote to former Ohio governor Salmon Chase, "Thank God! Lincoln is chosen. It is a joy to have lived to this day." Then he literally counted down the hours until the inauguration. "Only 47½ hours—and then! Hurrah for President Lincoln!" he wrote to his brother.[31]

By now, even Giddings believed in Lincoln. After leaving the Whigs in 1848 to support the new Free Soil Party, he joined the Republicans in the wake of the Kansas-Nebraska Act. Despite his earlier concerns about his messmate's timidity, he now considered Lincoln as sound on the slavery question as the better-known Republican radicals Seward and Chase. Above all, he concluded, "I know him to be *honest* and faithful." In December 1860, Giddings visited the president-elect, this time on Lincoln's home ground, the house at Eighth and Jackson in Springfield, where they sat in the parlor and reminisced cheerfully about their time together at Mrs. Sprigg's. "I found Lincoln unaltered in his appearance, manners, &c.," he wrote to his daughter. "He laughs as heartily and tells as good a story as ever." Mary Lincoln, Giddings reported, "is *smart*, and speaks right out in plain terms what she thinks, but blushed much when I spoke to her of the White House." In a passage that may betray a lingering personal friction between the two from their days at Mrs. Sprigg's, Giddings observed less charitably that "Mrs Lincoln has grown more stout" over the intervening years.[32]

From the other side of the sectional divide, native Kentuckian Duff Green supported the Constitutional Union Party and its nominee, John Bell. A passionate promoter of southern economic development who was equally devoted to the Union, Green rejected any hint of sectionalism that might provoke secession. After the election, at the behest of President Buchanan, he paid a secret visit to Lincoln in Springfield to solicit a commitment to a constitutional amendment that might avert the impending civil war, probably a guarantee of slavery in the southern states. After they met, Lincoln wrote Green bluntly that "I do not desire any amendment of the Constitution." Green was disappointed but remained convinced that Lincoln meant to treat the South fairly. After secession, he left Washington and settled in Georgia to support the Confederacy in the name of southern economic independence. His mines and mills in Georgia and Tennessee proved crucial to the Confederate war effort, producing almost one-half of the South's output of iron for rifles, shot, horseshoes, and railroads. In his absence, the U.S. government commandeered Duff Green's Row as the property of a secessionist and put it to use in the Union war effort. Green never returned to Washington.[33]

Like Green, Georgia's Alexander Stephens, Lincoln's onetime confidant and fellow Young Indian, also feared disunion. Anxiously awaiting the election of 1860, Stephens avowed, "My greatest desire is to defeat Lincoln and thus prevent the evils that such an event might precipitate upon us." Resolving to support Stephen Douglas instead, he predicted, "Should Mr. Breckinridge get the entire South and Lincoln the entire North no earthly power could prevent civil war." Even this pragmatic southern moderate concluded that "I do not know that it can be anyhow should Lincoln be elected." After opposing secession, he became vice president of the Confederacy.[34]

PART II

"Cleaning the Devil
Out of Washington"

CHAPTER FIVE

"A Wide Spread and Powerful Conspiracy"
Warnings and Threats from Washington

O N FEBRUARY 11, 1861, Abraham Lincoln stood at the rear of a train as it was about to pull away from the Great Western railroad depot in Springfield at the beginning of his journey to Washington, DC. "Here I have lived a quarter of century, and have passed from a young to an old man," he told the thousand friends, neighbors, and well-wishers who had gathered to see him off. "Here my children have been born, and one is buried," he continued, commemorating little Edward Baker Lincoln, or Eddie, who had died in 1850, less than a year after Lincoln concluded his congressional term in Washington. After noting this touching, premature death, Lincoln ominously forecast another—his own. "I now leave, not knowing when, or whether ever, I may return," he told the crowd, "with a task before me greater than that which rested upon Washington."[1]

Lincoln had good reason to question his own survival. After his election, he received a flood of hate mail from enemies and worrisome warnings from political supporters and friends. The deluge began just two days after he was elected, when "A Citizen" in Pensacola, Florida, sent him an ambiguous telegram that said simply, "You were last night hung in effigy in this city." Less enigmatically, a well-wisher wrote from Philadelphia to warn Lincoln that "I firmly believe that some reckless culprit will attempt to assassinate both you & Mr. Hamlin either at your own home on your way to Washington or there even at the time of the inauguration if not before."

Threatening letters from the Deep South confirmed that impression and reflected the mounting anger of slaveowners who feared the impending loss of their slaves and the way of life that slavery supported. "God damn your god damned old Hellfired god damned soul to hell god damn you and goddam your god damned family's god damned hellfired god damned soul to hell and god damnation god damn them and god damn your god damn friends to hell god damn their god damned souls to damnation god damn them and god dam their god damn families to eternal god damnation god damn souls to hell god damn them," ran one signed letter from Louisiana. While southerners issued their threats openly, letters from the North were usually anonymous. One note read succinctly, "May the hand of the devil strike you down before long—You are destroying the country Damn you—every breath you take."[2]

A slaveowner from Tennessee sent a runaway notice that began "On the 27th of December, 1860, my negro man left my residence in this place, no doubt with the intention to escape to a free State." The notice provided a detailed description of the fugitive slave and offered a $50 reward for his return. A handwritten note told Lincoln, "You damned old negro thief if you dont find the above described slave, you shall never be inaugurated President of the United States—You old cuss—When you find him you must send him right home." The vilest letter told Lincoln that "you are nothing but a goddam Black nigger" and warned him that "if you don't Resign we are going to put a spider in your dumpling and play the Devil with you." Revealing the personal animosity that racism infused into many of the threats Lincoln received, the writer called the president-elect a "mighty god dam sundde of a bith" and told him "go to hell and buss my Ass suck my prick." John G. Nicolay, Lincoln's newly appointed private secretary who screened all of his incoming mail, found it "infested with brutal and vulgar menace." Lincoln undoubtedly read many of these troubling missives himself but apparently did not consider them important. Before leaving for Washington, he decided to destroy them. After collecting an "armful" of sinister letters, he carried them downstairs from his law office to the cabinetmaker's shop below to toss them unceremoniously into a stove. When the cabinetmaker asked if he could keep them, Lincoln good-naturedly complied, unwittingly preserving this legendary collection of "hot stove letters" for posterity. Mary Lincoln received similar disturbing threats, including a portrait of her tarred and feathered husband with chains on his feet and a rope around his neck that arrived from South Carolina.[3]

Much more ominous, however, were the letters that not only damned Lincoln to hell but disclosed specific plans to assassinate him and seize the capital. "Caesar had his Brutus. Charles the First his Cromwell. And the President may profit by their example," read a sinister letter from Washington. The author claimed membership in "a sworn band of 10, who have resolved to shoot you in the inaugural procession." Writing from Baltimore to confirm the validity of this threat, "A Lady" warned that "I think it my duty to inform you that I was advised last night by a gentleman that there existed in Baltimore, a league of ten persons, who had sworn that you should never pass through that city alive." From the other side of the Potomac, a well-intentioned Virginian warned that "I have heard several persons in this place say that if you ever did take the President Chair that they would go to washington City expressly to kill you." The writer called himself "a friend of yours" and offered to "go to washington City and raise a body of men to guard you." Some of Lincoln's hate mail constituted assassination attempts in their own right. "You would explode with laughter," legal colleague Henry C. Whitney related, "to hear him tell about the southerners trying to assassinate him. He has got stacks of preserved fruit and all sorts of such trash which he is daily receiving from various parts of the south, sent to him as presents." Lending gravity to Lincoln's complacent reaction, Whitney reported, "He had several packages opened and examined by medical men who found them to be all poisoned."[4]

Writing from the capital, Joseph Medill, the Washington correspondent of the *Chicago Tribune*, confirmed the severity of the threats, informing Lincoln that "the secessionists are seriously contemplating resistance to your inauguration in this Capitol." Raising the specter of the spontaneous mob actions that littered the city's history, Medill reported that "the Union & loyal sentiment of her citizens is gradually

giving way, and the vicious rabble are getting control." He predicted
that by the time of the inauguration "the city will be under complete control of Disunion vigilance committees and a reign of terror
will domineer." Broadening the scope of the conspiracy well beyond
the "10 sworn men" of the anonymous missives, Medill concluded,
"There is certainly a secret organization in this city numbering several hundred members having that purpose in view—sworn armed
men." Elihu Washburne, an Illinois congressman and Lincoln's old
friend, relayed a credible report of "*a wide spread and powerful conspiracy to seize the capitol.*" He questioned the loyalty of the southern-
dominated federal bureaucracy, declaring that "all the Departments
are now filled with traitorous clerks, who would do all in their power
to surrender up the buildings to a hostile force." His proposed solution was reinforcing Washington with a formidable military force
before the president-elect arrived. "Now the only thing to prevent
the attempt will be the presence here of a sufficient force to hold
the city against all comers," he advised, suggesting that "in addition
to the 600 or 700 regulars now here, there should be at least 10,000
volunteers."[5]

Some of Lincoln's friends considered bypassing the military
authorities, whom they distrusted, and mounting a vigilante action
of their own. Major David Hunter wrote from Fort Leavenworth
to warn of a conspiracy to use the army and navy to "keep possession of the government." Hunter was a thoroughly trustworthy ally
whose grandfather had signed the Declaration of Independence. A
Republican stalwart during the recent election campaign, Hunter
now suggested using the party's paramilitary arm, the Wide Awakes,
to secure the fruits of victory. "Would it not be well, to have a hundred thousand Wide Awakes, wend their way quietly to Washington,
during the first three days of March: taking with them their capes
and caps?" he wondered. "By a *coup-de-main* we could arm them in
Washington." James Watson Webb, a New York newspaper editor,
warned that Washington "can and will be taken from us if they desire
it; & they would indeed be *fools* were they not to seize it." He urged
Lincoln to "arrange to have at least five thousand persons in Wash-

ington, a week previous to the inauguration, ready in case of necessity." In Washington, a critic of these plans noted that the city had ten thousand men eager to come to its defense and dismissed the idea of "a counter Northern mob invasion," which he ascribed to "timid Republicans." More pointedly, a resolution adopted by the National Rifles, a volunteer unit comprising federal employees, warned against arming the Wide Awakes, because "these sympathizers with John Brown may make similar assaults upon life and property in this city." Property, of course, meant slavery.[6]

A more judicious solution was to summon Lincoln to Washington before the situation could escalate beyond anyone's control. Lincoln's choice for his secretary of state, New York senator William Seward, suggested just that. "There is a feverish excitement here which awakens all kind of apprehensions of popular disturbance and disorders, connected with your assumption of the governmt," Seward warned Lincoln. "Habit has accustomed the public to anticipate the arrival of the President elect in this city about the middle of February and evil minded persons could expect to organize their demonstrations for that time," he reasoned. "I beg leave to suggest whether it would not be well for you Keeping your own counsel, to be *prepared* to drop into the City a week or ten days earlier.—The effect would probably be reassuring and soothing." Joseph Medill proposed a combination of the Hunter and Seward plans, in which Lincoln would arrive in Washington early—and unannounced—to rally the city's Unionists and attract others from the northern free states. "Would it not be a *coup d etat*, were you to quietly, with only a carpet sack, get on the cars, and drop down in this city some day next week or very soon," he asked Lincoln. "Would it not knock over and discourage all the plans of the traitors, and show them they had a second Jackson to deal with. Thousands of our friends would then flock here from all parts, and Maryland would remain loyal." Medill cut to the heart of the matter when he declared, "It is all important that you take the oath of office here on the 4th of March on the steps of the capital. The moral effect will be worth an army of 10,000 men."[7]

Friends had good reason to fear "violence on the person of Lincoln" not only via the mails but in the national capital itself. As the president-elect knew all too well from his personal experiences as a congressman, Washington, DC, was a dangerous place to live even during the best of times. As an artificial community that was the focus of national political contention, the capital was subject to frequent civil and partisan upheavals that periodically disrupted its tenuous social fabric. Like most other antebellum cities, Washington suffered a series of race riots and anti-abolition actions beginning in the 1830s. In 1835, a week-long riot erupted after a slave tried to murder the widow of William Thornton, the architect of the U.S. Capitol building. The primary target of the mob action, a free African American restaurant owner, Beverly Snow, lent his name to the episode, which became known as the "Snow Riot" or "Snow Storm." This outbreak of racial violence, which required intervention from the federal government and the District of Columbia's militia, prompted enactment of a harsher Black Code and probably contributed to adoption of the congressional gag rule, silencing congressional debate over slavery, in the following year. Lincoln's memories of the April 1848 "*National Era* Riots" undoubtedly fed his doubts about the prospects for emancipation in the national capital and his apprehensions about the city's propensity for spontaneous proslavery violence.[8]

Washington's fundamental problem was its inadequate, politically infused, and racially biased police force. Since its founding, the city had suffered an insufficient tax base, because the federal government owned so much of the land and buildings. The constant, bitter complaint was that "nearly half the property in the city—that is to say, all Government property, including public buildings and public grounds—is exempt from taxation." Even the wide avenues and geometric pattern of spacious city squares that distinguished Pierre L'Enfant's original plan diminished the amount of land that was subject to taxation, leaving city services, including the police, underfunded and understaffed. "We never could comprehend the object of the original projectors of this city in laying out the city on such a plan as it presents," ran one complaint. The diagonal pattern of the wide avenues, fetching on paper, created hundreds of triangles that sat empty through disuse. "There is not a city in the country where the proportion of land occupied by streets, avenues, and alleys occupy so great a proportion of area, as in this city."⁹

At its founding, Washington joined other American cities in establishing a paid, albeit underpaid, daytime force of constables supplemented by a voluntary night watch or "patrol." This customary "constabulary-watch system" left the national capital, like other cities, insecure after dark. When arson destroyed the Capitol Library in 1825, Congress stepped in at last and provided a federally funded night watch. Originally a mere force of two restricted to guarding the Capitol building and its grounds, in 1842 the night police expanded into an Auxiliary Guard charged with "the protection of public and private property" after sunset. This federal overlay gave the city its "dual police system" of daytime and nighttime police forces but also created a perennial and troublesome tug-of-war between municipal and congressional responsibility for protecting Washington. Too often, neither level of government took responsibility for securing the city.¹⁰

Within this patchwork system of policing, corruption—both financial and political—reigned. To supplement their deficient salaries, the police grew dependent on collecting fines, which they were allowed to pocket as fees for enforcing the laws. The police kept fees even if a case was dismissed, so they had every incentive to make an arrest on the slightest of pretexts. The mayor himself recognized the abuses inherent in this antiquated fee system, arguing with considerable understatement that "a strong inducement is held out to the officers to take out legal processes without due examination of the grounds of action." The predictable result was "oppression on the poor and the ignorant, particularly on the free negroes." A primary function of the constables was control of the city's African Americans, both slave and free, through enforcement of the law that prevented any "black person or person of colour" from assembling or even "walking about" after the 10:00 P.M. curfew subject to a $10 fine. "The day and night police of Washington city are worthless. They protect no one's person or property—prevent no fires or burglaries, and detect none of the offenders," one bitter Washingtonian charged. "Instead of vigilantly watching the property of the citizens, they are generally engaged to preserve order at negro dances, getting $2 50 a night each, in addition to their city pay, and being white gemmen, have the first choice of the liquor."[11]

Any slave violating the Black Code was liable "to receive any number of stripes, on his or her bare back, not exceeding thirty-nine, but it shall be optional with such slave, to have the punishment commuted for the payment of the fine." Fines were therefore "commutation fees," on which the city depended to fund the police. When the constables administered a whipping, they received a fifty-cent fee. (During Lincoln's second month in the White House, a group of visitors explained that they "were late getting here, as their driver, who was a constable, had to stop to whip a nigger!") The police grew dependent on this "whipping fee," gleaned from scourging both men and women, to supplement their salaries. Any free African American who refused to pay a fine under the Black Code was sent to the city's "work-house" for up to six months to pay it off, so the city used the Black Code as a vital source of revenue. In the decade before the Civil War, the Washington police arrested African Americans at three times the rate of whites. The provisions of the Black Code, according to the Washington *Evening Star*, "certainly afford opportunities for extortion from and oppression of negroes by unprincipled magistrates, county officers and policemen, who will always exist where the law affords them such opportunities." Rampant arbitrary arrests, which targeted African Americans, turned the county jail, the infamous "Blue Jug," into a veritable slave pen. A U.S. senator from Iowa decried the fee system, charging that "if a slave wandered a certain distance from the master's residence, even to pick berries or visit a friend, there were harpies lying in wait who arrested and imprisoned the slave, and when weeks afterwards the master discovered the condition of his servant he could not reclaim him without paying jailor's fees, justice's fees, constable's fees, and an 'apprehension' fee, which was the temptation for such arrests." After passage of the Fugitive Slave Law in 1850, federal fees for the arrest of runaways became available, heightening the temptation to arrest African Americans. The police now became "engaged in the *procurement of the arrest of negroes* as fugitive slaves, for the purpose of realizing the apprehension fees."[12]

The fee system also turned the police force into a lucrative source of patronage appointments for Washington's mayors. In response to this endemic police corruption, in 1851 the city raised police salaries and ended the fee system, and Congress doubled the federally funded Auxiliary Guard. Still, political, ethnic, and religious divisions plagued the police throughout the 1850s. As immigration mounted, nativist movements, including the American Party, or "Know Nothings," attempted to force recent immigrants and Catholics out of the American political system. In 1854, Washington's Know Nothings exploited rising ethnic tensions to elect a mayor who politicized the police, producing a series of election-day riots. Riddled with partisan appointees, originally Know Nothings and later Democrats, the police not only ignored election-day violence but often abetted it. At the same time, Washington's underfunded fire department depended on volunteers, who organized six rival engine companies that reflected political and ethnic divisions and functioned as undisciplined gangs beyond any police control.[13]

During the mayoral election of 1857, the police force fomented a riot designed to subvert the political process and consolidate the Know Nothings' power. Washington's fire companies and nativist "Plug Uglies" from Baltimore joined the police in disrupting the election and intimidating immigrants and Catholics at the polls. During this predictable eruption of political violence, President Buchanan called out one hundred marines to restore order. The Plugs, who commanded a six-pound cannon, threw stones and fired revolvers at the marines, who fired back, killing eight rioters and wounding more than twenty. The resulting turmoil, which one newspaper labeled "a perfect hell," continued for weeks. With firemen rioting, vigilantism raging, and the captain of the Auxiliary Guard surviving an assassination attempt, the city outlawed the carrying of weapons, enumerated as "dagger, pistol, bowie-knife, dirk-knife or dirk, colt slung-shot or brass or other metal knuckles."[14]

In the following year, Washington enlarged its police force and attempted to instill needed discipline by adopting a uniform, consisting of a blue frock coat, blue pantaloons with a white stripe, and a cap bearing a badge labeled CITY POLICE. To prevent another election-day riot, the city appointed thirty additional policemen to every precinct, authorized them to carry arms, and banned anyone else from carrying a weapon. During this relatively peaceful election, a major shift in Washington politics occurred when a Democrat, James Berret, defeated Richard Wallach, who ten years earlier had helped Duff Green secure the release of Henry Wilson from the Alexandria slave pen. Berret responded by politicizing the newly expanded police force by packing it with Democrats. During the 1860 mayoral election, a mysterious "target company," including members of the police and Auxiliary Guard, appeared in the city. Armed with muskets and bayonets and conducting public military drills, they systematically disrupted Republican Party meetings. In a vote that was marred by corruption, intimidation, and police intervention, Berret defeated Wallach a second time, leaving the city, as the *Evening Star* cautioned, "at the mercy of a murderous mob." Even the fiercest political opponents, Senators William Seward and Stephen Douglas, could agree on one thing, that "life is not safe in this city at present."[15]

In a challenge that was unique to the capital, presidential inaugurations had always prompted both the threat and reality of civil disruption. The city routinely expanded its police force and hired plainclothes detectives from New York and Philadelphia to try to head off trouble, but the sectional crisis and the debate over slavery only heightened the danger. The inaugurations of the Whig Zachary Taylor and the Democrat James Buchanan were particularly contentious. During Buchanan's inauguration, the city appointed an "extra police force" of one hundred men to supplement the permanent complement of sixty. Now, in this politically, racially, and ethnically charged atmosphere, and in the midst of disunion, the inauguration of the nation's first Republican president promised to be even more chaotic and potentially explosive.[16]

While threats and warnings poured into Springfield from across the country, Washington exhibited a heightened level of political conflict of its own that accentuated its traditional culture of civil violence and made the city an exceedingly dangerous place to live. As the nation divided in the wake of Lincoln's election, so did Washington. On election night, yet another of Washington's fabled riots erupted. During the presidential campaign, supporters of Southern Democratic nominee John Breckinridge organized a militia unit, the National Volunteers, to campaign on his behalf. As election night ended, fifty to sixty members of the unit met at the Breckinridge campaign headquarters on Pennsylvania Avenue and resolved to march to the Republican headquarters and "wreck the shanty." Republicans had taken over the editorial offices of the *National Era*, which folded the year before when its editor, Gamaliel Bailey, died. Washington Republicans dubbed the press building the "Wigwam" in honor of the famous temporary structure in Chicago where their party had nominated Lincoln in May 1860. As the National Volunteers moved toward the Wigwam, they gathered up 250 or 300 of their members, who lined up in formation and marched in ranks to their target. To shouts of "Burn it down," they fired pistols and threw stones, smashing the windows on the front of the building. They broke inside, destroyed flags and banners, demolished the furniture, and forced the occupants to scramble onto the rooftop. When the police arrived fifteen minutes later, three Republicans asked to be arrested for their own protection. The Night Watch's "gray coats" arrested just five of the rioters and allowed the rest to carry off two banners, presumably as trophies. After their "sack" of the Wigwam, the Volunteers reassembled, received the commendation of their captain, obeyed an order to "fall in and move off," and marched away. The melee, dubbed the "Wigwam Riot," joined the Snow Riot of 1835 and the *National Era* Riots of 1848 among the most violent episodes of civil disorder in Washington's history. Unlike the earlier outbreaks, however, the Wigwam Riot was a carefully orchestrated, partisan action organized with military precision by proslavery Democrats protesting the outcome of the presidential election and, more broadly, intimidating Lincoln supporters. Ostensibly an arm of the Breckinridge presidential campaign, the National Volunteers continued to muster and drill long after the election was over.[17]

During the months to come, a wave of political violence swept the city. At the National Hotel, a Washington lawyer who supported Lincoln argued with a Democrat, pulled a knife, and tried to stab him. "Politics was the cause of the difficulty," according to the *National Republican*. In a beer saloon, a Republican partisan was "knocked flat" by a Douglas supporter during a political melee. During another political dispute at the National Hotel, Illinois congressman William Kellogg attacked Lincoln's colleague and confidant Joseph Medill, who "received some pretty severe blows about the head and face." Two rowdies confronted a German immigrant peddling balloons to children in front of the hotel, cut his balloons loose, hit him, and called him a "d——d Black Republican." On Christmas Day, thirty to forty Plug Uglies fomented a riot, throwing stones, swinging clubs, and firing pistols when police arrived. On the same day, a second riot erupted near the Navy Yard. A hundred rowdies wielding fence pickets, stones, clubs, and brickbats tried to fight off the police, who shot one of the rioters.[18]

After South Carolina seceded on December 20, 1860, "Palmetto" badges and cockades began appearing on lapels, caps, and bonnets, sporting blue rosettes and ribbons fastened with gilt buttons bearing an image of the palmetto tree. Even more ominously, Virginia and Maryland cockades soon proliferated. Opponents of secession answered with their own Union badges and shields. The Union cockade was a double rosette—white silk on red silk—trailing blue ribbons, all held together by a gilt button featuring an eagle and a ring of stars. When the New York 7th Regiment's band serenaded the Lincolns, Willie and Tad stood on the South Portico wearing Union badges on their jackets. Starting a process that would soon escalate beyond anyone's imagination, Washingtonians began paying a price for expressing their political opinions. When a cabinet officer asked a subordinate about the badge he was wearing, he replied, "Sir, that is a Palmetto badge and signifies that I am for secession." He was fired immediately. After a mechanic working on the new Capitol dome expressed his approval of Lincoln's election, his foreman let him go. When a Connecticut military unit, the Putnam Phalanx, arrived in the capital, a bystander was arrested for calling them "a set of abolition sons of b——hs." Mimicking—or mocking—the newly adopted police badge, Plug Uglies now donned "secession badges" of their own and rioted with a purpose. Already bitter rivals, fire companies adopted formal resolutions declaring their allegiances.[19]

While Washington's secessionists openly paraded their disunion emblems, the more secretive adopted the city's traditional and stealthy tool of protest, fire. Lincoln's election provoked a wave of arson that the city's police were unprepared to combat. "Scarcely a night passes but there is one or more fires," a Washington businessman warned, "and some of them very destructive." He proposed the formation of a citizen patrol on every public square to "curb this spirit of incendiarism." Amid constant complaints that the official night watch, the congressionally established Auxiliary Guard, was insufficient, Washingtonians expressed "despair of any aid from Mayor Berret or his police in putting an end to the incendiaries so rife in this city." The vigilantes took action, dividing their wards into districts and appointing watch captains. Confirming the ineffectiveness of the police, the patrolmen reported "a standing topic of surprise that they never by any chance encounter a watchman." Only after the patrols were established and proved their effectiveness, including one on Pennsylvania Avenue, did Berret agree to commission the vigilantes as a special voluntary police force. Amid the escalating and increasingly strident political conflict, the *Evening Star* reported, "Yesterday, a young man, who probably possesses an average share of brains when in the use of his faculties, was observed passing about the streets of the city and the various public places, wearing a large label on his breast, which at first was mistaken for the sign of a peddler, who might have trinkets of some sort for sale; but upon closer inspection, it proved to be a placard announcing his political proclivities."[20]

In the absence of a coordinated defense among the army, the navy, and the marines or any precautionary measures on the part of the Buchanan administration, some Lincoln supporters suggested turning to the northern states to provide help in securing the capital. Lincoln's old messmate from "Abolition House," Joshua Giddings, agreed on the necessity of military action to protect Washington but proposed a more practical approach. "Sir. I would respectfully suggest, that the time has arrived when the free states should pre-

pare for concerted and efficient action to insure your inauguration at
the federal city," Giddings advised. "Of course you cannot act officially; but your secretary of war may with great propriety express
his desire to see a specific programme of preparation carried out by
the states." Lincoln's designated secretary of war was Pennsylvanian
Simon Cameron, one of his rivals for the Republican nomination. At
the beginning of January, Cameron met with Buchanan's general-
in-chief, Winfield Scott, and decided that he was committed to preventing disunion, safeguarding Washington, and protecting Lincoln
during his inauguration. "I have seen Genl. Scott, who bid me say
he will be glad to act under your orders, in all ways to preserve the
Union," Cameron reported. "He says Mr Buchanan, at last, has called
on him to see that order shall be preserved at the inauguration in
this District." Noting that Scott promised to assume the role of city
constable if necessary, Cameron assured Lincoln, "The old warrior is
roused, and he will be equal to the occasion." Elihu Washburne also
met with Scott but was less sanguine than Cameron. "It appears to
be well understood that there now exists a formidable conspiracy to
seize the capitol," he reported. "In it are men of high public position."
Fortunately, both Buchanan and Scott were at last taking action to
allay the danger. "Every possible means," Washburne assured Lincoln, "will be taken to protect the city." Following up his meetings
with Lincoln's emissaries, Scott wrote to Lincoln personally. "The
President elect may rely, with confidence, on Genl. S's utmost exertions in the service of his country (the *Union*) both before & after the
approaching inauguration."[21]

BEYOND WASHINGTON'S untrustworthy police department and the
volatility of its citizens, the city sat virtually undefended. The nearest military stronghold, Fort Washington, fifteen miles south on the
Potomac, was designed to repel a foreign rather than domestic invasion and had sat ungarrisoned for years. The city's military force, in
the words of its wartime provost marshal, "consisted chiefly of General Scott, his staff and orderlies, and the marine band." Some of
Lincoln's closest advisors also doubted the loyalty of the army itself

under the Buchanan administration. Despite Scott's assurances to the contrary, Lincoln's allies—and possibly Lincoln himself—continued to worry that neither Scott nor President Buchanan was fully committed to securing Washington during the upcoming inauguration or even holding the city as the Union capital. Before the November election Scott had counseled Lincoln to pursue "moderation" in dealing with secession and confided that he preferred the Constitutional Union ticket of Tennessee's John Bell, who was committed to compromise. Scott's own chief of staff had defected to the Confederacy. Now, New York editor James Watson Webb heard through Scott's private secretary that "the Genl. *expects* to see the capital fall, & that Buchanan peremptorily refuses to furnish the means to protect & defend it." Joseph Medill was equally alarmed and assured Lincoln, "It is the plan of the disunionists to have an army in this city within five weeks, to drive out the Republican members and to prevent your inauguration by force."[22]

Foreshadowing one of his key roles during the first year of the Lincoln administration, Seward took both decisive and clandestine action to safeguard Washington's—and Lincoln's—security. In December, he had received direct warnings of an assassination plot, including a letter disclosing that "there is a combination to prevent the inauguration of the Prest elect even at the peril of his life. What an exposed situation he would be in for 15 minutes on the Eastern Portico!" He now proceeded on three fronts to get to the bottom of the suspected conspiracy and try to head it off. First, he worked with a handful of other Republican congressmen to hire two New York City police detectives to investigate the rumors. Second, he developed a secret relationship with an informant inside the Buchanan administration who provided him with confidential details about the president's policies and the inner workings of the cabinet. None other than Edwin Stanton, Buchanan's own attorney general and Lincoln's second secretary of war, communicated with Seward daily through an intermediary, who passed on the administration's most sensitive secrets to the incoming secretary of state. Stanton, who considered himself the only voice of reason in an otherwise treasonous cabinet, allowed Seward to apprise Lincoln about the secret arrangement.

This extraordinary partnership between Stanton and Seward, which became public knowledge five years after the war ended, foreshadowed the secretive relationship that the two later developed within the Lincoln administration to monitor potentially treasonous behavior within Washington during the Civil War.[23]

Seward's third initiative centered on a congressional inquiry to expose and therefore quash any conspiracy that might be brewing in the capital to prevent Lincoln's inauguration by assassinating him or seizing the city. On January 9, at the likely behest of the newly forged team of Seward and Stanton, the House of Representatives established a committee of five members to investigate the Buchanan administration's response to South Carolina's secession. Seward quickly converted this Select Committee of Five into a Republican tool for exposing subversive activities in both Washington and Baltimore in advance of the inauguration. By the end of the month, the House adopted a resolution that Seward had drafted instructing the committee "to inquire whether any secret organization hostile to the government of the United States exists in the District of Columbia." Popularly dubbed the "Treason Committee," the panel began investigating, in the words of its chair, "those ten thousand rumors that are afloat, and which may do mischief, if ever so false, and which will certainly do mischief if true."[24]

The testimony of the committee's first witness, James Berret, Washington's Democratic mayor and a Breckinridge supporter during the election, exuded complacency but could hardly have inspired confidence in the capital's security. While admitting that he had heard reports of a threatened secessionist conspiracy within his own city, Berret dismissed them out of hand. "I have so frequently received anonymous communications, threatening myself and the President and other people," he testified, "that I never attach any consequence to anonymous communications." Minimizing any threats from within Washington, Berret diverted the focus to the possibility of an external attack from Maryland or Virginia. "I have not been able to ascertain the slightest ground for any apprehensions that there has been contemplated, or that there is likely to be contemplated," he assured the committee, "any foray or raid upon the city of Washington." As for internal security during Lincoln's inauguration, Berret announced coolly that "I shall deem it wholly unnecessary to add one solitary man to the police force of this city." His rhetorical confidence in the police belied the long-standing tradition of augmenting the force during presidential inaugurations, and he himself admitted that he had appointed two hundred special police officers during a far less dramatic event, the "inauguration of the statue of Washington," just a year before. Those police, he reported, were appointed primarily "to keep the streets clear of carriages." Overlooking his city's long history of spontaneous mob violence at the hands of proslavery rowdies and nativist Plug Uglies, Berret concluded that "I do not believe there is a solitary man in this city, with any claims to decency and standing, who would attempt to place the slightest impediment in the way of the peaceable inauguration of Mr. Lincoln." Still, he admitted that he had not investigated the possibility of a secret organization of less respectable character operating within the city. When asked about the National Volunteers, Berret overlooked their election-night raid on the Wigwam and dismissed them as "a mere political organization." He argued that they did not operate in secret and therefore did not fall under the committee's charge to investigate "any secret organization." As for the Washington police, Berret characterized them, ominously, as "perfectly loyal—as perfectly within my command," meaning perfectly loyal to the mayor.[25]

General-in-Chief Scott, who had already pledged his personal fealty toward Lincoln, challenged Berret's rosy assessment of the city's security. "I have received innumerable letters from probably, thirteen to sixteen States, three and four, and up to seven, a day," he testified, "since it was known that I had been charged by the President with the peace and security of this city." Half of the communications were anonymous. He concluded judiciously, "Some sort of conspiracy obviously exists, either for mischief or creating a false alarm." There were "several objects," in his opinion—seizing control of the Capitol and other government buildings, disrupting the counting of the electoral votes on February 13, and preventing Lincoln's inauguration. Scott reviewed in detail the security measures that he had undertaken, such as the posting of eight military companies— roughly five hundred soldiers—at key points during the inauguration and mustering 240 marines at the Navy Yard. Limiting his responsibility to securing the national capital, Scott disclosed, disturbingly, that he had not ordered an escort for Lincoln between Springfield and Washington. The president-elect remained vulnerable throughout his journey to the capital, particularly during his passage through Baltimore, where he would need to change trains.[26]

The committee's final witness, Maryland governor Thomas H. Hicks, signaled the precarious condition of his border state when he refused to come to Washington to testify. Hicks was a mercurial politician who had pursued a circuitous route through the Democratic, Whig, Know Nothing, and Constitutional Union parties but remained a steadfast Unionist throughout. (In Maryland, which was heavily Catholic, Know Nothings substituted Unionism for the national organization's obsession with nativism and religious intolerance.) As a slaveowning Unionist, Hicks nevertheless harbored a grievance against the North for its haphazard enforcement, and indeed obstruction, of the Fugitive Slave Law. In the face of the escalating secession movement, Hicks struggled mightily to keep Maryland neutral, within the political and cultural "Middle Ground" that the Border State traditionally occupied. He snubbed an emissary from the Deep South, who was a personal friend, and refused to convene the legislature for fear of precipitating secession, actions for which he himself, like Lincoln, courted assassination. When the Committee of Five traveled to Annapolis to hear his testimony, Hicks confirmed the reports of an organized movement to attack the government in Washington but insisted that it had disbanded to pursue secession rather than a forcible takeover of the capital. He also acknowledged "secret organizations now in the city of Baltimore" but characterized them as "limited in numbers and in power." After giving up the idea of a direct attack on Washington, they still hoped to disrupt the government. Other witnesses from Baltimore reported the formation of military companies to resist a "northern invasion" and "prevent northern volunteer companies from coming through." More diplomatically, Governor Hicks characterized these efforts as "thwarting the regular course of public affairs."[27]

The Committee of Five ended its mission to identify "secret organizations hostile to the government" by issuing the overly legalistic conclusion that the military companies drilling in Washington and Baltimore were "in no proper sense secret" and had no intention of acting "as a mere mob." They would act only under "the sanction of State authority, to attack the Capitol," meaning at the official behest of Maryland if that state seceded. Simply put, no secret organization would attack Washington or the government "upon its own responsibility." On the existence of any organized threat within the city, the committee was utterly silent. As the *Evening Star* put it, the committee "developed nothing to lead to the impression that there has existed anything like an organization for such a purpose." Their final report also overlooked the imminent threat to federal troops who might need to pass through Baltimore to come to the capital's defense. In fact, Washington's secessionists had refocused their efforts on Maryland, whose secession would render the capital strategically untenable. The goal, according to the editor of the *National Intelligencer,* was "hurrying Maryland out of the Union [whereby] they will inaugurate the new 'Southern Confederacy' in the present capital of the U. States." In this sense, the threat was no longer internal to Washington but external, dependent on the success of Maryland and Virginia's secessionists.[28]

As Seward himself acknowledged after the war, however, the true purpose of the committee was not to disperse disloyal organizations in the capital but to notify them that the government was aware of their existence and their plans and activities. From this perspective, the Committee of Five represented the first step in creating a comprehensive security apparatus that would monitor and detain pro-southern dissidents in Washington and Maryland throughout the course of the war. Well before Lincoln began his twelve-day journey from Springfield to Washington, the team of Seward and Stanton had effectively taken control of the defense of the capital, and Lincoln's allies had recruited General-in-Chief Scott into the devoted service of the incoming administration. After learning of a plot hatched in Baltimore to assassinate Lincoln before he could reach Washington, for example, Scott notified neither Buchanan nor the governor of Maryland nor the mayor of Baltimore, but relayed the warning directly to Lincoln's advisors, indeed to William Seward himself. In this fashion, the newly forged triumvirate of Seward, Stanton, and Scott solidified Republican control of Washington's security apparatus under the nose of the Buchanan administration months before Lincoln even reached the capital. Working clandestinely, they cleverly subverted a suspected southern, proslavery conspiracy into a northern, Republican takeover of the city.[29]

CHAPTER SIX

"The Way We Skulked into This City"
Claiming the Presidency

━━━━◆◆◆━━━━

GENERAL WINFIELD Scott's commitment and ability to maintain order in Washington was essential to Lincoln's safe arrival. Leaving nothing to chance, the president-elect sent a personal emissary, Illinois adjutant general Thomas Mather, to the War Department to gauge Scott's reliability. Despite his age and debilitating infirmities, the War of 1812 veteran and former Whig presidential nominee assured Mather that he was fully prepared to secure Washington in time for the inauguration. "His hair and beard were considerably disordered," Mather reported, and "the flesh seemed to lay in rolls across the warty face and neck, and his breathing was not without great labor." Still, the seventy-four-year-old general-in-chief exuded bravado, swearing that "I'll look after those Maryland and Virginia rangers myself; I'll plant cannon at both ends of Pennsylvania avenue, and if any of them show their heads or raise a finger I'll blow them to hell." Scott himself wrote to Lincoln, with what he called a "sick hand," to assure him that both President Buchanan and the secretary of war were now cooperating in the defense of the capital during both the counting of the electoral votes in mid-February and the inauguration on March 4. He also offered to "prepare" Lincoln for his new role as commander-in-chief by providing advice on military affairs. The next day, the secretary of the navy garrisoned Fort Washington at last but provided only 48 of the full complement of 400 men. By the end of the month, there were 250.[1]

The next step for Lincoln's team was to deliver him safely over the eight hundred miles that separated Springfield from the White House, a journey that meant traversing a dozen regional railroad lines that required repeated transfers between trains. Rumors circulated that Lincoln might bow to the mounting hate mail, take the oath of office in Springfield, and undertake the trip to Washington as a sitting president. Determined to assume the ultimate responsibility for his own security, Lincoln weighed the various risks himself. Dismissing the idea of arriving early in Washington or taking the oath in Springfield and arriving later, he identified what he considered a greater concern. "I have been considering your suggestions as to my reaching Washington somewhat earlier than is usual," he told Seward. "It seems to me the inauguration is not the most dangerous point for us. Our adversaries have us more clearly at disadvantage, on the second Wednesday of February, when the votes should be officially counted." As a good lawyer, Lincoln was more worried about disrupting the constitutionally mandated counting of the electoral votes than about his own personal safety. "In view of this," he instructed Seward, "I think it is best for me not to attempt appearing in Washington till the result of that ceremony is known."[2]

Given the cascading secession movement in the South and the escalating hostility in Virginia and Maryland, the choice of his route to the capital would be crucial. Lincoln assumed personal command of that decision as well. After his election, he received a flood of letters from railroad executives offering free transportation to Washington along with assurances of their ability to guarantee his safety. Lincoln himself preferred a direct and defiant route to Washington, along the Baltimore and Ohio line, that would take him through both Virginia and Maryland. "I think Mr. Lincoln's preferences are for a southerly route, via Cincinnati, Wheeling and Baltimore," Henry Villard, a journalist who befriended the president-elect, reported, "doubtless to demonstrate how little fear he entertains for his personal safety." Many supporters, however, advised him to avoid the southern route at all costs. The editor of the influential *New York Tribune*, Horace Greeley, reminded Lincoln that "your life is not safe, and it is your simple duty to be very careful of exposing it." He cautioned that "I doubt whether you ought to go to Washington via Wheeling and the B. & O. Railroad unless you go with a very strong force. And it is not yet certain that the Federal District will not be in the hands of a Pro-Slavery rebel army before the 4th of March." In Washington, secessionists opposed the southern route for a different reason, calling it a threat not to Lincoln but to Virginia, "a sort of bravado, inviting disturbance." Villard acknowledged the overwhelming opposition to the southerly route, noting that "there is great pressure brought to bear on him in favor of a more northerly one, via Pittsburgh and Harrisburg, and it is most likely that this will be ultimately determined upon."[3]

The greater security and political value inherent in the northern route were unarguable, and Lincoln agreed to more than double the distance of the direct route to Washington in exchange for these two advantages. His final itinerary therefore took him on a circuitous 1,900-mile journey—what he called his "winding way"— through more reliable Republican territory, where he delivered 101 speeches to immense crowds along the route. "He knows that those who elected him are anxious to see how he looks," Villard concluded, "and hence is willing to gratify this, their excusable curiosity." The goal was to introduce the largely unknown Lincoln to the nation while rallying support for the beleaguered Union. As one result of the safer, northern route, Lincoln announced that he would travel without a military escort, which he considered an unwarranted exercise of "ostentatious display and empty pageantry," a predilection that he would demonstrate time and again throughout his presidency, to his own peril.[4]

Even along the northern route, Lincoln could not avoid running a final, harrowing gauntlet through secessionist Maryland. The danger was real. After the war, Samuel M. Felton, the president of the Philadelphia, Wilmington, and Baltimore Railroad, which Lincoln would need to traverse, disclosed, "It came to my knowledge in the early part of 1861, first by rumors and then by evidence that I could not doubt, that there was a deep-laid conspiracy to capture Washington, destroy all the avenues leading to it from the East, North, and West and thus prevent the inauguration of Mr. Lincoln in the Capitol of the country." Even more ominously, the conspirators planned "if this plot did not succeed, then to murder him on his way to the capital." An army captain who was familiar with Baltimore, fittingly named George W. Hazzard, wrote to Lincoln to explain the dangers he would face in changing trains. He dismissed the Baltimore police force as unreliable and declared that "there are men in that city who, I candidly believe, would glory in being hanged for having stabbed a 'black republican president.' " Captain Hazzard outlined three possible scenarios for covering the mile-and-a-quarter distance between Baltimore's train stations. The first, "Going publicly through the city," would expose Lincoln to marksmen firing from windows and rooftops and require a military escort of 50,000 men. The second, "Avoiding the city of Baltimore," would entail crossing the Potomac River twice to make a detour through Virginia, a harrowing passage in its own right. The third option involved "Passing through Maryland incognito" in the middle of the night, disguised by a "false mustache, an old slouched hat and a long cloak or overcoat for concealment." Heightening the danger, Baltimore proved the only major city on Lincoln's route that did not issue a formal invitation to visit or speak. Neither Baltimore's mayor nor Maryland's governor asked to meet with Lincoln or created a committee to greet him. This lack of any official endorsement could only encourage hostility in the city, which cast only 1,083 votes for Lincoln, or 4.5 percent, in 1860.⁵

Despite every warning to the contrary, Lincoln's entourage did not include a formal military escort, and his itinerary, which was public knowledge, had him passing openly through Baltimore during the daytime. The superintendent of arrangements for the journey was William S. Wood, a New York railroad and hotel executive selected for his detailed knowledge of train schedules and hotel accommodations across the Northeast rather than any security expertise. Through the complacence of military authorities in Washington, including General Scott, Lincoln's personal safety fell to his friends and colleagues. In Illinois, supporters implored him to adopt a military guard and even offered their personal services. Three officers of the Springfield Zouaves—named after the French infantrymen who served in

North Africa—including Second Lieutenant John G. Nicolay, Lincoln's private secretary, volunteered to provide a "special escort" for the journey eastward. Lincoln rejected so conspicuous an escort and instead handpicked five friends and relatives to serve as an unofficial security team. Major David Hunter, a West Pointer who was Fort Leavenworth's paymaster, had earned Lincoln's trust by writing to him in December to report disloyalty in the U.S. Army. Captain John Pope, an army topographer, was a descendent of George Washington and one of Mary Lincoln's in-laws. He came aboard to act as a scout of sorts, assaying the railway lines for potential threats, both geographical and human in character. Captain George Hazzard, another West Pointer, had provided political intelligence to Lincoln during the presidential campaign by cultivating Democratic leaders and infiltrating their meetings. After Lincoln's election, he volunteered military advice about disloyalty in the army and potential threats on the route to Washington.[6]

The youngest member of the bodyguard was Colonel Elmer Ephraim Ellsworth, a twenty-two-year-old Lincoln family friend. In early 1860, he began reading law under the tutelage of Lincoln's law partner, William Herndon, studying in their law office during the exciting election year. Exuberant and ambitious, he mastered military drill, wrote a *Manual of Arms for Light Infantry*, and founded a militia company, the U.S. Zouave Cadets of Chicago, leading them on a twenty-city tour during the summer of 1860, during which they performed dazzling gymnastic drills before rapt audiences. The colorful Zouave uniform heightened both their showmanship and their popular appeal. Befriending the young Robert Lincoln, the flamboyant Ellsworth became a surrogate family member and campaigned for the Republican nominee, with the Zouave Cadets in tow. The fifth member of the security team, Colonel Edwin V. Sumner, like Lincoln a veteran of the Black Hawk War, was a career army officer who commanded the Department of the West under General Scott and was the general-in-chief's only representative on the Lincoln Special.[7]

The sixth and most conspicuous member of the informal security detail was Ward Hill Lamon, one of Lincoln's longtime friends and legal colleagues, and a distant relative of Mary Lincoln. Although he was a thoroughgoing Republican, Lamon's Virginia roots prompted an instinctive revulsion to abolitionism that Lincoln was willing to overlook in exchange for his fierce personal devotion. For this occasion, he wore a self-fashioned uniform that he had donned as an aide to Illinois's Republican governor, Lincoln's friend Richard Yates, and sported a pair of revolvers tucked into his belt. A garish blusterer by nature, Lamon relieved the tedium of the journey by singing and playing a banjo. Nicolay called Lamon, who was known as Hill in recognition of his imposing physical stature, "a man of extraordinary size and herculean strength." An exemplar of southern bravado and masculinity, Lamon provided the "muscle," whenever necessary, as the Lincoln Special chugged onward. A clutch of Illinois officials, including the governor, who had just commissioned him a colonel of artillery for this occasion, led him into a room and locked the door. "We intrust the sacred life of Mr. Lincoln to your keeping," they told him, "and if you don't protect it, never return to Illinois, for we will murder you on sight." Lamon accepted this charge somberly and acted, almost obsessively, as his friend's personal bodyguard for the next four years.[8]

Lincoln's security team, which represented one-sixth of the thirty-five-member entourage, observed extraordinary caution in preventing railway accidents and sabotage. On the first day of the journey, February 11, a group of supporters near Decatur, Illinois, blocked the track with a rail fence to force the train to make an unscheduled stop. From then on, "pilot trains" ran ahead over every stretch of track to test its safety and remove any barricades. Scout teams "spiked and guarded" every switch until the Lincoln party passed to ensure that none could be thrown in an attempt to divert the Lincoln Special into an ambush or a railway disaster. The railroads posted guards and signalmen within sight of each other along the entire length of their lines. In New York, the crews planted American flags along every section of secure track to signal the "all safe." These precautions were effective, but poison remained a preeminent concern. Four years earlier, President-Elect Buchanan, along with most of his cabinet and forty members of Congress, had suffered "violent purging, inflammation of the large intestines and a swollen tongue" while staying at the National Hotel. *Harper's Weekly* popularized the notion that the two-week epidemic, which killed two guests and sickened a thousand others, was the result of poison. Growing in legend into a failed assassination attempt, the episode reputedly frightened Buchanan enough to convince him to knuckle under to southern demands for the remainder of his term. As one Lincoln well-wisher warned from Washington, "The remarkable and peculiar disease of our National Hotel is yet fresh in the memories of the public, and too sadly so, to those who mourn departed friends, who fell victims to it." After learning that his own party was scheduled to stay at the National, Lincoln requested alternate accommodations, telling Elihu Washburne that "Mrs. L. objects to the National on account of the sickness four years ago."[9]

When the Lincoln Special reached Philadelphia on February 21, the four-month litany of amorphous threats suddenly acquired a frightening substance. As the apprehensive entourage weaved its way methodically toward Baltimore, two independent investigations were uncovering compelling evidence that the danger to Lincoln's life was genuine. In January, Congressman Washburne had warned him that "certain it is, there are traitors everywhere" but simultaneously assured him that "we are in a way to find out the thread of the conspiracy." In the absence of administration or congressional alarm over any potential threat outside the city of Washington, Seward and Washburne, acted on their own initiative. Reflecting their justifiable lack of confidence in the Baltimore authorities, they turned to New York, a reliable northern state and Seward's home turf, for help. With the possible assistance of General Scott, they asked the superintendent of the New York City police, John A. Kennedy, to dispatch "some of the most trustworthy officers" under his command to Baltimore. Not only were the New York police a model for the modern law enforcement methods that were beginning to safeguard American cities, but Kennedy himself earned praise for his oversight of security during Lincoln's stopover in the city, where his vice presidential running mate, Hannibal Hamlin of Maine, now joined the entourage. Kennedy detailed plainclothes detectives to Baltimore to pose as secessionist sympathizers in an effort to probe the validity and scope of the dangers that Lincoln might well encounter during his impending passage through Maryland.[10]

Simultaneously but independently, Samuel M. Felton, the president of the Philadelphia, Wilmington, and Baltimore Railroad, who had earlier warned Lincoln about the dangers inherent in the change of trains in Baltimore, continued to worry about the security of the Lincoln Special as it passed over his line. He imported a northern detective of his own, Allan Pinkerton, Chicago's pioneering sleuth who had almost single-handedly invented the field of private detective work and coined the term "private eye." Under the cover of an array of aliases and code names that included E. J. Allen, J. H. Hutcheson, and "Plum," Pinkerton assembled a team of operatives to infiltrate the Baltimore underworld of "Bullies" and "Plug Uglies" that gave the city its ominous nickname, "Mobtown." During his month-long investigation, Pinkerton and a dozen of his best operatives gathered evidence of a plot among secessionists to assassinate Lincoln through one of three possible methods. Two rumored threats were the obstruction of the railroad line to derail the Lincoln Special and the destruction of Lincoln's car with an "infernal machine" or grenade. A third strategy involved surrounding his carriage as he left Baltimore's Calvert Street Station to begin his journey across town to board the Baltimore and Ohio train. Under this third scenario, which was the simplest and therefore most foolproof, Lincoln would be surrounded by "a large and organized crowd of roughs," who had already drawn straws to decide which of them would have the honor of committing the assassination. Pinkerton reported the plot to Felton but also decided to establish contact with a member of the president-elect's entourage, Norman Judd, an Illinois attorney and politician who had helped orchestrate Lincoln's nomination at the Republican convention in Chicago. During the trip, Judd received a letter from Pinkerton in Cincinnati and a clandestine visit from one of his operatives in New York. Convinced that a team of assassins would be awaiting the arrival of the train in Baltimore, Pinkerton rushed to Philadelphia to warn Lincoln.[11]

After Seward's detectives, led by New York police superintendent Kennedy, reached a similar conclusion, he dispatched his son Frederick to Philadelphia on an identical mission. By coincidence, Allan Pinkerton and Frederick Seward converged on Lincoln's hotel simultaneously on the night of February 21. Judd decided that Lincoln should meet Pinkerton personally. Without sharing Pinkerton's revelations, or even his involvement, with any other member of the party, Judd summoned Lincoln to his hotel room at 11:00 P.M. and introduced him to the famous detective. The president-elect, who considered Pinkerton a colleague of sorts through their mutual work for Illinois railroads, sat and listened calmly and patiently as he laid out the evidence of the conspiracy in all of its stark details. Pinkerton implored Lincoln to leave Philadelphia immediately, forgo any public appearances in Baltimore, and make a secret journey to Washington that night, which he considered "the only way to save the country from Bloodshed." Lincoln was equally firm in refusing. He told Pinkerton succinctly that "I cannot consent to do this." He was determined to complete his full schedule in Philadelphia, which had been timed to coincide with George Washington's birthday, and then visit Harrisburg, Pennsylvania's capital. "I shall hoist the Flag on Independence Hall to-morrow and go to Harrisburg to-morrow," he insisted, "then I have fulfilled all of my engagements." Only then would he consider any change of schedule.[12]

Norman Judd advised Lincoln to ponder the public impact of a clandestine journey, which would likely elicit "sneers and scoffs" from both friends and enemies. In essence, he was asking Lincoln to weigh the damage to his reputation against the danger to his life. As Judd remembered it, he told Lincoln that "I am convinced that there is danger—Presdt Felton says there is danger—Pinkerton says there is danger—There's danger, but you must prepare to be laughed at by friends and foe." Only Lincoln could decide, because "you are to bear the burthen of the thing." Lincoln understood the implications of the plan but calmly assured Judd that he "could stand anything that was necessary." In fact, he doubted that the Baltimore Plot was real. "I could not believe that there was a plot to murder me," he told an old friend from Illinois, Congressman Isaac Arnold, nearly four years later. "I made arrangements, however, with Mr. Judd for my return to Philadelphia the next night, if I should be convinced that there was danger in going through Baltimore."[13]

LINCOLN BECAME convinced soon enough. After leaving Pinkerton, who fully appreciated his "firmness of tone," he pushed his way through the hotel throng and encountered Frederick Seward, who was anxiously awaiting him. Seward had approached young Robert Lincoln to ask for a meeting with his father. Unknown to Judd, Ward Hill Lamon escorted him to see Lincoln. "When I was making my way back to my room, through crowds of people," Lincoln told Isaac Arnold, "I met Frederick Seward. We went together to my room, when he told me that he had been sent, at the instance of his father and General Scott, to inform me that their detectives in Baltimore had discovered a plot there to assassinate me." Seward's father had asked him to locate Lincoln and personally hand him three letters. In the first, the New York senator disclosed that in the face of mounting security concerns General Scott wanted him to reconsider his plans for entering the capital. "I concur with General Scott in thinking it best for you to reconsider your arrangements," Seward advised. The second was a letter from Scott himself introducing a report from Colonel Charles P. Stone, the inspector general of the District of Columbia militia, who had "an important communication to make." The third was Stone's report itself, which relayed the results of Superintendent Kennedy's investigation of a possible conspiracy. During his three weeks in Baltimore, Kennedy had uncovered "threats of mobbing and violence" and observed "rowdies holding secret meetings." Stone concluded that "there is serious danger of violence to and the assassination of Mr Lincoln in his passage through that city should the time of that passage be known."[14]

The similarity between Colonel Stone's conclusions and the warning that Allan Pinkerton had just delivered must have astounded Lincoln. Still, Frederick Seward could detect "no sign of surprise" in the face that was studying the letters. "All risk might be easily avoided," Stone advised, "by a change in the travelling arrangements which would bring Mr Lincoln & a portion of his party through Baltimore by a night train without previous notice." This was precisely the plan that Captain Hazzard, now a member of Lincoln's personal bodyguard, had presented the previous month, before the Pinkerton and Kennedy investigations had even begun. Lincoln had now heard reports of the identical danger in Baltimore and received similar recommendations about how to avoid it from three unrelated, trustworthy sources. To verify the independence of the reports, Lincoln asked Frederick Seward if he was familiar with the name Allan Pinkerton. The answer was no. "They knew nothing of Pinkerton's movements," Lincoln told Arnold. "I now believed such a plot to be in existence." As Lincoln reasoned, "I thought it wise to run no risk, where no risk was necessary."[15]

Lincoln did indeed "hoist the Flag on Independence Hall" in Philadelphia on February 22, its additional thirty-fourth star commemorating the Republican Party's six-year struggle to admit Kansas into the Union as the newest free state. Lincoln seized this apt opportunity, the anniversary of Washington's birth, to reiterate what he considered America's founding mission. Like the Founders, the Republican Party and now Lincoln's presidency were dedicated to the never-ending extension of the core principles of the Declaration of Independence, freedom and equality, throughout the nation, and indeed the world, on into the future. "I have never had a feeling politically that did not spring from the sentiments embodied in the Declaration of Independence," he proclaimed. "It was that which gave promise that in due time the weights should be lifted from the shoulders of all men, and that *all* should have an equal chance." The Declaration made this promise, in his estimation, "not alone to the people of this country, but hope to the world for all future time." The heaviest weight of all, of course, was slavery, and Lincoln now stood inside Independence Hall promising to remove all weights, as he put it, "in due time." The unsettling events of the previous evening must have prompted his bold decision at Independence Hall to offer up his own life in full devotion to this ideal and, in effect, issue a public challenge to anyone lying in wait for him in the pandemonium of Baltimore. "But, if this country cannot be saved without giving up that principle," he announced, "I was about to say I would rather be assassinated on this spot than to surrender it." As always, Lincoln meant what he said, and his words proved all too prophetic. "I have said nothing but what I am willing to live by, and, in the pleasure of Almighty God, die by."[16]

On the same day, in Washington, Secretary of War Joseph Holt, a steadfast Unionist, and General Scott held a Washington's Birthday parade to emphasize the capital's readiness and rally national unity around an admired patriotic symbol. The "grand parade" of virtually all of the city's military forces—army, marines, and militia—was meant to send a message to potential plotters and secessionists. At the last minute, former president John Tyler, a Virginian, pressured Buchanan into canceling the parade. A crowd of thousands watched the city's fifteen militia companies, which Buchanan did not control, march as scheduled in the morning, while the regular troops were confined to their barracks on the president's order. Daniel Sickles, a fiery Democratic congressman from New York who later lost his right leg commanding Union troops at Gettysburg, met with Buchanan and persuaded him to approve a second, belated parade in the afternoon. The regulars marched up Pennsylvania Avenue and past the White House to receive Buchanan's salute. Afterward, the president apologized to Tyler for allowing the parade to proceed. (After Virginia seceded, Lincoln's commissioner of public buildings removed Tyler's portrait from the Capitol Rotunda.) By all accounts, the parade had its desired effect. "Previously, the question of whether we had spunk enough at the Federal Capital to make a creditable turn out of well drilled officers and men," the *Evening Star* confirmed, "was a debated one." Still, after the parade, a Lincoln supporter was attacked with stones and clubs by a group of drunken men shouting "kill the d——d republican son of a bitch." In self-defense, he pulled his revolver, fired twice, and ran into the north entrance of the Capitol and through its entire length, escaping through the south entrance. His pursuers did not dare to follow him into the Capitol but pelted the building with "a perfect storm of brickbats and paving stones."[17]

Meanwhile, in Philadelphia, Pinkerton had met with Lincoln's security team to devise a final plan for traversing Baltimore, which had him leaving Harrisburg on the evening of February 22, during the concluding governor's reception, and traveling surreptitiously through "Mobtown." Mary Lincoln and the boys would follow the next day. Scott's representative, Colonel Sumner, voiced the loudest objections to slipping through Baltimore overnight, calling the proposal "a d——d piece of cowardice." Under Scott's orders to secure Lincoln's passage to the capital, he swore that "I'll get a Squad of Cavalry Sir, cut our way to Washington Sir." Of course, Lincoln rendered the final decision. "Unless there are some other reasons besides ridicule," Lincoln decreed, "I am disposed to carry out Judd's plan." (Accentuating the wisdom of the plan that he now accepted, Lincoln's running mate, Hannibal Hamlin, and his wife, worried about their own safety, had decided to leave the entourage ahead of schedule. That very afternoon, they had ridden through Baltimore, where a gang of roughs pushed through their car looking for the president-elect.) The fiery Sumner then announced that he must accompany Lincoln to Washington himself. "Such were my orders from General Scott," he insisted, "and I'm going to carry them out." Instead, Lincoln selected Ward Hill Lamon, who enjoyed his—and his wife Mary's—entire confidence. More than up to the task, Lamon displayed his own formidable cache of weaponry, including a "brace of fine pistols, a huge bowie knife, a black-jack and a pair of brass knuckles." When the brash Lamon offered Lincoln a revolver and a bowie knife, Pinkerton objected that he "would not for the world have it said that Mr. Lincoln had to enter the National Capitol Armed." Presaging the coming confrontation at Fort Sumter, Lincoln wanted to avoid violence and proceed peaceably, allowing his adversaries to strike the first blow. As Pinkerton recommended, "If fighting had to be done, it must be done by others." His mind made up, the president-elect assured the gathering that he "had no fears."[18]

Accompanied only by Lamon and Pinkerton, Lincoln boarded his train wearing a broad-brimmed felt hat that he could pull down over his eyes and a "Gentleman's shawl" that he could pull up over his face. The three rode a regularly scheduled train on an ordinary sleeping car and had to endure thirty scheduled stops during the four-and-a-half hour trip. Stooping to disguise his conspicuous six-foot-four-inch height, Lincoln arrived at Baltimore's Calvert Street Station at

3:30 A.M., nine hours before 15,000 Baltimoreans crowded the depot to witness his arrival. Sealed inside their sleeping car, the trio listened intently to the "profound repose" of a sleeping Baltimore as a team of horses jostled them about for the forty-five minutes it took to lumber through the city to the Camden Street Station. Pinkerton described a relaxed Lincoln "joking in rare good humor" and "as full of fun as ever." Once hitched to a Baltimore and Ohio train, the sleeper continued its clandestine journey to Washington and at 6:00 A.M. arrived uneventfully in the bitterly divided capital.[19]

Meeting him at the depot, Lincoln's friend Congressman Elihu Washburne found him thoroughly satisfied with "the complete success of his journey." A waiting carriage whisked the quartet through the silent early morning streets of Washington to the Willard Hotel, which sat three blocks from the White House. Avoiding the conspicuous Pennsylvania Avenue entrance, Lincoln entered unobserved through a side door. He telegraphed immediately to confirm the safety of his wife and three sons, who were traveling the scheduled inaugural route through Baltimore. Then he met with William Seward, who took him to see President Buchanan at the White House and General Scott at the War Department next door. With a justifiable sense of relief, Pinkerton sent a wire to his operatives, reporting that "Nuts," his whimsical code name for Lincoln, had arrived safely. The man who twelve years earlier proposed an emancipation plan for Washington's slaves had slipped discreetly into the capital through a "side door" of his own device. He could not have known, and probably never did know, that there was a baby boy in Washington named Abraham Lincoln Hawkins. His mother, Mary Ann Hawkins, a twenty-five-year-old house servant and slave, had delivered him a month earlier. She named her son in honor of the president-elect just as he was preparing to make his inaugural journey to Washington, and doing his utmost to arrive safely.[20]

Lincoln later confessed to his friend Lamon that "the way we skulked into this city, in the first place, has been a source of shame and regret to me, for it did look so cowardly!" His secret midnight flight from Harrisburg to Washington contradicted the message that he had delivered during his 101 speeches across the North, in which he had exuded a calm confidence for the future and a forthright faith in the country's ability to avoid violence and, if it came, to meet it nobly. Sparking what proved a public relations nightmare for his fledgling administration, the final, impetuous twelve-hour passage into Washington threatened to subvert all of the precise planning and prudent rhetoric of the preceding twelve-day journey. As Norman Judd had warned, friends and enemies alike, including the usually forgiving Republican press, now viciously excoriated Lincoln through both words and images. The anti-Republican *Baltimore Sun* struck first and set the tone for the vicious reaction that was to follow. Trumpeting the news of the "Great Lincoln Escapade," the *Sun* declared solemnly that "we do not believe the Presidency can ever be more degraded by any of his successors than it has been by him, even before his inauguration." Less solemnly, the newspaper lampooned Lincoln's "wretched comicalities" and prompted readers to picture him entering the Willard Hotel "with a 'head-spring' and a 'summer-sault,' and the clown's merry greeting to Gen. Scott, 'Here we are!'" More cowardly than clownish, however, Lincoln violated the basic tenet of southern manhood by hiding behind the skirts of a woman. As the *Sun* related, "While Mr. Lincoln went by another route, he affectionately left Mrs. Lincoln to come by that on which the cars were to be thrown off the track." With mock relief, the paper rejoiced that "there is to be some pluck in the White House, if it is under a bodice."[21]

While the prevailing charge was simply cowardice, some critics accused Lincoln of hypocrisy while others questioned his masculinity, insisting that his disguise included women's apparel and even his wife Mary's clothing. A New York newspaper impugned his character merely through its spelling of the presumed danger that he had averted—"ASS-ASS-IN-ATION." Some newspapers, including the *Baltimore Sun*, lampooned his opposition to slavery by labeling his route to the safety of Washington an "Underground Railroad" all his own. The former slave and abolitionist Frederick Douglass poignantly turned the metaphor around, as only he could, to highlight the human dimensions of the journey that Lincoln had endured. "He reached the capital," Douglass declared, "as the poor, hunted fugitive slave reaches the North, in disguise, seeking concealment, evading pursuers by the underground railroad." Throughout his harrowing twelve-hour flight, Lincoln was indeed a fugitive from the same defenders of slavery who routinely pursued runaways along the back roads of Maryland.[22]

For the most part, contemporaries who heaped ridicule on him in 1861 regretted their words after his assassination at the hands of a Marylander in 1865. As the war unfolded, the president himself gained faith in the reality of the Baltimore Plot, as he confided to Congressman Isaac Arnold just four months before his death. Most historians have confirmed his own prudent assessment of the danger. At the beginning of the twelve-day gauntlet that Lincoln ran across the North and then through Baltimore, he displayed a studied indifference, and at times a jocularity, toward the threats that allowed him to shrug off even the vilest "hot stove" letters as inconsequential. Rejecting offers of a military escort, a decision that he heedlessly announced to the public, he instead assembled a handpicked cadre of trusted friends and relatives to safeguard his security. As president, he recognized the devotion of three of the five military officers on the Lincoln Special—David Hunter, John Pope, and Edwin Sumner—by granting them the rank of general. Ellsworth became adjutant and inspector general of militia two weeks after reaching Washington. Lincoln rewarded Lamon by appointing him marshal of the District of Columbia to safeguard Washington's—and his own—security throughout the war.[23]

Meanwhile, as he slowly approached his destination, an informal security apparatus began to envelop the dividing capital. Bypassing the military, which had earned his distrust, William Seward seized the opportunity that the Baltimore Plot presented to assemble a shadow government to safeguard Lincoln and his incoming administration. Without the president-elect's knowledge, Seward enlisted the help of Buchanan's attorney general, secured the loyalty of the general-in-chief, orchestrated a congressional inquiry into treason, and marshaled a team of plainclothes police and detectives, even before Lincoln had taken office. Unaware of the danger through his first eleven days on the Lincoln Special, the president-elect embraced and indeed celebrated the public openness of his inaugural journey.

During the final twelve hours, however, he reluctantly accepted its secretive dimension as well, to safeguard the completion of that harrowing journey. Despite his oft-voiced contrition, the way he "skulked" into Washington soon became the wartime capital's second nature, and his own, an inescapable imperative for survival. At the beginning of his journey, security was a mere distraction from the "the task before me" that he identified in his Farewell Address at Springfield. By the time he reached Washington thirteen days later, security had become an indispensable dimension of that task. Throughout the war, and at the ultimate cost of his life, he continually disdained and often transgressed the boundaries that his own personal safety in Washington demanded. But he never shrank from the imperative to safeguard the capital's—and the nation's—security.

After reaching Washington, Lincoln spent the last week of February holding court in the opulent rooms of Parlor No. 6 at the Willard Hotel, quickly dubbed "the Lincolnian chambers," where he received government officials and a prodigious and "hungry-looking" crowd of office seekers. Consulting with his former rivals for the presidency, he received Stephen Douglas and John Breckinridge and walked two miles before breakfast one morning to hold a long meeting with John Bell. He met with conspicuous advocates of compromise including Maryland governor Thomas Hicks, and dined with General Winfield Scott. In an ironic twist on the numerous proslavery threats that Lincoln had received, one of his visitors warned him about a possible African American uprising on Inauguration Day. When Judge Horatio Taft, the Patent Office's chief examiner, visited Parlor No. 6, he found few of Washington's socialites present and concluded that the Lincolns were "not welcome." Venturing out, however, Lincoln took pains to embrace the government and the city that he would soon need to master as president. In the Capitol, he attended a reception for both houses of Congress and another for the Supreme Court justices. When Mayor Berret and the city councils visited, Lincoln extended his friendship, acknowledging Washington's "ill feeling" toward a northern president but assigning it to "a misunderstanding between each other which unhappily prevails." He raised the question of slavery immediately but assured the mayor that "I have not now, and never have had, any disposition to treat you in any respect otherwise than as my own neighbors." In response to a serenade the next day, he acknowledged even more forthrightly his understanding that he was assuming the presidency "amongst the people, almost all of whom were opposed to me, and are yet opposed to me, as I suppose." Members of the crowd shouted, "No, no" and "You are mistaken in that, indeed you are."[24]

Still, Washington's military authorities and police, receiving reports that an "organized band of five hundred men have sworn that Mr. Lincoln shall never sleep in the White House," took action. During the week before the inauguration, police officers were assigned as detectives "who, for the occasion, lay aside the uniform and appear in the guise of citizens." An additional force of detectives arrived "from abroad"—New York, Philadelphia, and Baltimore—to watch the city. (The *Evening Star* complained that the detectives "confined their labors chiefly to sampling liquors at our drinking shops, etc. etc.") Plainclothes police rode the trains connecting Philadelphia, Baltimore, and Washington "to prevent the congregation of disorderly characters." General Scott, who commanded the regular army, and Colonel Stone, who commanded the District's militia, were determined to oversee a peaceful inauguration. On March 4, two thousand soldiers, comprising infantry, cavalry, and artillery, assembled at strategic points throughout the city. Stone, whose letter describing the Baltimore Plot had convinced Lincoln that the threats were genuine, had begun purging the militia of secessionists to ensure their loyalty. Lining the mile-long stretch of Pennsylvania Avenue between the Willard Hotel and the Capitol, riflemen joined the crowd of thousands who waited—on foot, in carriages, and on horseback—to watch the presidential procession pass by. The patent examiner, Horatio Taft, refused to allow his wife and children to go near the Capitol, where "trouble was really expected." Instead, they sat in the window of a hardware store on Pennsylvania Avenue. "As we took our places a file of green-coated sharpshooters went up through the roof," Taft's daughter Julia remembered. "The whisper went round that they had received orders to shoot at any one crowding toward the President's carriage." (Snipers regularly wore green to blend in with surrounding foliage.) Police milled through the crowd—"passing amongst them ever and anon"—to break up any clumps of "suspicious looking individuals." Riflemen loomed from the windows of the Capitol's East Front, and Stone's militamen surrounded the platform where Lincoln delivered his Inaugural Address before an audience of 30,000. Standing on the East Portico under the unfinished Capitol dome, Lincoln faced across First Street toward Duff Green's Row and spoke "with a clear, loud, and distinct voice, quite intelligible by at least ten thousand persons below him."[25]

Despite the all too visible threats, Lincoln's address was conciliatory. The Confederacy consisted of seven states in the Lower South, but eight slave states in the Upper South remained in the Union. Lincoln's primary goal was to keep them there. Conditional Unionists in the Upper South were willing to wait for an act of aggression against the South or slavery before seceding from the Union. "Apprehension seems to exist among the people of the Southern States, that by the accession of a Republican Administration, their property, and their peace, and personal security, are to be endangered," Lincoln acknowledged. He assured them, "There has never been any reasonable cause for such apprehension." He then offered a list of concessions to the South, endorsing "the right of each State to order and control its own domestic institutions according to its own judgment exclusively," promising to support a constitutional amendment protecting slavery in southern states, and pledging to enforce the Fugitive Slave Law with amendments protecting the basic rights of accused fugitives. He resolved to maintain federal functions in the seceded states, including mail delivery, but only if he could do so peaceably. "In doing this, there needs to be no bloodshed or violence," he reasoned, "and there shall be none, unless it be forced upon the national authority." On the legality of secession, however, Lincoln refused to compromise, declaring that "the Union of these States is perpetual" and "the central idea of secession, is the essence of anarchy." Overall, he advocated "a peaceful solution of the national troubles, and the restoration of fraternal sympathies and affections." His plea for peace and reconciliation ended with an appeal to the historic "mystic chords of memory" that had held the Union together for so long through shared triumphs and sacrifices. Above all, Lincoln hoped to forestall the spread of secession. Keeping the eight remaining slave states in the Union might allow the long-looked-for "sober second thought" to bring the seceded states back to their senses. Ultimately, Lincoln managed to keep four of the eight in the Union.[26]

After delivering his Inaugural Address, Lincoln took his oath of office from Chief Justice Roger B. Taney, the conservative Mary-lander whose infamous *Dred Scott* decision had ignited outrage across the North and boosted the popularity of the Republican Party. The procession retraced its steps up Pennsylvania Avenue toward the White House. Thousands of well-wishers passed through the Executive Mansion to shake the new president's hand. Ten days after Lincoln slipped through the side door to enter the Willard Hotel, General Scott had delivered the newly inaugurated president to the White House at last. After playing an indispensable—and no doubt exhausting—role in making those momentous events even possible, Scott swore solemnly in relief, "Thank God, we now have a government." Scott, like most other Washingtonians, believed that the crisis was past and the capital secure. "At the present moment, when all is quiet, it is difficult to realize the state of alarm which prevailed when the troops were first ordered to this city," the complacent Buchanan reflected. "This alarm instantly subsided after the arrival of the first company, and a feeling of comparative peace and security has since existed, both in Washington and throughout the country." The War Department shifted the troops that had been guarding the capital back to their peacetime stations.[27]

CHAPTER SEVEN

"This Big White House"
The Lincoln Family

F ROM ITS initial occupation by John and Abigail Adams in
November 1800, the White House was known formally as the
"Executive Mansion." Throughout Lincoln's presidency, the home
retained that official name, as it did until President Theodore Roosevelt replaced it with "White House" in 1901. Before coming to
Washington, Lincoln had never used the nickname "White House"
in any of his letters or speeches that have survived, but within two
months of moving in he wrote a memo referring to "what is called the
White House." After that, he began to use the label more freely and
frequently, emphasizing the simplicity, rather than splendor, of the
home that, as he put it, he temporarily occupied. As he told the 166th
Ohio Regiment in August 1864, "I happen temporarily to occupy this
big White House. I am a living witness that any one of your children may look to come here as my father's child has." The Lincolns
quickly settled into the White House with their children Willie and
Tad. The Executive Mansion mirrored their own Victorian home in
Springfield through its mingling of both public and private areas and
functions, albeit on a much grander scale. The first floor was entirely
public in character, and, in fact, with only a single doorkeeper to
monitor and announce visitors, the general public had virtually the
run of all the "state chambers," ranging from the State Dining Room
on the west end through the Green Room, Blue Room, and Red
Room (also called the Scarlet or Crimson Room), which served as

intimate parlors, and on to the cavernous East Room, which hosted public ceremonies, performances, and receptions.[1]

The White House was therefore much more public than private in character. In August 1861, Prince Napoleon of France visited and observed in disbelief that "one goes right in as if entering a café." So many visitors "went right in" during the receptions that the windows were converted into exits to allow them to leave. When the poet Walt Whitman attended a levee, he found "a compact jam in front of the White House—all the grounds fill'd, and away out to the spacious sidewalks," with the crowds surging through the hallways and reception rooms. Lincoln stood patiently for hours, "drest in black, with white kid gloves, and a claw-hammer coat, receiving, as in duty bound, shaking hands." Reporter and Lincoln friend Noah Brooks remembered that "so vast were the crowds, and so affectionate their greetings, that Mr. Lincoln's right hand was often so swollen that he would be unable to use it readily for hours afterward." The white kid glove on his right hand "always looked as if it had been dragged through a dust-bin."[2]

Abraham Lincoln worked upstairs on the south side of the second floor in a massive 25-by-40-foot room, which doubled as his office and the cabinet's meeting room. (There was no Oval Office until William Howard Taft created it in 1909.) Lincoln's cabinet included only seven members, so the heavy walnut table at the center of his office could easily accommodate them all at their weekly Tuesday afternoon meetings. This was an austere and utilitarian workplace. William Stoddard, one of Lincoln's secretaries, noted, "There is hardly an ornamental or a superfluous article of furniture in the room." A sofa and two chairs lined one of the walls, with military maps hanging above, along with a "slave map" that reflected the president's interest in emancipation as a potential tool for winning the war. Lincoln worked at an old mahogany desk in one corner, above which pigeonholes facilitated his idiosyncratic filing system. (One of the pigeonholes contained eighty threatening letters that his secretaries considered serious enough to pass along.) Working models of proposed new weapons sat randomly around the office, including a hand grenade that Lincoln used as a paperweight. (Stoddard called the invention "of no practical use in these days of long-range rifles.") Lincoln personally selected a portrait of Andrew Jackson to hang overhead. A longtime critic of Jackson's imperious exercise of executive authority, Lincoln nevertheless admired his predecessor's impassioned and effective devotion to the Union. Subsequent first families called the room the Lincoln Study, until 1945 when Bess Truman turned it into the Lincoln Bedroom. As president, Lincoln slept in a small bedroom in the southwest corner of the family quarters.[3]

Despite his working at home for the first time during the couple's marriage, Lincoln's wife and family saw less of him than ever. "The number of times that Mrs. Lincoln herself entered his business-room at the White House," according to one of his secretaries, "could probably be counted on the fingers of one hand." Although his office was just a few steps away from the family quarters, his new responsibilities were vast, and the Lincolns continued to observe the rigid Victorian separation of home and work. The president began the war with two private secretaries, John Nicolay and John Hay, both of whom came with him from Illinois. They had offices adjacent to his on the second floor of the building and actually lived there, sharing a bedroom to assist Lincoln as necessary twenty-four hours a day. A bell cord hung in Lincoln's office to summon them whenever needed. After arriving in Washington, the president added a third secretary, William Stoddard, whose official appointment was in the Patent Office, to sort his mail. One of the secretaries' primary responsibilities was screening the "never-ending stream" of office seekers—and later pardon seekers— who haunted the White House's hallways and stairways, intent on seeing the president. The ever mischievous and enterprising Tad set up a toll gate and solicited donations, five cents at a time, from the waiting supplicants, who became known as "Tad's clients."[4]

The initial throng of job and favor seekers required Lincoln to keep a twelve-hour day, from breakfast until late evening. "He has not had an opportunity to ride out since his inauguration, and yesterday he stepped out into the grounds of the White House for the first time," the *Evening Star* reported one week into his presidency. "His family only see him at dinner, he being compelled from fatigue to retire to his room as soon as he leaves his office." Eventually, he could limit his daily reception hours to five (10:00 A.M.–3:00 P.M.) and finally a mere three (10:00 A.M.–1:00 P.M.). Still, Lincoln spent most mornings and evenings in his office attending to the crush of wartime business. "The President's capacity for work was wonderful," remembered one of his secretaries. "Each hour he was busy." He made only two concessions to preserve his family's privacy and provide a few more moments of time alone with them. First, he erected a partition in the reception room—a ground-glass and bronze screen—that allowed him to slip between his office and the family quarters without being seen, which was the only change that he ordered to the White House during his entire presidency. Second, he insisted that Nicolay and Hay take all of their meals a few blocks away at the Willard Hotel to avoid any unnecessary intrusions into the family's meals, which they took in the State Dining Room.[5]

One unfortunate oversight in the White House's accommodations was the lack of a direct telegraph connection. To centralize control over his burgeoning and far-flung army, Lincoln made innovative use of the recently invented telegraph, but had to walk to the War Department next door to read and reply to messages from his generals. There, he could confer with Stanton while scanning the latest war news. During major engagements, he spent many a night huddled next to the telegraph reading and writing dispatches as part of his growing personal direction of the war. As one of his bodyguards marveled, "It would never have occurred to Mr. Lincoln to regard his own personal dignity and wait for his Secretary to come to him." The route between the White House and the War Department took Lincoln through a grove of shade trees that separated the two buildings, along a brick walkway protected only by a low brick wall and lit by a few flickering gas lamps. His bodyguards considered this secluded spot an ideal setting for assassination but quickly learned that "he hated being on his guard, and the fact that it was necessary to distrust his fellow-Americans." On top of all of her other apprehensions, Mary Lincoln had to worry constantly about her husband's safety as he trudged back and forth to the War Department at all hours, at least twice a day throughout the war.[6]

Previous first families had allowed the White House to deterio-

rate over time, rarely spending all or even most of the funds that
Congress provided for upkeep and improvements. Still, the home
boasted several genteel refinements. Gas had just been added to the
building to supplement the traditional candlelight. Abraham Lincoln's office had two gas jets with glass globes high on the walls. (On
one occasion, a gas leak nearly suffocated him before it was located
and repaired.) A furnace in the basement relieved the household from
tending the inefficient and unsafe fireplaces, with the attendant soot,
that sat in every room. Running water had just been added to the family quarters. Each bedroom had a sink with a faucet, and the family
had two toilets in their second-floor family quarters. (Everyone else
made do with a row of outhouses on the eastern end of the building.)
A new layer of white paint on the exterior made the White House
whiter than ever. Abraham Lincoln's predecessor, James Buchanan,
had made another welcome addition to the home, a greenhouse on
the west end—the new White House Conservatory, which became
Mary Lincoln's favorite locale. She delighted in brightening the
home with arrangements, especially during social functions, presenting bouquets to visitors, and sending flowers to the hospitals to cheer
the wounded soldiers. "The conservatory attached to this house is
so delightful," she confided to a friend. "We have so many choice
bouquets."[7]

Mary Lincoln believed that she bore a vital civic responsibility
of her own as part of her husband's administration. She considered
the White House an important symbol of national power and pride,
more crucially than ever during a civil war. She was determined to
restore the building, which had fallen into considerable disrepair, to
its former grandeur, adopting President Jefferson's stately but elegant
adornments and entertainments as her model. (Indeed, since the
Polk administration a bronze statue of Jefferson, now weathered a
dull green, had stood on the front lawn to welcome visitors onto the
White House grounds.) Yet a higher goal was to set a standard of
grace and refinement that the entire nation might envy and emulate
as befitting the chief executive of a nation that, as her husband put it,
was "worth fighting for." Mary Lincoln was determined to use every
resource at her disposal to help elevate the presidency that her hus-

band now occupied and truly earn the novel label "First Lady of the Land." (Although used informally on occasion as early as her distant relative Dolley Madison's tenure in the White House, the label First Lady gained currency during the Civil War, with reference to Mary Lincoln.) Mary's years of experience hosting Springfield's social and political elites in her comfortable home had prepared her to preside as hostess at the most elegant address in America.[8]

Even before traveling to Washington for the inauguration, Mary Lincoln journeyed to New York City to shop. Traveling to the major centers of culture and fashion—Philadelphia, New York City, and Boston—assured that she would uphold her self-imposed standards of quality and style as a worthy First Lady for the divided nation. Shopping trips gave her the opportunity to escape both the literal and figurative heat of Washington, exercise her symbolic and indeed real authority as the nation's new fashion leader, and attempt to reinstate the White House as a symbol of national pride and, by extension, power. "I must dress in costly materials," she explained to her dressmaker, Elizabeth Keckly. "The people scrutinize every article that I wear with critical curiosity." This was also an arena in which no man, no matter how imperious, vain, or refined, could compete with her.[9]

She shopped not only for herself but for the White House, which she was determined to resurrect to its former glory as a presidential mansion. During her first shopping trip for household furnishings, William S. Wood, the acting commissioner of public buildings, and her cousin Elizabeth Todd Grimsley accompanied her to New York City. Every president received a $20,000 congressional appropriation for the White House furnishings, for his entire four-year term. Previous first families spent the funds overcautiously, so the White House languished in threadbare condition. Mary Lincoln now went overboard in refurbishing a mansion that she considered something of a national disgrace. Her most expensive purchases were a $2,500 carpet for the expansive East Room, a seven-hundred-piece set of cut glass tableware, a large set of gold-trimmed china, and $6,800 in French wallpaper. She later spent almost $6,000 on silverware, china, and chandeliers through a New York importer and $7,500 on carpeting and wallpaper from a Philadelphia merchant, and this was only the beginning. A rosewood grand piano from Philadelphia facilitated performances at White House entertainments, as well as music lessons for Willie and Tad. The First Lady completed her renovations in October 1861.[10]

In Illinois, Mary had always depended heavily on female companionship to relieve her inveterate loneliness and compensate for her husband's long absences while riding the legal circuit and stumping for office. True to form, she invited a dozen of her relatives to visit Washington during her first month as First Lady. Back in Springfield, her best friend, Mercy Levering Conkling, observed with some exaggeration, "Half the town seems to have gone to Washington." She gained the greatest comfort from her oldest sister, Elizabeth Edwards, and Elizabeth Grimsley, or "Cousin Lizzie," who spent the most time with her in Washington over the course of the war. Lizzie originally planned to stay a month or so in Washington but ended up keeping Mary company for half a year. Mary also cultivated some of the most powerful men in her husband's administration, offering the kinds of character assessments of potential appointees at which she believed she excelled. To Lincoln's legal mentor and campaign manager, David Davis, she counseled against a cabinet appointment for Chicago newspaperman Norman Judd. "*Judd* would cause trouble & dissatisfaction," she insisted, especially "in *these times*, when honesty in high places is so important." (Lincoln ultimately appointed Judd to serve as minister in Berlin.) She was particularly anxious to have the right kind of men overseeing the White House grounds and budget. She reported to Ward Hill Lamon that the applicants for commissioner of public buildings "are very unsuitable, deficient in intelligence, manners, and it may be, morals. May I ask the favor of you, to speak to Mr L. on the subject." She usually got her way but of course made enemies in the process.[11]

Once in the White House, Mary Lincoln quickly assembled her own White House staff that included Mary Ann Cuthbert, who served as both a seamstress and a "dressing maid" and eventually rose to the position of head housekeeper. Two African American women, Rosetta Wells and Hannah Brooks, performed "plain sewing" for the First Lady. Rebecca Pomroy, a nurse at the Union Hotel Hospital in

Georgetown and later Columbian College Hospital, also served as the Lincoln family's nurse. Mary's most important personal assistant and later trusted confidante was Elizabeth Keckly, who began as one of her dressmakers but quickly attained the status of "regular modiste." Born in Virginia in the same year as Mary Lincoln, Keckly was a slave for the first thirty-seven years of her life. After her owner hired her out as a seamstress in St. Louis in 1847, she perfected her skill as a dressmaker and used her earnings to purchase her own freedom and that of her sixteen-year-old son, George. Relocating to Washington in the spring of 1860, she built an exclusive clientele that included Jefferson Davis and his wife, Varina. Mary Lincoln hired her on the strength of her reputation, considered her "a very remarkable woman," and grew to depend on her even more for her advice and companionship than for her considerable skills as a dressmaker. Lincoln himself called her affectionately "Madam Elizabeth."[12]

Mary Lincoln's initial forays into the Washington social scene could not have gone better. The inaugural festivities—an afternoon reception at the White House followed by an inaugural ball—were both well-attended, and Mary was beautifully attired, thanks to the dressmaking entourage that she had so painstakingly assembled. She delighted in dancing until 4:00 A.M. in the immense ballroom, a temporary structure built expressly to house the inaugural gala. At the ball, all eyes were on Mary as she savored her first dance on the arm of her ironic partner for the evening—Stephen A. Douglas. Twenty years earlier in Springfield, Lincoln and Douglas had competed for Mary Todd's affection. She later claimed that she had turned Douglas down when he proposed to her, spurning the "Little Giant" for the big one. Lincoln's satisfaction with the inaugural ball must have been personal as well as political. Always careful to defer to the lady of the house, however, after a mere two hours—at 1:00 A.M.—Lincoln slipped out of the ballroom and left the Todd women to celebrate until dawn.[13]

One of the First Lady's formal duties was hosting a demanding round of receptions and levees on behalf of her husband at which attendance was virtually unrestricted. The Lincolns' Tuesday evening receptions ran from 8:30 to 10:30 P.M. Mary Lincoln also held her own Saturday Matinee between 1:00 and 3:00 P.M., which the president was expected to attend, "when his public duties permit." Ironically, in light of future events, Washingtonians were initially more apprehensive about Mary Lincoln's western heritage than her southern roots. Harriet Lane, Buchanan's niece and his White House hostess, feared that she would prove "awfully *western*, loud & unrefined." Still, the Lincolns' first formal social event, an evening levee at the White House, earned widespread praise as a "monstrous success" and the "most successful party" ever held at the White House. "The crowd was so great in the House that hundreds left without seeing the Prest," Horatio Taft reported. "It was a perfect *jam*." Mary's private entertainments were equally popular. "This is certainly a very charming spot & I have formed many delightful acquaintances," she boasted with satisfaction during her first month in Washington. "Every evening our *blue room*, is filled with the elite of the land, last eve, we had about 40 to call in, to see us *ladies*." She wrote a friend cheerfully that "I am beginning to feel so perfectly at home, and enjoy every thing so much."[14]

BEYOND HER conspicuous public role as White House hostess, of course, Mary Lincoln's primary responsibility was raising her children. Just like the Lincoln home at Eighth and Jackson in Springfield, the White House became a playground for Willie and Tad, now ten and eight. Abraham and Mary Lincoln cherished their boys beyond measure and gave them the run of the White House, often to the consternation of the president's secretaries and other officials. The Lincolns hired a tutor for the boys and turned the family's second-floor sitting room, the Oval Room, into a makeshift schoolroom during the afternoons. They discovered that Horatio Taft had two sons and invited the Taft boys—Horatio Jr., called Bud, and Halsey, called Holly—to play. The four immediately became fast friends and nearly constant companions. Bud and Holly's older sister, Julia Taft, was sixteen and often accompanied her brothers to the White House, to the delight of Abraham Lincoln, who loved to tease her, and even more so Mary, who had always wanted a daughter.[15]

The family included the three Taft children in their school lessons, as well as in many of their more private moments together. Julia withdrew from Madame Smith's French school to join her brothers in the White House, where she undoubtedly learned a lot from Mary Lincoln. Julia later reminisced that beyond their lessons in the Oval Room, the Lincolns resolved simply to "let the children have a good time" in the White House. "Often I have heard Mrs. Lincoln say this with a smile," she remembered, "as her two sons and my two brothers rushed tumultuously through the room, talking loudly of some plan for their amusement." The boys had the run of the White House, its grounds, and in fact beyond. When they disappeared one afternoon, Lincoln dispatched his security team to look for them late into the evening. They were found exploring the basement of the Capitol, the site of an immense bakery, where they reported excitedly that they had discovered rats. Surrounded by thousands of armed soldiers, the boys invested many of their games with a military theme. On the White House roof, which Julia Taft labeled "the favorite playground of the boys," they mustered with decommissioned rifles to watch for any enemy advance. "The Boys are having a nice time on *top* of the White House," Horatio Taft wrote with satisfaction. "The Roof is copper, flat & with a high stone Ballistrade all round." They turned the roof into a ship, "The Ship of State," complete with a cabin and spyglasses to scan the Potomac. "Let 'em come," Tad boasted. "Willie and I are ready for 'em."[16]

Tad was the younger and more mischievous of the brothers. Noah Brooks, who knew him well, called him a "boisterous, rollicking, and absolutely real boy." His best-known exploits were designed to draw his distracted father into the boys' games. When Tad prepared to execute the toy soldier Jack for falling asleep on guard duty, for example, Abraham Lincoln intervened to grant him a pardon. This humorous interlude must have brightened the day for a president who had to make hundreds of real life-and-death decisions of that character. Tad's most legendary prank was waving a Confederate flag on the White House grounds during a troop review. Tad stood behind his father brandishing the Stars and Bars until Lincoln noticed and put an end to the display. The boy's overindulgent parents tolerated and sometimes even abetted his misadventures. When Tad wanted goats, the Lincolns bought him a pair, Nanny and Nanko, who had the run of the South Lawn. Tad chased them through the gardener's flower beds and drove them, pulling an overturned chair, through the East Room. The president and Mary Ann Cuthbert, the housekeeper, tolerated the animals until Mary and Tad took an extended trip and left Nanny and Nanko in their care. "Tell dear Tad, poor 'Nanny Goat,' is lost," Abraham wrote Mary, "and Mrs. Cuthbert & I are in distress about it. The day you left Nanny and Nanko was found resting herself, and chewing her little cud, on the middle of Tad's bed. But now she's gone! The gardener kept complaining that she destroyed the flowers, till it was concluded to bring her down to the White House. This was done, and the second day she had disappeared, and has not been heard of since. This is the last we know of poor 'Nanny.' " The president's message, which he entitled "Letter about 'Nanny goat,' " raises the suspicion that Nanny did not disappear entirely of her own volition. Later, however, Abraham telegraphed Mary, "Tell Tad the goats and father are very well—especially the goats."[17]

Climbing into the attic, Tad found the controls for the bell-pull system, tripped all of the wires, and sent every servant in the White House rushing into his father's office simultaneously. In more tender moments, however, the president genuinely enjoyed his quiet time together with his children. Julia Taft remembered Lincoln lingering in the Oval Room in a familiar role, as storyteller, with all of the boys. "Tad perched precariously on the back of the big chair, Willie on one knee, Bud on the other, both leaning against him," she recalled. "Holly usually found a place on the arm of the chair, and often I would find myself swept into the group by the long arm which seemed to reach almost across the room." At odd moments, Lincoln slipped out of his office to play horsey or blind man's bluff with little Tad through the numerous rooms of the family quarters. Julia Taft recalled Tad's disappointment whenever he reported that "Pa don't have time to play with us now."[18]

The greatest drawback to life in the White House, which had tragic consequences, particularly for the two boys, Willie and Tad, was sanitation. Of the city's 127 streets, only one was paved, Pennsylvania Avenue, known simply as "the Avenue." A wartime resident lamented that "the streets of Washington were always either mud or dust," and Mary Lincoln agreed that "*dust*, I presume we will never be freed from, until *mud*, takes its place." During a typical wartime winter, the *National Republican* declared, "The mud is at least a *foot* deep in almost any street in the city; in some localities (still worse) it is ankle deep, and we have suspicions that in the back streets it is knee deep." Running from the Capitol northwestward to the White House, the Avenue boasted the city's Center Market and its most fashionable shops, on its northern side, and the notorious red-light district popularly known as Murder Bay—and during the war, Hooker's Division—on its southern side.[19]

Just south of Pennsylvania Avenue and the White House ran the notorious Washington Canal. The canal that bore his name was the most visible remnant of George Washington's dream of turning the national capital into a commercial metropolis by creating a water route connecting the Potomac and Ohio rivers. The Chesapeake and Ohio Canal was designed to run from Georgetown to Wheeling, Virginia, to funnel midwestern produce and raw materials to the Atlantic coast via Washington. The Washington Canal would bring this immense trade into and through the city itself, giving Center Market—standing between the Capitol and the White House—regional, even national, importance as an entrepôt. Expediency recommended creating a channel from two existing creeks: Goose Creek (later renamed Tiber Creek to comport with the classical Roman architectural surroundings) and James Creek. L'Enfant's plan accordingly incorporated a city canal running from Georgetown on the Potomac, between the White House and the National Mall, and then bending southward just west of the Capitol, to connect with the Anacostia River, or Eastern Branch. Flowing along what is now Constitution Avenue just south of the White House (an old gatehouse still stands there as part of the White House grounds), the canal emptied into the Potomac at the "watergate." Overlooking the fundamental principle that water flows faster through a narrow channel, the final plan produced a canal that was 160 feet wide, four times the width of the Erie Canal. The result was a slow-moving and often stagnant stream that allowed sediment to settle and mosquitoes to breed.[20]

Washington's rival city, Baltimore, created a connection with the Ohio River of its own but built a railroad, the Baltimore and Ohio, rather than a canal. When the B&O Railroad beat the C&O Canal to Wheeling, Baltimore captured the lucrative Ohio Valley trade. The Chesapeake and Ohio Canal stopped halfway to the Ohio River at Cumberland, Maryland. Suddenly, the Washington Canal lost its original purpose, and Congress let it fall into neglect for the next half century. Center Market became not a grand entrepôt but a "mean combination of ugly looking cabins." During the Civil War, the Washington *Daily Chronicle* called for construction of a new city market, complaining, "The present structure is an eyesore. It has always been the ugliest blotch on our beautiful avenue." The canal itself, however, provoked even more disgust as an "abominable sink of filth," a "stink-trap, man-trap and mud-hole," and a "breeder of disease and death." In the absence of a sewage and drainage system, the canal collected the debris of the city, both human and animal, including corpses and horse and cattle carcasses. "Dead animals, of all descriptions and sizes," the Washington *National Republican* complained, "are thrown in and suffered to lay exposed to the rays of the sun, and the pestilential stench is borne by every breeze into the nostrils of all within reach of the place." The grand canal envisioned by George Washington and Pierre L'Enfant had degenerated into a "shallow, open sewer." The condition of the canal provoked such resentful bitterness that one Washington resident declared that "those who are responsible for it ought to die from its effects." Wartime proposals for rehabilitating the nuisance included creating a system of dams and sluice gates to produce a constant flow, strengthening the canal's current by narrowing it to one-half of its width, arching it over to create an enclosed sewer, or simply filling it in completely. Lincoln's quartermaster general, Montgomery C. Meigs, proposed dividing the canal along its length, creating a sewer on one side and a stream on the other. Each half would be narrower and therefore run faster. Under the press of wartime events, Congress and the city did nothing.[21]

The canal's influence on the city, as well as on the White House and its occupants, was profound. The channel created an artificial, low-lying island, cut off from the rest of Washington by a handful of bridges and walkways. Dubbed simply "the Island," the area was densely populated by African Americans and Irish immigrants, who constantly contested for living space. The poor bathed in the canal, swam in it, and frequently drowned in it. Compounding the pestilence, the Union Army on the Virginia side dispensed with latrines and instead dug ditches to facilitate the runoff of sewage into the Potomac, which backed up into the canal with every high tide. The White House's South Lawn, labeled the "White Yard" in honor of its conspicuous white picket fence, was essentially Willie and Tad's backyard and slanted downward toward the pestilent canal. The overflowing water created "sewage marshes" that turned the National Mall into what Benjamin Stoddard called a "great slope of grass and weeds and rubbish." A visitor complained that the White House "is rendered very unhealthy by the accumulation of refuse and garbage, which the tide washes to and fro." Benjamin Brown French, the wartime commissioner of public buildings, noticed an offensive "effluvia" pervading the rooms and hallways. William Stoddard reported "rats, mildew and foul smells" and detected "the air of an old and unsuccessful hotel." John Hay called the Executive Mansion the "White pest-house." During his year of living there, Willie suffered measles, scarlet fever, and typhoid fever, from which he died. Tad survived measles, typhoid fever, and malaria, for which he took quinine daily. Abraham Lincoln himself suffered a mild form of smallpox upon his return from Gettysburg in November 1863. Life in Washington was so precarious that the British Foreign Office designated the city a hardship posting.[22]

Despite his administration's extraordinary efforts to secure the capital as both a military stronghold and the seat of government, Lincoln himself was never truly safe in Washington. Midway through the war, a reporter lamented that while living in the White House, "It took Mr. Lincoln very little while to discover that he need not go ten rods at any time to find a man who would gladly take his life." As the war began, White House security was notoriously lax. Initially unguarded, the White House grounds invited mischief. Ten days after the inauguration, Allan Pinkerton's detectives watched (but did not arrest) a burglar casing the building's windows and doors with a set of skeleton keys and a jimmy. Initially, the interior of the White House was little safer. Soon after arriving in 1861, John Hay was disgusted to discover that "a young and careless guard loafed around the furnace fires in the basement." Only a doorkeeper at the entrance and a messenger outside Lincoln's office stood between the president and assassination. The doorkeeper, Edward McManus, described as "undersized," was an elderly Irish immigrant who had held that position since the Taylor administration. Visitors overran the first floor and vandalized Mary Lincoln's elegant furnishings with abandon. They snatched flowers from vases, clipped the cords and tassels from the curtains, removed swatches of carpeting, pulled down wallpaper, and cut whole yards of fabric from the windows. "It is easy enough to do this here," Noah Brooks explained, "for though there are always one or two watchmen about the house, a thief can have an accomplice to engage the attention of the watchmen elsewhere." During receptions, the souvenir hunters sliced the buttons from Mary Lincoln's gowns. "The stealing was all done well and successfully," William Stoddard mused. In December 1864, Commissioner of Public Buildings French asked Congress to appoint a single watchman to prevent the vandalism, but they refused.[23]

Heedless of his personal safety, Lincoln put his own life at risk through his very accessibility. His sober fatalism convinced him that "if any one wanted to murder him no precaution would avail." Insisting on an open-door policy in the White House, he exposed himself to the entire range of Washington's intrepid humanity through a process that the provost marshal labeled "public-opinion baths." His doorkeeper observed that "Lincoln seldom if ever declined to receive any man or woman who came to the White House to see him." Presidential secretary William Stoddard marveled at the motley assemblage who enjoyed access to Lincoln in his private office. "Mingled with men of worth, energy, efficiency, and highly meritorious political services," he recalled, "were the broken-down, used-up, bankrupt, creditless, worthless, the lame, the halt and the blind." Exhibiting

"marvelous self-control," only rarely and reluctantly did Lincoln ter-
minate an interview. White House secretary John Nicolay became all
too familiar with the swarm of "self-appointed advisers" and adopted
Lincoln's strategy of hearing them out as the most humane response.
"Lunatics and visionaries are here so frequently that they cease to be
strange phenomena to us," he recalled, "and I find the best way to
dispose of them is to discuss and decide their mad projects as deliber-
ately and seriously as any other matter of business."[24]

Fearing "eavesdroppers and traitors lurking about the White
House," Ward Hill Lamon advised Lincoln to restrict access to his
office. "I would suggest that no one be allowed up stairs except such
as you permit, after their sending up their cards," he warned. "Some
visit there I fear who have no expectation of obtaining an interview
with you—whose sole object is to pick up such information as they
can." Still, the interruptions continued. A detective arrested one tres-
passer "for hanging about the White House and annoying the President." Another intruder, described as "evidently insane," was charged
with "creating a disturbance at the President's House." Late in the
war, a "crazy man" gained access to Lincoln's office and launched into
a speech. Only when he insisted that he had been elected president
was he arrested and lodged in the Central Guardhouse. Yet Lincoln's
determination to listen to everyone yielded compensating, positive
results. In one of his more poignant moments, he was accosted by a
soldier near a tree as he was walking between the White House and
the War Department. The patient president considered the soldier's
request and then "sat right down under the tree, took out his pencil,
and then and there 'acted upon it,' by indorsing and referring it favor-
ably to the proper department."[25]

CHAPTER EIGHT

"White and Black, All Mixed Up Together"
The African American Community

━━◆◆◆━━

A FTER LEAVING Congress in 1849, Lincoln spent the next twelve years in Illinois fighting the spread of slavery into the territories, building a Republican Party founded on the doctrine of free soil, and running for the Senate and then the presidency on that principle. Simultaneously, slavery in Washington continued to deteriorate. During the 1850s, the number of slaves in the city fell by one-sixth and their proportion of the population from 5 percent to just 3 percent. Meanwhile, the free black community continued to grow. Increasing by one-eighth during the decade, the proportion of African Americans in the city reached 15 percent by 1860. When the Civil War began, nearly four-fifths of Washington's African American residents were free. Slavery's weakening position in Washington reflected its more general decline in the Chesapeake region. Former slaves, including runaways, sought out the city, where they could blend in with the black community, take shelter in free families, and hope, if possible, to move northward with the help of the region's long-established underground railroad. The Fugitive Slave Law of 1850 made the prospect of successful flight northward increasingly remote, while the capital's Black Code continued to constrict the lives of free African Americans. The arrival of European immigrants, which fueled the city's 50 percent population growth during the 1850s, heightened racial discrimination and constricted economic opportunities for African Americans. Nativism and anti-

Catholicism, embodied in the election of a Know Nothing mayor in 1854, forced immigrants, primarily Irish and German in origin, into menial livelihoods, putting them into direct and often intense competition with African Americans for both jobs and housing along the margins of Washington society. By 1860, there were more foreign immigrants than free African Americans, a majority of them Irish.[1]

Segregation did not exist in its modern form in early Washington. In the prewar pedestrian or "walking" city, Americans preferred to live near their workplaces, which was one reason that Congressman Lincoln selected Mrs. Sprigg's boardinghouse, across the street from the Capitol, "20 to 40 rods" away, as Joshua Giddings put it. To go to work, Lincoln had to walk no more than two hundred yards, as he had done in Springfield. All classes and races mingled together in every part of Washington but clustered around major centers of activity, including the Capitol, the White House, City Hall, and the Navy Yard. Only with the advent of streetcars, which Washington adopted during the Civil War, could anyone choose to live in a neighborhood any distance from his or her place of work. Property values were highest on Capitol Hill, the city's core, so there whites predominated. Slaves were required by law to live with their masters, as part of the city's regime of severe racial control and surveillance. Slaveowners devised a unique arrangement to keep their slaves on their property, as the law required, yet physically separated from their homes. They built slave quarters—often no more than sheds, shacks, and even stables—behind their houses, where slaves could come and go through the city's alleyways, out of sight but always close at hand. A courtyard separated the slave quarters from the "front lots," which faced the street. Slaves worked in the courtyard and passed through it when necessary to the back entrance of their master's house. The back courtyard and slave quarters were fenced in together and called euphemistically "the area."[2]

Free blacks could not afford to rent houses in the core around Capitol Hill, so they lived farther out toward the edges of the city, walking greater distances to work and eventually hopping the city's segregated streetcars. Skilled workers and the narrow slice of the middle class could rent and even own houses that fronted on the streets, but many African Americans had to crowd into the shabby but proliferating alley housing. With the arrival of European immigrants beginning in the late 1840s, some property owners built new apartments or row houses in the alleyways to rent to these low-paid, unskilled workers. Immigrants, often Irish women, began supplanting African Americans as domestic servants and rented homes in the alleys from their employers, especially after emancipation deprived Washingtonians of their slaves. Soon two thirds of alley dwellers were white. Before the Civil War, there were forty-nine inhabited alleys in Washington, but that number more than doubled as the process of emancipation brought 40,000 former slaves crowding into the city.[3]

Midway through the war, a soldier patrolling "Tin Cup Alley" found the pathway "occupied by white and black, all mixed up together." The *Evening Star* characterized one alley as "a notorious resort of the 'roughs,' black and white." Eventually, African Americans dominated the "black alleys," as they became known. Here, they could congregate and avoid the nightly "pick up" after the 10:00 P.M. curfew that banned them from the city streets. While the unpaved alleys had no official names, city directory compilers often christened them informally. They thus assumed the names of the landlords who built the housing that their denizens occupied—Snow's Alley, Brown's Alley, Carlin's Alley, Bate's Alley, Prather's Alley—or received imaginative but deceptively picturesque names, such as Marble Alley, Soap Alley, Goat Alley, and Pear Tree Alley. Other names sprang from the alleys' unique social and cultural character, as in the aptly labeled Fighting Alley. One of the most notorious, Light Alley, drew its name from the German immigrant family of habitual thieves and prostitutes who ruled it during the Civil War. In this fashion, the city came to occupy two coexisting urban grids, the famous streets and squares of L'Enfant's imagination and the all too forbidding reality of the alleys, one-fourth of the city, overlaid geographically but socially and economically far distant.[4]

The White House itself sat encircled by a racially and ethnically diverse neighborhood, the First Ward, which contained the highest proportion of African Americans anywhere in the city. When the Lincoln family moved into the White House, more than one-quarter of the First Ward's residents were African Americans, one-tenth of them slaves. The wartime community that surrounded the White House exhibited a spectrum of minutely drawn distinctions of race, ethnicity, and legal status that were enforced by both law and custom. White citizens, resident aliens, naturalized immigrants, free blacks, mixed-race African Americans, and slaves all occupied unique social and economic niches but were geographically "all mixed up together," as the Union soldier patrolling Tin Cup Alley noticed. Implanted artificially from Maryland and Virginia to help with the construction of Washington even before it became the national capital, slavery had slowly degenerated into a vestigial institution. At its peak in 1810, the institution claimed almost one-sixth of Washington's population but then declined steadily to just over 3 percent in 1860. Over the intervening half century, whites and blacks worked together to undermine slavery through self-purchase, "freedom suits" in court, and the creation of an illicit—and feared—underground railroad. John Quincy Adams's petition campaign, Joshua Giddings's "Abolition House," Duff Green's legal representation, Gamaliel Bailey's editorial efforts, the attempted escape on the *Pearl*, the Compromise of 1850, and even Lincoln's emancipation proposal were representative of the mounting campaign that gradually wore away at slavery in Washington by making it less secure. By 1860, the nation's capital was inhospitable toward slavery, an increasingly dangerous and unprofitable place for slaveowners to keep their slaves.[5]

The 255 slaves who continued to live and labor in the First Ward when the Lincolns arrived were a remnant of a once flourishing system of slavery that played a diminishing economic role in the city but remained symbolically important for its defenders. In 1860, 94 percent of the white families in the First Ward no longer owned slaves. Now a luxury rather than a perceived necessity, slaves served a small minority of the area's wealthiest families, about one in twelve. These masters were five times as wealthy as the average white resident, as measured by real property ownership. Signifying their elite economic standing, most of these ninety-four masters—60 percent of them—owned more than one slave and, in an extreme instance, as many as twelve. In keeping with the trend toward hiring out, one-quarter of the ward's slaves, like Henry Wilson, the waiter at Mrs. Sprigg's, were not owned but "rented" by the families they served. The Chesapeake region's slaveowners increasingly hired out their slaves to generate a monthly cash income rather than putting them to work in their own homes. Many of the "rented" slaves were hired out by the Virginia and Maryland planters who were shifting from tobacco production toward wheat and other grains. In an urban setting, hiring out, as the slaves at "Abolition House" had demonstrated, facilitated freedom through either self-purchase or flight, further eroding an already beleaguered institution.[6]

By 1860, Washington's slaves were concentrated in the hands of a diminishing elite. One-fourth of all slaves in the District of Columbia belonged to a mere fifty residents who claimed ten or more. The largest slaveowner in the District owned sixty-nine. In the First Ward, slave masters either owned or rented an average of 2.7 slaves as part of their household staffs. Symbolizing the concentration of the residual institution in the hands of this southern-born elite, seven lawyers and seven clerks together owned one-fifth of the First Ward's slaves. Generally youthful, the slaves ranged in age from ten months to eighty years but averaged age twenty-six, with one-quarter in their twenties, the peak age for physical labor. Two-thirds were female, evincing the city's prevalent demand for domestic servants. More cynically, one contemporary wrote that a "large proportion of the slaves here are females. The reason of this is obvious. They are the most profitable. They allow of an increase of numbers." Male slaves were therefore much more susceptible to sale in the lucrative slave markets of Baltimore and Alexandria for ultimate shipment to New Orleans and Natchez, where they were in high demand as field hands in the proliferating cotton fields of Mississippi, Louisiana, and Arkansas. (The Compromise of 1850 outlawed the sale of slaves within the District of Columbia but did not forbid their removal to Maryland or Virginia for eventual sale.) At age twenty-two, the typical male slave was six years younger than his female counterpart, suggesting that owners were seizing the opportunity to sell them southwestward at the peak of their physical condition and monetary value.[7]

Slaves practiced a wide range of manual tasks for their masters.

Females were relegated to the traditional "indoor" work, duties performed within the home or behind it in the "area." Described collectively as domestic labor, these tasks were an extension of the kinds of "women's work" that many of their mistresses would have otherwise performed. One primary task was creating and cleaning clothing for the household as seamstresses, sewers, washers, and ironers. They prepared and served food at mealtimes as cooks and waitresses. Maintaining the newly prescribed cleanliness of the Victorian home meant cleaning and scrubbing as chambermaids. They helped with pregnancy and childrearing as midwives and nurses. Slaveowners distinguished between "family servants" and "body servants," who catered to the grooming and other personal needs of their mistresses. In the "area," female slaves performed the family's gardening and dairying chores.[8]

Slaveowners often characterized servants as a "housegirl" or a "house woman" or simply a "domestic," but sometimes enumerated their specific skills as "cook and washerwoman," "cooking, washing and ironing and plain sewing," "dining room servant and chambermaid," "pastry cook and laundress," "dairy maid," and so on. A relative few were described as "efficient in every branch of house work," "generally useful," or "knows all about housekeeping." The overburdened Sarah Dover, under five feet two inches in height, was valued as "a cook, washer, ironer, dining room servant, chambermaid, seamstress and parlor servant." Accordingly, some female slaves could rise to positions of domestic importance and personal trust within white households. One master attested that two of his slaves, a mother-daughter team, "had charge and management of his house." Another slaveowner, who kept a domestic staff of ten, called one of his slaves an "excellent cook" who "has charge of the keys and the whole management of his house." Slaveowners, of course, grew dependent on their slaves, sometimes for everything. One older mistress, Ann Kelley, described her thirteen-year-old slave girl as "faithful and truth telling" and avowed that "she relies on Laura for domestic comforts and attendance in her infirm state of health." Indeed, Laura was her "only companion, attendant and nurse both night and day." In an unusual gesture of appreciation, Kelley had arranged to set Laura free upon her death. Some female slaves acquired skills that could serve them well in freedom, such as Louisa Forrest, who could "cut and make men's or women's clothing."⁹

Male slaves performed "indoor" work as cooks, waiters or "dining room servants," gardeners, florists, or simply "a hand about the house," but also a wide range of "outdoor" roles, such as carriage drivers, cartmen, hostlers or horse tenders, and draymen, who delivered beer. Unlike females, however, they could practice a range of skilled crafts, especially if they were fortunate enough to be hired out. Thirty-one-year-old Barney Clark was "capable of all kinds of work, especially as relates to saw mills and boats." Leander Prout was "a butcher by trade and a first-rate hand" who was capable of earning $30 a month when hired out. Dick Massi was "a good farm and garden hand and an excellent coachman and driver" as well as "a complete manager of horses and cattle." Carpenters, upholsterers, teamsters, drivers, nurserymen, plowmen, farm hands, blacksmiths, painters, brick burners, and stable hands could work for wages—and potentially their freedom—outside their owners' homes. Like longtime domestic servants, hirees could earn positions of responsibility and trust. Sixty-year-old John Sepas became a farm manager described by his owner as "invaluable" and such "as is rarely found." Twenty-year-old Frank Digges was a "good engineer" who ran a steam engine in a printer's shop. A cook and waiter, Adam Lee oversaw "the dining room in the most fashionable restaurant and eating saloon" in Washington. After achieving their freedom, skilled and experienced slaves possessed valuable although limited occupational abilities. Along with racism, their early training restricted them to largely manual occupations during their initial years of freedom.¹⁰

The Black Code enjoined masters from overworking or injuring their free African American servants but did not regulate the treatment of slaves. Employment in unpaid, manual labor subjected slaves to unusual physical hazards, in kitchens, shops, and stables, as well as severe punishments that produced a gruesome range of disabilities and infirmities. A frightful number of slaves, both men and women, bore scars that betokened the routine dangers of their labor, as well as the lack of legal restraints on their punishment. Scars abounded on their faces, shoulders, hands, and feet as the result of cuts and burns. Working outside and tending animals, men and boys suffered the worst afflictions, including lameness, missing limbs or fingers, and broken teeth. Women and girls suffered similar infirmities while working indoors. A wide variety of household accidents could abruptly claim fingers and eyes. Slave women bore the additional burden of childbirth and nursing and rearing their own children, as well as those of their masters. Thirty-year-old Louisa Gantt had borne three children of her own, aged eight, six, and seven months. "She is not of perfect health and has been reduced in flesh by nursing her infant and, probably," her owner wrote either candidly or callously, "by overwork, and her condition is not free from danger." The inevitable neglect of slave children while their parents worked maimed many of them for life. John Brooks was "lame in one hip from its dislocation in infancy or youth," and Sandy Diggs was "a little lame in his left foot and has had only one eye from the age of three or four." Slaveowners clearly rued the impact of an injury on the aesthetic appearance of their slaves and ultimately its effect on their market value. When Lewis Dade suffered an injury, his owner lamented that he "had his hand burned about seven months ago, but whether it will leave a scar or not is not known." How much of the scarring, lameness, and blindness arose not through accidents and overwork but rather the kinds of punishments that the lack of legal protection and the abuse of complete control allowed masters to inflict on their own slaves is now impossible to assess. Beyond doubt is whites' ruthless disregard for the hidden, emotional scars that they inflicted upon both slaves and free African Americans, as when Louisa Warren's owner reported that she was "subject at times to depression of spirits that, as a Physician, I consider as not of the least importance."[11]

AS SLAVERY in the District declined, white families increasingly took advantage of the burgeoning free African American community as domestic laborers. During the half century that preceded the Civil War, Washington's labor pool had shifted from slaves to free workers. By 1860, one-eighth of the families in the First Ward employed live-in servants, either white or black. In the First Ward, one-sixth of employed African Americans were servants living within white families. One-half of those lived in a household where they were the only African American. The growth of domestic service favored females, who represented 70 percent of black servants living in white homes. One-third of them were of mixed racial ancestry, confirming whites' often stated preference for lighter-skinned African Americans. A majority of African American servants were adults, and their average age was twenty-seven, signifying that domestic servitude would be a lifelong rather than transitory occupation. Their three most common roles were house servant, which claimed one-half of them, cook, which occupied about one-fifth, and waiter, a smaller number. The remainder served their masters as coachmen, gardeners, nurses, bakers, laborers, sailors, and hostlers. Despite the deterioration of slavery in Washington, slaves remained the mainstay of servitude in the First Ward. Almost one-half of domestic servants were slaves, one-quarter free blacks, and about one-quarter whites, often immigrants. African Americans, both free and slave, therefore represented three-fourths of live-in domestic servants in the First Ward. As a result, about one in seven households—like the White House itself—was racially mixed. Whites and blacks were accordingly "mixed up together" not only in neighborhoods but in individual homes.[12]

The District's Black Code regulated not only slaves but also free African Americans. Any found "living idle"—without employment— or simply "going at large" were subject to six months of unpaid service, their wages accruing to the county treasury. This law virtually required African Americans to enter into the service of whites in the absence of other opportunities. To prevent servants from running away, they were prohibited from boarding any sailing vessel for longer than one hour. (Fines accumulated during every additional hour they were on board.) The severe discipline under which black servants were expected to work, as well as the extraordinary power that whites held over them, was clear in the provision prohibiting their mistreatment. Masters were admonished to provide African American servants with adequate meat, drink, housing, clothing, rest, and sleep. They were also prohibited from injuring them through overwork, excessive beating, and abuse, as well as punishment consisting of "above ten lashes for any one offense." In freedom, Washington's African Americans were a large, dependent class that remained subservient and under the rigid control of whites, even as slavery itself declined. The legacy of enslavement, the restrictions imposed by the Black Code, and the poverty engendered by their relegation to menial labor fragmented Washington's free black families. One-third of African American families were female-headed, and one-sixth contained at least one "embedded family," through the widespread practice of subletting a room to accommodate an entire tenant family.[13]

Although Washington was not yet geographically segregated, occupational divisions between the races were glaring. Whites living in the First Ward practiced the entire range of pursuits, from U.S. senator, bank president, lawyer, physician, navy captain, and "gentleman" at the top of the occupational ladder to teamster, huckster, hostler, orange vendor, lamplighter, and laborer at the bottom, a total of 233 different occupations. African Americans, however, were restricted to the menial end of the spectrum. Male household heads plied only 47 different occupations and filled five economic niches in particular—laborer, waiter, hackman, wagoner, and porter. These five pursuits accounted for more than one-half of African American employment in 1860. With the exception of ministering to the black community and teaching their children, professional and clerical roles were forbidden. (One minister and two teachers in the First Ward were African Americans.) Whites dominated the neighborhood's skilled crafts and retail sales. All of the ward's tailors, stonecutters, machinists, bricklayers, plasterers, engineers, bakers, confectioners, clerks, grocers, druggists, and merchants were white, as were at least nine-tenths of blacksmiths, butchers, painters, carpenters, and cabinetmakers. African Americans, including slaves, were sometimes employed as retail clerks to wait on other members of their own race. All of the ward's porters were blacks, as were all but two of the forty-eight cooks, all but one of the fifty-three waiters, and all but three of the nineteen washerwomen. One-third of African American men were laborers, and four-fifths of African American women were servants or cooks. In freedom, only three African Americans—the two teachers and the minister—practiced occupations that were forbidden to slaves. Former slaves, of course, enjoyed their freedom but recoiled from the bitter reality of the exploitation that they experienced daily even as free men and women. "He had been a slave, and although liberty was sweet, yet he would say that he got along much better when he was a slave than he did now," one freedman admitted. "Then he had nothing to look for, now he had to look forward all the time to some day when he would not have a job." In 1860, 6 percent of the First Ward's African American household heads were unemployed.[14]

Complicating class divisions and blurring the distinction between the races was the growing employment of immigrants, notably the Irish, in menial occupations. Mirroring the racism that restricted economic and social opportunities for African Americans, nativism imposed a parallel although far less severe regime of discrimination upon immigrants. By 1860, more than one-quarter of household heads in the First Ward were immigrants, 60 percent of them Irish. The Irish community suffered similar kinds of economic barriers as African Americans. Their occupational choices were actually far more limited. They occupied the same lower rungs of the occupational ladder, pursuing only 43 of the 223 occupations available to whites, fewer than African Americans practiced. Just two occupations, laborer and grocer, accounted for almost two-thirds of Irish immigrant employment in the First Ward in 1860. Their primary economic role was providing unskilled labor for the growing city. One-third of African American men were laborers, but one-half of Irish household heads joined them in that occupational niche. Their arrival liberated most native whites from the same plight, so four-fifths of all white laborers were Irish. As Catholics, their experiences during the nativistic 1850s differed dramatically from those of the largely Protestant German and English immigrant communities, who represented one-fifth and one-tenth of the ward's foreign-born men. Astoundingly, just 2 percent of German and English household heads were laborers, a total of three Germans and one Englishman, as compared to 52 percent of the Irish. Such severe occupational segregation produced differences in accumulated wealth. In 1860, Irish families owned just one-eighth as much real property as non-Irish whites, on average. Still, Irish immigrants could achieve, on a very limited scale, an occupational status that was off-limits for African Americans—lawyer, surveyor, manufacturer, ship master, grocer, stone mason, tailor, and even one astronomer. Unable to achieve independence, even in one of the shacks that increasingly lined Washington's dismal alleyways, one-fifth of Irish families lived in embedded households. In this fashion, the recent arrival of European immigrants combined with nativism to foment intense competition with African Americans for both economic opportunities and housing, further diminishing their prospects for the future.[15]

While Lincoln was still in Springfield, a well-wisher had written from Washington warning him that "should he keep the same servants in the house, who are there now, and have been for the last sixteen or twenty years, it is feared he will meet the same fate as Generals Harrison and Taylor"—poison. "The President should bring his steward along with him—a man he knows and who can be trusted," ran the advice. "Before he takes possession of the Whitehouse, he ought to appoint the Commissioner of Public Buildings, whose first duty should be to renovate the house, and employ an *entirely* new corps of servants." Lincoln did not remove the entire White House staff, but he did bring one servant with him from Springfield. His personal valet, William H. Johnson, had accompanied the family to Washington, tending to the president-elect during the twelve-day railway journey. Lincoln planned to employ Johnson in the White House, "attending to his wardrobe, shaving him and acting as a handy man and private messenger for the family," African American folklorist John E. Washington, who knew some of the Lincolns' White House servants, related eighty years later. The incumbent staff, however, "so fearful that they would lose their jobs, instantly began to make trouble for any newcomer." In this instance, they rejected Johnson because of his appearance. "In his case there was almost an open rebellion, not only for the regular reasons, but also because of a social distinction," Washington explained. "Johnson's color was very dark and White House servants were always light."[16]

According to the prevailing racial ideology, darker African Americans would have been more "fitted" to physical labor than domestic service. Although one contemporary described Johnson as "a likely mulatto," there is no telling where the White House staff might have placed him along the full spectrum of Washington's subtle hues. According to John E. Washington, Johnson "was mistreated in such a way that it became necessary for the President to look elsewhere for employment for him." Reluctant to challenge the capital's entrenched racial hierarchy, which had become self-enforcing within the African American community itself over decades of elaboration, Lincoln deferred to the White House staff's "color talk." He put Johnson to work keeping the fire in the furnace room in the basement of the White House, out of sight, at a salary of $50 per month. Three days after entering the White House, he wrote a letter of reference for Johnson, addressed "To Whom It May Concern," in hopes that he could find him another position somewhere in Washington. "William Johnson, a colored boy, and bearer of this, has been with me about twelve months," Lincoln attested, "and has been, so far, as I believe, honest, faithful, sober, industrious, and handy as a servant." As John E. Washington put it, "Openings were difficult to find but President Lincoln felt that since he had brought to Washington this Negro who had loyally served him and his family, it was absolutely necessary that Johnson be found work." After more than a week passed with no results, Lincoln penned a personal letter to his new secretary of the navy, Gideon Welles, making a direct request for help. The Navy Department was renowned—or notorious—for enlisting African Americans as sailors at sea and laborers ashore. "The bearer (William) is a servant who has been with me for some time & in whom I have confidence as to his integrity and faithfulness," Lincoln told Welles. "He wishes to enter your service. The difference of color between him & the other servants is the cause of our separation. If you can give him employment you will confer a favour on Yours truly A. Lincoln."[17]

Nine months later, Lincoln was still trying to secure an honorable situation for Johnson somewhere beyond the White House. After writing another reference letter with no result, he then approached the Treasury Department, which sat next door, to the east of the White House. "You remember kindly asking me, some time ago, whether I really desired you to find a place for William Johnson, a colored boy who came from Illinois with me," Lincoln wrote Treasury Secretary Salmon Chase in November. "If you can find him the place shall really be obliged." Chase, who was busily turning the Treasury Department into an enclave of abolitionism within the wartime bureaucracy, did oblige. The next day, he appointed Johnson as a messenger in the Treasury Department with a $600 annual salary, the highest rank available to African Americans in the federal government. In 1861, the Treasury Department employed one messenger, whose salary was $900, and an assistant messenger, who earned $700 a year. Johnson, like other African Americans who entered federal service, was therefore underpaid, earning no more than he had stoking the furnace in the basement of the White House.[18]

Indispensable to Lincoln, Johnson stopped at the White House every morning to attend to the president's wardrobe, shave him, and perform other personal duties before rushing off to the Treasury Department next door, where he acted as a messenger for the librarian during the afternoon. This was not an unusual arrangement. "Nearly everyone not only did the work required by the Government," John E. Washington related, "but also served as house servants and valets for their chief without extra compensation." Johnson, however, was exceptional in serving as one of Lincoln's private White House messengers. Messengers were a ubiquitous and vital feature of the federal bureaucracy in Washington because of the "magnificent distances" that separated its various components, particularly the Capitol and the White House, with its cluster of executive departments, a mile and a half to the west. "Who but a slaveholder in laying out the plan of the national buildings would have dreamed of locating all the departments and offices of the government in which are employed at least one thousand clerks, assistants, etc., at such a great distance from the capitol!" abolitionist Theodore Dwight Weld complained to his wife while boarding at Mrs. Sprigg's. "Thousands of dollars are spent every year and *years* of time lost in going and sending from the Offices of the Capitol and vice versa. All of which might have been saved if they had been located in each others vicinity." The jumble of messengers who continually crisscrossed the city was an inevitable result. Employers favored age and experience over youth and energy, and above all reliability, because of the responsibility and confidentiality that the work entailed. Messengers living in the First Ward, around the White House, were forty-six years old, on average, and ranged in age from thirty-six to sixty-two. One-sixth of them were African Americans. Johnson was considerably younger, in his mid-twenties, when he arrived in Washington.[19]

"Although he deemed it undiplomatic to force Johnson's presence upon the resentful servants of the White House," John E. Washington concluded, "Lincoln felt it a bounden duty to look out for him." Lincoln meant it when he avowed that Johnson "is a worthy man, as I believe," and once entrusted him to hand-deliver an envelope containing $900 in greenbacks, half again as much as his entire annual salary in the Treasury Department. Johnson, in turn, devoted his "untiring vigilance" toward the president's needs, according to a *New York Times* correspondent. Like most other members of Washington's free African American community, however, the rising ranks of government employees had trouble making ends meet. "Most of the colored men then in Government service as laborers and messengers," John E. Washington observed, "depended on outside work to help them in supporting their families." William Johnson was no exception. At times, Lincoln asked the Treasury Department to grant him one or two days' leave, to assist Lincoln or perhaps to earn additional wages. He endorsed a $150 loan for Johnson and, when all else failed, provided him with extra cash, including a personal check for $5 made out to "William Johnson (colored)." In this fashion, on his first day in the White House Lincoln began forging a racial compromise on a small scale. Characteristic of the man, he labored to forge a pragmatic solution, quelling the White House staff's "almost" rebellion by bowing to the capital's prevailing racial hierarchy, yet finding a way to retain William Johnson as his half-time valet and confidential messenger.[20]

CHAPTER NINE

"A Swift and Terrible Retribution"
Striking the First Blows

———◆◆◆———

W HEN LINCOLN became president, the Confederacy had captured all but two forts in the seceded states, Fort Pickens at
Pensacola, Florida, and Fort Sumter in South Carolina's Charleston
Harbor. A truce left Fort Pickens under federal control, but both the
North and South considered Fort Sumter a crucial symbol of Union
defiance sitting just offshore from the heart of southern secessionism.
On the day after his inauguration, Lincoln learned that the Union
garrison at Fort Sumter under the command of Major Robert Anderson was about to run out of provisions. General-in-Chief Scott told
Lincoln that the Union could not reinforce the fort. Cabinet members offered conflicting and often shifting advice, with only Secretary of State Seward and Secretary of the Interior Smith challenging
Lincoln's personal resolve to hold the fort. Seward believed that his
vast political experience fitted him alone to lead the nation through
the secession crisis. With Scott addressing him as the "chief" of the
cabinet, Seward went one step further and considered himself the
"premier" of the Lincoln administration. On April 1, he wrote an
impudent letter to Lincoln charging that after a month the president
had developed no domestic or foreign policy and that a cabinet member should devise one and "pursue and direct it incessantly." He then
proposed a plan for provoking a war with a foreign enemy that would
reunite the nation. Appalled, Lincoln replied that he had enunciated
a response to southern secession in his Inaugural Address and that if

any change were necessary, *"I* must do it." After putting Seward in his place, Lincoln crafted a plan to use unarmed ships to resupply, but not reinforce, Fort Sumter. Possibly the most important letter that Lincoln sent during his presidency was his April 1861 warning to Governor Francis Pickens of South Carolina that he intended to resupply Fort Sumter "with provisions only." Lincoln sent a "special" messenger, who reached Charleston in forty-eight hours, read the letter to Pickens, handed him a copy, and refused to accept the governor's reply, on Lincoln's order. Sending an unarmed relief expedition to resupply Fort Sumter with provisions but not arms placed the onus of starting a war on the Confederates, if they chose to fire on the ships.[1]

As Lincoln's resupply vessels steamed southward toward Charleston Harbor, Confederate president Jefferson Davis decided to take Fort Sumter before they could arrive. On the morning of April 12, 1861, General P. G. T. Beauregard's batteries unleashed three thousand shells on the fort in a barrage that lasted thirty-three hours. The garrison surrendered, without a single casualty, on April 14. The next day, Lincoln called 75,000 state militiamen into federal service to suppress what the Constitution labeled a "domestic insurrection," prompting four additional slave states in the Upper South—Virginia, North Carolina, Tennessee, and Arkansas—to embrace secession. Washington's situation between two secessionist states, Virginia and Maryland, posed unique security concerns for the nation's capital. Two days after Lincoln's call for troops, Virginia's secession convention—which had been watching events unfold for two months— voted to secede from the Union, subject to a popular referendum to be held on May 23. Maryland, to Washington's rear, was even more critical to the capital's security. In the midst of the secession crisis, Governor Hicks hoped for compromise and supported the Washington Peace Conference, a last-minute attempt to address the looming impasse. Virginia sent commissioners to Maryland to try to negotiate a "defensive" alliance. Meanwhile, Maryland hedged its bets by sending commissioners to the seceded states to discuss cooperation but adopted a policy of "armed neutrality," to prepare for any eventuality.[2]

Allies advised Lincoln to strike preemptively against Maryland to avoid isolating and even losing Washington. The *Chicago Tribune*'s Joseph Medill warned Lincoln that "if Maryland gives way your friends will have to fight their way with the sword from the Pa. line to the capital" and proposed "to lay waste Maryland." In early April, Winfield Scott wrote to Lincoln, with incredible understatement, that "I have nothing of special interest to report today; but that machinations against the Government & this Capital, are secretly going on, all around us—in Virginia, in Maryland & here, as well as farther South." Still, Scott demonstrated a singular inability to gauge the precise nature of the threat. He explained that "I have no police man, at my service, & no fund for the payment of detectives. But, under the circumstances, recommend, that such agents should be, at once, employed in Baltimore, Anapolis, Washington, Alexandria, Richmond & Norfolk." Indeed, at one point the befuddled Scott confessed to Lincoln that "nothing of military importance has reached me to day except thro' the news-paper." If still capable of managing the army, he showed no inclination to assemble a covert security apparatus within the War Department and blithely turned that responsibility over to Lincoln.[3]

As for the defense of the capital, Scott was not yet ready to call up the District's militia but warned that "the necessity of such call, however, may not be very distant." Three days later, Scott had moved closer toward mustering the militia. He informed the president of "a growing apprehension of danger, here," yet he lacked troops on hand to meet the threat to the capital. Reinforcements were on their way but "may be too late for this place." Another concern was the growing list of slave-state army officers who were reluctant to fight Confederate forces, had to be reminded to obey their oaths, and had begun resigning. "Officers of the Federal Army and Navy, had resigned in great numbers," Lincoln put it succinctly, "and, of those resigning, a large proportion had taken up arms against the government." On April 8, Scott asked the District's militia commander to ascertain the number of "*reliable* volunteers" and concentrate them around the White House. The next day, Secretary of War Cameron met with Scott and the District commanders and recommended calling up ten volunteer companies. Lincoln ordered them to muster.[4]

The muster was disappointing, because the militiamen were required to take an oath of allegiance to the United States. Many of the District's militiamen refused to take the oath and resigned. When their companies fell below effective strength, they could not muster. All but fifteen members of the National Rifles, originally comprising seventy federal employees, stood down. On April 22, they crossed the Potomac into Virginia and formed the Beauregard Rifles, named in honor of General P. G. T. Beauregard, who had ordered the firing on Fort Sumter ten days earlier and later commanded Confederate troops at the First Battle of Bull Run. When Scott and Stone refused to provide arms for the National Volunteers, who had shot up the Republican campaign headquarters on election night, they too crossed the Potomac and joined the 1st Virginia Infantry. Many of the District's militiamen agreed to serve only in defense of the capital, refusing to march beyond its borders to take part in offensive operations against Virginia or Maryland. After Major Irvin McDowell, the District's assistant adjutant general, assured them that their role would be defensive only, they agreed to serve. Scott asked Cameron to call up more militiamen to safeguard the capital, for a total force of six companies of regulars and fifteen companies of volunteers.[5]

On April 19, two days after Virginia seceded, a riot broke out in Baltimore when regular army forces from the North tried to pass through the city along the same route that Lincoln had followed to Washington two months earlier. The nine hundred men of the 6th Massachusetts Regiment were making the harrowing transfer between railroad depots when they discovered the tracks obstructed by paving stones, a pile of sand, and anchors. The troops resolved to run the mile-and-a-half-long gauntlet on foot, carrying a white flag, amid a jeering crowd of two thousand to three thousand who pelted them with paving stones. Shooting erupted from both sides, killing four soldiers and twelve civilians. Government officials in Maryland burned railroad bridges and cut telegraph lines to prevent the passage of any other troops through Baltimore, which they justified as a defensive measure. The troops following behind were ordered back into Pennsylvania. In Washington, there were immediate calls to burn Baltimore to the ground. Lincoln's secretary, John Hay, awoke the next morning to discover that the "streets were full of the talk of Baltimore" and abuzz with "feverish rumours about a meditated assault upon this town." Major David Hunter, who was bivouacked in the White House with a brigade of Kansans while continuing his duties as Lincoln's bodyguard, told Hay bluntly that "the troops should have been brought through Baltimore if the town had to be leveled to the earth." Eighteen of the soldiers wounded in Baltimore went to Washington's only hospital, the City Infirmary, located in the former jail and run by the Catholic Sisters of Mercy. Eight suffered head injuries inflicted by paving stones, bricks, and brickbats, and two lost fingers to gunfire.[6]

Lincoln knew that any military response would prove disastrously counterproductive to his goal of keeping Maryland in the Union and tried to court the state's conservatives. "He thoroughly believed in the loyalty of Maryland," Hay observed. "The President seemed to think that if quiet was kept in Baltimore a little longer Maryland might be considered the first of the redeemed." Governor Hicks, however, had already called a special session of the legislature to convene one week after the Baltimore Riot, stoking fears that the state might secede. Lincoln insisted emphatically that the movement of troops through Baltimore was purely defensive and not meant as a threat to Maryland or Virginia: "I *do* say the sole purpose of bringing troops *here* is to defend this capital." When Governor Hicks wrote Lincoln that "it is my solemn duty to inform you that it is not possible for more soldiers to pass through Baltimore unless they fight their way at every step," the president proposed a compromise. "For the future, troops *must* be brought here," he answered, "but I make no point of bringing them *through* Baltimore." General Scott devised a plan to bypass Baltimore by shipping troops to Annapolis by water and then bringing them overland the rest of the way to Washington, which Lincoln now relayed to Hicks. "By this, a collision of the people of Baltimore with the troops will be avoided," he reasoned, "unless they go out of their way to seek it." Governor Hicks, however, wanted no more troops crossing his state, through either Baltimore or Annapolis, and rejected the compromise. Four days later, he wrote to Scott that "I feel it to be my duty to advise the President to order elsewhere the troops now off Annapolis and also that no more may be sent through Maryland." The president, of course, could agree to no such "advice." On the same day, Scott informed him that twenty miles of railroad between Annapolis and Washington had been torn up.[7]

When a committee of fifty from Baltimore came to ask Lincoln not to send any more troops through Maryland, Hay observed that "the whining traitors from Baltimore were here again this morning. The President I think has done with them." Lincoln told them bluntly that "your citizens attack troops sent to the defense of the Government, and the lives and property in Washington, and yet you would have me break my oath and surrender the Government without a blow." He reiterated that "I have no desire to invade the South; but I must have troops to defend this Capital." Then, with exasperated logic, he laid out the inescapable imperative that the troops must pass through Maryland. "Our men are not moles, and can't dig under the earth; they are not birds, and can't fly through the air. There is no way but to march across, and that they must do." He offered them, in blunter language, the same compromise that their governor had rejected: "Keep your rowdies in Baltimore, and there will be no bloodshed. Go home and tell your people that if they will not attack us, we will not attack them; but if they do attack us, we will return it, and that severely."[8]

With the railroad and telegraph lines to Baltimore interrupted, the capital spent the next week virtually cut off from the North, waiting anxiously for troops to arrive via the gerrymandered route through Maryland. Meanwhile, Scott told the president that 1,500 to 2,000 Virginia troops were installing a battery near Mount Vernon to close off the Potomac, with only one "small War steamer," the USS *Pawnee*, patrolling the river. Another force was preparing to attack Fort Washington fifteen miles southward. He expected 10,000 Virginia troops to launch "a general attack on this Capital," which he anticipated "at any moment," but believed that the 7,000 District Volunteers could hold them off. Yet he confessed to Lincoln that "I do not fully know what troops are in the Capitol, what in the Treasury, what arrived today or the exact positions of the battalions of District volunteers." Lincoln told Hay that "it seemed there was no certain knowledge on these subjects at the War Department, that even Genl. Scott was usually in the dark in respect to them." In the midst of the crisis, he asked Vice President Hannibal Hamlin "to write him a daily letter in regard to the number of troops arriving, departing, or expected, each day."[9]

Above all, the capital awaited the arrival of more troops from the North, particularly the New York 7th Regiment. In the interim, seventy-six veterans of the War of 1812 met to "offer their services to the Government for the defense of the city." Lincoln himself climbed onto the White House roof, which Hay called "the battlements of the Executive Mansion," to watch for friendly or hostile troop movements. From his office window, the president sat with his feet up, peering through a telescope resting on his toes, gazing southward. The most exasperating sight was a "Secession flag" flying over the Marshall House, a hotel across the river in Alexandria, which was visible from the White House. As the week wore on, Hay confided to his diary that "the North is growing impatient." Lincoln grew discouraged, shrouded in "gloom and doubt," as he too waited in vain for the "relief of Washington." At one point, he announced pessimistically, "I don't believe there is any North. The Seventh Regiment is a myth." Amid the grueling suspense, he sat in the White House asking, "Why don't they come? Why don't they come?"[10]

Suspense and fear mounted as the capital's isolation dragged on. With the railroad to Baltimore cut and the Potomac blockaded, Washingtonians ran low on food, missed out on mail, and read three-day-old newspapers from the North. Aggravating the impasse in Maryland, Virginians stopped selling food in Washington's markets. In Alexandria, an "impromptu vigilance committee" of secessionists intimidated local farmers, and when wagons from Virginia did cross the Potomac, government troops stopped and searched them. "Housekeepers here," John Hay wrote, "are beginning to dread famine." On April 25, the New York 7th Regiment arrived at last and the railroad connection to Baltimore resumed. "The Seventh marched up Pennsylvania avenue, preceded by their band, looking magnificently and causing the wildest demonstrations of pleasure on the part of our citizens," the *National Intelligencer* reported. "They went as far as the President's House, where they passed in review before the President and the Secretaries of State and War." Equally portentous as the arrival of troops in the capital was the first appearance of fugitive slaves. "All through Maryland," according to John Hay, slaves seeking freedom followed the soldiers, "begging to be allowed to come with them as servants." A former slave who had bought his own freedom, Hay reported, told the soldiers that "If I had known you gun men was acoming, I'd a saved my money." The arrival of troops and fugitives became a familiar sight in Washington and foreshadowed the future of both the city and the Civil War.[11]

WHILE NO longer a direct military threat, Maryland could obstruct an effective defense of Washington, abetting its capture and occupation by Virginia. Advisors urged Lincoln to take that possibility seriously. General Benjamin Butler, whose brigade had made a harrowing passage through the state, much of it on foot, requested permission "to bag the whole nest of traitorous Maryland Legislators and bring them in triumph here." On April 25, Secretary of the Treasury Salmon Chase implored Lincoln to subdue Maryland, whose secession, he believed, would triple the strength of the rebellion. "Do not, I pray you, let this new success of treason be inaugurated in the presence of American troops," he asked. "Save us from this near humiliation." He suggested an order to Scott to secure Maryland for the Union. "A word to the brave old commanding General," he concluded, "will do the work of prevention, and you alone can give the word." On that same day, Lincoln told Scott, "The Maryland Legislature assembles to-morrow at Anapolis; and, not improbably, will take action to arm the people of that State against the United States." Acknowledging the pressure he felt "to arrest, or disperse the members of that body," he concluded judiciously that "I think it would *not* be justifiable." Instead, he asked Scott "to watch, and await their action, which, if it shall be to arm their people against the United States, he is to adopt the most prompt, and efficient means to counteract it, even, if necessary, to the bombardment of their cities—and of course in the extreme necessity, the suspension of the writ of habeas corpus."

Lincoln's order made clear that he considered suspending the writ of habeas corpus a more severe measure than bombardment. Two days later, he explicitly authorized Scott to suspend the writ and make arbitrary arrests, if resistance made it necessary, to protect the military line between Washington and Philadelphia. As he often did early in the war, Lincoln left the final decision to his military commander. Within two days, however, Scott declared Washington secure. When Governor Hicks called the heavily Democratic Maryland legislature into session, a Unionist majority blocked consideration of an ordinance of secession.[12]

The army's arrest of a Maryland secessionist, John Merryman, accused of drilling troops for service in the Confederate Army, prompted Chief Justice Taney's opinion of June 1, 1861, challenging the president's authority to suspend the writ of habeas corpus, an opinion Lincoln ignored. In July, he expanded his order to Scott to include the entire military line between Washington and New York City. When Congress convened on July 4, he explained that the Constitution was silent on the question of whether they alone or the president possessed the power to suspend the writ of habeas corpus. But, he asked, even if he had violated the law in suspending it, which he did not believe, "are all the laws, *but one*, to go unexecuted and the government itself go to pieces, lest that one be violated?" Lincoln considered this potential breach of the Constitution a justifiable executive response to the "dangerous emergency" posed by secession. Congress agreed with him that "this authority has purposely been exercised but very sparingly" and voted to approve his actions retroactively. Lincoln eventually extended the military line northward to Bangor, Maine.[13]

WITH THE military line through Maryland secure, the focus turned to Virginia. The first proposal to invade Virginia came from Major General George B. McClellan, who commanded the military forces in Ohio. McClellan was a thirty-four-year-old West Pointer who had graduated second in his class. He was one of the most highly respected tacticians in the army, who had served with distinction in the Mexican-American War, spoke four languages, and studied military doctrine in Europe. An admirer of Emperor Napoleon, McClellan was a former chief engineer of the Illinois Central Railroad who had mastered the latest modern organizational skills. From his command in Ohio, McClellan wrote a presumptous letter to Winfield Scott proposing an attack on Richmond with an army of 80,000. "The movement on Richmond should be conducted with the utmost promptness, & could not fail to relieve Washington, as well as to secure the destruction of the Southern Army," he wrote. "I know that there would be difficulties in crossing the mountains, but would go prepared to meet them." Scott was appalled and probably threatened by McClellan's audacity.[14]

In an unusual move, he sent McClellan's letter to Lincoln with a critique of the plan and a proposal of his own. A premature attack on Richmond, he advised the president, would undermine Virginia's Unionists, who had an important foothold in the western third of the state that lay beyond the Blue Ridge, and "probably insure the revolt of Western Virginia." In short, McClellan's plan ran counter to Lincoln's strategy of keeping slave states in the Union. (Virginia's referendum on secession was still three weeks away.) Scott seized this opportunity to propose a more comprehensive plan than McClellan's. "His plan is to subdue the seceded states, by piecemeal, instead of enveloping them all (nearly) at once," Scott advised Lincoln, "by a cordon of posts on the Mississippi to its mouth, from its junction with the Ohio, & by blockading ships of war on the sea-board." Thus was born Scott's famous proposal for surrounding the South through a coastal blockade and control of the Mississippi and Ohio rivers, which the press quickly dubbed the "Anaconda Plan," after the South American snake that encircles its victim and then slowly crushes it to death. While McClellan's proposal was impractical, as well as counterproductive, the idea of defending Washington by attacking Virginia made sense. Lincoln now turned the capital's perilous geographic location into a decisive military advantage. After securing Maryland to the rear, he turned Virginia into an offensive front and Washington into the most strategic military position in the Union.[15]

The defense of Washington required securing the Virginia side of the Potomac. Two strategic bridges spanning the Potomac River represented not only essential routes for any crossing into Virginia but also potential gateways for an enemy advance into the city. The Long Bridge, aptly named after its mile-long span, received a federal charter in 1809 as a toll bridge linking the capital with Virginia. Its economic value in peacetime was immense, and its strategic value in wartime even more so. During the British invasion of the capital during the War of 1812, the Americans burned the Virginia end of the timber structure to keep the enemy from crossing over, and the British burned the Washington side to keep the Americans from reentering the city. When flooding and ice damaged the Long Bridge in 1831, the government bought it from the Washington Bridge Company and reconstructed it, erecting eight masonry arches to give it more stability. Before the war, the commissioner of public buildings labeled the bridge "very rickety," and a single boat driven by a gale disabled it. Still, 325,000 people, 83,000 vehicles, 7,300 riders on horseback, and 10,000 cattle crossed the Long Bridge between Washington and Virginia in 1860. During the war, it could take an hour to cross because of the immense military traffic. "On arriving at the Long Bridge, we found it covered with carriages, & men on foot & horseback from one end to the other," the commissioner of public buildings reported. "We got into the line as soon as possible, & moved slowly about ½ way over, when Major Gen. McC. escorted by about *two miles* of cavalry passed us. All had to stop till they had passed across. Then came a parcel of baggage wagons from the other side, & we had to wait for them to pass, then a vessel came up and the draw was opened, & we had to wait for *that.*" Farther upriver, the Chain Bridge connected Georgetown with Virginia. Before the war, six different bridges had occupied the same site in succession, the third of which was one of the world's earliest suspension bridges, held up by chains rather than cables, hence its name. The Civil War–era structure was made of timber trusses sitting on seven stone piers, but the name had taken hold.[16]

In early April, responding to the "talked-of raid of the secessionists upon Washington," militia units began patrolling the approaches to the city, particularly the Potomac bridges. Union engineers crossed

stealthily into Virginia and surveyed the ground for future fortifications. During the Maryland crisis, Virginia initiated the process of
expelling northerners who refused to take an "oath of allegiance."
Thus began the flood of Unionist refugees who crossed the Long
Bridge into Washington throughout the course of the war. After taking an oath of allegiance to the Union, they received parole and were
free to go on their way. Any civilians who wanted to cross the bridge
in the opposite direction needed a pass from General Joseph Mansfield, Commander of the Department of Washington. On the Washington side of the bridge, the government erected a special telegraph
line to maintain instant communication. Meanwhile, Virginians tore
down the telegraph line that connected the bridge with Alexandria,
rolling up the wires and hauling off two cartloads for reuse. On May
3, Winfield Scott informed Lincoln that Virginia had installed artillery batteries on Arlington Heights, the Lee estate that commanded
a breathtaking view of Washington across the river, representing a
natural defensive position. Scott warned Lincoln that "the Presidents' square & all the western part of this city, with Georgetown are
within the reach of heavy gun batteries on the Arlington heights."[17]

George Washington Parke Custis, Martha Washington's grand-
son and the adopted son of George Washington, established the Lee
estate at Arlington in 1802. After Robert E. Lee married Custis's only
daughter, Mary, in 1831, the couple settled on the 1,100-acre estate
and lived there for the next thirty years. One of the army's most
talented combat engineers, Lee graduated second in his class from
West Point in 1829. He spent most of his military career designing
fortifications, improving rivers and harbors, and surveying. During
the Mexican-American War, he served with distinction as an aide
to General Winfield Scott and worked alongside Ulysses S. Grant.
After the war, he was superintendent of West Point before accepting his first field command in Texas in 1855. During the secession
crisis, in March 1861, the War Department recalled Lee from his
post in Texas to receive a promotion to full colonel, which he considered a contrivance to encourage his loyalty to the Union. Winfield
Scott, now general-in-chief, urged him to side with the Union. "I
shall never bear arms against the Union," Lee concluded, "but it may

be necessary for me to carry a musket in favor of my native state." Lee spent the month of March pondering his—and the nation's—fate. On the day after the Virginia Convention voted to secede, Lee crossed the Potomac and met with Scott, who wanted him to lead the army as his second in command. Scott may have believed that appointing the South's finest military officer to head the Union Army might forestall secession. When Lincoln's personal emissary, the Marylander Francis Preston Blair, asked Lee to oversee the defenses of Washington as a major general, Lee feared that meant leading an invasion of the South. He ultimately decided that "though opposed to secession and deprecating war, I could take no part in an invasion of the Southern States." Scott advised Lee that he was making a mistake but that if he was determined to resign he should do so immediately.[18]

Two days later, on April 20, Lee resigned from the Union Army and within days accepted command of Virginia's military forces. (Ironically, some commentators believed that Lee's command over the Virginia militia would prevent an attack on the capital, because he was too experienced to believe that it had much chance of success.) Upon his appointment as major general and commander-in-chief of Virginia's army, Lee understood that Arlington would become a prime military target because of its strategic value in defending the capital and Washingtonians' bitter reaction to his resignation. General Scott sent a member of his staff, Orton Williams, who was Mary Lee's cousin, to warn her to leave Arlington while she could. Mary Lee watched in wonder as Union engineers surveyed her estate even before the invasion began. (As for Williams, when he tried to resign from Scott's staff, he was arrested for fear that he might disclose the impending plan of attack on Virginia. After he promised not to enter the Confederacy for a month, he was released on parole. To avoid provoking Scott, Lee sent Williams to Tennessee as soon as his one-month parole ended. Two years later, he put on his U.S. Army uniform, forged orders from General William Rosecrans, and asked to inspect the enemy's fortifications. He was hanged as a spy.) Writing from Richmond, Lee cautioned his wife that she "had better prepare all things for removal." Watching the military movements in Washington from her perch on the heights, Mary Lee dutifully packed their belongings, including George Washington's personal papers, but could not take everything and left several relics inherited from Martha Washington. She fled from Arlington with loathing and only to ease her husband's mind, telling Scott, "Were it not that I would not add a feather to his load of care, nothing would induce me to abandon my home." As a sign of things to come, the Lee family slaves began disappearing. Pessimistically, her husband advised her, "Make your plans for several years of war." After the Union's confiscation of Arlington from the Lees, the Confederate government retaliated by seizing General Scott's Virginia estate on their side of the front.[19]

As the May 23 referendum on secession approached, Virginians began to view the Union sentinels on the Virginia side of the Long Bridge and the Chain Bridge as invaders of their sovereign soil. "For the second time, the Virginia pickets stationed at the Chain Bridge were fired upon last night on the Virginia side, by a party of northern troops, and forced to leave their posts," the *Alexandria Sentinel* complained. The *Sentinel* warned, "These acts of aggression cannot longer be borne with impunity." Union troops were growing restive as well. Army scouts began crossing the bridges to reconnoiter on the Virginia side. Elmer Ellsworth led his dashing Zouaves, newly mustered into federal service, across the Long Bridge and encountered a band of "secession scouts" but did not engage them. The flamboyant Ellsworth had taken Washington by storm, symbolizing the energy and elan of the looming war effort. After reaching Washington aboard the Lincoln Special, he had headed straight to New York City to recruit a regiment of 1,100 firemen. They agreed to join him on his mission to defend the capital and donned the exotic and colorful Zouave attire with zest—red shirts and caps and gray jackets and pantaloons. When he first encountered the firemen, Hay called them "the largest, sturdiest, and physically the most magnificent men I ever saw collected together." Ellsworth himself wore a sword and revolver in his belt, along with "an enormously large and bloodthirsty-looking bowie knife, more than a foot long in the blade and with body enough to go through a man's head from crown to chin as you would split an apple." In Washington, they camped in the House Chamber and committee rooms surrounded by polished marble, towering mirrors, elegant chandeliers, and brilliant frescoes, smoking, playing cards, joking, reading letters, and writing home. They slept in the Rotunda on pieces of carpet with knapsacks or carpetbags under their heads. A few days later, the Zouaves ensconced in their permanent quarters just east of the Capitol in a bivouac dubbed "Camp Lincoln." The Zouave uniform grew so popular that eight-year-old Tad Lincoln wore one on a trip to New York with his mother.[20]

In May, as the Union prepared to cross the Potomac, Lee resigned himself to ceding Alexandria County, including his beloved Arlington House. He advised his officers that "it is not expected possible with the troops presently under your command, that you will be able to resist successfully an attempt to occupy Alexandria." The commander at Alexandria ordered its residents to evacuate at the first sign of Union troops approaching. On May 21, the Confederacy made Richmond its capital, but Lincoln waited to strike until Virginia officially seceded. Two days later, the long-awaited referendum ratified secession with 78 percent approval. At 2:00 A.M. the following morning, under a full moon, Union forces crossed the Potomac. Assuring the Virginians of their peaceful intentions, two columns marched over the Chain Bridge from Georgetown and the Long Bridge from Washington. A third contingent, under Ellsworth's command, crossed the river on two steamers and landed at Alexandria. As Lee had planned, the Confederate forces decamped peaceably for Manassas Junction, and the Union took "quiet possession" of Alexandria and Arlington.[21]

The invasion produced one casualty on each side. For weeks, the secession flag floating above the Marshall House had been "impudently flaunting" Virginia's defiance from across the Potomac in full view of Washington. It seemed that every soldier in the capital coveted the honor of single-handedly tearing it down. "Night before last one of the Rhode Island Regiment started on foot and alone for Alexandria, for the purpose of cutting down the secession flag over the Marshall House," the *Evening Star* reported a few weeks earlier. "His comrades getting wind of it, started in pursuit, and overtaking him at the Long bridge, succeeded in making him return to the city." Just five days before the invasion, the Zouaves had crossed into Maryland, where they confiscated a secession flag from a known Confederate sympathizer, to great acclaim. Now, Ellsworth made it his personal mission to tear down the hated Marshall House flag. When he asked the hotel keeper, James Jackson, to lower the flag himself, he refused. (Jackson had earlier gained renown for cutting down a Republican flag in a neighboring town. As Union troops approached Alexandria, Jackson's neighbors urged him to lower the secession flag, but he remained defiant.) Ellsworth then climbed to the roof, pulled the flag down himself, and trampled it beneath his feet. As he descended the stairs, Jackson reappeared with a double-barreled shotgun, which he fired into Ellsworth's chest. Another Zouave sent a musket ball into Jackson's head and then pinned him to the stairs with his bayonet. "Colonel Ellsworth dropped his sword and seizing hold of his clothing over his breast tore it entirely off," according to the witnesses, "and looking down upon the wound closed his eyes and fell dead without uttering a word." The dashing Zouave had become the first Union war hero and, a few moments later, its first martyr. The death of his former law clerk, as the first Union officer to die during the Civil War, was Lincoln's brutal introduction to the horrible cost of the long conflict that lay ahead. As Ellsworth lay in state in the White House, the president somberly composed the first of many condolence letters that he would send to the families of the fallen. "In the untimely loss of your noble son, our affliction here is scarcely less than your own," he assured Ellsworth's parents. "So much of promised usefulness to one's country, and of bright hopes for one's self and friends, have rarely been so suddenly dashed as in his fall." The press commemorated the victory and mourned the loss by announcing "A Swift and Terrible Retribution."[22]

Within hours of occupying the opposite shore, the army began fortifying the Virginia foothold, "sending immense quantities of tools and fortification implements and requirements across the Long Bridge in train after train of wagons on their way to Arlington." Construction of Fort Ellsworth, commanding the approaches to Alexandria, began just hours after the fallen hero had died. The next day, the first of many signals warning of an attack—the sound of three guns firing—called the troops in Washington to arms. "The streets, house tops, and every eligible seeing place in the city" filled with spectators, as soldiers came running to join the first skirmish on the other side. The army's chief engineer, John G. Barnard, who was tasked with fortifying Washington, oversaw the construction of five forts to defend the Potomac bridges, along with breastworks, blockhouses, rifle trenches, and military roads radiating outward. Long lines of rifle pits connected all of the forts along the defensive line. At the foot of Arlington Heights, the Alexandria Canal ran northward along the Potomac and crossed an aqueduct bridge before joining the Chesapeake and Ohio Canal at Georgetown. The army drained the aqueduct and laid down a roadbed of planks to carry heavy military traffic. This quarter-mile-long Aqueduct Bridge joined the Long Bridge and the Chain Bridge as the three most important wartime connections between Virginia and the capital.[23]

In the months that followed, infantry, cavalry, and wagons by the thousands poured across the three bridges onto the Virginia side, including a cavalry train that had to stretch out for four miles to cross the narrow Long Bridge. Engineers replaced the telegraph line between the Long Bridge and Alexandria and strung an "immence amount" of wire between the War Department and all of the Virginia camps. In mid-June, Lincoln, Secretary of War Cameron, and Secretary of the Treasury Salmon Chase inspected the fortifications and "left highly pleased with the completeness and perfection of the arrangements for defense." A ring of sentries two miles in radius guarded every entry into the city, including the bridges, roads, railroads, and the Chesapeake and Ohio Canal. Still, saboteurs plagued the foothold. Secessionists tried to blow up the Long Bridge with four kegs of powder. When the Virginia end collapsed, fifty steers crossing into Washington fell into the Potomac. The telegraph line between Arlington and the War Department was cut, and the U.S. flag that had replaced the secession banner over the Marshall House was torn down. For the rest of the war, "wonder-mongers" who lived near the Potomac would haunt windows on the Washington side, watch every troop movement in the Virginia camps, and send "sensation rumors" rippling across the city.[24]

When Congress convened on July 4, Lincoln justified the military movement into Virginia, excusing it as a response to the state's secession. "The people of Virginia have thus allowed this giant insurrection to make its nest within her borders," he told Congress, "and this government has no choice left but to deal with it, where it finds it." He immediately faced pressure to use the new foothold not just to defend Washington but to attack Virginia. He received reports from the front that Virginia was teeming with "thousands of loyal citizens who are only waiting for arms and an opportunity." "Every one here is impatient and anxious for orders to move" was the prevailing sentiment. The northern press, as well as Washington's newspapers, demanded an offensive through the insistent cry "On to Richmond!" The army now assumed a second mission, charged not only with defending the Union capital but with launching an offensive into Virginia, with the Confederate capital as its ultimate goal. Lincoln created the Department of Northeastern Virginia and appointed the newly promoted General Irvin McDowell to command it with a force of 35,000 men. (Although McDowell had never commanded troops in battle, Lincoln appointed him on Treasury Secretary Chase's recommendation.) Confederate General P. G. T. Beauregard had an army of 20,000 concentrated at Manassas, a vital railroad junction just south of Bull Run, a tributary of the Potomac. The two armies, twenty-five miles apart, skirmished constantly, but Lincoln's gravest fear was a Confederate counterattack on Alexandria. When he ordered McDowell to submit a plan for attacking Manassas, the inexperienced general asked for more time to train his men. "You are green, it is true, but they are green also," Lincoln counseled. "You are all green alike."[25]

Hearing "a thousand different rumors," in early July Washingtonians watched reinforcements pour over the Long Bridge day after day and knew that a battle was looming. Four thousand troops crossed over at a time, led by regimental bands and followed by dozens of supply wagons. The mood was festive, and when General Ambrose Burnside rode across the bridge with his 4,600 men, festooned with bouquets, their regimental bands played "Dixie." There were, however, more ominous signs of things to come. Military units scoured the city by night rounding up "stragglers" who had decamped to seek out the city's many saloons. "Several hundred army ambulances have been sent over the river in the last few days," the *Evening Star* reported, "and others are constantly on the way." Despite the certainty of "comparatively severe" casualties, the prevailing opinion held that the "dislodgement of the enemy from his works at Bull Run can only be, with such an army as Gen McDowell has, a question of hours." Spectators, including congressmen, rode toward Manassas to "see the Rebels get whipped."[26]

The inexperienced troops betrayed their lack of discipline by spending two and a half days marching twenty-two miles. Meanwhile, Confederate general Joseph Johnston had moved his 12,000 troops from the Shenandoah Valley to Manassas by railroad. On Sunday, July 21, McDowell's men mobilized at 2:00 A.M. and crossed Bull Run. For the next twelve hours, they advanced against the Confederate soldiers, who fell back in confusion. In midafternoon, however, the tide turned when Virginia's General Thomas J. Jackson rallied the army and, "standing like a stone wall," gained the nickname that he made famous. Despite a conspicuous display of personal bravery, McDowell failed to rally his own exhausted men, and they fell back across Bull Run. As they retreated, they panicked and began running in a veritable "stampede of teamsters, spectators, and demoralized soldiers." Jefferson Davis arrived at Manassas in time to witness the Confederates win a decisive victory. He wanted his generals to pursue the retreating army into Washington, but Johnston told him that the Confederate troops were "more disorganized by victory than that of the United States by defeat," which was hard to imagine. Beauregard later blamed Davis for the decision not to assault Washington when they had the opportunity.[27]

Lincoln monitored the battle from the War Department next to the White House, where he spent most of the day poring over dispatches, which arrived over the newly installed military telegraph every twenty minutes or so. At the very moment that the troops were careening back toward Washington in disarray, Lincoln received word that "We have carried the day—Rebels accepted battle in their strength but are totally routed." Two hours later, Seward told him the awful truth. Retreating through a driving rain, McDowell's men reached the capital in the early morning hours, "straggling into the city, by way of the Long Bridge, in squads," where onlookers peppered them with questions. General Scott himself came to the White House at 2:00 A.M. to insist that Mary Lincoln and her sons leave Washington immediately and head north to avoid the impending danger. She refused to leave without her husband. Through it all, the Union's chief engineer believed that Beauregard and Johnston's army could have breached the fortifications and reached the capital. On the day after the battle, Lincoln appointed George McClellan to command the defenses of Washington.[28]

The surprising defeat found the city entirely unprepared to receive and treat the wounded, who exceeded one thousand. Before the war, Washington had just one general hospital, the City Infirmary on E Street, which treated fewer than two hundred patients a year, mostly government workers and charitable cases. During the Battle of Bull Run, the federal government took control of the infirmary and put an army surgeon in charge. The Catholic Sisters of Mercy stayed on as nurses. Just two weeks earlier, the government had leased the Union Hotel in Georgetown and converted it into Georgetown Hospital. Sometimes called more forthrightly the Union Hotel Hospital, the 230-bed facility's poor ventilation, narrow hallways, and crumbling woodwork were ill-fitted for medical service. Its staff comprised one doctor and six unpaid nurses, selected from the 150 northern women who had volunteered. Before the advance toward Manassas, the army had cleared its camps of "all but men in perfect health," perhaps one-fifth of the volunteers, so Washington's hospitals were already overflowing before the Battle of Bull Run began. With ambulances sitting abandoned on the battlefield, however, many of the wounded at Bull Run never even reached the capital, so civilians spent two or three days trekking out toward Manassas to pick them up in wagons and carriages. Families took wounded men into their homes and gave them coats, hats, and other garments to replace the ones that they had lost as they retreated. They sent soup to the infirmary, where a hundred of the wounded lay, while the Willard Hotel fed ninety-five of Elmer Ellsworth's Fire Zouaves. The *Evening Star* declared that "hundreds of private houses in this city have been converted into temporary hospitals for the soldiers by the kind-hearted citizens." One family opened its home to seventeen wounded soldiers. The enemy refused to allow army surgeons and ambulances to cross their lines but promised to provide medical care to wounded prisoners.[29]

Along with Union stragglers, Confederate prisoners trickled into Washington. They went to the Old Capitol Prison, across the street from the Capitol and a block north of the onetime Mrs. Sprigg's boardinghouse in Duff Green's Row. After the British burned the Capitol building in 1814, Washington hastily threw up a temporary building across the street, where Congress convened for several years until the Capitol was restored. Dubbed the "Old Brick Capitol," the building became a school, a hotel, and finally Hill's Boarding House, which hosted, among other congressmen, John C. Calhoun. When the Civil War began, the government commandeered the building as a military prison. Over the course of the war, untold thousands of Confederate prisoners, Union soldiers, suspected spies, southern sympathizers, and political dissenters inhabited its cells, where one-eighth of them died. As the first group of prisoners arrived after Bull Run, a crowd that included veterans of the battle jeered, threw stones, and shouted, "Kill them!" Marines pushed them back with bayonets. "At the Capitol, the Sergeant, finding his men so hard pressed, made a halt and prepared for extreme measures before proceeding to the prison," according to a reporter who witnessed the scene. "It is probable that no more will be carried through the city so openly." Union deserters from Bull Run, including ambulance drivers, who were civilians, joined the Confederates in the Old Capitol. The army also posted a guard at the railroad depot to arrest soldiers "who were trying to get away in the cars," which became a daily ritual throughout the war.[30]

Lincoln reorganized the Army of the Potomac to include northeastern Virginia, Washington, and Baltimore, with a force of 100,000 men. In August, he appointed General George McClellan, who had achieved conspicuous military success in western Virginia, to command the new army. As most of the original "three-month men" that he had called up in April began heading home, Lincoln ordered 30,000 of the new "three-year men" to assemble in Washington. The Bull Run disaster also prompted the city to raise a regiment for offensive rather than merely defensive purposes, the 1st Regiment District Volunteers. "The war spirit which sprung up anew throughout the country immediately upon learning of our repulse at Bull Run," the *Evening Star* reported, "has already formed the nucleus of a fine regiment in this city." Ninety-day militiamen whose terms were expiring formed the core of the new three-year regiment. Their first mission was guarding the crucial military line between Washington and Baltimore—the B&O Railroad. In February 1862, the 2nd District Regiment, called the Home Guard, formed to help defend the capital, which was McClellan's first priority. Although the 2nd Regiment saw action as sentries in the Battle of Antietam in September 1862, they spent most of the war serving in Washington's Provost Guard and providing security in the city's hospitals.[31]

Chief Engineer Barnard observed, "When, after the disaster of Bull Run, it became apparent that the war was to be a struggle of long duration, the necessity of the thorough fortifying of Washington ceased to be doubtful." Above all, the "national capital was in danger." Barnard understood the magnitude of the challenge involved in defending Washington. "Not compact and concentrated, like most European capitals, the objects to be not only defended, but protected from distant artillery fire, were dispersed over an extensive area." McClellan considered the defenses on the Virginia side, which his superior General-in-Chief Scott thought "impregnable," insufficient to protect Washington, and Barnard considered them "exceedingly weak." The force at McClellan's command, both defensive and offensive, numbered 50,000 infantry, 1,000 cavalry, and 650 artillerymen on both sides of the Potomac. Hoping to free up most of those men for offensive rather than defensive operations, McClellan felt that "it was necessary, besides holding the enemy in check, to build works for its defense strong and capable of being held by a small force." Congress had already mandated completion of the defenses on the Virginia side of the Potomac. Barnard now urged construction of a similar line of fortifications north of the city "so as to reduce to a minimum the number of troops required for the protection and defense of the capital." New forts arose between the Potomac and the Eastern Branch to defend vital road and rail approaches leading northward. Fort

Stevens, Fort Totten, Fort Reno, and Fort Lincoln commanded the hills, with rifle pits and artillery batteries stretching between them. Barnard's ultimate goal was "surrounding Washington by a chain of fortifications," which would reduce the number of defensive forces required to secure the city while ensuring security if the offensive forces faltered. The defensive system eventually included sixty-eight forts connected by twenty miles of trenches and ninety-three artillery positions boasting eight hundred cannons. By itself, each fort was undermanned, garrisoned in one instance by a single sergeant and two sentries. But as Barnard explained, the "fronts not attacked may contribute the larger portion of their garrisons to the support of those threatened." As long as Washington faced attack from only one direction, the defenses would hold. The War Department held "mock alarms" to test their readiness. Barnard may have doubted the offensive capabilities of the Army of the Potomac, but he believed in the defenses. "With our army too demoralized and too weak in numbers to act effectually in the open field against the invading enemy," he reasoned, "nothing but the protection of defensive works could give any degree of security."[32]

Two days after the Battle of Bull Run, Lincoln and Seward visited the camps on the Virginia side and reviewed the progress of the fortifications. When they encountered Colonel William Tecumseh Sherman, Lincoln joked that "we heard that you had got over the big scare, and we thought we would come over and see the 'boys.' " That evening, Senator Charles Sumner of Massachusetts visited Lincoln in the White House. Sumner told Lincoln that "the country was aroused to intense action" and urged him to consider emancipation at this opportune moment. The two men sat talking until midnight, but Lincoln was not yet prepared to move against southern slavery as one of his war aims or military strategies.[33]

CHAPTER TEN

"Order out of Confusion"
Preparing for War

LEE'S PREDICTION of "several years of war" now seemed judicious, and the capital prepared for a war of unprecedented dimensions. Through its proximity to the front, Washington assumed the role of "grand depot of supplies" for the Eastern Theater. When the Maryland bottleneck reopened at the end of April, troops, weapons, horses, and supplies began pouring into Washington. Almost overnight, 20,000 men enveloped a city whose peacetime population was only 60,000. Housing, feeding, and outfitting the troops, most of them ill trained and poorly supplied volunteers, was the order of the day. Washington's thirty-three militia units had armories of their own in which to muster and drill, but the flood of new recruits had to make do. The first troops to arrive were considered honored guests and found accommodations in the East Room of the White House (the first sentence of John Hay's diary was simply "The White House is turned into barracks") and later its lawn, the Capitol, Georgetown College, Columbian College (now George Washington University), the Washington Arsenal, churches, and a profusion of buildings that the government rented for the purpose. (All of the city's tinners were engaged in constructing cooking facilities for these new quarters.) Soon "temporary canvas cities" surrounded the Capitol for a radius of three miles. The Capitol building itself accommodated seven thousand troops at a time, filling the Senate and House chambers, galleries, committee rooms, and hallways. Before Congress could convene on July 4, layers of "grease, tobacco, and filth" had to be scrubbed away with soap, water, and sand. By the end of the war, the Quartermaster's Department had erected more than four hundred new buildings and structures, so housing even the initial arrivals was a gargantuan task. The summer weather was perfect for camping in the public squares, fields, and groves on the edge of the city, where soldiers threw up improvised shelters, such as the "wedge tent," two planks leaned against a ridge pole and nailed together. Troops bivouacked and drilled in the inaugural ballroom, a temporary structure behind City Hall. The press lamented, "Their quarters are subject to a complete drenching whenever it rains." All of the camps around the city were connected to the War Department with telegraph lines.[1]

Arming the soldiers was the next task. The Ordnance Department lost one of its two main suppliers of arms when Union troops burned the federal arsenal at Harpers Ferry after Virginia seceded. The army expanded production at the Springfield Armory in Massachusetts tenfold to compensate for the loss. The Washington Arsenal, the largest arsenal in the Union, also provided an immense supply of weapons. Situated a mile south of the Capitol, at the confluence of the Potomac and Eastern Branch rivers, the Arsenal aimed its rows of cannons toward Virginia on the opposite shore before hauling them off to the Union Army. A massive assemblage of cavernous buildings filled with workshops, the Arsenal produced an artillery battery of six to twelve cannons every week, and every day turned out 100,000 minie cartridges, 36,000 minie balls, and hundreds of cannon shot, shells, and grape canisters. The heavily guarded Arsenal did not produce rifles but stored a quarter million of them at a time. In addition to the immense production of weaponry that went on within its walls, the Arsenal routinely received arms by railroad and the river. A single shipment before the Battle of Bull Run brought seven carloads of 24-pound cannonballs, totaling five thousand. Its enormous stores of combustible powders of all varieties, employed in the production of artillery shells and minie cartridges, made the Arsenal the most dangerous place in Washington. In April 1862, the first of many gruesome wartime accidents presaged the carnage that was to come. "In the room where they were preparing fuses some of the combustible matter accidentally became ignited and communicated to other parcels of the compound," the *National Intelligencer* reported, "the explosion of which seriously burnt and injured six or eight persons, but none of them fatally, it is hoped." The eight munitions workers, who were filling paper fuses for artillery shells, all survived, but their faces and hands were "very much burnt." As production increased and men entered the army, women, boys, and girls replaced them in the Arsenal, with even more tragic consequences.[2]

The Arsenal's companion, the Navy Yard, sat a mile southeast of the Capitol along the Eastern Branch, employing 1,800 men in the production of naval ordnance. Like the Arsenal, the Navy Yard produced cannons, shot, shells, and caps and bullets for rifles. Most of the iron cannons came from northern foundries to be turned and bored, painted, and fitted with gun carriages in Washington for the U.S. Navy, but the yard produced brass howitzers from scratch. Its forge molded massive four-ton anchors. The Navy Yard also ran a copper mill that turned out tons of the metal each day for use in shipbuilding and ordnance production. Among other wartime duties, the Navy Yard repaired and refitted the USS *Monitor* after its fabled engagement with the CSS *Merrimack*—and put it on display for Washingtonians to examine. As a result of the navy's long tradition of employing African Americans, both free and slave, the neighborhood that grew up around the Navy Yard was one of the centers of their community. When fugitive slaves began arriving in Washington from the seceded states, they were initially housed—and later put to work forging anchors—at the Navy Yard. Littered with barrels and boxes of powder, the Navy Yard, like the Arsenal, saw its share of wartime disasters. A few days after Bull Run, an explosion in the "rocket house" burned one worker "to a crisp," killed another, and injured two more.[3]

The arsenals began employing women in October, initially former department clerks, to free up men for military service. The District of Columbia Armory originally stored rather than manufactured "various paraphernalia of war"—muskets, rifles, cartridges, and sabers. Soon, however, the Armory was employing three hundred women and one hundred men and boys to produce cartridges, the "missiles of death," at the rate of 150,000 to 200,000 a day. The "nimble fingers of the gentler sex" were perfect for the task of cutting paper into the right shape and size, rolling it into a cylinder, adding the ball and the requisite amount of powder, and then pinching the top of the cartridge to close it. The women bundled them into packages of ten or twelve, along with a roll of percussion caps, and packed them into boxes of one thousand to two thousand cartridges of various sizes. Soldiers bit off the end of each cartridge and poured the shot and premeasured gunpowder into their muzzle-loading muskets. The Armory's commanding officer claimed another motive for employing women—saving them from dependence on charity—and "always made it a rule to favor the most needy applicants." During the first few months of 1862, almost three thousand women and girls sought employment in the Armory, "many of the applicants coming on to Washington, from the large cities of the North, in hopes of finding employment." For their daily wage of fifty cents to one dollar, each of them made a thousand to twenty-five hundred cartridges. In Victorian America, most women earned praise rather than money for the labor that they performed outside of their homes. Surrounded by immense quantities of "terribly explosive powder," these women's greatest reward was the satisfaction they earned "for aiding to suppress the rebellion which has ruined so many happy firesides, and sent bitterness and sad desolation into the hearts of so many females in our land!"[4]

In June 1864, after a long series of fatal arsenal accidents at the Washington Arsenal, 250 women and girls were charging cartridges in a massive shed when an explosion left 21 of the workers "mangled, scorched, and charred beyond the possibility of identification" and 30 others burned, blind, or disfigured. Three days later, on a Sunday afternoon, the government held a funeral service at the Arsenal, which Lincoln attended. A train of mourners followed a procession of 150 carriages up Seventh Street and then up Pennsylvania Avenue past the White House toward the Congressional Cemetery, where a throng of 25,000 witnessed the interment. After a government inquiry faulted the Arsenal's pyrotechnist for gross negligence, causing his removal, Congress took the unprecedented step of appropriating $2,000 for the treatment of the injured women. A private subscription raised $3,000 to erect a memorial in the Congressional Cemetery to honor the victims. A marble shaft rising twenty feet, supporting a stylized statue of a grieving woman, contained the names of all of the known victims of the explosion.[5]

Just as essential as arming the troops, supplying them with consumables ranging from food to firewood proved a herculean and unending task that dramatically altered the face of the capital. The quartermaster general, Montgomery C. Meigs, was responsible for providing clothing, supplies, transportation, horses, mules, and forage for the entire Union Army. Born in Georgia, as a boy Meigs moved to Pennsylvania with his family and attended West Point. A talented engineer, during the 1850s Meigs worked on expanding the U.S. Capitol, including construction of the new cast-iron dome, completed during the war at Lincoln's insistence, the Patent Office, and the magnificently designed and constructed Washington Aqueduct. Lincoln appointed him quartermaster general after his predecessor, Joseph Johnston, resigned to command the Confederate forces in Virginia. Widely admired for his professionalism, incorruptibility, and devotion to the Union, Meigs ran the Quartermaster's Department effectively and efficiently throughout the entire war. His basic strategy was letting out many contracts to smaller firms, which increased competition, lowered prices, and kept a steady stream of provisions flowing into Washington's supply depots. His first challenge was clothing the volunteers, many of whom arrived in the capital without uniforms. At the start of the war, the army bought all of its uniforms from a single firm in Philadelphia that employed 10,000 seamstresses. As demand mushroomed, Meigs let out contracts to smaller producers of civilian clothing across the North, who used their cloth on hand to produce black, brown, and gray uniforms, resulting in confusion and friendly fire at Bull Run and allowing enemy troops to single out the volunteer regiments. In September, McClellan suggested prohibiting volunteers from wearing gray, "the color generally worn by the enemy." Secretary of War Cameron went one step further and recommended a blue uniform "as readily distinguishable from that of the enemy." The army's traditional hand-sewn uniforms quickly gave way to mass production made possible by the recently invented sewing machine, which reduced the time needed to produce a soldier's blouse from fourteen hours to only one. As the army exceeded 300,000 men, Meigs told Cameron that "I fear that there is neither the wool nor the indigo in this country to make the cloth we need" and began importing uniforms from Europe.[6]

Provisions reached Washington from the North by railroad—a "tide of cattle, horses, and freight" that turned the capital into the Army of the Potomac's primary supplier. "The movements of military trains have been rapid and continuous, going and coming, loaded and empty, in almost endless lines, in every direction," a visitor reported. "This rumbling is hardly ever out of our ears night or day." Horses had always posed a problem for American cities, dropping thirty to fifty pounds of manure per day, fouling the streets and the air and spreading disease. Their carcasses became a public nuisance and a sanitation problem. Runaway wagons and carriages were a constant danger, and stables were both unpleasant and a fire hazard, as Washingtonians discovered tragically throughout the war. The Lincolns personally endured three carriage accidents and a mysterious stable fire. In peacetime, horses were a ubiquitous feature of life in Washington, plagued as it was by L'Enfant's "magnificent distances," which ironically produced "long lines of filthy livery stables" befouling his carefully delineated streets. In wartime, they acquired even more importance. Key components of the government's war machine were remote from Capitol Hill—the White House a mile and a half to the west, the Arsenal a mile to the south, and the Navy Yard a mile to the southeast. Above all, the army demanded horses by the thousands as mounts for its cavalry and, along with mules, draft animals for its vast fleet of wagons and ambulances. Just weeks after the firing on Fort Sumter, the government's corral in the First Ward stabled 2,000 horses. Soon herds of 500 were arriving from across the North, with 300 hitched into working teams each day. Up to 100 young horses, some unbroken, could be seen—and heard—racing through the streets, "fastened in couples to a long rope, which passed down between the files," essentially a single 100-horse team. (By itself, McClellan's Army of the Potomac needed 46,000 horses to function, three-fourths of them draft animals.) By October 1861, the mammoth Government Stock Depot corralled 10,642 horses and 2,718 mules, with 1,200 wagons and 133 ambulances on hand. Washington's forage master put up 150 tons of hay and 8,000 bushels of oats each week. One hundred carloads—3,300 bales—of hay from Baltimore arrived at the depot just north of the Capitol every day, along with 50 carloads of oats and corn for fodder. All of it had to be hauled across town by wagon—2,800 pounds per load—to the government stables.[7]

The continually expanding depot eventually encompassed stables, shops, and yards that accommodated 15,000 horses, corralled into three herds of cavalry mounts, artillery teams, and draft animals. One-half of the animals driven to the depot were deemed unfit for military service and turned away—"the contractors endeavoring to foist all sorts of stock upon the Government." The army was selective, preferring dark-colored geldings that were six to eight years old and fifteen to sixteen hands high at the withers, representing, according to reputation, "a very superior class." Once purchased, they were branded as "government horses" and shod by one hundred blacksmiths, with a team of eight hundred saddlers harnessing and saddling the cavalry mounts. Unbroken horses went to the depot's expansive breaking and training ground. The depot's most laborious task was outfitting the 1,300 sutlers' wagons that supported the troops in Washington and the Army of the Potomac. Worn-out teams and wagons came in continually for refitting. Saddlers repaired harnesses, carpenters restored wagons, and wheelwrights re-tired them. With a fresh team of four or six horses—all of them used-up cavalry mounts—hitched up, the wagon was fit to return to service. When parked, the supply wagons covered 100 acres and, if driven end-to-end, would stretch out for eighteen miles. Sick horses and mules went to the veterinary hospital—or *"Horse*-pital"—which eventually comprised seven stables that each treated a specific disease. Accommodating nearly one thousand sick horses at a time, the horse hospital could treat nearly four thousand horses a month. By itself, the task of watering the animals was herculean, and everyone living within earshot was "tortured to constant wakefulness by the eternal screech of abominable pump handles." At another government workshop near the Potomac, three hundred blacksmiths specialized in shoeing mules, at the rate of a thousand per day. Slipping two straps under each mule's belly, they lifted it off the floor and tied its hooves to a beam. Farriers, working in a team of four, each filed and shod one hoof, reducing the entire process to a mere five minutes. Later in the war, as horses and mules grew scarce, the army rode through Maryland impressing them, compensating only those owners who could prove their loyalty. Upon hearing that a Union general and some mules had been captured, Lincoln reportedly quipped that he could "make another general in five minutes," but mules cost $200. He eventually banned the export of horses—and later hay—from the United States as essential articles of war.[8]

All told, the army purchased one million horses and mules over the course of the war. Once they were "used up," they remained a valuable resource. At the height of the war, three thousand horses wore out in the Eastern Theater every month, through lack of proper feed, exposure to heat and cold, and hard riding, which caused lameness. The army sent them to the horse hospital in Washington, where they underwent a triage at the hands of a veterinary surgeon, who decided which to keep on hand, rehabilitate, or sell. The Quartermaster's Department auctioned up to one thousand horses at a time for agricultural use on farms across the North, at an average price of $25 to $30. At one auction, a horse went for 37½ cents. After the purchaser drove him home, the worn-out horse, "disgusted with the value placed upon him, quietly laid down and gave up the ghost." Horses and mules that went unsold were shot and sold as carcasses for less than $2 apiece, at the rate of three thousand a month. One visitor to Washington witnessed horses being led down to the river one by one, shot, and thrown onto a pile of fifty carcasses. They were loaded onto barges and floated to a "bone factory" near the Long Bridge. The horseshoes were removed for scrap iron, the hooves used to make haircombs and glue, the hides sold to tanners, and the hair from the manes and tails exported to Europe for weaving into horsehair cloth. The shinbones were valued as imitation ivory for use in cane heads, knife hilts, and pistol handles. Once skinned, the carcasses were boiled in a huge vat, 140 at a time, and the oil skimmed off and barreled for sale as a lubricant and an ingredient in soap. The bones were ground into "bone dust" fertilizer. The sale of dead horses netted the government $60,000 a year.[9]

Horses and stables were favorite targets for saboteurs throughout the war. In December 1861, the government corral in the First Ward caught fire, destroying five of the ten massive stables, each hundreds of feet long, that held 1,500 horses. Five regiments, along with civilians, rushed into the stables, cut the horses' halters, and let a thousand run free. Chased by dogs, the frenzied horses stampeded throughout the city in all directions, jumping, kicking, and breaking their legs as they ran. Civilians who had guns shot the most badly injured. In the morning, two hundred blackened corpses lay where the government stables once stood. On the following night, a saboteur tried to burn the remaining stables by throwing a lighted candle inside, and a few days later the government stables at the railroad station were set ablaze. In 1863, an arsonist set fire to the massive forage shed near the Washington Monument, killing a dozen horses and destroying 1,500 bales of hay. Within weeks, incendiaries tried to burn down the stable of Washington's provost marshal. To improve security and allow expansion, the government relocated its corral to Giesboro Point on the Maryland side of the Eastern Branch. Giesboro occupied nearly a square mile and could accommodate 1,000 horses, with 15-acre corrals each holding 1,000 animals. The depot employed 5,000 government workers, included a camp of instruction and barracks for apprentice cavalrymen, and produced 700 tons of manure each day. Two years into the war, the general-in-chief reported that a half million horses had already been sacrificed to the Union military effort.[10]

While the Quartermaster's Department supplied and fed the horses, the Subsistence Department fed the men, an equally gargantuan task. The Capitol boasted a bakery in its basement, in which 150 bakers produced 50,000 loaves of bread a day, soft bread for camp and hard bread for campaigns. Two hundred forty barrels of flour lined the Capitol's corridors, "leaving only sufficient space for two men to pass abreast." The vault beneath the floor of the Rotunda, designed to accommodate George Washington's tomb, was said to hold an incredible eight thousand barrels in reserve. Fourteen hundred gallons of yeast manufactured daily in huge vats of boiled potatoes leavened the flour. In the "kneading room," forty bakers, dusted from head to toe with white flour, continually pounded the dough into loaves, sliding fifteen loaves at a time into six huge, barrel-arched brick ovens. After baking, the bread went through the Capitol's windows into wagons that backed up for lading before heading off for the camps and hospitals. By October 1862, the Army of the Potomac was building its own bakery in Alexandria that could turn out 100,000 loaves a day. When Congress ordered the bakery in the basement of the Capitol removed, the commissioner of public buildings feared that military authorities would object. By necessity and inclination a "hands on" president, Lincoln intervened and personally ordered the dismantling to proceed.[11]

Leftover bread was ground up and fed to the cattle that grazed around the half-finished Washington Monument. Beef was the most important staple of the Union soldiers' camp diet. The standard ration of meat was a pound and a half of salted or fresh beef or three-quarters of a pound of bacon or pork per day. In camp, soldiers received a ration of fresh beef on seven out of every ten days. Throughout the war, more than a thousand cattle—"destined for the Army"—could arrive at any one time from Baltimore, either on the hoof or by train, thundering through the streets as they headed to the Monument corral. "A regiment of beef cattle made its appearance in our streets yesterday," the *National Republican* reported in 1862. "They were a fine drove of about 1,000, all in excellent order and well fitted to feed our big uncle's boys in the field." Early in the war, the Monument stockyard was slaughtering 150 steers every day. Lincoln's White House office looked southward over this scene, with its attendant smells, flies, and mosquitoes. The city's commissioner of health asked the army to move all of its slaughterhouses outside the city to alleviate the "bone and offal nuisance," but the Monument stockyards and slaughterhouse remained.[12]

Less perishable rations, including "dessicated" potatoes and vegetables, came in by train from New York and Philadelphia via Baltimore. A single provision train carrying "immense cargoes of military stores" could pull into the railroad depot and spill out twenty car-loads of flour, rice, bacon, hams, sugar, dried apples, and coffee. To stockpile the tons of provisions carried by steamers chugging up the Potomac River and the narrow canal boats that plied the C&O, the government built twenty huge warehouses along the city's wharves. By August 1861, the Subsistence Depot at the wharves contained three million military rations, including 18,000 barrels of flour, 9,000 barrels of salted beef and 3,000 of salted pork, 500,000 pounds of coffee, 500,000 pounds of sugar, and 1,500,000 pounds of hard bread, along with the tons of candles, soap, and ice required to supply the entire army. Typically, a regiment of one thousand men waited for two or three hours in line for their turn to receive a ration of two slices of bread and beef or pork, dished onto a tin plate and followed by soup or coffee in a tin cup, repeated dozens of times a day across the city. The army's medical director ordered coffee immediately after reveille—5:00 A.M. in summer or 6:00 A.M. in winter—for every soldier. At the Government Mess House in the First Ward, the men broke up into squads, each headed by a sergeant, sat in rows at the mess tables, and pulled their tin plates, cups, knives, and forks out of their haversacks (spoons did not become standard issue in the army until 1863). Too often, troops who arrived from their home states "half-starved, living on crackers and cold water," could not wait until they reached their mess and began foraging immediately. Farmers complained that "our fruit trees have been stripped, our cornfields have been overrun and plucked, our cows milked, our fences torn down. Our potatoes are pulled up half-grown and useless, celery plants plucked up and strewn about the ground, young cabbages uselessly destroyed, and turnips carried off by the bushel."[13]

As the war began, the soldiers who descended on Washington taxed the city's antiquated system of water supply. Traditionally, Washingtonians carried buckets to draw their water from the public wells, located at street corners and on the squares, or the natural springs that watered the White House and the Capitol. In 1860, the city began pumping unfiltered water from the Potomac into homes and government buildings, including the White House. The poorest residents could not afford to pay the water rent and continued to depend on the pumps, which quickly fell into disrepair. As the pumps failed, one by one, they fetched their water from the city's natural springs, which were enclosed and capped but deteriorated during the war. The "elegant" spring that fed the War and Navy departments, known to be inhabited by a large frog for years, went foul when a gang of boys pried the lid up and killed the frog with sticks, leaving it to float in the water and decompose. Much more gruesome were the discoveries in the drinking-water supplies that lay to the north of the city. "Many of our citizens have been made sick, *not* by the Potomac water," one account ran, "but by reports in circulation of dead soldiers and horses, in a state of decomposition, having been fished from the reservoirs, circumstances being minutely detailed." In 1853, two years after a fire consumed the Library of Congress, the federal government initiated a decade-long project to build a serpentine, twelve-mile-long aqueduct to carry fifty million gallons a day from the fresher Potomac water above the Great Falls, for both drinking and firefighting. A masterpiece of hydraulic engineering overseen by Montgomery Meigs, the aqueduct was completed in 1863, halfway through the war. Until then, pure drinking water was always scarce in Washington.[14]

"The soldiers arriving during the hot weather are anxious to find bathing places as soon as possible," the press noted, "in order to relieve themselves of the dust which accumulates upon them and keeps them in misery until it is removed by a refreshing bath." The initial 20,000 soldiers, however, taxed the pumps immediately. "Many of the pumps about town seem to be incapable of service," the *Evening Star* complained, "and, in fact, now that so many soldiers are stationed here, there seems a necessity for some fuller provision in the way of hydrants." Damming Tiber Creek to collect the water, the soldiers blithely violated the city ordinance prohibiting public bathing between sunrise and sunset, "shocking the delicacy" of the Victorian city. Unfamiliar with the condition of the pestilent canal, soldiers bathed in it, "ignorant of the fact that it is hardly more than a drain for the most populous portion of the city, into which all the sewers empty." Almost immediately, a soldier drowned in the filthy canal—widely known as a "delectable pool of filth, dead carcasses, and kindred abominations"—while bathing in it.[15]

Another military necessity, firewood, resulted in the virtual deforestation of the Virginia side of the Potomac. The forests of Alexandria County provided "skulking places" for Confederate sharpshooters who continually plagued Union sentries. The 6th Maine Regiment specialized in cutting down "acres and acres of woodland" in Virginia to thwart the snipers. They felled the trees in uniform rows facing outward to create abatis that stopped both infantry and cavalry from advancing, earning the nickname "The Woodchoppers" as a result. As Chief Engineer Barnard put it, "This fallen timber (most of which still lies on the ground) rendered an enemy's approach to the lines difficult." For the moment, the ax replaced the rifle in defending the city, and the press reported that "an immense number of axes have arrived, and are being taken across the river for the felling of trees carried on there so extensively just now." The engineers consumed entire forests in constructing the twenty-three Union forts on the Virginia side. They also stripped the heights of all of their trees, up to two hundred acres at a time, to improve the army's range of vision. One Union soldier watched "the simultaneous felling of a whole hillside of timber," which may have been the 800-acre forest at Arlington Heights. Of course, the Confederate army was doing exactly the same thing on the other side of the front. One Virginia family whose forest contained enough firewood "for hundreds of years" watched in dismay as their own army "cut down every last bit of it." A Confederate soldier considered the country "ruined for at least fifty years," and a Union soldier wondered "what the poor mortals subsisted upon." Campfires, however, were the great despoiler on the Virginia side. Union soldiers initially tore up fences for their campfires and then turned to the forests to meet the army's enormous demand for fuel. "As each regiment is allowed two hundred and fifty cords for its winter consumption," according to one estimate, "the entire amount required is immense." Choppers cut wood along the Chesapeake and Ohio Canal as far westward as Cumberland, Maryland, 150 miles away, and then shipped it to Washington on canal boats. Barnard concluded, "It is impossible, at present, to indicate the exact extent of forest cut down," while complaining that the troops, always short of fuel, tore up the fortifications for "tent floors and fire-wood." When he visited the field hospitals, Walt Whitman found Virginia "Dilapidated, fenceless, and trodden with war."[16]

Beyond the military use, and misuse, of the Virginia forests, the government allowed wood dealers to operate behind Union lines, targeting the shores of the Potomac and the lesser rivers and creeks that drained into it. Two years into the war, the forests north of Washington began to fall victim to the chopping. In late 1863, the Washington *Chronicle* reported that "great bodies of forest, from a distance of five to nine miles in that direction, have been cut down under contract with the Government, and at this time as many as one hundred and fifty wagons, with four horses each, are engaged traversing the roads in that quarter, hauling in the wood." As forests disappeared, the price of firewood in Washington grew "extortionate." During the blockade of the Potomac, September 1861–March 1862, wood-boat pilots were willing to run the Confederate artillery to meet the demand. With the onset of winter, thieves pilfered cordwood from government piles and, by the end of the war, were hauling it off by the wagonload. Government teamsters sometimes abetted the thefts. "The Government will lose nothing by keeping an eye to the teams which haul wood to the various military posts," a reporter advised. "We hear of logs falling off occasionally; and what is a little remarkable about such accidents is, that they always occur near the shanty of some friend of the drivers." Milled lumber for construction, which included the four hundred new structures that the government began building in the capital, arrived by railroad via Baltimore. During a two-month period, the B&O trains delivered 15 million feet of lumber, as well as 12,000 cords of firewood and 10,000 tons of coal for fuel, reconfirming the critical importance of the "military line" connecting Washington with Baltimore, Philadelphia, and New York City. By 1862, Washington's supply depots were delivering six hundred tons of provisions a day to the Army of the Potomac in horse-drawn wagons. Overall, the Union spent more money during the Civil War than the total of all previous federal expenditures combined. Whatever its offensive capabilities, the Army of the Potomac was, as Barnard attested, "well armed and supplied."[17]

*   *   *

MOST OBSERVERS faulted lack of discipline for the sobering Union defeat at Bull Run. The flood of volunteer soldiers into the city in the midst of disunion posed an unprecedented challenge to keeping the peace in the already turbulent capital. The day after the Baltimore Riot erupted in April, an uneasy Mayor Berret issued a proclamation reminding Washington's citizens and soldiers of their obligation to preserve the public order. "The presence of large bodies of troops, though it gives to the city an unaccustomed aspect," Berret reasoned, "in no manner supersedes or intercepts the regular and orderly administration of the municipal government." He was over-optimistic. The abrupt introduction of so many northern volunteers to a community that was overwhelmingly southern in character and sympathies was bound to produce a volatile and even explosive mixture of emotions. During his two months of command, General McDowell tried to control his 20,000 new recruits, but his efforts were unsystematic and virtually doomed to failure. Exercising "petty tyranny," overzealous soldiers assumed the task of personally ridding the city of secessionists. "We hear numerous complaints of respectable families being grossly insulted by some of the volunteers now here, and it is quite time the officers should put these men under stricter discipline," the *Evening Star* complained. "A too free use of liquor seems to be at the bottom of this mischief." Acting without authority, the soldier-vigilantes patrolled Washington, arresting known secessionists as spies and warning others to leave the city. A sergeant who "had a clue to a man who was acting with the secessionists" formed ten of his men into a squad, marched them to the home of the suspected disunionist, and shot him dead. In the absence of an effective provost guard, or military police, civil authorities took the men into custody.[18]

Soldiers bullied and sometimes terrorized citizens in unpredictable ways. Thirty soldiers on leave descended on a restaurant five blocks from the White House, kicked the doors open, broke in the windows, and riddled it with bullets from their revolvers. Once inside, they smashed "everything they could lay their hands on," including tables, chairs, and bottles of liquor. They emptied the cash drawer and threw the money into the street. Then they attacked the crowd that had gathered to watch. The police were useless, because they were "in such bad odor with the soldiers as to be entirely inadequate to suppression of any kind of disturbance." The press noticed that "riots" of this character were bound to break out just after payday and concluded, "Our local day police of twenty-five men is wholly insufficient to hold drunken volunteers in check. The services of a military police force are absolutely required." This imperative became obvious when the police shot and killed a soldier that they were arresting for disorderly conduct. Responding to breaches of discipline, McDowell imposed the traditional "drumming out." Witnessing the ritual humiliation, a reporter "heard the drum and fife discoursing the doleful strains of the 'Rogue's March,' and soon saw a procession which consisted of a drum corps and two files of men with reversed arms. Between these files was the subject of military ejection." He was escorted across the Long Bridge and unceremoniously "left to his fate" in Washington.[19]

Lesser infractions included public drunkenness and the cavalier misuse of firearms. A drunken private made a scene by "reeling about Pennsylvania avenue, musket in hand." As pedestrians passed, "he amused himself for some time with snapping it, to the infinite terror of ladies." Then he slammed the gun on the pavement repeatedly until it broke. Unregulated target practice produced another grievance. Initially, Washingtonians took delight in demonstrations of weaponry within the city, as when a corps of fifty Zouaves showed off the accuracy of their new long-range rifles in a public park, and the Rhode Island Rifle Flying Artillery fired shells near the unfinished Washington Monument. Careless and casual gunfire, however, angered civilians. An entire regiment took target practice beside the Eastern Branch of the Potomac, unaware that their musket balls were crossing the river and raining down like hail upon farmers on the other side. Orders went out prohibiting the firing of guns within the city limits and inside or near quarters, but they were rarely enforced.[20]

While soldiers occasionally killed each other through carelessness, the theft of guns undoubtedly cost even more lives. Civilians haunted the camps, stealing equipment, especially pistols, from the soldiers.

Many of the thieves were "fast boys" who sneaked into barracks and stole up to half a dozen revolvers at a time. As the problem spread, the secretary of war ordered soldiers who lost their pistols to pay the government $20, the typical cost of a revolver—and more than a month's pay. Some organized gangs specialized in stealing government stores, including a wide variety of weapons. One ring made off with "almost every article used in the military service—such as muskets, rifles, pistols, sabres, carbines, swords, sword-belts, cartridge-boxes, bayonets and bayonet sheaths, military caps and clothing of all descriptions, commissary stores—in fact, everything except artillery pieces and gunboats." Government employees stole pistols for sale on the open market. Civilians had easy access to pistols at the gun shops that dotted the city, including one on Pennsylvania Avenue that advertised "Pistols, Pistols, Pistols! Colt's Navy and Pocket Revolvers, Latest Improvement. Also, Sharp's Repeating Pistols, with the necessary appendages. For sale low." The proliferation of firearms in Washington made an already dangerous city even less safe.[21]

Firearms fell into the hands of children, who contracted "military fever" during the war. A reporter noticed one of them shooting robins on the White House grounds. When two friends were playing with a pistol, which became a favorite pastime for boys, one of them received a bullet through the chest and died. Secretary of War Stanton reportedly gave Tad Lincoln twenty-five unloaded guns for his mock military maneuvers. While visiting the Tafts' house, Tad discovered six loaded muskets in a closet and fired one of them out the window, hitting the house next door and narrowly missing the head of an African American servant, who was washing clothing in the "area." In May 1863, Lincoln himself requested an unloaded pistol from the Washington Arsenal for the ten-year-old boy to play with. When Mary Lincoln took Tad with her on a trip to Philadelphia, her anxious husband sent her a two-sentence telegram that read simply, "Think you better put 'Tad's' pistol away. I had an ugly dream about him." His apprehension was justified. While two brothers were playing with a loaded gun, one accidentally shot the other, "blowing his head to pieces and scattering his brains over the floor of the room."[22]

General McClellan shared the widespread opinion that the army's chief deficiency was lack of discipline. When he took command in July 1861, he resolved to discipline his troops, secure the capital, and restore order to the city. "The result of the first battle of Manassas had been almost to destroy the *morale* and organization of our Army, and to alarm Government and people," he believed. "Many soldiers had deserted, and the streets of Washington were crowded with straggling officers and men, absent from their stations without authority, whose behavior indicated the general want of discipline and organization." Now began "the labor of bringing order out of confusion." One of his first actions was the appointment of Colonel Andrew Porter as Provost Marshal for the city, with one thousand infantry, a cavalry squadron, and an artillery battery at his command. His principal task was the "restoration of order in the city of Washington." The army's provost marshal system had a long history but had fallen into virtual disuse in peacetime. Porter embarked on a campaign to use the four hundred regular army troops under his command to reestablish "peace in the streets" and achieve "a return of all stragglers to their appropriate quarters."[23]

Drunkenness was a special target. Porter immediately promised to "put an end to the frequent disgraceful scenes resulting from the intoxication of soldiers who roam about the streets." Within days, Congress outlawed the provision of liquor to any soldier in the District of Columbia. Saloons posted signs announcing, "Nothing sold to soldiers." Smugglers invented a wide range of techniques for sneaking liquor past the sentries at the Long Bridge to sell in the Virginia camps. The most ingenious was a "submarine wire and tackle system" that conveyed jugs and bottles of liquor across the river under the water. Porter later addressed the nagging problem of civilian drunkenness by imposing a 9:30 P.M. curfew on barrooms in Washington—"the night grog-shop nuisance"—a few days before New Year's Eve. After the initial six-month cleanup of the city, he responded to complaints from hotel and restaurant owners by relaxing the curfew. They could sell liquor to officers but not enlisted men and keep a "side door" open until midnight to sell both food and spirits, but the barrooms themselves still had to close at 9:30. One private tried to evade this rule by wearing "stripes" that he had bought from a first lieutenant. He ended up in the guardhouse.[24]

In the wake of the Battle of Bull Run, the press faulted not the men but the army officers for habitual absence from their posts and inattentiveness to their troops. "If they would forego doing duty around the Washington hotels for but twenty-four hours," the *Evening Star* complained, "and attend at once to the duty we mention, much, indeed, would be gained." Under McClellan, officers faced a draconian scrutiny that produced a wave of resignations. The volunteer regiments that had poured in from the North during the spring had elected their own officers, as the *Star* put it, "on the devilish-clever-fellow principle." The imposition of regular army discipline under McClellan's command produced a "quiet purging" of officers throughout the summer of 1861, in some cases to escape the disgrace of courts-martial. The result was the appointment of a new class of regimental and company commanders who understood and enforced military discipline. As soon as he took command, McClellan began requiring passes for all officers and men leaving their camps for Washington. Porter's Provost Guard began patrolling the city in squads, stopping soldiers on the streets and examining their passes. Initially, senior officers challenged the authority of the guard but were reprimanded and later arrested for "discourtesy" or "insubordination."[25]

McClellan then issued a series of orders that created a rigorous pass system for the District of Columbia. Civilians needed a pass signed by the provost marshal or issued by army headquarters to cross over into Virginia. If they were residents of Virginia, they needed to provide certificates of loyalty endorsed by a "well-known, loyal and responsible" person. Civilians crossing the bridges from Virginia into Washington did not need passes. No one needed a pass to travel within Washington itself unless "suspected of disloyalty." The new pass system, which was rigidly enforced, prompted a "rush of people" to the Provost Marshal's Pass Department. "Young and old, white and black, they form a crowd and string extending out beyond the door for a hundred feet, from 7 A.M. until 1 P.M., daily." McClellan also regulated military traffic within the city of Washington, empowering the provost marshal to prevent the "fast riding" of government horses on the streets. "Officers dispatching mounted messengers conveying papers will state upon the envelope of the dispatches the gait the messenger is to take—whether a walk, a trot, or a gallop," he directed. "The same directions may be indicated by the seals on an envelope—one seal for the walk, two for the trot, and three for the gallop." To avoid interrupting pedestrian traffic in the city, teamsters were required to leave a gap in their wagon trains between every ten wagons.[26]

The Provost Guard enforced McClellan's general orders "to the letter" to eliminate every distraction from military discipline. "General McClellan has cleared the streets of Washington of loafing officers and rowdy soldiers," the press observed with approval. "But it now appears that it is equally necessary for him to rid the army of them. Otherwise, our every battle in this quarter may reasonably be expected to be a Bull-run affair over again." Targets ran the gamut from desertion, a potentially capital offense, to the relatively trivial. "Yesterday the crowd of lemonade, pie, cake, fruit, and whisky venders about Camp Anderson were made to vacate their stands in that vicinity by summary process," the *Evening Star* reported. In response to the continual threat of incendiarism during the war, Provost Marshal Porter took control of the undisciplined fire companies in an effort to run them with military efficiency. The press quickly embraced the new system, reporting that "since the disastrous 21st of last month, a remarkable change for the better has been steadily and rapidly progressing. The current condition of the streets of the Federal metropolis prove the fact." By the end of 1861, Barnard considered McClellan's army "tolerably well-disciplined."[27]

The provost marshal's responsibilities expanded during the war to include supervision of the draft, the arrest of deserters, responsibility for fugitive slaves, and the suppression and detention of political dissenters, the pervasive "state prisoners." In August 1861, McClellan ordered Porter to embark on "the surveillance of all persons in this city who are disposed inimically to the Government," whether soldiers or civilians. As the imperative for military discipline and control over the civilian population grew, in February 1862 McClellan created the Provost Marshal's Department and appointed Porter as provost marshal general over the Army of the Potomac. Each division of the army had its own provost marshal and provost guard. The provost marshal system originated in Washington during the unprecedented circumstances that the city faced during the summer of 1861. An ad hoc response to the Bull Run crisis, the system grew incrementally and then followed the army wherever it went, continually expanding along with the Union military effort.[28]

CHAPTER ELEVEN

"*I Was Slow to Adopt the Strong Measures*"
Loyalty and Disloyalty

———◆◆◆———

After safeguarding the external security of the capital against an attack from the Confederacy and disciplining the troops, the government turned its focus to security within the city, what Lincoln called "cleaning the devil out of Washington." With mounted patrols riding "street to street" throughout the night, the Provost Guard supplemented the overburdened federally funded Auxiliary Guard or Night Watch, which had never proved effective. The city built a new guardhouse during the secession crisis that, for efficiency's sake, combined a courtroom and a jailhouse in one. The guardhouse was originally designed "as a place of temporary confinement for soldiers arrested in the streets who were without passes, or who had overstaid their passes, or who were drunk or disorderly, and after a detention of twenty-four or forty-eight hours they were usually returned to their regiments," sometimes more than one hundred a day. The building, which was surrounded by a 9-foot brick wall, featured a hearing room at the front of the first floor with seven temporary holding cells behind it. The second floor housed a 30-by-40-foot drill-room in the front for target practice and seven "lodgers' cells" to the rear. The guardhouse boasted Washington's first bell tower, symbolizing its stature as a bastion of regularity and control. Initially, violators were tried before Washington's civil magistrate. Upon conviction, civilians were committed to the county jail, and military offenders were lodged in the guardhouse.[1]

The military and civil authorities began clashing, however, over jurisdiction in military cases. Early in the war, the U.S. attorney for Washington charged that Joseph Mansfield, the military commander of the District, was arresting, trying, and sentencing civilians without authority. In the ensuing clash between civil and military authorities, Generals Mansfield and Scott claimed that they had ordered only three civilians arrested. Lincoln settled the matter, for the moment, with a simple decree: "Unless the *necessity* for these arbitrary arrests is *manifest*, and *urgent*, I prefer they should cease." As the war proceeded, of course, the necessity grew more "manifest and urgent," and Lincoln enunciated the simple, wartime logic that the writ of habeas corpus "relieves more of the guilty, than of the innocent." Lincoln personally supported the military arrests. In October 1861, the District's deputy marshal tried to serve an injunction against Provost Marshal Porter and appealed to Secretary of State Seward, who oversaw military arrests during the first ten months of the war. Seward told him bluntly, "The President instructs you that the habeas corpus is suspended in this city at present and forbids you to serve any process upon any officer here." Then he turned to Lincoln's private secretary, John Hay, and asked, "That is what the Prest says, is it not, Mr. Hay?" Hay answered, "Precisely his words." In the struggle between military justice and the civil authorities in Washington, the military had won out, at Lincoln's behest.[2]

In February 1862, Provost Marshal Porter decreed that he had complete authority over all infractions of military regulations in Washington, whether committed by soldiers or civilians, and that he considered Washington "a military encampment, and therefore subject to military laws." Two days later, Secretary of War Stanton, who had assumed control over the Union's security apparatus, confirmed the War Department's power to make "extraordinary arrests" of civilians. Lincoln ultimately conceded that "instances of arresting innocent persons might occur, as are always likely to occur in such cases." But he justified the arrests by arguing that "thoroughly imbued with a reverence for the guarranteed rights of individuals, I was slow to adopt the strong measures, which by degrees I have been forced to regard as being within the exceptions of the constitution, and as indispensable to the public Safety."[3]

From that point forward, the Provost Guard exercised jurisdiction over both soldiers and civilians, and both went into military prisons upon conviction. With the elimination of civil trials, the army's Provost Guard arrested prisoners, tried them, and passed sentence under its own authority. Thus began the escalating military arrests of civilians that gave Lincoln his reputation for violating civil liberties in the name of suppressing the rebellion. By March 1862, the guardhouse contained 170 prisoners—"entirely too many prisoners for the capacity of the prison"—four-fifths of them permanent rather than temporary detainees, including civilians. The provost marshal converted a building in Georgetown, which became Forrest Hall Prison, to supplement the guardhouse. Eventually, Forrest Hall was receiving 1,500 prisoners a month, many of them arrested by provost marshals outside the District and sent to Washington for confinement and trial. Most of them were ultimately discharged "for want of evidence." Midway through the war, a soldier and six accomplices were arrested for trying to burn down the new prison.[4]

Addressing the wartime threats to the capital's civic order, in August 1861 Congress reformed Washington's antiquated and corrupt police force at last. They fashioned the Metropolitan Police Department along the model that New York City adopted in 1845, which was itself inspired by London's Metropolitan Police Service, the fabled Scotland Yard. During the secession crisis, disunion sentiment had infested the Washington police. Rumor held that only a dozen members of "Mayor Berret's police" were reliably loyal and that many belonged to the secessionist National Volunteers. When the city required the police to take an oath of loyalty in May, many of them deserted or "eloped." The mayor allowed them a "reasonable time" to return and then replaced them. The Metropolitan Police reform consolidated the forces of Washington, Georgetown, and rural Washington County into a single entity, the Metropolitan Police District. Five federally appointed commissioners, nominated by the president and confirmed by the Senate, administered the new department. The Board of Police included the mayors of Washington and Georgetown as ex officio members with no direct authority over the police. Police officers had to be U.S. citizens and residents of the District for at least two years. Congress eliminated the infamous "fee system," including the long-decried "whipping fee" that traditionally rewarded policemen for making arbitrary arrests, targeting African Americans in particular. The act stipulated that "no member of the board of police, or of the police force, shall receive or share in, for his own benefit, under any pretence whatever, any present, fee, or emolument, for police services, other than the regular salary and pay provided by this act, except by consent of the board of police." Any incidental fees or profits from confiscated property went into a "policeman's fund," which provided aid to officers disabled in the line of duty. The act also eliminated the federally funded and never effective Auxiliary Guard, while explicitly prohibiting the police from inflicting "personal violence" against voters. "The corporation does not pay this organization, it did not create it, nor does it appoint its officers," one observer put it simply. "Not only this, but it actually is, and was intended to be, independent of their influence."[5]

The reformed police department afforded Lincoln the opportunity to appoint Unionists, as well as conspicuous opponents of slavery, to the new Police Board. His appointees included Sayles J. Bowen, an antislavery activist, who was the business manager for the only "school for colored girls"—which slaveowners derided as a "nigger school"—in Washington before the Civil War. Bowen had come to Washington as a Democrat to work in the Treasury Department during the Polk administration but lost his job when he supported the Free Soil Party, later becoming a Republican. After the war began, Bowen proposed legislation to establish public schools for African Americans in Washington and wrote a bill to undermine enforcement of the Fugitive Slave Law. (David Wilmot sponsored the bill in the Senate.) He later became a leader of the National Freedmen's Relief Association and advocated African American suffrage. Lincoln later appointed Bowen as Washington's postmaster and collector of internal revenue. After the war, Bowen was a member of the Board of

Trustees of Colored Schools. Elected mayor of Washington, he supported integration of the public school system and appointed African Americans to key positions in city government. Washington attorney Richard Wallach, another Lincoln appointee to the police board, had helped to secure the release of Henry Wilson after he was snatched from Mrs. Sprigg's boardinghouse in 1848. Wallach was a leading Republican who had twice run against James Berret for mayor, losing both times. At their first meeting, the Board of Police Commissioners elected Wallach its president. When Wallach was absent, Bowen was president pro tem. Lincoln personally sent another of his appointees, Zenas Robbins, to New York City to investigate their policing methods. With the passage of the Metropolitan Police Act, Mayor Berret had lost his authority over Washington's police force, and his chief political rival was now president of the Police Board. Republican control over security in the District of Columbia was nearly complete.[6]

The Board of Police received 1,500 applications for the 160 positions on the force. When appointing the new officers, the board sought "the very best material for policemen in our community." While not all Republicans, they were uniformly "zealous Union men, loyal to the Government, and true to the old flag." Most of them were veterans of three months' service in the District militia. The new superintendent of police, William B. Webb, promised "a standard of excellence which has heretofore been considered unattainable in this city." His first decree to his men was that "they must not be seen loafing upon the corners or elsewhere on the streets." The patrolmen's uniforms, modeled after New York City's, were double-breasted dark blue coats with two rows of gilt buttons, blue shirts, and blue pantaloons with white worsted cords running along the seams. They were directed to keep their coats buttoned whenever on duty. The patrolmen carried polished rosewood staffs, but the Police Board sent to the War Department for revolvers. Their silver badges, worn on the breast, read METROPOLITAN POLICE. The new force joined the Provost Guard in cleaning up the city, focusing on liquor sales to soldiers and "clearing the public squares, streets and corners of the vagrants by which they were infested." The new police enforced the Sabbath law that closed businesses on Sundays, and "All the beggars which have been such a nuisance to citizens and strangers have been made to 'move on.' " The Metropolitan Police made an astounding 22,000 arrests during its first year and more than 70,000 over the course of the war. (An ambrotypist took a photograph of every thief arrested, creating a "Rogue's Gallery" of all known criminals in the city.) Still, the Police Board considered the force that Congress authorized "much smaller than is desirable, especially during the present national troubles, when a population so large and changeable is about." Congress limited the police to only 150 patrolmen, one for every 570 residents. The police commissioners wanted 545 and complained that patrolmen earned less than lamplighters. Washington's 307 miles of streets and alleys produced a beat, or "round," of four miles in length, and in one instance seven miles, taking up to two hours to traverse.[7]

Throughout the war, the missions of the Provost Guard and the Metropolitan Police overlapped. In addition to their oversight of the civilian population, the Metropolitan Police devoted considerable effort to monitoring soldiers, who accounted for one-sixth of all arrests during the war. The police turned them over to the military authorities for discipline. Simultaneously, however, the Provost Guard scrutinized and arrested civilians accused of violating military regulations or suspected of disloyalty. The provost marshal prosecuted civilians in his custody under military law. In one instance, the Provost Guard intervened when police attempted to arrest a soldier who was fighting with a civilian. The soldier ended up in police custody and the civilian in the guardhouse. In their first Annual Report to Congress, the Police Board accused the provost marshal of "persistently refusing to act in concert with the police force, and in several instances declining to communicate with the board of police and its officers." Considering the entire city a "military encampment," Porter in fact did not recognize "the legal existence of the board of police." According to the report, the Police Board had "endeavored to arrive at an understanding with the Provost Marshal, in order to make both forces as efficient as possible by acting in concert to prevent crime." Calling on the president or Congress to "define the duties of each force," they feared an eruption of "a conflict between them." Lincoln, of course, took the side of the military authorities, who imposed nearly absolute federal control over the District for the duration of the war.[8]

In a cabinet meeting less than two weeks after the firing on Fort Sumter, Attorney General Edward Bates proposed requiring all employees in the executive branch—"from the head Secretary to the lowest messenger"—to retake their oaths of allegiance. The entire cabinet agreed. The oath of allegiance, required of all federal employees upon appointment, was originally a simple declaration that "I will support the Constitution of the United States." Never before controversial, the oath was the first act passed by the first Congress in 1789. The next day, Lincoln issued a general order requiring all army officers to resubscribe to their oaths of allegiance. Bates himself was the first official to retake the oath, followed by a host of government clerks. Some of them wondered if the promise to support the Constitution was a pledge of military service but accepted reassurances to the contrary. A minority of federal appointees refused to take the oath. On the first day, thirty-four employees in the Patent Office, Census Bureau, Pension Bureau, and Land Office refused to take the oath and resigned. The press reported every instance, heightening fears for the security of Washington. The oath immediately acquired potent symbolic and real value in safeguarding the government from disloyalty. A Treasury Department clerk who was arrested for "conspiracy with secessionists" was absolved after taking the oath, setting the precedent that the mere act of oathtaking could allay the gravest suspicions of disloyalty. Even an accused spy could win release simply by taking the oath. Five days after convening on July 4, 1861, the House created a committee to investigate federal employees "who are known to entertain sentiments of hostility to the Government" and refused to take the oath. After three weeks of inquiry, the chair of the committee, Republican John F. Potter of Wisconsin, told Congress that he was "astonished at the number of well-authenticated cases of disloyalty to the Government."[9]

Congress responded by lengthening and strengthening the oath in August. The revised oath replaced "support the Constitution" with "support, protect, and defend the Constitution and Government."

Oathtakers also had to forswear "any ordinance, resolution, or law of any State Convention or Legislature to the contrary." Thus began a second round of oathtaking among all the federal employees, along with a second wave of resignations. The Potter Committee divided disloyalty into three categories—overt sympathy for the rebellion, questionable support for the Union, and failure to take the oath—and requested the names of all federal employees who refused to take the oath but remained in office. During its first four months, the committee heard more than 450 "respectable and responsible" informants testify about disloyal employees in the government and investigated more than 550 charges of disloyalty. When the committee's final report came out, the press described "quite a stampede, from this city of witnesses before that Committee, they not being quite prepared to face the parties they have testified against." Potter sent two lists of employees to every executive department, the unquestionably loyal and the doubtful supporters of the Union. Each department head decided how to respond to the list. Edwin Stanton, who replaced Simon Cameron as Secretary of War in January 1862, was enthusiastic and met personally with Potter on his first day in office. Secretary of the Treasury Salmon Chase was skeptical, allowing Potter's targets to present letters of support and insisting on examining all of the evidence himself before dismissing anyone. Seward chose to conduct his own investigation in the State Department. The Potter Committee met in secret, did not notify suspects that they were under investigation, and collected no rebutting testimony. Admitting that much of the testimony "amounted to mere opinions or impressions," the committee justified the secrecy and sweep of the allegations. "It may happen that loyal men have become the victims of unjust suspicion, and the fact is to be regretted," they acknowledged. "But they cannot complain if the government should feel constrained to remove them from public employment at a moment when its very existence is imperiled by treachery and violence." In all, the Potter Committee identified 320 government employees that they considered disloyal to some degree. Potter's greatest weapon was publication of the lists in congressional records and the newspapers in hopes of goading the government to take more aggressive action.[10]

Despite the popular judgment that "there seems but little doubt that no inconsiderable portion of this evidence is a bundle of malicious perjuries," the tactic worked, and the oaths spread beyond federal employees. There were immediate calls for administering the oath to municipal appointees, government contractors, and schoolteachers. Stonecutters working on the Capitol, teamsters, wharfmen, and applicants for passes to cross the river were eventually required to take the oath. Anyone who requested a pass and then refused to take the loyalty oath fell under suspicion and was arrested. Early in 1862, Congress prescribed an oath for voting in the District. Upon a challenge to their loyalty, voters were required to take an oath promising not only future loyalty but also past loyalty, known as a "test oath," that included a final pledge that "I have always been loyal and true to the Government of the United States." The *National Republican* suggested that government clerks living in "rebel boarding houses," which were kept by "the most notorious of that contemptible class, rebel women," be required to take the oath. As oathtaking spread beyond Washington, military officers, acting without congressional sanction, imposed it on civilians in occupied areas of both the Confederacy and the Border States. Telegraph operators, steamboat pilots (including the young Mark Twain), the crews of warships, and military pensioners were required to pledge their loyalty. The oath gained such immediacy that for $1 Washingtonians could purchase a 2-foot-square engraving, "The Family Record, or Oath of Allegiance," for their own homes as a "parlor ornament." Boasting portraits of Lincoln surrounded by eleven of his military commanders, as well as Stephen Douglas, George Washington, Thomas Jefferson, and John Hancock, the engraving was nonpartisan. Family members could inscribe their own names on the ornate lithograph. "Every loyal family should have a copy as a record for posterity," the *National Republican* enthused, "and those who are suspected of disloyalty cannot do better to vindicate themselves, than to purchase a copy."[11]

During the summer of 1862, Congress strengthened the oath yet again and required every federal official, including members of Congress, but neither the president nor vice president, to swear to it. The new Ironclad Test Oath closed loopholes by requiring pledges that the subject had never voluntarily borne arms against the United States, voluntarily given aid to the enemy, or held office under the Confederacy. (The famous ironclads, the *Monitor* and the *Merrimac*, had engaged in their epic naval battle four months earlier.) Two weeks later, Congress barred rebels from ever again holding federal office. Opponents of the Ironclad Oath argued that it violated the Constitution by imposing ex post facto qualifications for holding office, obstructed the president's power of pardon, and curtailed the Fifth Amendment's due process clause. Washington Provost Marshal William Doster labeled the oath of allegiance "the most perfect farce," observing that "prisoners used to take the oath under duress and considered themselves not bound to observe it because they were not free agents when the obligation was assumed." Despite its clear deficiencies, the Ironclad Oath was the most important avenue to freedom for civilians under "arbitrary arrest" for simply "using treasonable language," "uttering seditious and treasonable sentiments," or "cheering for Jeff Davis." The Washington press acknowledged that the system of arresting civilians under military law was "imperfect" and "liable to abuse" but characterized the government's policy of "imprisoning the advocates of secession in the North" as a "necessary act." They saw the evidence everywhere—"the seat of Government is almost in the enemy's country," "the whole city of Washington swarms with spies and rebels," "information and aid, sometimes of a very important character, are constantly being afforded to the enemy," and "the life of the President is supposed by many to be in danger." The conclusion seemed inescapable that "we are, in short, surrounded by active, untiring, bitter enemies." During the war, almost three hundred Washington residents spent time in the Old Capitol Prison under suspicion of disloyalty.[12]

The secession movement and loyalty campaign indeed produced an army of exiles from Washington, mostly men, many of whom—more than four hundred—joined the Confederate military and government. They included Buchanan's secretary of war, John B. Floyd, who accepted a commission as a brigadier general in the Confederate army; Robert Ould, a former district attorney who was the Confederacy's assistant secretary of war; Dr. Alexander Garnett, who became Jefferson Davis's personal physician; Charles Wallach, the brother of Washington's mayor Richard Wallach and W. D. Wallach, editor of the *Evening Star*, who joined the Confederate Quartermaster's Department; and former Washington mayor Walter Lenox, who entered the rebel government. The exiles' ingratitude and shortsightedness received unrelenting scorn from the city they left behind, symbolized by an anecdote about an Episcopal minister who fled south and left his cat locked in the cellar with just enough food to last until Washington fell to the Confederacy and he could return. "The minister's cellar was opened a short time since," according to the *Evening Star*, "and the poor cat was found in a pitiable condition, having devoured everything edible in her place of confinement." The cat resembled the Confederacy, confined, hungry, and barely alive.[13]

The government confiscated the exiles' personal property outright, putting their household furnishings up for auction, but claimed the use of their real estate only for the duration of the war. Giesboro, the country estate of the largest slaveowner in the District, George Washington Young, was converted into a massive government horse corral across the Eastern Branch from Washington. Harewood, the rural home of Washington banker W. W. Corcoran, who spent the entire war in Europe, became Harewood Hospital, strewn with tents that accommodated three thousand patients. Corcoran's almost completed art gallery, a block from the White House, was converted into a warehouse for army clothing and later the newly established Army Medical Museum. After the war, Corcoran returned to Washington and opened the Corcoran Art Gallery in the same building. Congress converted the estate of Georgetown's Richard Cox into an orphanage for African American children. After Duff Green fled to Georgia, the government purchased Duff Green's Row, to create, in succession, a women's prison, a home for fugitive slaves, a government laundry, and a smallpox hospital.[14]

The southward flight of the secession exiles, many of whom left their families behind, shifted the onus of dissent onto the capital's women. In August 1861, Rose Greenhow, a Washington widow and socialite, was arrested as a spy and charged with providing plans for the Battle of Bull Run. Greenhow was born in southern Maryland to a slaveowning plantation family. When she was young, one of their slaves killed her father, turning her into an outspoken opponent of abolition. Her three-story house sat in Lafayette Square across from the White House, and she became one of the leading lights of the Washington social scene. She was a confidante of leading Democrats, including President James Buchanan, whom she herself considered "unfit to grapple with the terrible events," and Senator Stephen Douglas, who married her niece in 1856. During the spring of 1861, a War Department employee with southern sympathies, who later joined the Confederate Army as a lieutenant colonel, recruited Greenhow. She organized an undercover network in Washington that included seventeen spies and couriers, most of them government clerks. Greenhow funneled the information that her agents collected to the newly formed Confederate secret service via couriers who carried the "rebel mail" to Richmond across the Potomac bridges or through southern Maryland. Throughout the war, government detectives intercepted and even infiltrated the rebel mails, called the "underground mail" and the "grape vine telegraph," running primarily between Washington and Port Tobacco, Maryland. The superintendent of the Old Capitol Prison claimed that his agents actually took control of the underground mail, reading the letters before sending them on to Richmond. One confiscated document, prepared by a member of Greenhow's ring, a wealthy Washington banker, provided "full particulars of the numbers and condition of the union troops in the vicinity of Washington, a complete and elaborate description of the fortifications, the number of guns they mounted, their location, &c., with other information valuable to the enemy."[15]

In addition to the stronger Provost Guard and the reformed police department, the Union was creating a secret service, as Winfield Scott had recommended. The new detective corps was headed by Allan Pinkerton, who had accompanied Lincoln on his midnight journey through Baltimore. Pinkerton began his government service working for George McClellan when he was commanding the Department of the Ohio. When McClellan took command of the Army of the Potomac in August 1861, he brought Pinkerton to Washington. Lincoln personally asked Pinkerton to organize a new secret service, in part to protect the president. As McClellan attempted to secure the capital, Pinkerton and his agents interviewed spies, fugitive slaves, refugees, deserters, and prisoners of war from Virginia while running a "detective police force" that monitored disloyal activities in Washington. "Shadow detectives" tailed suspected spies and saboteurs, as well as any suspicious-looking strangers in the city. No one escaped scrutiny. Walt Whitman came to Washington to attend his wounded brother and stayed to nurse thousands more Union and Confederate soldiers during the war. A friend recalled that while walking home from Carver Hospital the bearded poet "was accosted by a policeman and ordered to remove that 'false face,' his name for a mask. Walt quietly assured him that the only face he wore was his very own, but added, 'Do we not all wear false faces?' "[16]

Greenhow fell under a cloud through her associations with high government officials and military officers, her outspoken southern sympathies, and her familiarity with southern Maryland, through which several important rebel mail routes ran. (On the day of Greenhow's arrest, Ward Hill Lamon, the marshal of the District of Columbia, wrote to Lincoln that "so far as I am able to judge—I believe that more than one half of the *women* in Maryland are secessionists.") Using the alias E. J. Allen, Pinkerton ordered his operatives to shadow Greenhow, trail the visitors to her home, and arrest any of them who tried to cross the military lines. In August 1861, Pinkerton arrested Greenhow, confined her in her house, and seized her papers. (She had written them in a code that Pinkerton's agents were able to break.) Before the Battle of Bull Run, Greenhow had obtained military plans, including McClellan's orders, from Winfield Scott's personal secretary and Senator Henry Wilson of Massachusetts. She boasted that "I employed every capacity with which God has endowed me, and the result was far more successful than my hopes could have flattered me to expect." Sending the intelligence she had gleaned to General Beauregard, she received the reply, "Let them come: we are ready for them. We rely on you for precise information. Be particular to us with descriptions and destinations of forces, quantity of artillery etc."[17]

Five months later, after Greenhow attempted to communicate with members of her ring, she was transferred to the Old Capitol Prison. (When she had first come to Washington, she had lived in the Old Capitol while it was still a boardinghouse.) When Greenhow arrived, the Old Capitol contained sixty-five Confederate prisoners, who were held in the basement, and five fugitive slaves, along with a dozen or so women, including several "notorious prostitutes." The inmates were just beginning to suffer the outbreak of disease that led to so many deaths after the prison filled with southern blockade runners, smugglers, rebel mail carriers, Union deserters, bounty jumpers, political prisoners, and hostages. Throughout the war, the prison's superintendent was William P. Wood, an aide to Secretary of War Edwin Stanton, one of Lincoln's former legal adversaries. In 1858, Wood had served with Lincoln on the legal team that argued the famous Manny Reaper Case. Cyrus McCormick sued a rival reaper manufacturer, John H. Manny, for patent infringement. Manny hired a defense team that included Stanton, a prominent Pittsburgh lawyer before he became Buchanan's attorney general, and Lincoln. When Lincoln arrived in Cincinnati with a carefully prepared argument, Stanton asked, "Where did that long-armed creature come from, and what can he expect to do in this case?" Dismissed from the case, Lincoln sat through the trial anyway, learning from the arguments. Stanton hired Wood to locate and alter an early McCormick reaper to make it look less like Manny's. Introduced as evidence, the modified reaper helped Stanton win the case. Despite the personal snub and the legal subterfuge, three years later Lincoln appointed Wood as superintendent of the Old Capitol.[18]

The wily Wood used a range of ruses to obtain information from his prisoners, including befriending Greenhow to win her confidence, which meant allowing her daughter to join her as an inmate of the prison. (While she was in the prison, her daughter helped her sneak messages to Confederate agents.) After leaving Washington on a flag-of-truce ship through a prisoner exchange in June 1862, Greenhow went to Europe to raise money for the Confederacy. In England, she published a book, *My Imprisonment and the First Year of Abolition Rule at Washington*, which recounted and romanticized her experiences as a spy while excoriating the conditions that she endured in the Old Capitol Prison. During her voyage home in October 1864, Greenhow drowned when her boat, a blockade runner, ran aground off the mouth of the Cape Fear River in North Carolina. She was carrying $2,000 worth of gold in a bag chained around her neck that she intended to donate to Confederate relief. The gold weighed her down, and she was the only casualty of the wreck.[19]

Greenhow's arrest in August 1861 (she was never tried) cast suspicion on the city's most fashionable women. Early in the war, the government had overlooked women as threats to the security of either the capital or the army. In August 1861, for example, Lincoln's military guard was forming across the street from the White House in Lafayette Square when an "evidently deranged" woman "with a bundle in her left hand, and a pink calico scarf thrown gracefully over her shoulder and the end waved in her right hand for oratorical effect, lectured in loud tones for ten minutes, denouncing the President, blackguarding the soldiers, and extolling Jefferson D." The president's escort did not arrest her. "I cannot but wonder why women are allowed to express treasonable sentiments so freely, and also to make such ostentatious displays of their sympathy for rebel prisoners, and their perfect *hatred* of Union soldiers," one Washingtonian marveled, "right under the noses of our military authorities." Pinkerton himself admitted that "little attention was paid to these grand dames of the old regime, as it was not deemed possible that any danger could result from the utterances of non-combatant females." After Greenhow's arrest, however, the public viewed women, including the most outwardly respectable, as the most stealthy enemies, because they were the last to arouse suspicion. One Washingtonian challenged the obsession with men's loyalty, pointing out that "the husband *may be loyal* while the wife and children *may be traitors*." Arresting only "suspicious characters" seemed fruitless, because "the traitors in our midst belong generally to the very respectable classes," as did Greenhow. "A lady friend tells us that the arrangement of red and white in a lady's attire, so as to imitate in any manner the 'bars' of the secesh flag, indicates a secession sympathizer," a reporter explained. "Two red and one white rose on the bonnet marks the wearer as a rebel. The rebel milliners in this city use their best endeavors to sell all the bonnets of this style they can." When the government used Greenhow's house to imprison several other women, they called it "the House of Detention for Female Rebels." The press dubbed it "Fort Greenhow."[20]

Confirming the new stereotype of the "secesh female," a second scandalous arrest in July 1862 snared Belle Boyd, a legendary Confederate spy and mail carrier. Born in western Virginia in 1844, Boyd belonged to a family of Confederate spies—two uncles and a cousin—and began her own espionage career at the age of eighteen. On July 4, 1861, she shot and killed a Union soldier who, emulating Elmer Ellsworth, had come to her family's home in western Virginia to remove their Confederate flags and raise the Stars and Stripes. Amid the early wartime climate that excused the disloyalty of women, Boyd was released without a trial. During the Battle of Front Royal in May 1862, she collected intelligence from Union soldiers and delivered it to General Stonewall Jackson, helping to achieve a Confederate victory. She continued working as a spy and mail courier in eastern Virginia for the next year, until she was captured and imprisoned in Baltimore, where she convinced the prison warden to release her. Rearrested in July 1862, she landed in the Old Capitol Prison a month after Rose Greenhow's release. When Duff Green abandoned Washington, the government converted what was now called his "row of sleazy wooden edifices" into the women's wing of the Old Capitol, known as the Carroll Annex. Boyd now spent fifteen months jailed in the same row of houses where Lincoln had lived while in Congress.[21]

In December 1863, Boyd was released during a prisoner exchange but soon gained new notoriety. Like Greenhow before her, she sailed for England to aid the Confederate cause. She was captured, however, and lodged on a U.S. warship for the return trip, during which she seduced a naval lieutenant, Samuel Wylde Hardinge, who helped her escape and, as a result, found himself in the Old Capitol. Banished from Union territory, Boyd was rearrested when Lee's army retreated through her hometown. Instead of following the Confederate Army, she stayed and was discovered living behind federal lines. After another stint in the Old Capitol, where she was "an incessant singer of rebel songs," the government exiled Boyd to Canada. True to form, on the trip northward, she "was very noisy, and attracted general attention by the loud voice in which she detailed her adventures." From Canada, she went to England and performed dramatic readings, centered on her career as a spy, on the London stage. After he was court-martialed for aiding Boyd, Hardinge joined her in England, where the couple married. They returned to America in 1864 and worked as a husband-and-wife team of spies for the Confederacy. The luckless Hardinge was captured and found himself in the Old Capitol yet again, where he died from one of the diseases that infested the prison. Boyd ended her infamous espionage career as a widow at the age of twenty-one. The public's fascination with the vivacious Boyd seemed endless. "Perhaps there is no Southern woman who has gained more notoriety during this war than has Belle Boyd," the press confirmed. "Traitors and sympathizers with traitors have surrounded her name with a romantic heroism almost equal to that of Joan of Arc." After the war, she too wrote a book, *Belle Boyd, in Camp and Prison*, traveled the country giving dramatic readings based on her exploits, and died while on tour in 1900.[22]

The flood of exiles to the Confederacy divided families but also facilitated the flow of sensitive information from the wives they left behind. In addition to infiltrating and suppressing the rebel mail, the Greenhow and Boyd arrests prompted the War Department to strengthen the supervision of its own postal service. In December 1861, Cameron ordered that all letters addressed to anyone in the Confederacy, except Union prisoners of war, be sent to Washington's Dead-Letter Office. His successor, Edwin Stanton, also prohibited letters from going into the Confederacy under the aegis of flag of truce, except to Union prisoners, "on account of the privilege having been abused." A year later, stricter regulations required that all mail traveling between Washington and Richmond go through Union-held Fortress Monroe in Virginia and consist of no more than one page, limited to "purely domestic matters." The Washington press boasted that "the rebel sympathizers here are in trouble, and do not obtain private news as easily as they used to do" and resorted to ingenious methods to keep the mail moving. "The rebels in the lower counties of Maryland are so closely watched by the Union troops," the *National Republican* reported, "that they find it difficult to communicate with their friends in Virginia with as much freedom, or as openly, as formerly." Their latest "dodge" was tying letters to the tail of a kite, sailing it over the Potomac, and then cutting the string. Subversive language among "secession women" earned equal attention from the provost marshal. In a typical episode, a woman, aptly named Virginia Douglass, "paid a visit to the Cliffburne Barracks, and in the presence of some of the officers of the Second District regiment, made use of some violent secesh language, and also gave the officers a tongue lashing." The provost marshal confined her for twenty-four hours and then released her. At the end of 1862, the government began rounding up the wives and children of Washington's exiles and shipping them to the Confederacy by flag-of-truce ship. On Christmas Day 1862, five hundred of them went southward "to join their relatives and friends." The *Daily Chronicle* wrote with undisguised bitterness, "They will, no doubt, be a most acceptable christmas gift to a number of chivalric gentlemen who are doing their best to merit this favor from the Government by doing all in their power to overthrow it." Still, one-fifth of the women did not appear on the appointed day.[23]

Lincoln turned a third sensational arrest to his own advantage. The act that created the Metropolitan Police District required the mayors of Washington and Georgetown to take a loyalty oath as ex officio members of the Police Board. In August 1861, Washington mayor James Berret refused to take the oath. The press reported that at least ten members of his administration had fled Washington to join the Confederate Army, the loyalty of many others was dubious, and War Department detectives had been monitoring his "conduct and associations." Provost Marshal Porter, under orders from the War Department, arrested him at his home at 4:00 A.M. Two hours later he was on a train heading to New York City. After three weeks of confinement in Fort Lafayette, a military prison in New York Harbor, Berret agreed to resign as mayor and take the loyalty oath to gain his release. In short, the government considered him loyal enough to go free but too disloyal to continue serving as mayor. As the *Evening Star* explained, "while there can exist no valid reason why he may not be restored to his liberty on taking the oath of allegiance, there *does* exist valid reason why he may not be restored to official power, by the misuse of which he may, if so inclined, prove almost as dangerous an enemy to the United States as Beauregard at the head of his army."[24]

Berret's wife, Julia, wrote to Lincoln personally to insist that the charges against her husband were politically motivated and "cruelly false." She claimed that nativists were angry with her husband for recommending Montgomery Blair for a cabinet post at the expense of fellow Marylander Henry Winter Davis, one of their own. She asked Lincoln to allow Berret to resign rather than removing him from office. In reply, Lincoln explained that the arrest, "though made by my general authority," occurred without his specific knowledge. Berret accepted the terms of his release, moved to New York, and lived as an "exile" from Washington for the duration of the war. The city councils elected Richard Wallach, president of the Police Board, to replace Berret. After narrowly losing to Berret in the previous mayoral election, Wallach headed the Unconditional Union Party that had emerged to support the war effort in Washington. Like the party itself, Wallach supported the Union without question but, as a slaveowner from Virginia, opposed general emancipation efforts. He went on to win the next three mayoral elections. Lincoln's hand-picked guardian of public order in Washington was the city's mayor for the rest of the war. The administration's control over security in the District was complete.[25]

THE ESCALATING loyalty campaign spared no one and soon intruded into the White House. Immediately after her husband's election, rumors began circulating in Washington that Mary Lincoln was a "pro-slavery woman," and gossips dubbed her "Lady Davis." Soon both sides, North and South, found reason to distrust her. Southerners saw a traitor to her section who moved to the North, married a Republican "abolitionist," and now helped preside over a war of aggression against the South. Northerners distrusted her as a suspected southern sympathizer with deep roots in the slave South and a family full of not only rebel supporters but Confederate soldiers as

ABRAHAM LINCOLN in his first known photograph, just before his election to Congress in 1846 at age 37. Below is Duff Green's Row. Congressman Lincoln lived in Mrs. Sprigg's boardinghouse, the fourth building from the right, dubbed "Abolition House." Across the street in the Capitol, Lincoln flirted with "political suicide" through his outspoken critique of the Mexican-American War and his votes against slavery in the District of Columbia. *(Photos courtesy of the Library of Congress)*

The combative Joshua Giddings, an abolitionist congressman from Ohio, who championed emancipation in the District of Columbia. Giddings argued about slavery at the dinner table with his fellow boarders at Mrs. Sprigg's and, across the street on the floor of the House, with both Whigs and Democrats. He encouraged Lincoln to devise a plan to end slavery in the national capital but privately considered the effort futile.

The eccentric Duff Green, who owned Mrs. Sprigg's boardinghouse. A southern slaveowner related by marriage to John C. Calhoun, Green was also Lincoln's in-law. He proved a surprising supporter of slaves seeking their freedom in Washington. He later fled to the Confederacy and ultimately produced one-half of the iron that went into its wartime armaments, railroads, and horseshoes. *(Photos courtesy of the Library of Congress)*

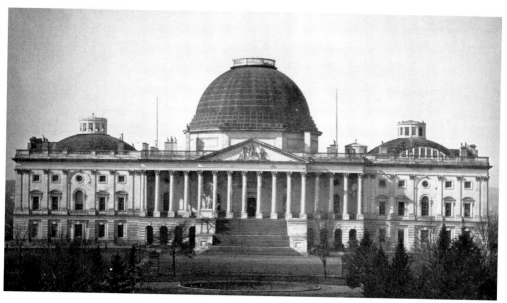

The Capitol's original "mustard pot" dome,
under which Lincoln served while in Congress.

South Carolina Senator John C. Calhoun (*left*) considered Lincoln's
emancipation proposal an example of northern "aggression and
encroachment." Lincoln's closest friend in the 30th Congress, Georgia Whig Alexander Stephens (*right*), became the vice president of
the Confederacy. *(Photos courtesy of the Library of Congress)*

Soon after Lincoln's election, Senator William Seward (*above left*) began working with Edwin Stanton (*above right*), President Buchanan's attorney general, and the army's general-in-chief, Winfield Scott (*left*), to secure Washington as the national capital and investigate threats to the president elect's safety. As Lincoln's Secretary of State and Secretary of War, Seward and Stanton devised a security apparatus that eventually encompassed the entire Union. (*Photos courtesy of the Library of Congress*)

When Lincoln returned to Washington in 1861, the Capitol was undergoing a major expansion that included a new, iron dome. Above, the unfinished dome looms over the pestilent Washington Canal. As president, Lincoln insisted on completing the Capitol as a symbol of democratic government and national resolve. Below, the north front of the Lincoln White House sits behind the bronze statue of Thomas Jefferson. *(Photos courtesy of the Library of Congress)*

As First Lady, Mary Lincoln (*above left*) did her utmost to make the White House an exemplar of genteel fashion and hospitality. The Lincolns' oldest son, Robert (*above right*), visited his family during vacations from Harvard College. Willie and Tad Lincoln (*below*) enjoyed the run of the White House, from basement to attic to rooftop, where they scanned the horizon for any enemy advance. (*Photos courtesy of the Library of Congress*)

Death stalked the Lincolns. The dashing Elmer Ellsworth, Lincoln's young law clerk from Springfield, Illinois, raised a regiment of Zouaves (*above left*). In May 1861, he became the first Union officer to die in the Civil War. Five months later, Edward Baker (*above right*) one of Lincoln's oldest and closest friends, became the only U.S. Senator to die in the war.

After 11-year-old Willie Lincoln succumbed to typhoid fever in February 1862, the grief-stricken family sought refuge in this cottage at the pastoral Soldiers' Home. (*Pencil drawing and photos courtesy of the Library of Congress*)

Three symbols of disloyalty. Spy Rose Greenhow languished in the Old Capitol Prison with her daughter, Little Rose (*above left*), while the Lincoln administration arrested Washington's mayor, James Berret (*above right*). The Union turned the Lees' estate across the Potomac into a military encampment, a freedmen's village, and Arlington National Cemetery. (*Photos courtesy of the Library of Congress*)

The heavily guarded Chain Bridge (*above*), connecting Georgetown with Arlington, Virginia, was one of the Army of the Potomac's links to the national capital as well as a potential route for a Confederate attack. Below, newly forged cannons line the yard at the Washington Arsenal. They always pointed west, toward Virginia. (*Photos courtesy of the Library of Congress*)

Lincoln Hospital (*above*), one of the "pavilion" medical facilities that the Union army hastily erected to treat the hundreds of thousands of sick and wounded soldiers who flooded wartime Washington. Below is the airy, tent-like interior of one of Armory Square Hospital's pavilions. (*Lithograph and photo courtesy of the Library of Congress*)

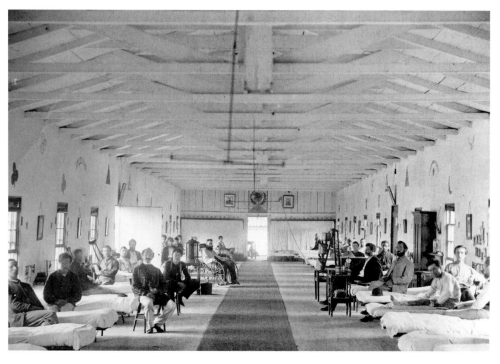

Dorothea Dix (*above left*), the noted medical reformer, who rushed to Washington to coordinate the appointment of female nurses, and the poet Walt Whitman (*above right*), who came to locate his wounded brother and stayed on to comfort tens of thousands more in the city's hospitals. Rebecca Pomroy (*left*), one of Dix's nurses, attended Willie Lincoln as he lay dying from typhoid fever. (*Photos courtesy of the Library of Congress*)

A group of fugitive slaves in Virginia. After Union General Benjamin Butler (*below left*) declared them "contraband of war," forty thousand sought freedom in Washington. Abolitionist Sojourner Truth (*below right*) came from Michigan to help them adjust to freedom and campaign for their rights. (*Photos courtesy of the Library of Congress*)

George McClellan (*above left*), Winfield Scott's successor as general-in-chief, hoped to end the war without disturbing slavery. After abolitionist General James Wadsworth (*above right*), military commander of the District of Columbia, obstructed enforcement of the Fugitive Slave Law, McClellan called him "a vile traitorous miscreant."

The District of Columbia's African American infantry regiment became the 1st Regiment United States Colored Troops after the Union army created the Bureau of Colored Troops in May 1863. *(Photos courtesy of the Library of Congress)*

Arlington Freedman's Village, established on the Lees' confiscated estate across the Potomac in Virginia to accommodate thousands of former slaves. *(Pencil drawing courtesy of the Library of Congress)*

Inside the White House, the First Lady's modiste, Elizabeth Keckly (*above left*), and the President's private messenger, William Slade (*above right*), spearheaded efforts to provide relief and education to former slaves and African American soldiers. *(Photos courtesy of the Abraham Lincoln Presidential Library & Museum)*

Throughout the war, abolitionists, including former slave Frederick Douglass (*above left*) and Senator Charles Sumner (*above right*), urged Lincoln to end slavery, recruit African American soldiers, and establish equal rights.

Secretary of the Treasury Salmon Chase (*above left*), the most radical member of Lincoln's cabinet, and Postmaster General Montgomery Blair (*above right*), the most conservative. Lincoln removed both of them while running for reelection in 1864. *(Photos courtesy of the Library of Congress)*

The plaster cast of the Statue of Freedom. During the 1850s, Jefferson Davis insisted on replacing its slave cap with a Roman war helmet. In 1863, the statue crowned the new, 300-foot-tall Capitol dome. A former slave, Philip Reid, was instrumental in converting the model into bronze before opening a foundry of his own in Washington. Today, the plaster cast is on display in the U.S. Capitol Visitor Center.

President Abraham Lincoln in February 1865. The war took a terrible physical toll on Lincoln. The awesome responsibilities of his office, incessant overwork, an endless stream of job- and pardon-seekers, the death of his son Willie, and a personal bout of smallpox wore him down as the war dragged on. When Harriet Beecher Stowe visited the White House, Lincoln told her, "I have the impression that I sha'n't last long." *(Photos courtesy of the Library of Congress)*

well. In truth, the younger of Mary's full brothers, George, served in the Confederate Army, as did all three of her half brothers. Three of her half sisters were married to Confederate officers, including Emilie, whose husband, Benjamin Hardin Helm, was a Confederate general. Betsey Todd, Mary's stepmother, was a distant relative of John C. Breckinridge, the Southern Democratic nominee for president in 1860 and major general of the Confederacy's 1st Kentucky Brigade. Before the firing on Fort Sumter, Mary had entertained him in the White House, which proved an impolitic blunder in hindsight. In short, her southern, slaveowning heritage and the bitter division of the Todd family now caught Mary Lincoln in the middle between the two warring sections. "The President's wife is venomously accused of being at heart a traitor," Lincoln's secretary William Stoddard discovered, "and of being in communication with the Confederate authorities, to whom, it is said, she sends information as to the plans of Union generals, as these are minutely confided to her by Mr. Lincoln."[26]

Mary's answer was simple and straightforward. As she asked Elizabeth Keckly, "Why should I sympathize with the rebels? Are they not against me? They would hang my husband to-morrow if it was in their power." Later, she told Emilie Helm in a panic that "I seem to be the scape-goat for both North and South!" Lizzie Grimsley noticed that old Washingtonians began to shun the First Lady. Soon, she wrote, "we ceased to meet at our informal receptions the Maryland and Virginia families who had always held sway, and dominated Washington society." Socialite Elizabeth Blair Lee, daughter of Maryland Republican Francis Preston Blair, tried to rally public support around the Lincolns. "The women kind are giving Mrs. Lincoln the cold shoulder in the City," she complained, "and consequently we Republicans ought to Rally." The northern press quickly turned on Mary Lincoln, exaggerated her influence on administration policy, and dubbed her "Madame President" and the "Presidentess."[27]

A sign of trouble ahead was the hostility Mary Lincoln encountered in her own White House. Abraham Lincoln's secretaries—known as "snobby and unpopular"—resented her potential influence with the president. State Department protocol demanded a fixed regimen of formal state dinners, dominated by government officials and foreign dignitaries, which supported a traditional rhythm of sedate White House functions throughout the Washington social season. As Abraham Lincoln's private secretary, John Nicolay was charged with overseeing these and all other White House social events. Mary Lincoln, however, decided to replace the traditional state dinners with a series of three public receptions that she would orchestrate, on the grounds that receptions would be larger, less expensive, and more inclusive. She talked her husband into supporting the plan and, in the process, undermined Nicolay's authority over the White House social calendar and, by implication, his overall standing with the president. Now expert at shielding Abraham Lincoln from supplicants of all varieties, Nicolay and Hay resolved to protect the president from undue influence from his own wife. These two young and overeager secretaries saw themselves, quite patronizingly, as the stewards of the president's time, energies, and indeed best interests, even to the point of denying the First Lady access to her husband, as they deemed appropriate. They labeled her "the hellcat," and as the rivalry between the secretaries and the First Lady escalated, John Hay observed, "The Hell-cat is getting more Hell-cattical day by day." Toward the end of the war, she became "Her Satanic Majesty." In her own turn, Mary Lincoln grew to resent Nicolay and Hay's exaggerated influence on the president.[28]

Mary Lincoln's quest for allies produced even more suspicion. She insisted that her husband appoint William S. Wood, whom she had befriended when he organized their inaugural journey, as commissioner of public buildings, overseeing the management of the White House. In addition to his official duties, Wood accompanied her on shopping trips to New York, which predictably spawned rumors of marital discord and even infidelity. As her bills for White House furnishings mounted and she overspent the congressional appropriation of $20,000 for her husband's four-year term, she withheld the most distressing information, the true extent of her outstanding debts to the merchants who were refurbishing the White House. After Wood refused to help her hide her debts, Mary Lincoln turned to the White House gardener, John Watt, who had earned a reputation for corruption since his appointment during the Pierce administration. When the First Lady enlisted his help in disguising her mounting debts by shifting them to other White House accounts, he eagerly agreed and received a lieutenant's commission at her insistence. Congressional oversight committees zeroed in on the mounting White House intrigues, targeting both Wood and Watt. After a congressional committee accused Wood of financial impropriety, the Senate refused to confirm his appointment, and Lincoln asked him to resign in September.[29]

Simultaneously, Congressman Potter wrote to Lincoln with evidence of Watt's disloyalty. "I do this from a sense of public duty," Potter insisted. "As the evidence will be laid before the House of Representatives, the committee deem it proper and respectful to submit the same to you, in order that you may take such action in the premises as in your judgment you may deem proper." According to informants, Watt associated with known secessionists, called Jefferson Davis "the best and bravest man in America," and immediately after Bull Run declared that "the federal army was composed of rubbish, and that the soldiers were cowards." Lincoln informed the adjutant general that "Lieut. John Watt who, I believe, has been detailed to do service about the White-House, is not needed for that purpose," and the gardener was summarily dismissed and ordered to join his regiment in the field. When the *New York Herald* obtained an advance copy of Lincoln's annual message to Congress, Watt admitted to leaking it and lost his lieutenant's commission as a result. Although denying any role in the scandal, Mary Lincoln faced widespread suspicion as the ultimate source of the security lapse. After the House Judiciary Committee investigated the episode, the president, who had always reviewed his major speeches and decisions with his wife, cut her off from any role in his decision making.[30]

Wood's replacement was Benjamin Brown French, a New Hampshire native who had lived in Washington for three decades. His friend Franklin Pierce appointed him commissioner of public buildings in 1853, but as French gravitated toward the Know Nothings, he fell from favor, lost his job, and embraced the Republican Party. His experience, reputation as "an ultra Union man," antislavery sympathies, and admiration for "honest old Abe" made him a natural fit for the appointment. French proved incorruptible and bemoaned "the 'Republican Queen'—who plagues me half to death with wants with which it is impossible to comply." Still, Mary Lincoln at length convinced him to intercede with the president on her behalf after mounting debts came to light. When he did so, according to French, Lincoln was "inexorable." Confronting his wife, he railed that "it would stink in the land to have it said that an appropriation of $20,000 for furnishing the house had been overrun by the President when the poor freezing soldiers could not have blankets, & he *swore* that he would never approve the bills for *flub dubs for that damned old house*." Lincoln felt honor-bound to make good the debt and "pay it out of his own pocket!" In his diary, French mused dryly that it "was not very pleasant to be sure, but a portion of it very amusing." Eventually, Congress made two additional appropriations to cover the overdrafts. Meanwhile, Lincoln and his secretaries practiced extreme frugality in appointing their own offices. A mahogany sofa, six chairs, and four mounted wall maps cost the government a total of $44.50. Through it all, French concluded that the First Lady was "more sinned against than sinning." His loyalty to the Lincolns echoed in the next generation. Fifty years later his nephew, Daniel Chester French, sculpted the statue that graces the Lincoln Memorial.[31]

A particular target of the Potter Committee was the Department of the Interior. Members charged that Secretary Caleb Smith was harboring both family members and disloyal employees, who "would rejoice to see JEFF. DAVIS in possession of Washington." After taking the Ironclad Oath in April, Horatio Taft, chief examiner in the Patent Office and father of Willie and Tad's playmates, had considered his position in the Interior Department secure. "*Treason* is in our midst," he acknowledged. "One hardly knows whom to trust. But I speak my own sentiments freely as I have all the time and denounce 'seceders' as Traitors." Still, Taft was a Democrat, and many of his original supporters had fled to the Confederacy. The Tafts knew Rose Greenhow, who often visited and asked Bud and Holly about what they overheard Lincoln saying during their visits to the White House. Before her arrest, one of Pinkerton's detectives came to their house and warned them to "say nothing." In the fall of 1861, Taft lost his job. A lawyer, he immediately secured a more lucrative position in New York, but Mary Lincoln pleaded with the family to stay in Washington. "My wife went today to pay her respects to Mrs Lincoln before leaving the City," Taft's diary recorded. "Was very graciously received by Mrs L. and assured that if *she* could do anything to keep our Family here she would do it as she was anxious to have our boys come there as companions & playmates for hers." The family agreed to stay and moved into a smaller house while the Lincolns tried to find Taft another government position. Armed with a recommendation from John Hay and a bouquet from the White House conservatory, Taft received a fruitless interview with Secretary Chase. Taft despaired. "Perhaps *I* am to be humbugged[,] as a *Democrat* does not, in reality, stand much chance." After Abraham Lincoln wrote a letter to the secretary of the interior and Mary sent Julia and Bud Taft with bouquets, Secretary Smith gave Taft a lower-paying position as a second-class clerk in the Land Office. The loyalty campaign was omnipresent, even in the White House, where Mary Lincoln had to fight her popular perception as a "secession lady" and Abraham Lincoln concluded wearily that he had "very little influence in this administration."[32]

The unrelenting hunt for subversives operating in the midst of the besieged capital reflected the horrific reminders of the war that Washingtonians encountered daily. In October 1861, McClellan ordered a reconnaissance in force—"a slight demonstration"—against a Confederate stronghold forty miles up the Potomac at Leesburg, Virginia. What should have been a routine mission turned into another debacle when the men encountered an ambush at Ball's Bluff. The Battle of Ball's Bluff hit Lincoln hard, perhaps hardest of all. One of his oldest friends, Senator Edward Baker, commanded the reconnaissance. A longtime legal colleague, Baker worked with Lincoln to build the Whig stronghold in central Illinois and preceded him in representing Springfield in Congress. Although friendly rivals, over the years the two men drew so close that Lincoln named his second son Edward Baker Lincoln, the ill-fated Eddie. During the Mexican-American War, Baker resigned from Congress, served as a colonel, and fought at the Battle of Cerro Gordo. A committed Free Soiler and Republican, he moved westward to Oregon and won election to the Senate in 1860. When Lincoln arrived in Washington, Baker was there to welcome him, riding in the presidential carriage during the inaugural parade and introducing him before he delivered his Inaugural Address.[33]

Lincoln rewarded Baker's friendship with an appointment as a brigadier general, which he declined. (Congress had decided that none of its members could accept commissions as generals, so Baker fought as a colonel instead.) He was not supposed to be at Ball's Bluff, but after coming up from Washington to observe the movement, he assumed command. Baker led his brigade into the ambush on a plain that sat on top of the bluff, surrounded on three sides by forest. Hidden in the trees, the enemy fired from three sides and shot him eight times. The newspapers reported that the "process of embalming was made very difficult by the shattered condition of the body." Lincoln's friend received a large wound in the left temple, a small musket ball above the right ear, another in the back of the neck, a fourth through his chest, another that passed through both of his thighs, a sixth that smashed his left arm, and another in his left breast. The final ball, apparently delivered while he was lying face down, entered the back of his shoulder and traveled the length of his body. (As gruesome as the mutilation of Baker's body seemed at the time, worse was to come. Two years later, a soldier who received twenty-three distinct wounds lived long enough to reach a hospital in Washington.)[34]

Baker's embalmer managed to make him look "life-like," and "if lying upon a couch, he would be easily mistaken for a sleeping soldier." A large glass window in his coffin allowed friends to view his face for one final time. Lincoln reportedly "felt the loss as if of a brother, and walked the floor of his room through the night in the greatest grief." McClellan came to the White House the next day, and the two "talked sadly over it." McClellan was philosophical about the loss. "There is many a good fellow that wears the shoulder straps going under the sod before this thing is over," he told Lincoln. "There is no loss too great to be repaired." Even he as commanding general could be replaced. "If I should get knocked on the head, Mr. President, you will put another man immediately into my shoes." Shocked and saddened by the death of his friend, Lincoln told McClellan, "I want you to take care of yourself." A few days later, Baker's funeral procession, which included the president, the cabinet, and members of Congress, trudged solemnly past the White House on its way to the Congressional Cemetery. William Stoddard thought that, "except for the death of 'little Willie,' the loss of Col. Baker touched him most deeply of all."[35]

During the ambush, Baker's men had their backs to the Potomac, and after losing their commander the soldiers were forced to retreat down the bluff. Lacking enough boats to cross the river, they poured into the water, where dozens were shot or drowned. The casualties totaled one-third those of the Battle of Bull Run. Two weeks later, a freshet rushing down the Potomac gave Washingtonians a first-hand revelation of the hideous realities of the war. Floodwaters from upstream swirled down the river, damaging the ramshackle Long Bridge and choking it with debris. "Great quantities of drift wood, and a large number of pumpkins, have come down with the flood and are banked against the bridge, and a number of people are engaged in securing the material for pies, as well as laying in fuel for the winter," the *Evening Star* reported. They made a gruesome discovery. "A soldier, supposed to have been drowned near Leesburg, with a light blue woolen uniform, is lying on a huge pile of drift wood." Over the next few days, more bodies, all in uniform, floated down, one by one. "At least eighteen dead bodies were taken from the river yesterday, between the Chain Bridge and the Long Bridge," the *Star* disclosed. "All were in uniform, and all are supposed to be a portion of the force drowned near Leesburg." They were buried on an island in the middle of the river. "Only one of them had a gun-shot wound, and he was shot through the head."[36]

Colonel Baker was known to emulate President Lincoln by keeping important papers lodged safely in his hat. When his body was retrieved from the battlefield, his bloodstained orders to advance were found in the accustomed place. In the wake of the Ball's Bluff disaster, and particularly Senator Baker's death, recriminations rippled throughout the War Department and Congress. Baker's friends blamed his commander, General Charles Stone (the same officer whose report on secessionism in Baltimore had convinced Lincoln to alter his inaugural route in February), for sending his brigade on what they considered a suicidal mission. Stone responded by questioning Baker's military competence. "Had his eye for advantage of ground in posting troops equaled his daring courage," he wrote bluntly, "he would have been to-day an honored, victorious general of the Republic, instead of a lamented statesman lost too soon to the country." Congress saw disloyalty or incompetence at the root of the disaster. "The massacre at Ball's Bluff," an officer in the State Department concluded, "is the work of either treason, or of stupidity, or of cowardice, or most probably of all three united." Describing Washington as "gloomy & despairing" in the aftermath of Ball's Bluff, radical Republican senator Benjamin Wade complained that McClellan was keeping his 200,000 men in the shelter of their entrenchments while "occasionally sending forth a *bulletin* announcing that 'the *Capital* is *safe*.' " Radical Republicans urged a more aggressive military strategy, including an attack on southern slavery, and worried about the medical condition of the army and the defense of Washington. When Congress reconvened in December 1861, Republicans debated a resolution requesting the secretary of war to provide information about the defeat at Ball's Bluff. The result was the creation of the Joint Committee on the Conduct of the War. Wade, who was Joshua Giddings's law partner for thirty years in Ohio, chaired the committee. For the rest of the war, the joint committee voiced congressional Republicans' demand that Lincoln pursue more aggressive measures against both the Confederate Army and the institution of slavery. They supported the appointment of Republican generals, a strong defense of the capital, and the uprooting of disloyalty in all its guises.[37]

CHAPTER TWELVE

"If I Were Only a Boy I'd March Off Tomorrow"
The Tide of Sick and Wounded

———◆◆◆———

IN SEPTEMBER 1861, Rebecca Pomroy, a forty-four-year old Massachusetts widow with a son in the army, read a newspaper advertisement calling on women to volunteer as nurses in military hospitals. "I can answer these requirements; what is to hinder my going?" she wondered. A family friend answered her question by urging, "Write your letter on the spot to Miss Dix." Dorothea Dix was the Union Army's superintendent of nurses, and her "requirements" called for women aged thirty-five to fifty who were "matronly" and exuded "habits of neatness, order, sobriety and industry." More specifically, the imperious Dix stipulated, "All nurses are required to be plain looking women." Pomroy received a reply three days later asking her to report to Washington immediately. Dix appointed her to the staff of the Union Hotel Hospital. Her first assignment was a ward of fifty typhoid fever patients, and, she wrote, "what with the odor and moans of the dying, it did seem to me unbearable."[1]

The firing on Fort Sumter found the Union, and Washington, DC, in particular, entirely unprepared to accommodate the more than one million sick and wounded soldiers who would need hospital treatment during the war ahead. In 1861, there were only thirty surgeons in the entire U.S. Army. (Eventually there were 11,000.) At the beginning of the war, the army commandeered the U.S. Capitol as Washington's first military hospital to supplement the city's single general hospital, the City Infirmary, which like most hospitals of the age was a charitable institution. As a result of its deficiencies—in this instance a defective furnace flue—the "old Infirmary building" burned down less than five months into the war. The prevailing medical theory focused on foul airs or "miasmas" that were thought to carry poisons—"organic emanations" and "carbonic acid"—that caused disease. Army doctors preferred to treat soldiers in "field" or regimental hospitals, consisting of tents, which were close to the front, mobile, and well ventilated. "The experience of all armies has shown, and my personal observation has convinced me of the fact, that the sick do much better in these regimental than in the general hospitals," the Army of the Potomac's medical director, surgeon Charles S. Tripler, insisted. "I consider general hospitals general nuisances, to be tolerated only because there are occasions when they are absolutely necessary." Despite his aversion to the city hospitals, the unprecedented scale of the Civil War forced the army to abandon the regimental tent hospitals and adopt "general" hospitals that collected the hundreds or thousands of casualties from a single battle, regardless of regiment, in a central place. Underestimating the length and scale of the war, the army began acquiring antiquated structures and converting them into general hospitals. The Union Hotel in Georgetown, the District's first posh hotel dating back to the days of John Adams and Thomas Jefferson, became the Union Hotel Hospital. In July, after the Battle of Bull Run poured casualties over the Potomac by the hundreds, the scope of the looming "hospital crisis" became all too apparent. A month later, the army converted Miss English's Seminary, also in Georgetown, into Washington's second military hospital, Seminary Hospital.[2]

Washington continued to gain about one new military hospital a month for the rest of 1861. In August, the C Street Hospital opened in two converted brick dwelling houses, which the *Evening Star* judged "entirely unsuitable for hospital purposes." The rooms were "small, dark, and badly ventilated," the kitchen too small, and the neighborhood congested. Its only advantages were large porticoes on which patients could take fresh air and an excellent well that provided cold water. The army supplemented its new hospital at Columbian College by pitching enough tents around it to accommodate five hundred patients, turning it into a large field hospital following the traditional regimental plan. When the army's medical director inspected Washington's hospitals in September, he judged them "totally inadequate." In his judgment, "It is impossible to ventilate them properly, and their interior is always so arranged that, while there is great waste of space, the sick are always crowded, and at the same time a larger number of surgeons, cooks, stewards, &c., are required for the administration than in the well-arranged hospitals that modern science and experience have devised."[3]

During the Crimean War of the mid-1850s, England and France had developed a new style of military hospital, the "pavilions," inexpensive wood-frame buildings that could be constructed quickly where they were needed and proved far more sanitary than the existing masonry structures that were unventilated, difficult to keep clean, and expensive to repair. The new pavilion hospitals were designed to reproduce the virtues of regimental treatment by mimicking large tents, providing "ridge" ventilation that collected foul air up to fourteen feet above the floor and released it through a vent that ran the length of the building. Airy wards, 25 feet wide and 150 feet long, radiated diagonally from a central building, resembling literal wings. Spurning the "large buildings of masonry" that the government had provided, the medical director advocated the new pavilion plan. "They admit of more perfect ventilation," he argued, "can be kept in better police, are more convenient for the sick and wounded and their attendants, admit of a ready distribution of patients into proper classes, and are cheaper."[4]

Still, the short-sighted conversions continued, with hospitals using barns as storerooms and cattle sheds as bakeries. In October, the government took over the city's schoolhouse in Judiciary Square and created Judiciary Square Hospital. Federal employees from Indiana opened a hospital on the second floor of the Patent Office, which the government took over and called Indiana Hospital. Walt Whitman found the patients lying in two large rooms among the "ponderous glass cases, crowded with models in miniature of every kind of utensil, machine or invention, it ever enter'd into the mind of man to conceive." When Abraham and Mary Lincoln visited, a volunteer walked by distributing tracts. Hearing one of the soldiers laughing, Lincoln told him, "My good fellow, that lady doubtless means you well." The soldier explained, "She has given me a tract on the 'Sin of Dancing,' and both my legs are shot off." After Senator Stephen Douglas died in June, the government leased his longtime Washington home and converted it into Douglas Hospital, which accommodated three hundred patients. By the end of 1861, Washington's general hospitals held slightly more than one thousand sick and wounded soldiers. In April 1862, Congress considered the city's hospital facilities ample enough to begin accommodating "transient paupers," in addition to soldiers, at government expense.[5]

Staffing the hospitals in Washington, however, proved no problem at all. Across the North, women spontaneously volunteered as nurses, even those who had no medical training or experience. There were no nursing programs in the country, but after sending sons and brothers off to fight, women of all ages felt compelled to help in any way they could. In Concord, Massachusetts, twenty-eight-year-old Louisa May Alcott cheered the Concord Company as they marched off to war, confiding to her journal that "I long to be a man, but as I can't fight, I will content myself with working for those who can." For the first year of the war, that meant "sewing and knitting for 'our boys' all the time," studying a medical manual on gunshot wounds, and musing wistfully, "If I were only a boy I'd march off tomorrow." Not content with crocheting bandages, knitting socks, and raising money to provide for the troops, eventually Alcott and 21,000 other women fulfilled their dreams of "marching off" to work in the army hospitals. "The examples of Florence Nightingale in the Crimea and the fame of Miss Dix brought many young women to Washington," the District's provost marshal recalled. "I used to send them all to Miss Dix, until this lady came and requested me to send none that were unable to turn a full grown man round in bed, and could do the most menial work. This thinned the ranks of applicants very much." During the first year of the war, seven thousand soldiers' aid societies, most of them organized by churches and led by women, emerged in towns and cities across the North. In New York City, Dr. Elizabeth Blackwell, America's first formally trained female physician, devised a plan to orchestrate this impulsive and chaotic outpouring of charitable contributions. The director of the New York Infirmary for Women and Children, Blackwell created the Woman's Central Association of Relief (WCAR) to "organize the whole benevolence of the women of the country into a general and central association." Her goal was to coordinate the relief efforts of the spontaneous charities, encourage the formation of others, work with the army's Medical Department to help meet its specific needs, and select and train female nurses to staff the Union's military hospitals.[6]

As women sought opportunities to volunteer, the "Woman's Central" grew quickly. Blackwell sent the Reverend Henry Whitney Bellows, a Unitarian minister, to Washington to meet with army medical officials and Secretary of War Cameron in hopes of gaining their approval and cooperation. There, Bellows met Dorothea Dix, America's most celebrated female reformer, who had crusaded for two decades to modernize the treatment of mental illness and create asylums for the indigent. Bellows discovered that the fifty-nine-year-old Dix had already used her celebrity to begin the process of organizing the recruitment of female nurses into army hospitals. Like Blackwell, Alcott, and thousands of other American women, Dix idolized Florence Nightingale, the English nurse who had worked unrelentingly during the Crimean War to improve sanitary conditions in the British Army and lend a feminine dimension to the care of sick and wounded soldiers. Her popular medical manuals, *Notes on Hospitals* and *Notes on Nursing*, had swept America just before the war began, and her declaration that "every woman is a nurse" became a call to action that inspired the wartime generation of women to emulate her by volunteering to serve in the Union's army hospitals.[7]

For many women, the Baltimore Riot on April 19 provided a more poignant motivation than the firing on Fort Sumter, because it produced the first casualties of the war, representing a portent of many more to come. When Dix heard about the casualties, she rushed immediately from her home in New Jersey to volunteer her own services in treating the wounded in Washington. Leaving a mere three hours after the melee in Baltimore, Dix wrote with understatement that it "was not easy to cross the city—but I did not choose to turn back." That very evening, she was at the White House meeting with Lincoln to volunteer the services of "myself and some nurses" to aid the War Department and the surgeon general. "Miss Dix called today, to offer her services in the Hospital branch," John Hay wrote in his diary. "She makes the most munificent and generous offers." Within four days of her arrival, Secretary of War Cameron had accepted Dix's "free services" and enlisted her to help organize military hospitals, provide nurses to staff them, and distribute the supplies that were pouring in from across the North. Washington's hospitals were the most strategically located in the Union. Close to the Army of the Potomac, they offered "first treatment" for many casualties, unlike the military hospitals in Baltimore, Philadelphia, and New York, which received convalescent soldiers upon their release in Washington. They were also situated under the eye of the surgeon general, the War Department, Congress, and the president, providing an important example of how best to treat the sick and wounded during the unprecedented national crisis.[8]

Upon arrival, Dix found medical care in Washington's hospitals in disarray. Although most soldiers preferred the ministrations of women, the military insisted on employing convalescent soldiers as nurses. As a result, on the day before the Battle of Bull Run, the army recalled "every cook, nurse, and wardmaster" to the front lines without any warning, leaving the hospitals stripped of their staffs at the very moment when they would be needed most. Working for the state associations that provided relief only for their own citizens, "state agents" lobbied for discharges to allow "their boys" to return home to convalesce. Once at home, they could obtain a certificate of discharge from any "physician in good standing." The surgeon general accused the medical inspector of selling blank certificates bearing his signature. Among the first militiamen to reach Washington, 30 percent went on the "sick list" during the summer of 1861. The army, of course, wanted to keep convalescing men in Washington to return them to their regiments as soon as they recovered. Convalescent soldiers also represented a potential defensive force. As Tripler put it, "Many of those left sick in the general hospitals would be able in a short time to serve in the works in case of an attack upon Washington, and they might be considered as forming a part of the garrison to be left." In 1863, the War Department created an Invalid Corps to assume exactly that responsibility.[9]

Only when McClellan took charge in July were soldiers required to undergo examination by their regimental surgeons before entering the hospitals or going home. The army's medical director found ambulances, whose drivers were civilians, "in general use as pleasure carriages for idlers and accommodation cabs for conveying officers and men from their camps to the city of Washington." Measles and smallpox were prevalent in both Washington and Georgetown. Washington's smallpox hospital was located two blocks from the Capitol in the center of the city, where soldiers infected the civilian population. "Everyday, inmates of the hospital appear on the streets," the *Evening Star* lamented, "and visit the shops in the neighborhood, just in the condition to spread the disease!" In September, the smallpox hospital moved to the outskirts of town and became the Kalorama Hospital for Eruptive Diseases. While in their camps, the press reported, soldiers lived in poorly ventilated quarters and ate inferior rations, and "changes in clothing are in many cases not provided." The army's Medical Bureau had no inspector general until April 1862, so Washington's Board of Health asked the surgeon general to inspect the sanitary conditions of the soldiers' quarters and order necessary changes.[10]

IN RESPONSE to the medical chaos, Dix began organizing a Society for the Relief of Volunteer Soldiers. She borrowed the reformed hospital regulations that had been adopted in New York and presented them to the women that she assembled. Meeting with Secretary of War Cameron, Dix volunteered to organize a "corps of nurses" to help with army sanitation and medical care. Dix's approach to nursing differed philosophically from Elizabeth Blackwell's. Like Florence Nightingale, Dix embraced a romantic vision of women as nurses, emphasizing the inherent value of their moral qualities and reputations more than their medical expertise. She hoped to reproduce the nurturing atmosphere of middle-class homes while instilling an emphasis on the patients as heroic figures. In the experience of one soldier in Washington, only female nurses could provide "the close watching, the numberless little attentions, the cheering and lightening of the heavy hours of pain by various sweet, womanly devices." Rejecting Dix's demand for "matronly" nurses, however, the soldier added that "I am in favor of women who are full of hopefulness and cheerfulness, who are sensible, and, withal, (O, forgive it!) young and pretty." As a physician with a medical degree, Blackwell prescribed formal training for skilled nurses as a prerequisite for hospital service. Blackwell proposed a real salary for nurses (the army paid them forty cents a day) to recognize and reward them as professionals rather than volunteers. But Dix was in Washington, and her reputation as an effective reformer carried the day.[11]

As a renowned medical reformer, Dix received permission to inspect the military hospitals and army camps around Washington, and Bellows joined her when he arrived. Forming a benevolent partnership, they expanded on Blackwell's ideas and proposed "*a sanitary commission to keep the whole question of Army health constantly stirred up here at headquarters*," envisioning "a resident organization in Washington" to supervise the relief effort and staff the city's hospitals with female nurses. In early June, Cameron endorsed the creation of "A Commission of Inquiry and Advice in respect of the Sanitary Interests of the United States Forces"—the United States Sanitary Commission. The USSC was to possess no executive authority but, as a civilian advisory group, would investigate medical conditions in the army and propose rules and regulations subject to the approval of the Secretary of War. On the following day, Cameron appointed Dix as superintendent of women nurses, authorizing her to "select and assign women nurses to general or permanent military hospitals."[12]

Endorsing Dix's approach to army nursing, Cameron advised that "during the present war, the forces being made up chiefly of volunteers, public sentiment and the humanity of the age requires that the services of women as nurses should be made available in the general hospitals, where, except in a very humble capacity, they have heretofore been excluded." He ordered that "women be adopted or substituted for men now in the general hospitals, whenever it can be effected." On June 13, Lincoln approved the plan of civilian reform and oversight through an executive order. Bellows was president of the USSC, and Frederick Law Olmsted, renowned as the designer of New York City's Central Park, was its general secretary, exercising supervisory control over its operations. Originally headquartered in the Treasury Building, the USSC moved into the Adams House, where John Quincy Adams had lived while serving in Congress.[13]

Several basic changes benefiting the care of soldiers occurred immediately. Olmsted inspected the camps and found one-half of them deficient in sanitation and camp police. General Mansfield, the military commander of the District, ordered an immediate cleanup and regular policing of all camps. In August, the provost marshal ended the abuse of ambulances, ordering that "ambulances shall not be used for any purpose except for the transportation of the sick and wounded." Congress staffed the ambulances with a Corps of Cadets, who were wound dressers in the hospitals and ambulance attendants in the field, with the same rank and pay as West Point cadets. Troops often arrived in Washington from their home states "in a deplorable condition." In July, William S. Wood, the commissioner of public buildings, commandeered the temporary building constructed to host the Inaugural Ball and converted it into the Soldiers' Rest to provide meals and baths for arriving troops, a pressing but unmet need. "They are all to march directly to it from the depot," which was nearby, "and will find there every necessary convenience, including huge vats or reservoirs in which large numbers can bathe at the same time." A permanent building, which the Sanitary Commission inspected and approved, was 300 feet in length with dining accommodations for 2,000 men. During a typical month, the Soldiers' Rest served 26,000 men, including 677 recruits, 1,471 soldiers on furlough, 1,269 convalescents, 19,494 men returning home, and 749 detached parties and "stragglers," along with thousands of laborers from the fortifications, Confederate deserters, and newly exchanged prisoners just arriving from Virginia.[14]

The United States Sanitary Commission was the first and only official relief organization of the Union Army during the Civil War. Many of the early donations of military provisions had been directed toward home-state troops and even specific individuals. Olmsted envisioned the USSC as a way to collect supplies from local aid organizations and direct them where needed most regardless of their point of origin. As a national commission, the USSC therefore circumvented the state associations that had been looking after their own soldiers in the absence of any centralized authority. Under Olmsted, the all-male commission organized the efforts of a dozen regional bureaus that were headed by women. The commission assumed the recruitment and assignment of nurses in military hospitals, pointedly recommending "an adequate corps of male and female nurses." They countered the feminine ideal of nurture that Dix tried to instill in her nurses with the admonition that "the first sanitary law in camp and among soldiers is military discipline." Dix viewed this arrogation of authority as a personal slight and began cutting her ties with the USSC, just as she had earlier rejected the philosophy of Blackwell's WCAR. Dix paid a price for her independence. She appointed only one in seven of all female hospital workers during the war, and her nurses earned just over one-half as much as the Sanitary Commission appointees. Dix's preference for older, "matronly" nurses created conflict when army doctors found them less willing to respect their authority and follow orders to the letter. For this reason, among others, USSC nurses needed letters of reference written by "two physicians and two clergymen of standing" before they were considered for appointment. In short, Dix became increasingly marginal to the war effort as the army's male-dominated medical bureaucracy developed. Midway through the war, she had become superintendent of female nurses in name only.[15]

Meanwhile, the Sanitary Commission grasped at power and eventually overstepped its bounds. When the medical director, Charles Tripler, devised a plan for erecting new pavilion hospitals in Washington, he discovered that he had to negotiate with the USSC. Tripler insisted on "putting up cheap frame buildings, expressly designed for hospitals, in preference to relying upon hotels, school houses, and the like, as seemed to be the existing plan." He reasoned that "it is easily seen that there are not buildings enough in Washington that are likely to or can be procured to meet our wants." Assuming that the 200,000-man army would fight a decisive engagement—the expected "great battle"—he wanted a minimum of 20,000 hospital beds in Washington to accommodate the wounded. His estimate took into account the novel weaponry of the Civil War, "the destructive power of rifled muskets and cannon." The Sanitary Commission, however, recommended only 5,000 beds. The city's hospitals already had 6,000 beds, so the commission's recommendation was far too modest. After Tripler met with the commissioners to explain the army's needs, they compromised and agreed to endorse 15,000 beds, which was 5,000 short of what he considered acceptable. After he submitted his own recommendation to the army, the government objected to the cost. "Subsequent events have shown that if it had been done," he wrote in hindsight, "much inconvenience and suffering might have been spared." Washington's hospital capacity did not reach the level of Tripler's recommendation for another three years, at the end of 1864.[16]

To magnify its role in framing medical policies within the army, the Sanitary Commission used its wide public popularity to challenge military authority. With the support of army doctors, the USSC campaigned for the appointment of a new surgeon general, William Hammond, who was known for his independence and commitment to medical reform. In April 1862, the commission got its way, and Secretary of War Stanton appointed Hammond, a lukewarm supporter of Dorothea Dix and her female nurses, to the post. Hammond directed that "there shall be one woman nurse to two men nurses," ensuring a male majority in every hospital. Within a year, surgeons were choosing their own nurses independently of both Dix and the Sanitary Commission. During the summer of 1862, the USSC shifted its focus to improvements in transporting the sick and wounded from the battlefield to Washington by steamers, essentially floating hospitals, and from Washington by railroads to the growing number of convalescent hospitals in Philadelphia and New York. Meanwhile, public attention shifted to the commission's regional branches, run by women who organized Sanitary Fairs in cities across the North, selling or auctioning handmade items to raise funds for the provision of amenities to sick and wounded soldiers in the hospitals.[17]

The civilian initiative to relieve Union soldiers and staff military hospitals suffered many internal divisions. Rival philosophies and organizations rent the recruitment effort. Dix and Blackwell disagreed about the qualities that made women good army nurses. When Dix's philosophy won out, New York's WCAR receded into a local organization, and before they entered the military hospitals nurses never received the kind of rigorous training that Blackwell envisioned. The temporary alliance between Dix and Bellows produced the ambitious plan for a sanitary commission, but the USSC proved male-dominated and excluded women from leadership at the national level. The army's Medical Department had its own priorities and gradually assumed nearly complete control over wartime nursing at the expense of the civilian Sanitary Commission and the female volunteers. Above all, the army preferred the employment of male nurses, preferably soldiers who would enforce military discipline and obey orders without question. Class lines also divided female nurses. Middle-class women could afford to forgo wages—which were pitiably low—preferring to emphasize their altruistic service as patriotic volunteers rather than as paid employees. Even paid hospital workers were called "volunteers," and many of them donated their wages back to the hospitals in which they served. Along with women's traditional role as self-sacrificing nurturers in their own homes, the volunteer spirit undoubtedly depressed the wages of army nurses significantly. The chief surgeon at Armory Square Hospital, which boasted Washington's largest nursing staff, adopted a policy of dismissing paid workers and replacing them with volunteers whenever possible.[18]

Other surgeons preferred to appoint Catholic nuns—representing the Sisters of Charity, the Sisters of Mercy, the Sisters of St. Joseph, and the Sisters of the Holy Cross—because they worked without pay and were generally more obedient. This economic incentive, combined with the era's pervasive anti-Catholicism that had produced the Know Nothings, injected religious divisions into the provision of medical care. "We can get female nurses through Miss Dix and from among the Sisters of Charity," Medical Director Tripler confided in an official report. "It is a very damaging position for any one to take and avow, but in the honest discharge of my duties, though a Protestant myself, I do not hesitate to declare that in my opinion the latter are far preferable to the former, being better disciplined, more discreet and judicious, and more reliable." He recommended dividing each hospital equally between the two. From her perspective as a ward nurse, Rebecca Pomroy confirmed that the "surgeons say generally that they prefer Catholics to Protestants, and I feel ashamed to hear that." Pointing to another advantage of employing Catholic sisters, she noted, "Many of our Protestant nurses get married, and that troubles Miss Dix and the surgeons." The Sisters of Charity also gained a reputation for assuming any hospital task, no matter how menial or distasteful. Still, surgeons could employ them only under "special instructions" from the Surgeon General's Office. Dix personally succumbed to anti-Catholicism and adopted a policy of never hiring a Catholic nurse "if a Protestant could be substituted."[19]

Race drew the starkest dividing line among the nurses. Most white nurses exhibited the prevailing racial attitudes of the age. As the front moved southward and former slaves increased in number, many African Americans entered hospital service. Initially resistant, the War Department officially authorized the employment of African American men and women as nurses and cooks in all of the army's general hospitals in January 1864. Over the course of the war, one-tenth of female nurses were African American. Like the United States Colored Troops, they received lower wages than their white peers, $10 per month. In its infancy, the title of "nurse" concealed an array of duties beyond the care of patients, and one-half of nurses worked as cooks, laundresses, matrons, and chambermaids, with all of these tasks overlapping at times. In the segregated "colored" hospitals, African Americans predominated as caregivers, but in the hospitals for white soldiers they were generally laundresses, chambermaids, and cooks. White women abhorred menial tasks and were all too willing to assign them to African Americans, many of whom were fugitive slaves. One-third of all cooks in army hospitals were African American women.[20]

Rebecca Pomroy was appalled by the racial attitudes that she experienced at Columbian College Hospital, where she worked after the Union Hotel Hospital closed in May 1862. During Lincoln's visit to her ward, Pomroy "sent down into the kitchen and cook-room and ordered colored Lucy and the two male colored servants to wash their hands and make ready to come up." On his way out of the ward, Lincoln noticed them standing side by side with Pomroy and asked, "And who are these?" Pomroy told him, "This is Lucy, formerly a slave from Kentucky. She cooks the nurses' food." Lincoln held out his hand and asked, "How do you do, Lucy?" After he left, Pomroy "became aware of a feeling of intense disapprobation and disgust among the officers." Her own assistant confronted her to ask, "Mother, what could you be thinking of to introduce those niggers to the President!" One of the surgeons told a colleague, "Anybody would know she was a Massachusetts woman, for no one else would do such a mean, contemptible trick as to introduce those d——— niggers to the President." The surgeon in charge of the ward agreed, observing that "it was in Massachusetts that the first *abolition egg* was laid." Pomroy later asked Lincoln if her impulsive introduction had offended him. "Hurt? No, indeed!" he answered, "it did my soul good. I'm glad to do them honor."[21]

In the fall of 1862, Louisa May Alcott at last received her opportunity to "march off to war." Although she was not yet thirty, an acquaintance who had experience as an army nurse helped her win an appointment from Dorothea Dix, who invited her to come to Washington. During a process that must have left her crestfallen, Alcott received an assignment to Armory Square Hospital, one of the new, efficient, and clean pavilion facilities that the government was just beginning to build. Ultimately, she found herself at the notoriously ramshackle Union Hotel Hospital, which she quickly dubbed "Hurlyburly House." There she encountered the realities of war in the oldest military hospital that Washington had to offer. As for Dix, Alcott found her a "kind soul but very queer & arbitrary," concluding that "no one likes her & I don't wonder." If Alcott was anything like the heroine of her novel *Hospital Sketches*, her first revelation upon entering the Union Hotel Hospital was "a regiment of the vilest odors that ever assaulted the human nose." She soon discovered that two-thirds of all Civil War casualties suffered disease, not wounds, and despite her compassion for her patients she soon decided that she preferred to tend the wounded, because they made her feel "heroic." Her attitude was widespread throughout the army. One soldier complained with considerable justice that "the comfort of the wounded is promoted in preference to that of the sick. From the attendants of our hospitals to those visitors who make it their business to distribute necessaries and luxuries among their suffering inmates, nearly all seem possessed with the feeling, whether consciously or not, that their sympathies should be bestowed in largest measure upon the wounded."[22]

Soon after her arrival, Alcott received her chance at heroism in the spring of 1863 when the disastrous Battle of Fredericksburg sent more wounded soldiers pouring into Washington than the hospitals could handle. Just after the New Year in 1863, both Alcott and her supervisor, or "matron," Hannah Ropes, contracted typhoid fever from their patients. When Ropes died, Alcott's father traveled from Concord, Massachusetts, to bring her home after just six weeks of service in Washington. Her brief time nursing in the nation's capital had provided her with enough insights and empathy to write a novel that inspired other women, like her, to dedicate themselves to nursing the sick and wounded, just as Florence Nightingale's *Notes on Nursing* had moved Alcott herself. Above all, during her brief wartime experience, Alcott had seen more than her share of death, come close to dying herself, and finally made her peace with war's realities. She surely justified Mark Twain's appraisal that "in the late war we saw the most delicate women, who could not at home endure the sight of blood, become so used to scenes of carnage, that they walked the hospitals and the margins of battle-fields, amid the poor remnants of torn humanity, with as perfect self-possession as if they were strolling in a flower garden." In this same fashion, Alcott was able to lend her perspectives, both real and romantic, to the task of building support for the war, and fostering appreciation for the nurses, across the North.[23]

PART III

"An Unknown Something Called Freedom"

CHAPTER THIRTEEN

"Tinkering Experiments"
Toward Emancipation

M ARY DINES was born a slave in Maryland. When her owner
died, his will freed her, but his family had it set aside and put
her to work keeping house and raising their children. For the first
time in her life, she was whipped to break her spirit. Like thousands
of other slaves before the Civil War, she decided to flee to the nation's
capital. As she traveled by moonlight, other slaves on the route helped
her on her way. When she reached the Navy Yard Bridge, she encountered a "pick-up" wagon carrying fugitive slaves into Washington.
Hidden under a load of hay, she crossed the bridge over the Eastern
Branch of the Potomac and entered Washington. The hay wagon carried her to a way station on the underground railroad, a stable in an
alley on Capitol Hill, which collected runaways waiting to escape to
the North. After a few days, Dines decided to stay in Washington
instead and blend in with the capital's free African American community, settling on the "Island," the densest free black community in the
city. "Here many of them occupy small wooden tenements, as they
do in other places in the District, with garden patches attached," a
New York reporter observed. "Here they keep their horses and hacks,
used for hire, having small barns or stables attached to their premises.
These properties are their own, generally, the products of hard earnings, obtained in small sums, by public and private service." There
she lived with other African Americans and worked for "a little pay
and keep."[1]

Even before the war began, many of Washington's African Americans were already refugees, of some variety, from Virginia and Maryland. In 1860, about one-half of them were from Maryland and Virginia, with a slight preponderance of Virginians. Maryland's slaves were more likely to gain their freedom, but they enjoyed a wider range of refuges beyond Washington, including Baltimore and Philadelphia. The underground railroad ran through Maryland, so slaves could connect with white and black "conductors" more readily and reach cities farther north and even Canada, like Poor Robert from Mrs. Sprigg's. When fugitive slaves did arrive in Washington, they found antislavery advocates pursuing a form of "practical abolitionism." For decades, they had been chipping away at slavery through a variety of devices, including the underground railroad, freedom petitions filed with the help of lawyers such as Duff Green, purchases supported by northerners such as Gerrit Smith, and self-purchases, as in the case of Henry Wilson. Washington was also unique among southern cities in hosting defiantly antislavery newspapers, the *National Era* and its wartime successor, the *National Republican*. Several antislavery societies, including the Washington Free Soil Association, founded in 1848, and the National Republican Association, founded in 1855, supported emancipation. When in session, Congress boasted a growing number of antislavery advocates, in the tradition established by John Quincy Adams and Joshua Giddings. They included Senators Charles Sumner and Henry Wilson of Massachusetts, James Grimes of Iowa, Lot Morrill of Maine, and Benjamin Wade, Giddings's longtime law partner.[2]

In the wake of Lincoln's election, northern control of the government made Washington an even safer refuge for fugitive slaves. The creation of the Metropolitan Police Department put the police under the authority of a board of five presidential appointees and eliminated the fee system that had encouraged racially biased arrests. The provost marshal system, which substituted the army's will for a civil government dominated by southerners, heightened northern control. Mayor Berret's removal in August 1861 and his replacement by Richard Wallach also eliminated a powerful Democratic obstructionist. The outbreak of war gave Lincoln and Congress an unexpected opportunity and incentive to free slaves. The war created an immense demand for laborers, in both the city and the military camps across the Potomac, and ultimately new sources of soldiers for the advancing army. Throughout the conflict, Lincoln and his administration faced the conundrum of accepting 40,000 fugitive and newly freed slaves into the capital without promoting social and political disruptions that would impair the efficiency of the war effort or diminish support for the Union. This balancing act between freeing slaves and winning the war dominated Lincoln's unfolding emancipation policy throughout his presidency. When a delegation of Bostonians visited the White House to urge him to act more aggressively against slavery, he likened himself to a man walking a tightrope over Niagara Falls with a crowd of onlookers shouting "a step to the right!" and "a step to the left!" Only when he believed that freeing slaves would help restore and not endanger the Union would he fully embrace emancipation as a wartime goal and military strategy.[3]

In June 1862, Congress implemented the free soil principle, banning slavery from the western territories under the leadership of Lincoln's friends and allies from Illinois, Representatives Isaac Arnold and Owen Lovejoy. Through that act alone, the Republicans fulfilled their primary campaign promise of 1860 and achieved the goal that Lincoln had pursued relentlessly for more than a decade. Lincoln, however, felt legally bound to enforce the loathsome Fugitive Slave Law until Congress repealed it. Throughout the 1850s, he had consistently maintained that "under the Constitution of the United States, the people of the Southern States are entitled to a Congressional Fugitive Slave Law." He just as consistently called the 1850 law "objectionable" and urged revision to release private citizens from any legal obligation to enforce it and above all to protect the basic rights of accused runaways. In his Inaugural Address, he proposed observance of "all the safeguards of liberty known in civilized and humane jurisprudence," but agreed to enforce "all those acts which stand unrepealed." Congress, however, did not repeal the law until June 1864.[4]

As president, Lincoln felt obligated to attack slavery only where he had an unquestioned power to do it. With the outbreak of war, he gained that power under the guise of military necessity. On May

23, 1861, three fugitive slaves approached Fortress Monroe, a Union stronghold at Hampton, Virginia, at the mouth of Chesapeake Bay, and "delivered themselves up." The fort's commander, General Benjamin Butler, interviewed them and discovered that they were expecting to go to South Carolina to aid the rebel forces. Reluctant to leave their families and to support the Confederacy, they turned themselves in to the Union Army. Butler believed that the Confederate Army was employing slaves to build batteries nearby, and he needed laborers to maintain his own defenses, so he "confiscated" the slaves as "material of war." When a Confederate major asked for their return, Butler refused. The major asked Butler to fulfill his "constitutional obligations to deliver up fugitives under the fugitive-slave act." Butler replied that Virginia was now, by its own declaration, a "foreign country," to which the Fugitive Slave Law did not apply. Considering his action "of very considerable importance both in a military and political aspect," he asked General Winfield Scott for advice. Two days later, Butler informed Scott that more slaves had arrived, this time with their families. "As a military question it would seem to be a measure of necessity to deprive their masters of their service," he told Scott. "As a political question and a question of humanity can I receive the services of a father and mother and not take the children?" Butler decided to employ the "able-bodied" slaves as masons at Fortress Monroe and to provide food, clothing, and shelter for the "non-laborers." Thus began the momentous designation of fugitives as "contrabands of war," who could be "confiscated" to deprive the Confederacy of laborers and aid the Union military effort. Soon one hundred slaves were arriving at Fortress Monroe in "squads" of twenty to thirty in a single day. By July, the fort harbored nine hundred contrabands, three hundred of whom were men between the ages of eighteen and forty-five—considered "military age."[5]

After Lincoln discussed the question with his cabinet, Secretary of War Simon Cameron informed Butler, "Your action in respect to the negroes who came in your lines from the service of the rebels is approved." In Cameron's opinion, the suppression of the rebellion superseded the enforcement of the Fugitive Slave Law. Cameron ordered Butler not to interfere with slavery, as established by Virginia law, but not to return "any persons who may come within your lines." As for the slaves' legal status, "The question of their final disposition will be reserved for future determination." Personally savoring "the half whimsical satisfaction and the relief" that the proposed solution produced, Lincoln cheerfully approved the contraband policy, calling it "Butler's fugitive slave law." The "contraband" policy proved an effective method of freeing the Confederacy's slaves under the guise of military law. Here at last was a fugitive slave law that the president would be more than happy to enforce. So would more conservative Republicans. The racially conservative postmaster general, Montgomery Blair, wrote Butler to endorse the policy of confiscating the secessionists' slaves, concluding with bemusement that the "removal of the negroes from among them will make them all emancipationists." Blair's motives, however, were entirely pragmatic rather than humanitarian. An anti-abolitionist from Maryland, Blair called the fugitive slaves "secession niggers" and urged Butler to retain only the "working people," leaving the Confederacy to feed the women and children. He also suggested that "you can get your best spies from among them." But his endorsement signaled that even an opponent of abolition could embrace emancipation when imposed "under the logic of military law." As one of Butler's subordinates observed, "He is reluctant to have slaves declared freemen, but has no objection to their being declared contrabands."[6]

"The effect upon the public mind," Butler observed with satisfaction, "was most wonderful." The new label lent authority to the novel transition from slavery to freedom that it described, and "Never was a word so speedily adopted by so many people in so short a time," according to a New York lawyer and army officer. Union soldiers began implementing their own unofficial "contraband policy," harboring fugitives in their camps, employing them as servants, and seizing the opportunity "to lead them from the house of bondage never to return." The most celebrated episode involved a woman from Rockville, Maryland, Caroline Noland, who claimed that two of her slaves had taken shelter with the 1st Ohio Volunteers on the Virginia side of the Potomac. When she entered the camp, the colonel assured his superiors that "I do not believe Mrs. Noland has a negro in this camp and from the lying propensities of her sons I am now in doubt if she ever owned a negro." The army conducted a perfunctory inquiry that proved fruitless. As soldiers returned from Fortress Monroe, they brought fugitives—and the developing contraband system— to Washington. When the colonel commanding the 5th New York Regiment defied Butler's direct orders and took nine slaves to Washington, the general notified Scott that "This is a question of difficulty with departing regiments and one upon which I ask instructions," which he apparently never received. The army camps on the Virginia side of the Potomac soon became a shelter for fugitive slaves. During the hunt for yet another "contraband," an officer reported with seeming approval that the Ohio regiments occupying Arlington Heights were practicing "a little of the abolition system in protecting the runaway." The Army of the Potomac's official policy, however, upheld the Fugitive Slave Law. Both General McDowell and his successor, General McClellan, excluded slaves from Union lines. Upon assuming command, McClellan issued a proclamation assuring Virginians that his army had no intention of interfering with slavery and indeed that "All your rights shall be religiously respected." The greatest danger to slavery in Virginia, from his perspective, was not emancipation but the possibility of a servile insurrection. "Notwithstanding all that has been said by the traitors to induce you to believe that our advent among you will be signalized by interference with your slaves understand one thing clearly," his proclamation read, "not only will we abstain from all such interference but we will on the contrary with an iron hand crush any attempt at insurrection on their part."[7]

In July 1861, however, the House of Representatives endorsed Butler's contraband policy, absolving all army officers and soldiers from any moral, if not legal, obligation to return runaways. They approved a nonbinding resolution, introduced by Illinois Republican Owen Lovejoy, a political supporter and personal friend of the president. Lovejoy's resolution declared that "in the judgment of this House it is no part of the duty of the soldiers of the United States to capture and return fugitive slaves." One month later, the contraband policy acquired the force of law when Congress passed the Confiscation Act, which freed any slave required to take up arms against the United

States or work in any capacity in the service of the Confederacy. Now slaves employed by the Confederate Army and Navy would gain their freedom when they crossed Union lines rather than inhabiting the gray area between slavery and freedom as "contrabands" who were "confiscated" by the army and were, in effect, owned by the U.S. government. Two days later, Lincoln issued a formal rationale for freeing slaves employed in Confederate service. He declared that the army must uphold slavery in states and territories that remained loyal to the Union. In rebellious regions, however, "where the laws of the United States are so far opposed and resisted that they cannot be effectually enforced it is obvious that rights dependent on the execution of those laws must temporarily fail." In short, by supporting secession, slaveowners had forfeited their constitutional rights, including federal protection of slavery, as embodied in the Fugitive Slave Law. Fugitive slaves crossing into Union lines, in Lincoln's opinion, were "thus liberated." Despite his objections to the contraband policy, McClellan still needed laborers. In September, Secretary of War Cameron sent an order to Fortress Monroe: "You will as early as practicable send to General McClellan at this place all negro men capable of performing labor accompanied by their families. They can be usefully employed on the military works in this vicinity." In this fashion, emancipation began rippling through the army, including the Army of the Potomac, on the grounds of military necessity.[8]

The government now began the process of deciding what to do with the fugitive slaves who reached Washington. The District of Columbia, one of the loyal regions in the South, did not lie under the military umbrella of "Butler's fugitive slave law." Maryland, as a loyal Border State, could reclaim its runaways who reached the national capital. Despite their belief that they would be free "if they could get into Washington," fugitives from Maryland were returned to their owners. Typically, they were captured by the sentries guarding the Navy Yard Bridge—the same span that Mary Dines had crossed under a load of hay when making her escape into the city before the war—and held at the nearby Navy Yard. To reclaim their slaves, Marylanders had to present proof of ownership and convince the army that they were loyal "Union men." When General Daniel Sickles, the former Democratic congressman, harbored five runaways in his Maryland camp, McClellan ordered them arrested. A detail of Zouaves secured them and lodged them in the Washington county jail. As the number of fugitives in Washington swelled during the summer of 1861 and soldiers grew more reluctant to surrender them, the District's constables assumed the responsibility for rounding them up. When some of Sickles's soldiers seized three slaves from a Maryland secessionist and brought them into Washington, a patrolman tried to arrest the contrabands, but they escaped and "he was laughed at by the soldiers." Despite orders to the contrary, Sickles continued to apply the contraband policy on the Maryland side, employing fifty fugitives, whose owners had abandoned their plantations. In December, he sent thirty-one women and children to Washington, "twelve women, (six with infants in arms,) seven small boys, and six girls," whom their owners had left in "almost a destitute condition." The boys went to work in the government stables. All fugitive slaves who could not prove their state of origin or the disloyalty of their owners were treated as runaways who were subject to return under the Fugitive Slave Law. Slaves arriving from Maryland adopted the sensible practice of avoiding return simply by refusing to name their owners. As a result, the jail began filling up with "contrabands."[9]

Virginia's slaves met a far different reception. They were fleeing from owners who were presumed to be disloyal, and they often possessed valuable military intelligence. One week before General Butler improvised his "contraband" policy at Fortress Monroe, a Virginia slaveowner encountered one of his slaves on a street in Washington. The slave ran to the nearest army bivouac, where he found himself surrounded by bayonets. He asked the soldiers, "You are not going to let this man take me away in this manner?" They did. Then the contraband policy changed everything. A mere three weeks later the *Evening Star* reported, "It seems to be understood that the Maryland fugitives can be regained by their masters; but the Virginia masters may have to wait a while." Upon reaching the city, slaves from Virginia typically underwent the kind of "interview" that General Butler had originated at Fortress Monroe and then were absorbed into the army. If they were arrested by the police, they were usually released to the provost marshal on the grounds that they "possessed valuable information." The army's need for labor and intelligence gradually elevated the value and status of the contrabands. Instead of rounding up runaways on the streets of Washington, the army began escorting them into the city from Virginia. "This morning a squad of thirteen contrabands, men and women, with one or two children, passed up the avenue in the direction of the Provost Marshal's office, in charge of two Cavalry soldiers dismounted," the *Evening Star* observed. "It was said they came from the Virginia lines." In November 1861, an army steamer ran the Potomac batteries expressly to deliver fifty-five Virginia contrabands to the Navy Yard.[10]

The army began routinely accepting and soliciting intelligence, known as "negro authority," from fugitives who had served as slaves in Confederate army camps. "Having the run of the camps, as servants, and waiting upon all grades of officers, they have a chance to see all that is going on," Union spymaster Allan Pinkerton maintained, "and to hear the conversations of those likely to be best posted on the strength, condition, and position of the army." In January 1862, for example, John Hay wrote in his diary that "At evening came the news of Manassas being evacuated; this came through contrabands." As laborers, contrabands grew increasingly welcome and indeed indispensable to the army. Reputedly, there were "ten applications for the labor of every contraband brought into Washington." The Quartermaster's Department, which employed more than a thousand men, began hiring contrabands as teamsters. The teamsters, in turn, hired African American cooks, the "non-laborers" that the army spurned, in lieu of taking meals at the Mess House. New boardinghouses arose near the government depot to house the women, taking on names that included "Tuscan Hall" and the "Black Diamond." When a constable jailed an African American teamster as a suspected runaway—"leaving the team standing in the street"—the Provost Guard arrested the constable and released the teamster.[11]

THE FREQUENT sight of contrabands trudging into Washington, according to the press, "was one to excite the sympathy of lookers-on at their apparent helpless condition." Through their direct observations of slavery in Virginia and their personal contacts with slaves and runaways, often "so destitute and suffering as no tongue can tell," the soldiers quickly developed sympathy for African Americans and abhorrence for slavery. "As a general thing, our soldiers have not seen much of slavery; but they have seen a good deal of the effects of slavery, and the impression produced upon them has been profound," the *National Republican* concluded. "Certain things need to be seen in order to be realized; and all the books which have ever been written, even if such books were universally read, would not produce the effect upon the Northern mind which has been produced by the actual observation of slave-labor regions by hundred of thousands of Northern soldiers. It is this which has abolitionized the army, and will abolitionize the whole population of the North, when these soldiers return to their families." The men in the camps on the Virginia side of the Potomac did their best to feed, house, and clothe the contrabands in their midst, providing rations, tents, and the only clothing that they had available, army uniforms. Thus in August 1861 appeared on the streets of Washington a prelude to the army's future, "negroes in uniform." The Provost Guard issued a warning and promised to arrest them if the "nuisance" persisted. Eventually, African Americans in uniform would seem not a nuisance but a godsend.[12]

In December 1861, at Lincoln's direction, Seward informed General McClellan, Marshal Lamon, and Mayor Wallach that contrabands from Virginia were now entitled to "military protection" under the Confiscation Act and could not be arrested by civil authorities. In fact, the military was obligated to arrest anyone apprehending them as fugitive slaves. Simultaneously, Washington became a virtual armed camp for slaves from Maryland, who were fleeing a loyal state and therefore did not constitute "contrabands." The ever scrupulous Lincoln, still desperate to keep Maryland in the Union, decided to "carry out to the fullest all constitutional obligations" owed to that ever insecure Border State. The soldiers, however, recognized no such distinction and welcomed fugitives indiscriminately into their camps. Responding to repeated protests from Maryland slaveowners and public officials, Lincoln himself directed the army to keep fugitive slaves from crossing the Potomac to the camps on the Virginia side. "Various complaints have come to me relative to the difficulties of our citizens retaining their slaves at home in consequence of the tempting offers made to them by some of the volunteer regiments," Maryland congressman Charles B. Calvert protested in July 1861. Calvert advised that an order banning slaves from army camps "would at once calm down the public mind and prevent a great deal of bad feeling."[13]

In response, Scott ordered "stringent measures to prevent any fugitive slaves from passing over the river particularly as servants with the regiments." After Lincoln asked Scott, "Would it not be well to allow owners to bring back those which have crossed[?]," the general-in-chief urged McDowell to uphold the Fugitive Slave Law by helping Maryland slaveowners retrieve their slaves from the Virginia side. At the same time, the army guarded the bridges across the Eastern Branch and arrested fugitives when they tried to cross from Maryland. The Provost Guard watched the railroad depot to keep them from escaping northward, and the Baltimore and Ohio Railroad turned away any African American lacking written permission to travel. "Egress is not absolutely denied to negroes, but it is rendered so difficult, that it may fairly be said to be substantially denied," according to the *National Republican*. "The District of Columbia, in short, is to negroes an easy place to get into, but a hard place to get out of."[14]

During the summer of 1861, the Washington jail filled and then overflowed with fugitives from Maryland, who were held until reclaimed by loyal owners. Since its erection in 1839, the county jail, located in the current Judiciary Square, had served primarily as Washington's unofficial "slave pen," confining fugitive slaves and free African Americans who violated the Black Code. Neglecting the jail, Congress had never appropriated funds for its repair during its twenty-year history. In 1860, the commissioner of public buildings repeated his long-standing request that Congress build a new jail. When the District's grand jury made its twice-yearly inspection during the summer of 1861, they judged it "a badly ventilated, unwholesome building, unfit in nearly every respect for the purpose for which it was designed." At the same time, they praised the "intelligence and fidelity" of the jailor, John Wise, who they believed had "made the best of a bad case; and the jail presents an unusual appearance of cleanliness and order." A reporter for the *Evening Star* visited a month later and found the jail "probably about as clean as could be expected." The reporter, however, labeled the building itself "an architectural abortion—its repulsive appearance outside fitly shadowing forth the lack of comfort and convenience within." The cells, which were "small, dark, damp and disagreeable," were segregated by race and gender and held eighteen to twenty runaway slaves, in addition to 130 accused criminals and soldiers, both Union and Confederate.[15]

The marshal of the District of Columbia, Lincoln's legal colleague, bodyguard, and friend, Ward Hill Lamon, was the jail's custodian. Just after taking office, Lincoln consulted a committee of Washington Republicans for advice on choosing a marshal for the District. William P. Wood, the superintendent of the Old Capitol Prison, was a member of the committee. Lincoln told him that Lamon was "a good fellow, and calculated to make friends wherever he went." Wood asked him to appoint Lamon. Lincoln replied that he "did not want to make an appointment against the wishes of the people of the District." Wood then volunteered to secure endorsements for Lamon by circulating a petition recommending his appointment, which he presented to Lincoln. Lamon secured letters of support from prominent Washingtonians and received Senate confirmation. The marshal, however, proved just as neglectful of the jail as was Congress, spending most of the summer raising several regiments in western Virginia, where he was born. The press labeled the jail "Lamon's hotel," and Lamon himself considered it a "machine" through which he earned fees of over $4,000 a year while trusting his deputy marshal to run it. Passionate about defending Washington—and Lincoln—he wrote from Martinsburg, Virginia, that "I will try to clean out Martinsburg—*purge* it if possible, so it will have none of the unclean thing in it." Soon, however, Lamon gained notoriety for running the most "unclean thing" in wartime Washington, the infamous "Blue Jug."[16]

At the end of 1861, the Commissioner of Public Buildings, William S. Wood, reiterated the need for a new jail. "The old jail is now crowded with more than double the number of persons of different colors and sexes than can be kept there with any regard to cleanliness or health," he reported to Congress. "It is unfit for the purposes of a jail, and wholly inadequate to the demands made upon it." By December 1861, the number of inmates had nearly doubled to 235, four times its intended capacity, and up to ten prisoners shared an 8-by-10-foot cell. More than two-fifths of the inmates were African Americans, one-half of whom were held on civil charges, mostly larceny but also assault, arson, and riot. (A long-practiced subterfuge in the District was accusing suspected runaways of theft or other crimes as a pretext for lodging them in the "Blue Jug.") The other half—fifty-one of them—were held explicitly as runaways, including five women. According to Lamon's accounting, one-fourth of them had been arrested in July, but one of them had been in the jail for over a year. Two of them were in custody for "safe-keeping," presumably at the behest of their owners to prevent them from running away. Among the whites, one-tenth were soldiers, mostly held for insubordination and desertion. Another white inmate was accused of "Enticing slaves to escape."[17]

In December 1861, congressional radicals recruited Chicago detective Allan Pinkerton, who had helped fugitive slaves escape before the war, to inspect the jail. Pinkerton wrote a detailed report, which Senator Henry Wilson, a Massachusetts abolitionist and later vice president under Ulysses S. Grant, submitted to Congress. Pinkerton discovered sixty accused runaways, male and female, held without charge and denied legal representation. He claimed that several were free African Americans, who had come to Washington with northern regiments or under government employment and then were mistakenly arrested as runaways. Others were contrabands from Virginia, who had worked for the Confederate Army, were pressed into service with the Union Army and then were arrested on the streets of Washington. A handful were "committed to jail by the agents of disloyal parties now in the rebel service, *'for safe-keeping until the war is over.'*" In some instances, in short, the jail was still performing its prewar function as a "holding cell" for slaveowners' convenience. The report's most inflammatory claim was that runaway slaves who went unclaimed were "sold" to pay for their jail fees. Pinkerton made two recommendations. First, he called for the immediate release of all of the African Americans who had not been charged with crimes, "to engage in the numerous useful and remunerative situations open for them, in the city," after reporting to the Provost Marshal's Office for questioning. Second, he proposed that all accused runaways seized in the District be transferred from the civil courts directly to the Provost Marshal's Office. "Those that are not found strictly 'contraband,' " he suggested unsympathetically, "can be otherwise properly disposed of after examination." Pinkerton was doing in miniature what the government had been doing in general—welcoming the literal "contrabands" from Virginia, who were militarily valuable, and forsaking the fugitives from loyal slaveowners in Maryland. His final argument was entirely pragmatic. "Besides, if it becomes known abroad that contrabands are arrested and committed to jail immediately on arriving here," he reasoned, "it will of course deter them from coming here, if not from leaving the rebel service, and in this way, also, the Government will be deprived of the benefit of the information possessed by this valuable class of deserters."[18]

Although an abolitionist, Pinkerton argued for the transfer of the fugitives primarily in the name of military security, not humanitarianism or justice. Now a detective and spy for the Union, he emphasized the contrabands' value to the successful conduct of the war. Echoing Butler's argument for confiscating runaways at the front on the grounds of military necessity, Pinkerton justified their release from the Washington jail for a similar reason. They possessed important intelligence about the condition and movements of the rebel army and the operation of disloyal citizens within Union lines. "When it is taken into consideration that this District is the grand center to which deserters and fugitives from all quarters of the rebel service tend," Pinkerton argued, "I think that the importance of acting on this suggestion will not go unperceived." By arresting contrabands under civil authority, in short, the Washington police were "traitorously interfering with the internal economy of the Army, if not materially crippling its efficiency." Foreshadowing Lincoln's later Emancipation Proclamation, Pinkerton was arguing from military necessity to support a plea for freedom.[19]

Opponents of emancipation, however, criticized the report as "full of monstrous statements utterly destitute of foundation." They depicted Pinkerton as gullible, "imposed upon by crazy abolitionists on the one hand, and runaway slaves on the other." Cynically, they argued that slaves were abusing the contraband system. "Nearly all who now run away from their owners set up the plea that they were employed by their masters in military service against the Union, of course," their rebuttal ran. "That plea on their part is no proof of the fact." Nine-tenths of the fugitives in the jail, they argued, had been lawfully arrested. With justification, the same critics blamed the conditions in the "Blue Jug" on the District's Black Code, for encouraging arbitrary arrests, and Congress, for refusing to provide funds for repairs, let alone a new jail. Calling the place a "black hole," the *Evening Star* noted bitterly that "our grand juries, local committees before Congress, and newspapers, have year after year directed the attention of Congress to the matter—namely: that the jail of Washington county is miserably constructed, badly lighted, and poorly ventilated; and that it is inhuman to confine even the vilest criminals in its reeking cells." Still, African Americans were "confined there for no offence against the laws, unless having no master is such an offence."[20]

Senator Wilson submitted a resolution calling for the unconditional release of all accused runaways in the jail and requiring the provost marshal to provide them with assistance, including provisions and clothing, until they could become self-supporting. Arguing from compassion rather than necessity, Wilson depicted scenes of "degradation and inhumanity" at the jail that demanded the fugitives' release as an act of justice. He claimed that the oppression of African Americans in Washington had increased during the war but faulted the District's constables, who were independent of the Metropolitan Police, for arresting the runaways. Abolitionist senators, all New Englanders, supported Wilson's resolution but tempered his argument. Maine's William Pitt Fessenden faulted the District's legal system, not specific individuals, for oppressing African Americans.

"I have long been of opinion that the administration of justice, so-called, in this city, was an administration of injustice," he insisted. John P. Hale of New Hampshire agreed that "there is not a community, calling itself civilized, that has a worse administration of justice than this District." Seizing on the political value inherent in Pinkerton's report, however, he pointed out that the discovery of secessionists' slaves languishing in the jail for the duration of the war at public expense would rally northern support behind the war effort. The far-sighted Charles Sumner, Wilson's senior colleague from Massachusetts, called for revocation of the Black Code, which fostered the inequities, and beyond that, the abolition of slavery itself, which he labeled "the root of all this noisome inhumanity." In December 1861, the Senate approved Wilson's resolution and called for additional investigation of Pinkerton's charges.[21]

Wilson's address in the Senate prompted immediate action. A few days later, the jail's warden released all of the fugitives from the "Blue Jug," including twelve Virginia contrabands and the fifty or so runaways from Maryland. The *National Republican* rejoiced that "the country will no longer be disgraced by maintaining a negro pen." Resenting charges of "dereliction of duty," however, the combative Lamon escalated the controversy into a clash between the executive and legislative branches by preventing members of Congress from inspecting the jail. When Lamon refused to admit James Grimes, the Iowa senator went straight to the White House. Lincoln turned Grimes away, just as Lamon had barred him from the jail. "When, for the first time in six months, I attempted to approach the footstool of power at the other end of the avenue," Grimes informed the Senate, "I was told that the President was engaged, and his servants declined to convey my name to him." In response, the Senate unanimously approved a resolution holding Lamon in contempt. To defuse the standoff, Lincoln seized the initiative. Exerting executive authority over the jail, he asked Lamon to draw up formal regulations for visitors. Under the new rules, the president and cabinet members would be admitted "at their pleasure." Congressmen could enter the jail upon a pass issued by the President of the Senate or the Speaker of the House. In January 1862, Lincoln personally prohibited Lamon from holding fugitive slaves who were not charged with a crime for more than thirty days, producing a practical route to freedom for many Maryland slaves once they reached the District. After enduring what was in effect a thirty-day "waiting period" in the county jail, fugitive slaves from Maryland would go free.[22]

Still, the Senate was not done with Marshal Lamon. Grimes, the chair of the Committee on the District of Columbia, conducted an inquiry into the "conditions and management" of the jail, turning the controversy into a personal feud with Lamon. The committee's report concluded that "a barbarous system of punishment had been practiced upon colored persons in the jail," originating long before the war began, which they characterized as "torture." While the committee acknowledged that Lamon did not personally mistreat prisoners, they faulted him for lax supervision of the jail, a reluctance to correct the abuses when they came to light, and his appointment of John Wise as jailor. The report portrayed Wise as "the cruelest and most successful negro catcher in the District" who, according to Senator Wilson, "visits the various regiments and portions of the country about here, and steals negroes whenever he can lay his hands upon them." At the same time, the committee conceded that the jail building was inadequate to hold the number of prisoners admitted and that "the duties of the marshal of the District have become quite too onerous and his responsibilities too extensive." In response, Lamon faulted Congress for letting the jail run down, denied any knowledge of the physical abuse, and blamed the jailor and the eight guards for keeping it a secret from him. His primary defense, however, was the legacy of "immemorial usages having the force of law, in relation to the negro population of this District." When he assumed his office, he argued, he simply perpetuated customary practices that had become fixtures of law enforcement in Washington long before his appointment as marshal. Hence, he "was bound to receive and safely keep every negro committed to my custody as a *runaway*, or placed there by his master for safe-keeping." Hopelessly impolitic, the boorish Lamon construed the congressional disgust with the "Blue Jug" as a personal and perhaps political assault on his honor rather than a genuine effort to address the racism inherent in the District's Black

Code and the barbarity of the institution of slavery itself. Instead of embracing the long-overdue reforms in the capital's administration of justice, he defended himself against what he viewed as "the present movement against me."[23]

Throughout the conflict, Lamon argued that he was simply enforcing the Fugitive Slave Law, an act of Congress, and therefore did not merit congressional censure. "The law remained in force," he wrote, "and no attempt was made by Congress to repeal it, or to provide for the protection of the Executive officers whose duty it was to enforce it." He claimed that "the subject gave Mr. Lincoln great concern, but he could see no way out of the difficulty except to have the law executed." As Lamon put it, "Congress having made the offensive laws, it was the President's duty to execute them." Lincoln assured Lamon that he, and not the marshal, was the true target of the Senate inquiry, telling him that "we shall have to stand it whatever they send." Still, the bumbling Lamon imprudently conducted a public campaign to clear his name and restore his reputation. After Republican newspaper editors in the North excoriated his conduct in managing the jail, he sought vindication by suing Horace Greeley, editor of the influential *New York Tribune*, for libel. Attempting to heal this potential rift in the Republican Party and undoubtedly solicitous of Greeley's support for his administration, Lincoln personally intervened and managed to persuade Lamon to drop the suit. Greeley was confident that he would have prevailed in court but thanked Lincoln "heartily" for his help in settling the dispute. Still, Lamon's feud with Congress continued for the duration of the war.[24]

The controversy over the jail dramatically improved its condition and secured the release of the fugitive slaves held there. Its greatest legacy, however, was solidifying congressional opposition to slavery in the District of Columbia. During the debate over conditions in the Washington jail, Republican senators had proposed eliminating both the Black Code and slavery itself within the District. Even supporters of slavery recognized that the Grimes Committee report spelled the end of the institution in Washington. "The report in question is evidently being used to bring about the legal abolition of negro slavery in the District of Columbia," one of them shrewdly concluded.

The repeal of the Black Code by itself would produce "revolutionary changes" in Washington and represent a de facto emancipation in its own right. "Instead of a free negro population of perhaps 14,000," the writer prophesied, "in the current anomalous condition of the country the District of Columbia cannot fail to become at once the harbor for at least 50,000 negroes, practically freed as an incident of the war." In the absence of a Black Code, he predicted, "Washington will be rendered almost uninhabitable to the white man." He felt certain that abolitionists in Congress "will of course continue their tinkering experiments upon the local affairs of the District of Columbia, until they make it nothing less than a hell upon earth for the white man." Congress hastened that hell in March 1862 when they approved an article of war prohibiting any member of the military from returning fugitive slaves to their owners, on penalty of court-martial and dismissal from the service. Meanwhile, the president had begun pursuing "tinkering experiments" of his own.[25]

CHAPTER FOURTEEN

"Freedom Triumphant in War and Peace"
Emancipation in Washington

———◆◆◆———

DURING THE summer of 1861, Lincoln endorsed General Butler's "contraband" policy and signed the Confiscation Act into
law but had little faith in either process as a strategy for instigating
a permanent end to southern slavery. Both were temporary military
measures that were limited in scope and would vanish the moment
the war ended. In addition to these initial thrusts against slavery
in the Confederacy, Lincoln looked for opportunities to end slavery permanently in loyal regions. The Border States, where many
slaveowners valued the Union over slavery, seemed a far more sensible place to initiate emancipation. If nothing else, the accelerating
erosion of slavery was perfectly apparent to residents of the Upper
South, who might well accept compensation for the slaves whose
freedom seemed increasingly inevitable. "You can not if you would,"
Lincoln told them, "be blind to the signs of the times." Inducing
them to free their own slaves through state action would be unquestionably constitutional and would disarm critics who opposed any
federal interference with slavery as either a military strategy or a new
goal of the war. Above all, Lincoln told Congress, initiating emancipation in the Border States would bind them to the Union, dash any
hope that the Confederacy could lure them into seceding, and thus
help to achieve victory.[1]

Reasoning that gradual and compensated emancipation would be most acceptable to the Border States, Lincoln crafted a voluntary plan modeled on the one that he had proposed for the District of Columbia twelve years earlier. He told Congress "that the United States ought to co-operate with any state which may adopt gradual abolishment of slavery, giving to such state pecuniary aid, to be used by such state in it's discretion, to compensate for the inconveniences public and private." He also declared that "in my judgment, gradual, and not sudden emancipation, is better for all." He began by targeting Delaware, which contained the fewest slaves of any southern state, 1,800 or 1.6 percent of its population. (Before proceeding, he personally asked the superintendent of the census to compile a table of the population of slaves in the state.) In November 1861, he proposed a plan for the gradual abolition of slavery in Delaware that would provide time for the two races to adjust their new social and economic relationship. Lincoln's plan freed all slaves older than thirty-five immediately and all others when they turned thirty-five, in exchange for $500 per slave, a total of $719,200.[2]

Lincoln considered his Delaware "proposition" largely symbolic, "merely initiatory, and not within itself a practical measure," but an important beginning to a wave of emancipation that he hoped would sweep the South. "I do not speak of emancipation at once," he insisted, "but of a decision at once to emancipate gradually." Committing even one slave state to eventual emancipation would provide an apt example for the others. "If I can get this plan started in Delaware I have no fear but that all the other border states will accept it," Lincoln told the state's largest slaveowner, emphasizing, "This is the cheapest and most humane way of ending this war and saving lives." In its endorsement of the plan, the *National Republican* declared, "The great, transcendent fact is, that for the first time in two generations we have the recommendation from the presidential chair of the *abolition of slavery*." Viewing emancipation as a prelude to social and political equality, Delaware quickly rejected Lincoln's plan, declaring that "when the people of Delaware desire to abolish slavery within her borders, they will do so in their own way." (In fact, Delaware proved the only Border State to refuse to emancipate its slaves, who became free only upon ratification of the Thirteenth Amendment in December 1865.) Lincoln was disappointed but persevered and extended his plan to the remaining Border States.[3]

To make the prospect of emancipation more palatable to a region that was increasingly fearful of its free African American population, Lincoln included a colonization program as part of his Border State Plan. Colonization was a national movement that sought to eliminate blacks from American society by sending them in "colonies" to either Africa or Latin America. The American Colonization Society formed in Washington, DC, in 1816, mounting a campaign to create an overseas colony for African Americans. The founding members were mostly southerners, and Henry Clay presided over the meeting that organized the society. Their motives varied. Some of them were simply racists who strove to eliminate all African Americans, both slave and free, from American soil. Others hoped to undermine the institution of slavery by creating a viable alternative for slaveowners who might free their slaves if they knew those slaves would leave the country rather than remaining as free blacks. Still others genuinely believed that African Americans would be better off if they voluntarily left a predominantly white country and created a black society of their own in a tropical climate. Generally viewed as a threat to the continuation of slavery, the movement produced local colonization societies in every state except South Carolina and culminated in the creation of the new African nation of Liberia in 1822, settled by former slaves from the United States.[4]

Emulating his political idol Henry Clay, Lincoln had endorsed voluntary colonization during the 1850s, which he viewed as one way to undermine slavery indirectly by making eventual abolition more acceptable to whites in both the South and the North. Colonization might lead to the ultimate extinction of slavery, improve the lot of African Americans, and even benefit Africa, without threatening the bonds of Union that guaranteed freedom to white Americans. Lincoln labeled such a result "a glorious consummation" for all. He viewed voluntary colonization as a middle ground between the extension of slavery on one hand and abolitionism on the other. While he was never a member of the American Colonization Society, as his political star rose, in 1857 the Illinois Colonization Society elected him one of its eleven managers, which proved an entirely honorary appointment. In his Annual Message to Congress in December 1861, however, Lincoln endorsed colonization, reasoning that the Confiscation Act was producing a swelling population of free African Americans who, "thus liberated, are already dependent on the United States, and must be provided for in some way." He was undoubtedly aware that the results of that process, including conflicting military policies, overlapping jurisdictions, and overcrowding, were most plainly visible and divisive in the national capital itself. He recommended that Congress assume financial responsibility for the former slaves while simultaneously offering them the opportunity to emigrate voluntarily, "so far as individuals may desire," to one or more colonies. His ultimate rationale was preventing emancipation from turning the Civil War into "a violent and remorseless revolutionary struggle." Up to this point, he told Congress, "I have, therefore, in every case, thought it proper to keep the integrity of the Union prominent as the primary object of the contest on our part, leaving all questions which are not of vital military importance to the more deliberate action of the legislature." Hence, he was content to let Congress take the lead as the nation moved toward emancipation, while portraying colonization as an indispensable ingredient of any successful process and therefore an "absolute necessity" for the perpetuation of the Union. Beyond any personal commitment to transporting former slaves abroad, Lincoln recognized that a simultaneous colonization proposal would help any plan move forward.[5]

Lincoln's cabinet offered three distinct views on colonization. At one extreme, Attorney General Edward Bates of Missouri, a Border State, was a longtime member of the American Colonization Society and supported "compulsory deportation" of former slaves. He advocated their "emigration" to other countries as individuals but opposed "colonies" that would remain dependent on the United States for protection and aid. At the other extreme, Secretary of War Stanton and Secretary of the Navy Welles never supported colonization, perhaps eyeing former slaves as eventual recruits into the military. Four cabinet members occupied the middle of the spectrum, like Lincoln, supporting voluntary colonization. Postmaster General Montgomery Blair of Maryland, another Border State, was "strongly for deportation," arguing that it "would be necessary to rid the country of its black population, and some place must be found for them." The Blair family had begun championing colonization in Latin America even before the war began. Secretary of the Interior Caleb Smith of Indiana, whose department would implement any colonization plan, actively pursued a variety of projects that he urged upon the president, with whom he had served in Congress. The two radicals, Seward and Chase, were initially lukewarm but eventually acquiesced in the idea. Lincoln made clear to his cabinet that he "objected unequivocally" to compulsory colonization and believed that the government should provide support to former slaves. His experience, including his youth in Kentucky and Illinois and his two years living in Washington while serving in Congress, had convinced him that racial tensions might prevent whites and blacks from ever living together peaceably. Pessimistically, he told his cabinet that it was "essential to provide an asylum for a race which we had emancipated, but which could never be recognized or admitted to be our equals." This position put him in the middle of the spectrum within his cabinet.[6]

Lincoln inherited an ill-fated Central American land development contract from the Buchanan administration, in which the Chiriqui Improvement Company promised to deliver coal to the U.S. Navy and build a railroad across the Isthmus of Panama. (Bates called it "a rotten remnant of an intrigue of the last administration.") Secretary of the Interior Smith resurrected negotiations with the company as a potential military supplier. When Welles told Lincoln that he had "no confidence" in the project and wanted nothing more to do with it, the president turned the contract over to Smith as a possible opportunity "to secure the removal of negroes from this country." Lincoln also worked with the Senate to extend formal diplomatic recognition to Liberia and Haiti as possible locations for colonies. Seward came on board when Lincoln asked him to negotiate with other nations to identify alternate locations for colonies. Investors in the Chiriqui company, originally a "commercial and naval" venture, naturally seized upon congressionally funded colonization as an additional rationale for approval of the coal contract. One of the investors characterized colonization as "a duty of Christian Charity, and a political necessity to provide promptly & efficaceously for those thus helpless and homeless to the last degree—who are besides a severe tax upon the nation and are even at this early period becoming, from improvident and reckless habits an intolerable nuisance."[7]

Washington's antislavery newspaper, the *National Republican*, endorsed the Chiriqui project for contrabands, "a portion of whom would gladly accept an offer to be assisted in emigrating." The *Republican*, however, emphasized that colonization was no substitute for general emancipation, declaring that "we cannot believe that anything short of the unconditional emancipation of the slaves of rebels, meets either the necessities of the case, or the demands of public opinion." As an adjunct of emancipation, the Chiriqui initiative received the dismissive label "the Colony of Linconia." Meanwhile, conservatives repeated their traditional argument that African Americans were incapable of surviving in, let alone creating, a free society of their own. The *National Intelligencer* portrayed both colonization and immediate emancipation as unfair to southern slaves. "The 'institution' has reared them in habits of dependence and attendance upon the whites; it has given them no capacity for self-maintenance and self-government," their argument ran. "The transformation of domestic servants, accustomed life-long to none but indoor employments, into tamers of tropical forests and successful cultivators of new and unaccustomed regions, may be effected in a long course of years; but not without some little preparation and some skill in the arts of self-support."[8]

Many Border State Unionists, like Bates, advocated the compulsory emigration of former slaves. "The negroes that are now liberated, and that remain in this city," Kentucky senator Garrett Davis argued, "will become a sore and a burden and a charge upon the white population." Missouri representative Francis P. Blair Jr., the brother of Lincoln's postmaster general, introduced a congressional plan that combined confiscation with colonization, mandating apprenticeship and deportation for the Confederacy's slaves. "As regards colonization," the *National Republican* responded, "the President's recommendation that provision be made to assist the emigration of such people of color as are 'willing to emigrate,' seems to be going far enough in that direction." Still, the newspaper admitted that the growing population of contrabands from Virginia and fugitives from Maryland was heightening racial prejudices in the North and would lead to exclusion laws if it continued. "We know of but two ways to arrest the progress of this unholy feeling towards the colored race, and they are: First, universal emancipation, which would induce the blacks to remain in the South, after we shall have conquered the rebellion; and second, by providing a new and good home for those who have enterprise enough to avail themselves of it." There lay the conundrum. The piecemeal freedom provided by the contraband and confiscation policies demanded a colonization component to prevent a racist backlash that would hinder emancipation and undermine the war effort.[9]

"An American Negro" summed up the prevalent attitude toward colonization among Washington's African Americans when he explained to the conservative *Evening Star*, "We do not want to be exiled beyond the ocean to look for a home when there is land enough on the American continent. We are colored Americans, and we want a home on the American soil." Yet Lincoln persevered, and at his urging Congress appropriated $500,000 in July 1862 to support voluntary colonization efforts. In August 1862, he appointed James Mitchell, a Methodist minister and former agent of the American Colonization Society, as commissioner of emigration in the Interior Department. With no ties to the African American community, Mitchell took the simple step of advertising for emigrants in Washington's newspapers. Meanwhile, a handful of "emigration agents," both white and black, competed for the congressional funding by proposing colonization programs targeting Haiti and Liberia. James Redpath was a journalist and antislavery advocate who had reported the Kansas conflict of the mid-1850s and encouraged free-state emigration into that territory. In 1860, after investigating conditions in Haiti, he became the island republic's official lobbyist in Washington, campaigning for diplomatic recognition and African American emigration. Two years later, he arrived with emigration agents in tow to persuade the contrabands to leave Washington for Haiti. One of his former agents, Joseph E.

Williams, an African American, resented the Haitian government's treatment of the emigrants, cut his ties with Redpath, and embraced the Chiriqui initiative. An effective organizer, Williams held a series of public meetings and circulated petitions that received hundreds of signatures calling for congressional support for a Central American colonization project.[10]

Targeting leaders within the city's black churches, Williams generated substantial support. The Reverend Henry McNeal Turner of the Israel Bethel African Methodist Episcopal (AME) Church on Capitol Hill, the second-largest African American congregation in the city and a center of the underground railroad before the war, embraced Lincoln's Chiriqui proposal. Freeborn in the South Carolina upcountry, Turner began his remarkable odyssey in life after taking a job sweeping out a law office. Impressed with his abilities, the lawyers and clerks taught him to read and write. Undergoing a religious conversion, Turner gravitated toward the all-black AME Church. The senior bishop of the church, Daniel Payne, recruited him to Baltimore, where he studied theology, Hebrew, Greek, Latin, and German. In April 1862, the twenty-eight-year-old Turner assumed the pulpit at Washington's Israel Bethel Church, Payne's former congregation. An eloquent advocate of emancipation, Turner gained the confidence of Lincoln intimates Charles Sumner, Salmon Chase, and Owen Lovejoy.[11],

Most of Washington's African Americans, however, greeted the wartime colonization program with contempt. After Turner received what he called "a heavy tirade of denunciations," he muted his public support for emigration. The most controversial of the promoters was Liberia's emigration commissioner, John D. Johnson, a former member of the Liberian legislature. Many African Americans resented Liberia's association with the white-dominated American Colonization Society. During the spring of 1862, Johnson confirmed suspicions about the society's motives by suggesting that contrabands submit to compulsory colonization. Washington's leading opponent of colonization was the Social, Civil, and Statistical Association (SCSA), a mutual aid society that included many of Washington's elite African Americans. The association's purpose was to gather information about the city's African American community to demonstrate its achievements and support their advocacy of emancipation. The members' affiliation with the Fifteenth Street Presbyterian Church, founded by the Reverend John F. Cook Sr., a legendary leader of Washington's African American community, pitted the SCSA against the pro-emigration stance of Henry McNeal Turner of the Israel Bethel AME Church. Launching a campaign to rid the city of "emigration agents," the SCSA targeted Johnson, accused him of "acts inimical and treasonable to the interest of the colored people of this community and of the country generally," and asked him to leave the city. Two members of the association beat Johnson at his boardinghouse and were convicted of assault. The day after their conviction, for which they were sentenced to ten days in jail and fined $50, Lincoln issued a pardon, releasing them from the jail, in which they had spent one night, but allowing the fines to stand. Lincoln's pardon suggests that he felt some responsibility for creating the conflict and at the very least understood it, if not sympathized. As the opposition to emigration agents of all varieties intensified, opponents charged Joseph Williams with fraud and self-aggrandisement, and he received a "severe beating" of his own at the National Hotel.[12]

Prompted by Turner, in August 1862 Lincoln asked his commissioner of emigration to gather a group of African American leaders to meet with him personally at the White House. This initiative, according to one African American correspondent, "very nearly made some of our citizens frantic with excitement." Mitchell notified African American religious leaders and called a meeting at Union Bethel AME Church. The group adopted a resolution labeling emigration "inexpedient, inauspicious, and impolitic" but selected a delegation of five, including three members of the SCSA, to meet with Lincoln. Lincoln met with them at the White House on August 14, 1862. Rather than discussing anything with this assemblage of prominent Washington African Americans, however, the president did all the talking, and even his questions were entirely rhetorical. His plea on behalf of his emigration experiment was heartfelt but betrayed many of the racial biases that he had yet to overcome. At one point, he referred to Africa as "your native land." Still, his audience with Afri-

can Americans in the White House was unprecedented, signifying
both his sense of urgency in initiating emigration and the growing
importance of black Americans as a constituency to be addressed, if
not consulted, directly and personally. He began by acknowledging
the all too apparent racial prejudices that plagued African Americans,
which he labeled a "great disadvantage" to both races. "Your race
are suffering, in my judgment, the greatest wrong inflicted on any
people," he told the delegation, referring to slavery. "But even when
you cease to be slaves, you are yet far removed from being placed on
an equality with the white race." After admitting his own inability to
ameliorate racial prejudice, which he considered "a fact with which
we have to deal," he shifted responsibility for the present Civil War
onto the shoulders of African Americans themselves. "But for your
race among us," he reasoned, "there could not be war." His conclusion was simple, far too simple: "It is better for us both, therefore, to
be separated." He presented emigration to Liberia or Central America as an opportunity for the delegation not just to better their own
condition but to set an example for the even less fortunate former
slaves to improve their lot in life.[13]

Historians have looked for subtle signs in Lincoln's soliloquy to
suggest that his address to the delegation, like his colonization program itself, was largely rhetorical in character, designed to suppress
white resistance to emancipation while the process was unfolding.
If so, he was asking African American leaders to help him in that
effort by demonstrating "a successful commencement" to his colonization program, while admitting candidly that "I am not sure
you will succeed." He began by pleading for a "hundred" emigrants,
quickly reduced that goal to "fifty," and then concluded by asking
for a mere "twenty-five." When Edward M. Thomas, the chairman
of the delegation, announced that they would "hold a consultation
and in a short time give an answer," Lincoln's parting words were
surprisingly ambivalent. "Take your full time," he answered, "no
hurry at all." Thomas, the president of the Anglo-African Institute
for the Encouragement of Industry and Art, did not consult with
the other members of the delegation, nor did he take his time. Just
two days later, he single-handedly wrote a letter to Lincoln embrac-

ing colonization. He reported that the group "was entirely hostile to the movement until all the advantages were so ably brought to our view." He proposed sending delegates to visit African American leaders in Philadelphia, New York, and Boston to share the president's perspective and begin cooperating with them on the emigration movement.[14]

Washington's African American church leaders, however, felt slighted by the SCSA members within the delegation and particularly Thomas's premature response and precipitous approval of the president's plan. Expected to provide a report at Union Bethel AME Church two weeks later, none of the delegation appeared, reportedly because of the negative reaction that their audience with Lincoln had provoked. Once again, the prospect of government-supported colonization had divided Washington's African American community. Washington's antislavery newspaper, the *National Republican*, like the city's African Americans themselves, was critical of what it labeled "the President's little speech." Above all, the paper found "extraordinary" Lincoln's suggestion that whites suffered from the "presence" of African Americans. "It is not the 'presence' of the negro that we suffer from, but it is from our own guilt and folly in enslaving him," the editorial declared. "The negro does not injure us, if we let him alone." Still, the *Republican* acknowledged the practical value of aiding, "to a reasonable extent," truly voluntary emigration. "It is not likely to be extensive," the editorial reasoned, "but even if not so, it will allay the fears which are entertained by some, of injury from the presence of free negroes in large numbers." Many whites continued to support colonization under the guise of improving both African American and African society. Among the city's white ministers, the leading advocate of colonization was the Reverend Phineas D. Gurley, pastor of the Lincolns' New York Avenue Presbyterian Church. In 1864, more than a year after the Emancipation Proclamation, Gurley's church hosted the annual meeting of the American Colonization Society. In his address to the society, Gurley reasoned that "when the slavery question shall have been solved, and solved it may be, in blood, *the negro question will remain.*" He proposed Liberia as "a house of refuge to which thousands and tens of thousands of the colored people of this land and of other lands will yet be seen fleeing every year with gratitude and gladness."[15]

Ultimately, however, Lincoln's first colonization venture never materialized. During the summer of 1862, he appointed Senator Samuel C. Pomeroy of Kansas as the colonization agent for the Chiriqui project. As a member of the New England Emigrant Aid Society, Pomeroy had promoted free-state settlement in Kansas and therefore had both experience aiding emigrants and a reputation as a radical Republican to lend to the Chiriqui initiative. Pomeroy exuded a rare combination of radical zeal for emancipation and philosophical commitment to voluntary colonization. On the floor of the Senate in June 1862, he declared that African Americans "are not offensive to any body that I know of in their slavery, but the moment they are free they have all the difficulties about them." He then suggested expanding the colonization program to include "rebel masters," along with their slaves. "If they are so lovely together, if one cannot exist without the other, for I am assured on all hands that the slaves cannot take care of themselves and that the masters cannot take care of themselves," he insisted, "I think that is a good reason why, when we undertake a system of colonization, we should keep them together." Pomeroy's enlistment in the Chiriqui project brought Salmon Chase, his political ally, on board, and the radical secretary of the treasury endorsed colonization at last. By September, the enterprising Pomeroy had identified 13,000 potential emigrants, 500 of whom were prepared to voyage to Panama immediately. Snags arose, however, when Honduras, Nicaragua, and Costa Rica opposed the colonization plan and Joseph Henry, the secretary of the Smithsonian Institution, concluded that the vaunted coal deposits in Chiriqui contained nothing more than worthless lignite. Lincoln drafted a letter authorizing Pomeroy to plant the colony but never signed it. Lincoln's ambivalence suggests that he never viewed colonization as a realistic method for ending slavery, but only a way to undermine resistance to emancipation in the Border States. Originally an advocate of emigration, Henry McNeal Turner ultimately decided that Lincoln's proposal was a "strategic move" designed to defuse objections to emancipation. "Mr. Lincoln is not half such a stickler for colored expatriation as he has been pronounced," Turner declared. "The President," he concluded, "stood in need of a place to *point to*."[16]

WHILE SERVING in Congress, Lincoln had recognized the District of Columbia as the best place to begin the process of freeing America's slaves. For decades, abolitionists had considered the nation's capital the "grand point of attack" against southern slavery. John Quincy Adams and Joshua Giddings's petition campaign of the 1830s and 1840s had focused on the District of Columbia as the institution's weakest point and the most promising place to instigate emancipation. While living in "Abolition House," Lincoln had briefly joined that futile effort by proposing voluntary, gradual, and compensated emancipation in the District. During the 1850s, the free soil movement shifted his attention to the territories as a more promising arena for arresting the spread of slavery and eventually ending it. As president, his first emancipation initiative targeted the Border States to keep them out of the Confederacy and therefore undermine the southern war effort, win the war, and reunite the nation. With the ascendance of the Republican Party, the secession of eleven southern states, and the outbreak of the Civil War, the abolition of slavery in the District of Columbia became attainable at last. During the controversy over the Washington jail, radicals in Congress, led by Senator Henry Wilson of Massachusetts, resolved to address the root of the problem.[17]

During the summer of 1861, Republican senators from the Northeast—Henry Wilson and Charles Sumner of Massachusetts, and Lot Morrill and William Pitt Fessenden of Maine—began campaigning for abolition as both a war aim and a strategy for defeating the Confederacy. In December 1861, Wilson submitted a bill proposing the immediate and compulsory emancipation of the District of Columbia's 3,200 slaves. To win the support of Democrats and conservative Republicans, particularly representatives of the Border States, Wilson's plan compensated slaveowners and included a voluntary colonization program for the former slaves. The plan not only freed the slaves in the nation's capital but abolished the institution of slavery itself in the District of Columbia, prohibiting the admission of any new slaves to take their place. Opponents raised a sweep of objections, denying congressional power to end slavery in the District of Columbia, arguing that emancipation would generate support for the Confederacy in the Border States, portraying slaves as unfit for freedom, predicting a race war, and decrying the economic competition that free African Americans would impose on white workers. Border State senators championed compulsory colonization for the emancipated slaves. Two members of the House Committee on the District of Columbia, a Unionist from Maryland and a Democrat from New York, filed a minority report opposing the compensated emancipation plan, distinguishing between Congress's local jurisdiction over the capital and its national jurisdiction. Adopting the very argument that abolitionists had offered for decades, they predicted that abolition in the District would initiate a movement toward national emancipation. Calling the boundaries of the District "imaginary lines," they warned that "hosts of free blacks, fugitive slaves, and incendiaries would be assembled in the work of general abolitionism: and that from such a magazine of evil every conceivable mischief would be spread through the surrounding country with almost the rapidity of the movements of the atmosphere."[18]

Wilson's proposal allotted an average of $300 per slave to all slaveowners who were loyal to the Union, for a total payment of $900,000. Wilson allocated an additional $100,000 to support the emigration of any African Americans who voluntarily chose to leave the country for Haiti, Liberia, or any other foreign destination, raising the total cost of the plan to $1,000,000. Another radical senator, Lot Morrill of Maine, submitted a revision of Wilson's bill that compensated only slaveowners who could prove their allegiance to the Union by subscribing to an oath and procuring two witnesses who could testify to their loyalty. Morrill estimated that there were 3,200 slaves in the District, and two hundred or more disloyal slaveowners. He characterized the bill as the natural consequence, if not the inevitable result, of the prohibition of the slave trade enacted in the Compromise of

1850. "The logic and morality of a law, applicable to any country or locality, providing that slaves are not to be regarded as subject to transfer and sale is," he reasoned, "*virtual abolition.*" The conservative *National Intelligencer* conceded the premise but challenged the conclusion. "As slavery has dwindled down to so inconsiderable a point in the District, it was doomed by the operation of the same causes to an early quiet extinction, which few among the people of the District would have regretted," the paper reasoned. "It is, therefore, only to this sudden, forcible, and total act of emancipation, and the instant turning loose upon society of two thousand liberated slaves, together with the alarm and apprehension with which the act will naturally inspire the border Slave States, that will form the subject of regret." In other words, slavery was on the verge of disappearing, so any additional government action was unnecessary.[19]

Radical senator Samuel Pomeroy of Kansas opposed compensating slaveowners and argued that Congress should indemnify the slaves themselves as the victims of an institution that the government had tolerated and even abetted for so long. Likening compensation to a "ransom," clearly unjust but necessary to win the slaves' freedom, Charles Sumner justified the payment as the only practical way to achieve majority support for the plan. Opponents of emancipation declared that the radical senators were "acting as legislators for the District" and called the plan " 'the entering wedge' of projects destined to be more sweeping in their scope and radical in their application." They called for a referendum on the bill before passage, reminiscent of Lincoln's proposal from twelve years earlier, and endorsed the gradualism embodied in his Border State Plan. In March, the conservative *Evening Star* published seven objections to abolition in the District and two days later expanded the list to twenty. The *Star*'s primary argument was precedent, as embodied in the Compromise of 1850, Maryland law, which had governed the District for six decades, and Lincoln's campaign pledges not to disturb slavery in the nation's capital. Another cluster of objections portrayed congressional intervention as unwarranted, because abolition was a moral reform that no one outside Congress, including the slaves themselves, had demanded. The *Star* portrayed the measure as counterproductive, certain to strengthen the resolve of the Confederacy and heighten sympathy in the Border States and therefore undermine the war effort. The emancipation plan was unjust to slaveowners, because the appropriation significantly undervalued the District's slaves. Finally, emancipation in Washington was "the beginning of a social and political revolution in our midst" that would lead ultimately to equal rights. "The same power that can liberate our negroes against our will," the *Star* declared, "can and perhaps will confer upon them equality in civil and political privileges with the whites, so, for instance that negroes may vote for municipal or other officers; may hold such offices themselves; and sit as jurors, magistrates and judges in our courts." This, of course, was exactly what Republicans in Congress intended and soon achieved.[20]

While Congress was debating emancipation, rumors circulated that slaveowners were removing or "running out" their slaves from the District, generally to Maryland. According to the *National Republican*, slaveowners were removing their most valuable or "likely" slaves, leaving behind those for whom they considered $300 in compensation a fair price. A Washington slaveowner denied that slaves were leaving the District, simply because they were no longer a "marketable commodity" and the emancipation act therefore represented "the only hope we can reasonably indulge of ever getting anything whatever for our negroes." Another denial claimed that the reported "exodus" represented Maryland owners removing slaves that they had hired out in the District, fearing that they would lose their slaves under the act if they could not prove their loyalty to the Union. Blaming proslavery opponents of emancipation for spreading the rumors, the *Republican* insisted, "Slaves are sent out of this District, not because $300 is not far beyond their average value, but principally by secessionists, to whom no compensation is to be paid." There were genuine instances of slaves who were forcibly removed or "kidnapped." One slave was seized when he came to the emancipation commission's office to pick up his "free papers." General James Wadsworth, the commander of the Military District of Washington, arrested the county constable who committed the abduction. Despite exaggerated predictions that one-half or more of the District's slaves would end up in Maryland or even that "there will be no negroes to be freed by the bill when it shall have become an act," the number freed matched almost exactly Senator Morrill's original estimate of 3,200.[21]

During the debate over emancipation and equal rights in the national capital, Washington's abolitionists and radical members of Congress mounted a public campaign to influence public opinion, congressional dialogue, and Abraham Lincoln himself. Creating the Washington Lecture Association (WLA) during the fall of 1861, local reformers sponsored a lecture series at the Smithsonian Institution that hosted appearances by the most prominent northern antislavery advocates. Joseph Henry, America's most renowned scientist and the secretary of the Smithsonian, was a conservative New Yorker who had developed southern sympathies after his appointment in 1846 and even refused to fly the American flag over the Smithsonian Castle. Suspicious of the WLA's motives, he initially hesitated to allow political discussion within the Smithsonian's lecture hall. The organizers enlisted the aid of Illinois representative Owen Lovejoy, a Lincoln ally and friend, who considered Henry "an old traitor" and talked him into approving the lecture series, while disavowing any endorsement of its content. Twenty of the twenty-two lecturers were abolitionists who seized this opportunity to prod both Lincoln and Congress toward a more aggressive prosecution of the war that would ultimately end slavery.[22]

Speaking in January 1862, with Lincoln, Salmon Chase, and radical congressmen Henry Wilson, Owen Lovejoy, and Thaddeus Stevens sitting beside him on the stage, *New York Tribune* editor Horace Greeley delivered a combative attack on slavery as the underlying cause of the Civil War. Declaring that "the implacable enemy that is lifting the dagger to the heart of the nation is slavery, the most horrible legacy of evil that has ever fallen to a people," Greeley insisted that the war could only be won by attacking that institution. "And now, if the Union is to be restored, it is only on the basis of freedom or slavery—and the thing most to be dreaded in the settlement is compromise." With dramatic force, Greeley announced that *"it is time to look the enemy in the eye. It has declared, 'I am slavery.'"* Greeley's message was clear: "Compromise is impossible." The lecture received thunderous applause from the audience of one thousand.[23]

Following appearances by Ralph Waldo Emerson and Gerrit Smith, Boston abolitionist Wendell Phillips delivered the most anticipated lecture. Phillips was widely known and often reviled for rejecting any hint of compromise with slavery, even at the cost of disunion. The day before he spoke, however, Lincoln invited him to the White House, where they talked for an hour. When Phillips urged the president to mount a more decisive assault on slavery, Lincoln cited the imperative of keeping the Border States, who "loved slavery," in the Union. He then surprised Phillips by confiding that "he hated it and *meant it should die.*" The abolitionist left the White House feeling "rather *encouraged*," in fact now willing to trust the president's judgment. The next day, his lecture included a moving endorsement of Lincoln's recent antislavery initiatives. He told the audience that he was "not acquainted with rail splitting, but understood that a small thin wedge was first applied." He then compared the compensated emancipation proposal embodied in the Border State Plan to a wedge—"a small wedge, but still a wedge." Lincoln's plan had created an opening in the bulwark of slavery that would continue to widen until abolitionists would eventually "drive right through." Phillips exhorted northerners to support and encourage Lincoln to proceed even more aggressively.[24]

"The President goes on the thin ice as far as he dares; let us tell him the ice is thick, and go on." Agreeing with Greeley's assessment of the cause of the war and its ultimate solution, he concluded, "Slavery began the war, and the Government had the right out of rebellion to smite slavery to the dust." Conservatives, including Border State congressmen, denounced the lectures. Joseph Henry signaled his own disapproval by shutting the windows in the lecture hall and allowing the audience to "roast." Learning that the WLA intended to invite African American abolitionist Frederick Douglass to deliver the last lecture, he decreed that he "would not permit the lecture of a coloured man to be given in the room of my Institution." When the WLA agreed to substitute radical abolitionist William Lloyd Garrison in his place, Henry refused. While not canceling the lecture series, Henry restricted the topics to "courses on science and other subjects, which might be of service to those who desired actual instruction rather than mere amusement."[25]

The gravest threat to passage of the Compensated Emancipation Act was the opposition of Washington's city government itself. In February 1862, the Board of Police Commissioners asked the city councils to rescind the portion of the Black Code that imposed a curfew on African Americans. The curfew was one of the principal methods for restricting their freedom and subjecting them to arrest. The request provoked a heated debate over emancipation and legal equality that ended in a 6–4 negative vote and prompted city council members to pass a resolution denouncing the compensated emancipation plan. The aldermen declared that emancipation contradicted majority sentiment in the District, which opposed not simply "the unqualified abolition of slavery" but the influx of fugitives and free African Americans that seemed sure to follow. Their resolutions warned against "converting this city, located as it is between two Slaveholding States, into an asylum for free negroes, a population undesirable in every American community, and which it has been deemed necessary to exclude altogether from some even of the Nonslaveholding States." Every member of the city councils who voted against emancipation, however, went down to defeat in the next election, prompting the *National Republican* to crow triumphantly, "The days of pro-slavery domination in Washington are gone, never to return."[26]

The District of Columbia Compensated Emancipation Act won decisive passage on April 12, 1862, in a vote of 29–14 in the Senate and 92–38 in the House. Lincoln signed the bill into law four days later. "I have never doubted the constitutional authority of Congress to abolish slavery in this District, and I have ever desired to see the national capital freed from the institution in some satisfactory way," he told Congress. "Hence there has never been, in my mind, any question upon the subject except the one of expediency arising in view of all the circumstances." He specifically commended inclusion of compensation and colonization, which were key components of his Border State Plan. "I trust I am not dreaming," Frederick Douglass told Senator Charles Sumner, "but the events taking place seem like a dream." Under the Compensated Emancipation Act, all slaves in the District of Columbia were free immediately. Slaveowners had ninety days to submit a petition, which consisted of a preprinted form, requesting compensation for their slaves. The petitions, which were written by the slaveowners, identified each slave, provided a personal description, including the slave's "age, size, complexion, health and qualifications," and presented an estimated value of the slave for purposes of compensation. Many of the slaveowners provided additional information, including the slaves' family relationships, personal histories, and occupational skills. The petitions also included proof of ownership, such as bills of sale, deeds of trust, and wills, that reveal details about how the institution of slavery functioned before the Civil War, the slaveowners' attitudes toward their slaves, and above all the personal constraints on their freedom that the slaves were forced to endure and rise above. All of the petitioners were required to take an oath of allegiance to the United States and to provide two witnesses to verify their loyalty to the Union.[27]

Under the act, the president nominated a three-member commission to review the petitions, assess the claims of ownership and loyalty, and set the level of compensation for each slave. Lincoln's nominations were designed to mute sectional and partisan opposition and inspire confidence in the emancipation process. To chair the commission, he chose North Carolinian Daniel R. Goodloe, a rare southern Republican, abolitionist, and advocate of compensated emancipation. To encourage bipartisan faith in the process, Lincoln extended an olive branch to former mayor James Berret by nominating him to the commission. In his letter to Lincoln declining the appointment, Berret portrayed his imprisonment and removal as "wholly undesserved" and solicited Lincoln's assurance that he considered him loyal. Lincoln told Berret that he had confidence in his loyalty but that the former mayor had "made a mistake" that had prompted and justified his arrest. In his place, Lincoln appointed Horatio King, a longtime Democrat from Maine who was James Buchanan's postmaster general. The third member was Samuel Vinton, a lawyer, eleven-term member of the House of Representatives, and former Whig from Ohio. The commission appointed Ward Hill Lamon, marshal of the District of Columbia, as its deputy, "to attend upon the commission, and to execute its processes." Lamon was, in effect, Lincoln's representative on the commission. As the commission began its work, the sixty-nine-year-old Vinton died of a stroke, and Lincoln appointed John M. Brodhead, a Washington physician and native of New Hampshire, to replace him.[28]

In an effort to free the greatest number of slaves while compensating the greatest number of slaveowners, the commissioners were liberal in their interpretation of the emancipation act. Many slaves left the District immediately on the day that the act was passed, so their owners could take an oath testifying to their inability to produce them and their "due diligence" in trying to locate them. The commissioners also compensated slaveowners whose slaves had fled no more than two years before the passage of the act and then stipulated that they could not use the Fugitive Slave Law to recapture them. In two instances, slaveowners from Maryland asked the commission to rescind the free papers of slaves that they had hired out in the District. The commissioners ruled in favor of the slaves. Another slaveowner worked a farm that straddled the boundary between the District and Maryland. A few days before the emancipation act took effect, he moved his slaves across the line into Maryland. The commission heard evidence indicating that the slaves frequently crossed the line back into the District, and they received their freedom. Few claimants were denied compensation on the grounds of disloyalty. The commission applied a rigid definition that required "an overt act of 'aid and comfort' to the rebellion," rather than mere evidence of sympathy with secession or even residence in the Confederacy. Thirteen petitions that were filed after the deadline, despite the best efforts of the claimants, were referred to Congress with a recommendation for approval. Overall, the commissioners applied the principle that when slaves were entitled to freedom, their owners should receive compensation.[29]

The congressional appropriation represented only about one-third of the market value of the slaves, so the average compensation was almost always far less than the slaveowners requested. Because the Compromise of 1850 had outlawed slave sales in the District of Columbia, the commissioners hired Bernard M. Campbell, a slave dealer from Baltimore, to appraise the slaves' value. The commissioners recognized that Washington's slaves had lost considerable market value since the start of the war. Campbell himself had not bought a single slave since May 1861. They therefore asked him to appraise the relative value of the slaves according to prewar values. During the three-month process, 966 slaveowners filed petitions and testified before the commission. They had to present their slaves for examination or, if the slaves were fugitives, produce witnesses who could testify to the ownership and personal characteristics of the slaves. The commissioners approved 94 percent of the petitions, providing compensation for 2,981 slaves. They considered 111 slaves too young, too aged, or too infirm to merit compensation, so their freedom was uncompensated. They rejected a relative handful of petitions because the ownership of the slaves was questionable, the slaveowners were considered disloyal, or the slaves had run away more than two years earlier and were therefore considered unrecoverable. All told, 3,100 slaves received their freedom under the Compensated Emancipation Act. Most of the former slaves left their owners immediately and found work in Washington, where the wartime demand for labor was ample, moved to the North to join long-established African American communities, went to work for the Union Army, or, later, served as soldiers and sailors. In 1866, the Freedmen's Bureau found only seventy-seven of the emancipated slaves still working for their former owners. By the end of the decade, 70 percent of them had left the District entirely.[30]

Among the 966 petitioners, four were themselves African American. Henry Hatton, a blacksmith in Prince George's County, Maryland, had managed to purchase three of his own children—Martha, Henry, and George—during the 1840s for $220. Before the war, they were living together as a free family in Maryland. By 1862, Hatton's children were young adults and working in Washington as a seamstress, blacksmith, and servant. Hatton's twenty-two-year-old son and namesake, Henry, a skilled blacksmith, who was already living the life of a free craftsman in Washington, was the most highly valued of the slaves freed under the Compensated Emancipation Act. Henry Hatton Sr., received $700, more than twice the average payment, for his son. The Hatton family received a total of $1,839 under the emancipation act. In 1870, like most of the former slaves, Henry Hatton Jr. was no longer living in Washington, but his younger brother, George, was working in the office of the *Congressional Globe*. Forty-five-year-old Betsy Roberson had purchased her ten-year-old son John in 1847 for $150. Now twenty-six—his mother called him "a polite well behaved man"—he supported the family in Washington. The Robersons received $613, more than twice the average payment, for his freedom. In this fashion, African Americans who purchased family members, but did not free them, received a substantial boon from the emancipation act, representing partial payment for the years that they had spent in slavery.[31]

The white petitioners who received the greatest compensation under the act owned slaves with profitable skills. Beyond Henry Hatton, the most highly valued were a group of thirty men who were young and unusually skilled. They included cooks, dining room servants, coachmen, gardeners, blacksmiths, brickburners, and farmhands. Exclusively male, they were twenty-four years old on average, and many of them had proved their value through hiring out for wages. At the other extreme, the commissioners judged fifty slaves, three-fifths of them female, of "no value." Adult women were more likely to assume that status through age and were sixty-two years old on average. The adult men were only forty-nine years old on average but often suffered disabilities, including paralysis, lameness, and deformities that reflected the physical hazards involved in their labor. The children averaged seven years of age.[32]

The most uniquely skilled of the capital's slaves was Philip Reid, who worked for the government completing the new iron dome on the U.S. Capitol. When Lincoln served in Congress, the Capitol was crowned by a low, wooden, copper-sheathed dome—reviled as a "mustard pot"—that had begun rotting and leaking rain into the ornate Rotunda below. In 1853, Secretary of War Jefferson Davis appointed Captain Montgomery Meigs, a superb engineer, to complete the Capitol building, adding expansive marble wings for the two houses and raising the lofty dome—one hundred feet taller than the old one—that would loom over Washington for the next century and a half. Meigs and Davis, who were friends, worked well together. Meigs addressed the fundamental challenge—how to raise a 300-foot-high dome over the floor of the Rotunda—by erecting a wooden tower in the center from which a winch lifted the iron arches piece by piece to be bolted into place. The only conflict arose over the design of the bronze statue that would cap the dome. Meigs proposed a 19½-foot statue designed by Thomas Crawford, *Freedom Triumphant in War and Peace*, which depicted Lady Liberty wearing the classical Roman "liberty cap" that designated a freed slave. Appalled by the design, Davis dismissed the idea of an emancipated slave standing atop the capitol of what he considered a slaveowning republic, telling Meigs that the liberty cap "is the sign of a freedman and that we were always free, not freedmen, not slaves just released." Believing that the liberty cap was "inappropriate to a people who were born free and would not be enslaved," the secretary of war substituted a Roman military helmet in its place.[33]

As the Civil War approached, even the casting of the *Statue of Freedom* became a sectional issue. Northerners wanted it cast in a Massachusetts foundry, but southerners championed Clark Mills, a South Carolina sculptor whose most famous works were the equestrian statue of Andrew Jackson that sat across from the White House in Lafayette Square and the bronze of George Washington that graced Washington Circle. At the insistence of South Carolina's congressional delegation, the assignment went to the talented Mills. (Meigs later commissioned Mills's son Theophilus Fisk Mills to sculpt the bronze effigy that covered the tomb of his own son at Arlington Cemetery.) With the outbreak of war, a reporter encountered "a queer superstition that the dome is never to be finished, and that the coming crash of the Republic will leave the Capitol in the hands of those who will tear it down." Despite objections to the expense, as well as Meigs's personal opposition, Lincoln insisted that the work continue. He told General John Eaton that "the finishing of the Capitol would be a symbol to the nation of the preservation of the Union. If people see the Capitol going on, it is a sign we intend the Union shall go on." At his urging, Congress provided additional funding. (For his part, the defiantly patriotic Meigs wanted to cast the statue from captured Confederate cannons, but to no avail.) Mills depended on his slave, forty-two-year-old Philip Reid, whom he described as "not prepossessing in appearance, but smart in mind, a good workman in a foundry," to perform the labor. The casting required the disassembly of the plaster model into its five pieces, a task that Mills could not accomplish. After Mills gave up in frustration, Reid devised an ingenious method for gradually applying tension to the plaster to separate the five pieces just enough to allow disassembly. Mills and Reid completed the casting on November 19, 1863, the day that Lincoln delivered the Gettysburg Address. When a crane swung *Freedom* into place at the apex of the dome on December 2, a former slave shouted, "Three cheers for the Goddess of Liberty!" The immense crowd watching from below complied with enthusiasm. In an unusual recognition of his expertise, the government paid Reid for his work, in addition to the commission that went to Mills. In his request for compensation for Reid under the emancipation act, Mills stated that he had bought him in South Carolina for $1,200 "because of his evident talent for the foundry business." Asking $1,500 for Reid, Mills received $350. In freedom, Reid was able to set up a shop of his own in Washington.34

Two of the *Pearl* fugitives of 1848 received their freedom under the emancipation act. The owner of Eleanora Bell, one of Daniel and Mary Bell's daughters, who was now twenty-five, described her as young and healthy, "a good cook, washer, and ironer and generally a good worker." The emancipation commissioners awarded $394 to her owner. Eleanora's younger sister Caroline, now sixteen, belonged to a Maryland slaveowner who considered her "valuable, strong, faithful, honest, obedient and intelligent." He received $481 in compensation. One of the most poignant instances of emancipation was the freedom granted to Abraham Lincoln Hawkins, the president's namesake, born two months before his inauguration. Charles Homiller, a master butcher who kept a shop in Center Market, had bought his mother, Mary Ann Hawkins, as a child two decades earlier and considered her a "good, thorough house servant." Homiller called her now eighteen-month-old son "healthy & sound," and after examining him the commissioners allotted $43 to set him free.[35]

More than 150 slaveowners did not request compensation for their slaves, typically because they were openly disloyal to the Union, they lived in Maryland while their slaves lived in the District of Columbia, or their slaves were fugitives living in Washington. At Lincoln's urging, on July 12, 1862, Congress approved a "supplemental act" that allowed all of those slaves to file petitions for their own freedom. In addition to filling out a form, the slaves provided evidence to support their claims, usually written and oral testimony from witnesses who could verify their ownership, residence in the District, and other personal circumstances. The supplemental petitions are particularly valuable for providing insights into the experience of slavery and freedom as recorded by the slaves themselves rather than their white owners. One of the legacies of the supplemental act of July 1862 was the granting of freedom for slaves without any provision for or expectation of compensation for their owners, a principle that infused the long-overdue blanket emancipation of slaves embodied in the Emancipation Proclamation that Lincoln issued eight months later, and ultimately the Thirteenth Amendment, ratified two and a half years later. The supplemental act was also extraordinary in representing the first instance in which the federal government allowed African Americans to testify as both petitioners and witnesses in a formal judicial proceeding. The act therefore set a precedent that soon resulted in the admission of African Americans to federal courts as plaintiffs, witnesses testifying against whites, and jury members, promising not only freedom but eventually legal equality. During the commission's proceedings, the testimony of whites, free African Americans, and slaves was afforded equal weight. When the slaves established their right to emancipation, they received freedom certificates or "free papers" from the federal government, which cost them fifty cents. The commission evaluated 166 supplemental petitions and approved 86 percent of them.[36]

The primary avenue to freedom for slaves who filed their own petitions was evidence that they had lived in the District of Columbia on April 16, the day that the Compensated Emancipation Act became law, with their owners' knowledge and consent. Largely illiterate, the slaves were represented by white lawyers, notably George E. H. Day, who specialized in challenging the Fugitive Slave Law by defending runaways. Most of the slaves originated in Maryland and Virginia and claimed that they had lived in the capital for at least a year but sometimes as long as a quarter century. Jane Butler, for example, claimed residence "from her early childhood" and Fatima Milton "for a long time." Men often stipulated that they had been continuously employed in the District. In every instance, the supporting testimony, provided by both whites and blacks and sometimes slaves, was vital. George Robertson, for example, received the support of a white police officer, who testified that Robertson had worked in a livery stable and driven a cart in his neighborhood for the previous fifteen years. The witness claimed that he had "never missed him" in Washington and that he was present on April 16. Several petitioners claimed a temporary absence on the day that Lincoln signed the act but received their freedom anyway. Fifty-five-year-old Alice Addison, for example, left Washington with her two daughters and three grandchildren three days before passage of the bill "because they feared they would be colonized in Africa." After spending five months with her father, a slave in Maryland, the cautious Addison decided to bring her family back to Washington to receive their freedom under the supplemental act.[37]

A substantial minority of owners contested their slaves' claims, and the board denied 22 of the 166 petitions. Matilda Blaney's owner had hired her out in Washington for nine years before moving to Maryland and leaving her behind, according to two witnesses, one of them African American. Her owner, however, claimed that Blaney was a fugitive and that she had made an effort to locate her, without success, before passage of the emancipation act. The commissioners accepted the owner's claim and denied Blaney's petition. Caroline Noland, the Maryland slaveowner who had challenged "Butler's Fugitive Slave Law" by besieging the army camps in pursuit of her runaways, managed to reclaim Elizabeth Johnson. Two African

American witnesses testified that Johnson was a longtime resident of Washington. William Brown attested that "I have known Eliza for last 6 years. Near neighbor of mine. Was here on 16 April. Was not out of this city." Johnson's niece, Maria Stevenson, herself one of Noland's slaves, told the commissioners that "I have been living in District 16 years & Eliza came here before I did." In the absence of any testimony that Noland had consented to Johnson's residence in the capital the commissioners denied her petition. Stevenson, however, established her own right to freedom, with the help of her aunt's testimony.[38]

The board granted freedom to the five-member Beckett family after testimony indicated that they had lived in the capital for more than three years. After their owner labeled them fugitives, the commissioners considered the Becketts' petition. In a split 2–1 decision, they voted to sustain the family's freedom on the grounds that "their alleged legal owner has made no legal effort to reclaim them." In deference to the owner's challenge, however, they recommended compensation for the loss of her slaves. At the opposite extreme, thirty-three-year-old Washington Childs received support from his Virginia owner, presenting a solicitous letter that wished him "good health." Childs had lived in Washington for five years with permission to hire himself out as a hack driver and send his wages to his owner as payment for his freedom. Because Childs still owed $60, the owner asked him to send a supply of "good sugar & sacks of coffee and 2 bolts of cotton & pound of best tea that is if you can." He ended his forlorn attempt to wring some last-minute value out of Childs with the plea that "I know you can't think hard of this if you knew my circumstance & you will be at liberty for life. Your friend, Thos. A. Withers." Notwithstanding the plaintive request, the commissioners awarded Childs his freedom without compensating Withers.[39]

Slaves rarely cited the disloyalty of their owners, which was difficult to document. Before approving a petition on those grounds, the commissioners required evidence of an "overt act of aid and comfort" to the Confederacy. Leah Upshur claimed freedom because her owner had left Washington in August 1862 and "at last account was in Richmond," but without convincing evidence of disloyalty, the board denied her petition. Eliza Ann Blair had arrived in Washington two months after passage of the emancipation act but claimed that her Virginia owner was a "Rebel." The board denied her petition for lack of evidence of overt disloyalty. Philip Meredith, however, successfully petitioned for his own emancipation as one of Robert E. Lee's slaves. The thirty-year-old Meredith was already living as a free man in Washington with Lee's consent. Working as a waiter, he had built a family that included his wife, Lidia, and eight children, all of whom were born in the capital. Represented by antislavery lawyer George E. H. Day, he claimed that he had lived in Washington for twenty-five years with Lee's knowledge and indeed blessing. Testifying on his behalf was Lee's former legal agent, James Eveleth, a white clerk in the city who attested that he knew Meredith "perfectly well and have for 30 years as servant of Robert E Lee formerly of U.S. Army now in Rebel service." Not only was Meredith's owner openly disloyal, but he sanctioned his residence in the capital. "He has been here for years with masters knowledge—When Gen Lee went south he left servant in District," according to Eveleth, who claimed "frequent conversations with Gen Lee in which Gen Lee expressed regret that he owned servant & wished he was free." Accepting Eveleth's testimony, the commissioners granted Meredith a freedom certificate.[40]

All told, the slaves emancipated in the nation's capital represented about one-tenth of 1 percent of all of the slaves held in bondage in the American South during the Civil War. Yet opponents and supporters of slavery alike viewed the Compensated Emancipation Act as the beginning of the end of the institution, an experiment in freedom that would undermine slavery everywhere and point the way to a broader emancipation. Lincoln had already tried—and failed—to end slavery in the District of Columbia. He personally considered Delaware, which contained even fewer slaves, a more logical place to begin the emancipation process. Instead, Congress targeted Washington, where its power to end slavery was undisputed. "This is the best place to try the experiment of emancipation," Republican John Sherman of Ohio told the Senate. "I have always thought, since I could reason on this subject, that the law of God proclaimed emancipation as the ultimate end of this question. Here we have the power to try the experiment. Let us try it."[41]

Beyond the long-overdue impact of their emancipation on their own lives and those of their family members, the greatest legacy of this "first freedom" was to set an example of how the government could provide for the blanket emancipation of an entire group of slaves through an "act of justice," as Lincoln put it in the Emancipation Proclamation that followed eight months later. Senator Charles Sumner called the District of Columbia "an example for all the land" that could become the vanguard of freedom, equality, and justice as the nation fought the Civil War and rededicated itself to those founding principles. Five weeks after emancipating the capital's slaves, Congress repealed the District of Columbia's Black Code, taking the next step forward toward equal rights.[42]

CHAPTER FIFTEEN

"We Must Use What Tools We Have"
Toward Total War

———◆◆◆———

Lincoln's law partner, William Herndon, declared that Lincoln's ambition "was a little engine that knew no rest." If so, the president found his equal in the commander of the Army of the Potomac, George McClellan. Hailed as the "Young Napoleon" upon his arrival in Washington, McClellan basked in accolades from Congress, the cabinet, the press, and his own men. General-in-Chief Scott commended his "intelligence, zeal, science and energy" and promised him a "principal part" in prosecuting the war. "I find myself in a new & strange position here," McClellan marveled, "President, Cabinet, Genl Scott & all deferring to me—by some strange operation of magic I seem to have become *the* power of the land." While assuring Scott, "All that I know of war I have learned from you," privately McClellan considered his superior "a perfect imbecile" and told his wife, "He understands nothing, appreciates nothing & is ever in my way."

In August 1861, McClellan provoked a conflict by warning that Washington was in immediate danger of attack and that its defenses were "entirely insufficient" to meet the threat. The "vital importance of rendering Washington at once perfectly secure and its *imminent danger*," in his opinion, demanded a defensive force of 100,000. (A War Department commission later recommended a permanent garrison of 34,000, allowing two soldiers for every three feet of the outer perimeter.) McClellan's estimate reflected his inherently defensive mentality and his penchant for overestimating the strength of the opposing forces, which combined to produce an almost paralytic inaction within the Army of the Potomac, as well as his aspirations to replace Scott. The same general who six months earlier had surprised the general-in-chief by proposing a premature attack on Richmond was now faulting him for an insufficient defense of the Union capital.[2]

Stunned, Scott declared that "I have not the slightest apprehension for the safety of the government here" and then resigned. After Lincoln intervened, McClellan apologized to Scott, who withdrew his resignation. But the two generals' disagreement over the defense of Washington was symptomatic of McClellan's natural arrogance and long-standing insubordination. McClellan continued his campaign against Scott, concluding that "I presume war is declared— so be it. I do not fear him." Scott complained that McClellan was an "ambitious junior" who exhibited "indifference" toward him, routinely went over his head by communicating directly with the president and cabinet, and neglected his orders to the point of disobedience. Above all, McClellan began publicly blaming Scott for his own inaction. He assured radicals in Congress and the cabinet that Scott's departure would facilitate the long-awaited offensive and advance toward Richmond. In October, the dispirited and outmaneuvered Scott surrendered at last, announcing that "I shall definitely retire from the Army." On November 1, 1861, Lincoln informed McClellan that he was now general-in-chief. McClellan assured him that "I can do it all."[3]

The next to go was the secretary of war. Cameron's approval of Butler's "contraband" policy angered McClellan, who had promised not to disturb slavery in Virginia. "Help me to dodge the nigger— we want nothing to do with him," the racially conservative Democrat urged political allies. "I am fighting to preserve the integrity of the Union." In his annual report to Congress, Cameron endorsed the wisdom of the contraband policy "as too plain to discuss." (He also recommended altering the boundaries of Virginia, Maryland, and Delaware, surrounding the District of Columbia within a shield of loyal territory to guarantee its safety during any future insurrection.) Despite his reputation as inept and corrupt, Cameron seemed genuinely committed to using the Confederacy's slaves as a "military resource." On January 14, 1862, Lincoln replaced Cameron with another Pennsylvanian, former attorney general Edwin Stanton. Lincoln had appointed Cameron only reluctantly and now suppressed his personal misgivings toward Stanton, who had treated him so shabbily during the Manny Reaper trial seven years earlier. "I have made up my mind," the pragmatic Lincoln concluded, "to sit down on all my pride, it may be a portion of my self aspect, and appoint him to the place." Stanton, who was Cameron's legal advisor, had already formed a personal alliance with fellow Democrat McClellan that frequently found the general "concealed" at his house "to dodge all enemies in shape of 'browsing' Presdt, etc."Harewood, the site of fifteen new pavilions, exemplified the placement of new hospitals in park-like settings on the outskirts of the city.[4]

Soon, however, Stanton too grew impatient with McClellan's inaction. On January 27, Lincoln issued General War Order No. 1, requiring McClellan to advance on Richmond by February 22. "One thing I can say, that the army will move," Lincoln insisted, "either under General McClellan or some other man and that very soon." Lincoln preferred an overland movement that would simultaneously defend Washington, but McClellan proposed an amphibious assault on the James River Peninsula that would leave the capital exposed. To ensure Washington's safety during the risky expedition on the Peninsula, Lincoln divided McClellan's command into four corps, three of which were led by Republican opponents of the Peninsula plan. He then appointed a reliable ally, Brigadier General James S. Wadsworth of New York, as commander of the newly created Military District of Washington.[5]

Wadsworth was a politically connected and militarily astute Republican from a prominent family in the Geneseo Valley. He had inherited so much land that he reputedly could drive in a straight line for sixty miles without ever leaving his property. Although a wealthy lawyer who studied at Harvard and Yale and owned a house on New York's Fifth Avenue, he always considered himself no more than a simple farmer. Originally a Democrat, he embraced abolitionism, helped to found New York's Free Soil Party during the late 1840s, and became a Republican during the 1850s. After the Baltimore Riot of April 1861, Wadsworth personally organized and funded a relief expedition to bring supplies to the beleaguered capital by ship from New York City. The governor of New York appointed him, at age fifty-three, to his first military command as major general of a division of New York volunteers. After seeing action as an aide to General McDowell at the Battle of Bull Run, Wadsworth assumed command of a brigade in the newly formed Army of the Potomac. He became one of Lincoln's most trusted political and military advisors, and later John Hay's daughter married his son. Lincoln reportedly appointed him the District's military governor through their mutual distrust of McClellan's abilities and intentions. He immediately skirmished with McClellan, who wanted to pull enough troops from the defenses of Washington to field an army of 100,000 on the Peninsula. Eyeing Stonewall Jackson's forces in the Shenandoah Valley, Lincoln was adamant that any advance leave the security of the capital intact. "No change of base of operations of the Army of the Potomac," he ordered, "shall be made without leaving in, and about Washington, such a force as, in the opinion of the General-in-chief, and the commanders of all the Army corps, shall leave said City entirely secure."[6]

Wadsworth was unable to obtain estimates of troop strength from McClellan and, like Scott before him, had to resort to the press for help. To secure an accurate count of the men under his own command, he published an order in the newspapers asking his subordinates to report to him. (He later established a system of weekly troop-strength reports.) Fretful over Washington's security while Scott was general-in-chief, McClellan was now so cavalier that he waited until he had embarked for the Peninsula before informing Lincoln that 77,000 men were protecting the capital. McClellan included troops stationed up to sixty miles away, as well as units still en route to Washington. Wadsworth counted only the 19,000 under his direct command. Relying on the advice of Stanton, Wadsworth, McDowell, and members of the Joint Committee on the Conduct of the War, Lincoln withheld McDowell's corps from the Peninsula Campaign, reducing the strength of McClellan's army from the 100,000 he had demanded to 85,000. McClellan concluded that a cabal in Washington—"probably Pope, McD, & Wadsworth"—was working to ensure his defeat. Further embarrassment ensued when Confederate forces abandoned Manassas Junction, leaving behind "Quaker guns," pine logs disguised as artillery, that had been holding the Army of the Potomac at bay for months. In March, before McClellan could advance, Lincoln relieved him as general-in-chief to allow him to focus on his field command. The Peninsula Campaign lasted five months, from March to July 1862, and encompassed fifteen major battles. Throughout the campaign, Lincoln left the position of general-in-chief vacant and personally oversaw military operations.[7]

At the outset of the Peninsula Campaign the army embarked on construction of five new pavilion hospitals, "one story high, arranged in the form of a hollow square, row within row." Washington's model pavilion hospital was Armory Square, located along the National Mall on the Island, a mile southeast of the White House (on the current site of the National Air and Space Museum). Completed in August 1862, Armory Square Hospital consisted of ten pavilion wards, each a "hospital by itself" complete with its own ward masters, nursing staff, attendants, and one surgeon in charge. The wards, each with fifty beds, were 25 feet wide and 183 feet long, spaced 25 feet apart, and connected by covered walkways to a large central building that held the surgeons' offices. The 8-foot-high windows had sashes at the top and bottom that could be adjusted to facilitate ventilation. Window locks ensured that only the surgeons could control the airflow. The plan would allot each patient 1,260 cubic feet of fresh air. Ridgepoles ran down the center of the ward, and the beds sat 4 feet apart between the windows, eliminating "dark nooks and corners." A 1-square-foot sliding door at the head of each bed provided ventilation for individual patients as prescribed. Every morning, the surgeon would make his rounds, accompanied by the ward master and a nurse. Each hospital patient wore a card, the Civil War equivalent of a dog tag, indicating his name, rank, and unit. Another card at the foot of each bed listed the diagnosis and treatment, and a color-coded card prescribed the soldier's diet. A "diet kitchen" with hot and cold running water, chaplain's office, knapsack room to hold the patients' possessions, stable, guardhouse, and inevitable "dead-house" rounded out the complex. Other new hospitals were true "tent" hospitals, consisting of up to an acre and a half of field tents, which post surgeons considered preferable to barracks. Harewood, the site of fifteen new pavilions, exemplified the placement of new hospitals in park-like settings on the outskirts of the city. The construction of the pavilion and tent hospitals allowed the closing of some of the older makeshift facilities, including the Union Hotel Hospital in Georgetown and the temporary wards in the Patent Office.[8]

The surgeon in charge of Armory Square was a native New Yorker aptly named Doctor Willard Bliss (in honor of Dr. Samuel Willard, a Massachusetts physician during the Revolutionary Era). Taking a personal interest in the new hospital's administration, Lincoln met weekly with Bliss, a ballistic surgeon renowned for his energy in administering the hospital and his affability in cheering the patients and staff. "He is kind to patients, approachable to subordinates, courteous to strangers and gentlemanly to all," a frequent visitor wrote. "Being a thorough disciplinarian, without austerity or capriciousness, he has just enough of the 'governing' quality about him to manage well without the useless 'red tape' which encumbers most officials." Despite its location beside the pestilent Washington Canal, which provided "dirty water" for the hospital, Armory Square boasted grass lawns, gravel walks, and a vegetable garden. At Lincoln's suggestion, Bliss planted flowers provided by the Department of Agriculture in beds between the wards. One of Bliss's innovations was a railway, with "full diet" and "special diet" cars, which carried meals from the kitchen to all of the wards. The heated cars kept the food warm and did the work of sixty attendants.[9]

A printing office produced the *Armory Square Hospital Gazette*, a weekly newspaper that published news and original literary pieces. Patients and staff produced the *Gazette* on a press provided by Dr. Bliss. Edited by one of the nurses, the paper recorded the arrival and departure of patients, mourned their deaths, profiled hospital staff, and provided advice, both practical and spiritual. Articles examined the derivation of "bayonets" from the name of the French town, Bayonne, where they were first produced, celebrated donations to patients and staff, trumpeted the success of physician Dr.

Leon Alcan in treating wounded and disabled soldiers with electricity, and extolled the value of achieving a "good death" when medical treatment failed. "Tell my mother that I was brave, that I never flinched a bit" were the last words that one pious soldier ever spoke. "His trust was in God, and he was not afraid to die." Poems, contributed by patients, mingled patriotic fervor with religious faith. The *Gazette*, of course, supported the war effort, rebuked "copperheads," and endorsed Lincoln during his reelection campaign. (Despite Bliss's professional dedication and open commitment to the Union, when he inadvertently transgressed army regulations, he endured arrest and a brief confinement in the Old Capitol Prison. One of his nurses called this a "little earthquake" that underscored the military's dominion over wartime medical care.) Bliss eventually gained fame, along with a dose of notoriety, for his unsuccessful treatment of President James A. Garfield's bullet wounds, at Robert Lincoln's request, in 1881.[10]

Fielding an amphibious force on the Peninsula 150 miles south of Washington posed new challenges for treating the sick and wounded. The secretary of the Sanitary Commission, Frederick Law Olmsted, spearheaded a campaign to procure and staff a fleet of seven hospital transport ships to treat soldiers while carrying them to Washington's hospitals. Originally employing freighters, Olmsted envisioned and soon secured floating hospitals that provided a homelike setting of care and comfort. Continuing the precedent that the commission set in the general hospitals, Olmsted employed female nurses, fifteen of them to begin with, to afford the kind of individualized, feminine attention that soldiers craved. To collect the wounded on the Peninsula, the government commandeered one of Robert E. Lee's estates, "The White House," on the southern bank of the Pamunkey River. Once the possession of the widowed Martha Custis while she was being courted by George Washington, the estate descended to her great-granddaughter, Mary Custis Lee and her husband, Robert E. Lee. After losing Arlington in May 1861, Mary Lee had moved to the White House, where she spent the first Christmas of the war, only to flee yet again in the spring as McClellan's massive army approached. Union soldiers, in fact, captured Mary Lee, released her, and then captured her again, before granting her safe passage to Richmond to rejoin her husband, at her request.[11]

White House Landing, near the Lee estate, where a railroad bridge crossed the Pamunkey, became a major supply depot for the Army of the Potomac. The government had long eyed the White House plantation as an "evacuation hospital" for its spacious grounds, pure water, and commodious rooms, but McClellan had reportedly promised Lee that the army would not seize it. According to the *National Republican*, "when Mr. Lincoln heard how our soldiers were without shelter, except such as afforded by negro huts and barns, and subjected to drink impure water, while the rooms of Col. Lee's house were empty, and guarded by United States soldiers, he said 'the order must come. If Gen. McClellan has made a promise to Col Lee which he cannot break, *I will now break it for him.*' " Although McClellan ordered his men not to damage the Lees' house, they burned it down and destroyed all the outbuildings and fences. The new military hospital that arose in its place accommodated five hundred patients.[12]

Fought on May 31 and June 1, the Battle of Seven Pines or Fair Oaks produced five thousand Union casualties. The army transported the wounded to the White House by train, where contraband laborers carried them to the landing and loaded them onto the hospital steamers. "There were eight hundred on board," one of the female nurses reported. "Passage-ways, state-rooms, floors from the dark and foetid hold to the hurricane deck, were all more than filled; some on mattresses, some on blankets, others on straw." The water journey down the Pamunkey and up Chesapeake Bay took three to five days, during which the men endured "suffering in almost every form" and death, of course, took its toll. Confined on board with hundreds of suffering and often dying men, one army nurse resolved to "put away all feeling. Do all you can, and be a machine—that's the way to act; the only way."[13]

Waiting in Washington and scanning the Potomac with telescopes, a team of Sanitary Commission volunteers manned the Sixth Street Wharves. When a hospital transport came into view, they sprang into action to prepare for its arrival. The "commission boats" were met by surgeons, attendants, and ambulances that ran night and day to carry the casualties to the general hospitals. In a single day, the *State of Maine*, the *J. P. Warren*, and the *Elm City* deposited a total of 1,180 men, some of whom died while they waited on the wharves. "It was a sad sight to witness the maimed soldiers as they lay stretched out on their sacks," wrote one observer, "some with wounds in the head and face, others losing an arm and leg, or a foot, and then to reflect that these poor fellows but a few hours before were in full health and vigor." The same transports could spill out one hundred injured army horses and mules upon arrival. The press reported that "the ceremony of removal took place with order and rapidity, in each case, witnessed by a large crowd of citizens, attracted to the spot by sympathy or curiosity." Meeting one of the boats as it delivered its wounded, the poet Walt Whitman observed, "All around—on the wharf, on the ground, out on side places—the men are lying on blankets, old quilts, &c., with bloody rags bound round heads, arms, and legs." Ambulances backed up one by one to carry the men to the hospitals. Laden with supplies, the hospital ships turned back to repeat the seemingly endless process of picking up and transporting hundreds more wounded.[14]

Despite the efforts of the army's Medical Department and the Sanitary Commission, the unprecedented flood of casualties taxed Washington's medical facilities. After the arrival of the wounded from Seven Pines, the summer heat fostered disease, primarily malaria, dysentery, and typhoid fever, which sent thousands more to the hospitals in Washington. To make room for the new patients, the government sent convalescent soldiers by train to Baltimore and Annapolis and later Philadelphia and New York City. Relieving the congestion in the city, the army established Hammond Hospital, named for the surgeon general, at the mouth of the Potomac River at Point Lookout, Maryland. Located eighty-five miles south of Washington, Point Lookout cut the water journey from the Peninsula in half and could accommodate four to five thousand sick and wounded men. When the commander of the Confederate Army of Northern Virginia, General Joseph Johnston, was wounded in the Battle of Seven Pines on June 1, Robert E. Lee assumed command and turned the tide of the campaign. At the end of June and the beginning of July, the hideous fighting of the Seven Days, which encompassed a series of eight engagements, produced more than 15,000 Union casualties. Despite all of the preparations for transport and treatment, Washington could not accommodate them all. Compounding the problem, the medical corps gathered up the Confederate wounded, who had been abandoned on the battlefield by their own army, and transported them to Washington. "Let them be well cared for," the popular reasoning ran, "that they may see that we can be magnanimous, and even generous to a fallen foe." To treat their own wounded, the Confederate Army sent "a dozen secesh surgeons and nurses" on the transports under a flag of truce but also under heavy Union guard.[15]

Overwhelmed, the District's military commander, General Wadsworth, turned to the city's churches for help and met a magnanimous response. Among the numerous churches that were offered as temporary hospitals, the government accepted four—Trinity, Ascension, Epiphany, and E Street Baptist—and laid wood flooring over the pews to protect them and accommodate the beds. The New York Avenue Church, the Presbyterian congregation in which the Lincolns worshipped, was one of the first selected for conversion, but the Baptists offered theirs in its place. (The Baptist church had collapsed during a storm, and the congregation worshipped at the New York Avenue Church while building a new one. They volunteered their new building to the government to spare their benefactors.) Other churches that escaped conversion offered their buildings to displaced congregations for use on Sunday afternoons. The House of Representatives followed suit and turned over its chamber in the Capitol for religious services on Sundays until the hospital crisis subsided. The only discord arose when Protestants condemned the Catholic Church for withholding its own buildings from hospital service, concluding that "the Roman Catholic edifices are too *holy* to be thus desecrated!"[16]

After the Army of the Potomac stalled a mere five miles from Richmond and then retreated to Harrison's Landing in July 1862, Lincoln abandoned the Peninsula Campaign. But worse was to come. He appointed Henry Halleck, a West Point graduate and respected military theorist, as general-in-chief. (When Halleck proved indecisive, Lincoln judged him little more than "a first-rate clerk" and continued to oversee military strategy himself.) He also created a new army of 50,000 men, the Army of Virginia, under the command of General John Pope, his in-law and former bodyguard. After ordering the new army to march overland toward Richmond, Lincoln expected McClellan to reinforce Pope. Instead, McClellan sent a telegram proposing "to leave Pope to get out of his scrape & at once use all our means to make the capital perfectly safe." Aghast, Lincoln considered McClellan "a little crazy" and concluded that he "wanted Pope defeated." After calling for reinforcements for his own army for months, the petulant McClellan now withheld troops from the Army of Virginia and sneered that "Pope will be thrashed." His prediction proved all too accurate. On August 30, Lee's army dealt Pope a stunning defeat at the Second Battle of Bull Run, which killed eight thousand Union soldiers and wounded an equal number, the worst casualties yet inflicted during the war. Early the next morning, Lincoln walked into John Hay's bedroom at the White House and announced that "we are whipped again, I am afraid."[17]

"The field of the last Bull Run battle presents a most sickening scene," according to one witness. "The fields are strewn with dismantled gun carriages, caissons, clothing, shot, shell, and the dried mummy-like remains of slaughtered horses, which appear on almost every hand. The limbs of the half-buried dead are seen protruding from the earth; arms and legs are frequently found upon the surface of the ground, with the muskets, and portions of the flesh still adhering to the bones, and in some instances bearing the marks of dogs and buzzards." A shortage of ambulances and the civilian drivers' lack of discipline left thousands of wounded soldiers to suffer unattended on the battlefield. (The ambulance drivers had gone on strike the year before when their pay was reduced.) Compounding the misery, the Confederates captured thirty-seven nurses and seized forty wagons loaded with medical supplies.[18]

On the day of the battle, Secretary of War Stanton issued a national call for doctors and nurses to relieve the shortage of medical personnel. His well-meaning gesture backfired, however, when a flood of unqualified volunteers inundated Washington, which John Hay called "a vast army of Volunteer Nurses" and then pronounced "probably utterly useless." The provost marshal watched helplessly as "an incessant stream of ambulances carrying commissary stores, medicines, liquors, doctors, nurses, and curious citizens" crossed the Long Bridge to the battlefield thirty miles distant. "When the ambulances had gone, the crowd seized carriages, cabs, omnibuses, dog-carts, horses, and many walked to the field." General Wadsworth, who was expected to supervise the volunteer nurses, ended up guarding the bridges leading into the city to keep them out. Compounding the problem, the railroads provided free, one-way transportation to Washington, leaving the volunteers stranded in the capital. Now the wounded arrived in Washington not by steamer but by railroad, with trainloads of up to six hundred arriving at a time. On arrival, the *National Republican* reported, "a large number who were not so very badly wounded were necessarily neglected so long that they began to straggle off, and were taken in by kind-hearted citizens and well cared for." The popular symbol of the resulting chaos was a hapless trainload of wounded soldiers who traveled for two days by rail, arrived in Washington on a Saturday evening, and found "neither ambulance or wagon, surgeon or attendant," in fact "not the slightest evidence of preparation for our arrival." They depended on "the kind people of the neighborhood" to move them to hospitals and private homes.[19]

THE 6,000 hospital beds available in Washington, Baltimore, and Philadelphia proved tragically insufficient to accommodate the flood of wounded. In a ruthless mathematics of suffering, 7,000 convalescents were sent north to make way for 10,000 wounded from battlefields in Virginia. The government had decommissioned the church hospitals a few weeks earlier but during the renewed medical crisis had to take them over again. This second wave of confiscations included two Catholic churches and a synagogue. When the rectors of St. Aloysius Church asked permission to construct a barracks instead of surrendering their church, the medical director agreed and gave them one week to build it. Hotels, schools, warehouses, fraternal lodges, the former Republican campaign headquarters, and govern-

ment buildings, including Washington's City Hall, the recently evacuated Patent Office, and the Smithsonian Castle, became makeshift
hospitals. In the Capitol, the Rotunda, the House and Senate chambers, and all the corridors were lined with hospital beds and cots.
Lincoln personally offered half of the White House for use as a hospital. In the wake of the Peninsula Campaign, a total of twenty-two
hospitals, including thirteen converted churches, sprang up virtually
overnight and operated until January 1863.[20]

On September 2, three days after the second defeat at Bull Run,
Lincoln reinstated McClellan to his command in the Eastern Theater. Labeling the troops "utterly demoralized," he was counting
on McClellan to "reorganize the army and bring it out of chaos" to
secure the capital. He informed the general "that there were 30,000
stragglers on the roads; that the army was entirely defeated and falling back to Washington in confusion." Defending the appointment in
a cabinet meeting, Lincoln "seemed wrung by the bitterest anguish—
said he felt ready to hang himself." Ever the pragmatist, however, he
concluded that "we must use what tools we have." McClellan crowed
that "my enemies are crushed, silent & disarmed," declaring that
"under the circumstances no one else *could* save the country." His
army absorbed Pope's forces into the newly reorganized Army of the
Potomac, retreated toward Washington, and occupied the southern
line of defenses to shield the capital from attack. As in the aftermath
of the First Battle of Bull Run, panic now ensued in the wake of
rumors that the Confederate Army was headed toward Washington.
To help defend the capital, Lincoln ordered all government employees in the city to be armed and organized into military companies
under General Wadsworth. "For the first time," the *New York Tribune*'s Washington correspondent wrote, "I believe it possible that
Washington may be taken." Instead, Lee consolidated his forces with
those of Stonewall Jackson from the Shenandoah Valley and crossed
the Potomac into Maryland. Pessimists raised the specter of a rebel
army "liberating" Maryland by fomenting secession and rebellion
and even threatening the capital from the rear. The more optimistic
surmised that the government was luring Lee across the Potomac to
attack his army with its back to the river. In either event, "It is not

enough that we beat these invaders," ran the consensus. "We must annihilate them. If they ever recross the Potomac, save as prisoners, we are disgraced and humiliated."[21]

Shadowing the rebel movement northward, McClellan purged his army's field hospitals, dropping off thousands of wounded at Washington's doorstep for transportation and treatment. The city's military hospitals discharged their patients—seven thousand of them—into a huge "convalescent camp" on the Virginia side two miles south of the Potomac, literally within view of the capital. Considered a temporary camp, the collection point, described as "a sort of pen, into which all who could limp, all deserters and stragglers, were driven promiscuously," festered in obscure isolation for the next nine months. Lacking even an official name, its inmates dubbed it "Camp Misery." Within a month, the squalid camp held the seven thousand convalescents surrounded by "an area of over three acres, encircling the camp as a broad belt, on which is deposited an almost perfect layer of human excrement." The camp's unfortunate location, at the foot of a slope, accumulated water after every rain, which began freezing with the onset of winter. In December, the lack of adequate clothing, blankets, and firewood produced several deaths from exposure. The army's medical director put out a call for help in housing the convalescents, asking everyone who could take them in to "please inform this office of their names, residence, and number of such convalescents as they can receive and provide for." The commander of the Washington garrison closed the camp and built a new one, dubbed "Camp Convalescent," with fifty barracks that accommodated five thousand recovering soldiers.[22]

With the retreat from the Peninsula, the Sanitary Commission's steamer transport campaign came to an end, and a new cohort of female "field nurses" appeared, epitomized by Clara Barton. The daughter of a former militia captain who had fought in the Indian wars in the Old Northwest, Barton grew up in Massachusetts imbibing a strong sense of patriotic duty that compelled her to spearhead new opportunities for women in government service. After attending New York's Clinton Liberal Institute, she opened her own public school in New Jersey but found herself replaced by a male schoolteacher in the school that she had founded. Drawn to government service in Washington, she became the first female clerk within the federal bureaucracy in 1854 under the patronage of the commissioner of the Patent Office, who admired her clerical skills, particularly her "rapid perfect round handwriting." As an outspoken Republican during the sectional crisis of the late 1850s, she lost her position when Buchanan took office in 1857, returned to Massachusetts, and mounted a letter-writing campaign to get her job back. With the aid of Massachusetts senators Henry Wilson and Charles Sumner, she finally succeeded after Lincoln's election but considered her low-level job, which was a demotion, a mere "crumb."[23]

Like so many other northern women, Barton's patriotic fervor took flame after the Baltimore Riot of April 1861, when Rhode Island regiments bivouacked in the three-story white marble Patent Office, where she worked. She took wounded soldiers from Massachusetts into her own home, provided supplies to the troops who had lost their equipage in Baltimore, and visited the Capitol, where she took delight in reading the *Worcester Spy* to the troops encamped in the Senate Chamber. Put off by the severe supervision of "Dragon Dix," Barton rejected the idea of hospital nursing, filled her own home with medical supplies, and contented herself with visiting the hospitals, where women were slowly finding acceptance as caregivers. As a Washington newspaper advised a year into the war, women should feel free to visit the sick and wounded without male escorts now that there were female nurses—"Ladies of the first respectability"—on hand.[24]

Barton quickly tired of the condescending view of women as mere adjuncts to medical service whose greatest contribution was bringing "soups, jellies, fruits, fresh and preserved berries, fresh butter and cream" to the soldiers, along with "all the worn shirts and drawers, night shirts, dressing gowns, hose, slippers, &c., which are lying useless in your houses." One of the poems that she wrote early in the war lampooned the official advice to women to "pick some lint, and tear up some sheets, and make us some jellies, and send on some sweets, and knit some soft socks, for Uncle Sam's shoes, and write us some letters, and tell us the news." She was determined to challenge the notion that "the place for the women was in their own homes, there to patiently wait until victory comes." Witnessing firsthand the chaotic flood of victims of the Peninsula Campaign into the Patent Office and hospitals, Barton observed somberly that "everything is sad, the very pain which is breathed out in the atmosphere of this city is enough to sadden any human heart. 5000 suffering men, and room preparing for 8000 more, poor fevered, cut up wretches, it agonizes me to think of it." Springing into action, she solicited enough contributions from friends in Massachusetts and New Jersey to fill three warehouses with medical provisions. When she offered to help the Quartermaster's Department distribute supplies at the front, the officer in charge told her, "That's no place for a lady," but changed his mind when he discovered the quantity of goods that she intended to donate. General Wadsworth approved her extraordinary request "to travel on any military R.R. or Govt. boat to such points as she may desire to visit" just in time for the Second Battle of Bull Run.[25]

Barton now challenged the army's year-long policy that "Women nurses will not reside in the camps nor accompany regiments on a march." She rode a train to the battlefield in a uniform of her own device, a dark skirt, a bonnet, and a white blouse with a red bow around her neck, suggesting the symbol of the American Red Cross that she would later found. Working in the field hospitals, she distributed supplies, dressed wounds, comforted the dying, foraged for food, and prepared it when necessary. Following the army during its movement northward toward Maryland, she gained a reputation for organization, dedication, and sacrifice that convinced the commissioner of the Patent Office to grant her a leave of absence from her job. A colleague agreed to take her place and donate half of his salary to support Barton and her war work. Overall, Barton spent six months laboring in the Virginia Theater, reporting inefficiencies, and gaining the confidence and support of field commanders, including General Ambrose Burnside. The shortage of medical personnel and efficient transport that Barton observed produced two major reforms.[26]

The army created a new system of field hospitals that assigned a permanent medical staff to each division, consisting of thirteen doctors—a chief surgeon and twelve assistants—and a team of male nurses. A new ambulance system provided three ambulances for each regiment under a lieutenant who commanded military drivers and stretcher-bearers. The goal was removing the wounded from the battlefield immediately and delivering them efficiently to nearby field hospitals. "Heretofore, worthless and disabled soldiers have been detailed for these purposes," the press reported with approval. "When relieved from military restraints, they have become intemperate, careless, and unmanageable, and have proved wholly unfit for the duties to which they have been assigned. Able, humane, and patriotic men, will now be enlisted, mustered into the United States service, instructed and drilled for hospital duty."[27]

Assuming more control of its own hospitals, the Medical Department dispensed with the help of the Sanitary Commission in appointing nurses, turning it into merely an "advisory organization, which will amount to nothing," as one critic forecast, "as its advice will never be asked or thankfully received." For the rest of the war, the USSC's national office remained largely investigative in character and frequently critical of the government's provision of medical care. Responding to reports that a "large number of women are constantly arriving from the North, who come here for the purpose of looking after their husbands or other relatives who may be sick in the various hospitals," the commission established a "hospital directory" to help them locate their family members. They announced that their office was open daily from 8:00 A.M. to 8:00 P.M., but "in urgent cases applicants ringing the door bell, will be received at any hour of the night."[28]

Washington also hosted twenty-five unofficial relief associations, sixteen of which were the "state associations" that sent agents to the capital to attend to the needs of their own soldiers. After Second Bull Run, they combined to create the Union General Relief Association to investigate conditions in the army, both in the field and in hospitals, lobby for reforms, and "secure the co-operation of all the States for the amelioration of the condition of our sick and wounded soldiers who are disabled in the service of our common country." At the outset, the organization was "very severe on certain surgeons, stewards, attendants, and nurses" and created a committee comprising one member from each state association to present a report to the surgeon general. The committee cited uncleanliness in some hospitals, "the details of which were most disgusting," the "miserable" quality of the hospital food provided by the commissary general, the necessity of transferring control of the ambulance corps from the quartermaster general to the surgeon general, the "offensive arrogance and self importance of some *small* surgeons," and the chronic shortage of medical supplies. The bitter experiences of the preceding summer prompted one member of the association to declare, "Our soldiers feel that they are treated like dogs, and as no interest is manifested in them, they lose their interest in the great issue which they are dying to achieve."[29]

To its credit, the Medical Department made a genuine effort to respond. The surgeon general promised "a thorough inspection of all hospitals with a view to correct all existing abuses," replaced the surgeon in charge at Carver Hospital on the grounds of lax sanitation, agreed to request control over the ambulance service, and began stockpiling an immense quantity of medical stores to avoid another shortage. Within six months, the Medical Purveyor's Office had acquired five two-story warehouses, each 200 feet long, lined from floor to ceiling with crates full of blankets, cotton wadding, bed linen, surgical tape, bed pans and chamber pots, water basins, stomach warmers, razors and strops, mustard pots, wooden buckets, tin funnels, feeding cups, and medicine spoons. Medical stores poured in and streamed out to the field hospitals in Virginia and the general hospitals in the city. In a single year, 23,533 cartons of medicine, 68,195 blankets, 20,110 iron beds and wooden cots, 891 bedside tables, 1,754 chairs, and 5,622 brooms passed through Washington's warehouses. The appointment of regimental surgeons and the establishment of more field hospitals, which the military commanders favored over general hospitals, contributed to the decentralization of the medical system away from Washington. The state associations campaigned for the dispersal of convalescent hospitals to northern cities in an effort to bring their wounded "boys" home sooner—and often permanently. The Medical Department also created "convalescent camps" to empty the hospitals on short notice in anticipation of major battles. Washingtonians learned to watch the movements of the convalescents for clues to impending military movements. "Quite a number of convalescent patients were removed yesterday to new quarters," one newspaper reported in October and concluded that "This is indicative of a battle proceeding, or soon to come off." The temporary "Camp Misery" soon became the more substantial Camp Convalescent, where recuperating soldiers waited to be declared fit to rejoin their units in Virginia. Under congressional oversight, new barracks, kitchens, and dining halls made the camp livable, while a church, library, and post office provided amenities. The men worked three hours a day, published a newspaper, the *Camp Convalescent Gazette*, and organized plays and temperance meetings. Within Washington itself, new hospital construction favored pavilions and tents in the parklike "suburbs" on the outskirts of the city. In September 1862, the medical director designated Seminary Hospital in Georgetown as an officers-only facility. Wounded officers—more than 1,800 in 1862 alone—had previously received treatment individually, often in hotels, which all retained staff surgeons. Two months later, the president, who had personally inquired into the condition of the soldiers during the hospital crisis, received a tribute when Lincoln Hospital, located just east of the Capitol, opened with accommodations for 1,500 of the sick and wounded.[30]

As casualties mounted during the Peninsula Campaign and a discouraged public grew critical of the Union's military strategy, Lincoln decided to call for more volunteers to replace the recent losses and boost the army's offensive capacity. In July 1862, as a face-saving device, he arranged to have the northern governors "request" him to issue a call for 300,000 three-year volunteers. When the result was disappointing, a consensus emerged that replenishing and strengthening the army would require conscription. On July 17, Lincoln signed the Militia Act, which mandated the enrollment of all male citizens of military age, eighteen to forty-five, to facilitate a draft. The act empowered the president to call state militiamen into federal service for nine months, meeting a quota that was based on the population of each state. A few weeks later, Secretary of War Stanton issued a requisition for another 300,000 men, this time nine-month militiamen apportioned to the states under the Militia Act's quota system. Any states failing to meet their quotas of new volunteers would be forced to undergo a draft to make up the shortfall. The War Department appointed provost marshals in all of the loyal states to enforce conscription and arrest draft evaders and deserters, who had no recourse to civil courts. Hoping to avert a draft, which would call their loyalty into question, the states mounted aggressive recruitment campaigns, offering enlistment bounties of up to $1,000 to volunteers. They also appropriated the state quotas to cities, towns, and counties, to engage them in the recruitment effort, boost voluntary enlistments in the name of local pride, and help maintain the community basis of army units. Cities and counties began offering bounties of their own to attract volunteers.[31]

Along with the states, the District of Columbia received a quota for new nine-month men. A "great war meeting" that boosted enlistments in the 1st and 2nd regiments helped the District fulfill its July quota, but recruiting for the August requisition lagged. "As yet no draft has been ordered in this District, but we have good reason to believe it will be made unless the enlistments come up promptly," the *National Republican* warned. "We rejoice at the evidences now being manifested that the District will not be subjected to conscription. The issue is with our people." Washington's city government appropriated $40,000 toward a bounty to encourage enlistments—initially a mere $25 per volunteer. A controversial feature of the draft allowed any recruit to provide a substitute to take his place in the army. "Substitute brokers" soon descended on Washington to pay men of military age to go to other states, including Maryland, to help them fill their quotas, for a fee that eventually ran as high as $1,000. "Those engaged in the substitute business are interfering seriously in the recruiting business in this city for our District regiments," the *Republican* complained, "and it should be stopped at once."[32]

Stanton's call for nine-month men included a national suspension of the writ of habeas corpus to allow the arrest and imprisonment of the expected wave of draft evaders and deserters. Over the next month, the War Department made at least 354 "arbitrary arrests" of northern civilians, the highest rate of the entire war. On September

24, 1862, Lincoln himself issued a proclamation suspending the writ of habeas corpus throughout the entire nation, targeting "all rebels and insurgents, their aiders and abettors" and "all persons discouraging volunteer enlistments, resisting militia drafts, or guilty of any disloyal practice." The city's exertions, combined with Lincoln's determination to raise troops at any cost, helped the national capital avert a draft, for the moment.[33]

CHAPTER SIXTEEN

"On the Soil Where They Were Born"
The Former Slaves

———◆◆◆———

G ENERAL JAMES Wadsworth, commander of the Military District of Washington, awoke early one morning in May 1862 expecting to find his breakfast. Instead, he summoned his aide and ordered him "to take about 30 cavalrymen, mounted, and ride to the city jail and release therefrom every escaping slave, also his black woman cook, who, he had just learned, had been arrested by the police as a contraband, and she was needed to get breakfast for him and his family." Alethia Lynch, like hundreds of other fugitive slaves in the capital, had a "military protection" signed by Wadsworth guaranteeing her immunity from recapture by civil authorities, including Washington's police and the District of Columbia's constables. Slaveowners in Maryland, which remained in the Union, insisted on their right to retrieve their slaves from the District, with the assistance of the local authorities, under the Fugitive Slave Law. As the number of fugitives swelled during the first year of the war, however, their owners grew more aggressive in trying to reclaim them, and the civil courts grew more compliant in coming to their aid. In May 1862, forty of them went en masse to the circuit court to obtain warrants for the arrest of their fugitives. The press reported that a "gang of negro-catchers" were seizing fugitives, depositing them in the county jail, and collecting a $50 fee when their owners reclaimed them. The result was an upsurge in what a growing number of Washingtonians labeled "kidnapping." Wadsworth ordered Ward Hill Lamon, the

marshal of the District, to notify him whenever a fugitive slave possessing a military protection arrived at the jail. Lamon ignored the
order, arguing that he was obligated to enforce the Fugitive Slave
Law until Congress repealed it. Supporting Lamon, Attorney General Bates issued an opinion declaring that, short of a declaration of
martial law in Washington, the military authorities were subordinate to the civil government. Wadsworth was equally determined
to enforce another federal law, the Confiscation Act of 1861. He
insisted on verifying the loyalty of slaveowners before surrendering
their slaves and knew that Alethia Lynch's owner was disloyal. The
fate of the fugitive slaves had at last provoked the long-awaited clash
between the military and civil authorities.[1]

Arriving at the jail with a squad of cavalry, Wadsworth's aide, Lieutenant John Kress, discovered "quite a crowd of contrabands," including Alethia Lynch. He presented a written order from Wadsworth
demanding their release. After the jailor and the assistant marshal
refused to surrender the fugitives, Kress arrested them and sent them
to the Central Guardhouse. When the lawyer representing Lynch's
owner arrived with a five-member "posse," Kress arrested all of them
as well. Lamon rushed to the White House to enlist Lincoln's support, but the president was unavailable to receive him. He sent word
to all of the police stations to send patrolmen to the jail, but when he
arrived he found it under military control, with a sergeant in charge
and a sentry "pacing back and forth before the door." He immediately
placed the sergeant and sentry under arrest. A standoff now ensued.
Wadsworth was holding Lamon's assistant marshal and jailor at the
Central Guardhouse, and Lamon was holding Wadsworth's sergeant
and sentry at the jail.[2]

The next morning, Wadsworth defused the confrontation by
releasing Lamon's men. Lamon immediately released the soldiers
but continued to assert civil authority over fugitive slaves. Despis-
ing Lamon's obstinate devotion to the Fugitive Slave Law, congressional radicals sided with Wadsworth. "I have consulted several of
the Senators in regard to the demand of Marshall Lamon and they
all say you should pay no regard to his commands," Senator Henry
Wilson assured Wadsworth. "If the president sends you the orders

you will have to obey it, but I advise you to pay no regard to W. H. Lamon." Wilson's letter was endorsed by radical senators Charles Sumner, Benjamin Wade, and David Wilmot. Emboldened, Wadsworth renewed his commitment to end "the abduction without process of Law, of col'd persons within this Dist. which had long been practiced to the disgrace of the Capital." The elimination of slavery in the District of Columbia increased the flow of fugitives into Washington. Just weeks after Congress enacted the Compensated Emancipation Act, the governor of Maryland protested that "large numbers of slaves owned in Maryland are daily making their way into the District of Columbia from neighboring counties." Attorney General Bates replied dryly that he was "not at all surprised to hear that slaves in the border States are using all available means to escape into free territory." He told the governor that he considered it "very probable" that the Fugitive Slave Law remained in effect in Washington. Nine days later, Maryland slaveowners sent a delegation to see Lincoln personally to protest the "non-enforcement" of the Fugitive Slave Law, the "hindrances" to recapturing fugitives that Wadsworth imposed, and his policy of accepting "the evidence of the slaves." Supporting the general, Lincoln expressed his "entire confidence in Gen. Wadsworth's ability and intention to do right" but promised to "take their representations into consideration, and see that no injustice was done."[3]

As slavecatchers grew more daring and devious, public support for the Fugitive Slave Law quickly eroded. Armed with legal writs from conservative judges, "professional kidnappers" broke into homes in the middle of the night, offered employment to fugitives and then drove them to the jail in handcuffs, and monitored the army camps for runaways. "Slaveowners and slave stealers are now quite numerous in the city," the *National Republican* warned, "and prowl around the contraband depots like so many ravenous hyenas." Seizing an entire family in their own home, a gang of slavecatchers scoffed at their military "passes" and warned them to "get ready to return to slavery, and to prepare themselves, when they returned home, for a dose of 'cat o' nine tails.' " Slaveowners often appeared at the jail to claim their slaves with lawyers or even a legal team in tow. The defenseless fugitives, who had evoked the sympathy of white Washingtonians, now gained their support. "The distinction in morals between keeping a human being in bondage and kidnapping, is shadowy," the *National Republican* reasoned. "Slavery is nothing but a continuous kidnapping." Before the Civil War, abolitionists had employed habeas corpus petitions to impede enforcement of the Fugitive Slave Law. Now they revived that tactic to protect fugitive slaves in the capital.[4]

A Freedom Committee organized by philanthropic Washington residents engaged John Dean, a lawyer from Brooklyn, New York, to challenge the validity of the law in the District of Columbia. Dean's employers filed writs of habeas corpus against Marshal Lamon to produce a series of test cases designed to undermine the law. The Fugitive Slave Law commissioners, appointed by the District's conservative circuit court, refused to consider the loyalty of slaveowners when deciding whether to return their slaves, "except where the claimant resides in a State in open rebellion against the Government." Dean argued that justice, common sense, and national self-preservation all demanded consideration of the owners' loyalty. "A disloyal man, in a loyal State," he argued, "is a more dangerous enemy of the Government than one in a rebellious State." The commissioners also rejected the testimony of the jailed fugitives while allowing slaveowners to produce any number of white witnesses of dubious reliability, claiming "the right to use their discretion in the manner of examination." As for Dean's argument that the Fugitive Slave Law applied only to states and not the national capital, the commissioners disagreed. His final argument, that fugitives employed by the government should be exempt from the Fugitive Slave Law, was disallowed. During the habeas corpus hearings, Dean won only a single concession, the right to conduct a "reasonable" cross-examination, but only at the pleasure of the court.[5]

The most infamous of the habeas corpus cases involved ten fugitives employed by officers of the 76th New York Regiment. In May 1862, two policemen tried to enter the regiment's camp but were turned away. The regiment was deployed the next day and marched through the city with the fugitives, wearing army uniforms, within their ranks. When the policemen tried to apprehend the slaves, the regiment resisted, a large crowd gathered, a scuffle broke out, and several soldiers threatened to fire their weapons. The police seized two of the slaves and hauled them into the circuit court. Despite Dean's defense, they were sent back to Maryland. Complying with the commissioners' ruling, the provost marshal ordered the regiment to deliver up every fugitive that the court demanded. The soldiers refused, swearing that they "would see him in h-ll before they would deliver the negroes to him or any other person." While achieving no legal victories, the habeas corpus cases served an important purpose by subjecting the injustices inherent in the Fugitive Slave Law to public scrutiny. "The claimant may be in rebellion against the Government, still the law gives him his slave," the *National Republican* observed bitterly. Slave seizures began attracting angry crowds of both blacks and whites, producing "constant brawls and fighting in our streets." Concluding that "the Fugitive Slave Law cannot be enforced here without excitements and collisions, which will be lamentable, and may even be dangerous to the public peace," the newspaper called for the repeal of the law or at least its suspension for the duration of the war.[6]

Writing from the Virginia battleground, where she worked with contrabands daily, Clara Barton addressed an open letter to Lincoln beseeching him to reconsider his stance toward fugitive slaves from the Border States. "Slavery is on trial," she insisted, "the verdict is left to slave holders in the border States." Although repeal of the Fugitive Slave Law would wait another two years, in July 1862 Congress took another step to undermine slavery within the Confederacy. The Second Confiscation Act granted freedom to fugitives from rebellious states, including Virginia, without requiring them to prove that they had been employed in the Confederate war effort. Once they entered Union lines, they could gain their freedom. The act addressed one of the major deficiencies in the Fugitive Slave Law by requiring anyone attempting to reclaim a slave to take an oath of loyalty to the Union. (Lincoln the lawyer signed the Second Confiscation Act but remained attentive to the rights of the seceded states. "It is startling to say that congress can free a slave within a state," he insisted, "and yet if it were said the ownership of the slave had first been transferred to the nation, and that congress had then liberated, him, the difficulty would at once vanish.") Congress included a clause endorsing Lincoln's policy of employing African Americans for military service "for the purpose of constructing entrenchments or performing camp service," while extending it to include "any other labor or any military or naval service for which they may be found competent." On the same day, Congress passed the Militia Act, which authorized Lincoln to recruit African Americans into the army and navy and to free them and their families—their mothers, wives, and children—if their owners were disloyal.[7]

The *National Republican* exulted that the Second Confiscation Act "settles all difficulties about the treatment of contrabands, as all slaves who now come within the lines of our army, are not to be thrust back at the point of the bayonet, but are to be received, and are to be made FREE FOREVER!" Privately, Lincoln told allies that he approved of the enlistment of African Americans into the army, including slaves in the loyal states. After signing the Militia Act, he wrote a memo to himself declaring, "To recruiting free negroes, no objection. To recruiting slaves of disloyal owners, no objection. To recruiting slaves of loyal owners, *with their consent*, no objection." Publicly, he readily agreed to "employ, as laborers, as many persons of African de[s]cent, as can be used to advantage" but, still worrying about the loyalty of the Border States, not yet as soldiers. When a delegation from Indiana met with him to request permission to raise two African American regiments, Lincoln told them that he "would employ all colored men offered as laborers, but would not promise to make soldiers of them." He explained that arming African Americans "would turn 50,000 bayonets from the loyal Border States against us that were for us." Frederick Douglass declared bitterly, "The government consents only that Negroes shall smell powder in the character of cooks and body-servants in the army."[8]

As increasing numbers of contrabands from Virginia and fugitives from Maryland continued to flow into Washington, one observer reasoned that "a reservoir without outlets and into which streams constantly run, must finally become full and overflow." Citing the "alarming" growth of Washington's refugee population, he lamented,

"As yet, however, we have no word from anybody as to a possible remedy." As commander of the Military District of Washington, General James Wadsworth, an abolitionist, was committed to establishing a more enlightened and efficient system for accommodating the contrabands. Upon arriving in Washington, contrabands came under the authority of Wadsworth's newly appointed provost marshal general, Colonel William Doster. A twenty-five-year-old Pennsylvanian, Doster had first laid eyes on Lincoln as a law student, when the president-elect stopped in Philadelphia during his inaugural journey. "I stood in the crowd at the corner of Ninth and Chestnut streets to see him drive from the Reading Station to the Continental," Doster recalled. "He came, seated in an open carriage, a person of very large, lean frame, dark complexion, jet black hair, full beard, no mustache, wearing a high silk hat and brown overcoat." Under Wadsworth's command, contrabands arriving in Washington received a military escort and immediately underwent an interview, conducted by detectives, to determine their owners' loyalty and residence and extract any military intelligence that they possessed. "Now, when these slaves are claimed by their masters under the Fugitive Slave Law," the press explained, "General Wadsworth maintains that it is his duty to see that the claimant is a loyal citizen, and not a rebel." If their owners were disloyal and lived in the Confederacy, the slaves became official contrabands and received a certificate signed by Wadsworth stating that "The bearer, A—— B——, colored, is under the protection of the military authorities of the District," which became known as a "military protection."[9]

After the resolution of the jail controversy, the government lodged contrabands, numbering between fifty and one hundred, in the Old Capitol Prison, along with Confederate prisoners, smugglers, counterfeiters, and accused spies. Worried about the outbreak of smallpox, an army doctor recommended removing the contrabands, not for their sake but to segregate them from "respectable white people." Wadsworth immediately moved them to Duff Green's Row, which included Lincoln's former boardinghouse, across the street from the Capitol and just south of the prison. ("Abolition House" had earned its name at last.) The contrabands continued to receive food and fuel from William Wood, the superintendent of the Old Capitol. To meet their remaining needs, Wadsworth and Doster provided stolen goods, including blankets and uniforms, confiscated from blockade runners and the ubiquitous thieves who pilfered and resold government goods in the capital. Under Wadsworth's interpretation of "government protection," no slaveowners were permitted to prowl through the new "contraband depot" looking for fugitives, unlike the county jail.[10]

Whether through experience or pessimism, Doster viewed the contrabands who reached Washington as unwelcome outsiders. "The free colored negroes at Washington hated them as rivals," he wrote. "The slaves despised them for being runaways." In his diary, he recorded seeing "groups of contrabands in butternut sitting in a melancholy mood along the curbstone, as if they thought themselves an inferior order of negro." A wartime visitor to the capital confirmed Doster's impression that "Some of the tinctured natives of Washington affect great disgust towards their more pure blooded, but less aristocratic contraband brethren and sisters." Finding employment for the fugitives was the government's highest priority. The quartermaster's department "drafted" squads of twenty apiece as military laborers on the defenses, where they received wages of $15 to $25 a month and earned a reputation as "willing and anxious to be employed." The army hospitals paid them $4 to $10 a month as attendants performing the most menial medical duties. Washington residents who wanted to hire one or more of them individually had to prove their loyalty, demonstrate "good intentions," and promise to treat them fairly. Although Doster himself insisted that "as they were farm hands, nobody cared to have them," the press reported that "Large numbers of the contrabands in this city are finding good places," generally women and girls employed as domestic servants.[11]

Presaging one of the functions of the future Freedmen's Bureau, Wadsworth established an employment policy under which "Any person needing help is permitted to make a bargain with such 'contraband' as he may select, and the Government agent looks it over simply to see that the fugitive is not cheated." In this fashion, contrabands began replacing the slaves who were newly freed under the Compensated Emancipation Act. Amid the wartime labor shortage, a northern market for contrabands quickly emerged. "As fast as we could get the contrabands employment we shipped them North and made room for others," Doster explained. "If it were not for the fact that large numbers of them continue to flock in from the rebellious portions of Virginia," according to the *National Republican*, "there would not be very many remaining at Duff Green's row now." The idea was to keep the number of contrabands in Duff Green's Row at fifty, but every day during its four-month existence an average of twenty fugitives entered while only fourteen left. Within two months, 360 fugitives were occupying the newly subdivided rooms.[12]

REMINISCENT OF the partnership between the army and the Sanitary Commission to reform medical care in the city, the government worked with private charitable organizations to develop a system for housing, feeding, clothing, employing, and ultimately educating the newly freed slaves. The freedmen's relief associations were a natural outgrowth of the prewar antislavery societies, the wartime soldiers' relief efforts, and both national and local religious societies. Most of the private relief agencies had roots in the northeastern cities that had long-standing traditions of antislavery advocacy and philanthropic reform. In May 1862, the Reverend Danforth Bliss Nichols, a Methodist minister and agent of the American Missionary Association, arrived in Washington to provide any help that he could. Founded in 1846, the AMA was a church-based antislavery society supported by New York philanthropist Lewis Tappan, an abolitionist who had helped fund Washington's underground railroad and was rumored to be involved in the escape on the *Pearl*. Throughout the war, the AMA sent agents, generally ministers and teachers, to Union-occupied regions of the South to offer material and spiritual aid to contrabands. They ran contraband camps, clothed, housed, and fed the fugitives, organized church services, founded hospitals, and opened schools.[13]

As soon as Nichols arrived from Boston, he received a rude introduction to the kind of racial prejudice that prevailed throughout the slave South. Visiting the Capitol with an African American minister, Nichols was shocked when they had to enter through a side door. Nichols embraced the city's African American churches, listened to sermons, preached, and gained a newfound respect for their ministers. He discovered that a local organization, the National Freedmen's Relief Association, had formed just a week before his arrival to coordinate donations for contrabands, help educate them, provide religious support, afford them protection, and overall turn Washington into a "city of refuge." Washington's NFRA was a branch of the National Freedmen's Relief Association that had been founded in New York City in February 1862. Dominated by women, the national organization hoped to "colonize" the contrabands, "not by deportation out of the country, but by giving them the facilities to live in it—that is, land and implements to till the soil." Founded by a small group of federal clerks, Washington's NFRA hoped "to teach them Christianity and civilization; to imbue them with notions of order, industry, economy, and self-reliance; to elevate them in the scale of humanity, by inspiring them with self-respect." Attending one of the NFRA's meetings, Nichols discovered that beyond their relief efforts the organizers were plotting a secret, mass escape of contrabands that was reminiscent of the flight on the *Pearl*. Coordinated by Lewis Tappan, the plan entailed obtaining a ship to carry the fugitives to Philadelphia and New York "to get them out of the clutches of southern hounds."[14]

Within a month of Nichols's arrival, the NFRA convinced General Wadsworth to appoint him as superintendent of the new Department of Contrabands and put him in charge of Duff Green's Row. Nichols discovered that the "contraband depot," which was intended to accommodate no more than fifty fugitives, held four hundred and sometimes received that many in a single day. Judging Duff Green's Row "hostile to health," he learned that the death rate averaged three and a half per day and during his first visit discovered the bodies of four dead contrabands. To improve sanitation, he provided soap, water, washtubs, and lime. Amid the overcrowding, however, an epidemic was inevitable. Smallpox was largely an "urban" disease that was endemic in eastern cities, including Baltimore, Philadelphia, New

York, and Boston but rare in Washington before the war. The city controlled it by requiring vaccinations of all public school students and vaccinating the poor, who rarely could attend school. The city's few smallpox patients were quarantined in a hospital for contagious diseases on Capitol Hill. Exposure provided immunity, so most victims were rural in origin, including the contrabands who were fleeing the Virginia countryside. Along with army recruits from rural areas, they probably contracted smallpox from troops arriving from the northeastern cities. To treat infected white soldiers, the government created a general hospital for eruptive diseases on Kalorama Hill on the edge of town, which grew in size and importance as the wartime epidemic widened. Lax enforcement of the quarantine, however, allowed both white and black patients to spread the disease. "Persons are daily seen on the avenues, in the cars, not only with traces of the disease, but with the disease itself," the press lamented. "We heard the other day of one who caught the disease by being jostled against a small-pox patient on Pennsylvania avenue."[15]

Washington residents routinely reported such heartrending sights as "a barefooted, half-dressed man on the street suffering with the small-pox," a patrolman escorting two smallpox patients to the hospital on a public streetcar, an infected mother and child lying on a street corner, and the body of a young smallpox victim found abandoned in a cemetery. "There are, doubtless, hundreds of deaths attributable to the practice of allowing persons to walk the streets whose faces exhibit the marrings and scarring of the variola," the *National Republican* complained. Mayor Wallach ordered Washington's physicians to revaccinate the students in the all-white public schools, but African Americans went unvaccinated, so more of them contracted the disease. Authorities ignored repeated calls for "having all contrabands, now daily pouring in from Virginia, vaccinated *immediately* on their arrival, otherwise we are nursing a hot-bed for the continual production of this loathsome disease." The resulting toll on the African American community left Washingtonians aghast. They found an African American woman sitting in a fence corner "very badly broken out with small pox" and another lying in a gutter on Pennsylvania Avenue "suffering with small-pox of the most virulent character." Police came to the aid of an African American smallpox victim driven out of the army camps in Virginia and left to fend for himself on the Washington side of the river. A seventy-year-old former slave, "infirm and dreadfully afflicted," was found lying in a pile of manure. He was sent to the almshouse.[16]

In June, amid a smallpox epidemic in Duff Green's Row, Wadsworth commandeered a cavalry barracks in northwest Washington formerly occupied by General McClellan's bodyguard, the McClellan Dragoons. Located on a prewar cemetery and brickyard, the cavalry camp took its name, Camp Barker, from Major Charles W. Barker, the commander of the dragoons. In July, Nichols moved the healthy contrabands to the camp at Vermont Avenue and Twelfth Street, a mile north of the White House, leaving the smallpox victims at Duff Green's Row, which became known as the "smallpox hospital" or the "hospital for contrabands," serving as both simultaneously. In addition to housing fugitives, Camp Barker was a literal "depot" where slaves could register as official contrabands, obtain a "military protection" from Wadsworth, and seek employment. The camp was a rectangle lined with barracks on three sides, all facing inward. The forty-eight barracks, twelve feet square, each held ten to twelve fugitives. Surrounding the camp, William Stoddard noted, was "a tight barrier of six-foot pine boards to keep out, for instance, any attempt on the part of the Fugitive Slave Law to play wolf with the sheep of this fold."[17]

Camp Barker began with three to four hundred contrabands living in army tents, but every major battle in the Eastern Theater sent hundreds more pouring into Washington. After the Second Battle of Bull Run, four hundred fugitives from Virginia arrived over a mere two days. Some Virginians began sending their slaves into the Union lines simply because they could no longer feed them. During its first four months, the camp received an average of 30 contrabands a day and accommodated 675 by the end of October. During that period, however, almost 3,000 fugitives came through the camp. One-half of them found employment working for the government, the men as laborers, teamsters, and camp servants, the women as hospital attendants, laundresses, and domestic servants. The predominant employers were the Quartermaster's Department, which hired thousands of teamsters to drive government wagons, and the Commissary Department, in which the contrabands worked on the wharves. These were the best jobs, paying $15 to $25 a month. Officers' camp servants earned $8 to $10 a month. Woodcutters earned seventy-five cents per cord and common laborers forty cents a day. The commissioner of public buildings, Benjamin Brown French, put contrabands to work cleaning Pennsylvania Avenue and the streets around the Capitol, carting off the tons of mud that had perennially plagued Washington. Others were detailed to purge the city of the animal carcasses that had proliferated during wartime. Responding to a recommendation from the Sanitary Commission, still others were put to work filling in the pits where the "city scavengers" deposited night soil as part of Washington's primitive sanitation system.[18]

More than one-half of the contrabands arrived as families. "Among them are persons of all hues, ages, and sizes, including a sprinkling of infants barely a week old," one witness reported. "The women, for the most part, lugged the children, Indian fashion, and the men bore on their shoulders immense bundles of baggage." Others, however, "presented a grotesque picture, attired as they were in the plantation uniform, and the plantation mud still on the cart and oxen." When the men went to work for the army, they had to leave their wives and children behind. Mothers with dependent children stayed in the camp and went out every day to work in the hospitals and government laundries. One of Nichols's goals was to make the camp pay for itself to silence "the cry raised by alarmists, about 'contrabands' being a burden to the Government." The women who did not work outside the camp took in laundry from the army "to defray their own expenses" and were allowed to keep any excess. Children were taught "every kind of employment in which they can be serviceable, picking lint for wounded soldiers, &c., &c." Twenty residents worked for the camp itself for forty cents a day, the standard wage for contrabands in government service. Only a "small balance," according to Nichols, were too old or infirm to work. Nichols also tried to dispel the fear that the contraband policy would send a flood of freedmen to inundate the North. "I have not been able to persuade more than fifteen or twenty to go North, notwithstanding the most liberal offers have been made to them," he reported. "They desire to remain on the soil where they were born, if they can do so and enjoy their freedom." A visiting Quaker discovered that the women refused to leave Camp Barker as long as their husbands were working for the army. "This is not strange," she concluded. "This perpetual dread of separation of family ties, has been the part of bondage most painful to its victims." By April 1863, two or three families, and in one instance twenty-six contrabands, were sharing the 12-foot-square cabins.[19]

Intended to relieve overcrowding, improve the health of the con-trabands, and prevent epidemics from spreading within the heart of the city, Camp Barker suffered its own smallpox outbreak. "It is well known that the small-pox is raging frightfully in our midst. The con-traband camp is one vast charnel house; deaths are occurring there at the rate of twelve to fifteen a day," the *National Republican* reported. "A poor fellow who managed to escape from there says little, if any, medical attendance is paid to them; they are without bedding, lying on boards, &c., imperfectly fed." A delegation of Quakers found the hospital "ill-ventilated, and disgusting in the extreme." Rather than stemming the disease, this kind of treatment merely spread it fur-ther through the city. Once convalescent, the contrabands were "glad to escape, and before they are fitted to mingle with the community, they spread the contagion broadcast." Throughout the war, smallpox proved more virulent among blacks than whites. Once they entered the Union army, African Americans were five times more likely to die from the disease than were white soldiers. By April 1863, 4,860 fugitive slaves had passed through Camp Barker. Three thousand were put to work, mostly as laborers and servants. Seven hundred had died, leaving a thousand in the now overcrowded camp. During the summer of 1863, at the peak of the smallpox outbreak, twenty-five deaths occurred at Camp Barker each week. The government grouped smallpox victims into three classes: contrabands, soldiers, and paupers. Patients from Camp Barker went to the "hospital for contrabands" in Duff Green's Row. Soldiers who contracted the dis-ease received treatment at Kalorama Hospital. The city maintained its own smallpox hospital for paupers on East Capitol Hill, in a reputedly "low, malarious-breeding spot." Described as a "small shanty, having two apartments," the city hospital was maintained by a married couple and experienced three or four deaths a day. Designed to accommodate only fourteen patients, the hospital overflowed at times with up to fifty.[20]

Because of the overly bureaucratic classification system, grounded in both race and social class, "when the authorities are informed of a new case of this loathsome disease, the question has to be settled to their own satisfaction as to which of these classes they belong." The ambiguous status of fugitives in Washington made them difficult to categorize, so "By the time this question is settled the chances are that half a dozen persons in the vicinity have become infected by the disease." The body of a woman who died of smallpox, according to a newspaper report, lay in her house for three days "infecting the entire neighborhood with the loathsome disease, merely because the question as to whether she is a contraband or not has not been decided!" Aggravating the epidemic, the city refused to provide any treatment to white nonresidents, labeled "strangers." In March 1863, only after the disease had spread beyond the contrabands and soldiers in the army camps, the city at last appropriated $500 for the care of smallpox patients. When one council member proposed exempting nonresident paupers from treatment, the *Chronicle* asked incredulously, "Is it a crime not to be a permanent citizen of Washington?" Meanwhile, most white smallpox victims received treatment in their own homes, further dispersing the contagion across the city. In January 1864, there were 1,200 smallpox patients in Washington, and 150 contrabands died every month during the first half of the year. The NFRA provided a full-time physician for Camp Barker and by the end of the year moved the patients from the tent hospital into a converted church building. The two-hundred-bed Freedmen's Hospital assumed the responsibility for treating all of the city's African Americans.[21]

At Camp Barker, local and national relief organizations supplemented the meager provisions that the government provided. Noting that the army provided only food to the contrabands, the NFRA's female members raised funds, including $93 from U.S. senators, to buy cloth and sew it into clothing. Within the first month, they provided two hundred garments. The *National Republican* reported that "several of the colored churches have contributed liberally of their limited means," but "no white church has contributed a cent." Henry McNeal Turner's Israel Bethel AME Church created the Union Relief Association to raise funds for feeding, clothing, educating, and employing the fugitives. The members of Zion Methodist Church delivered a wagonload of "potatoes, cabbage, onions, squashes, beets, tomatoes, fresh pork, cheese, white sugar, apples, oranges, lemons, pipes, tobacco, stockings, &c." directly to the camp. The Friends' Freedmen's Relief Association of Philadelphia provided clothing, and national relief organizations, including the American Tract Society, the American Baptist Free Mission Society, the New England Freedmen's Aid Society, and Henry Highland Garnet's New York–based African Civilization Society, sent clothing and even missionaries—ministers and teachers—to help. The American Tract Society had operated Washington's first free school for African Americans in Duff Green's Row and now opened a larger one in Camp Barker. Although the society sent three teachers to conduct the school, the "constant change of new comers and departures" prevented its effective operation. Nichols discovered that "not *one* in a *hundred* could read before they came inside the Union lines, and but few can read yet." The NFRA sponsored an orphanage for African American children, and Nichols himself preached on Sundays and held prayer meetings during the week for the contrabands, whom he considered "the *most religious* people I have ever known." A reporter who visited the camp on a Sunday watched a round of preaching by several white ministers followed by the singing of two hymns, "Go Down, Moses" and "Jesus Is Coming." The ministers, he wrote condescendingly, "seemed to understand the character and capacities of their hearers." Afterward, a crowd of fugitives gathered in front of the church, held their own service, and "sang several pieces in their own style, keeping time with bodies and feet." Mystified, the outsider concluded that "their movements were ludicrous enough to excite a smile on one not accustomed to such a performance."[22]

By the end of 1862, 700 contrabands were living at Camp Barker, one-third of them children. Six hundred of them lived in the former cavalry barracks, which had been subdivided into fifty dwellings, each accommodating twelve people. Another 120 residents, one-sixth of the total, were in the gender-segregated hospitals. One hundred male patients were crowded into a 25-by-75-foot ward. (A typical wing in a pavilion hospital was twice as large but held half as many soldiers.) The death rate was two per day. The day school, run by two American Tract Society missionaries, met in the church and boasted an average attendance of seventy-five children. The night school attracted about one hundred adults. Most of the contrabands who lived at Camp Barker worked for the army as teamsters or laborers in the city's fortifications, earning $15 a month. In September 1862, Secretary of War Stanton began deducting $5 a month from their pay to create a Contraband Fund to support the residents of the camp who could not labor, which provoked frequent complaints. All contrabands employed in the Quartermaster's Department had to contribute to the fund whether or not they or any family members lived in the camp. In November, the government tried to reduce the camp's expenses still further by authorizing Nichols to apprentice contraband children into "good homes, where they will be well cared for and instructed in useful employments." For families—husbands and wives, mothers and children—that had persevered through slavery, the "perpetual dread of separation" continued.[23]

CHAPTER SEVENTEEN

"The Step Which, at Once, Shortens the War"
The Emancipation Proclamation

·

A S HE did so often, Lincoln waited for Congress to take a half-step forward before leapfrogging them and making a giant stride of his own in the same direction. Although he signed the Second Confiscation Act in July 1862, he doubted its effectiveness in freeing anyone. Because of constitutional limits on the power of the government to seize property, including slaves, implementation would require a hearing in federal court to prove the slaveowners' disloyalty, potentially 350,000 separate legal proceedings to render all of the slaves "forever free," as the act promised. Two months after its passage, Lincoln confessed that "I cannot learn that that law has caused a single slave to come over to us." After the debacle of the Peninsula Campaign, Lincoln embraced a new approach to waging the Civil War that came to be called "total warfare." He realized that the kind of classical warfare that the Union Army had been conducting by focusing on conventional battlefield victories was proving ineffective.[1]

The Confederacy's three million slaves represented its greatest economic and military resource. During the summer of 1862, Lincoln adopted what historians have labeled "abolitionist arithmetic," the simple logic that "Every slave employed by the army or navy represented a double gain, one subtracted from the Confederacy and one added to the Union." The hideous bloodlettings of the Peninsula Campaign and Second Bull Run, all too apparent within Washington's overflowing military hospitals, produced a shortage of man-power as well as a growing popular disillusionment with the war. Lincoln believed that he had no constitutional authority as president to free slaves as a humanitarian measure, carefully distinguishing between his *"official* duty" and his "oft-expressed *personal* wish that all men every where could be free." As commander-in-chief during wartime, however, he could emancipate the enemy's slaves under the guise of military necessity. At the outset of the war, Senator Charles Sumner had advised him that "under the war power the right had come to him to emancipate the slaves." Lincoln gradually concluded that emancipation was indeed a military necessity, "the step which, at once, shortens the war."[2]

Five days after signing the Second Confiscation Act, Lincoln told his cabinet that he had drafted an emancipation proclamation. While expressing surprise, all but two of the cabinet members, the most radical and the most conservative, welcomed the news. Secretary of the Treasury Salmon Chase, a longtime abolitionist, worried that the invocation of the president's war powers might set a dangerous prec-edent. "The measure goes beyond any thing I have recommended," he told Lincoln. He suggested instead that Lincoln empower his mil-itary commanders to free the slaves in areas of the South that they controlled and then "organize and arm the slaves." The conservative Attorney General Edward Bates of Missouri, one of the Border States, wanted to impose compulsory colonization on all slaves freed under the proclamation, which he called "deportation." Lincoln rejected both recommendations. Secretary of State Seward was supportive but advised Lincoln to postpone his proclamation until after a northern victory, presenting emancipation as an act of Union strength rather than weakness. Lincoln agreed and left the draft in his desk drawer until the right time to issue it arrived. On September 4, 1862, Lee led his army across the Potomac into Maryland. No longer worried about the defense of Washington, Lincoln ordered McClellan to "Destroy the rebel army, if possible." On September 17, the Battle of Antie-tam resulted in the bloodiest day of the entire war, killing 6,000 men and wounding another 15,000 on both sides. Rather than destroying Lee's army as Lincoln had ordered, McClellan achieved a stalemate.

Still, McClellan considered the result "a complete victory," indeed "a masterpiece of art," because he had forced the Confederates to retreat from Union territory.[3]

Despite his self-promoting bravado, McClellan had a point. Lincoln seized upon the Battle of Antietam as the long-awaited victory that would allow him to issue his proclamation. Five days after the battle, on September 22, 1862, the Preliminary Emancipation Proclamation put the Confederate states on notice that they had one hundred days, until January 1, 1863, to return to the Union or they would lose their slaves. Placating conservatives, Lincoln declared that the war would continue to be fought to restore the Union, not free the slaves. As he had famously written one month earlier in Horace Greeley's *New York Tribune*, "If I could save the Union without freeing any slave I would do it, and if I could save it by freeing all the slaves I would do it; and if I could save it by freeing some and leaving others alone I would also do that." At the same time, Lincoln reiterated his Border State Plan. In the loyal slave states, where he believed that he had no power to free any slaves under military necessity, compensated emancipation combined with voluntary colonization would need to suffice. In short, he was trying to save the Union "by freeing some and leaving others alone." Still, Lincoln's proclamation inaugurated a much more aggressive war effort that was intended, as he put it, to "strike more vigorous blows" against "the heart of the rebellion," which was slavery. Undermining slavery in advance of the Union armies would weaken the Confederacy and make victory that much easier to achieve. As the *National Republican* explained Lincoln's logic, "If it was really necessary to conquer the rebels before taking away their slaves, we never could conquer them."

McClellan, however, through both words and actions, made clear that he was unwilling to pursue the kind of total warfare that Lincoln now deemed necessary. Instead of pursuing Lee's army across the Potomac after the Antietam stalemate, he contemplated the spoils of victory and imagined himself forcing Stanton's removal as secretary of war and resuming his position as general-in-chief. McClellan's inaction enraged Lincoln, but with typical patience he wrote him a fatherly letter offering detailed strategic advice. Characterizing the general as "overcautious," he chided him for failing to defeat Lee's army at Antietam or at least pursuing the enemy after the bloody stalemate. "In coming to us, he tenders us an advantage which we should not waive," he reasoned. "We should not so operate as to merely drive him away. As we must beat him somewhere, or fail finally, we can do it, if at all, easier near to us, than far away."[4]

Privately, however, Lincoln was losing patience. Visiting McClellan's headquarters at Antietam with an old friend from Illinois, Lincoln looked around at the encampment and asked, "Do you know what this is?" The friend answered, "It is the Army of the Potomac." Lincoln replied derisively, "So it is called, but that is a mistake; it is only McClellan's bodyguard." When McClellan blamed his inaction on tired horses, Lincoln had heard enough. "I have just read your despatch about sore tongued and fatiegued horses," he replied. "Will you pardon me for asking what the horses of your army have done since the battle of Antietam that fatigue[s] anything?" Livid, McClellan told his wife, Nelly, "There never was a truer epithet applied to a certain individual than that of the 'Gorilla.' " Even worse, McClellan reiterated his opposition to both emancipation and total warfare, accusing Lincoln of "inaugurating servile war" and "changing our free institutions into a despotism." Lincoln suspected that McClellan's goal was to promote a prolonged stalemate that would end in a compromise, allowing the seceded states to rejoin the Union with slavery intact. In early November, after the congressional elections, he removed McClellan from command. One of the general's admirers, Washington's provost marshal, William Doster, shrewdly identified his conservative, defensive mentality as his greatest strength and his greatest weakness. As Doster recognized, "his part in the war was to change citizens into soldiers,—a vast and motley multitude of individualities into a machine, and to fortify Washington," he observed. "This he did excellently well." But he lacked the temperament, perhaps the ability, and certainly the will to lead a forceful offensive campaign. "This goes by different names: 'incompetency,' 'timidity,' 'over-caution,' 'hesitation,' " Doster mused. "It is only—non-combativeness." Committed to securing the capital as his highest priority, in the tradition of classical European warfare, McClellan had made an essential, indeed admirable, defensive contribution. "The army organized, Washington fortified, McClellan had really played his part," Doster concluded. "To ask him further to go and lead the army to Richmond was unreasonable." Lincoln put it more succinctly: "If he can't fight himself, he excels in making others ready to fight."[5]

The Washington press reflected the public's ambivalence toward emancipation. "This proclamation is the beginning of the end, or rather it is the end," the solidly antislavery *National Republican* declared, predicting that "it will restore to the President all his old friends." Noting that Lincoln had exceeded every congressional initiative, the newspaper rejoiced, "He has proclaimed the freedom of all slaves, as well of loyal owners as of rebels, and whether they escape to us, or not." The pro-Lincoln *Chronicle* savored the irony that "Slavery, caused the war: it is with the sword of his war power under the Constitution that President Lincoln now destroys the right arm of the rebellion—African slavery." Underestimating the resolve of African Americans to free themselves under presidential aegis, the ever cautious *National Intelligencer* dismissed the document as not "self-enforcing" and predicted that it would have "no practical effect." Questioning Lincoln's motives—and judgment—the paper suggested that he issued the proclamation as a worthless sop to abolitionists who would soon realize the futility of pursuing emancipation as a war aim. "On any other theory than this," the editorial concluded cynically, "the proclamation may be said to open issues too tremendous, and to be fraught with consequences too undeveloped, to admit of calculation or forecast by any intelligence we can command." The proslavery *Evening Star* ignored the document and said absolutely nothing. On Thanksgiving Day 1862, Washington's African American community provided a feast for the contrabands at Camp Barker. The Reverend Henry McNeal Turner, minister of the Israel Bethel AME Church, organized the banquet "in grateful acknowledgement to Almighty God for his kind and beneficent providence, who has thus led the Chief Executive of the nation to a deed so heroic and magnanimous." The Freedmen's Hospital at Camp Barker, which was the former church, became a dining hall lined with portraits of antislavery reformers and other notables, including General Wadsworth,

Horace Greeley, Senator Samuel Pomeroy, and Horace Mann. At the end of the hall hung a portrait of the president ringed with the inscription "God bless Abraham Lincoln—Liberty to the captive." The Reverend William Henry Channing, a leading Transcendentalist reformer and pastor of Washington's Unitarian Church, presided over the gathering of two thousand guests, among them Harriet Beecher Stowe. The speakers included AME bishop Daniel Payne, the former minister of Israel Bethel; William Stoddard, Lincoln's private secretary; and Senator Pomeroy, who advocated voluntary colonization. The Ladies' Contraband Relief Association, which was led by Mary Lincoln's seamstress, Elizabeth Keckly, provided a large pyramidal cake in the center of the hall to honor Washington's fugitives, now numbering 10,000, who were "impelled hither by military necessity or personal aspirations for an unknown something called freedom."[6]

On January 1, 1863, Lincoln signed the final Emancipation Proclamation. During the one hundred days since he had issued the preliminary draft, he made four additions, two that were meant to soften its rhetoric and two designed to strengthen its impact. First, to answer the widespread charge that the proclamation was intended to provoke a "servile insurrection" within the Confederacy, Lincoln decided to "enjoin upon the people so declared to be free to abstain from all violence, unless in necessary self-defence." Second, to allay fears that emancipation would leave the postwar South destitute by eliminating its most important source of labor, he initiated the coming transition to a free labor system by urging that "in all cases when allowed, they labor faithfully for reasonable wages." Third, he expanded implementation of the Militia Act to enlist former slaves into the military, as he put it, "to garrison forts, positions, stations, and other places, and to man vessels of all sorts." This provision put the teeth into the proclamation that the *National Intelligencer* had found wanting. Over the next two years, with the help of African American troops, the document would become, in large measure, "self-enforcing."[7]

Finally, Charles Sumner insisted "that there must be something about 'justice' & 'God.'" Salmon Chase proposed a further invocation of military necessity and the authority of the Constitution. These two suggestions produced the final sentence of the proclamation: "And upon this act, sincerely believed to be an act of justice, warranted by the Constitution, upon military necessity, I invoke the considerate judgment of mankind, and the gracious favor of Almighty God." The concluding sentence therefore grounded Lincoln's actions not only in military necessity, familiar to Americans since General Butler's decision to confiscate the contrabands at Fortress Monroe, but also in the justice that African Americans and abolitionists had striven for so long to achieve and a moral imperative transcending the limits of human events and mortal actions here on earth. The final proclamation also featured a significant omission. The preliminary proclamation contained a clause urging voluntary colonization, which Lincoln deleted from the final version. The final proclamation contained no hint of compromise with the rebels. At the same time, the document exempted all slaveowners in loyal parts of the Union, where Lincoln believed that he had no power as commander-in-chief to free slaves. Specifically, he spared the Border States, Union-occupied territory in Louisiana and Virginia, and the state of Tennesee, which was moving toward emancipation on its own. Looking to the future, however, Lincoln qualified the exemption by adding that the "excepted parts are, *for the present*, left precisely as if this proclamation were not issued."[8]

On New Year's Day, Lincoln held a levee at the White House that drew an immense crowd of well-wishers. After spending three hours shaking hundreds of hands, he sat down, signed his name to the proclamation, smiled, and said simply, "That will do." Finding "a multitude of people" gathered at his Israel Bethel AME Church, the Reverend Henry McNeal Turner rushed out to the office of the *Evening Star*, where a crowd was waiting for copies of the proclamation. Turner and several others tore up a newspaper as they all grabbed for it at once. He came away with the piece that contained the proclamation. "Down Pennsylvania Ave. I ran as for my life," he recalled, "and when the people saw me coming with the paper in my hand they raised a shouting cheer that was almost deafening." Crowds of men, black and white, marched up and down in front of the White House, cheering and congratulating Lincoln. Turner watched as "Men squealed, women fainted, dogs barked, white and colored people shook hands, songs were sung, and by this time cannons began to fire." He concluded that "nothing like it will ever be seen again in this life." Lincoln agreed, calling the Emancipation Proclamation "the central act of my administration, and the great event of the nineteenth century." As he told Charles Sumner, "I know very well that the name which is connected with this act will never be forgotten."[9]

For the moment, however, fugitives from Maryland, like Alethia Lynch, remained subject to arrest and return until Congress repealed the Fugitive Slave Law a year and a half later. In November 1862, General Wadsworth and Marshal Lamon squared off for one last skirmish between the military and civil authorities. Sandy Sutherland, an attendant at the Patent Office Hospital, was abducted and jailed despite possessing a military protection from Wadsworth. When his wife, Rachel, the chief laundress at Harewood Hospital, went to the jail looking for her husband, she was also arrested. Provost Marshal Doster sent a lieutenant and ten soldiers to the jail to release them and return them to Camp Barker, where they lived. Producing a warrant from the Fugitive Slave Law commissioners, Lamon refused to hand them over. According to Doster, "Lamon then called for a *posse comitatis*, but no one responded." Doster and Lamon agreed to let Lincoln resolve the standoff. After hearing both sides, Lincoln refused to intervene but told Doster that if he wanted to release the Sutherlands, "Lamon could not prevent it." Lamon freed them under protest. The next day, Doster arrested the slavecatchers who had jailed the couple and sent them to the Old Capitol Prison for six weeks of solitary confinement. Wadsworth resigned his command of the Military District of Washington one week later. He had originally accepted the position to get out of the Army of the Potomac because he had doubted George McClellan's abilities as a general. (Privately, McClellan deemed Wadsworth "a vile traitorous miscreant.") When Lincoln replaced McClellan, Wadsworth eagerly accepted a new field command. After leading his infantry division in the Battles of Chancellorsville and Gettysburg, Wadsworth was shot in the forehead during the Battle of the Wilderness in May 1864. He lingered unconscious for two days and then died, six weeks before Congress repealed the Fugitive Slave Law at last.[10]

After relieving General McClellan for his reluctance to pursue Lee's army into Virginia and to embrace total warfare, including emancipation, Lincoln appointed General Ambrose Burnside to command the Army of the Potomac. Burnside's mission was to mount the counterattack against the Confederates that McClellan had refused to launch. The disastrous result was the Battle of Fredericksburg in mid-December 1862, during which the Army of the Potomac suffered more than 12,000 casualties, more than twice the Confederate losses, while attempting to cross the Rappahannock River. Through the winter of 1862–63, the Army of the Potomac sat along the Rappahannock, where they had been repulsed from Fredericksburg. Facing criticism from his own generals, in the spring Burnside offered his resignation, which Lincoln accepted. The popular General Joseph Hooker was Burnside's most severe critic. He had also rebuked the army and the Lincoln administration for incompetence and stupidity, calling for the installation of a "dictator" to direct the war. Overlooking Hooker's intemperate bluster, Lincoln considered him the best choice to lead the Army of the Potomac and appointed him to succeed Burnside. "Only those generals who gain successes," he told Hooker, "can set up dictators. What I now ask of you is military success, and I will risk the dictatorship." Hooker's army nearly outnumbered Lee's by two to one. Emphasizing the imperative to fight a total war, Lincoln told Hooker, "In your next fight, put in all your men." On April 30, 1863, Hooker executed a daring plan in which he left one-third of his army facing Fredericksburg while the other 70,000 men crossed the Rappahannock upriver and came up behind Lee's army near Chancellorsville. Executing a brilliant maneuver, Lee attacked Hooker's forces, resulting in yet another disastrous loss for the Union. Over the four-day Battle of Chancellorsville, the Army of the Potomac suffered 17,000 casualties before Hooker ordered a retreat back across the Rappahannock. When Lincoln heard the news, he exclaimed, "My God! My God! What will the country say?" Lincoln's strategy of total warfare, which included the recruitment of African American troops, had become imperative.[11]

*   *   *

THE MOST visible immediate impact of the Emancipation Proclamation was the enlistment of African Americans, eventually 179,000
of them, in the Union Army. Ten days after the surrender of Fort
Sumter, Jacob Dodson, a Washington, DC, African American, had
written to Secretary of War Cameron that "I desire to inform you
that I know of some 300 reliable colored free citizens of this city who
desire to enter the service for the defense of the city." Describing his
military experience, Dodson told Cameron that "I have been three
times across the Rocky Mountains in the service of the country with
Frémont and others." A servant of Missouri's Senator Thomas Hart
Benton, John C. Frémont's father-in-law, Dodson had accompanied
the "Pathfinder" on his expeditions to the West during the 1840s,
including California during the Mexican-American War. Frémont
described Dodson as "a free young colored man of Washington City,
who volunteered to accompany the expedition and performed his
duty manfully." Dodson's estimate of three hundred potential soldiers represented one-sixth of the city's African American men of
military age. A week later, Cameron rejected Dodson's offer in a
single sentence: "I have to say that this Department has no intention at present to call into the service of the Government any colored soldiers." The U.S. Navy observed a long tradition of enrolling
African American seamen and began accepting black volunteers in
September 1861. Congress, however, had restricted militia service to
whites beginning in 1792. African American men volunteered to fight
or raise regiments across the North, including two from Ohio who
requested "the poor priverlige of fighting—and (if need be dieing)"
for the Union. Unable to fight as an African American, in August
1861 Elizabeth Keckly's fair-skinned son, George, had joined the 1st
Missouri Volunteers as a white man. He lost his life just weeks later
in his first battle at Wilson's Creek.[12]

Black and white abolitionists, Republican radicals, and a handful
of Union generals supported their efforts in the name of military
victory and racial equality. The War Department approved limited
mobilization of African American soldiers on the South Carolina

coast and in Louisiana and Kansas when generals recommended it "in cases of great emergency." The Militia Act that authorized Lincoln to recruit African Americans into the army counted them toward the enlistment quotas that were assigned to each state as part of the Union's first draft. Under Governor John A. Andrew, Massachusetts passed a law enrolling both blacks and whites as eligible for the draft. The crucial turning point for Lincoln, however, was the bloodletting in the Eastern Theater during the summer and fall of 1862, prompting his embrace of total warfare, conscription, and emancipation as essential ingredients of his military strategy. Endorsing the recruitment of African American soldiers, Lincoln had concluded, "To now avail ourselves of this element of force, is very important, if not indispensable."[13]

After his Emancipation Proclamation urged African Americans to join the army, the War Department sanctioned the formation of regiments in Massachusetts, Connecticut, and Rhode Island. Two men from Washington enlisted in Colonel Robert Gould Shaw's famed 54th Massachusetts Regiment Volunteer Infantry, formed in March 1863, and ten in its companion regiment, the 55th Massachusetts. The Confederacy, however, contained eighteen times as many potential African American soldiers as the free states, nine-tenths of them slaves. The South therefore possessed the greatest potential for mobilization, which was one of Lincoln's motives for issuing his proclamation. The northern states had an incentive to enroll African Americans to help fill their draft quotas, but Lincoln viewed the recruitment of slaves as doubly beneficial to the army, reasoning that it would "help us where they come from, as well as where they go to." Personally urging Governor Andrew Johnson of Tennessee to raise African American troops in March 1863, Lincoln confided that the "bare sight of fifty thousand armed, and drilled black soldiers on the banks of the Mississippi, would end the rebellion at once. And who doubts that we can present that sight, if we but take hold in earnest?" Simultaneously, at Lincoln's request, Stanton issued an order emphasizing "the importance attached by the Government to the use of the colored population emancipated by the Presidents proclamation, and particularly for the organization of their labor and military strength."

Six months later, Lincoln approved the removal of a Union general who was "disinclined to raise colored troops." The Bureau of Colored Troops, created in May 1863, coordinated the recruitment and enlistment of African American soldiers and the selection of their commanding officers who, at Stanton's behest, were exclusively white.[14]

Washington had more military-age African American men than eleven of the free states, and just 150 fewer than the entire state of Massachusetts. In the wake of the Emancipation Proclamation, the city's African Americans called immediately for the raising of a regiment, as both a contribution to the war effort and a step toward equal rights. "I think the result would go far towards breaking down the prejudices here, against the negroes," African American community leader William Slade predicted. "In my opinion, the placing of colored men in the attitude of soldiers will bring men more to a level than anything else." Henry McNeal Turner declared, "Abraham Lincoln can get any thing he wants from the colored people here, from a company to a corps." In April 1863, two white ministers, the Reverend J. D. Turner and the Reverend W. G. Raymond, who had extensive experience as hospital chaplains, proposed the formation of a volunteer regiment of African Americans in the capital. "I would respectfully ask your Excellency to appoint me to the command of a Regiment of colored troops, or give me authority to raise a Regt in connection with W. G. Raymond in this District," Turner wrote Lincoln. "I have always, since my earliest recollection, sympathized with the oppressed colored race. And have earnestly labored for their elevation not unfrequently at considerable personal sacrafice." Turner had served for a year and a half as a chaplain in the 4th Pennsylvania Cavalry during the Peninsula Campaign and the Seven Days. Raymond, a lieutenant in the 86th New York Regiment, had spent four months as an officer in Washington's Provost Guard and eight months as post chaplain at Trinity Church Hospital until it closed in April. Turner and Raymond had numerous supporters, including three Washington hospital chaplains, the governor of Pennsylvania, Turner's home state, and the governor of Minnesota. The Reverend William Henry Channing, minister of Washington's Unitarian Church, attested to the two men's "moral and Christian character

and integrity." Lincoln's own minister at the New York Avenue Presbyterian Church, Phineas D. Gurley, recommended Raymond as
"faithful and effective." Turner and Raymond, who had worked with
Washington's African American congregations for three months,
assured Lincoln that they enjoyed wide support within the city's
African American community. Raymond believed that the example
of an African American regiment in Washington "would go through
the rebel states like electricity!" Southern slaves would "rise *en masse*,
and come away as fast as they could."[15]

LINCOLN APPROVED the formation of Washington's 1st Regiment of
Colored Volunteers and appointed Turner and Raymond as colonel
and lieutenant colonel. They announced an organizational meeting
and declared that "the colored men who feel that now is the time to
demonstrate their manhood, are earnestly invited to be present." The
meeting assembled at Asbury Church on May 4, 1863, under the guard
of the 39th Massachusetts Regiment, assigned by the provost marshal
as sentries at the door and in the aisles "to prevent any unfavorable
demonstration by the negro-hating, rowdy Copperheads who might
be disposed to obstruct or defeat the objects of the meeting." Among
other threats, a city police officer had reportedly announced that
he "would put as many bullets through a nigger recruit as he would
through a mad dog." Another motive was preventing the recapture of
contrabands by slavecatchers, who would be sure to lurk about. "The
President was anxious to do all he could for this people, but he had
become somewhat discouraged," Turner told the volunteers from the
pulpit. "Prominent men would go to him and ask authority to raise
colored troops, and then go away, make a feeble effort, and return
and ask for something else." He challenged his audience to "take Mr.
Lincoln at his word and bring forward the men." An African American minister, Adolphus Winkfield, endorsed Turner and Raymond as
"the men of our choice." Alluding to the Emancipation Proclamation,
he reasoned that the American flag "is now *my* flag, and I will die for
it." To loud applause, he professed, "Our people are free, and let us go
and defend them. We now have an opportunity to be men." Pointing

out the Provost Guard at the door, succeeding speakers declared that "the Union bayonet protected the black man," that "God had raised up Abraham Lincoln," and that "practical efforts would do more than all abolition speeches in the world." One hundred forty men enlisted before the meeting ended. On the same day, Turner and Raymond visited Camp Barker, where they recruited another thirty volunteers. The *Washington Chronicle* marveled that the "hatred of the negro and the approval of slavery with which we have been tainted, and which have been the work of three generations of politicians and writers, have disappeared like an April snow before the inexorable and practical necessity of freeing the slaves and turning them into soldiers." The newspaper asked in amazement, "Who would have believed a year ago that such could be the case?" The answer seemed simple— "every drafted colored man saves a white man."[16]

A second meeting two nights later at Henry McNeal Turner's Israel Bethel AME Church produced even more progress. Turner offered his church as the recruiting headquarters for the regiment, and his aide, Thomas H. C. Hinton, became recruiting sergeant. "I am for the war; I am for fighting, too," Turner urged. "If we would be freemen we must fight." Anthony Bowen, a former slave who had purchased his own freedom and then helped to operate Washington's underground railroad, declared that "Mr. Lincoln is a Moses to lead us out of Egypt." The assembly appointed an executive committee of seven African American leaders, including Presbyterian minister John F. Cook Jr., to hold additional rallies, post announcements, recruit volunteers within their communities, and solicit donations to support the soldiers until they were mustered in. The meeting produced another two hundred volunteers raised by the city's literary societies. Two more meetings at the Fifteenth Street Presbyterian Church and the Union Bethel AME Church increased the enrollment to eight hundred. Turner and Raymond met with Lincoln to present the enlistment rolls and make a formal request for quarters. Lincoln instructed Stanton to "do the best for them you can" pending their medical inspection. While the men were drilling, some white soldiers asked, "How is it that you colored people can drill so well?" Their sergeant major answered that "the colored people had been pretty well '*drilled*' for years." Then he declared that he "had put on the uniform, and he did not intend to put it off until he could be recognized as a citizen." A white captain advised him that African Americans would need to "rise and *take*" their rights, that "the shortest and quickest road to liberty, is by the use of the sword." Even more pointedly, Hinton believed that the regiment would "show secession sympathizers in the District that their predictions as to the impracticability of making soldiers of 'niggers,' as they ignorantly and sneeringly remarked, has turned out, and will continue to be just the reverse." In mid-May, the first company to be mustered in marched through the streets of Washington. Forty to fifty in number, the "negroes in uniform" wore red, white, and blue badges and cockades.[17]

Overseeing the medical examinations of the volunteers was Major Alexander T. Augusta, one of the Union army's first African American officers. Freeborn in Philadelphia, Augusta emigrated to Canada, "on account of prejudice against colour," as he put it, which prevented him from studying medicine in the United States. He earned a medical degree at Trinity College, Toronto, and maintained a practice for six years. One week after Lincoln issued the Emancipation Proclamation, Augusta wrote to him to request an appointment as "surgeon to some of the coloured regiments, or as physician to some of the depots of 'freedmen.' " In March, the Army Medical Board rejected his request on the grounds that he was "a person of African descent" and a British subject. After traveling to Washington, Augusta insisted that "I have come near a thousand miles at a great expence and sacrifice, hoping to be of some use to the country and my race." The board relented and ruled him "qualified for the position of Surgeon in the negro regiment now being raised," and he became one of only eight African American physicians to receive an officer's commission during the war. A month later, as he passed through Baltimore by train in his Union Army uniform, a crowd gathered and followed him through the streets. One of the onlookers, James Dunn, assaulted him and cut off his shoulder straps. When the Provost Guard arrived, three members of the crowd attacked its commander. The guard took Augusta into custody, but after he produced a copy of his commission, they released him. The guard then arrested Dunn instead and charged him with striking an officer. The other three were charged with assaulting and interfering with the Provost Guard. Only then could Augusta board the Washington train. As the 1st Regiment's surgeon, Augusta supervised the medical examination of the volunteers, which was conducted by a white physician. On the first day, 151 passed the exam and were immediately mustered into service. The *National Republican* boasted, "The whole country is looking on this regiment with interest." Soon African American soldiers were arresting whites who challenged their authority. In July 1863, a squad from the 1st Regiment ostentatiously marched a white man, who had tried to attack them, down Pennsylvania Avenue and lodged him in the Central Guardhouse.[18]

A few days later, on May 22, 1863, the army created the Bureau of Colored Troops, located in the basement of the War Department. That evening, during another "war meeting" to raise volunteers, Turner and Raymond announced that the government had removed them from command and replaced them with an "under officer who knew nothing of their wants and feelings as colored men." They reasoned that there was intense competition among white officers to secure commands, so the new African American regiments were tempting prizes. In response to its first call for regimental commanders, the bureau's Board of Examiners received 140 applications in Washington alone. (William Stoddard noted that "it was astonishing how large a number of second lieutenants were willing to sacrifice themselves for the good of the service as majors and colonels.") Insistent on local control over the 1st Regiment, whites in the capital resented the leadership of the Pennsylvanian and the New Yorker. "A desperate fight is being made to get District men in over the colored men," Turner and Raymond concluded, reporting that they were forbidden to visit their own regiment under penalty of arrest. That very afternoon, Lincoln himself "was riding around the streets with his wife, for the purpose of finding the two companies already mustered in, and he could not find them," they announced. "They were where even the President could not go to them without a pass."[19]

The two officers discovered that their regiment had been moved to a 75-acre island in the middle of the Potomac River. Mason's Island bore the name of George Mason, the Virginia planter who was best known for originating the idea of a Bill of Rights in the Constitution. During the Civil War, the Union Army occupied the island, which was owned by one of the directors of the Chesapeake and Ohio Canal. Accessible by a causeway from the Virginia side but only by ferry from Washington, Mason's Island was also called Analostan Island during the Civil War. (It became Theodore Roosevelt Island in 1932 as a memorial to the twenty-sixth president.) The move to the island was never explained but may have been undertaken to protect the African American soldiers from the increasing hostility of white Washingtonians and to reduce the visibility of the regiment as a symbol of looming racial equality. The escalating racial tensions became apparent when a white soldier confronted Private William James, a Washington blacksmith who had enlisted two weeks earlier, and demanded that he remove his military insignia. When James refused, a crowd assaulted him. Fearing a riot, police arrested James but released him when the evidence showed that he had been attacked. A week later, Corporal John Ross experienced similar treatment when a crowd of whites surrounded him on the street, shouting, "Take the straps off him!" and "Stop the raising of nigger regiments!"[20]

The army called the Mason's Island bivouac Camp Greene in honor of Elias M. Greene, chief quartermaster of the Military Department of Washington. The army provided a row of barracks, a parade ground, a firing range, an infirmary, and quarters for the regimental band. The regiment's new colonel was William Birney, the son of James G. Birney, a founder of the Liberty Party and its presidential candidate in 1840 and 1844. Birney's appointment was part of the army's effort to centralize and professionalize control over its African American regiments. A lawyer by profession, and later the U.S. attorney for the District of Columbia, Birney served in all of the major actions of the Army of the Potomac during the first two years of the war. With the creation of the Bureau of Colored Troops, Birney recruited and assumed simultaneous command of six African American regiments in addition to the 1st Colored District Volunteers. Rapidly promoted to major general, he was an experienced field commander and possessed far more military expertise than either Turner or Raymond. After his removal, Turner himself admitted that organizing the regiment "had worn upon his mind to such an extent as to cause his health to give way temporarily, and he was now quite ill."[21]

The *Daily Chronicle* concluded that the "Colored troops must be commanded by white men, and it is the determination of the Board to select for them the very best officers to be had." Unlike Turner and Raymond, Birney was able to get his men fully equipped and uniformed, and within two weeks they were marching up Pennsylvania Avenue. No longer arrested for wearing uniforms, they received applause from a crowd that included Lincoln, who murmured with approval, "It'll do. It'll do!" Headed by a drum corps, they elicited praise, according to the *Chronicle*, "from even those who affect to despise them and their cause." Abolitionist Jane Grey Swisshelm agreed that "People here are becoming accustomed to see them in United States uniform, and they are more frequently hailed with signs of approbation and approval." Turner and Raymond had done an admirable job of recruiting the regiment and, above all, helping to work what seemed a miraculous change in Washington. "Less than two years ago any colored man wearing a military cap, or in fact anything pertaining to the army, was taken in charge by the military authorities," the *Chronicle* marveled. "These are, indeed, progressive times." To his credit, Turner accepted his replacement magnanimously, telling the next "war meeting," which Birney chaired, that he "had always been with the colored people, and whether he was sacrificed or not, he should always remain with them."[22]

On June 30, 1863, the 1st District Colored Volunteers became the 1st Regiment United States Colored Troops (USCT), the first African American regiment mustered into federal service. No longer "volunteers," they were regular army soldiers. On that very day, the poet Walt Whitman wrote to his mother in his typical meandering prose that "There are getting to be *many black troops*—there is one very good reg't here black as tar—they go armed, have the regular uniform—they submit to no nonsense—others are constantly forming—it is getting to be a common sight." After visiting Camp Greene, he concluded that "no one can see them, even under these circumstances—their military career in its novitiate—without feeling well pleas'd with them." When the 1st USCT reached its full strength of one thousand men, Birney turned over field command to Colonel John H. Holman, a Maine native and ardent abolitionist. Now a general, Birney focused on recruiting and training African American regiments and was engaged in raising a brigade comprising several regiments from Washington and Baltimore, assuring Secretary of War Stanton that he could "raise a regiment in less than ten days." The hands-on Lincoln personally monitored Birney's recruitment efforts in specific states and counties.[23]

Emblematic of the regiment's mission, as well as the changing character of the war, the marching song that their new commander wrote began, "Let the North rally forth / In resistless might. / Let her send her legions forth / For liberty and rights!" Liberty and rights did not go hand in hand, however, and the 1st Regiment suffered the kinds of racial discrimination that were endemic to the USCT. When raising three regiments in Massachusetts, Governor John Andrew had deferred to the War Department's insistence on white officers. In a compromise, Andrew was allowed to appoint African American chaplains as officers, as long as they wore simple black suits instead of uniforms. Already the 1st USCT's unofficial chaplain, Henry McNeal Turner sought a formal appointment before the soldiers deployed. Armed with the endorsement of Birney and Holman, as well as five of Washington's black and white ministers, he submitted his application to Stanton. After "having been kept in suspense for some time," he wrote to Stanton again, not only reiterating his own request but demanding to know "ONCE FOR ALL whether it is the intention of the government to have colored chaplains or not." A month later, after Secretary of the Treasury Salmon Chase and Lincoln's friend Illinois representative Owen Lovejoy interceded on his behalf, Turner received Stanton's assent. Major Augusta encountered similar resistance. After the USCT transferred him to Maryland as a Senior Surgeon, half a dozen white officers objected to serving under him. While professing to support "the elevation and improvement of the Colored race," they refused to "willingly compromise what we consider a proper self respect." In response, the War Department assigned Augusta to "detached duty" with no subordinates. He eventually attained the brevet rank of lieutenant colonel, making him the highest-ranking African American officer to serve during the Civil War.[24]

When Lincoln named Turner the 1st USCT's chaplain in September 1863, he became one of only fourteen African American chaplains appointed during the entire war. The remaining 119 chaplains serving USCT units were white. Although commanded by white officers, throughout their service the 1st Regiment looked to Turner as their spiritual leader. His primary role was presiding over religious services, visiting his men in the army hospitals, comforting the dying, and sanctifying the dead. During his two years of military service, Turner was also a regular correspondent of the *Christian Recorder*, the official journal of the AME Church, published in Philadelphia. He recounted the regiment's combat experiences, advocated racial equality inside and outside the army, and commented on military affairs and national politics, providing a rare African American perspective on the war. Chafing at the lack of a uniform, he petitioned Secretary of War Stanton to provide insignia for regimental chaplains, because "not having any badge or mark by which we are known, subjects us to a thousand inconveniencies, especially at Hospitals where we are the most needed, unless the guards know us personally, we are often treated below a private, not allowed to enter where we have important business, and some times driven away." Turner shared in all of the soldiers' trials and victories, both under fire and in camp, many of them unique to the USCT. Among other tribulations, after joining his regiment near the front in Portsmouth, Virginia, he immediately contracted smallpox, probably while attending a sick soldier. "For many days we thought we had lost him," one of the men wrote, "he having been reported several times as dead. But God raised him up." After a three-month leave, Turner served with the regiment during their six battles in Virginia, including Wilson's Wharf, Petersburg, and Fair Oaks, and their five engagements in North Carolina, including two at Fort Fisher. They took part in Sherman's march through North Carolina, which culminated in General Joseph Johnston's surrender. A Washington resident later recalled "the cries of the newspaper boys, who used to shout, after any battle in which the colored men were engaged, 'the colored troops fought nobly.' "[25]

African American soldiers endured racial discrimination from both the Union and Confederate armies. The Militia Act of 1862 set black privates' pay at $10 a month, minus a $3 clothing allowance. White privates received $13 a month, plus a $3.50 allowance. White chaplains received $100 a month, while African American chaplains received a private's pay. The 54th and 55th Massachusetts regiments rejected their state's offer to supplement their pay and refused to accept any salary until they were paid equally. As protests mounted, soldiers in the 3rd South Carolina Infantry stacked their arms, refusing to serve until they received equal treatment. The army executed their leader, Sergeant William Walker, for mutiny. As chaplain of the 1st Regiment USCT, Turner counseled the men to serve patiently but used the columns of the *Christian Recorder* to register a public protest. After their conspicuous service at Wilson's Wharf, he wrote, "The universal expression among the white soldiers was, *That it was a burning shame for the Government to keep these men out of their full pay.*" With typical candor, Turner declared that "I do not care if Congress and the entire administration see the remark."[26]

Secretary of State Seward advised African Americans to serve without regard to "pay or place." When Secretary of War Stanton submitted an equal-pay bill, the Senate refused to pass it. Frederick Douglass, who was recruiting soldiers and whose three sons were serving in the army, campaigned forcefully for equal treatment. In August 1863, he visited the White House to discuss the inequities. Citing "popular prejudice" against arming black soldiers, Lincoln defended the lower pay. He told Douglass that African American enlistment "could not have been successfully adopted at the beginning of the war," and that the public still "needed talking up" before they would accept racial equality in the army. Lincoln reasoned that "the fact that they were not to receive the same pay as white soldiers seemed a necessary concession to smooth the way to their employment at all as soldiers, but that ultimately they would receive the same." As Lincoln predicted, Congress equalized the pay for enlisted men in June 1864. His meeting with Lincoln convinced Douglass that "slavery would not survive the war." While visiting Washington, however, Douglass discovered that as an African American even he needed a pass to travel freely. The secretary of the interior and Senator Samuel Pomeroy provided one that Lincoln endorsed on the day that he met with Douglass. "The bearer of this, Frederick Douglass, is known to us as a loyal, free, man, and is, hence, entitled to travel, unmolested," it read. "We trust that he will be recognized everywhere, as a free man, and a gentleman."[27]

As soldiers, African Americans faced a unique danger, execution or enslavement if captured. In June 1863, the Union halted all prisoner exchanges to protest the Confederacy's threatened execution of black troops and their white officers. In July, Lincoln issued an executive order pledging to execute one Confederate prisoner for every African American soldier killed in violation of the recognized laws of war. After their surrender at the Battle of Fort Pillow in Tennessee in April 1864, African American soldiers were executed, reenslaved, and forced to labor on Confederate fortifications. The exact number is unknown, but Confederate general Nathan Bedford Forrest boasted, "The river was dyed with the blood of the slaughtered for 200 yards." Still, Lincoln could not bring himself to enforce his retaliation order. "Having determined to use the negro as a soldier, there is no way but to give him all the protection given to any other soldier," he reiterated. "The difficulty is not in stating the principle, but in practically applying it." As he explained to Frederick Douglass, he considered his retaliation order a "terrible remedy" and "very difficult to apply— that, if once begun, there was no telling where it would end." The legalistic Lincoln did not want to punish soldiers for crimes committed by others. None of Lincoln's cabinet members advised executing enemy prisoners arbitrarily, unless the Confederate government officially acknowledged the massacre. Although the 1st Regiment USCT adopted the popular battle cry "Remember Fort Pillow," Turner insisted on the humane treatment of Confederate prisoners.[28]

Perhaps because of their prominence as the 1st USCT, the regiment attracted recruits from twenty-two states and five foreign countries. Fewer than one-tenth of the enlisted men were born in the District, while over one-half originated in the Confederacy, reinforcing the power of African American military recruitment to undermine southern slavery. Two-fifths of the enlistees were born in Virginia, but eight other Confederate states were represented. Turner continued his recruitment efforts while stationed in North Carolina, which contributed one-tenth of the regiment's total strength. The Border States, primarily Maryland, contributed almost one-third of the men, mostly former slaves. One in twenty hailed from ten free states, ranging from New York and Massachusetts to North Dakota and California, but primarily Pennsylvania. Thirteen soldiers were born in Canada or Latin America. The recruits from the District reflected the capital's traditional occupational segregation. More than one-half of them were laborers or waiters before enlisting. Overall, laborers represented about one-fourth of the regiment and waiters about one-tenth, but the predominant occupation was farming, accounting for about three in ten of the recruits. By the time they were mustered out in October 1865, the 1st Regiment had lost 185 men, including five officers, a 15 percent fatality rate, almost two-thirds of which resulted from disease.[29]

The enactment of a comprehensive conscription law in March 1863 reiterated both Lincoln's commitment to total warfare and the incorporation of African American men into the military. The Enrollment Act mandated the enrollment of all male citizens, without reference to race, between the ages of twenty and forty-five, including immigrants who had applied for citizenship. African American leaders, including Henry McNeal Turner, supported the provision that subjected black men to conscription, and Turner himself was drafted five months later. The act therefore established the principle of universal eligibility for military service as an essential obligation of citizenship. (Attorney General Bates had declared African Americans U.S. citizens in November 1862.) In response to the soaring price of substitutes, the new law allowed draftees to commute their service by paying a commutation fee of $300, which was meant to keep the cost of substitutes below that level. The loyal states were divided into 185 enrollment districts, in each of which an enrollment board identified eligible draftees, held a draft lottery, and exempted recruits on the basis of physical disability or personal hardship.[30]

The Enrollment Act governed the last six troop calls of the war, which were designed to raise an astounding 1,685,000 men between June 1863 and December 1864. Despite its coercive features, including the suspension of the writ of habeas corpus, the draft spared most eligible recruits. The enrollment boards exempted a majority of the men of military age through disability—they recognized forty-one specific infirmities—or personal hardship. The commutation feature was immensely popular, and a majority of draftees paid the $300 fee in place of serving. States and communities continued to fill most of their quotas by raising volunteers through bounties and appeals to patriotic duty and local or personal pride. "What young man of this generation," a Washington newspaper asked, "will not be ashamed to own to his children and grandchildren that he had no part or lot in the imperishable glory which will enshrine the names and memories of those who risked all in this holy cause?" The draft was therefore more an inducement to enlist volunteers than an effective conscription mechanism. During the entire war, only 13 percent of Union soldiers were draftees or substitutes. In February 1864, Congress revised the Enrollment Act to incorporate all African American troops into the regular army as members of the USCT rather than in state militia units. In this fashion, conscription, a creation of military necessity, promoted broad public acceptance of African American soldiers by helping states and communities fulfill their quotas and, above all, saving white men from the draft.[31]

CHAPTER EIGHTEEN

"Defend What Is Our Own"
The Limits of Freedom

I N T H E wake of the Emancipation Proclamation, tens of thousands more fugitive slaves sought freedom in the national capital. James Wadsworth's successor as commander of the Washington Military District, General John H. Martindale, initially lacked his predecessor's emancipationist zeal and allowed conditions at Camp Barker to deteriorate. In December 1862, a new outbreak of smallpox forced the camp's school to close. During its first six months, nearly one-tenth of Camp Barker's contrabands had died, including one-half of its hospital patients, at the rate of five a day. During January 1863, five hundred more contrabands arrived, doubling the population of the camp. The death toll resulted in the transfer of Freedmen's Hospital to the army's medical director. After the NFRA replaced the camp's physician with one of its own members, Dr. Daniel Breed, a longtime Washington abolitionist and Quaker reformer, mortality in the hospital fell from one-half to one-fifth. Losing faith in Danforth Nichols's administration, Martindale recruited Captain James I. Ferree, a Methodist minister and chaplain at Fortress Monroe's U.S. General Hospital, as military commander of Camp Barker. Ferree had earned the trust of the contrabands at Fortress Monroe, who called him "Captain Free." Amid all the turmoil in the camp, Nichols, Ferree, and Breed clashed. Martindale tried to defuse the conflict by replacing Breed with Major Alexander Augusta as the camp's physician. Augusta's appointment put Ferree in a quandary. "Knowing that Dr Agusta ranked as Major, & that I ranked only as Captain," he reported to Stanton, "I felt at a loss as to what I should do, doubting my right to assign to duty an officer who ranked me."[1]

In the same way that the army decentralized medical care away from Washington, Nichols proposed establishing a new contraband camp south of the Potomac on the Virginia side. Camp Barker could not provide the "preparatory training and guardianship" that he felt the former slaves needed to prepare them for freedom. He believed that the current policy of "scattering them among the whites generally" would do nothing to remold their character and "elevate the race." Instead, he suggested establishing a farm where companies of three hundred to five hundred contrabands would learn the "arts of life," replacing the culture of dependence that the fugitives brought into the camp with a spirit of self-reliance. Only then would they be "pushed out into the world to fill their places in society." Chief Quartermaster Elias M. Greene, a New Yorker, endorsed the proposal as "a scheme to give employment to all of the Contrabands in this Department, and make such employment profitable both to them, and to the Government." In May 1863, he oversaw the transfer of contrabands from Camp Barker across the Potomac to abandoned farms in Virginia. In the "pure country air," they would live as families, plant crops to feed themselves, and learn a new culture of freedom. Within a month, six hundred contrabands were raising vegetables, hay, and corn at seven Virginia farms scattered around three new contraband camps: Camp Rucker, Camp Wadsworth, and Camp Springdale, which was situated just south of Arlington House on the Lees' estate. Nichols left Camp Barker to become superintendent of the new "Contraband Farms." Camp Barker retained only convalescent women and children who could not work on the farms, leaving Freedmen's Hospital its only functional remnant, under the care of Dr. Augusta. In response to a call to donate blankets and clothing for the patients, Dr. Breed's wife, Gulielma, who was active in the NFRA, collected the items.[2]

Conditions in the Virginia camps were at first abysmal, with two or three families sharing a single tent. Farming former slave plantations for $10 a month minus the cost of shelter, clothing, and even the food that they grew themselves, all the while "protected" by a mounted guard, the fugitives could not "see much difference between this condition and their former one," according to the contrabands' physician. When the "government farms" proved profitable, generating a reported $80,000 a year, Nichols decided to create a more permanent village consisting of one-and-a-half-story wooden houses, each accommodating four families. Every family occupied one room with its own door leading outside, and a common chimney served the four apartments. Greene added two more farms totaling 900 acres and planned to grow vegetables for the military hospitals. Workshops would allow the fugitives to produce manufactured items, including baskets and clothing, during the winter months when they were not farming. In September, Greene went to New York to buy cloth for the 879 contrabands to turn into clothing, including uniforms for themselves. Thus, the new Freedman's Village on the Lee estate at Arlington Heights was born.[3]

Meanwhile, Camp Barker languished in neglect. The contrabands dug a well to provide drinking water and to supply the laundry. Dr. Augusta believed that the well water was contributing to disease in the camp, which was located on an old cemetery. His request for access to Potomac water from the recently completed Washington Aqueduct went unanswered. During the second half of 1863, nearly five hundred fugitives died at Camp Barker. Beyond the neglect, in June 1863 competition with contrabands produced an ugly conflict with white teamsters, who kept their wagons in nearby "wagon parks." Gathering at midnight, twenty teamsters lit a bonfire near Camp Barker, which was a prearranged signal for an attack on a foraging party of contrabands. Carrying pistols, the mob of teamsters stoned the fugitives with slingshots, wounding several, two of them nearly fatally. Notoriously "desperate and unprincipled," many of the teamsters were Union and Confederate deserters who refused to take the oath of allegiance and lost their jobs as a result. "There is no cause alleged for these deadly assaults upon these people," the *National Republican* reported, "but the fact that they have black skins." In December 1863, the government decided to close Camp Barker, move its residents to the Virginia farms, and maintain a "small depot" in Washington to receive and process contrabands. "So complete are the arrangements now for their reception," the *Chronicle* reported, "that promptly on their arrival at Col. Greene's headquarters, they are conveyed to Freedman's Village, and from that moment they are in the charge of the Government."[4]

As the contraband children prepared to move from their temporary tents to the permanent village, they recited a poem written expressly for the event:

> To Freedmensville we soon shall go, / And there
>   still let the people know
> That we have minds that do expand / Beyond the
>   scope of "Contraband."
> Oh, "Contraband!" that lawyer's crook, / By
>   which Ben Butler (wise in look)
> Took us from slavery, and then / Full hearts
>   rushed forth to greet us—"men."
> And men we'll be in all respects, / Nor will we
>   yield to base neglects.
> We will defend what is our own, / And look for
>   help to Father's throne.

On December 3, 1863, as cannons boomed to emphasize the military character of the enterprise, Superintendent Nichols presided over the formal dedication of Freedman's Village. The event attracted a flood of congressmen and other visitors from Washington, armed with passes and riding in carriages and ambulances that came "jolting and rattling" over the Aqueduct Bridge. They found a literal village, whose main street gave the settlement its horseshoe pattern. Connecting with Hamlin Street were Lincoln Park, Seward Park, Stanton Street, Rucker Street, School Street, and Wadsworth Row. The village, which claimed over one thousand contrabands, contained fifty houses, with room for two hundred families, a building with five hundred seats that doubled as a school and a church, and a massive 72-by-30 foot, two-story barracks to accommodate infirm and aged contrabands who could no longer work—"the halt, the lame, the maimed, and the blind." In effect an almshouse for the indigent, the Providence Home for Aged and Infirm Freedmen was administered by the American Tract Society and named in honor of the $1,000 donation from the residents of Providence, Rhode Island, that made it possible. (The Quartermaster's Department dismissively called the inmates "infirm old darkies.")[5]

The schoolhouse, funded by the American Tract Society, the Boston School Board, and the government, eventually admitted up to nine hundred children during the day, who studied reading, writing, arithmetic, and geography. Adults, up to 125 in number, attended night school on Mondays, Wednesdays, and Fridays. The quaintly named "tailor shop" was a large workshop where 140 women and girls sewed clothing when not engaged in farming. Inside, according to one visitor, "the girls are being taught the use of the sewing-machine and the needle by some young ladies from the North." A dozen of the ninety or so contrabands operated machines, but most of them sat on wooden benches sewing by hand for eight hours a day. For their six-and-a-half-day workweek, the "sewing girls" earned $6 a month plus board. The army erected a carpentry shop to employ the men. Freedman's Village later boasted a small, fifty-bed hospital, Abbott Hospital, an orphanage, and its own water system, complete with fireplugs. During the winter, the contrabands harvested ice from the village's reservoir for the military hospitals, which was essential during the summer to preserve bodies until interment. During January 1864, the contrabands stockpiled 800 tons of ice for the hospitals and 150 tons for their own use.[6]

In his address, Nichols emphasized the healthfulness of the community, which had experienced only ten deaths during the preceding month, a mortality of less than 1 percent. Overall, the move from Camp Barker to Freedman's Village reduced the daily death rate from five to two. To accommodate the residents of Camp Barker at Freedman's Village, in January 1864 Colonel Greene began building new houses on the original four-room plan on Arlington Heights, newly renamed Greene Heights in his honor. Four-fifths of the 650 residents of Camp Barker, however, refused to move to Freedman's Village, preferring to remain in Washington near family and friends.

The government farms' appearance and management reminded them of nothing so much as a prewar southern plantation. Some of the contrabands told a missionary that "they would rather starve in Washington than go to Arlington to be under Nichols." One former resident informed the government that "Mr Nichols was not kind to the people under him in the camp; he used to knock them about and kick them right smart." According to William Slade, president of Washington's Social, Civil, and Statistical Association, the contrabands considered Nichols "better suited to an overseer of a Southern Plantation." The 1st Regiment's recruitment officer, Thomas Hinton, publicly denounced Nichols as a "perfect tyrant" for turning away elderly fugitives. "I'll follow him up, if I live and have the power," Hinton pledged. "The brute beast! He is paid to take care of those poor people. They are treated like dogs over there. Hear that, Uncle Sam?" Even after the Quartermaster's Department tore down Camp Barker's buildings, more than five hundred of its residents continued camping in the area, "homeless, helpless, and starving," according to the NFRA. Financed by the Contraband Fund and a 1 percent "hospital tax," the newly renamed Freedmen's Hospital and Asylum moved into a vacated military facility, Campbell Hospital, which had been built a year earlier. After the war, the Freedmen's Bureau absorbed Freedmen's Hospital as part of its mission to provide medical care to former slaves. In 1869, Howard University's Medical School, which Alexander Augusta helped to found, assumed control and turned it into a teaching hospital.[7]

CONCEIVING OF freedman's village as a "little colony," Nichols and Greene were determined to impose order, instill discipline, and above all ensure that the camp paid for itself and indeed produced a profit. The camp's highest priority was clearly labor. Under the detailed regulations that governed the village, "The Superintendent of Contrabands will without delay select the most intelligent of the young men and women and assign them to duty in the workshops; have the able-bodied field hands transferred to the superintendent of Government farms; send the children to school; the sick to hospital, and the aged and infirm to the home provided for them." Able-bodied men were required to work for ten hours every day, either on the nine farms surrounding the village or in the workshops, for $10 a month, $5 of which went into the Contraband Fund. Women earned $6 a month. A running account kept track of their "credits"—the number of days they labored—and their "debits," which included rations, clothing, fuel, and their quarters, for which they paid a monthly rent of $1 to $3. (Nichols himself admitted, "They work hard but their wages are all taken for board, cooking utensils &c.") Able-bodied adults who refused to work were reported to the superintendent, "who shall take steps as will insure obedience to these regulations."[8]

The contrabands could only be hired out with their consent, and only to potential employers who guaranteed to treat them fairly and employ them for at least a year, under penalty of a $100 fine. Residents needed a pass to leave the village, however, and after leaving to work for another employer were forbidden to return without proof that they were treated "cruelly or unjustly" or had been defrauded. Nichols did his best to match contrabands with employers who made specific requests, such as "a bright mulatto boy about twelve years old," "a girl from 12 to 13 years of age (black colored preferred) to act as household servant," and "either an aged couple without children, or a woman with a half grown boy." In the camp, corporal punishment was forbidden. "Mild offenses" earned a "reproof" from the superintendent, while "idleness or disposition to shrink from labor, or untidiness or uncleanliness in person or habitation" resulted in the withholding of passes and sugar rations for five days.[9]

During its lifetime, Freedman's Village performed several functions. From a practical perspective, it provided a refuge for the growing number of fugitive slaves entering Washington in the wake of the Emancipation Proclamation. Symbolically, the camp was an experiment in liberty looming above the capital on Arlington Heights, visible from every part of the city. As one of the founders of the NFRA confided, he "never expected the experiment to be first tried upon the estate owned by the rebel Gen. Lee" and "believed that such contrasting scenes emanated from the workings of an all-wise Providence." Militarily, however, Freedman's Village grew in value as a supplier of labor and provisions for the increasingly insatiable Union Army engaged in total war. Superintendent Nichols and Chief Quartermaster Greene struggled to balance the welfare of the refugees, the symbolic importance of the village's location on the Lee estate, and the needs of the army. Nichols generally privileged the humanitarian mission of the camp, while Greene viewed it primarily as a military asset.[10]

Overprotective of the contrabands, the paternalistic Nichols often detained African American visitors whose legal status was ambiguous. Increasingly, however, Greene emphasized the profitability and military contributions of the camp at the expense of the contrabands' needs. At one point, he diverted enough clothing, including shoes, hats, and blankets, from the village to supply 1,500 contrabands working at the cavalry depot. On another occasion, he abruptly ordered Nichols to "have 48 shot bags made up, out of ticking, and sent in *tomorrow morning without fail.*" When Washington's hospitals needed additional nurses, Greene demanded thirty contrabands. "I do not ask if there are such *willing to go*, but whether there are thirty suitable persons," he told Nichols. "If so, the detail will be made whether they are willing or not. Answer at once." Greene later ordered Nichols to begin hiring out contrabands with dependents whenever possible to "entirely relieve the government of the charge of the family." As trees grew scarce in Virginia, Greene prohibited the contrabands from cutting firewood on the Arlington estate without special permission, a decision that he announced in the dead of winter. He shipped in firewood from Camp Convalescent but instructed Nichols to inform the contrabands, "with as much humanity as possible," that if they didn't pay for the wood they must leave the village. "Their sufferings are most heart rending," one visitor wrote. "The weather is cold; they have little or no wood." In February 1863, the contrabands grew so desperate for fuel that a local African American acquired one of the "Quaker guns" from Manassas—a log painted black to resemble a cannon—and donated it to be cut into firewood.[11]

Reflecting these military priorities, a reporter who visited Freedman's Village in April 1864 observed little evidence of order or industry, finding a "jumble of houses," a proliferation of tree stumps, "an inexcusable absence of gardens," and unimproved streets bearing grandiose names. "The hills upon which the village is situated abounds in beds of gravel, which should be used for the improvement of the streets, and especially the sidewalks," he complained. Tree stumps obstructed the roads, rendering them nearly impassable. "Grubbing is a branch of civil engineering with which the inhabitants are particularly well acquainted," he wrote with condescension, "and it would not be a hardship to require them to remove the stumps and roots in front of their doors." Sidewalks, shops, grid-like streets, and garden plots to produce vegetables and flowers would have made the spot more livable. Instead, the village bore a "camp-like appearance in which no one has anything to do." Still, the reporter had to admit that the residents "feel perfectly secure where they are, and are apprehensive that in leaving they would run the risk of being taken back into slavery." Under Nichols's supervision, Freedman's Village had one final role to play. In March 1864, the Quartermaster's department informed Nichols that 407 former slaves had arrived from the Île à Vache off Haiti and would arrive the next day. In December 1862, Lincoln had signed a contract to fund a colony of five thousand African Americans there. Proponents of the plan included his emigration commissioner, James Mitchell; Republican Senators Samuel Pomeroy of Kansas and James Doolittle of Wisconsin; James Holly, an African American Episcopal priest; the Haitian government; and the Île à Vache's self-styled "governor," who was in reality a land developer. Operating under the aegis of the Preliminary Emancipation Proclamation, which urged voluntary colonization to make emancipation more palatable to racial conservatives, Lincoln approved the plan. In April 1863, 453 former slaves, wearing Union army uniforms, sailed to the Île à Vache, supported mostly by private investors but also $50 apiece from the congressional emigration fund. Their plan was to create a self-sustaining and profitable community by growing cotton and cutting timber as citizens of the world's first self-governing black republic.[12]

After the colonists arrived, the Haitian government renounced the enterprise, dooming the Île à Vache colony to failure from its beginning. The island's governor refused to pay the wages that he had promised and actually borrowed money from the colonists, which he never repaid. The American investors fired him, leaving the colonists to fend for themselves and endure near-starvation and disease, including the smallpox that they brought with them, for more than three months. When they asked to return to the United States, Lincoln immediately sent a warship to rescue them and ordered that they "be employed and provided for at the camps for colored persons." Despite their year-long ordeal as the only government-sponsored colonists in American history, Greene ordered Nichols to treat them no differently from any other contrabands. "The returned Haytian Colonists are on just the same footing as other Freedmen," he decreed. "If they labor, they will be classed with laborers,—if not, they will be classed with dependent Freedmen." Within ten days of their arrival, Greene had forged an agreement with the Union Pacific Railroad to hire them as laborers. He insisted that the railroad pay all of their expenses at Freedman's Village and support their families as well. His goal was to "guarantee that aid to families will never hereafter be a burden upon the United States Government." Instead, most of the men, more than two hundred of them, enlisted in the Union Army. In fact, after he issued the Emancipation Proclamation and the recruitment of African American soldiers into the Union Army became imperative, Lincoln's interest in colonization diminished. Lack of interest, indeed hostility, among African Americans and the disastrous results of the Île à Vache experiment prompted him to abandon his public support for colonization as a concession to white racism. All told, Lincoln spent $38,000 on his colonization efforts, just 6 percent of the funds that Congress had provided. In June 1864, Congress rescinded its funding for colonization.[13]

After issuing the Emancipation Proclamation, Lincoln created a commission to study the fate of the former slaves and forge a policy for helping them adjust to freedom. Robert Dale Owen, a Scottish social reformer, chaired the Freedmen's Inquiry Commission. Owen had come to America in 1825 to found an experimental utopian community at New Harmony, Indiana. An outspoken abolitionist whom Lincoln considered "an intelligent, disinterested, and patriotic gentleman," Owen was a rare utopian who was also politically astute. He served two terms in the House of Representatives, where he wrote the bill that created the Smithsonian Institution, held an ambassadorial post under Franklin Pierce, and was uncannily attuned to Lincoln's strategic vision. Shortly before Lincoln issued his Preliminary Emancipation Proclamation, he received a letter from Owen urging him to free the slaves. Owen understood Lincoln's refusal to attack slavery as a moral wrong when he had no constitutional power to do so. "But the time has come when it *is* Constitutional to redress it," Owen insisted. "The rebellion has made it so. Property in man, always morally unjust, has become nationally dangerous." Owen's simple "abolitionist arithmetic" justified emancipation as a strategy to strengthen the Union and weaken the enemy. "You can declare emancipated his slaves, the suppliers of his commissariat," he reasoned. "Gradually you can deprive him of these; and for every hundred thousand productive laborers he loses, you may have a hundred thousand soldiers." Three days later, Lincoln issued his preliminary proclamation, which was designed to do just that.[14]

Labeling emancipation "one of the gravest social problems ever presented to a government," Owen's commission investigated the condition of former slaves in the District of Columbia and Union-occupied regions of the Confederacy. In June 1863, the commissioners, all of whom were abolitionists, reported that the contrabands were loyal, hardworking, peaceable, and temperate. Any deficiencies in their character were the temporary result of their enslavement and would quickly disappear once their rights were fully recognized, after which the typical contraband would learn "readily and quickly, to shift for himself." They therefore required only a brief period of "guidance and protection" before exercising their rights and enjoying their freedom. The commissioners praised and endorsed the employment of contrabands in farming abandoned lands, laboring for the army, and serving as soldiers—recommending the recruitment of "two hundred thousand or more colored troops"—as a genuine benefit for both the former slaves and the Union. Government aid was essential "for a season" but should be temporary only, rather than "a permanent institution." After the war, when the abandoned lands that they were farming became available for purchase, the contrabands should become landowners, working their own farms, which the commission considered their highest aspiration. The unequivocal recommendation was that "all 'contraband camps' (as they are usually called) be regarded as places of reception and distribution only," temporary way stations on the road leading from slavery to freedom that would provide "encouragement and direction" but not government support. Any program of long-term aid and supervision would perpetuate the slaves' traditional dependence, substituting the government in place of the soon-to-be-defunct institution of slavery.[15]

As the contraband camps' mission grew less humanitarian and more military in focus, Nichols lost much of his influence and indeed his relevance at Freedman's Village. In what must have seemed eerily reminiscent of Captain Ferree's earlier arrival at Camp Barker, in May 1864 Greene installed Captain Joseph M. Brown, his assistant quartermaster, to act as his "representative" at the village. Brown eventually replaced Nichols as superintendent of the camp, just as Ferree had superceded him at Camp Barker. (Brown later headed the army's "Freedmen's Department," the forerunner of the postwar Freedmen's Bureau.) Displaced from Freedman's Village by military authorities, in May 1864 Nichols moved to yet a third camp located inconspicuously on Mason's Island. The new camp was precisely the kind of "reception and distribution" camp that the Freedmen's Inquiry Commission had recommended. Holding about 1,200 contrabands, the same number as Freedman's Village, the camp occupied the barracks vacated by the 1st Regiment USCT when they deployed to Portsmouth, Virginia. Uninviting and unhealthy—subject to "malignant fevers of every type"—the Mason's Island settlement was not a village at all but a "hiring-out depot," which was by now the primary function of Washington's contraband camps. Awaiting dispersal, generally to the North, the residents performed no labor. With the completion of the fortifications around the capital in mid-1863, employment opportunities for contrabands in Washington diminished. During the last year of the war, only thirty-three contrabands found employment in the District of Columbia each month. Instead, Greene and Nichols began contracting out laborers in groups to large employers in the North, including state employment agencies and the Union

Pacific Railroad. "Very few single men are on the island," a visitor reported, "as they are disposed of as fast as they arrive." Separate barracks held single women, single men and boys, married women with children, and widowed women with families. The elderly and infirm were processed at Mason's Island and then sent to Providence Home at Freedman's Village. The camp comprised seven barracks, two hospital wards, a messhouse, a stable accommodating fifty horses, and a large icehouse. The Mason's Island depot, which never even acquired a name of its own, closed two months after the war ended. The dejected Nichols resigned as superintendent at the end of January 1865 and went to work as a clerk in the Treasury Department. He eventually resumed his humanitarian mission by working at Freedmen's Hospital, which he had helped to create as Superintendent at Camp Barker. In all, 11,000 contrabands had passed through the government camps in the Washington area over the course of the war.[16]

Beyond the founding of Freedmen's Hospital, the most visible legacy of Washington's contraband camps was the continuation of an African American community at Arlington. After the war, the Freedmen's Bureau took possession of the contraband camps. When wartime employment opportunities ended, the bureau discouraged migration to Washington and emphasized resettlement in the rural countryside and the Midwest. Freedman's Village, however, was more homelike than the other camps, and many of its residents wanted to stay. While abandoning most of the contraband camps, Congress viewed the symbolic value of former slaves living and laboring in freedom on the Lee estate as too valuable to forgo. The government allowed the residents to stay under "the direct understanding that they are to acquire no title to the land, and are to move when required." No longer "contrabands," they became "villagers" who farmed to feed themselves and worked for the government at nearby Fort Whipple or the new Arlington National Cemetery to pay the rent on their land and houses. As Washington grew, however, real estate developers coveted the land around Arlington as the site of potential suburban communities connected with the city by streetcar. Succumbing to the economic pressure to reclaim land on the former Arlington estate for private development and government use, in 1887 the War Department ordered the villagers to move, calling them "squatters on the reservation, who have no rights or privileges whatever there." The villagers, numbering 800 former slaves living in 170 families, challenged the decision but also requested $350 in compensation for each homeowner. Three years later, the government evicted the residents. In 1900, Congress allocated a total payment of $75,000 to the former villagers, in part to compensate them for their contributions to the wartime Contraband Fund. Most of the dispossessed villagers moved to other parts of Alexandria County. Construction of the Pentagon at the beginning of World War II obliterated the last vestiges of the wartime experiment embodied in Arlington's Freedman's Village.[17]

CHAPTER NINETEEN

"Never Forget What They Did Here"
Honoring the Fallen

———— ◆•◆•◆ ————

L IVING IN the White House, the Lincoln family was subject to many of the same trials that other Washington residents, both white and black, endured throughout the Civil War—separation, threats of violence, tests of loyalty, personal loss, disease, death, and mourning—all within the confines of a city under siege. Bound to the White House by the obligations of his office, the president could rarely escape the rigors of the war, personified by the horde of supplicants who continually lined the stairway leading up to his office, as well as the family friends who too often lay in state within the grandeur of the East Room. The First Lady, however, had recourse to both physical and mental refuges to muffle the booming cannons that the family could often hear echoing from the other side of the Potomac. Mary Lincoln could leave Washington on extended forays farther north and throw herself into the social swirl of the Washington scene that represented one of her primary functions as First Lady. As she explained to a friend before fleeing the White House in August 1861, just after the First Battle of Bull Run, "I have passed through so much excitement, that a change is absolutely necessary." Her northern forays lasted two, three, or four months at a time, and she was usually accompanied by one or more of her sons, as well as her closest female companions, at first Elizabeth Grimsley and later Elizabeth Keckly. Favoring summers to escape from Washington, she often combined shopping with recuperation in mountain resorts in New York and New Hampshire. When he could get away from Harvard College, Robert Lincoln would sometimes join his mother and brothers.[1]

Throughout these extended separations, Abraham and Mary Lincoln kept in constant contact, preferably by telegraph, usually to inquire about each other's health and safety and that of their sons. A typical note from Mary read, "Your telegram received. Did you receive my reply[?]" A typical reply from her husband read simply, "All doing well." So regular was their communication that any interruption was sure to produce anxiety. On one trip to New York, for example, Mary wrote the president impatiently that "I have waited in vain to hear from you, yet as you are not *given* to letter writing, will be charitable enough to impute your silence, to the right cause." She followed this indulgent tone with a mild rebuke: "Strangers come up from W- & tell me you are well." On a later trip, she telegraphed Lincoln, "Do let me know how Taddie and yourself are," but then promptly telegraphed the White House doorkeeper, "Let me know immediately exactly how Mr. Lincoln and Taddie are." The preoccupied president was clearly less communicative, and Mary might send a succession of messages before receiving a reply, as when he wrote, "Your three despatches received. I am very well; and am glad to know that you & 'Tad' are so." Increasingly, however, Mary Lincoln wrote to ask her husband to send money, as when she telegraphed from New York City, "We reached here in safety. Hope you are well. Please send me by mail to-day a check for $50."[2]

When in Washington, Mary performed another of her functions as First Lady, holding the traditional White House levees and receptions that were overseen by the secretary of state. After losing his struggle with Mary Lincoln to control the White House social schedule, John Nicolay wrote derisively to his fiancée that " 'La Reine' has determined to abrogate dinners and institute parties in their stead. How it will work remains to be seen." Mary scheduled the first of three planned receptions for February 5, 1862. The large, public gathering was meant to show off the lavish renovations to which she had devoted the White House budget—and more. "Half the city is jubilant at being invited," John Hay quipped with seeming satisfaction, "while the other half is furious at being left out in the cold." When Senator Benjamin Wade, chairman of the Joint Committee on the Conduct of the War and a leading critic of Abraham Lincoln, received his invitation, he asked, "Are the President and Mrs. Lincoln aware that there is a civil war?" He then declined the invitation. In the end, the Lincolns expanded the guest list to make the affair even more inclusive and paid for it out of the president's private funds. Undeterred, Mary prepared a flowing white silk dress with bare shoulders and a plunging back in the style of the French empress Eugénie, the true "La Reine" and the current exemplar of European fashion. Critics joined Senator Wade in faulting her for holding a gala in the midst of a bloody and costly civil war. When her son Willie fell sick on that very day, she took it as divine retribution for her heedless pride and extravagance.[3]

Both Willie and Tad contracted typhoid fever, probably through the new plumbing that piped Potomac River water into their bedrooms—from the reservoirs that held the decaying bodies of Union soldiers—or the pestilent canal that flowed, and sometimes overflowed, literally in their own backyard. That winter, Washington's physicians labeled the canal more pestilent than ever, and Benjamin Brown French, the commissioner of public buildings, warned that the "canal has been very rapidly filling up during the past year, and never has been in anything like so offensive a state as it now is." Tad eventually recovered from the typhoid, but Willie had suffered measles and scarlet fever the previous winter, which undoubtedly weakened his immune system and left his body more susceptible to the ravages of the disease. Both parents sat by his bedside almost constantly during his two-week illness. Visiting the White House, Dorothea Dix discovered that the Lincolns were personally caring for their children, with the assistance of "poor old aunt Mary, a colored nurse." The Lincolns' nurse was Mary Dines, the runaway slave from Maryland who had crossed over into Washington before the war. Dines had left the Island and taken refuge at Camp Barker, quite probably for her own protection. President Lincoln, Dines later reminisced, frequently stopped "to visit and talk" with the fugitive slaves at Camp Barker. Dines was a talented soprano who led the former slaves in song as Lincoln listened. "He was no President when he came to camp," she emphasized. "He just stood and sang and prayed just like all the rest of the people." On one occasion, according to Dines, the former slaves sang "Swing Low, Sweet Chariot," "Go Down, Moses," "Been in the Storm So Long," and other spirituals and hymns. "President Lincoln actually joined in singing every piece," according to her reminiscence, "and he was so tenderhearted that he filled-up when he went over to bid the real old folks good-by." Dines became the Lincolns' cook and, in the midst of their medical crisis, their only nurse. After a year of sending Maryland fugitives back to their owners to appease secessionists, the president had now taken one of their runaway slaves into his own home.[4]

Physicians urged Lincoln to accept more help, so he asked Dix to provide the services of a good nurse. Dix recommended Rebecca Pomroy, who was still nursing at the old Union Hotel Hospital. Lincoln asked Dix to assign Pomroy to the White House for two weeks. When she arrived, she found Willie near death and his little brother Tad "tossing with typhoid." After Willie's death, the grief-stricken Lincoln murmured, "My poor boy, he was too good for this earth," and declared, "It is hard, hard to have him die!" The boy's body lay in state in the Green Room for four days before a funeral procession carried him to the Congressional Cemetery. Pomroy remembered the half-mile-long funeral train—"the hearse, drawn by two white horses; the President's carriage, drawn by two black horses; the secretaries and their families, a large number of private carriages, and last of all, the colored help." Mary Lincoln could not bring herself to attend the funeral, but Lincoln did and wept openly. Both parents suffered dreadfully when Willie died, but Abraham Lincoln had a war to manage and returned to work after two days of grieving. The devout Rebecca Pomroy consoled Lincoln as Tad recovered from the disease that had claimed his brother. Calling her "one of the best women I ever knew," out of gratitude Lincoln asked Secretary of War Stanton to promote her son to second lieutenant. Still, Lincoln's grief took its physical toll on his usually robust physique. "His hair is grizzled, his gait more stooping, his countenance sallow," a reporter observed, "and there is a sunken, deathly look about the large cavernous eyes." Long after Lincoln forced himself back to work, his wife practiced mourning with a vengeance. She well knew the Christian consolation literature that enjoined survivors to place their faith in God and look forward to a heavenly reunion with the departed, condemning excessive mourning as evidence of a doubter's lack of faith. Such a refusal to submit to God's will was itself a defiant act of pride. Still, she blamed herself for holding the gala reception and feared that Willie's death was the result of her own self-indulgence. Succumbing to "paroxysms of grief," she spent the next three weeks virtually incapacitated in bed. According to Elizabeth Keckly, who emerged as Mary's closest companion during this period of prolonged mourning, Lincoln—himself devastated by Willie's death—led his wife to a window, pointed out St. Elizabeth's insane asylum, and implored her, "Mother, do you see that large white building on the hill yonder? Try and control your grief, or it will drive you mad, and we may have to send you there."[5]

Mary Lincoln grieved with abandon. Banishing all mementoes of Willie from the White House, she collected all of his belongings and shipped them back to Springfield. "Please keep the boys home the day of the funeral," she instructed the Tafts; "it makes me feel worse to see them." In fact, she excluded Tad's playmates, Bud and Holly Taft, from the White House forever. (In their place, Tad befriended Perry Kelly, whose father was a tinner on Pennsylvania Avenue.) Although mourning manuals called for no more than six months of "deep mourning" for the loss of a child, Mary Lincoln observed first-degree mourning for an entire year. She ordered lavish mourning regalia, including black crepe dresses, bonnets, and veils, and even black jewelry, from the suppliers of mourning goods that had proliferated as the wartime casualties mounted. Then she entered six months of half-mourning, wearing gray at first, followed by lavender and eventually a "touch of white at the wrist." Her sister Elizabeth Edwards came from Springfield to console her and observed with understatement that "Mary is so constituted as to present a long indulgence of such gloom." Imposing her own grief on the wartime city, she forbade the Marine Band from performing its traditional Saturday afternoon concerts on the South Lawn for over a year.[6]

Mary Lincoln gradually overcame the depths of her grief, what she termed her two-year-long "fiery furnace of affliction," and on New Year's Day 1864 shed her mourning garb at last. Resolving to restore the conviviality and optimism of the early war years, the Lincolns celebrated the New Year with an evening levee that surpassed, by all accounts, any of their previous social events. "Between the hours of 8 and 11 o'clock," the *National Republican* reported, "a steady stream of human beings, of all classes in society, the high and low, young and old, beautiful and ugly, rich and poor, bold misses and modest retiring maidens—to the number of about eight thousand, passed the President and Mrs. Lincoln and paid their respects." The First Lady was "never more richly and tastefully or more appropriately attired." The report declared, "We have not seen the President looking in better health than last night." The First Lady was determined to resume her role as White House hostess, recognizing that "My position, requires my presence, where my heart is *so far* from being." Her personal grief had prompted her to view the sacrifices of those around her, both individuals and the nation itself, from a fresh perspective. "I had become, so wrapped up in the world, so devoted to our political advancement," she observed, "that I thought of little else besides." Above all, she now focused on the health and safety of her remaining family members, husband Abraham and sons Tad and Robert. The war was taking a terrible toll on Abraham Lincoln, who told Harriet Beecher Stowe during her visit to the White House, "Whichever way it ends, I have the impression that I shan't last long after it's over."[7]

At the beginning of the war, Washington, DC, was no more prepared to bury and mourn its dead than were the Lincolns. In 1860, the city maintained only one general hospital, the City Infirmary, which treated 192 patients during the entire year. In 1864, at the peak of the fighting, Washington's hospitals were treating more than 18,000 soldiers at a time. In 1860, only 17 of the City Infirmary's patients died. In 1864, the army was burying almost 600 dead a month, and sometimes 60 a day. Incapable of even imagining the unprecedented toll that the war—let alone the next battle—would exact, the Union Army continually confronted burial of the dead as a disturbing but supreme necessity. During the first half of the nineteenth century,

Americans redefined the meaning of death. The colonial era's Calvinistic conception of death as an unavoidable expression of God's wrath gave way to the Second Great Awakening's promise of eternal salvation for the truly righteous. Rather than a tragic end to life on earth, death became the majestic beginning of a meeting with God and a reunion with loved ones.[8]

Mount Auburn Cemetery, established in Cambridge, Massachusetts, in 1831, symbolized Americans' reconception of death. Once confined to the dreary solitude of churchyards and family plots, interment took on a more hopeful and hallowed aspect that merited public commemoration in pleasant, pastoral surroundings. Popularizing the word "cemetery," which was derived from the Greek for "sleeping place," Mount Auburn was a memorial park where family members could gather to remember the dead, enjoy bucolic vistas, and even look forward to their own eventual interment as a reunion with the departed. This new and increasingly sentimental perspective on death emphasized the preservation, and even public display, of physical remains, as well as commemoration through permanent and often majestic headstones. Civil War soldiers carried these comforting expectations of a physical reunion with loved ones even as they entered battle in faraway and forbidding landscapes. One of the Civil War soldier's greatest dreads was dying alone and unidentified on a battlefield and spending eternity in an unmarked grave. In an era before dog tags, soldiers often pinned their own names to their uniforms before entering battle. As one soldier wrote home from his post in Virginia, "some how I have a horor of being thrown out in a neglected place or bee trampled on as I have seen a number of graves here."[9]

In the chaotic aftermath of a battle, that is exactly what happened to most of the fallen. On the rare occasions when Americans confronted mass deaths before the Civil War, expedience overcame sentimentality in the name of the common good. Cholera and yellow fever epidemics could leave bodies "lying piled on the ground, swollen and bursting their coffins, and enveloped in swarms of flies." The public's health demanded mass graves in shallow trenches, hurriedly covered over and unmarked. Similarly, throughout the Civil War, mass deaths generally necessitated mass burials. The Union Army was rarely prepared for the scope of the casualties each successive battle produced, treating them all as "emergencies." After First Bull Run, commanding officers were required to lay out burial plots complete with headboards, bearing names, if possible, but at least numbers. A register identified the graves in hopes of future reinterment or commemoration. A retreating army, like Lee's after Antietam, had to depend on the enemy to bury their dead, usually in mass graves, wrapped in blankets and unidentified. The 23,000 casualties at Antietam took ten days to bury. Always short on supplies, Confederate soldiers were known for stripping the Union dead of shoes and sometimes uniforms before burial. To bury its own dead, a defeated army had to request a flag of truce from the victors before returning to the battlefield with a burial detail, which could take one to three days to secure. Always anxious to follow up a victory, and even a defeat, with a new battle, after Cold Harbor Grant forced Lee to wait three days before recognizing a flag of truce. Lee was reportedly "on his knees begging for time to bury his dead," but Grant gave the Confederates twenty-four hours rather than the forty-eight they requested. Assignment to a burial detail was often considered a punishment, which mitigated against respectful treatment of the fallen. "They dig holes and pile them in like dead cattle," a soldier wrote somberly after the Battle of Shiloh, "and have teams to draw them together like picking up pumpkins."[10]

Receiving special treatment, officers' bodies were returned to their families whenever possible. (When not possible, officers and enlisted m en were interred in distinct mass graves.) Union officers who fell in battle were packed in charcoal, shipped to Washington, and then sent home in coffins by railroad, sometimes with an honor guard. The most famous retrieval brought General James Wadsworth home to New York from the Wilderness battlefield. Like many generals' deaths in battle, Wadworth's generated multiple accounts—an impausible eight in number—with a handful of Confederate soldiers claiming credit for the kill. Beyond dispute was the fatal wound to the head that splattered Wadsworth's brains over his aide, who assumed that the general had died instantly and left him lying on the field, along with the other 25,000 casualties of the Wilderness Campaign. A Confederate major discovered Wadsworth lying grievously wounded but still alive on the battlefield, pinned his name to his uniform, and ordered immediate treatment. At a makeshift field hospital, a captured Union Army surgeon attended him until he died two days after falling. Lee personally ordered his burial "by a large tree, the tree to be cut low and his name marked on it." The interment was meant to be temporary until the Union could retrieve the body. Four days later, Secretary of War Stanton ordered General George Gordon Meade, the commander of the Army of the Potomac, to try to retrieve Wadsworth's body, and those of other Union officers, from behind Confederate lines. Lee refused to grant a flag of truce but instead personally sent Major General Wade Hampton to convey Wadsworth's body to the Wilderness Church. Nine days after his death, the Union Army took possession of the remains, had them embalmed, and shipped them home. Lincoln told his secretary John Hay that "no man has given himself up to the war with such self-sacrificing patriotism as Gen¹ Wadsworth."¹¹

Ellsworth, Baker, and now Wadsworth—the deaths of three personal friends of the president set higher standards for the treatment of the Union dead. Ellsworth received acclaim as the first Union officer to fall and as one of the first beneficiaries of the infant science of embalming. Lincoln personally ordered that Ellsworth's body be embalmed by Dr. Thomas H. Holmes of Brooklyn, New York, widely recognized as the father of American embalming. Holmes had invented a new method of embalming corpses for dissection in medical schools without using dangerous chemicals, such as arsenic, mercury, and zinc. He now gained fame when newspapers reported that mourners were able to "take a farewell look at the remains" as Ellsworth lay in state in the White House, bearing both his Zouave uniform and "a pleasant and natural expression." Embalming gained immediate popularity, and Holmes contracted with three undertakers (two in Washington and one in Georgetown) to provide his services to the families and friends of Union soldiers. When Edward Baker died a few months later, Holmes gained additional renown for embalming his body. During the war, Holmes embalmed the remains of over four thousand soldiers. Embalming was available to only the wealthiest families, who paid $100 for the procedure and the cost of shipping the body home for viewing and burial. But newspaper readers also learned that Ellsworth's body was encased in an "expensive metallic coffin" of imitation rosewood. Such airtight zinc coffins allowed even unembalmed bodies to travel to their final resting places alongside their loved ones. The metallic coffins included a glass window over the face to facilitate viewing. The Adams Express Company began specializing in shipping the bodies of less celebrated soldiers home for burial. Two years later, the Staunton Transportation Company introduced a Transportation Case that used ice to create a "portable refrigerator" designed to preserve soldiers' bodies for the trip home, if not for eternity. Along with embalming, metallic coffins and express shipping allowed the families that were able to afford it a final glimpse of fallen soldiers in the comforting repose of "eternal slumber." The special treatment accorded officers such as Ellsworth and Wadsworth raised popular expectations for the return of the fallen to their families. "Concerning my husband's precious remains, if it is possible, how glad would I be to have him buried in the family burial-ground with his dear connections," one New York widow pleaded, "so that when I am done with the afflictions of this life, I can slumber sweetly by his side."[12]

The new science of embalming held out that promise. As casualties mounted, undertakers and embalmers competed fiercely for customers in the vulnerable throes of mourning. To demonstrate the superiority of his method, Holmes displayed the embalmed bodies of unknown soldiers and the body of a child. The Staunton Transportation Company not only shipped the dead but offered the services of "guides" and "exhumers" who promised to locate and retrieve long-buried bodies from distant battlefields. Disreputable embalmers were accused of preserving bodies without permission and then extorting exorbitant fees from grieving families. In late 1861, Holmes gained a competitor when the New York embalming firm of Brown and Alexander opened a parlor on Pennsylvania Avenue, practicing a rival method developed by a Frenchman, who used zinc chloride. His method purportedly gave the body a lustrous look akin to polished white marble. Brown and Alexander bought the American rights to the French method and received the Lincolns' endorsement in February 1862 when they chose the firm to embalm the remains of their cherished little Willie. "The embalmment was a complete success," the press reported, "and gave great satisfaction to all present." (Lincoln was said to have assuaged his grief by visiting Willie's crypt, opening the coffin, and gazing upon the lifelike visage of his son.) Holmes countered the favorable publicity for the French method by labeling his own method "no foreign invention, but purely American" and promising "No Poisons Used." But he was too late. Within days of Willie Lincoln's funeral, the War Department designated Brown and Alexander the official embalmers of the Union Army. They received the exclusive right "to march with the different columns of divisions of the army, and practice their profession in the field, when desired, to be remunerated by the friends of the deceased." The embalmers operated parlors in military camps for most of the war. (Before the institution of embalming in the field, disinterred bodies were shipped to Washington, embalmed, and then sent home.) At the same time, the government appointed an official undertaker, Frank T. Sands, to bury soldiers who were not embalmed and shipped home. Ominously, at $4.99 per burial, Sands was the low bidder.[13]

Sick and wounded soldiers who reached a general hospital had a 92 percent chance of surviving. Still, over the course of the war 87,000 soldiers died while undergoing treatment in Union Army hospitals. At the beginning of the war, Washington had one military cemetery, located at the Soldiers' Home three miles north of the White House. The government created the Soldiers' Home soon after the Mexican-American War as an asylum for disabled veterans. The main dormitory, Scott Hall, named after the general-in-chief who spearheaded the project, could accommodate 150 veterans. Four smaller buildings surrounded Scott Hall on the rustic and peaceful grounds. Previous first families had spent part of their summers at the Soldiers' Home, which sat on the highest point in the District of Columbia and was therefore the coolest and driest locale within commuting distance of the White House. Anderson Cottage, a fourteen-room Gothic Revival mansion on the grounds, was available for the Lincolns to occupy as they chose, but during their first summer in Washington the family elected to stay in the White House. In 1862, however, after Willie's death and the growing criticism of Mary's role in the White House, the Lincolns decided to summer at the Soldiers' Home. Mary Lincoln continued in mourning but benefited from the more pleasant surroundings that Willie had never inhabited. A half hour's carriage ride from the White House, the cottage became a welcome refuge from the heat, humidity, and germs of the city, as well as the lines of office and favor seekers who continued to plague the president. Lincoln made a daily commute on horseback or by carriage, arriving at the White House by 8:00 A.M. and returning in the evening, quite often after dusk. Here he found the kind of quiet solitude that he had always needed to think, reflect, and write, and here he produced his Emancipation Proclamation. He could also entertain his closest friends and advisors in privacy, read his favorite humorists—Petroleum V. Nasby, Artemus Ward, and Orpheus C. Kerr—and pore over his Bible, in which he increasingly sought wisdom and solace as the war progressed. Secretary of War Edwin Stanton also had a cottage on the grounds, and he became a close friend, trusted advisor, and confirmed admirer. All told, Abraham Lincoln spent three summers—thirteen months, or one-fourth of his presidency—commuting to and from the Soldiers' Home.[14]

The adjoining seven-acre cemetery was intended for veterans who died at the Soldiers' Home but soon became the resting place for the first five thousand soldiers who died in Washington's army hospitals. The Quartermaster's Department, which was responsible for burying soldiers and maintaining military cemeteries, kept detailed records. "The Soldiers' Burial Record" listed each soldier's name, age, citizenship, rank, company, original residence, marital status, nearest relative or friend, cause, date, and place of death, and the number of his burial plot. The registry encouraged the novel practice of relatives and friends coming to Washington to visit soldiers' graves. Death was not the ultimate sacrifice that any soldier could endure for the Union. There was one even greater—the unmarked grave. "Nameless are thousands of graves in this cruel war of the rebellion, scattered through the reedy swamps, among the mournful pines, and along the margins of the dark and sullen waters of the South," ran one mournful lament. Yet despite their best efforts, even Washington's military hospitals could not identify all of their dead. "The sad fact will not fail to be noticed that some of these soldiers are recorded as unknown," the *Daily Chronicle* conceded. "Despite every effort of the hospital attendants, they give no clue to their names or residences, nor can anything be found upon them betokening either, and many a brave soldier is laid in a lonely unknown grave."[15]

"The first duty of a Government is to protect the life of the soldier," the *National Republican* declared, while "the second is to give him honorable burial when he has fought his last battle." During the first two years of the war, the army too often fell short of meeting this second obligation. Washington's hospital chaplains bemoaned the inadequacy of the contract burial system. "Is it right to deliver the remains of those beloved ones of our country to such irresponsible characters as are employed by the undertaker to convey them to the place of interment?" Trinity Hospital's chaplain asked. Coffins were poorly constructed and difficult for the chaplains to seal. Military escorts often waited an hour for the "rickety" hearse to arrive and carry the coffins, sometimes stacked in a pile, to the cemetery. "The man who leaves all the endearments of home to serve his country in the hour of her peril, and who dies while in defence of her existence, should be buried decently," he concluded. "Anything short of this is a disgrace to the nation." In November 1862, the city's hospital chaplains created an Association of Chaplains and met to recommend improvements. They identified the contract bidding system as the primary culprit, reasoning that "the present undertaker furnished the shroud, the coffin, the vehicle, team and driver, had the grave dug and filled in, for all of which he only received $4.99." A single hearse made the rounds of all the city's twenty-five hospitals, carrying an average of twenty to thirty, and sometimes forty, coffins a day. The chaplains appointed a committee to make recommendations to the surgeon general and quartermaster general, who quickly announced that "an arrangement will be speedily made when a suitable coffin will be furnished for every deceased soldier, and a pall covered with the American flag, escort, and appropriate religious services at his funeral." Chaplains were assigned to the cemetery to perform burial rites. The War Department dismissed the government undertaker when his six-month contract expired and hired a new one. The reformed system used multiple hearses with cavalry escorting the flag-draped coffins to "well prepared" graves. At the beginning of 1864, the War Department ended the contract system and began burying its own dead.[16]

Another grievance was the proliferation of embalming parlors throughout the city. As both casualties and the popularity of embalming rose, the chemicals began appearing in apothecary's shops and the price of the procedure fell from $100 to $25 or $30. One competitive undertaker actually promised to perform the embalming for free. "The citizen of Washington can scarcely turn to the right or to the left," the *Chronicle* claimed, "but what is obtruded on his vision are the warning words, 'Embalming of the Dead.' " As the practice grew in scope, it became a health hazard, with the *Chronicle* complaining that "human bodies that have lain on the battle-field for several days, have been brought into the heart of the city and allowed to remain for forty-eight hours, while undergoing the 'embalming process.' " Labeling the embalming houses "stench-factories," the press asked, "Have these embalmers a right to ask such a sacrifice to their grim but profitable trade?" In June 1864, the Metropolitan Police acted and arrested Dr. Holmes himself for "creating a nuisance" by embalming bodies in the heart of the city. He went to jail with bail set at $300.[17]

The preservation of the dead became such a nuisance in the capital that the *Chronicle* ran a parody of Americans' newfound insistence on displaying departed family members in their homes. "Every one, however slightly acquainted with the family, may enter the house, and see the locked coffin laid in state on the dining-room table, and look at the once familiar features through the oval glass put for that purpose on the lid of the coffin," the grisly spoof ran. "Sometimes in the case of children the funeral is long delayed, and a loving mother will ask you *months* after her child's death, to look at their sweet Sally? and on your look of surprise and astonishment, will add quietly: 'We take in an extra dime of ice and charcoal every day, and she is quite beautiful.' " Proximity to the dead was understandably comforting, but transporting coffins became such a burden for the express companies that they eventually refused to ship any remains without a "written guarantee that they have been properly embalmed." The Quartermaster's Department prohibited the disinterment of soldiers for reburial during the warm months, May through September. General Grant ordered all repellent coffins removed from trains headed north and ultimately banned embalmers from the battlefield entirely. The ideal solution was a national cemetery near Washington in which fallen soldiers and their families would feel honored to have their bodies repose, a "memorial park" for the nation's dead.[18]

GETTYSBURG NATIONAL cemetery set the pattern. After the Confederates' decisive victory at Chancellorsville in May 1863, General Lee proposed an invasion of Pennsylvania, similar in design to his invasion of Maryland a year earlier. Following the Shenandoah River northward, Lee's army crossed the Potomac in mid-June, stripping the southern Pennsylvania countryside of food, livestock, and horses and the towns of store goods and even bank deposits. They seized hundreds of African Americans as "fugitives" and forced them southward into slavery, "just like we would drive cattle," according to one witness. Defending the capital, General Hooker kept his army between Lee and Washington. Hesitating to attack Lee, however, he proposed attacking Richmond while Lee was in Pennsylvania. A disappointed Lincoln told Hooker that "I think *Lee's army*, and not *Richmond*, is your true objective point." When Hooker submitted his resignation, Lincoln accepted it and appointed General George Gordon Meade to command the Army of the Potomac. Meade obeyed Lincoln's order to move against Lee, and three days after he assumed command the armies met at Gettysburg, a railroad junction in southern Pennsylvania. During three days of fighting, July 1–3, the Union and Confederate forces suffered a total of 47,000 dead, wounded, and missing men.[19]

Losing one-third of his army, Lee could never again contemplate another invasion of the North and stayed on the defensive for the rest of the war. Just as he had exhorted McClellan to pursue Lee after Antietam, Lincoln now ordered Meade to "push forward, and fight Lee before he can cross the Potomac," but the general proved as overcautious as his predecessor. Lincoln viewed the Confederate invasion not so much as a defensive challenge for Washington and the North as an offensive opportunity to destroy the enemy's army. When the rain-swollen river trapped Lee's army on the Maryland side at Williamsport, Meade let the unexpected opportunity to counterattack slip away. "We had them in our grasp," an exasperated Lincoln swore. "We had only to stretch forth our hands & they were ours. And nothing I could say or do could make the Army move." He was so dismayed that his son Robert found him in his office "in distress, his head leaning upon the desk in front of him, and when he raised his head there were evidences of tears upon his face." Lincoln wrote a letter to Meade telling him that through his inaction "the war will be prolonged indefinitely," but he never sent it. Both Meade and Lee offered their resignations to their commanders-in-chief. Both Lincoln and Davis refused to accept them. A week later, the bodies of eight Confederate soldiers floated down the swollen Potomac toward Washington.[20]

In addition to the 21,000 wounded soldiers from both armies, the 2,400 residents of Gettysburg had to confront the 7,000 dead who dotted the landscape. Labeling the town "one vast hospital," local newspapers also reported with bitterness that the retreating Confederates had "left behind them six drunken, inefficient and worthless surgeons and 11,000 wounded." Most of the fallen had been buried by their own armies during the three days of fighting, many in shallow graves. The wounded lay for three weeks in the buildings at Gettysburg College and the Lutheran seminary on Seminary Ridge and in churches, barns, and private homes, until the army created Camp Letterman, a model field hospital comprising four hundred to five hundred tents. Pennsylvania's Republican governor, Andrew Curtin, rushed to the scene to address the emergency, selecting Gettysburg lawyer David Wills to solve the problem of burying—and reburying—the dead. Wills, who had studied law under Thaddeus Stevens, rejected the local cemetery as inadequate to hold and honor the battle's victims and proposed the creation of Soldiers' National Cemetery at Gettysburg. He hired William Saunders, a botanist in the newly established Agriculture Department, to lay out a seventeen-acre memorial park resembling Mount Auburn Cemetery, which he had designed. While the townspeople and army surgeons gladly treated the northern and southern wounded without discrimination, the national cemetery would be restricted to the Union dead. Two embalming parlors shipped bodies home to families who could afford the procedure—"colonels, majors, captains and privates by the car-load"—but the remainder would rest in the hallowed ground of the newly conceived national cemetery. For the next five months, African American reburial teams exhumed six thousand bodies, moved the Union dead to the new cemetery, and reburied Confederate soldiers where they lay. Through their defense of secession, Confederates had surrendered their claim to repose in a "national" cemetery. "A considerable portion of the battle-ground is likely to be ploughed up this spring and summer," a Washington newspaper reported. "As a matter of course the Confederate graves must be obliterated."[21]

Governor Curtin invited Lincoln to deliver "a few appropriate remarks" to help dedicate the new National Cemetery in November. (Always a "hands-on" president, Lincoln summoned William Saunders from the Agriculture Department to review the design of the memorial park.) Wearing a mourning band around his famed stovepipe hat in memory of the tragically departed Willie, he held themes of sacrifice and remembrance uppermost in his mind. Interrupted five times by applause, Lincoln's lyrical address still took only three minutes for him to deliver. Lincoln had progressively shifted his own understanding of the war's meaning from Union during the first year to emancipation during the second and now equality during the third. The first sentence of his address reiterated that progression, as he declared, "Four score and seven years ago our fathers brought forth on this continent a new *nation*, conceived in *Liberty*, and dedicated to the proposition that all men are created *equal*." In keeping with the novel conception of death as an eternal slumber, Lincoln labeled the cemetery "a final resting place for those who here gave their lives that that nation might live." His reference to the "hallowed" and "consecrated" ground lent new meaning to what a burying place could and should do—honor the dead, not simply inter them, and thereby honor the cause for which they gave their lives. Surely aware that only Union soldiers lay in the cemetery around him, Lincoln by implication diminished the cause of the Confederate soldiers who had fought against nation, liberty, and equality. In his insistence that "The world will little note, nor long remember what we say here, but it can never forget what they did here," he recognized that the best way to honor the Union dead was above all to remember them. His Gettysburg Address signaled that the nation's terrible sacrifice had assumed a new and higher purpose that merited a greater devotion to commemorating the dead. A military turning point, the Battle of Gettysburg also transformed Americans' conception of the meaning of death in battle. The legendary dedication of the cemetery, framed within Lincoln's transcendent address, helped to transform the dehumanizing impact of the carnage into an ennobling, national exercise in honoring the fallen who had given their "last full measure of devotion" to the Union cause.[22]

The dedication of the National Cemetery at Gettysburg—and Lincoln's famous address— initiated a new commitment to honoring national service and sacrifice through somber reverence for the dead. By early 1864, after eight thousand burials, the cemetery at the Soldiers' Home was full. The Union Army had seized the Lee family's estate at Arlington in April 1861 but legally could only use the property temporarily during wartime. The government acquired permanent title to Arlington only after Congress passed a federal tax on Confederate land in June 1862. Southern landowners had sixty days to pay the tax or forfeit their land at auction. The law required Confederate landowners to appear in person to pay the tax, virtually guaranteeing that they would forfeit their land. The idea was to seize the estates of wealthy southerners for redistribution to poor whites. Under the law, Mary Lee owed $92.07 on the Arlington estate, which was valued at over $100,000. In January 1864, Lincoln authorized the War Department to purchase Arlington at auction for $26,800, restricting its use to "war, military, charitable, and educational purposes." In May, while touring the estate with Lincoln, Quartermaster General Montgomery Meigs observed dead soldiers at an Arlington hospital being loaded for shipment to the Soldiers' Home. He immediately suggested planting a new military cemetery in Arlington on the confiscated estate. As his former friend, Meigs felt personally betrayed by Lee's decision to support the Confederacy and by his "almost alone" prolonging the war through his battlefield victories. A Union cemetery on the Arlington grounds would prevent Lee from ever returning. He told Lincoln the "ancients filled their enemies fields with salt and made them useless forever, but we are a Christian nation, why not make it a field of honor?" After watching the cemetery at the Soldiers' Home fill up day after day, Lincoln readily embraced the idea. Meigs assured Stanton that "the grounds about the mansion are admirably adapted to such a use." The secretary of war authorized him to designate up to two hundred acres—"not interfering with the grounds occupied by the Freedmans camps"—as the site for a new military cemetery.[23]

Meigs personally supervised the first burials at Arlington in June 1864. He envisioned a conspicuous ring of graves "encircling" the Lees' mansion as closely as possible. The Union officers occupying the house, however, situated the first interments a half-mile away near the estate's original slave graveyard, directing one of the Lees' former slaves to dig the graves. Meigs angrily ordered reinterment on the land "immediately surrounding the Arlington Mansion" and personally marked out plots around Mary Lee's rose garden. He declared that if the Lees ever returned to Arlington "they should encounter the ghosts of their victims." When one of Meigs's own sons, Lieutenant John Meigs, died during a Confederate raid later in the year, he had him buried near the mansion at Arlington. After the war, Meigs ordered reburial crews to scour the Virginia countryside for thirty miles around Washington looking for makeshift graves. In September 1866, he dug a 20-foot-wide pit just southeast of the Lees' magnificent Greek Revival portico and deposited the remains of 2,111 of these unidentified soldiers, gathered from "the fields of Bull Run and the route to the Rappahannock." A large monument honors the unknown Civil War dead as a "noble army of martyrs."[24]

The government continued to rebury Union soldiers for five years after the war ended. A total of 11,623 reside in Arlington National Cemetery. In 1867, Congress passed the National Cemetery Act, under which seventy-two Civil War burial sites, both northern and southern, received designation and protection as national cemeteries. Overall, almost one-half of all soldiers who died during the Civil War lie in national cemeteries. Ultimately, the National Cemetery System included far more Confederate soldiers, because so many of the Union dead had been shipped home. In his final accounting of army burials, Meigs reported to Congress that Union soldiers lay in an additional 285 cemeteries scattered in cities, towns, and villages across the North, as monuments to "the last full measure of devotion" that they contributed to the war effort. Through his pensive eloquence and his conspicuous personal commitment to honor the dead, Lincoln had ignited a national redefinition of the ennobling power of service and sacrifice.[25]

PERSONALLY, THE Lincolns not only did their utmost to honor the dead, including their own, but did their best to commend the sick and wounded soldiers who abounded in wartime Washington. Abraham Lincoln, for example, spent part of July 4, 1862, riding with a train of ambulances carrying wounded soldiers from the Peninsula Campaign to a makeshift hospital at the Soldiers' Home. On Christmas Day, he visited Armory Square Hospital, shook hands with every patient, and offered "a suitable word of sympathy and consolation for every one." One of the nurses felt overwhelmed to "see him pass from bed to bed and give each occupant the warm, honest grasp for which he is noted," calling it "a grand thing for him to come and cheer our soldier boys." Two years later, he visited three hospitals and shook hands with a thousand wounded soldiers in a single day but still displayed compassion for individual patients. While visiting one of the hospitals, he watched the amputation of a wounded soldier's arm. After an attendant congratulated the surgeon, Lincoln interjected, "But how about the soldier?" Convalescents and their families often visited the Lincolns at the White House, to receive their thanks and to inspire them in return. When the "One-Legged Brigade" from St. Elizabeth's Hospital assembled outside the White House, Abraham Lincoln called them "orators," whose very appearance spoke louder than any words. The day before he left for Gettysburg, Lincoln reviewed 2,500 members of the Invalid Corps as they marched en masse up Pennsylvania Avenue past the White House.[26]

Mary Lincoln had more time to devote and, especially after Willie's death and Tad's illness, increasingly identified with the sick and wounded and their families. She not only visited the hospitals but raised funds to help them do their work. In June 1862, she brought "a profusion of magnificent flowers" to Mount Pleasant Hospital, which were distributed among the patients. She also raised money to buy fruit to help stave off scurvy. In August, she collected $1,000 during one of her visits to New York, bought fruit and "other needed comforts" for the men, and delivered them personally to the hospitals. She bought "a vast quantity" of turkeys and chickens for Christmas dinners and served them herself to the soldiers. In 1864, she contributed flower arrangements to the large Sanitary Fair held in the Patent Office for the benefit of the Washington hospitals. They were auctioned off and fetched $50 apiece. On her visits to the hospitals, she consoled the men, read to them, copied letters home, and attended musical performances and literary readings. As one of the newspapers put it, "Among the many ladies who visit the hospitals none is more indefatigable than Mrs. Lincoln." On one occasion, she brought flowers to a convalescing soldier at Campbell Hospital. On her next visit, she wrote a letter to his mother. "My dear Mrs Agen," she wrote, "I am sitting by the side of your soldier boy. He has been quite sick, but is getting well. He tells me to say to you that he is all right. With respect for the mother of a young soldier." She signed the letter "Mrs Abraham Lincoln." When the soldier, James Agen, reached home and read the letter, he told his family that he had no idea that his visitor had been Mary Lincoln. Her attention to the soldiers' medical needs gained so much publicity that secession sympathizers in the city derided her as "the hospital matron." One observer, however, concluded that she was able to "gradually overcome petticoat and political prejudices by her kindness of manner, her goodness of heart, and the generous devotion with which she has tenderly cared for the sick and wounded soldiers."[27]

After returning from Gettysburg, Lincoln himself fell ill with smallpox, like so many other residents of wartime Washington. "Nobody is supposed to know it," William Stoddard observed, "but the White House has suddenly been turned into a smallpox hospital." Diagnosed with a mild variety of the disease, varioloid, Lincoln underwent quarantine and recovered after three weeks. Like many other African Americans, however, his valet, William Johnson, contracted a severe form of the disease and died in January 1864. Although Johnson had accompanied him on his trip to Gettysburg, Lincoln insisted that he had not given him the disease—"at least I think not," and most certainly he hoped not. Still, the president took financial responsibility for Johnson and his family. When Johnson was unable to sign for his salary as a Treasury Department messenger, Lincoln secured it for him by "cutting red tape" and personally counted it out for him. He helped Johnson's family, paid for his coffin, and buried him in Arlington National Cemetery with the simple inscription "William H. Johnson, Citizen" on his headstone. Lincoln had suffered another personal loss to the war effort. In the spirit of his Gettysburg Address, he did his best to commemorate Johnson's service and sacrifice.[28]

Lincoln's rededication of the nation to the principle of equality also appeared in the closer personal ties that he developed with Washington's African American community. Lincoln appointed two new staff members to take Johnson's place. Solomon James Johnson, a twenty-two-year-old barber, had volunteered for the 54th and 55th Massachusetts regiments but could not meet their physical qualifications and joined Lincoln's presidential guard instead. When William Johnson died, Lincoln asked Salmon Chase to find a position for Solomon Johnson in the Treasury Department, where he received an appointment as a laborer, working part-time as the president's valet. One month before his assassination, Lincoln recommended a "little promotion" for Johnson, who received a clerkship in 1867 after studying law at Howard University. As his confidential messenger, Lincoln appointed William Slade, a leader within Washington's African American community. Slade kept a boardinghouse and was a clerk in the Treasury Department, possibly the first African American clerk in the federal government. Slade, a Virginia native in his late forties, became Lincoln's de facto White House steward as well as his messenger, with access to his own carriage to convey private presidential messages around the city by hand. According to Slade's daughter, "He was really a confidential and constant companion and was treated by Lincoln with the greatest intimacy."[29]

Considered "a gentleman well known to the community," Slade bridged Washington's racial divide, working with both African American and white reformers. He was president of the Social, Civil, and Statistical Association, which dominated the African American delegation that met with Lincoln to discuss colonization. In 1862, Slade became the founding president of the Contraband Relief Association. While working for Lincoln in the White House, Slade founded a free evening school for African Americans, taught by clerks in the Treasury and War departments. Funded by charitable donations, the school met twice a week in the basement of the First Colored Baptist Church, providing instruction in reading and spelling on Mondays and arithmetic and penmanship on Fridays. After a month, forty-eight students had joined the school, most of them former contrabands from Virginia. Along with Elizabeth Keckly, Mary Lincoln's confidante, Slade, his wife, Josephine, and their daughter were active members of the National Freedmen's Relief Association. Slade was one of the NFRA's commissioners, along with the Reverend James I. Ferree (Camp Barker's "Captain Free") and antislavery lawyer George E. H. Day. Josephine Slade was one of the founders of the Ladies' National Union Relief Association, a biracial organization formed to provide aid to African American refugees. In July 1866, when Congress established the position of White House Steward, Lincoln's successor, Andrew Johnson, appointed Slade to the post, which put him in charge of the entire White House staff.[30]

Seven of Lincoln's fourteen predecessors in the White House kept slaves as servants. During the early years of the White House, servants were personal employees of the president, so slaveowners could cut expenses by bringing their own slaves to Washington. Jefferson initiated the practice, employing three white servants as steward, chef, and coachman to supervise the other nine members of his domestic staff, who were slaves. Every succeeding slave-state president brought slaves to work in the White House. Before the Civil War, the best-known White House slave was Paul Jennings, James Madison's personal attendant, who published a memoir in 1865. As a widow living in Washington, Dolley Madison sold Jennings in 1846. Daniel Webster bought him ten months later and immediately freed him, keeping him on as a servant while he worked off his purchase price. In 1848, Jennings was one of a handful of free African Americans who helped to plan the escape on the *Pearl*. Lincoln's immediate predecessor, James Buchanan, employed eleven servants—six men and five women—none of them slaves but all of them white. In addition to his private secretaries, during Lincoln's presidency the Department of the Interior paid for a total of seven members of the White House domestic staff—a steward, messenger, doorkeeper, assistant doorkeeper, two watchmen, and a gardener. Employing her own personal staff, Mary Lincoln hired at least four African Americans, the seamstresses Rosetta Wells and Hannah Brooks, the cook Mary Dines, and the modiste Elizabeth Keckly. Beyond his three private secretaries, Lincoln brought William Johnson with him from Springfield and after his death replaced him with two African Americans, William Slade and Solomon Johnson, both of whom he befriended.[31]

Over time, the Lincolns' relationships with African Americans grew deeper and more personal. Having grown to adulthood in the slave South, Mary Lincoln had much more experience than her husband in interacting with African Americans, not only as servants but as people. Through her deepening connections with former slaves such as Mary Dines and Elizabeth Keckly, who rose to the presidency of the Ladies' Contraband Relief Association, Mary Lincoln increasingly developed a genuine interest in helping the freedmen. In Springfield, Mary had referred to African Americans crudely as "Kentucky darkies" and thought of them as nothing more than menials under the management of white people. In Washington, she gradually developed a greater appreciation and indeed respect for African Americans as independent individuals. Dines remembered that "Mrs. Lincoln contributed money and sent gifts to the older people" at Camp Barker. Making an unprecedented request, in 1864 a group of African American Sunday schools asked permission to hold an Independence Day celebration on the White House grounds. The Lincolns readily agreed and turned over the grove between the White House and the War Department to the immense crowd, who heard the students deliver recitations that included the Declaration of Independence, "Sufferings of the Poor," "The Soldier's Dream," and "The Stars."[32]

When Elizabeth Keckly sought support for the city's contrabands, Mary lent and donated funds to her directly and was eloquent in asking her husband to help as well. Keckly used her trips northward with the First Lady as opportunities to solicit support for her relief efforts from contributors in New York and Philadelphia. In November 1862, for example, Mary wrote to her husband from New York that "Elizabeth Keckley, who is with me and is working for the Contraband Association, at Wash is authorized by the *White* part of the concern by a written document—to collect any thing for them— *here* that, she can—She has been very unsuccessful." Mary went on to report that "the immense number of Contrabands in W—— are suffering intensely, many without bed covering," adding pointedly, "Many dying of want." Then she asked directly, "Please send check for $200," which he did. "The cause of humanity requires it," she assured him. On another occasion, Keckly asked Mary to lend her $30, and Mary asked Abraham Lincoln for $100. Traveling with Mary Lincoln to Boston on a visit to Robert at Harvard gave Keckly the opportunity to meet Wendell Phillips and help organize a local aid society. The abolitionist and feminist reformer Jane Grey Swisshelm actually concluded that the First Lady was now "more radically opposed to slavery" than even her husband. After inviting an African American schoolteacher to tea at the White House, Mary Lincoln was horrified to discover that she had been admitted through the servants' entrance. As her guest was leaving, she made a point of shaking her hand. Salmon Chase's daughter Kate was so horrified by the gesture that she disparaged her publicly for "making too much of the Negro."[33]

Through William Slade's and Elizabeth Keckly's influence, Lincoln himself met a wider range of African Americans, including Sojourner Truth, whom he invited to the White House. Lincoln gained a friend in Frederick Douglass, who recalled that "in all my interviews with Mr. Lincoln, I was impressed with his entire freedom from popular prejudice against the colored race." Emphasizing the impact of this friendship, on August 11, 1863, after meeting with Frederick Douglass, Lincoln wrote a check for $5 made out to "Colored man, with one leg." The Slades' daughter Katherine, or "Nibbie," reminisced that she and her brother and sister often visited the White House, where "they would spend the entire day playing with Tad in the basement, in the White House grounds, or in any other part of the house that the little son of the President wanted to use." Lincoln often returned these visits to the Slades' home about half a dozen blocks from the White House, leaving Tad behind "to spend the entire day with the children and their playmates on Massachusetts Avenue." According to Katherine Slade, "Tad played with all the children and he was a real boy in the midst of real boys and girls, white and colored." Deepening the two families' relationship, Mary Lincoln hired the wife of Slade's cousin, Hannah Brooks, as one of her White House seamstresses. After her husband's assassination, Mary Lincoln gave William Slade one of his canes and his familiar gray shawl. Josephine Slade received the dress that Mary wore on the night of the assassination, and Elizabeth Keckly her cloak and bonnet. Two national leaders of the swelling equal rights campaign, Frederick Douglass and Henry Highland Garnet, also received canes in recognition of their friendship with the president.[34]

CHAPTER TWENTY

"Worth More than a Victory in the Field"
The End in Sight

⊹⊱◈⊰⊹

C ASUALTIES WOULD escalate dramatically during 1864. In the Western Theater, General Ulysses S. Grant had emerged as the most effective commander in the Union Army. His early victories at Forts Henry and Donelson in Tennessee, his defiant repulse of the Confederate counterattack at Shiloh in April 1862, and his long siege of Vicksburg that ended in its surrender on July 4, 1863, had helped him rise to the command of the Western Theater. Early in the war, Lincoln declared that "I can't spare this man; he fights." He also admired a general who won battles, embraced total warfare, stayed clear of politics, and endorsed emancipation. "I have given the subject of arming the negro my hearty support," Grant wrote Lincoln. "This, with the emancipation of the negro, is the heaviest blow yet given the Confederacy." In March 1864, Lincoln transferred Grant to the Eastern Theater, appointed him general-in-chief, and promoted him to lieutenant general, the first to hold that rank since George Washington. Lincoln and Grant shared a strategic vision. Arguing that the Union's armies had "acted independently and without concert, like a balky team, no two ever pulling together," Grant devised a comprehensive military strategy for defeating the South. Echoing the advice that Lincoln had offered to McClellan in vain, Grant told Meade that "Lee's Army will be your objective point. Wherever Lee goes, there you will go also." As general-in-chief, unlike McClellan, Grant spurned the politically charged atmosphere of Washington and established his headquarters in the field with the Army of the Potomac.[1]

During May and June 1864, Grant's army moved seventy-five miles southward, advancing inexorably toward Richmond. In a mere five months, 68,000 wounded soldiers poured into Washington, many by steamers from the White House on the Pamunkey, as they had during the Peninsula Campaign two years earlier. Once again, the government resorted to temporary hospitals, this time fitting up barracks in the capital's defensive fortifications. By midsummer, the Army of the Potomac was laying siege to Richmond and Petersburg, a railroad hub twenty-three miles south of the Confederate capital. "Before Grant took command of the eastern forces we did not sleep at night here in Washington," Lincoln reportedly told one of Grant's generals. "We began to fear the rebels would take the capital, and once in possession of that, we feared that foreign countries might acknowledge the Confederacy. And now we sleep at night."[2]

Grant's relentless offensives and the resulting casualties severely stretched the North's ability to supply fighting men. As the national capital, Washington faced unique challenges in meeting its recruitment quotas and fell subject to two drafts, in July 1863 and September 1864. Many federal officials and employees were exempted from conscription, including congressmen and their staffs, arsenal and armory workers, and merchant seamen. City officials believed that one-third of all government employees in the capital were potentially exempt from the draft. Lawyers who specialized in drawing up exemption papers "in good legal style" eagerly offered their services for a fee. Thousands of government clerks in Washington paid the $300 commutation fee to escape the draft and continue doing their jobs. If they bought substitutes, however, the government credited the enlistments to their home states, not the District. The city's population tripled during the war, which inflated the enrollment lists by including thousands of temporary residents, the so-called floating population. These nonresidents should have been counted in the enrollments of their home states, because they were exempt from the draft in Washington. As a result, officials claimed that Washington's draft quotas were proportionally higher than those of any northern

state. Campaigning to have them lowered, the city sent a committee to meet with Lincoln and Provost Marshal General James Fry in
April 1864, after which the War Department agreed to base the draft
quotas on the 1860 census. Washington's location next to southern
Maryland, where secessionists used the former underground railroad
network to help draftees escape, also undermined conscription in the
District. The provost marshal's detectives monitored the railroad station and the bridges for draft evaders, who were sent to Camp Distribution in Virginia, where new recruits and convalescing soldiers
were processed before joining their regiments. Crossing the Potomac
remained the only escape route, despite the vigilance of the Potomac
Flotilla. "They cross by various ways," the *Daily Chronicle* reported,
"upon canoes, boats, and rafts, etc., and beg their way through the
country on getting into Maryland," where they were welcomed.[3]

Captain Henry A. Scheetz, now Washington's provost marshal,
was responsible for meeting the quotas by recruiting volunteers and,
when that effort failed, enforcing the draft. He opened four recruiting
offices and set out to offer "great inducements" to potential recruits,
which included bounties and enlistment balls with martial music.
Scheetz worked with a citizens' committee to encourage and organize the volunteers and raise funds for a more generous bounty. He
allocated the quota among the city's wards, which formed subscrip-
tion committees to fund bounties and pay commutation fees, dividing the wards into districts and going door-to-door. Washington's
perennial problem, its meager tax base, impaired recruiting. While
the city contributed $40,000 toward bounties, the financial induce-
ments remained low. "Since the larger cities offer very large bounties for volunteer enlistments," Washington officials noted, "numbers
of our residents are attracted thither for the purpose of joining the
ranks." Recruiting agents from northern states enticed Washington
residents away with promises of higher bounties. Washington officials called on Congress to authorize the city to borrow $500,000 to
raise the bounties. Civilians who recruited volunteers received a $15
premium for their efforts. African American recruits, representing
just over one-quarter of all eligible men, were credited toward the
city's quota and became instrumental in helping to forstall a draft. In

the First Ward, one-quarter of the draftees were African Americans, including William Johnson, Lincoln's valet and messenger. Eager to serve, African Americans held their own recruiting rally at Wesley Zion Church in September 1864 to "assist their white brethren in filling the quota." The Reverend Anthony Bowen declared that this "was a golden opportunity for the colored men to prove themselves worthy of the freedom they enjoyed. They ought to fight; they had greater reason to fight than any class of men in the world. Slavery was their enemy, and they must fight it down." Although Secretary of War Stanton recommended paying equal bounties to whites and blacks, Washington offered African American recruits only half as much, $25. "Special inducements should be offered to colored men to enlist, by giving them bounty and pay equal to white men," the *National Republican* insisted. "If money is wanting and it is necessary to levy a tax to raise it, let that be done." The War Department itself conducted an enrollment of African Americans working in the Army of the Potomac preparatory to a special draft of contrabands.[4]

"The Government needs men," the *Chronicle* wrote with resignation before the District's first draft in July 1863. "It is idle to say that the three hundred thousand men the Government needs could be raised by calling for volunteers. The time was when more than that number sprang to the rescue. But that could not go on forever." The first step was culling the enrollment lists of men with physical disabilities and noncitizens. "At the Provost Marshal's office hundreds of persons applying for exemption from the draft are collected daily, the majority of whom, after waiting frequently as long as three hours at a time, discover that the complaints upon which they seek exemption are not among those included in the list to which the present examination has reference," the *Chronicle* reported. "Alienage, unsuitableness of age, non-residence, erroneous enrolment, and physical disability, are the specific causes which entitle one to exemption at this time." On the day of the draft, the District's draft commissioner oversaw the ceremonious lottery at the office of the provost marshal, alongside the Enrollment Board, who sat at a table on a raised platform surrounded by a railing. The names of all eligible draftees were recorded on small red cards inside a box that was shaken repeatedly throughout the process. A blind man, with his shirt sleeves pushed above his elbows, drew out the cards one by one. As the draft commissioner called out the names, seven clerks filled out notification forms for delivery to the draftees, who had two days to report for duty or face arrest for desertion, which was potentially a capital offense. During the first draft, one soldier who failed to report was arrested as a deserter. While he was climbing out of a window to try to escape, a sentry shot him twice through the head and killed him. To set an example, during the city's second draft Abraham and Mary Lincoln each secured "representative recruits" from Washington to enlist on their behalf as their own personal contributions to the war effort.[5]

Responding to complaints of unfairness, at Lincoln's suggestion Congress eliminated commutation in July 1864, so substitutes remained the only way for draftees to avoid conscription. Recognizing that many of the drafted men would not personally serve, the city paid substitute agents $20 for every substitute they secured. To obtain substitutes, draftees could pay $300, cobbled together from federal and District bounties and voluntary contributions, to Mayor Wallach, who promised to "endeavor to supply substitutes for all who need them." Eligible recruits could also join an "exemption club," which would furnish a substitute for a $50 membership fee. Draft insurance, available for $30 to $100 per draft, guaranteed the provision of a substitute, or "sub." Substitution brokers opened offices in the city and announced, "The highest prices will be paid for Substitutes for Drafted men." In Washington, substitutes cost $200 to $250 plus the broker's fee and the bounties that went along with enlistment. "The numerous substitute brokers in this city are reaping a rich harvest in supplying the demand of the market," according to the *Chronicle*. "Their profit on nearly every sale is exorbitant, sometimes reaching one hundred dollars." Still, substitutes seemed preferable to commutation, because "they furnish to the Government what it needs more than money—soldiers." Substitution, however, created a wave of desertions toward the end of the war. Many substitutes were already deserters who intended to desert yet again after pocketing their fees and bounties. "We suppose that more than half the men who offer themselves as substitutes, are deserters from the army," the

Chronicle estimated, "and it is a fair presumption that not one of these intends to perform his duty."[6]

Desertion plagued Washington throughout the war. Secessionists in southern Maryland and even agents from Richmond dressed in civilian clothing were said to be encouraging and helping deserters. Critics faulted Lincoln for fostering a "culture of desertion" through a policy of "super-leniency" early in the war. Lincoln was renowned for his clemency, and John Hay noted "the eagerness with which the President caught at any fact which would justify him in saving the life of a condemned soldier." Benjamin Stoddard agreed that "Mr. Lincoln was always glad enough to find a good reason for the exercise of the pardoning power," but he could not abide spies or deserters who aided the enemy. "Such men got their hanging, or whatever it was," Stoddard noted, "with very little interference on the part of the President." To set an example for the troops, the Army of the Potomac ordered its first execution of a deserter in December 1861. William H. Johnson, a private in the Lincoln Cavalry, was executed because he offered military information to the enemy. He was carted through the camps of his division sitting on his coffin while the regimental bands played a funeral dirge. Seven thousand soldiers watched his execution before a twelve-man firing squad. The most common method of desertion was simply donning civilian clothing, slipping past the government detectives at the railroad depot, and catching the train to Baltimore. After the army began confiscating and destroying all civilian clothing in the camps, soldiers bought or borrowed civilian clothes while in Washington on passes. The Provost Guard arrested merchants who sold civilian clothing to soldiers and barbers who shaved them as an aid to desertion. One soldier paid a barber $10, almost a month's pay, to dye his whiskers as a form of disguise. Another enterprising deserter had himself closed up in a coffin for shipment home and escaped during the journey. The most unusual deserter was a woman in uniform who deserted after serving three months in a Pennsylvania regiment. Arrested wearing men's civilian clothing, she was sentenced to ninety days in the workhouse, not for desertion but "for leading a life unbecoming her sex." Male deserters sometimes wore women's clothing during their escapes.[7]

Early in the war, most deserters were treated no more harshly than "stragglers," who overstayed their passes in Washington and were sent to Camp Convalescent in Virginia before rejoining their regiments. After the institution of the draft in July 1862, however, desertions proliferated. With the Emancipation Proclamation and the recruitment of African American troops, desertions also changed in character. One Ohio private declared that "we did not enlist to fight for the negro and I can tell you that we never shall or many of us anyhow no never." Another soldier wrote to his wife, "If the nigger is the object, I am out of it forever and shall act conscientiously in leaving the army." Desertion could now be interpreted as a political statement in opposition to conscription, emancipation, and equality, as symbolized in the New York City Draft Riot of July 1863. The resentments of Irish immigrants facing conscription to fight in what they considered a "rich man's war" that was increasingly dedicated to emancipation produced a riot that targeted African Americans, Republicans, and antislavery advocates. Over four days, rioters destroyed the local draft office, mobbed the *New York Tribune* building, burned the Colored Orphan Asylum, and lynched a dozen African Americans. Lincoln sent in troops from the recently concluded Battle of Gettysburg, who fired on the rioters. The largest riot in American history, this episode of violent resistance to the draft claimed at least 120 lives.[8]

One month after Lincoln issued the Emancipation Proclamation, the army began depositing both deserters and stragglers in Forrest Hall, a military prison in Georgetown, up to 350 at a time. Two years later, Forrest Hall was remodeled and officially converted into "the prison-house for deserters, bounty-jumpers, and others who have no fear of God or their country." Sentences ranged from sixty days to five years at hard labor working on the fortifications around Washington. In February 1863, the government converted Stone Hospital from an "eye and ear" hospital into a hospital for sick and wounded deserters. After recovering, the deserters were sent to Forrest Hall or back to their regiments. In July 1863, the newly created Bureau of Deserters arrested six thousand men. "The almost certainty of arrest and punishment through the agency of the Provost Marshal

General's Department has become known throughout the army," the press reported, "and has resulted in a decrease of seventy-five per cent." Casting a wide net, Washington's provost marshal arrested one innocent soldier for every two actual deserters. Meanwhile, the provost marshals in the northern states grew more expert at rounding up deserters and sending them back to the Army of the Potomac through Washington. Considered "desperate and unprincipled," deserters could be dangerous. A deserter shot a government detective in the back with a Sharps revolver in front of Ford's Theatre. The detective grabbed the pistol and shot the deserter twice.[9]

The army made an example of the most incorrigible deserters by marching seventy-five of them, shuffling in leg irons and handcuffs, up Pennsylvania Avenue in a grand Rogue's March. Public pressure demanded even more stringent measures. "Desertion is the greatest and most dangerous crime a soldier can commit, and less than any other ought to have leniency shown to it," the *Daily Chronicle* reminded readers. "No army is safe where desertion becomes habitual." In February 1863, when Lincoln and his cabinet discussed shooting a deserter, "the necessity of an example to check a rapidly increasing evil was unanimously assented to." To provide fair notice to the soldiers, on March 10 Lincoln proclaimed an amnesty for all recruits and draftees who were absent from their regiments without leave and gave them until April 1 to return. Rather than faulting the deserters themselves, Lincoln condemned the "evil disposed and disloyal persons" who encouraged them to desert, such as the Peace Democrats or Copperheads. However, any deserter who did not return would be arrested and punished "as the law provides."[10]

In August, General George Gordon Meade ordered the execution of five substitute deserters and bounty jumpers in the Army of the Potomac. Hearing their appeals, Lincoln could find no grounds for mercy and let the sentences stand. "I understand these are very flagrant cases," he told Meade, "and that you deem their punishment as being indispensable to the service." The *National Republican* reported that "the wife of one of these unfortunate men was at the White House to implore mercy of the President, but she was too late. The stern edict had gone forth." Trying to balance justice, clemency, and duty, in February 1864 Lincoln commuted all death sentences for desertion into imprisonment in the Dry Tortugas off Florida for the duration of the war. At the same time, he empowered commanding generals to restore convicted deserters to duty, "when in their judgment the service will be thereby benefited." One month before the war ended, with victory in sight, Lincoln extended a pardon to all deserters and gave them sixty days to return to their regiments or lose their U.S. citizenship.[11]

Intense competition for troops brought state recruiting agents from the North to enlist African Americans, often as substitutes, routinely offering them more than the meager bounties they received for enlisting in Washington. Under the premise that contrabands were not permanent residents of the capital, they had the option of joining regiments in the loyal states, where they could then establish legal residency. This procedure fulfilled the government's goal of encouraging the former slaves to move northward to permanent homes but also diminished the capital's ability to meet its own quota. When a recruiting agent contracted to take twenty contrabands to New York, the provost marshal's detectives commandeered them to work for the Quartermaster's Department, promising them a wage of $40 a month, quadruple what they would have been paid in the army. The provost marshal began arresting the "foreign" recruiting officers, many of whom were African Americans themselves.[12]

The revised Enrollment Act of February 1864 allowed agents from northern states to recruit former slaves in the Union-occupied regions of the Confederacy, as well as slaves in the Border States. In this fashion, conscription became yet another tool for undermining the institution of slavery. The District of Columbia entered the competition for former slaves in the South by sending recruiting agents to Union-occupied regions of Virginia, North Carolina, South Carolina, Georgia, Alabama, Mississippi, and Florida. In the Border States and occupied areas of the Confederacy, slaves who enlisted with their owners' consent received their freedom. Their owners, if loyal, received compensation, capped at $300, which came from the "commutation fund." Slaveowners also pocketed the $100 bonus that the federal government awarded African American enlistees. In effect, the much reviled draft provided a mechanism for implementing the kind of compensated emancipation in the Border States that Lincoln himself had proposed, without success, two years earlier. Overall, the District of Columbia provided 3,269 African American soldiers for the Union war effort, behind only Pennsylvania, New York, Ohio, and Massachusetts among the free states.[13]

To free up fighting men for active duty, in April 1863 the War Department created the Invalid Corps, which enrolled sick and wounded soldiers who were considered fit for garrison or "light" duty. Clad in a pale shade of sky blue, the corps provided an emergency force for the city's defense, replaced able-bodied men as provost guards and hospital sentries, and represented a form of charitable support for soldiers disabled in the service of the Union. The sturdiest Invalids carried muskets, with the rest restricted to sabers and pistols. By October 1863, the city's hospitals and Camp Convalescent in Virginia had provided enough disabled veterans to man five regiments, who bivouacked in a new Invalid Camp near Columbian College. By the end of the year, there were 12,000 Invalids in Washington, who did their best to develop a martial esprit, mounting military parades through the city, including the march of the One-Legged Brigade up Pennsylvania Avenue on crutches. An escort from the 1st Regiment Invalid Corps later accompanied Lincoln on his trip to Gettysburg. The army was so desperate to reassign able-bodied men, however, that many of the Invalids were clearly unfit for duty. A guard assigned to Armory Square Hospital was so sick when he arrived that he served only six days before dying of consumption. Another guard died at the hospital on the same day that he arrived. "Chester Sheldon came here from the Invalid Corps," the *Armory Square Gazette* reported, "was with us only one day, and was so sick when he was brought in, that it was with difficulty that his address could be obtained." As a military corps, the hapless Invalids quickly generated more than their allotment of contempt. "As a member of the Invalid Corps now on duty in this city, I do protest against the growing disposition to throw ridicule on this useful body," one soldier complained. Others were reduced to duty drumming disgraced comrades to the guardhouse to the sound of the "Rogue's March." (Their insignia read "I.C.," the same designation that the army applied to used-up horses as "Inspected and Condemned.") To raise their status and improve discipline, in March 1864 Secretary of War Stanton elevated one brigade to the rank of Veteran Reserve Corps, incorporating Invalids who were fit enough to carry muskets in defense of the capital.[14]

The city's defenses endured their first direct attack in July 1864. As General Grant slowly closed the Army of the Potomac's vise around Richmond and Petersburg, Lee decided to send General Jubal Early on a desperate raid into the Shenandoah Valley. His plan was to relieve the valley, draw off part of Grant's army, foment rebellion in Maryland, and threaten Washington. Early led a drive up the Shenandoah Valley all the way to Harpers Ferry on the Potomac, virtually unopposed. Under General David Hunter, Lincoln's former bodyguard, Union forces in the Valley refused to give battle and retreated into West Virginia. As Early's 10,000-man army turned eastward toward Washington, Grant warned of an attack on the capital and sent reinforcements. General Lew Wallace, commanding at Baltimore, had a mere 6,000 men to oppose Early's advance, most of them raw, hundred-day volunteers. He could do nothing to stop Early from taking over Frederick, Maryland, where he exacted $200,000 in tribute. Determined to prevent the Confederates from reaching Washington, Wallace engaged Early's troops at the Monocacy River on July 9. The Battle of Monocacy was a delaying action that provided an extra day for reinforcements to reach the capital. After losing one-fourth of his army, Wallace retreated back into Baltimore, leaving Early to advance on Washington unopposed.[15]

Wallace's defeat stunned the capital and sent stragglers and refugees pouring into the city. "Let us be vigilant and keep cool," Lincoln advised calmly. "I hope neither Baltimore nor Washington will be taken." Professing faith in Chief Engineer Barnard's meticulously designed fortifications, the *Daily Chronicle* crowed that "Washington is fortified. Engineering skill has made it one of the most thoroughly defended spots in the world. Independent of the thousands of trained soldiers who are here to beat back the enemy, it has able-bodied men enough in it to hold the united hosts of rebeldom at bay." In fact, the defenses were manned by the musket-wielding Veteran Reserve

Corps, and many of the forts had been converted into hospitals. The War Department quickly organized three thousand government clerks and quartermaster's employees into militia companies. Unaware of the scope of the Confederate assault but imagining the worst, Washingtonians feared another Antietam or Gettysburg campaign with Washington as its target. "The demonstration is not simply a raid, it is an invasion," the *Chronicle* decided. "It would seem as if the bulk of Lee's army will soon be on this side of the Potomac, if, indeed, it has not already crossed." With the telegraph and railroad lines cut, the city was eerily quiet. Crowds gathered around the newspaper offices waiting for every bit of news. Afraid to light even a lantern, they groped their way through the streets in total darkness.[16]

The next morning, July 11, a sentry spotted a cloud of dust approaching from the North and rode to nearby Fort Stevens. The Confederate Army was advancing down Seventh Street Pike, Washington's primary north-south artery. If Fort Stevens, just five miles north of the Capitol, fell they could march into Washington unopposed. Lincoln immediately mobilized eight regiments of the District of Columbia militiamen for sixty days' service. Just after noon, the enemy troops approached Fort Stevens, allowing Early to assess his target, where he found "exceedingly strong" fortifications. "The timber had been felled within cannon range all around and left on the ground," he discovered, "making a formidable obstacle, and every possible approach was raked by artillery." Early's men stormed the fort three times but were driven back. Reinforcements streamed into Fort Stevens, along with civilian spectators who had ridden the horsecars up Seventh Street to watch the day-long skirmish. Abraham and Mary Lincoln joined Edwin Stanton and Gideon Welles to watch the battle. Lincoln coolly mounted the parapet, refusing to take cover as Early's sharpshooters, a thousand feet away, fired volley after volley. According to legend, Captain Oliver Wendell Holmes Jr., a future Supreme Court justice, ordered the president, "Get down, you fool!" (Lincoln told John Hay that "A soldier roughly ordered him to get down or he would have his head knocked off.") Taking the initiative, the garrison counterattacked, forced the Confederates back into their lines, and spent the night skirmishing with pickets.

Repulsed, the Confederate cavalry spent the next day north of Washington, stealing horses and cattle, raiding farms, burning houses, and pillaging country estates, including the Maryland home of Francis Preston Blair. Ward Hill Lamon lost four horses that he was pasturing in Maryland. But Barnard's defensive system had met the test. Fort Stevens, the only point on the perimeter to face a direct attack during the entire war, had held. Still, when Early's army slipped back over the Potomac, just as Lee's had after Antietam and Gettysburg, John Hay reported that Lincoln was "disgusted."[17]

FROM THE BEGINNING of the war, Washingtonians marveled as they watched their city becoming "Northernized." With Richmond under siege, Early's army repulsed, and the war slowly grinding down to its conclusion, Washington's Republicans boasted of their success in turning the national capital into a progressive, northern city. Reviewing the unexpected opportunity that the war presented to free, first, the capital's slaves and, soon afterward, the Confederacy's, the *Daily Chronicle* announced that Washington is "to-day essentially a Northern city. We are perfectly aware that many of the old inhabitants look on the incoming tide of innovations with disfavor, and probably we might say disgust." Despite the entrenched resistance to racial progress, "the fact remains that Washington is rapidly losing its pro-slavery character." Beyond emancipation, the contrast between the prewar city and its emerging postwar incarnation justified the labor and resources invested and prompted additional reforms to come. "The rebellion has effected revolutions in many instances, and none more signally than in Washington," the *Chronicle* argued. "The outside American world begins to look in upon this microcosm." The wartime influx of newcomers set an example and issued a challenge to Washington's growing cadre of urban reformers. "For the most part, they come from Northern cities, and are accustomed to different laws and customs, to cleanliness in the streets, observance of law, order, and decency, regard for the Sabbath, local pride, and that determined opposition to everything that stands in the way of progress," the *Chronicle* thundered. "And having come here they have settled down and are beginning to look around them to find a dirty, squalid, neglected city, dirtier than any city they ever saw before." The paper offered a litany of reforms, on the northern model, that would benefit and indeed transform Washington—the city's water supply, paving, lighting, sanitation, police, and public schools. Heralding "the magic growth of Washington," reformers resolved that the "capital of a great Republic should not only be the freest, but the most progressive."[18]

As emancipation spread forth across the nation, Washington's African Americans insisted on legal equality as another unanticipated but imperative consequence of the war. Congress's newfound willingness to remake the city in a northern image facilitated the real and emblematic change, which initially focused on equal access to public transportation. At the beginning of the war, transit within Washington consisted of privately owned hackney carriages, or "hacks," and a public system of omnibuses, or "busses." Hacks were usually driven and sometimes owned by African Americans. (In the First Ward, almost two-thirds of hackmen were African Americans.) Hacks, like modern taxis, were licensed and heavily regulated. Hackmen had to wear badges displaying their license numbers, paint the numbers on their lamps, park only at the hack stands that were located on major thoroughfares and near hotels, control their horses when not engaged, and provide service to all paying passengers. Fares, which ran from twenty-five to fifty cents, depending on the distance, put hacks out of reach of most working people. Washington built its first omnibus line in 1830. Unlike hacks, which were "on-demand" vehicles, omnibuses ran a route on a fixed schedule. The seats ran lengthwise, facing outward, and passengers entered and exited through the rear, sometimes hopping on and off while the vehicle was moving. Much larger and heavier than hacks, omnibuses required a three- or four-horse team, severely damaging city streets. During the war, Commissioner of Public Buildings Benjamin Brown French complained that Pennsylvania Avenue was "pretty much cut to pieces by omnibusses." With a 12½ cent fare, half that of the hacks, omnibuses were more affordable and specialized in carrying government clerks to and from work. While hacks were considered luxury vehicles and omnibuses catered to the middle class, working people were still forced to walk Washington's "magnificent distances." Enforcing its Sabbath laws, Washington did not allow hacks or omnibuses to operate on Sundays.[19]

Northern cities had begun replacing their omnibuses in the 1830s, so Washington was three decades behind the times. In May 1862, the wartime Congress seized the opportunity to modernize Washington's transit system and chartered the city's first horse railway system, the Washington and Georgetown Railroad. The horse railway rode on iron tracks down the middle of the street on a level pavement rather than cobblestones. The smoother ride allowed them to operate with half as many horses as omnibuses, only two, lowering fares substantially. The horsecars carried three times as many passengers, up to forty, traveled faster, and went farther. The seats ran lengthwise, facing inward, and the middle aisle was lined with straw to collect mud and rain water. Washington's main horsecar line ran from the Navy Yard on the east, curved around the Capitol, and followed Pennsylvania Avenue to Georgetown on the west. Arriving at three-minute intervals, Washington's forty horsecars cost a "half dime" to ride. For the first time, the working classes could afford to ride to and from work. The horse railway, however, was segregated. Special cars for African Americans, which ran infrequently and often not at all, bore signs proclaiming "This car exclusively for colored people." Whites frequently rode in the segregated cars when convenient, but African Americans boarding a whites-only car had to ride outside, on the front and rear platforms.[20]

In August 1863, a group of African American ministers challenged the streetcar company's segregation policy. After the driver admitted them into a whites-only car, the conductor ordered them to move to the forward platform. When they refused, the conductor ordered them to get out, and a crowd gathered and insulted the ministers. After the newspapers called repeatedly for additional "colored cars" to accommodate more African American riders, the streetcar line converted six old omnibuses into one-horse streetcars. In a rhetorical concession, they bore signs announcing "Colored people can ride in this car." (With ironic symbolism, the new cars were painted a darker color.) Trying to defuse the conflict, Mayor Wallach reached an informal compromise with the streetcar line. The city would allow the cars to run on Sundays, if the streetcar company agreed to provide additional segregated cars. In another concession, the railway bought ten new two-horse streetcars to replace the old one-horse omnibuses, running them at fifteen-minute intervals. The National Freedman's Relief Association opposed the introduction of any additional "colored cars," which merely perpetuated "an odious distinction between the two classes" and represented a futile attempt to resurrect "the dead carcass of slavery." George Hatton, a member of the 1st Regiment USCT, announced that he "would not ride in the cars until he had his rights and could sit inside."[21]

In February 1864, the equal rights campaign escalated when Major Alexander Augusta, now a surgeon in the 7th Regiment USCT, was summoned to Washington to testify in a court-martial. When he boarded a whites-only streetcar, the conductor told him that he had to ride on the front platform with the driver. "I told him I would not ride on the front, and he said I should not ride at all," Augusta reported. "He then ejected me from the platform, and at the same time gave orders to the driver to go on." Augusta wrote a letter to the army's judge advocate, calling for the arrest and punishment of the conductor. The letter provoked outrage in the press and in Congress, and the segregated streetcar system immediately became the focus of a growing civil rights movement that demanded social equality for African Americans, not simply freedom. "The Government, endorsed by the great acclaim of the loyal people, has decided that the black man is not only free, but is entitled to wear, and shall wear, the Federal uniform," the *National Republican* declared. "Now let it promptly and emphatically declare that that uniform, by whomsoever worn, *must and shall be respected*, at all times and in all places." Calling segregation a "lingering relic of slavery," the newspaper cited the example of integrated streetcar lines in northern cities, including Boston, New York, and Philadelphia.[22]

In Congress, Charles Sumner read Augusta's letter on the floor of the Senate, called his ejection an outrage, and proposed an inquiry into "the exclusion of colored persons from the equal enjoyment of railroad privileges in the District of Columbia." Supporters called the segregated line an "offshoot of slavery" and a disgrace to both the national capital and the government. When opponents charged Sumner with pursuing social and political equality, Senator James Grimes retorted that he had ridden in the "colored cars" and "did not consider myself disgraced by riding to the Senate Chamber in a car with some colored people." Senator Samuel Pomeroy suggested extending the inquiry to the railroads leaving Washington, "to prevent the difficulties which colored men have in getting out of this District." The Senate passed Sumner's resolution overwhelmingly and ordered the Committee on the District of Columbia to conduct an inquiry. Responding to Sumner's resolution, the typically conservative Committee on the District recommended no action, arguing that anyone excluded from the horse railway had the right to sue the streetcar company. But Sumner did take action. In July 1864, when Congress granted a charter to a second streetcar line, the Metropolitan Railroad, he insisted on a clause forbidding "exclusion of colored persons from the equal enjoyment of all railroad privileges in the District of Columbia." The phrase "all railroad privileges" meant equal access to all cars. In exchange, the new line's charter did not forbid it to run cars on Sundays. Washington began prosecuting streetcar conductors and drivers for ejecting African Americans. The wartime integration campaign culminated in March 1865, when Congress approved Sumner's proposal to extend the equal access provision of the Metropolitan Railroad's charter to "every other railroad in the District of Columbia." Resistance was substantial, with the Senate divided 17–16.[23]

Washington's equal rights campaign grew directly out of the contraband relief movement. The National Freedman's Relief Association specialized in extending legal rights to former slaves, including free public education, while other organizations continued to provide material aid. Late in the war, the Ladies' Contraband Relief Association shifted focus from contrabands to the families of African American soldiers, changing its name to the Freedmen and Soldiers' Relief Association. The streetcar protest originated with African Americans' traditional leaders—particularly Baptist, AME, and Methodist ministers—and drew in African American soldiers, who were empowered by their military service. Even whites reasoned that "the United States uniform and the individual man who wears it must and shall be respected." These two groups formed the backbone of African Americans' postwar political leadership. A third cohort, northern reformers, many of them women, relocated to the Washington area during the war, providing national prestige and crucial organizational skills. Sojourner Truth, along with Harriet Jacobs, Lucy Colman, Jane Grey Swisshelm, and Anna Dickinson, brought reform credentials and a national reputation to the equal rights campaign. A former slave from New York, Sojourner Truth emerged as one of the best known antislavery speakers and women's rights advocates after delivering her "Ar'n't I a Woman" speech at the Ohio Woman's Rights Convention in 1851. In the wake of the Compensated Emancipation Act, the Emancipation Proclamation, and other antislavery advances, Truth decided to travel to Washington from her home in Michigan to "see the freedmen of my own race," as well as the "first Antislavery President."[24]

In Washington, Sojourner Truth worked with the National Freedmen's Relief Association and the new Colored Soldiers' Aid Society established by Henry Highland Garnet, a Presbyterian minister from New York who also relocated to Washington to support the relief effort. For the rest of the war, Truth worked at Arlington Freedman's Village, Mason's Island, and Freedmen's Hospital. While working at Freedman's Village, Truth and white reformer Lucy Colman received an invitation to meet with Lincoln in October 1864, with the help of Elizabeth Keckly. During their White House visit, Colman thought Lincoln too dismissive, addressing Truth as "Aunty," but Truth noted that he stood up and shook her hand, an unusual gesture of respect toward a black woman. After she called him "the best president who has ever taken the seat," Lincoln objected. "I expect you have reference to my having emancipated the slaves in my proclamation," he told her, explaining modestly that the war, not he, had freed the slaves. "If the people over the river had behaved themselves, I could not have done what I have," he explained, "but they did not, which gave me the opportunity to do these things." When Truth admitted that she had never heard of him before his election as president, he answered that "I had heard of you many times before that." Their meeting ended when an African American woman who was about to be evicted arrived and received the president's help.[25]

While riding the streetcars to her post at Freedmen's Hospital, Truth encountered the capital's entrenched segregation and joined the equal rights campaign. When two streetcar drivers refused to stop for her, she shouted, "I want to ride! I want to ride!! I want to ride!!!" A crowd of whites gathered, stopped the next streetcar, and cheered as she boarded it. The conductor ordered her to "Go forward to where the horses are, or I will throw you out." Truth refused. After Congress integrated the streetcars in March 1865, the struggle continued. One white woman asked the conductor, "Does niggers ride in these cars?" When he said yes, Truth answered, "Of course colored people ride in the cars. Street cars are designed for poor white, and colored, folks," and then told her that if she objected she should hire a hack. When Truth boarded a streetcar ahead of a white relief worker that she was traveling with, the conductor told her to "make way for the lady." Truth answered, "I am a lady too." Ultimately, a conductor tried to remove her from a streetcar forcibly, injuring her shoulder. After Truth secured his dismissal and arrest, he was convicted of assault and battery. "It is hard for the old slave-holding spirit to die," Truth observed. "But *die* it *must*."[26]

During her trip east, in the midst of the 1864 presidential election campaign, Sojourner Truth delivered speeches supporting Abraham Lincoln and wrote that "I hope all will do all they can in putting him in as President again." As the election approached, Lincoln faced tremendous pressure, even among his allies, to revoke or modify the Emancipation Proclamation to end the war sooner. Lincoln listened patiently but decided that any hint of retreat on emancipation would violate his "solemn promise" to African Americans. "As a matter of morals," he asked, "could such treachery by any possibility, escape the curses of Heaven, or of any good man?" Retreat would dash any hope of military victory, because "no human power can subdue this rebellion without using the Emancipation lever as I have done." Gauging the remarkable reversal of public opinion in the North, Lincoln confidently declared, "There is a witness in every white mans bosom that he would rather go to the war having the negro help him, than to help the enemy against him."[27]

Expecting the nomination of a Democratic candidate preaching a compromise on emancipation, in August Lincoln wrote a private memo predicting his own defeat. "This morning, as for some days past, it seems exceedingly probable this this Administration will not be re-elected," he confided. "Then it will be my duty to cooperate with the President elect, as to save the Union between the election and the inauguration; as he will have secured his election on such ground that he cannot possibly save it afterwards." Convinced that African American soldiers were essential to military victory, Lincoln viewed Union and emancipation as inseparable goals. With Lincoln standing firm on slavery, the *Washington Chronicle* concluded "Every vote for Abraham Lincoln is a vote to free the four millions of African slaves—a vote to elevate their condition by investing them with civil and ultimately political rights." That was exactly what southerners and northern Democrats suspected and feared. A week later, the Democratic Party nominated George McClellan for president and adopted a platform that proposed peace at the expense of emancipation. In accepting the nomination, McClellan promised a military victory followed by "conciliation and compromise." Making clear that emancipation would be open to negotiation, he declared, "The Union is the one condition of peace—we ask no more." Lincoln's old friend Alexander Stephens, now vice president of the Confederacy, called the Democratic platform "the first ray of light I have seen from the North since the war began." More bluntly, the *Chronicle* considered a vote for McClellan a vote for the Confederacy, concluding that "it is Abraham Lincoln or Jefferson Davis in the coming contest." When William Tecumseh Sherman's army captured Atlanta on September 2, Lincoln's reelection was virtually assured.[28]

While lacking even a single electoral vote, the capital played an important role in Lincoln's reelection. Republican-controlled states adopted "voting in the field," which allowed soldiers to cast ballots wherever they were stationed, without returning home on election day. The Union Army set up ballot boxes in the army camps around Washington and in the city's military hospitals to muster votes for

Lincoln. The soldiers and staff at Armory Square Hospital supported Lincoln. The surgeon in charge, Dr. Bliss, presided over a "Grand Gathering" for Lincoln and his running mate, Andrew Johnson, the military governor of Tennessee. The *Armory Square Gazette* endorsed Lincoln and offered fifteen reasons to "Stand by the Administration." To compensate, relief agents from Democratic states prowled the hospitals looking for McClellan voters. At the same time, Democratic-controlled states spurned voting in the field to suppress soldier votes for Lincoln, so the army furloughed Republican soldiers to allow them to vote at home. Along with federal employees furloughed for the same purpose, they jammed the trains leaving Washington by the thousands. In November, Lincoln and the Republicans won an overwhelming victory. Lincoln received 55 percent of the popular vote and 212 of 233 electoral votes. In Congress, Republicans won 145 of the 185 seats in the House of Representatives and secured a 41–10 majority in the Senate. McClellan won only three states—Delaware, Kentucky, and New Jersey. Among the soldiers who voted in the field, 78 percent supported Lincoln. Assessing the conclusive election results, General Grant declared that Lincoln's overwhelming reelection "will be worth more than a victory in the field." After his second inauguration in March 1865, Benjamin Brown French reported that "I went to the President's and attended the largest reception I ever saw. From 8 till ¼ past 11 the president shook hands steadily, at the rate of 100 every 4 minutes—with about 5,000 persons!" With the war concluding, Lincoln enjoyed more personal popularity than ever.[29]

"The Country Was Ready to Say Amen"

O N MARCH 4, 1865, Frederick Douglass stood before the Capitol among the crowd of 30,000 to 40,000 who assembled to hear Lincoln's Second Inaugural Address. Hoping to congratulate the president personally, Douglass went to the White House to attend the inaugural reception. Before the Lincolns, White House social events had banned African Americans. Now, when Douglass reached the White House, the guards told him that "no person of color" could enter. Believing that "No such order could have emanated from President Lincoln," Douglass insisted that "I shall not go out of this building till I see President Lincoln." When Lincoln caught sight of Douglass entering the East Room, he called out, "Here comes my friend Douglass," and took his hand. "I am glad to see you," he told the abolitionist. "I saw you in the crowd today, listening to my inaugural address; how did you like it?" Douglass demurred, but Lincoln insisted on an answer, assuring him that "there is no man in the country whose opinion I value more than yours." Douglass felt honored to hear "such expressions, from such a man" and told Lincoln "that was a sacred effort." Later, Douglass recalled that the episode left him feeling like "a man among men." When two other African Americans attended a White House levee, presidential secretary William Stoddard called it "a practical assertion of negro citizenship, for which few were prepared." Lincoln himself seemed prepared and "received them with marked kindness."[1]

As Lincoln delivered his Second Inaugural Address, he looked out over a city that had changed dramatically during his four years as president. In 1861, there were more than three thousand slaves in the District of Columbia. Now, slavery was a thing of the past in the nation's capital, which had become the South's first enclave of freedom in April 1862. The Emancipation Proclamation, issued eight months later, spelled the doom of the institution throughout the Confederacy. Largely through Lincoln's personal intervention, Congress approved the Thirteenth Amendment at the end of January 1865, which would achieve the "ultimate extinction" of slavery when it was ratified eleven months later. Lincoln delivered his First Inaugural Address before an audience that excluded African Americans, who were prohibited from entering the Capitol and even its grounds. The throng who listened to his Second Inaugural Address included many of the former slaves who had gained their freedom over the course of the war.[2]

In 1861, Lincoln delivered his inaugural address below the skeletal silhouette of the unfinished Capitol. At his insistence, the magnificent dome, capped by the *Statue of Freedom*, had risen to its full height as an emblem of the North's resolve to restore the Union and to secure Washington as its capital, come what may. In 1861, the Lees' estate on Arlington Heights looked down on the city, a symbol of the South's defiance of a northern president who stood committed to arresting the spread of slavery. Now, Arlington National Cemetery and Arlington Freedman's Village graced the 1,100-acre estate. The embattled Lee faced a siege in Petersburg and would surrender his army to General Ulysses S. Grant five weeks later. In 1865, Lincoln took the oath of office not from a slaveowner, Roger B. Taney, but from the recently confirmed Chief Justice Salmon P. Chase, an abolitionist and one of the founders of the Free Soil and Republican parties. The inaugural procession that marched from the White House to the Capitol included four companies of the 45th Regiment U.S. Colored Troops.[3]

Amid unprecedented challenges, Lincoln was the first president in thirty-two years to win a second term. He began his presidency by pursuing a policy of conciliation toward the South. Believing that southern civilians remained fundamentally loyal to the Union, Lincoln hoped that a spirit of moderation would bring them to their senses and convince the Confederate states to rejoin the Union voluntarily. Running for president in 1860, Lincoln promised to promote the gradual extinction of slavery in the states where it already existed, while preventing its spread into new territories. He initially pursued this policy as president. In his First Inaugural Address, he promised not to invade the seceded states unless attacked nor to disturb slavery where it already existed, including the District of Columbia. His campaign promises and constitutional scruples prevented him from attacking slavery within the states, even the seceded states of the Confederacy. Only when he believed that military victory required the destruction of slavery and the enrollment of African Americans as soldiers could he embrace emancipation as an additional imperative of the war.

During the first year and a half of his presidency, as military defeats and casualties mounted, Lincoln gradually realized that classical warfare, limited to the battlefield, could never subdue the South. Exemplified by General George McClellan's overcaution, traditional strategies left southern social and economic institutions, and above all slavery, untouched. The total warfare that he initiated during the summer of 1862 challenged southern slavery and mobilized all available resources, including more than two million soldiers, 179,000 of them African Americans. Beginning with General Benjamin Butler's "contraband" policy in May 1861 and concluding with the ratification of the Thirteenth Amendment, emancipation transformed the war by striking at the foundation of southern power, adding an additional, moral dimension to the Union military effort and turning slaves into soldiers. Under the new philosophy, Grant and Sherman's armies marched relentlessly into the heart of the Confederacy, seizing whatever they needed, destroying the rest, and recruiting African American soldiers in their wake.[4]

Now, with victory at hand, Lincoln advised restraint as the most effective approach to achieving his original war aim, the restoration of the Union. His Second Inaugural Address eschewed retribution, reproach, and even self-congratulation. Although the outcome of the war seemed certain, Lincoln modestly ventured "no prediction in regard to it," simply expressing "high hope for the future." In a spirit of reconciliation, he emphasized not the differences between the two sections but their similarities. Both North and South had feared civil war and striven to avert it. Ultimately, the South chose to "*make* war," while the North chose to "*accept* war." Neither section anticipated the long and bloody conflict that would result. "Each looked for an easier triumph, and a result less fundamental and astounding." Above all, both sections prayed to the same God. While acknowledging that slavery caused the war, Lincoln refused to grant northerners any claim to moral superiority—or to God's favor—as a result. Slavery was a curse that befouled the entire nation and in which both sections were complicit. Because slavery offended God, the war was a divine retribution that both sections must endure, "until every drop of blood drawn with the lash shall be paid by another drawn with the sword." In this sense, retribution was in no way the North's privilege to exact. Reunion would therefore proceed "With malice toward none, with charity for all." Lincoln ended by charging Americans with a twofold task—"to bind up the nation's wounds" and "to do all which may achieve and cherish a just, and a lasting peace."[5]

Commanding the Union, Lincoln's leadership strategy had always favored moderation. His fundamental achievement was ending slavery in a way that promoted both military victory and restoration of the Union. That task proved a perpetual and harrowing, and often heartrending, balancing act. Lincoln had to weigh the demands of radicals at one end of the spectrum against those of conservatives, including slaveowning racists, at the other. In January 1864, Harriet Beecher Stowe, who visited Lincoln in the White House, declared that "Surrounded by all sorts of conflicting claims, by traitors, by half-hearted, timid men, by Border State men and free State men, by radical abolitionists and conservatives, he has listened to all, weighed the words of all, waited, observed, yielded now here and now there, but in the main kept one inflexible, honest purpose, and drawn the national ship through." Maintaining that balance required Lincoln to move slowly, by degrees, but he almost always moved in the right direction. As Lincoln assured Frederick Douglass, while he proceeded cautiously toward the goal of emancipation, once he took any step forward he never retreated. "He has moved in the right path from the beginning," the *Washington Chronicle* concluded late in the war. "Some have chided him for being too fast; others for being too slow; but all must see that he has kept pace with the country, neither rising with its exultation, nor sinking with its depression, but steadily, calmly, constantly, directly moving on in the path of progress and liberty." Lincoln's gift, the newspaper concluded, was his understanding of what the nation was capable of achieving at any given moment—"to speak the right word at the right time, just as the country was ready to say amen."[6]

As the national capital, Washington, DC, proved the most strategic point within Lincoln's military and emancipation efforts. Southern and slaveowning in tradition, and now secessionist in orientation, Washington presented an unnerving range of potential threats to Lincoln personally, as well as to his effective prosecution of the war. The capture of the city, disruption of the inauguration, kidnapping of the president-elect, and his assassination as president all loomed as ever-present possibilities. From the moment of his election, Lincoln and his allies assumed command of the capital. Members of Lincoln's incoming administration and Buchanan's outgoing government created a security apparatus that could monitor suspected Confederate sympathizers. Upon his inauguration, Lincoln's first task as president was "cleaning the devil out of Washington." After Republicans in Congress reformed the city's antiquated and partisan police force, Lincoln appointed a reliable Unionist to lead it. The Metropolitan Police Department's 70,000 wartime arrests ended the city's storied tradition of spontaneous and organized mob actions. A rigorous Provost Guard, one of General George McClellan's achievements, assumed supremacy over the civil government, at Lincoln's behest. The administration's arrest and removal of Democratic mayor James Berret for alleged treasonous behavior allowed Richard Wallach, a Lincoln ally, to govern the city for the remainder of the war.[7]

Initially, Washington's geographical location between Confederate Virginia and loyal but slaveowning Maryland imposed severe military and political disadvantages. "Every step he has taken has been well considered, quite as much with regard to the time of taking it as to its provisions," a wartime reporter observed. "Radical measures are a necessity, but they may be premature and untimely in any given locality." Presiding over Washington, Lincoln always kept the capital's strategic situation in mind when framing or endorsing any new initiative. Facing the Army of Northern Virginia to their front, Lincoln and his general-in-chief, Winfield Scott, permitted no interference from Confederate sympathizers in Maryland to their rear. Making Washington a "grand depot" capable of supplying troops and provisions for the Army of the Potomac, Lincoln established a secure "military line" running northward through Baltimore. During the first two years of the war, Lincoln considered Washington a defensive liability, withholding up to 50,000 troops from offensive operations to keep the city secure. The completion of the capital's defenses in mid-1863 gave him the confidence to use the city as bait, an offensive asset that could lure Lee's army away from its base in Richmond. Closer to Washington, the Union Army could inflict crippling casualties upon the Confederacy. As Lincoln reasoned after the Union defeat at Second Bull Run, "We must hurt this enemy before it gets away." The victory at Gettysburg in 1863 and Lincoln's personal exhilaration as he watched the repulse of General Jubal Early's troops at Fort Stevens in 1864 confirmed the wisdom of the new strategy.[8]

Washington became the refuge for 40,000 fugitive slaves. Proximity to Virginia and Maryland, along with a tradition of anti-slavery activism coordinated by abolitionists, made the District of Columbia the most attractive destination for runaways fleeing the Confederacy. During his two-year congressional term, Lincoln had learned to move cautiously against slavery. Under the guise of military necessity, he embraced the emerging "contraband policy" that denied manpower to the enemy while providing laborers and eventually soldiers for the Union war effort. Always keeping Maryland's tenuous loyalty in mind, Lincoln mollified its slaveowners through enforcement of the Fugitive Slave Law, which Congress was painfully slow to repeal. The continual arrest of fugitives from Maryland heightened support for emancipation within Congress, the army, and the general public. After the Border States rejected his proposal for gradual, compensated emancipation, Lincoln endorsed the congressional initiative to free the capital's slaves, the first demonstration of the Union's resolve to end slavery where it already existed. Within months, Lincoln decided that the destruction of slavery throughout the Confederacy was essential to his goal of winning the war and reuniting the nation. Under his Emancipation Proclamation, the extinction of slavery joined the restoration of the Union as one of his primary wartime objectives.

Loyal Washingtonians reveled as they watched their city grow increasingly northern in outlook and character. As part of this budding urban transformation, northern reformers and congressional radicals joined African Americans—newly empowered through military service—in launching an aggressive equal rights campaign. The growing number of reformers, both white and black, who converged on the capital helped to spawn a new culture of equality and progress. Washington became the first southern city to achieve the elimination of its Black Code, the creation of public schools for African Africans, the integration of its streetcars, the empaneling of African Americans as jurors, and—once the war ended—the adoption of manhood suffrage and officeholding. Still, the war's immediate impact on the city was frightening. While the wartime capital tripled in size, Congress, which governed the District of Columbia, stubbornly underfunded its police force, neglected its buildings and streets, allowed its sanitation and public health to deteriorate, and above all failed to accommodate its burgeoning population of former slaves. The army provided housing for fugitives from Virginia, and later Maryland, but viewed the settlements as temporary "depots" for recruiting men into military service and women into domestic labor, rather than permanent homes for welcome newcomers. Only Arlington Freedman's Village, singled out as a poignant symbol of the stark contrast between slavery and freedom, ever resembled an enduring settlement of former slaves. This anomalous experiment in independence survived for a generation beyond the war but only through the persistence of its residents and their defiance of the government.[9]

Meanwhile, the hundreds of thousands of sick and wounded soldiers who flooded the wartime hospitals, as well as the city's proliferation of burials and embalming parlors, provided constant reminders of the horrific and heroic sacrifice that the eventual Union victory demanded. The Lincolns shared fully in the city's sacrifice and heroism, including Willie's death from typhoid fever and Lincoln's bout of smallpox. The Lincolns' decision to begin summering at the Soldiers' Home took them away from the pestilent White House—and the overbearing supplicants and ubiquitous vandals that haunted it— but exposed them to additional dangers. Lincoln's daily commute to and from the refuge invited assassination and kidnapping plots. After the war, Thomas Nelson Conrad of the Confederate Signal Corps revealed his involvement in a conspiracy to kidnap Lincoln during his half-hour-long ride. John Wilkes Booth's original plan was to kidnap Lincoln while he was commuting to and from the Soldiers' Home.[10]

Lincoln initially made his daily ride unescorted and without any protection. Secretary of State Seward injudiciously informed a correspondent that Lincoln commuted to the Soldiers' Home "on horseback, night and morning, unguarded." Focused on winning the war, Lincoln literally shrugged off all danger. "A stranger to fear, he often eluded our vigilance," Ward Hill Lamon recalled, "and before his absence could be noted he would be well on his way to his summer residence, alone, and many times at night." On one occasion, Lamon arrived at the White House only to learn that Lincoln had ridden off on his favorite horse, which his mounted guard donated and dubbed "Old Abe." Fearing an assassination attempt, Lamon borrowed the fastest horse on the grounds and rode after him. Fortunately, the president's horse "wouldn't go faster than a dogtrot if you beat him to death," so Lamon caught up with both Old Abes halfway to the Soldiers' Home. "Lincoln, far from suspecting that the Marshal was on his trail," according to reminiscence, "invited him to come along and have some fun." On another occasion, sentries at the Soldiers' Home heard a gunshot and were startled to see the president, on horseback, speed onto the grounds without his trademark stovepipe hat. When they investigated, they found the hat, shot through with a conspicuous bullet hole. Lincoln blamed the episode on a careless hunter—"some foolish gunner"—and shrugged off any concerns for his safety. The next day, he told Lamon about the episode, which he tried to laugh off while admitting that "just now I don't know what to think: I am staggered."[11]

In September 1862, at both Mary Lincoln's and Ward Hill Lamon's insistence, General James Wadsworth, commander of the Military District of Washington, assigned a mounted regiment, the 11th New York Cavalry, as Lincoln's permanent escort. "He always has a company of twenty-five or thirty cavalry, with sabres drawn and held upright over their shoulders," Walt Whitman, who lived along the route to the Soldiers' Home, observed. "They say this guard was against his personal wish, but he let his counselors have their way." Lincoln complained to his general-in-chief Henry Halleck that "he and Mrs. Lincoln 'couldn't hear themselves talk,' for the clatter of their sabers and spurs." Drawing on his fabled humor to defuse concerns over his safety, he claimed that "he was more afraid of being shot by the accidental discharge of one of their carbines or revolvers, than of any attempt upon his life." Lamon concluded that "he was always prepared for the inevitable, and singularly indifferent as to his personal safety."[12]

In 1863, a hundred-man cavalry company from Ohio, the President's Mounted Bodyguard, began patrolling the front entrance of the White House, while a Pennsylvania unit, Company K of the 150th Pennsylvania Infantry, guarded the south side. These defenses, however, remained all too porous. In the following year, the White House stables caught fire. When Lincoln arrived, he tried to save the animals himself, but the burning hay and straw, which produced a gas line explosion, made rescue impossible. Six horses, including those belonging to Lincoln, Nicolay, and Hay, along with the family's two ponies and all of Tad's goats, succumbed. Lincoln reportedly wept when he learned that little Willie's gray pony was one of the victims. Concluding that the fire was the work of an arsonist, the police arrested Mary Lincoln's former coachman, whom she had fired that very day, but later released him. Three fire companies tried to fight the blaze, but there was no fireplug near the White House. In addition to Washington's tradition of incendiarism, a series of carriage accidents afflicted the Lincolns. Abraham Lincoln suffered a minor accident while returning from the Navy Yard, but Mary Lincoln and William Seward suffered serious mishaps. In July 1863, Mary Lincoln was riding in a carriage near Mount Pleasant Hospital when the coachman's seat came loose and threw him to the ground. As the horses ran off with the carriage, the First Lady jumped out onto the roadway and hit her head. The wound festered and the infection spread. Her already bothersome headaches increased in frequency, and Robert Lincoln believed that his mother never entirely recovered. This suspicious accident may well have been aimed at the president, not his wife, but Abraham Lincoln typically minimized the episode. When Rebecca Pomroy, who was nursing the First Lady, asked him about taking additional precautions for his own safety, he answered with resignation that "I can do nothing different from what I am doing." His only official response was a memo directing that the "place on the road near Mt. Pleasant Hospital ought to be repaired."[13]

Beyond his cavalry escort, the government did not provide Lincoln with a personal bodyguard until November 1864, when Lamon had four members of the Metropolitan Police assigned to the White House. Two of them protected Lincoln during an eight-hour daytime shift, but he had only one bodyguard at night, who patrolled the upstairs corridor and listened to the president breathing as he slept. Still, Lamon continued his self-imposed duty of sleeping in front of Lincoln's bedroom door surrounded by his personal arsenal of pistols and bowie knives. The policemen carried revolvers, but Lincoln insisted that they pose as doorkeepers in civilian attire. Whenever he left the White House, he requested that they remain inconspicuous by walking astride him rather than trailing behind. Now Lincoln had an escort during his frequent treks to the War Department's telegraph office and his nightly trips to confer with Secretary Stanton. The police were ineffective, however, and a plainclothes detective lost $40 to a pickpocket when mingling with a crowd at the White House. (One of these four officers was guarding Lincoln on the night of his assassination.) The police did insist on building cloakrooms near the White House entrance to prevent visitors from concealing weapons. By this time, Washington's women, wearing voluminous wraps, were considered the prime suspects.[14]

Three years before nearly succumbing to an assassination attempt at the hands of John Wilkes Booth's co-conspirator, Lewis Powell, William Seward declared, "Assassination is not an American practice or habit." William Stoddard wrote complacently that the "idea of assassination has been held up before us until it is worn out and there is no more scare in it." Ward Hill Lamon knew better. In December 1864, he admonished Lincoln for neglecting his own safety, warning bluntly that *"you are in danger."* Begging him not to attend the theater without an escort, Lamon emphasized that "you know or ought to know that your life is Sought after, and will be taken, unless you and your friends are cautious—for you have many enemies within our lines." Suspecting that Lincoln would not act on his advice, five days later Lamon wrote a briefer and more pointed note to John Nicolay. "I may be unnecessarily frightened about Mr Lincoln's personal safety—but I do assure you I think I have good reasons for my uneasiness about him," he warned. "See that he don't go out alone either in the day or night time."[15]

In the last speech that Lincoln ever delivered, he joined the equal rights campaign by endorsing the adoption of limited African American suffrage. On April 11, 1865, two days after Lee's surrender at Appomattox Court House, Lincoln stood before an exuberant crowd assembled below a White House window. Before beginning, he told William Stoddard that "I am going to say something tonight that may be important." As in his Second Inaugural Address five weeks earlier, Lincoln forwent the opportunity to trumpet the success of the Union war effort and instead enjoined the country to reunite and look forward to the future. Acknowledging the congressional radicals' call for granting the vote to African Americans, he proposed a compromise. "I myself would prefer that it were now conferred," he declared, "on the very intelligent, and on those who serve our cause as soldiers." In these words, Frederick Douglass perceived yet another "entering wedge" that would challenge and potentially transform the now defeated South. "It was just like Abraham Lincoln," he concluded. "He never shocked prejudices unnecessarily. Having learned statesmanship while splitting rails, he always used the thin edge of the wedge first." As usual, Lincoln had counseled—and practiced—

patience before deciding to chart a new and controversial course, waiting until he believed that "the people were ready to say amen."[16]

Before delivering his speech, Lincoln had worried about "saying things that other people don't like." Standing in the audience under the window was a southerner who indeed detested what he had just heard. "That means nigger citizenship," John Wilkes Booth told co-conspirator David Herold. "Now, by God, I'll put him through. That's the last speech he will ever make." Three days later, on Good Friday, the Lincolns took one of their familiar afternoon carriage rides. Feeling free to dismiss their annoying cavalry escort at last, Abraham told Mary cheerfully, "I prefer to ride by ourselves to day." Enjoying the return of peace and the prospect of a placid second term, they too preferred to look forward rather than behind them to the heartrending past. Lincoln told Mary, "We must *both*, be more cheerful in the future—between the war & the loss of our darling Willie—we have both, been very miserable." But that cheerful future never came. At Ford's Theatre that evening, Washington, DC, surrendered its last, tragic casualty to the American Civil War.[17]

ACKNOWLEDGMENTS

Over the last decade, as I conceived, researched, and wrote this study of Lincoln's presidential leadership within the context of Washington, DC, as a wartime community, I have received generous support from numerous colleagues. In particular, I would like to single out Jean Baker, Gabor Boritt, Michael Burkhimer, Michael Burlingame, James Cornelius, Rodney Davis, Brian Dirck, Joseph Fornieri, Sara Gabbard, Matthew Gilmore, Allen Guelzo, Harold Holzer, William Miller, Lucas Morel, Phillip Paludan, James Rawley, Sylvia Rodrigue, Thomas Schwartz, Frank Williams, and Douglas Wilson for providing encouragement, advice, and insights at various points and in various measure. Simultaneously, dozens of archivists and librarians at repositories across the country, too numerous to single out, have generously contributed their time, energy, and insights to the never-ending search for source material.

At the University of Nebraska-Lincoln, Vice Chancellor for Research and Economic Development Prem S. Paul, Dean David Manderscheid of the College of Arts and Sciences, Dean Joan Giesecke of the University Libraries, the UNL Research Council, the Center for Digital Research in the Humanities, and the Department of History have consistently provided generous funding for documentary materials, computing equipment, travel, and research assistance. The digital project that I co-direct, *Civil War Washington*, received substantial funding from the National Endowment for the Humanities through a three-year Collaborative Research Grant that carries "We the People" designation. Beyond this indispensable institutional support, my co-directors, Susan Lawrence, Coordinator of UNL's Humanities in Medicine Program, and Kenneth Price, an eminent Walt Whitman scholar, have offered welcome encouragement and advice. Our three project managers, Wesley Raabe, Stacey Berry, and Elizabeth Lorang, have been instrumental in securing otherwise inaccessible documents. William G Thomas, III, Chair of the History Department at UNL, has proven more than collegial in sharing his insights into the Civil War Era, as well as his expertise in digital history.

From beginning to end, Steve Forman, Senior Editor and Vice President at W. W. Norton & Company, has offered crucial encouragement, advice, and insights with invariable good sense and perceptive wit, along with a welcome dose of collegial support, all of which I genuinely appreciate. Throughout the long process of research, writing, and revision that has culminated in *Lincoln's Citadel,* his outstanding staff of editorial assistants generously shared the kind of expertise that makes W. W. Norton such a respected publisher and a rewarding press to work with in all respects.

Of course, I bear the entire responsibility for the use that I have made of all of the support, advice, and encouragement that I have received over the years.

NOTES

ABBREVIATIONS

ALPLC   Abraham Lincoln Papers, Library of Congress

CG   *Congressional Globe*

CMPP   James D. Richardson, *A Compilation of the Messages and Papers of the Presidents, 1789–1897* (Washington: Published by Authority of Congress, 1899), 10 vols.

CW   Roy P. Basler, ed., *The Collected Works of Abraham Lincoln* (New Brunswick: Rutgers University Press, 1953), 9 vols.

CWS   Roy P. Basler, ed., *The Collected Works of Abraham Lincoln, First Supplement, 1832–1865* (New Brunswick: Rutgers University Press, 1974).

DBNS   D. B. Nichols Scrapbooks, 1853–1873, Library of Congress

EDC   "Emancipation in the District of Columbia," 38th Cong., 1st Sess., House Ex. Doc. No. 42

JRGP   Joshua Reed Giddings Papers, Ohio Historical Society

LOC   Library of Congress

LTDW   Gilbert H. Barnes and Dwight L. Dumond, eds., *Letters of Theodore Dwight Weld, Angelina Grimké Weld, and Sarah Grimké, 1822–1844* (New York: D. Appleton-Century Company, 1934), 2 vols.

MTL   Justin G. Turner and Linda Levitt Turner, *Mary Todd Lincoln: Her Life and Letters* (New York: Fromm International Publishing, 1987)

NARA   National Archives and Records Administration

OR   United States War Department, *The War of the Rebellion: A Compilation of the Official Records of the Union and Confederate Armies* (Washington: Government Printing Office, 1880–1901), 70 vols.

PCR   *Philadelphia Christian Recorder*
RBCES   Records of the Board of Commissioners for the Emancipation of
             Slaves in the District of Columbia, 1861–1863, NARA, Record
             Group 217.6.5, Records of the General Accounting Office
RCHS   *Records of the Columbia Historical Society*
WDC   *Washington Daily Chronicle*
WES   *Washington Evening Star*
WNE   *Washington National Era*
WNI   *Washington Daily National Intelligencer*
WNR   *Washington National Republican*

NOTE ON CURRENCY VALUES

To appreciate the current value of Civil War–era U.S. currency, readers should adjust dollar values in specific years by the following multiples, which are based on the percentage increase in the Consumer Price Index, as calculated by the currency inflator available online at http://www.measuringworth.com/uscompare/: 1847 (28), 1848 (29), 1849 (29), 1861 (26), 1862 (23), 1863 (18), 1864 (15), 1865 (14).

PREFACE

1. Walt Whitman, *Specimen Days* (Boston: David R. Godine, 1971), 60; Roy Morris Jr., *The Better Angel: Walt Whitman in the Civil War* (New York: Oxford University Press, 2000), 75; Daniel Mark Epstein, *Lincoln and Whitman: Parallel Lives in Civil War Washington* (New York: Ballantine Books, 2004), 114.
2. *CW*, VI, 226.
3. I am grateful to my colleague Susan C. Lawrence, coordinator of the Humanities in Medicine Program at the University of Nebraska–Lincoln, for providing this figure from the database of military hospital capacity and occupancy in Washington that she is compiling from Record Group 94, NARA.

CHAPTER ONE "Getting the Hang of the House"

1. Washington officials estimated that L'Enfant's plan could accommodate a city of 389,456 residents; 37th Cong., 3rd Sess., H. Exec. Doc. 1, Pt. 2, 649. William H. Herndon and Jesse W. Weik, *Herndon's Lincoln*, ed. Douglas L. Wilson and Rodney O. Davis (Urbana: University of Illinois Press, 2006), 192; Keith Melder, *City of Magnificent Intentions: A History of Washington, District of Columbia*, 2nd ed. (Washington: Intac, 1997), 138; Lois Bryan Adams, *Letter from Washington, 1863–1865*, ed. Evelyn Leasher (Detroit: Wayne State University

Press, 1999), 35; Elizabeth Smith Brownstein, *Lincoln's Other White House: The Untold Story of the Man and His Presidency* (Hoboken, NJ: John Wiley & Sons, 2005), 26.

2. Bob Arnebeck, *Through a Fiery Trial: Building Washington, 1790–1800* (Lanham, MD: Madison Books, 1991), 579; James Sterling Young, *The Washington Community, 1800–1828* (New York: Columbia University Press, 1966), 89, 98–99, 102; Paul Findley, *A. Lincoln: The Crucible of Congress* (New York: Crown, 1979), 85; Rachel A. Shelden, "Messmates' Union: Friendship, Politics, and Living Arrangements in the Capital City, 1845–1861," *Journal of the Civil War Era* 1 (Dec. 2011), 463.

3. *WNI*, Nov. 30, Dec. 1, 1847; Wilhelmus Bogart Bryan, *A History of the National Capital from its Foundation through the Period of the Adoption of the Organic Act,* (New York: Macmillan, 1916), II, 444–45; Young, *Washington Community*, 24, 98–99, 102; Shelden, "Messmates' Union," 457.

4. *WNI*, Nov. 30, 1847; Constance McLaughlin Green, *Washington, Village and Capital, 1800–1878* (Princeton: Princeton University Press, 1962), 108; Letitia Woods Brown, *Free Negroes in the District of Columbia, 1790–1846* (New York: Oxford University Press, 1972), 7; David R. Goldfield, "Antebellum Washington in Context: The Pursuit of Prosperity and Identity," in Howard Gillette Jr., ed., *Southern City, National Ambition: The Growth of Early Washington, D.C., 1800–1860* (Washington: George Washington University Center for Washington Area Studies, 1995), 20; Jean H. Baker, *Mary Todd Lincoln: A Biography* (New York: Norton, 1987), 103, 136.

5. William D. Haley, ed., *Philp's Washington Described: A Complete View of the American Capital, and the District of Columbia* (Washington: Philp & Solomon, 1861), 207–8; Samuel C. Busey, *Personal Reminiscences and Recollections of Forty-Six Years' Membership in the Medical Society of the District of Columbia* (Washington, 1895), 25–26; Donald W. Riddle, *Congressman Abraham Lincoln* (Urbana: University of Illinois Press, 1957), 8; Allen C. Clark, *Abraham Lincoln in the National Capital* (Washington: W. F. Roberts Company, 1925), 3; Arnebeck, *Through a Fiery Trial*, 26, 494–95, 500, 579; C. M. Harris, "Washington's Gamble, L'Enfant's Dream: Politics, Design, and the Founding of the National Capital," *William and Mary Quarterly* 56 (July 1999), 547; Richard M. Lee, *Mr. Lincoln's City: An Illustrated Guide to the Civil War Sites of Washington* (McLean, VA: EPM Publications, 1981), 43; Laura Bergheim, *The Washington Historical Atlas: Who Did What When and Where in the Nation's Capital* (Rockville, MD: Woodbine House, 1992), 91–92.

6. In 1813, Green married Lucretia Maria Edwards, sister of Ninian Edwards, territorial governor of Illinois and its first U.S. senator, who was the father of Ninian W. Edwards, who married Mary Lincoln's oldest sister, Elizabeth Todd; W. Stephen Belko, *The Invincible Duff Green: Whig of the West* (Columbia: University of Missouri Press, 2006), 24. Findley, *Crucible of Congress*, 85; Busey, *Recollections*, 26; Wendy Gamber, *The Boardinghouse in Nineteenth-Century America* (Baltimore: Johns Hopkins University Press, 2007), 8, 56–57, 90.

7. A rod is equivalent to 16½ feet. According to the U.S. Manuscript Census, Free Population Schedule, Washington, DC, 1860, Ann G. Sprigg was fifty-nine years old in 1860. To Angelina G. Weld, Jan. 1, 2, 1842, *LTDW*, II, 883–84; to "Boy" [Grotius Reed Giddings], Dec. 29, 1839, to "My Dear Wife" [Laura Waters Giddings], Jan. 1, 1843, Jan. 26, 1849, JRGP; James Brewer Stewart, *Joshua R. Giddings and the Tactics of Radical Politics* (Cleveland: Press of Case Western Reserve University, 1970), 195; Stephen Nissenbaum, *Sex, Diet, and Debility in Jacksonian America: Sylvester Graham and Health Reform* (Chicago: Dorsey Press, 1980), 139 n. 20.

8. Weld to Angelina G. Weld, Jan. 1, 1842, *LTDW*, II, 883; Busey, *Recollections*, 27; Riddle, *Congressman Abraham Lincoln*, 31–32.

9. To "Boy" [Grotius Reed Giddings], Dec. 29, 1839, Seth M. Green, Warsaw, New York, to Giddings, Dec. 5, 1843, to Lura Maria Giddings, Dec. 26, 1847, JRGP; Weld to Angelina G. Weld, Jan. 18, Feb. 9, 1842, *LTDW*, II, 897, 914.

10. Busey, *Recollections*, 26, 28; Gamber, *Boardinghouse in Nineteenth-Century America*, 90–91.

11. Busey, *Recollections*, 26; Riddle, *Congressman Abraham Lincoln*, 29.

12. *CW*, I, 423–29, 430; Busey, *Recollections*, 25.

13. *CW*, I, 454; Riddle, *Congressman Abraham Lincoln*, 27.

14. *CW*, I, 420–22; Springfield *Illinois State Register*, Jan. 7, 14, 1848; Springfield *Illinois State Journal*, Jan. 12, 1848; Riddle, *Congressman Abraham Lincoln*, 2; Mark E. Neely Jr., "Lincoln and the Mexican War: An Argument by Analogy," *Civil War History* 24 (March 1978), 5–24; G. S. Borit[t], "Lincoln's Opposition to the Mexican War," *Journal of the Illinois State Historical Society* 67 (Feb. 1974), 79–100.

15. *CW*, I, 430–31, 441–42, 446–47; Springfield *Illinois State Register*, April 11, 1845; Springfield *Illinois State Journal*, April 6, 1848; Herndon and Weik, *Herndon's Lincoln*, 179; Riddle, *Congressman Abraham Lincoln*, 56–69; Findley, *Crucible of Congress*, 152–53; Mark Neely, "Did Lincoln Cause Logan's Defeat?" *Lincoln Lore* 1660 (June 1976), 1–4.

16. *CW*, I, 465, 496; Busey, *Recollections*, 28; Baker, *Mary Todd Lincoln*, 120–21; Jennifer Fleischner, *Mrs. Lincoln and Mrs. Keckly: The Remarkable Story of the Friendship Between a First Lady and a Former Slave* (New York: Broadway Books, 2003), 163; Kenneth J. Winkle, *Abraham and Mary Lincoln* (Carbondale: Southern Illinois University Press, 2001), 57–60.

CHAPTER 2   "At War with Washington"

1. *U.S. Constitution*, Art. I, Sect. 8; Joseph Sturge, *A Visit to the United States in 1841* (London: Hamilton, Adams, 1842), 76; Brown, *Free Negroes in the District of Columbia*, 10–11; Arnebeck, *Through a Fiery Trial*, 57, 117, 205, 229, 597.

2. Sturge, *Visit to the United States*, 74–75; Allan Johnston, *Surviving Freedom: The Black Community of Washington, D.C., 1860–1880* (New York: Garland, 1993),

91; Mary Beth Corrigan, "The Ties That Bind: The Pursuit of Community and Freedom Among Slaves and Free Blacks in the District of Columbia, 1800–1860," in Gillette, *Southern City, National Ambition*, 70–71; Stanley Harrold, *Subversives: Antislavery Community in Washington, D.C., 1828–1865* (Baton Rouge: Louisiana State University Press, 2003), 2, 28.

3. Sturge, *Visit to the United States*, 74–75, 89; Solomon Northup, *Twelve Years a Slave. Narrative of Solomon Northup, a Citizen of New-York, Kidnapped in Washington City in 1841, and Rescued in 1853* (New York: Miller, Orton & Co., 1857), 40–64; Federal Writers Project, *Washington: City and Capital* (Washington: Government Printing Office, 1937), 69; Bergheim, *Washington Historical Atlas*, 315; Jesse J. Holland, *Black Men Built the Capitol: Discovering African-American History In and Around Washington, D.C.* (Guilford, CT: Globe Pequot Press, 2007), 28–29; Sandra Fitzpatrick and Maria R. Goodwin, *The Guide to Black Washington: Places and Events of Historical and Cultural Significance in the Nation's Capital*, rev. and illus. ed. (New York: Hippocrene Books, 2001), 46.

4. *WES*, Aug. 8, 1861; Green, *Washington: Village and Capital*, 180; Constance McLaughlin Green, *The Secret City: A History of Race Relations in the Nation's Capital* (Princeton: Princeton University Press, 1967), 29; Federal Writers Project, *Washington: City and Capital*, 69; Bergheim, *Washington Historical Atlas*, 315; Holland, *Black Men Built the Capitol*, 28–29; Fitzpatrick and Goodwin, *Guide to Black Washington*, 36, 46; Sturge, *Visit to the United States*, 89–91; Josephine F. Pacheco, *The Pearl: A Failed Slave Escape on the Potomac* (Chapel Hill: University of North Carolina Press, 2005), 33; James Brewer Stewart, "Joshua Giddings, Antislavery Violence, and Congressional Politics of Honor," in John R. McKivigan and Stanley Harrold, eds., *Antislavery Violence: Sectional, Racial, and Cultural Conflict in Antebellum America* (Knoxville: University of Tennessee Press, 1999), 173; Frederic Bancroft, *Slave Trading in the Old South* (New York: Frederick Ungar Publishing, 1931), 54.

5. Johnston, *Surviving Freedom*, 91; Brown, *Free Negroes in the District of Columbia*, 11–12, 14–15, 119; Corrigan, "Ties That Bind," 70–72; Harrold, *Subversives*, 5.

6. Louis Filler, *The Crusade Against Slavery, 1830–1860* (New York: Harper & Row, 1960), 99–100, 104; Ronald G. Walters, *American Reformers, 1815–1860* (New York: Hill & Wang, 1978), 80–85; Merton L. Dillon, *The Abolitionists: The Growth of a Dissenting Minority* (DeKalb: Northern Illinois University Press, 1974), 100, 102.

7. Throughout his congressional career, Giddings denied that he was technically an abolitionist, arguing that once the federal government stopped supporting slavery it would die its own natural death; Stewart, *Joshua R. Giddings*, 275. Stewart, *Joshua R. Giddings*, 5–7, 10, 25, 31; Filler, *Crusade Against Slavery*, 103; William Lee Miller, *Arguing About Slavery: The Great Battle in the United States Congress* (New York: Alfred A. Knopf, 1996), 339, 386–87; Stewart, "Joshua Giddings, Antislavery Violence, and Congressional Politics of Honor," 170; Giddings to "My Dear Wife," Jan. 7, 1846, Giddings-Julian Papers, LOC.

8. Miller, *Arguing About Slavery*, 405, 448; Eric Foner, *Free Soil, Free Labor, Free*

Men: The Ideology of the Republican Party Before the Civil War (New York: Oxford University Press, 1970), 73–87; Daniel Walker Howe, *The Political Culture of the American Whigs* (Chicago: University of Chicago Press, 1979), 168; Stewart, *Joshua R. Giddings*, 196.

9. Howe, *Political Culture of the American Whigs*, 174–75; Howard Jones, *Mutiny on the Amistad: The Saga of a Slave Revolt and Its Impact on American Abolition, Law, and Diplomacy*, rev. ed. (New York: Oxford University Press, 1987), 181, 193.

10. Miller, *Arguing About Slavery*, 404–5; Dillon, *Abolitionists*, 84; Harrold, *Subversives*, 34–35; Benjamin P. Thomas, *Theodore Weld: Crusader for Freedom* (New Brunswick: Rutgers University Press, 1950), 200; Stanley Harrold, *Gamaliel Bailey and Antislavery Union* (Kent: Kent State University Press, 1986), 81; Douglas E. Evelyn and Paul Dickson, *On This Spot: Pinpointing the Past in Washington, D.C.* (Sterling, VA: Capital Books, 2008), 48.

11. Weld to Angelina G. Weld, Dec. 27, 1842, *LTDW*, II, 947; to "My Dear Wife" [Laura Waters Giddings], Jan. 1, 1843, to "My Dear Boy" [Comfort Pease Giddings or Joseph Addison Giddings], Dec. 25, 1843, JRGP; Miller, *Arguing About Slavery*, 408; Harrold, *Subversives*, 66.

12. Giddings to "My Dear Daughter," Feb. 8, 1842, Giddings-Julian Papers; Weld to Angelina G. Weld, Jan. 25, 1842, *LTDW*, II, 903; Jones, *Mutiny on the Amistad*, 208, 211; Thomas, *Theodore Weld*, 200, 209, 211; Miller, *Arguing About Slavery*, 446–47, 449, 452, 453–54.

13. Brown, *Secret City*, 14–15, 106–8, 111–12; Corrigan, "Ties That Bind," 74–75; Mary Beth Corrigan, " 'It's a Family Affair': Buying Freedom in the District of Columbia, 1850–1860," in Larry E. Hudson Jr., ed., *Working Toward Freedom: Slave Society and Domestic Economy in the American South* (Rochester: University of Rochester Press, 1994), 163–91. T. Stephen Whitman, *The Price of Freedom: Slavery and Manumission in Baltimore and Early National Maryland* (Lexington: University Press of Kentucky, 1997), provides a detailed analysis of manumission, hiring out, and self-purchase in Maryland, whose slave code governed the District of Columbia.

14. Weld to Angelina G. Weld and Sarah Grimké, Feb. 17, 1842, Weld to Angelina G. Weld, Jan. 4, 1843, *LTDW*, II, 948, 956; to "My Dear Boy," Aug. 15, 1842, JRGP; Hilary Russell, "Underground Railroad Activists in Washington, D.C.," *Washington History* 13 (Fall/Winter 2001/2002), 28–49.

15. Thomas Smallwood, *A Narrative of Thomas Smallwood (Coloured Man)* (Toronto: By the Author, 1851), 60; Wilbur H. Siebert, *The Underground Railroad from Slavery to Freedom: A Comprehensive History* (New York: Macmillan, 1898), 88, 175; Harrold, *Subversives*, 29, 32, 34, 36, 54, 64, 66, 68–78; Pacheco, *The Pearl*, 55; Mary Kay Ricks, *Escape on the Pearl: The Heroic Bid for Freedom on the Underground Railroad* (New York: William Morrow, 2007), 32, 35; Mark S. Schantz, *Awaiting the Heavenly Country: The Civil War and America's Culture of Death* (Ithaca: Cornell University Press, 2008), 31; Russell, "Underground Railroad Activists," 30–31. Smallwood's pseudonym was Samivel Weller Jr.

16. S. M. Gates, Warsaw, New York, to Giddings, Dec. 5, 1848, JRGP.

17. According to Stewart, "Joshua Giddings, Antislavery Violence, and Congressional Politics of Honor," 183, "Mrs. Sprigg herself was actually a slaveholder but of a highly unusual and subversive sort: she retained this status simply for the purpose of releasing anyone she managed to acquire." Russell, "Underground Railroad Activists," 30, identifies Mrs. Sprigg as the keeper of one of two "anti-slavery boarding houses" within Washington's underground railroad network. S. M. Gates, Warsaw, New York, to Giddings, Dec. 5, 1848, William Slade, Troy, New York, to Giddings, Dec. 17, 1848, JRGP; Siebert, *Underground Railroad*, 63, 415, 416.

18. Joshua R. Giddings, *History of the Rebellion: Its Authors and Causes* (New York: Follet, Foster & Co., 1864), 267–68; Stewart, "Joshua Giddings, Antislavery Violence, and Congressional Politics of Honor," 169, 174, 183; Harrold, *Subversives*, 44, 108–9; Riddle, *Congressman Abraham Lincoln*, 104; Green, *Secret City*, 44.

CHAPTER 3 "A Western Free State Man"

1. Boston *Daily Whig*, Feb. 3, 1848; Cleveland *Daily True Democrat*, Jan. 24, 1848; Giddings, *History of the Rebellion*, 268–69; Harrold, *Subversives*, 108–9.

2. Boston *Daily Whig*, Feb. 3, 1848; Cleveland *Daily True Democrat*, Jan. 24, 1848; Weld to Angelina G. Weld, Jan. 2, 1842, *LTDW*, II, 885; Giddings, *History of the Rebellion*, 268–69; Harrold, *Subversives*, 109.

3. Giddings proposed the creation of a special committee, because the standing Committee on the District of Columbia contained a majority of slaveholders; *CG*, 30th Cong., 1st Sess., 179–80; Giddings, *History of the Rebellion*, 268–71; Boston *Daily Whig*, Feb. 3, 1848; *WNI*, Jan. 18, 1848; Cleveland *Daily True Democrat*, Jan. 25, 27, 1848; Harrold, *Subversives*, 109–11.

4. According to the U.S. Manuscript Census, Slave Schedule, 1830 and 1850, Washington, DC, Green owned five slaves in 1830 and one slave in 1850. Cleveland *Daily True Democrat*, Feb. 16, 1848; Belko, *Invincible Duff Green*, 157–59, 288–89, 411, 436; Shelden, "Messmates' Union," 460–61; Ricks, *Escape on the Pearl*, 98.

5. Armistead's surname is sometimes rendered as Armstead. Duff Green and Ben E. Green, "To the Hon. Judges of the Circuit Court of the United States for the District of Columbia," Jan. 1848, Duff Green Papers, Southern Historical Collection, University of North Carolina Library; Pacheco, *The Pearl*, 48–50; Ricks, *Escape on the Pearl*, 57–60.

6. The Greens referred to Eleanora Bell variously as "Ellenora Beall, or Bell" and "Eleanor Beall." Green and Green, "To the Hon. Judges"; Brown, *Free Negroes in the District of Columbia*, 105–6; Dorothy S. Provine, *District of Columbia: Free Negro Registers, 1821–1861* (Bowie: Heritage Books, 1996), 232.

7. Williams was a fifty-year-old native Virginian; U.S. Manuscript Census, Free Population Schedule, Washington, DC. 1850. To Mr. W H Williams, Washington, DC, Jan. 24, 1848, Wm H Williams, Washington, DC, to Green, Jan.

24, 1848, Green Papers; *WNE*, Feb. 24, 1848; Cleveland *Daily True Democrat*, Feb. 16, 1848; Harrold, *Subversives*, 110–11.

8. According to the U.S. Manuscript Census, Slave Schedule, Washington, DC, 1850, Wallach owned one slave. Richard Wallach, Washington, DC, to Green, Jan. 24, 1848, to Richard Wallach, Washington, DC, Jan. 24, 1848, Green Papers; *WNE*, Feb. 24, 1848; Cleveland *Daily True Democrat*, Feb. 16, 1848; Harrold, *Subversives*, 110–11.

9. According to Riddle, *Congressman Abraham Lincoln*, 174, "Giddings had been cultivating Lincoln, doubtless hoping to attach him to his coterie of free-soil associates." *CW*, I, 109; Leonard L. Richards, *"Gentlemen of Property and Standing": Anti-Abolition Mobs in Jacksonian America* (New York: Oxford University Press, 1970), 12, 14, 157.

10. *CW*, I, 75; Paul Simon, *Lincoln's Preparation for Greatness: The Illinois Legislative Years* (Urbana: University of Illinois Press, 1965), 132; Riddle, *Congressman Abraham Lincoln*, 174.

11. *CW*, I, 75.

12. *CW*, I, 74, 75, IV, 65; Simon, *Lincoln's Preparation for Greatness*, 131–34.

13. *CW*, I, 348.

14. *CW*, I, 505, II, 252; Riddle, *Congressman Abraham Lincoln*, 178; Findley, *Crucible of Congress*, 128; Lewis E. Lehrman, *Lincoln at Peoria: The Turning Point* (Mechanicsburg, PA: Stackpole Books, 2008), 216–17.

15. *WNI*, April 19, 1848; Pacheco, *The Pearl*, 48–55; Harrold, *Subversives*, 99, 102, 128, 140–41.

16. Washington's city councils consisted of two elected legislative chambers, the Common Council and the Board of Aldermen. *WNI*, April 19, 1848; Giddings, *History of the Rebellion*, 273; Pacheco, *The Pearl*, 56, 57, 58, 61, 63, 75.

17. According to Stewart, *Joshua R. Giddings*, 152, "Giddings had full knowledge of this risky enterprise beforehand and was anxious for its success." Giddings to "Dear Molly," April 23, 1848, Giddings-Julian Papers; Giddings, *History of the Rebellion*, 272–73; Harrold, *Subversives*, 124, 127, 129; Pacheco, *The Pearl*, 55.

18. Washington's city councils consisted of an eight-member Board of Aldermen and a twelve-member Common Council. *WNI*, April 20, 21, 22, 1848; Allan Nevins, ed., *Polk: The Diary of a President, 1845–1849* (New York: Longmans, Green, 1929), 320; Giddings, *History of the Rebellion*, 274; Pacheco, *The Pearl*, 73–74, 80, 86, 87; Harrold, *Subversives*, 54.

19. Giddings, *History of the Rebellion*, 274–75; *WNI*, April 22, 1848; Pacheco, *The Pearl*, 77–79.

20. To "Dear Molly," April 23, 1848, JRGP; from John C. Calhoun, undated, Green Papers; *WNI*, April 24, 1848; Harrold, *Subversives*, 132, 137; Pacheco, *The Pearl*, 127. Calhoun's letter is undated and annotated "[Jan. 1848?]" but clearly postdates the capture of the *Pearl*. Calhoun's list spells Eleanora's name as Ellañor.

21. Giddings, *History of the Rebellion*, 277–78; Harrold, *Subversives*, 137–38, 140–41; Pacheco, *The Pearl*, 230.

22. *CG*, 30th Cong. 1st Sess., 672–73; *WNI*, April 26, 1848; Giddings, *History of the Rebellion*, 276–77, 278; Findley, *Crucible of Congress*, 136.

23. Harrold, *Subversives*, 48, 146–47, 159–60, 162–63; Pacheco, *The Pearl*, 130–33, 217; Ricks, *Escape on the Pearl*, 192; Debby Applegate, *The Most Famous Man in America: The Biography of Henry Ward Beecher* (New York: Doubleday, 2006), 225–26, 229.

24. *CW*, I, 348, 448, 463, 468; Myrta Lockett Avary, ed., *Recollections of Alexander H. Stephens* (New York: Doubleday, Page, 1910), 21–22; Thomas E. Schott, *Alexander H. Stephens of Georgia: A Biography* (Baton Rouge: Louisiana State University Press, 1988), 81; David Herbert Donald, *Lincoln* (New York: Simon & Schuster, 1995), 126–27; Riddle, *Congressman Abraham Lincoln*, 86, 99; Findley, *Crucible of Congress*, 117.

25. *CW*, I, 480–90, 492, 501–16; to "My Dear Son" [Joseph Addison Giddings], Jan. 22, 1848, to "My Dear Son" [Joseph Addison Giddings], July 22, 1848, to Lura Maria Giddings, Jan. 26, 1847, JRGP; Stewart, *Joshua R. Giddings*, 152.

26. *CW*, II, 4, 9; Harry E. Pratt, *The Personal Finances of Abraham Lincoln* (Springfield: Abraham Lincoln Association, 1943), 101.

CHAPTER 4   "Is the Center Nothing?"

1. Findley, *Crucible of Congress*, 117, labeled Lincoln a "cotton Whig" at the outset of the 30th Congress. Harrold, *Subversives*, 114–15; Stewart, *Joshua R. Giddings*, 169; Findley, *Crucible of Congress*, 115–16.

2. Diary, Dec. 3, 4, 5, 6, 20, 1848, JRGP; Riddle, *Congressman Abraham Lincoln*, 71.

3. Diary, Dec. 12, 1848, JRGP; Giddings, *History of the Rebellion*, 284; Stewart, *Joshua R. Giddings*, 189 n. 2; Riddle, *Congressman Abraham Lincoln*, 71–72, 166; Findley, *Crucible of Congress*, 137.

4. To "My Dear Son" [Joseph Addison Giddings], Dec. 16, 1848, Diary, Dec. 15, 18, 25, 26, 1848, JRGP; Stewart, *Joshua R. Giddings*, 167–69.

5. *CG*, 30th Cong., 2nd Sess., 55–56; Diary, Dec. 18, 1848, JRGP; *WNE*, Dec. 28, 1848; Stewart, *Joshua R. Giddings*, 167–69.

6. Diary, Dec. 24, 1848, JRGP; *WNE*, Dec. 21, 1848; Miller, *Arguing About Slavery*, 458–59.

7. Donald, *Lincoln*, 136, views Lincoln's plan as "a compromise to end the debates that were beginning to tear his party apart just before a new Whig president was to be inaugurated." *WNE*, Dec. 28, 1848; Findley, *Crucible of Congress*, 137; Riddle, *Congressman Abraham Lincoln*, 169; Simon, *Lincoln's Preparation for Greatness*, 135–36.

8. Frederick Douglass, "The Address of Southern Delegates in Congress to Their Constituents or, the Address of John C. Calhoun and Forty Other Thieves," *North Star*, Feb. 9, 1849; Richard K. Cralle, ed., *The Works of John C. Calhoun* (New York: Appleton, 1851–56), VI, 285–313; Merrill D. Peterson, *The Great Triumvirate: Webster, Clay, and Calhoun* (New York: Oxford University Press,

1987), 447–48; William W. Freehling, *The Road to Disunion: Secessionists at Bay, 1776–1854* (New York: Oxford University Press, 1990), 479–80; Riddle, *Congressman Abraham Lincoln*, 170; Findley, *Crucible of Congress*, 139; Stewart, *Joshua R. Giddings*, 170–71.

9. *CW*, II, 20–22; Don Fehrenbacher and Virginia Fehrenbacher, *Recollected Words of Abraham Lincoln* (Stanford: Stanford University Press, 1992), 260.

10. *CW*, II, 260; Lehrman, *Lincoln at Peoria*, 122–23.

11. *CW*, II, 20–22.

12. *CW*, II, 20–22; Diary, Jan. 8, 9, 11, 1849, JRGP; Donald, *Lincoln*, 136; Eric Foner, *The Fiery Trial: Abraham Lincoln and American Slavery* (New York: W. W. Norton, 2002), 58.

13. *CW*, II, 20–22, Diary, Jan. 11, 1849, JRGP; Fehrenbacher and Fehrenbacher, *Recollected Words*, 260.

14. George H. Julian, *The Life of Joshua R. Giddings* (Chicago: A. C. McClurg and Company, 1892), 259, reiterated that "The object of these movements was to place before the country the fact that both the Whig and Democratic parties were committed to the support of slavery and the slave-trade in the District." Diary, Dec. 19, 1848, Jan. 8, 1849, JRGP; Giddings, *History of the Rebellion*, 285–86; Busey, *Recollections*, 26–27, 28; Stewart, "Joshua Giddings, Antislavery Violence, and Congressional Politics of Honor," 175; Filler, *Crusade Against Slavery*, 99–100, 107; Foner, *Free Soil, Free Labor, Free Men*, 112; Miller, *Arguing About Slavery*, 351–56; Pacheco, *The Pearl*, 200.

15. *CW*, IV, 391, VII, 454; Findley, *Crucible of Congress*, 106.

16. Weld to Angelina G. Weld, Jan. 1, 1842, *LTDW*, II, 883; Stewart, *Joshua R. Giddings*, 169; Stewart, "Joshua Giddings, Antislavery Violence, and Congressional Politics of Honor," 170, 172, 180; Barbara Jeanne Fields, *Slavery and Freedom on the Middle Ground: Maryland During the Nineteenth Century* (New Haven: Yale University Press, 1985).

17. Findley, *Crucible of Congress*, 92; Stewart, "Joshua Giddings, Antislavery Violence, and Congressional Politics of Honor," 172; Nicole Etcheson, *The Emerging Midwest: Upland Southerners and the Political Culture of the Old Northwest, 1787–1861* (Bloomington: Indiana University Press, 1996); Kenneth J. Winkle, *The Young Eagle: The Rise of Abraham Lincoln* (Dallas: Taylor Trade Publishers, 2001), 23–29.

18. *CW*, II, 54; Findley, *Crucible of Congress*, 198–208; Riddle, *Congressman Abraham Lincoln*, 213, 218.

19. *CW*, II, 253, 264.

20. Smallwood, *Narrative of Thomas Smallwood*, 63.

21. *CW*, II, 252; Diary, Jan. 8, 1849, JRGP.

22. David Potter, *The Impending Crisis, 1848–1861* (New York: Harper, 1976), 90–120; Freehling, *Road to Disunion*, 508–10; Harrold, *Subversives*, 164–67; Pacheco, *The Pearl*, 190, 200.

23. To "My Dear Wife" [Laura Waters Giddings], Dec. 2, 1849, JRGP; Harrold, *Subversives*, 148, 164–67; Sturge, *Visit to the United States*, 76; Stewart, *Joshua R. Giddings*, 195.

24. *CW*, II, 67, 260, 453, 492, 514; Potter, *Impending Crisis*, 90–120; Freehling, *Road to Disunion*, 508–10.

25. *CW*, II, 260, 263, 268, III, 5, 18, 40–42; Allen C. Guelzo, *Lincoln and Douglas: The Debates That Defined America* (New York: Simon & Schuster, 2008), 123–24.

26. *CW*, III, 254–55, 537; Harold Holzer, *Lincoln at Cooper Union: The Speech That Made Abraham Lincoln President* (New York: Simon & Schuster, 2004), 128–31; William C. Harris, *Lincoln's Rise to the Presidency* (Lawrence: University Press of Kansas, 2007), 186–87.

27. Potter, *Impending Crisis*, 405–47; Elting Morison, "Election of 1860," in Arthur M. Schlesinger Jr. and Fred L. Israel, eds., *History of American Presidential Elections, 1789–1968* (New York: Chelsea House, 1971), II, 1097–152; Reinhard H. Luthin, *The First Lincoln Campaign* (Cambridge: Harvard University Press, 1944), 136–67.

28. Harris, *Lincoln's Rise to the Presidency*, 201–6; Donald, *Lincoln*, 246–49.

29. David C. Mearns, *The Lincoln Papers* (Garden City, NY: Doubleday, 1948), I, 235–37; Luthin, *First Lincoln Campaign*, 139, 157–66.

30. *CW*, IV, 152, 182.

31. Hugh Davis, *Joshua Leavitt: Evangelical Abolitionist* (Baton Rouge: Louisiana State University Press, 1990), 266–67; from Gerrit Smith, Peterboro, New York, June 2, 1860, JRGP.

32. To George Julian, Jefferson, Ohio, May 25, 1860, JRGP; to "My Dear Laura," Springfield, Illinois, Dec. 2, 1860, Giddings-Julian Papers.

33. *CW*, IV, 162–63; *WDC*, Aug. 15, 1862; Belko, *Invincible Duff Green*, 443; Harold S. Wilson, *Confederate Industry: Manufacturers and Quartermasters in the Civil War* (Jackson: University of Mississippi Press, 2002), 22–23.

34. Ulrich Bonnell Phillips, ed., "The Correspondence of Robert Toombs, Alexander H. Stephens, and Howell Cobb," *Annual Report of the American Historical Association for the Year 1911* (Washington: American Historical Association, 1913), II, 496, 501.

CHAPTER 5 "A Wide Spread and Powerful Conspiracy"

1. *CW*, IV, 190; Harold Holzer, *Lincoln President-Elect: Abraham Lincoln and the Great Secession Winter, 1860–1861* (New York: Simon & Schuster, 2008), 296.

2. "A Citizen" to Lincoln, Nov. 8, 1860, Alfred W. Upham to Lincoln, Nov. 26, 1860, Unknown to Lincoln [1860], A. H. Flanders to John G. Nicolay, Jan. 27, 1861, ALPLC; Harold Holzer, *Dear Mr. Lincoln: Letters to the President* (Reading, MA: Addison-Wesley Publishing Company, 1993), 194, 231–32, 327, 340–42; Michael J. Kline, *The Baltimore Plot: The First Conspiracy to Assassinate Abraham Lincoln* (Yardley, PA: Westholme, 2008), 37, 228.

3. J. B. Long to Unknown, Jan. 18, 1861, ALPLC; Holzer, *Dear Mr. Lincoln*, 341; Kline, *Baltimore Plot*, 37, 228.

4. Unknown to Lincoln [1860] ALPLC; A. H. Flanders to John G. Nicolay, Jan.

27, 1861, ALPLC; Holzer, *Lincoln President-Elect*, 194, 231–32; Holzer, *Dear Mr. Lincoln*, 341, 342.

5. Joseph Medill to Lincoln, Dec. 1860, Elihu B. Washburne to Lincoln, Feb. 3, 1861, ALPLC; Holzer, *Lincoln President-Elect*, 194.

6. David Hunter to Lincoln, Dec. 18, 1860, James Watson Webb to Lincoln, Feb. 6, 1861, ALPLC; *WES*, Jan. 2, 11, 1861; Holzer, *Lincoln President-Elect*, 153.

7. William H. Seward to Lincoln, Dec. 28, 1860, Joseph Medill to Lincoln, Dec. 31, 1860, ALPLC.

8. Green, *Secret City*, 36–37; Green, *Washington: Village and Capital, 1800–1878*, 141–43; Harrold, *Subversives*, 33; Jefferson Morley, *Snow-Storm in August: Washington City, Francis Scott Key, and the Forgotten Race Riot of 1835* (New York: Nan A. Talese, 2012); Richards, *Gentlemen of Property and Standing*.

9. *WNR*, May 1, 1862; Kenneth G. Alfers, *Law and Order in the Capital City: A History of the Washington Police, 1800–1886* (Washington: George Washington University, 1976), iii, 12.

10. *WDC*, Jan. 28, 1863; Alfers, *Law and Order in the Capital City*, 3, 5, 8, 13, 14, 21.

11. Worthington Garrettson Snethen, *The Black Code of the District of Columbia, in Force Sept. 1st, 1848* (New York: American and Foreign Anti-Slavery Society, 1848), 41–42; *WES*, Jan. 22, 1861; Alfers, *Law and Order in the Capital City*, 6–7, 9.

12. Contemporaries often called the Washington county jail, erroneously, the "city jail." Snethen, *Black Code of the District of Columbia*, 41–42; John Hay, *Lincoln and the Civil War in the Diaries and Letters of John Hay* (New York: Dodd, Mead, 1939), 11; *WES*, Jan. 16, Feb. 21, 1862; Alfers, *Law and Order in the Capital City*, 6–7, 9; Green, *Secret City*, 48.

13. *WES*, Dec. 5, 1861; Alfers, *Law and Order in the Capital City*, 13, 15.

14. "Alleged Hostile Organization Against the Government Within the District of Columbia," 36th Cong., 2d Sess., H.R. Report No. 79, 18; Alfers, *Law and Order in the Capital City*, 17–18, 19–20.

15. Alfers, *Law and Order in the Capital City*, 18, 19, 20, 21.

16. "Alleged Hostile Organization," 9; Alfers, *Law and Order in the Capital City*, 15, 17.

17. *WNI*, Nov. 13, 16, 1860; *WNR*, Dec. 6, 13, 1860.

18. *WES*, Nov. 11, Dec. 7, 26, 1861, Feb. 16, 1861; *WNR*, Nov. 26, Dec. 3, 27, 1860.

19. *WES*, Dec. 6, 12, 13, 18, 19, 1860, Jan. 2, April 29, 1861; *WNR*, Dec. 14, 18, 1860; Norma B. Cuthbert, ed., *Lincoln and the Baltimore Plot, 1861* (San Marino, CA: Huntington Library, 1949), 149.

20. *WNR*, Dec. 21, 1860; *WES*, Jan. 7, 11, 17, 29, 1861.

21. Joshua R. Giddings to Lincoln, Jan. 1, 1861, Elihu B. Washburne to Lincoln, Jan. 4, 1861, Winfield Scott to Lincoln, Oct. 29, 1860, Jan. 4, 1861, ALPLC; David M. Potter, *Lincoln and His Party in the Secession Crisis* (New Haven: Yale University Press, 1862), 263; Benjamin Franklin Cooling, *Symbol, Sword, and Shield: Defending Washington During the Civil War* (Hamden, CT: Archon Books, 1975), 23.

22. Winfield Scott to Lincoln, Oct. 29, 1860, Joseph Medill to Lincoln, Dec. 31, 1860, James Watson Webb to Lincoln, Feb. 6, 1861, ALPLC; *WES*, Jan. 7, 1861;

John G. Barnard, *A Report on the Defenses of Washington* (Washington: Government Printing Office, 1871), 6; William E. Doster, *Lincoln and Episodes of the Civil War* (New York: G. P. Putnam's Sons, 1915), 9, 60.

23. Abram C. Randall to William H. Seward, Dec. 15, 1860, ALPLC; Potter, *Lincoln and His Party in the Secession Crisis*, 259–60.

24. "Alleged Hostile Organization," 16; *WES*, Feb. 4, 1861; Potter, *Lincoln and His Party in the Secession Crisis*, 261–62.

25. "Alleged Hostile Organization," 1, 3–5, 8.

26. Winfield Scott to Lincoln, Jan. 4, 1861, ALPLC; "Alleged Hostile Organization," 52–53, 61, 64.

27. "Alleged Hostile Organization," 87, 134, 177; Jean H. Baker, *The Politics of Continuity: Maryland Political Parties from 1858 to 1870* (Baltimore: Johns Hopkins University Press, 1973), 34, 47–49; Charles B. Clark, "Suppression and Control of Maryland, 1861–1865: A Study of Federal-State Relations During Civil Conflict," *Maryland Historical Magazine* 54 (Sept. 1959): 254; Kline, *Baltimore Plot*, 11, 14, 29, 61.

28. "Alleged Hostile Organization," 2; *WES*, Jan. 15, 30, 1861; Kline, *Baltimore Plot*, 11.

29. Potter, *Lincoln and His Party in the Secession Crisis*, 262, 264.

CHAPTER 6 "The Way We Skulked into This City"

1. Douglas L. Wilson and Rodney O. Davis, eds., *Herndon's Informants: Letters, Interviews, and Statements About Abraham Lincoln* (Urbana: University of Illinois Press, 1998), 709; Winfield Scott to Lincoln, Jan. 4, 1861, ALPLC; *WES*, Jan. 7, 28, 1861; Cooling, *Symbol, Sword, and Shield*, 21; John C. Waugh, *Lincoln and McClellan: The Troubled Partnership Between a President and His General* (New York: Palgrave Macmillan, 2010), 54.

2. *CW*, IV, 170; Holzer, *Lincoln President-Elect*, 195; Kline, *Baltimore Plot*, 39.

3. Horace Greeley to Lincoln, Dec. 22, 1860, ALPLC; *WES*, Jan. 25, 1861; *WNI*, Feb. 7, 1861; Holzer, *Lincoln President-Elect*, 196–97, 276; Kline, *Baltimore Plot*, 40.

4. Holzer, *Lincoln President-Elect*, 196–97, 281, 389; Kline, *Baltimore Plot*, 40.

5. George W. Hazzard to Lincoln, Jan. 1861, ALPLC; Kline, *Baltimore Plot*, 18, 29, 86, 143, 183, 347; Cuthbert, *Lincoln and the Baltimore Plot*, xiii.

6. Springfield Illinois Zouave Greys to Lincoln, Dec. 1860, ALPLC; Kline, *Baltimore Plot*, 50–56; Holzer, *Lincoln President-Elect*, 277, 279–80; Waugh, *Lincoln and McClellan*, 106.

7. Holzer, *Lincoln President-Elect*, 280; Kline, *Baltimore Plot*, 54–55, 57.

8. Lamon married Sally Logan, the daughter of Stephen T. Logan, a cousin of Mary Lincoln and Abraham Lincoln's second law partner. Ward Hill Lamon, *Recollections of Abraham Lincoln, 1847–1865* (New York: A. C. McClurg, 1895), 32–33; John G. Nicolay, *An Oral History of Abraham Lincoln: John G. Nicolay's Interviews and Essays*, ed. Michael Burlingame (Carbondale: Southern Illinois University Press, 1996), 113; Lavern M. Hamand, "Lincoln's Particular

Friend," in Donald F. Tingley, ed., *Essays in Illinois History in Honor of Glenn Huron Seymour* (Carbondale: Southern Illinois University Press, 1968), 19–21; Holzer, *Lincoln President-Elect*, 305, 400; Kline, *Baltimore Plot*, 57, 225.

9. R. C. Carter to Lincoln, Nov. 12, 1860, S. A. H. McKim to Aaron Gibbs, Dec. 1860, ALPLC; "Has There Been an Attempt to Poison the President?" *Harper's Weekly*, March 28, 1857, 194; Holzer, *Lincoln President-Elect*, 273, 278; Kline, *Baltimore Plot*, 62, 148.

10. Elihu B. Washburne to Lincoln, Jan. 4, 1861, ALPLC; Kline, *Baltimore Plot*, 70–71, 153.

11. Herndon and Weik, *Herndon's Informants*, 433; Holzer, *Lincoln President-Elect*, 377–78; Kline, *Baltimore Plot*, 30, 191, 229.

12. Allan Pinkerton, *The Spy of the Rebellion; Being a True History of the Spy System of the United States Army During the Late Rebellion* (Philadelphia: H. W. Kelley, 1883), 83, 85; Holzer, *Lincoln President-Elect*, 377–79.

13. Benson J. Lossing, *A Pictorial History of the Civil War* (Philadelphia: George W. Childs, 1866), I, 279–80; Wilson and Davis, *Herndon's Informants*, 433; Holzer, *Lincoln President-Elect*, 378.

14. William H. Seward to Lincoln, Feb. 21, 1861, Winfield Scott to William H. Seward, Feb. 21, 1861, Charles P. Stone, Feb. 21, 1861, ALPLC; Lossing, *Pictorial History of the Civil War*, I, 280.

15. Isaac N. Arnold, *The History of Abraham Lincoln and the Overthrow of Slavery* (Chicago: Clarke & Co., 1866), 171; Lossing, *Pictorial History of the Civil War*, I, 279–80; Holzer, *Lincoln President-Elect*, 380–81; Kline, *Baltimore Plot*, 346.

16. *CW*, VI, 240–41.

17. *WES*, Feb. 23, July 16, 1861; Cooling, *Symbol, Sword, and Shield*, 22, 27–28.

18. Wilson and Davis, *Herndon's Informants*, 434; Lamon, *Recollections of Abraham Lincoln*, 41; Holzer, *Lincoln President-Elect*, 388, 390–92; Kline, *Baltimore Plot*, 180–81, 226, 229, 249.

19. Wilson and Davis, *Herndon's Informants*, 435; Lamon, *Recollections of Abraham Lincoln*, 44–45; Holzer, *Lincoln President-Elect*, 394–95; Kline, *Baltimore Plot*, 183, 239, 249, 250, 257, 259.

20. RBCES, Petition No. 857; *WNI*, Feb. 25, 1861; Lamon, *Recollections of Abraham Lincoln*, 45–46; Holzer, *Lincoln President-Elect*, 395–96; Kline, *Baltimore Plot*, 266–67; Cuthbert, *Lincoln and the Baltimore Plot*, xiv–xv.

21. *Baltimore Sun*, Feb. 25, 1861; Lamon, *Recollections of Abraham Lincoln*, 266.

22. Holzer, *Lincoln President-Elect*, 397–99.

23. Lincoln appointed Ellsworth as adjutant and inspector general of militia two weeks after reaching Washington. Holzer, *Lincoln President-Elect*, 403, concluded that "verifiable evidence strongly suggests that some kind of threat did exist." Cuthbert, *Lincoln and the Baltimore Plot*, xxii; Mark E. Neely Jr., *The Abraham Lincoln Encyclopedia* (New York: McGraw-Hill, 1982), 102.

24. *CW*, IV, 246–47; *WES*, Feb. 28, March 1, 2, 1861; Earl Schenck Miers, ed., *Lincoln Day by Day: A Chronology, 1809–1865* (Washington: Lincoln Sesquicentennial Association, 1960), III, 22–23.

25. Diary of Horatio Nelson Taft, 1861–1865, LOC, I, March 4, 1861; *WNI*, March 5, 1861; *WES*, Feb. 21, 26, 27, March 4, 1861; Julia Taft Bayne, *Tad Lincoln's Father* (Lincoln: University of Nebraska Press, 2001), 7; Cooling, *Symbol, Sword, and Shield*, 12, 20.

26. *CW*, IV, 262–71.

27. *WNI*, March 5, 6, 1861; Holzer, *Lincoln President-Elect*, 452; Cooling, *Symbol, Sword, and Shield*, 30; Jerrold M. Packard, *The Lincolns in the White House* (New York: St. Martin's Griffin, 2005), 5.

CHAPTER 7 "This Big White House"

1. *CW*, VII, 512; Noah Brooks, *Lincoln Observed: Civil War Dispatches of Noah Brooks*, ed. Michael Burlingame (Baltimore: Johns Hopkins University Press, 1998), 81; William O. Stoddard, *Inside the White House in War Times: Memoirs and Reports of Lincoln's Secretary*, ed. Michael Burlingame (Lincoln: University of Nebraska Press, 2000), 47; Packard, *Lincolns in the White House*, 10–11, 71.

2. Walt Whitman, *Memoranda During the War*, ed. Peter Coviello (New York: Oxford University Press, 2004), 76–77; Noah Brooks, *Washington, D.C., in Lincoln's Time*, ed. Herbert Mitgang (Athens: University of Georgia Press, 1989), 69.

3. Stoddard, *Inside the White House*, 11, 21, 162; Ronald D. Rietveld, "The Lincoln White House Community," *Journal of the Abraham Lincoln Association* 20 (Spring 1999), 22, 32; William Seale, *The President's House: A History* (Washington: White House Historical Association, 1986), 758, 1005; Margarita Spalding Gerry, comp. and ed., *Through Five Administrations: Reminiscences of Colonel William H. Crook, Body-Guard to President Lincoln* (New York: Harper & Brothers, 1920), 11; Packard, *Lincolns in the White House*, 62.

4. Stoddard, *Inside the White House*, 187; Brooks, *Washington, D.C., in Lincoln's Time*, 248; Gerry, *Through Five Administrations*, 30; Packard, *Lincolns in the White House*, 63; Rietveld, "Lincoln White House Community," 27, 29; Brownstein, *Lincoln's Other White House*, 31.

5. *WES*, March 12, 1861; Brooks, *Lincoln Observed*, 80; Gerry, *Through Five Administrations*, 12; Rietveld, "Lincoln White House Community," 29–30, 32, 40; Packard, *Lincolns in the White House*, 27.

6. Elizabeth Keckley, *Behind the Scenes: Or, Thirty Years a Slave, and Four Years in the White House* (New York: G. W. Carleton, 1868), 42; Gerry, *Through Five Administrations*, 3, 10; David Homer Bates, *Lincoln in the Telegraph Office: Recollections of the United States Military Telegraph Corps During the Civil War* (Lincoln: University of Nebraska Press, 1995), 113–23; Smith Stimmel, *Personal Reminiscences of Abraham Lincoln* (Minneapolis: William H. M. Adams, 1928), 43–45; Packard, *Lincolns in the White House*, 62; Tom Wheeler, *Mr. Lincoln's T-Mails: The Untold Story of How Abraham Lincoln Used the Telegraph to Win the Civil War* (New York: Collins, 2006), 46–67.

7. *MTL*, 82; Stoddard, *Inside the White House*, 182; Gerry, *Through Five Adminis-*

trations, 12, 16; Rietveld, "Lincoln White House Community," 22, 36; Packard, *Lincolns in the White House*, 11–12, 51.

8. *WNR*, Dec. 11, 1860; Brooks, *Lincoln Observed*, 80; Packard, *Lincolns in the White House*, 9.

9. Mary Lincoln's modiste signed her name "Keckly," which is today the accepted spelling; Fleischner, *Mrs. Lincoln and Mrs. Keckly*, 327. Keckley, *Behind the Scenes*, 51; Baker, *Mary Todd Lincoln*, 229.

10. Packard, *Lincolns in the White House*, 53–54; Rietveld, "Lincoln White House Community," 26–27; Brownstein, *Lincoln's Other White House*, 41.

11. *MTL*, 71, 86; Baker, *Mary Todd Lincoln*, 203.

12. Keckley, *Behind the Scenes*, 20–22, 68; Fleischner, *Mrs. Lincoln and Mrs. Keckly*, 28, 125, 145, 147, 183–84, 207–8.

13. Packard, *Lincolns in the White House*, 6; *WES*, July 16, 1861.

14. *MTL*, 82; Diary of Horatio Nelson Taft, I, March 8, 1861; Benjamin Brown French, *Witness to the Young Republic: A Yankee's Journal, 1828–1870*, ed. Donald B. Cole and John J. McDonough (Hanover: University Press of New England, 1989), 385; Rietveld, "Lincoln White House Community," 42; Packard, *Lincolns in the White House*, 4, 29.

15. Bayne, *Tad Lincoln's Father*, 6; Packard, *Lincolns in the White House*, 77.

16. Diary of Horatio Nelson Taft, I, Jan. 11, 1862; Bayne, *Tad Lincoln's Father*, 6, 21, 28, 47, 65; Packard, *Lincolns in the White House*, 76, 77–78.

17. *CW*, VI, 371–72, VII, 320; Noah Brooks, *Washington, D.C., in Lincoln's Time*, ed. Herbert Mitgang (Athens: University of Georgia Press, 1989), 248; Bayne, *Tad Lincoln's Father*, 16; Michael Burlingame, *Abraham Lincoln: A Life* (Baltimore: Johns Hopkins University Press, 2008), 801.

18. Stoddard, *Inside the White House*, 27; Bayne, *Tad Lincoln's Father*, 16, 47–48.

19. 37th Cong., 3rd Sess., H. Exec. Doc. 1, pt. 2, 649: *WNR*, Jan. 23, 1862; Adams, *Letter from Washington*, 77–78; Ellen M. Calder, "Personal Recollections of Walt Whitman," *Atlantic Monthly* 99 (June 1907), 831; Alfers, *Law and Order in the Capital City*, 30; Packard, *Lincolns in the White House*, 9; Matthew Pinsker, *Lincoln's Sanctuary: Abraham Lincoln and the Soldiers' Home* (New York: Oxford University Press, 2003), 7.

20. 37th Cong., 3rd Sess., H. Exec. Doc. 1, Pt. 2, 649; *MTL*, 108; Joel Achenbach, *The Grand Idea: George Washington's Potomac and the Race to the West* (New York: Simon & Schuster, 2004), 159–60, 169; Harris, "Washington's Gamble, L'Enfant's Dream," 542–43; Robert Harrison, *Washington During Civil War and Reconstruction: Race and Radicalism* (Cambridge: Cambridge University Press, 2011), 245–46; Arnebeck, *Through a Fiery Trial*, 51–52, 54; Helen Tangires, "Contested Space: The Life and Death of Center Market," *Washington History* 7 (Spring/Summer 1995), 47, 51–52.

21. 38th Cong., 1st Sess., Senate Misc. Doc. No. 84; *WNR*, March 26, April 29, May 5, 8, 1862, May 30, 1863, May 2, June 2, 1864; *WDC*, Aug. 17, Dec. 14, 1863, Feb. 10, March 25, April 5, May 4, June 27, Aug. 13, 1864.

22. Burlingame, *Lincoln: A Life*, II, 251; Brooks, *Lincoln Observed*, 145; Brooks, *Wash-*

ington, D.C., *in Lincoln's Time*, 13; Stoddard, *Inside the White House*, 21; Packard, *Lincolns in the White House*, 7, 155–56.

23. *WES*, March 14, 1861, Dec. 24, 1864; *WDC*, Dec. 1, 1862, June 14, 1863; Hay, *Lincoln and the Civil War*, 4; Stoddard, *Inside the White House*, 151, 183; Brooks, *Lincoln Observed*, 82–83; Gerry, *Through Five Administrations*, 27.

24. John G. Nicolay, *With Lincoln in the White House: Letters, Memoranda, and Other Writings of John G. Nicolay, 1860–1865*, ed. Michael Burlingame (Carbondale: Southern Illinois University Press, 2000), 110; Stoddard, *Inside the White House*, 199; Doster, *Lincoln and Episodes of the Civil War*, 14; Gerry, *Through Five Administrations*, 3, 33; Rietveld, "Lincoln White House Community," 29.

25. *WDC*, Dec. 3, 1862, June 13, July 10, 1863, March 29, 1864; Ward H. Lamon to Lincoln, Aug. 17, 1861, ALPLC.

CHAPTER 8 "White and Black, All Mixed Up Together"

1. Joseph C. G. Kennedy, *Population of the United States in 1860* (Washington: Government Printing Office, 1864), xxxii; Green, *Secret City*, 33, 49; Kate Masur, *An Example for All the Land: Emancipation and the Struggle over Equality in Washington, D.C.* (Chapel Hill: University of North Carolina Press, 2010), 19–20.

2. To "Boy" [Grotius Reed Giddings], Dec. 29, 1839, JRGP; James Borchert, *Alley Life in Washington: Family, Community, Religion, and Foklife in the City, 1850–1970* (Urbana: University of Illinois Press, 1980), 5, 23, 25, 28; James Borchert, "Alley Life in Washington: An Analysis of 600 Photographs," *RCHS* 73–74 (1976), 244–45; James Borchert, "The Rise and Fall of Washington's Inhabited Alleys: 1852–1972," *RCHS* 71–72 (1975): 271.

3. Borchert, *Alley Life in Washington*, 5, 6–7, 12, 25, 26, 28; Borchert, "Alley Life in Washington," 245; Borchert, "Rise and Fall of Washington's Inhabited Alleys," 275.

4. 37th Cong., 3rd Sess., H. Exec. Doc. 1, Pt. 2, 649; *Boyd's Washington and Georgetown Directory, 1860* (Washington: Taylor & Maury, 1860), 32; *WNR*, Dec. 4, 1860, Feb. 24, May 23, June 18, 1862, Nov. 14, 1863, May 20, 1864: *WES*, Nov. 11, 1860, Aug. 19, 1861; Snethen, *Black Code of the District of Columbia*, 41.

5. Kennedy, *Population of the United States in 1860*, 588; Green, *Secret City*, 33.

6. U.S. Manuscript Census, Free and Slave Population Schedules, Washington, DC, 1860.

7. EDC, 17–71; U.S. Manuscript Census, Free and Slave Population Schedules, Washington, DC, 1860; *WNR*, March 29, 1863.

8. RBCES; Richard L. Bushman and Claudia Bushman, "The Early History of Cleanliness in America," *Journal of American History* 74 (March 1988), Petition No. 1-966, 1213–38.

9. RBCES, Petition No. 101, 408, 759, and passim.

10. RBCES, Petition No. 408, 704, 744, 872, 893, 948.

11. RBCES, Petition No. 122, 422, 657, 680, 868; Snethen, *Black Code of the District of Columbia*, 9.

12. The average real wealth of white families with slaves was $17,376, of white families with live-in servants $9,602, and of white familes with no domestic staff $2,531. U.S. Manuscript Census, Free Population Schedule, Washington, DC, 1860.

13. U.S. Manuscript Census, Free Population Schedule, Washington, DC, 1860; *WES*, April 28, 1862; Snethen, *Black Code of the District of Columbia*, 9, 19, 29–30.

14. U.S. Manuscript Census, Free Population Schedule, Washington, DC, 1860.

15. U.S. Manuscript Census, Free and Slave Population Schedules, Washington, DC, 1860.

16. S. A. H. McKim to Aaron Gibbs, Dec. 1860, ALPLC; John E. Washington, *They Knew Lincoln* (New York: E. P. Dutton, 1942), 127–28.

17. *CW*, IV, 277, 288; Washington, *They Knew Lincoln*, 128; Burlingame, *Lincoln: A Life*, II, 24; James Cornelius, "William H. Johnson, Citizen," http://www .alplm.org/blog/2010/07/lincoln-and-the-other-johnson/#comments; Steven J. Ramold, *Slaves, Sailors, Citizens: African Americans in the Union Navy* (DeKalb: Northern Illinois University Press, 2002), 6–24; Joel Williamson, *New People: Miscegenation and Mulattoes in the United States* (New York: Free Press, 1980), 35, 53, 63, 65, 67, 71, 75; Walter Johnson, *Soul by Soul: Life Inside the Antebellum Slave Market* (Cambridge: Harvard University Press, 1999), 139, 154, 156. According to Audrey Elisa Kerr, "Two Black Washingtons: The Role of Complexion in the Experience of District of Columbia Residents, 1863," Ph.D. diss., University of Maryland, College Park, 1998, 84–85, after the Civil War, African Americans in Washington adopted a "paper bag test," in which the color of a brown grocery bag marked the division between "light enough" and "too dark."

18. *CW*, IV, 474, V, 33, 446–47, VI, 69; *Register of Officers and Agents, Civil, Military, and Naval, in the Service of the United States* (Washington: Government Printing Office, 1862), 15; Cornelius, "William H. Johnson, Citizen"; Harrold, *Subversives*, 228; Ira Berlin, Steven F. Miller, Joseph P. Reidy, and Leslie S. Rowland, eds., *The Wartime Genesis of Free Labor: The Upper South*, Ser. I, Vol. 2 of *Freedom: A Documentary History of Emancipation, 1861–1867* (New York: Cambridge University Press, 1993), 245.

19. Weld to Angelina G. Weld, Feb. 9, 1842, *LTDW*, II, 914–15; Washington, *They Knew Lincoln*, 141; Cornelius, "William H. Johnson, Citizen." The amount of time that Johnson spent attending Lincoln is unclear. Roy Basler, who edited the *CW*, wrote (VI, 69) that he "tended to Lincoln's wardrobe, shaved him, and did other personal services in the mornings." More recently, James Oakes, "Natural Rights, Citizenship Rights, States' Rights, and Black Rights: Another Look at Lincoln and Race," in Eric Foner, ed., *Our Lincoln: New Perspectives on Lincoln and His World* (New York: W. W. Norton, 2008), 115, stated that "Lincoln had Johnson put on the Treasury Department payroll, though he worked exclusively for Lincoln in the executive mansion."

20. *CW*, V, 446–47, 474, VI, 8–9, 69, 125, VIII, 487; Washington, *They Knew Lincoln*, 32, 131, 132; Gabor Boritt, *The Gettysburg Gospel: The Lincoln Speech That*

Nobody Knows (New York: Simon & Schuster, 2006), 54; Burlingame, *Lincoln: A Life*, II, 24, 578.

CHAPTER 9 "A Swift and Terrible Retribution"

1. *CW*, IV, 323–24; Winfield Scott to William H. Seward, March 3, 1861, Winfield Scott to Lincoln, March 11, 1861, William H. Seward to Lincoln, April 1, 1861, Lincoln to William H. Seward, April 1, 1861, ALPLC; James M. McPherson, *Ordeal by Fire: The Civil War and Reconstruction*, 2nd ed. (New York: McGraw-Hill, 1992), 145–48; Potter, *Lincoln and His Party in the Secession Crisis*, 368–69; Russell McClintock, *Lincoln and the Decision for War: The Northern Response to Secession* (Chapel Hill: University of North Carolina Press, 2008), 236–37.
2. *CW*, IV, 331–32; McPherson, *Ordeal by Fire*, 145–48; Baker, *Politics of Continuity*, 52.
3. Joseph Medill to Lincoln, Dec. 26, 1860, Winfield Scott to Lincoln, April 5, 8, 13, 1861, ALPLC.
4. *CW*, IV, 422; Winfield Scott to Lincoln, April 5, 8, 13, 1861, ALPLC; Cooling, *Symbol, Sword, and Shield*, 32, 38.
5. Winfield Scott to Lincoln, April 13, 1861, ALPLC; *WES*, April 11, 13, 16, 1861; Cooling, *Symbol, Sword, and Shield*, 32; James H. Whyte, "Divided Loyalties in Washington During the Civil War," *RCHS* 60/62 (1960/1962), 108.
6. Thomas H. Hicks to Winfield Scott, April 22, 1861; *WES*, April 11, 20, 26, May 21, 1861; *WNI*, April 20, 22, 1861; Hay, *Lincoln and the Civil War*, 1, 4–5, 7; Baker, *Politics of Continuity*, 53; Cooling, *Symbol, Sword, and Shield*, 33; Mark E. Neely Jr., *The Fate of Liberty: Abraham Lincoln and Civil Liberties* (New York: Oxford University Press, 1991), 5; Fitzpatrick and Goodwin, *Guide to Black Washington*, 36.
7. *CW*, IV, 340; Reverdy Johnson to Lincoln, April 22, 1861, Winfield Scott to Lincoln, April 22, 1861, Thomas H. Hicks to Winfield Scott, April 22, 1861, Lincoln to Reverdy Johnson, April 24, 1861, ALPLC; Hay, *Lincoln and the Civil War*, 3–4, 7, 16; *WES*, April 22, 1861; Cooling, *Symbol, Sword, and Shield*, 34–35; Neely, *Fate of Liberty*, 6.
8. *CW*, IV, 341–42; Hay, *Lincoln and the Civil War*, 7.
9. Winfield Scott to Lincoln, April 8, 13, 22, 26, 1861, ALPLC; Hay, *Lincoln and the Civil War*, 19.
10. *OR*, Ser. III, I, 224; John G. Nicolay and John Hay, *Abraham Lincoln: A History* (New York: Century, 1890), IV, 151–52; Hay, *Lincoln and the Civil War*, 4, 11, 13, 15, 19; Bayne, *Tad Lincoln's Father*, 28.
11. *WNI*, April 26, 1861; *WES*, April 16, 25, 26, 1861; Hay, *Lincoln and the Civil War*, 8, 12; Cooling, *Symbol, Sword, and Shield*, 35.
12. *CW*, IV, 347, 419, 429–31; Salmon P. Chase to Lincoln, April 25, 1861, Abraham Lincoln to Winfield Scott, April 25, 1861, ALPLC; Hay, *Lincoln and the Civil War*, 11–12; Baker, *Politics of Continuity*, 55–56; Allen Guelzo, *Fateful Lightning: A New History of the Civil War and Reconstruction* (New York: Oxford University Press, 2012), 144.

13. On July 5, 1861, Attorney General Bates submitted an official opinion that the president had discretionary power to arrest anyone known or suspected to be engaged in "criminal intercourse" with secessionists and, if necessary, could refuse to obey a writ of habeas corpus; "Suspension of the Privilege of the Writ of Habeas Corpus," *Official Opinions of the Attorneys General of the United States* (Washington: Government Printing Office, 1873), X, 74–92. In September 1861, the administration ordered the arrest of sixteen members of the Maryland legislature to prevent another attempt at secession. General McClellan approved of the action, arguing, "Their arrest was a military necessity, and they had no cause of complaint"; George B. McClellan, *McClellan's Own Story: The War for the Union* (New York: Charles L. Webster, 1887), 147; James M. McPherson, *Tried by War: Abraham Lincoln as Commander in Chief* (New York: Penguin, 2008), 49. *CW*, IV, 429–31, 554; Neely, *Fate of Liberty*, 8, 10; Brian McGinty, *Lincoln and the Court* (Cambridge: Harvard University Press, 2008), 79, 83.

14. Winfield Scott to Lincoln, May 2, 1861, ALPLC; Carol Reardon, *With a Sword in One Hand & Jomini in the Other: The Problem of Military Thought in the Civil War North* (Chapel Hill: University of North Carolina Press, 2012), 20–21; Phillip Paludan, *A People's Contest: The Union and Civil War, 1861–1865* (New York: Harper & Row, 1988), 61–62.

15. Winfield Scott to Lincoln, May 2, 1861, ALPLC; *WES*, April 26, 1861; Cooling, *Symbol, Sword, and Shield*, 35, 41; Reardon, *With a Sword in One Hand*, 20–22.

16. *WES*, Dec. 31, 1860; Donald Beekman Myer, *Bridges and the City of Washington* (Washington: U.S. Commission of Fine Arts, 1974), 29, 3–5; Harry C. Ways, *The Washington Aqueduct, 1852–1992* (Baltimore: U.S. Army Corps of Engineers, 1996), 48–50; French, *Witness to the Young Republic*, 380.

17. Winfield Scott to Lincoln, May 3, 1861, ALPLC; Barnard, *Report on the Defenses of Washington*, 7; *WES*, April 13, 22, 23, May 3, 8, 27, June 20, 1861; Charles O. Paullin, "Alexandria County in 1861," *RCHS* 28 (1926), 111.

18. Douglas Southall Freeman, *R. E. Lee: A Biography* (New York: Charles Scribner's Sons, 1934–35), 425, 432–33, 436–37; Paul C. Nagel, *The Lees of Virginia: Seven Generations of an American Family* (New York: Oxford University Press, 1990), 237, 239, 265–69.

19. *WES*, April 23, Nov. 2, 1861; John Perry, *Mrs. Robert E. Lee: The Lady of Arlington* (Sisters, OR: Multnomah Books, 2001), 221, 223–25, 229–30; Mary P. Coulling, *The Lee Girls* (Winston-Salem: John F. Blair, 1987), 85–88, 89, 122–23; Paullin, "Alexandria County in 1861," 112.

20. Hay, *Lincoln and the Civil War*, 17, 20, 22; *WES*, May 3, 6, 7, 8, 10, 16, 18, Sept. 6, 1861.

21. *WES*, May 24, 25, 1861; Cooling, *Symbol, Sword, and Shield*, 44, 45–46.

22. Lincoln to Ephraim and Phoebe Ellsworth, May 25, 1861, ALPLC; *WES*, May 4, 22, 24, 25, 1861; Hay, *Lincoln and the Civil War*, 13.

23. Barnard, *Report on the Defenses of Washington*, 8, 124; *WES*, May 24, 25, 27, 28, 1861; Myer, *Bridges and the City of Washington*, 7, 11–12.

24. *WES*, May 28, June 1, 8, 15, 17, 25, Aug. 31, Oct. 14, Nov. 27, 1861; *WNI*, April

23, 1861; *WNR*, Jan. 2, 1862; Doster, *Lincoln and Episodes of the Civil War*, 68–69; Cooling, *Symbol, Sword, and Shield*, 46–47.

25. *CW*, IV, 427; McPherson, *Ordeal by Fire*, 209–10.

26. *WES*, July 9, 10, 14, 16, 17, 18, 19, 1861; Benjamin Franklin Cooling, "Defending Washington During the Civil War," *RCHS* 71–72 (1971–72): 316; Cooling, *Symbol, Sword, and Shield*, 51.

27. *WES*, July 22, 23, 1861; McPherson, *Ordeal by Fire*, 210, 212.

28. Manassas Virginia Telegraph, July 21, 1861 (Dispatches), ALPLC; Katherine Helm, *The True Story of Mary, Wife of Lincoln* (New York: Harper, 1928), 179; Reardon, *With a Sword in One Hand*, 25.

29. *OR*, Ser. I, V, 679; *WES*, Dec. 31, 1860, May 10, July 16, 21, 22, 23, 24, 25, 26, 30, Aug. 6, 10, 1861; Jane E. Schultz, *Women at the Front: Hospital Workers in Civil War America* (Chapel Hill: University of North Carolina Press, 2004), 80.

30. *WES*, July 24, 25, 30; Doster, *Lincoln and Episodes of the Civil War*, 63; Neely, *Fate of Liberty*, 118; Curtis Carroll Davis, "The 'Old Capitol' and Its Keeper: How William P. Wood Ran a Civil War Prison," *RCHS* 52 (1989), 207–8; Nina Silber, *Daughters of the Union: Northern Women Fight the Civil War* (Cambridge: Harvard University Press, 2005), 204; Roger Pickenpaugh, *Captives in Gray: The Civil War Prisons of the Union* (Tuscaloosa: University of Alabama Press, 2009), 6–7; Evelyn and Dickson, *On This Spot*, 19.

31. *OR* Ser. I, V, 5, 11; *WES*, July 8, 17, 22, 23, 24, 30, Nov. 29, 1861, Feb. 26, 1862; *WNR*, Jan. 3, April 2, Oct. 13, 18, 1862; *WDC*, Jan. 6, 1863; Cooling, "Defending Washington during the Civil War," 320.

32. *OR*, Ser. I, V, 8, 11–12, 678–79; Barnard, *Report on the Defenses of Washington*, 1, 6, 10, 12, 124–25; *WES*, July 22, 1861; Cooling, *Symbol, Sword, and Shield*, 119; Cooling, "Defending Washington During the Civil War," 320; Richard M. Lee, *Mr. Lincoln's City: An Illustrated Guide to the Civil War Sites of Washington* (McLean, VA: EPM Publications, 1981), 163.

33. William T. Sherman, *Memoirs of General William T. Sherman* (New York: C. L. Webster, 1892), 217; Edward L. Pierce, *Memoir and Letters of Charles Sumner* (Boston: Roberts Brothers, 1893), IV, 42.

CHAPTER 10 "Order out of Confusion"

1. Hay, *Lincoln and the Civil War*, 1; *WES*, Jan. 21, April 30, May 8, 28, June 8, July 16, 1861; *WNR*, April 15, 1864; Doster, *Lincoln and Episodes of the Civil War*, 60; Cooling, *Symbol, Sword, and Shield*, 43; Perry, *Mrs. Robert E. Lee*, 229; William Quentin Maxwell, *Lincoln's Fifth Wheel: The Political History of the United States Sanitary Commission* (New York: Longmans, Green, 1956), 39.

2. *WES*, June 21, July 2, 10, 1861, April 23, 1862; *WNI*, April 23, 1862; *WNR*, April 25, 1862; Mark R. Wilson, *The Business of Civil War: Military Mobilization and the State, 1861–1865* (Baltimore: Johns Hopkins University Press, 2006), 32; Kath-

ryn Allamong Jacob, *Testament to Union: Civil War Monuments in Washington, D.C.* (Baltimore: Johns Hopkins University Press, 1998), 21.

3. *WES*, June 26, July 29, Dec. 2, 1861; *WNR*, Oct. 28, 1862, July 30, 1863; *WDC*, Nov. 6, 1862, Nov. 13, 1863; Cooling, *Symbol, Sword, and Shield*, 35.

4. *WNR*, Feb. 26, April 2, 1862; *WES*, Oct. 31, 1861.

5. *U.S. Statutes at Large*, XIII, 38th Cong., 1st Sess., Res. 76, 416–17; *WNR*, June 17, 1864; *WDC*, June 17, 19, 20, 25, July 7, 28, Nov. 28, 1864; Brooks, *Lincoln Observed*, 116; Judith Giesberg, *Army at Home: Women and the Civil War on the Northern Home Front* (Chapel Hill: University of North Carolina Press, 2009), 89–90; Jacob, *Testament to Union*, 21–23.

6. *OR*, Ser. III, I, 453, 531, 608–9; Russell F. Weigley, *Quartermaster General of the Union Army: A Biography of M. C. Meigs* (New York: Columbia University Press, 1959), 158; David W. Miller, *Second Only to Grant: Quartermaster General Montgomery C. Meigs* (Shippensburg, PA: White Mane Books, 2000), 116–18; Wilson, *Business of Civil War*, 1, 23, 37; Guelzo, *Fateful Lightning*, 315–16.

7. *WES*, May 8, July 16, Aug. 31, Sept. 9, Oct. 7, 18, 1861; *WDC*, Jan. 28, 1863; *WNR*, Jan. 24, 1862; Adams, *Letter from Washington*, 36, 203; Doster, *Lincoln and Episodes of the Civil War*, 59; Clay McShane and Joel A. Tarr, *The Horse in the City: Living Machines in the Nineteenth Century* (Baltimore: Johns Hopkins University Press, 2007), 26, 27, 122; Ann Norton Greene, *Horses at Work: Harnessing Power in Industrializing America* (Cambridge: Harvard University Press, 2008), 145; Miller, *Second Only to Grant*, 120–21.

8. *CW*, VIII, 227; Abraham Lincoln, Executive Order on the Export of Arms and Ammunition, Nov. 21, 1862, ALPLC; Edwin M. Stanton, Order Concerning Purchase and Sale of Horses, May 13, 1863, ALPLC; *WNR*, Oct. 9, 21, 1862, May 2, 1864; *WES*, Aug. 32, Oct. 7, 14, 1861; *WDC*, May 13, Nov. 18, 1863; Wilson, *Business of Civil War*, 109; Miller, *Second Only to Grant*, 120; Greene, *Horses at Work*, 129, 143.

9. *WES*, Sept. 17, 18, 1861; *WDC*, April 24, 1863, Jan. 7, March 5, Oct. 2, 1864; *WNR*, Jan. 19, Feb. 26, 1864, Jan. 4, 1865; Adams, *Letter from Washington*, 131; Wilson, *Business of Civil War*, 1.

10. *WES*, Dec. 27, 1861, Jan. 1, 3, 1862; *WNR*, Oct. 19, Nov. 12, 1863; *WDC*, Oct. 20, Dec. 14, 19, 1863; Greene, *Horses at Work*, 142.

11. Abraham Lincoln, Order to Remove Bakeries from the Capitol, Oct. 14, 1862, ALPLC; *WES*, May 6, June 8, July 27, Sept. 21, 1861; Anna L. Boyden, *Echoes from Hospital and White House: A Record of Mrs. Rebecca R. Pomroy's Experience in War-Times* (Boston: D. Lothrop & Company, 1884), 141–42; Wilson, *Business of Civil War*, 32.

12. Through most of the war, the standard Union Army ration included twenty ounces of salted or fresh beef or twelve ounces of pork or bacon and twenty ounces of soft bread, a pound of hard bread, or twenty ounces of corn meal; Bell Irvin Wiley, *The Life of Billy Yank: The Common Soldier of the Union* (New York: Grosset & Dunlap, 1951), 224. *WES*, Aug. 23, Sept. 21, 1861; *WDC*, March 24, April 13, 1863; *WNR*, Aug. 24, 1862, Oct. 19, 1863.

13. *OR*, Ser. I, V, 110; *WES*, May 6, 8, 25, July 10, Aug. 16, 19, 21, 29, 1861; *WNR*,

Oct. 19, 1863; *WDC*, April 13, 1863; Cooling, *Symbol, Sword, and Shield*, 95–96; Wiley, *Life of Billy Yank*, 45.

14. *WES*, May 18, June 15, June 28, July 10, Aug. 10, Nov. 7, 25, 1861; *WNR*, July 30, 1863; *WDC*, Dec. 14, 1863.

15. *WES*, April 27, May 8, June 20, 1861; *WNR*, July 11, 1862; Michael A. Cooke, "Physical Environment and Sanitation in the District of Columbia, 1860–1868," *RCHS* 52 (1989), 290, 300, 303; Brehon Somervell, "Washington Water Supply," in John Clagett Proctor, ed., *Washington Past and Present: A History* (New York: Lewis Historical Publishing, 1930), II, 612.

16. *OR*, Ser. I, V, 679, 682, 699; *WES*, Sept. 5, Nov. 2, 1861, Jan. 8, 1862; *WDC*, Oct. 31, Dec. 5, 1863; Paullin, "Alexandria County in 1861," 125; Noel G. Harrison, "Atop an Anvil: The Civilians' War in Fairfax and Alexandria Counties, April 1861–April 1862," *Virginia Magazine of History and Biography* 106 (Spring 1998), 142, 161, 163; George Worthington Adams, *Doctors in Blue: The Medical History of the Union Army in the Civil War* (Baton Rouge: Louisiana State University Press, 1952), 11; Whitman, *Memoranda*, 52.

17. Barnard, *Report on the Defenses of Washington*, 125; *WES*, Oct. 2, 18, 23, 1861; *WDC*, Oct. 31, 1863, Oct. 29, 1864; *WNR*, Jan. 24, Feb. 8, 1862, Nov. 28, 1863; Weigley, *Quartermaster General of the Union*, 269; Wilson, *Business of Civil War*, 1.

18. *WES*, April 20, 29, 30, May 3, 5, 7, 1861; Wilton P. Moore, "Union Army Provost Marshals in the Eastern Theater," *Military Affairs* 26 (Autumn 1962), 121.

19. *WES*, May 8, June 27, 28, July 15, 1861.

20. *WES*, April 22, May 8, June 20, 22, July 6, 10, 29, 1861.

21. *WNI*, Jan. 21, 1861; *WES*, June 12, 18, 22, July 29, Aug. 19, Sept. 30, 1861, Aug. 2, 1862; *WDC*, April 3, June 16, 1863, Feb. 13, May 10, 1864; *WNR*, May 16, 1864.

22. *CW*, VI, 256; *CWS*, 187; *WDC*, Jan. 3, June 16, April 3, 1863; Bayne, *Tad Lincoln's Father*, 32; Gerry, *Through Five Administrations*, 21.

23. *OR*, Ser. I, V, 8, 11–12; *WES*, Aug. 1, 1861; Moore, "Union Army Provost Marshals," 120; Steven J. Ramold, *Baring the Iron Hand: Discipline in the Union Army* (DeKalb: Northern Illinois University Press, 2010), 304.

24. *U.S. Statutes at Large*, XII, 36th Cong., 1st Sess., Chap. XLIV, 291–92; *WES*, Dec. 26, 1861, Jan. 1, 1862; *WNR*, Feb. 13, 1862, July 17, 1863; *WDC*, Jan. 10, 1863; Brooks, *Washington, D.C., in Lincoln's Time*, 16.

25. *WES*, July 23, Aug. 1, 2, 3, Sept. 1, Oct. 17, 1861; Moore, "Union Army Provost Marshals," 121.

26. General Orders, No. 4, *OR*, Ser. I, V, 564–65; General Orders, No. 56, *OR*, Ser. I, V, 688–90; *WES*, Aug. 20, Sept. 2, Dec. 28, 1861.

27. Barnard, *Report on the Defenses of Washington*, 15; *WES*, Aug. 3, 6, 10, 1861.

28. *OR*, Ser. II, V, 2; Moore, "Union Army Provost Marshals," 121–22.

CHAPTER 11 "I Was Slow to Adopt the Strong Measures"

1. *CW*, VI, 226; "Central Guard-House," H.R. Exec Doc. No. 75, 37th Cong., 2d Sess., 1–2; *WES*, Dec. 1, 1860, Aug. 1, 5, Sept. 7, 1861.

2. *CW*, IV, 372; Hay, *Lincoln and the Civil War*, 30–31; *WES*, Oct. 1, 1861.

3. *CW*, IV, 430, VI, 263–64; *WNR*, Feb. 13, 1862; Neely, *Fate of Liberty*, 122.

4. "Central Guard-House," 1–2; *WES*, Aug. 26, 1861; *WNR*, Feb. 13, 1862; *WDC*, May 29, Nov. 9, 1863; Moore, "Union Army Provost Marshals," 124; Neely, *Fate of Liberty*, 19.

5. *U.S. Statutes at Large*, XII, 37th Cong., 1st Sess., Chap. LXII, 320–26; 37th Cong., 2nd Sess., S. Exec. Doc. 1, pt. 1, 912; *WES*, Jan. 17, April 29, May 2, 6, 15, July 31, Sept. 9, 1861; *WDC*, March 17, 1863; John P. Deeban, "To Protect and to Serve: The Records of the D.C. Metropolitan Police, 1861–1930," *Prologue: Quarterly of the National Archives and Records Administration* 40 (Spring 2008), 51; Alfers, *Law and Order in the Capital City*, 24, 25, 27.

6. A longtime Washingtonian and Republican, Robbins was an attorney who had represented Lincoln when he applied for a patent for an improved method of buoying boats in 1849; Zenas C. Robbins to Lincoln, April 13, 1849, ALPLC. *WES*, Aug. 16, 19, 1861; William Tindall, "A Sketch of Mayor Sayles J. Bowen," *RCHS* 18 (1915), 25–30; Harrold, *Subversives*, 174, 177, 186, 230, 240, 254; Masur, *Example for All the Land*, 80, 162–63, 172; Alfers, *Law and Order in the Capital City*, 24.

7. 37th Cong., 2nd Sess., S. Exec. Doc. 1, Pt. 1, 912; 37th Cong., 3rd Sess., H. Exec. Doc. 1, Pt. 2, 649–50; 38th Cong., 1st Sess., H. Exec. Doc. 1, Pt. 3, 719; *WES*, Sept. 10, 17, 19, Oct. 6, 7, Dec. 31, 1861, Jan. 13, 1862; *WNR*, Jan. 15, 1862; *WDC*, Jan. 7, March 23, June 9, 1863, Nov. 19, 1864.

8. 37th Cong., 2nd Sess., S. Exec. Doc. 1, Pt. 1, 912, 913; Alfers, *Law and Order in the Capital City*, 25.

9. General Orders No. 13; *OR*, Ser. III, I, 133–34; Howard K. Beale, ed., "The Diary of Edward Bates, 1859–1866," *Annual Report of the American Historical Association for the Year 1930* (Washington, DC, 1930), 187; *WES*, April 22, 23, 26, May 21, July 12, 1861; Harold Melvin Hyman, *Era of the Oath: Northern Loyalty Tests During the Civil War and Reconstruction* (New York: Octagon Books, 1978), 1, 163 n. 2.

10. *U.S. Statutes at Large*, XII, 37th Cong., 1st Sess., Chap. LXIV, 326–27; "Loyalty of Clerks and Other Persons Employed by Government," 37th Cong., 2nd Sess., House Report No. 16, Jan. 18, 1862, 3, 4; *WES*, Feb. 1, 1862; *WNR*, Feb. 2, 1862; Hyman, *Era of the Oath*, 1–3, 5, 7–9, 157.

11. *WES*, Nov. 27, 1861; *WNR*, Feb. 26, April 16, June 16, July 2, Aug. 13, 14, Sept. 11, Nov. 11, 1862; *WES*, Feb. 1, 1862; *WNI*, April 21, 1862; Hyman, *Era of the Oath*, 13–14.

12. *WES*, April 30, 1861; *WNR*, Aug. 8, Sept. 2, 1862; *WDC*, Dec. 12, 1862; Doster, *Lincoln and Episodes of the Civil War*, 104; Hyman, *Era of the Oath*, 22–24, 28–29, 158–59; Whyte, "Divided Loyalties in Washington During the Civil War," 114.

13. Whyte, "Divided Loyalties in Washington During the Civil War," 104, 110–12, 114; Margaret Leech, *Reveille in Washington, 1860–1865* (New York: Harper & Brothers, 1941), 438; *WES*, Nov. 25, 1861.

14. *WES*, March 26, 1862; *WNR*, July 19, 24, 1862; *WDC*, May 30, 1863; Brooks,

Washington, D.C., in Lincoln's Time, 17; John H. Brinton, *Personal Memoirs of John H. Brinton, Civil War Surgeon, 1861–1865* (Carbondale: Southern Illinois University Press, 1996), 182; Whyte, "Divided Loyalties in Washington During the Civil War," 117; Davis, "Old Capitol," 211; James I. Robertson Jr., "Old Capitol: Eminence to Infamy," *Maryland Historical Magazine* 65 (Winter 1970), 395.

15. *WNR*, Jan. 10, 1862; *WES*, Aug. 24, 1861; Ann Blackman, *Wild Rose: Rose O'Neale Greenhow, Civil War Spy* (New York: Random House, 2005), 27, 36–37, 161–62; Donald E. Markle, *Spies and Spymasters of the Civil War*, rev. ed. (New York: Hippocrene Books, 2004), 159–60; Davis, "Old Capitol," 5–6, 219, 221; William Gilmore Beymer, *Scouts and Spies of the Civil War* (Lincoln: University of Nebraska Press, 2003), 153.

16. Wilson's biographer argues that Greenhow obtained information not from the senator but from one of his clerks; Richard H. Abbott, *Cobbler in Congress: The Life of Henry Wilson* (Lexington: University Press of Kentucky, 1972), 117; Pinkerton, *Spy of the Rebellion*, xxvii, xxviii, 138–39, 245, 247; Calder, "Personal Recollections of Walt Whitman," 831.

17. Ward H. Lamon to Lincoln, Aug. 23, 1861, ALPLC; *WNR*, Jan. 29, 1862; Pinkerton, *Spy of the Rebellion*, 261; Markle, *Spies and Spymasters of the Civil War*, 160–64.

18. Herndon and Weik, *Herndon's Lincoln*, 220; William Lee Miller, *Lincoln's Virtues: An Ethical Biography* (New York: Knopf, 2002), 410–17; Davis, "Old Capitol," 210–12.

19. *WES*, Aug. 5, 12, 1861, Jan. 20, 1862; Robertson, "Old Capitol," 396–97, 398; Beymer, *Scouts and Spies*, 162–63; Blackman, *Wild Rose*, 297–301; Rose O'Neal Greenhow, *My Imprisonment and the First Year of Abolition Rule at Washington* (London: R. Bentley, 1863).

20. *WES*, July 6, Aug. 8, 1861; *WNR*, Jan. 2, June 21, July 1, 2, 1862, May 13, 1863; Pinkerton, *Spy of the Rebellion*, 138, 250–51; Blackman, *Wild Rose*, 188; Bayne, *Tad Lincoln's Father*, 62.

21. *WNR*, Aug. 2, 1862, March 21, 1864; Louis A. Sigaud, *Belle Boyd: Confederate Spy* (Richmond: Dietz Press, 1944), 14; Markle, *Spies and Spymasters of the Civil War*, 155–57; Belko, *Invincible Duff Green*, 443; Davis, "Old Capitol," 207, 211; Beymer, *Scouts and Spies*, 151.

22. *WNR*, Sept. 23, Dec. 3, 1863; Markle, *Spies and Spymasters of the Civil War*, 157–58; Belle Boyd, *Belle Boyd, in Camp and Prison* (New York: Blelock, 1865).

23. *OR*, Ser. III, I, 869; *WES*, Jan. 29, 1861, March 4, 1862; *WDC*, Dec. 20, 1862, Jan. 8, May 5, May 29, 1863; *WNR*, Jan. 22, 1862.

24. When Berret argued that he was exempt from the oath of allegiance because he had already taken a loyalty oath as mayor, Attorney General Bates submitted an official opinion that the secretary of the interior was obligated to administer the oath to all members of the Police Board; Edward Bates, "Metropolitan Police Board," *Official Opinions of the Attorneys General*, X, 104–7. *OR*, Ser. II, II, 596–99; *WES*, Aug. 20, 24, Sept. 13, 14, 18, 1861.

25. Julia W. Berret to Lincoln, Sept. 14, 1861, Lincoln to James G. Berret, April 22,

1862, ALPLC; *WES*, Feb. 1, Oct. 18, 1861; Harrison, *Washington During Civil War and Reconstruction*, 152.

26. *WES*, Nov. 27, 1860; Brooks, *Lincoln Observed*, 88; Stoddard, *Inside the White House*, 18; Bayne, *Tad Lincoln's Father*, 14; Fleischner, *Mrs. Lincoln and Mrs. Keckly*, 209.

27. Helm, *True Story of Mary*, 225; Rietveld, "Lincoln White House Community," 24; Fleischner, *Mrs. Lincoln and Mrs. Keckly*, 210, 214.

28. Nicolay, *With Lincoln in the White House*, 125; Brooks, *Lincoln Observed*, 83; Daniel Mark Epstein, *Lincoln's Men: The President and His Private Secretaries* (New York: Collins, 2009), 76; Baker, *Mary Todd Lincoln*, 224, 238; Rietveld, "Lincoln White House Community," 36; Packard, *Lincolns in the White House*, 45, 86.

29. Burlingame, *Lincoln: A Life*, II, 266–68, 273–74; Packard, *Lincolns in the White House*, 50, 90.

30. *CW*, V, 25; "Loyalty of Clerks and Other Persons Employed by Government," 28–29; Burlingame, *Lincoln: A Life*, II, 266–68, 273–74.

31. French, *Witness to the Young Republic*, 3, 7, 10, 361, 374, 382; Michael Spangler, "Benjamin Brown French in the Lincoln Period," *White House History* 8 (Winter 2002), 5–6, 9–10, 17.

32. *CW*, V, 28; *New York Times*, Jan. 20, 1862; Diary of Horatio Nelson Taft, I, April 12, 22, Sept. 25, Oct. 1, 11, 18, Nov. 23; Bayne, *Tad Lincoln's Father*, 60–62, 64, 65–66.

33. These actions are also known as the Battle of Leesburg, the Battle of Harrison's Island, and the Battle of Edward's Ferry. *OR*, Ser. I, V, 300–302; Neely, *Abraham Lincoln Encyclopedia*, 15–16.

34. *OR*, Ser. I, V, 300–302; *WES*, Oct. 29, 1861; *WDC*, Oct. 17, 1864; McPherson, *Ordeal by Fire*, 216–17.

35. *WES*, Oct. 22, 23, 1861; Hay, *Lincoln and the Civil War*, 30; Stoddard, *Inside the White House*, 167; McPherson, *Ordeal by Fire*, 217; Bruce Tap, *Over Lincoln's Shoulder: The Committee on the Conduct of the War* (Lawrence: University Press of Kansas, 1998), 21.

36. *WES*, Nov. 4, 7, 1861.

37. *OR*, Ser. I, V, 297, 301–2; Tap, *Over Lincoln's Shoulder*, 18, 22; Stewart, *Joshua R. Giddings*, 10; Neely, *Abraham Lincoln Encyclopedia*, 16.

CHAPTER 12 "If I Were Only a Boy I'd March Off Tomorrow"

1. Louisa May Alcott, *Hospital Sketches*, ed. Alice Fahs (Boston: Bedford/St. Martin's, 2004), 18; Boyden, *Echoes from Hospital and White House*, 13–15, 17, 21; Silber, *Daughters of the Union*, 198.

2. *OR*, Ser. I, V, 90, 109; *WES*, Aug. 10, Nov. 11, 1861; *WNR*, Jan. 9, April 2, Aug. 18, 1862; Harvey E. Brown, *The Medical Department of the United States Army from 1775 to 1873* (Washington: Surgeon General's Office, 1873), 215; Schultz, *Women at the Front*, 49; Adams, *Doctors in Blue*, 9, 149–50, 151; Maxwell, *Lincoln's Fifth Wheel*, 33.

3. *OR*, Ser. I, V, 90, 104; *WES*, Aug. 10, 16, Sept. 2, 1861.

4. *OR*, Ser. I, V, 100–101, 109; Adams, *Doctors in Blue*, 153.

5. *WES*, Oct. 10, Dec. 7, 18, 1861; *WNR*, April 2, June 30, 1862; Whitman, *Memoranda*, 11; Brooks, *Washington, D.C., in Lincoln's Time*, 17, 19.

6. Alcott, *Hospital Sketches*, ed. Fahs, vii, 11, 13, 15, 18; *WES*, May 20, 1862; Doster, *Lincoln and Episodes of the Civil War*, 158; Judith Ann Giesberg, *Civil War Sisterhood: The U.S. Sanitary Commission and Women's Politics in Transition* (Boston: Northeastern University Press, 200), 5, 22, 32, 33; Schultz, *Women at the Front*, 20; Silber, *Daughters of the Union*, 198.

7. *WES*, April 23, 1861; Alcott, *Hospital Sketches*, ed. Fahs, 15, 102; Silber, *Daughters of the Union*, 196; Giesberg, *Civil War Sisterhood*, 18, 23, 25, 31, 34, 36.

8. *OR*, Ser. III, I, 107; *WES*, Sept. 14, 1861; Schultz, *Women at the Front*, 25; Hay, *Lincoln and the Civil War*, 4; Giesberg, *Civil War Sisterhood*, 22, 34, 35.

9. *OR*, Ser. I, V, 76–77, 81, 82, 103; *WES*, May 20, Aug. 10, 1861; P. M. Ashburn, *A History of the Medical Department of the United States Army* (Boston: Houghton Mifflin, 1929), 81; Schultz, *Women at the Front*, 18, 19; Adams, *Doctors in Blue*, 13.

10. *OR*, Ser. I, V, 81, 84; *WDC*, May 9, 1863; Ashburn, *History of the Medical Department*, 69; Maxwell, *Lincoln's Fifth Wheel*, 64.

11. *WES*, May 14, 1861; *WNR*, June 7, 1862; Giesberg, *Civil War Sisterhood*, 34, 36–37, 44, 100.

12. *OR*, Ser. III, I, 258–59; Adams, *Doctors in Blue*, 7–8; Giesberg, *Civil War Sisterhood*, 38.

13. *CWS*, 187; *WES*, June 11, July 29, 1861; Giesberg, *Civil War Sisterhood*, vii, 34, 43, 100; Elizabeth Stevenson, "Olmsted on F Street: The Beginnings of the United States Sanitary Commission," *RCHS* 73–74 (1976), 129–30.

14. *WES*, May 25, July 23, 26, 27, Aug. 10, 13, Sept. 5; *WNR*, Oct. 3, Dec. 3; *WDC*, June 6, 1863; Maxwell, *Lincoln's Fifth Wheel*, 37–40.

15. *OR*, Ser. I, III, 1, 262, V, 102–3; *WES*, July 29, 1861; Giesberg, *Civil War Sisterhood*, 47, 48, 51, 116; Schultz, *Women at the Front*, 5, 15, 21, 25, 41, 61; Silber, *Daughters of the Union*, 216.

16. *OR*, Ser. I, V, 90–91, 103; Ashburn, *History of the Medical Department*, 88.

17. *WNR*, July 26, 1862; James Evelyn Pilcher, *The Surgeon Generals of the Army of the United States of America* (Carlisle, PA: Association of Military Surgeons, 1905), 49; Ira M. Rutkow, *Bleeding Blue and Gray: Civil War Surgery and the Evolution of American Medicine* (New York: Random House, 2005), 93–94; Giesberg, *Civil War Sisterhood*, 48–49; Schultz, *Women at the Front*, 18; Silber, *Daughters of the Union*, 213; Maxwell, *Lincoln's Fifth Wheel*, 29; Stevenson, "Olmsted on F Street," 129.

18. Schultz, *Women at the Front*, 25, 37, 39, 42, 100; Silber, *Daughters of the Union*, 199; Adams, *Doctors in Blue*, 183, 184.

19. *OR*, Ser. I, V, 102–3; *WNR*, July 26, 1862; Boyden, *Echoes from Hospital and White House*, 141.

20. *WDC*, Jan. 30, 1864; Schultz, *Women at the Front*, 21, 22, 33, 36–37, 39, 99; Silber, *Daughters of the Union*, 214–15.

21. *WNR*, May 14, 1862; Boyden, *Echoes from Hospital and White House*, 95–98.

22. *WDC*, June 30, 1863; Alcott, *Hospital Sketches*, ed. Fahs, 18, 20, 23, 24; Schultz, *Women at the Front*, 41.

23. Alcott, *Hospital Sketches*, ed. Fahs, 20–21, 28; Mark Twain, *The Gilded Age: A Tale of To-day* (New York: Harper & Brothers, 1915), 151; Schultz, *Women at the Front*, 41, 53, 86.

CHAPTER 13 "Tinkering Experiments"

1. The stable was probably the underground railroad station operated by African Americans John Bush and his wife east of City Hall; Russell, "Underground Railroad Activists in Washington, D.C.," 30–31. Washington, *They Knew Lincoln*, 82–83; *WNR*, March 29, 1862.

2. In Washington's First Ward in 1860, 47 percent of adult male African Americans had been born in the District of Columbia, 27 percent in Virginia, and 23 percent in Maryland; U.S. Manuscript Census, Free Population Schedule, Washington, DC, 1860. Louis Gerteis, *From Contraband to Freedman: Federal Policy Toward Southern Blacks, 1861–1865* (Westport, CT: Greenwood Press, 1973), 17; Whitman, *Price of Freedom*, 61; Harrold, *Subversives*, 169, 215–19.

3. Nicolay, *Oral History*, 49; Gerteis, *From Contraband to Freedman*, 5, 17; Harrold, *Subversives*, 225.

4. *CW*, III, 41, 317, 384, 435, 514, IV, 157, 182, 264; *U.S. Statutes at Large*, XII, 37th Cong., 2nd Sess., Chap. CXI, 432.

5. *OR*, Ser. II, I, 752, 754; Edward Pierce, "The Contrabands at Fortress Monroe," *Atlantic Monthly* 8 (Nov. 1861), 627, 630; Benjamin F. Butler, *Butler's Book* (Boston: A. M. Thayer, 1892), 256–58; *WES*, May 30, 1861; Gerteis, *From Contraband to Freedman*, 15; Glenn David Brasher, *The Peninsula Campaign and the Necessity of Emancipation* (Chapel Hill: University of North Carolina Press, 2012), 33–34. For the legal foundation of "military emancipation," see James Oakes, *Freedom National: The Destruction of Slavery in the United States, 1861–1865* (New York: W. W. Norton, 2012), 345–52.

6. *OR*, Ser. II, I, 754–55; Pierce, "Contrabands at Fortress Monroe," 626–27; *Private and Official Correspondence of Gen. Benjamin F. Butler* (Norwood, MA: Plimpton Press, 1971), I, 116–17; John Eaton, *Grant, Lincoln and the Freedmen: Reminiscences of the Civil War* (New York: Longmans, Green & Co., 1907), 92; Brasher, *Peninsula Campaign*, 37; Gerteis, *From Contraband to Freedman*, 14–15.

7. *OR*, Ser. II, I, 753, 757, 758–59, 761; Pierce, "Contrabands at Fortress Monroe," 628, 633; Butler, *Butler's Book*, 259; Johnston, *Surviving Freedom*, 114–15; Kate Masur, " 'A Rare Phenomenon of Philological Vegetation': The Word 'Contraband' and the Meanings of Emancipation in the United States," *Journal of American History* 93 (March 2007), 1051; Brasher, *Peninsula Campaign*, 44–45.

8. *OR*, Ser. II, I, 753, 759, 761–62, 771; *U.S. Statutes at Large*, XII, 37th Cong.,

2nd Sess., Chap. LX, 319; Gerteis, *From Contraband to Freedman*, 16; Ira Berlin, Barbara J. Fields, Thavolia Glymph, Joseph P. Reidy, and Leslie S. Rowland, eds., *The Destruction of Slavery*, Ser. I, Vol. 1 of *Freedom: A Documentary History of Emancipation, 1861–1867* (New York: Cambridge University Press, 1985), 162; Oakes, *Freedom National*, 201.

9. *WES*, May 8, June 1, 6, 27, Aug. 3, Sept. 11, 14, Dec. 9, 1861; Johnston, *Surviving Freedom*, 119; Green, *Secret City*, 59.

10. *WNR*, Feb. 7, 15, 1862, March 11, 1862; *WES*, May 20, June 11, 1861; March 10, 1862.

11. *OR*, Ser. I, VIII, 390; *CG*, 37th Cong., 2nd Sess., 10; Hay, *Lincoln and the Civil War*, 37; *WNR*, March 15, 1862; *WES*, Sept. 2, 5, Nov. 29, 1861.

12. *WES*, Feb. 16, 1862; *WNR*, Jan. 17, 29, 1862; Elaine Cutler Everly, "The Freedmen's Bureau in the National Capital" (Ph.D. dissertation, George Washington University, 1972), 33.

13. *OR*, Ser. II, I, 760, 764, III, 1, 324; *WES*, Sept. 14, Dec. 5, 1861; Lamon, *Recollections of Abraham Lincoln*, 254–55; Berlin et al., *Destruction of Slavery*, 162; David Taft Terry, "A Brief Moment in the Sun: The Aftermath of Emancipation in Washington, D.C.," in Elizabeth Clark-Lewis, ed., *First Freed: Washington, D.C., in the Emancipation Era* (Washington: Howard University Press, 2002), 76–77.

14. *OR*, Ser. II, I, 760, 764; *WNR*, April 8, 1862.

15. Senate Rep. Com. No. 60, 37th Cong., 2nd Sess., 6; *WES*, Dec. 5, 31, 1860, July 18, Aug. 19, 28, 1861.

16. "A Friend" to Lincoln, Feb. 1861, Washington, DC, Citizens to Lincoln, March 30, April 2, 1861, Ward H. Lamon to Lincoln, May 27, 1861, C. Beckwith to Lincoln, June 7, 1861, Ward H. Lamon to Lincoln, July 4, 1861, ALPLC; *WES*, June 15, Nov. 6, 1861; Senate Rep. Com. No. 60, 37th Cong., 2nd Sess., 26–27.

17. Senate Rep. Com. No. 60, 37th Cong., 2nd Sess., 6; "Report of the Marshal of the District of Columbia," 37th Cong., 2nd Sess., Misc. Doc. No. 2; *WES*, Dec. 4, 6, 1861, Jan. 13, 1862.

18. *CG*, 37th Cong., 2nd Sess., 10; Alfred G. Harris, "Lincoln and the Question of Slavery in the District of Columbia," *Lincoln Herald* 52 (Feb. 1950), 6.

19. *CG*, 37th Cong., 2nd Sess., 10; Waugh, *Lincoln and McClellan*, 53.

20. *CG*, 37th Cong., 2nd Sess., 10; *WES*, Dec. 5, 7, 31, 1861.

21. *CG*, 37th Cong., 2nd Sess., 10–13; 37th Cong., 3rd Sess., H. Exec. Doc. 1, Pt. 2, 652–53; *WES*, Dec. 7, 1861.

22. 37th Cong., 2nd Sess., H.R. Report No. 11; *CG*, 37th Cong., 2nd Sess., 310–11; *WES*, Dec. 10, 1861, Jan. 20, 1862; *WNR*, Jan. 16, Feb. 14, 1862.

23. Senate Rep. Com. No. 60, 37th Cong., 2nd Sess., 1–7, 27, 33, 34, 35, 37; *CG*, 37th Cong., 2nd Sess., 311; *WNR*, Feb. 14, 1862.

24. Horace Greeley to Lincoln, Jan. 6, 1863, ALPLC; Senate Rep. Com. No. 60, 37th Cong., 2nd Sess., 37; Lamon, *Recollections of Abraham Lincoln*, 254, 259.

25. *U.S. Statutes at Large*, XII, 37th Cong., 2nd Sess., Chap. XL, 354; *WES*, Dec. 11, 1861, March 17, 1862.

CHAPTER 14 "Freedom Triumphant in War and Peace"

1. *CW*, V, 144–46, 223; Allen C. Guelzo, *Lincoln's Emancipation Proclamation: The End of Slavery in America* (New York: Simon & Schuster, 2004), 55–56.

2. Lincoln used "it's" in his original message. *CW*, V, 144–46; Joseph C. G. Kennedy to Lincoln, Nov. 26, 1861, ALPLC; *WNR*, March 10, 1862.

3. *CW*, V, 144–46, 318, 324; *WNR*, March 10, 1862; William C. Harris, *Lincoln and the Border States: Preserving the Union* (Lawrence: University Press of Kansas, 2011), 160–61, 162; Harold Bell Hancock, *Delaware During the Civil War: A Political History* (Wilmington: Historical Society of Delaware, 1961), 107–8, 109–10; Foner, *Fiery Trial*, 183–84; Guelzo, *Lincoln's Emancipation Proclamation*, 57–59, 92–93.

4. P. J. Staudenraus, *The African Colonization Movement, 1816–1865* (New York: Columbia University Press, 1961), 27–29; Floyd J. Miller, *The Search for a Black Nationality: Black Emigration and Colonization, 1787–1863* (Urbana: University of Illinois Press, 1975), 54–90; Leonard P. Curry, *The Free Black in Urban America, 1800–1850: The Shadow of the Dream* (Chicago: University of Chicago Press, 1981), 232–37; Filler, *Crusade Against Slavery*, 20; George M. Fredrickson, *The Black Image in the White Mind: The Debate on Afro-American Character and Destiny, 1817–1914* (New York: Harper & Row, 1971), 6–32; Leon F. Litwack, *North of Slavery: The Negro in the Free States, 1790–1860* (Chicago: University of Chicago Press, 1961), 20–24; Douglas R. Egerton, "Averting a Crisis: The Proslavery Critique of the American Colonization Society," *Civil War History* 43 (April 1997), 142–56.

5. *CW*, V, 48–49; Winkle, *Young Eagle*, 265; G. S. Boritt, "The Voyage to the Colony of Linconia," *Historian* 37 (Aug. 1975), 627; Michael Vorenberg, "Abraham Lincoln and the Politics of Black Colonization," *Journal of the Abraham Lincoln Association* 14 (Summer 1993), 23–45.

6. Beale, "Diary of Edward Bates," 113, 263–64; Gideon Welles, *Diary of Gideon Welles* (Boston: Houghton Mifflin, 1911), I, 150–52; Vorenberg, "Abraham Lincoln and the Politics of Black Colonization," 31, 37–38; Eric Foner, "Lincoln and Colonization," in Foner, *Our Lincoln*, 147, 150; Kate Masur, "The African American Delegation to Lincoln: A Reappraisal," *Civil War History* 56 (June 2010), 122.

7. Ambrose Thompson to Lincoln, April 25, 1862, Ambrose W. Thompson to Gideon Welles, Aug. 8, 1861, Lincoln to Caleb B. Smith, Oct. 23, 1861, ALPLC; Welles, *Diary of Gideon Welles*, I, 150–52.

8. *WNR*, Jan. 13, 15, Aug. 26, 1862; *WNI*, April 7, 1862.

9. *WNR*, Jan. 13, 1862; Vorenberg, "Abraham Lincoln and the Politics of Black Colonization," 28.

10. *WES*, April 2, 25, 29, 1862; *WNR*, April 10, 23, May 12, Aug. 22, 1862; *WDC*, Dec. 31, 1862; Berlin et al., *Wartime Genesis of Free Labor*, 263–66; Burlingame, *Lincoln: A Life*, II, 384; Vorenberg, "Abraham Lincoln and the Politics of Black Colonization," 33–34; Masur, "African American Delegation,"

120–21, 123–24, 133; John McKivigan, *Forgotten Firebrand: James Redpath and the Making of Nineteenth-Century America* (Ithaca: Cornell University Press, 2008), 22, 67.

11. Turner eventually scorned wartime emigration, writing that "I suppose no colored man in the nation would have any objection to going any where, if this government pay them for their two hundred and forty years' work"; *PCR*, Aug. 30, Oct. 4, 1862. After the war, however, as an A.M.E. bishop, he responded to racial inequality by embracing emigration to Africa. *American Colonization Society, Addresses Delivered at Its Late Annual Meeting, in Washington, D.C.* (New York: T. R. Dawley, 1864), 16; Edwin S. Redkey, *Respect Black: The Writings and Speeches of Henry McNeal Turner* (New York: Arno Press, 1971), 42, 85, 131; Edwin S. Redkey, "Henry McNeal Turner: Black Chaplain in the Union Army," in John David Smith, ed., *Black Soldiers in Blue: African American Troops in the Civil War Era* (Chapel Hill: University of North Carolina Press, 2002), 337; Stephen Ward Angell, *Bishop Henry McNeal Turner and African-American Religion in the South* (Knoxville: University of Tennessee Press, 1991), 47, 119; Stephen W. Angell, "Henry McNeal Turner—Conservative? Radical? Or Independent?" in Peter Eisenstadt, ed., *Black Conservatism: Essays in Intellectual and Political History* (New York: Garland, 1999), 25–27, 43; Phillip W. Magness and Sebastian N. Page, *Colonization After Emancipation: Lincoln and the Movement for Black Resettlement* (Columbia: University of Missouri Press, 2011), 4; C. R. Gibbs, *Black, Copper, and Bright: The District of Columbia's Black Civil War Regiment* (Silver Spring, MD: Three Dimensional Publishing, 2002), 32, 104, 109; Russell, "Underground Railroad Activists," 36.

12. *CW*, VI, 194–95; *WDC*, April 30, 1863; *WNR*, May 12, 1862; Masur, "African American Delegation," 125–27; Angell, "Henry McNeal Turner," 29; *PCR*, Aug. 9, 30, 1862.

13. *CW*, V, 370–75; Masur, "African American Delegation," 128–31; *PCR*, Aug. 30, 1862.

14. *CW*, V, 370–75; Boritt, "The Voyage to the Colony of Linconia," 624–25.

15. *CW*, V, 371; *WNR*, Aug. 16, 1862; Masur, "African American Delegation," 135; *PCR*, Aug. 30, 1862.

16. Turner suggested that he had firsthand knowledge of Lincoln's motives by telling readers, "I do not wish to trespass upon the key that unlocks a private door for fear that I might loose it, but all I will say, is, that the President stood in need of a place to *point to*"; *PCR*, Aug. 30, Oct. 4, 1862; *CW*, V, 37; Joseph Henry to Frederick W. Seward, Sept. 5, 1862, ALPLC; *CG*, 37th Cong., 2nd Sess., 2997; *WNR*, Aug. 26, Oct. 16, 1862; Vorenberg, "Abraham Lincoln and the Politics of Black Colonization," 34, 35, 38.

17. Sturge, *Visit to the United States in 1841*, 76.

18. "Slavery in the District of Columbia," H.R. Report No. 58, 37th Cong., 2nd Sess., 8, 9, 10; Michael J. Kurtz, "Emancipation in the Federal City," *Civil War History* 24 (Sept. 1978): 251, 252–53, 254, 255.

19. *WNR*, Feb. 15, 1862; *WNI*, April 12, 1862.

20. *CG*, 37th Cong., 2nd Sess., 1338, 1449; *WNR*, March 1, 17, 19, 21, June 4, 1862; *WES*, March 19, 21, 1862; *WNI*, March 27, April 2, 1862; Kurtz, "Emancipation in the Federal City," 255–56.

21. *WNR*, March 24, 26, 31, April 2, 8, 17, Sept. 15, 1862; *WNI*, April 2, 7, 1862.

22. *WES*, Dec. 11, 1861, Jan. 4, 1862; *WNR*, Jan. 4, 1862; Michael F. Conlin, "The Smithsonian Abolition Lecture Controversy: The Clash of Antislavery Politics with American Science in Wartime Washington," *Civil War History* 46 (Dec. 2000), 301, 305, 307–10.

23. *WES*, Jan. 4, 1862; *WNR*, Jan. 4, 1862; Conlin, "Smithsonian Abolition Lecture Controversy," 312–13.

24. WES, March 15, 1862; *WNR*, Jan. 30, March 1, 1862; James Brewer Stewart, *Wendell Phillips: Liberty's Hero* (Baton Rouge: Louisiana State University Press, 1986), 236.

25. WES, March 15, 1862; Conlin, "Smithsonian Abolition Lecture Controversy," 316, 318–20.

26. *WNR*, March 5, 1862; *WNI*, March 27, 1862; *WES*, March 1, 1862; Kurtz, "Emancipation in the Federal City," 257.

27. *U.S. Statutes at Large*, XII, 37th Cong., 2nd Sess., Chap. LIV, 376–78; "Message of the President of the United States," 37th Cong., 2nd Sess., Senate Ex. Doc. No. 42; EDC, 2, 8; RBCES, Petition No. 1-966; Kurtz, "Emancipation in the Federal City," 254; David W. Blight, *Frederick Douglass' Civil War: Keeping Faith in Jubilee* (Baton Rouge: Louisiana State University Press, 1989), 108.

28. Abraham Lincoln to James G. Berret, April 22, 1862, ALPLC; U.S. Manuscript Census, Free Population Schedule, Washington, DC, 1860; *WNI*, April 17, 1862; *WES*, April 19, 1862; EDC, 1–2; Kurtz, "Emancipation in the Federal City," 259.

29. EDC, 5, 8–9, 10–11, 74; Kurtz, "Emancipation in the Federal City," 262, 266.

30. EDC, 2–3, 8, 17–70; U.S. Manuscript Census, Population Schedule, Washington, DC, 1870; Johnston, *Surviving Freedom*, 158.

31. Henry, Martha, and George Hatton appeared in the 1860 U.S. Census as "free inhabitants"; U.S. Manuscript Census, Free Population Schedule, Prince George's County, Maryland, 1860. RBCES, Petition No. 61, 460.

32. RBCES, Petition No. 1-966; EDC, 20.

33. RBCES, Petition No. 741; U.S. Manuscript Census, Population Schedule, Washington, DC, 1870; Guy Gugliotta, *Freedom's Cap: The United States Capitol and the Coming of the Civil War* (New York: Hill & Wang, 2012), 3, 6–7, 140, 383; Holland, *Black Men Built the Capitol*, 5; Miller, *Second Only to Grant*, 33; Jacob, *Testament to Union*, 30–31.

34. RBCES, Petition No. 741; U.S. Manuscript Census, Free Population Schedule, Georgetown, DC, 1860; *Boyd's Directory of Washington and Georgetown, 1867* (Washington: Hudson Taylor Book Store, 1867), 471; Stoddard, *Inside the White House*, 79; Eaton, *Grant, Lincoln and the Freedmen*, 89; Weigley, *Quartermaster General of the Union Army*, 157–58; Miller, *Second Only to Grant*, 46; Gugliotta,

Freedom's Cap, 357–58, 393; Holland, *Black Men Built the Capitol*, 6–9; Jacob, *Testament to Union*, 9, 155–56; Brooks, *Washington, D.C., in Lincoln's Time*, 21.

35. RBCES, Petition No. 13, 79, 857; U.S. Manuscript Census, Free Population Schedule, Georgetown, DC, 1860; *Boyd's Washington and Georgetown Directory, 1860* (Washington: Taylor and Maury, 1860), 88; Ricks, *Escape on the Pearl*, 321.

36. *U.S. Statutes at Large*, XII, 37th Cong., 2nd Sess., Chap. CLV, 538–39; EDC, 10; Brittany Jones, "Emancipation in Washington, DC, During the Civil War" (Senior Honors Thesis, Department of History, University of Nebraska–Lincoln, 2012); Kurtz, "Emancipation in the Federal City," 264. The act's final clause prohibited the exclusion of African American witnesses in all judicial proceedings in the District.

37. The supplemental petitions are not numbered but are generally filed sequentially by surname or date. Records of the U.S. District Court for the District of Columbia Relating to Slaves, 1851–1863, Records of District Courts of the United States, Record Group 21, NARA, Oct. 3, 6, 1862, Jan. 7, 1863; *WNR*, Nov. 16, 1863.

38. RBCES, Sept. 26, 27, 1862, Jan. 7, 1863; EDC, 10, 73.

39. Records of the U.S. District Court for the District of Columbia Relating to Slaves, 1851–1863, July 21, 29, 1862, Aug. 2, Oct. 3, 1862; RBCES, July 26, 1862; EDC, 73.

40. Meredith appeared in the 1860 U.S. Census as a "free inhabitant"; U.S. Manuscript Census, Free Population Schedule, Washington, DC, 1860. The census listed Meredith's age as thirty-five in 1860, but his petition gave his age as thirty in 1862. RBCES, Aug. 2, 15, Sept. 16, 1862; Records of the U.S. District Court for the District of Columbia Relating to Slaves, 1851–1863, June 30, 1862; EDC, 5; *Boyd's Directory of Washington and Georgetown, 1860*, 113; *Hutchinson's Washington and Georgetown Directory, 1863* (Washington: Hutchinson & Brother, 1863), 146.

41. *CG*, XII, 37th Cong., 2nd Sess., 1491; *WNI*, April 4, 1862.

42. *U.S. Statutes at Large*, XII, 37th Cong., 2nd Sess., Chap. LXXXIII, 407; Clark-Lewis, *First Freed*; Masur, *Example for All the Land*, 1, 26.

CHAPTER 15 "We Must Use What Tools We Have"

1. Herndon and Weik, *Herndon's Lincoln*, 231; Allan Peskin, *Winfield Scott and the Profession of Arms* (Kent: Kent State University Press, 2003), 258–60.

2. OR, Ser. I, XXI, 903–16; George B. McClellan to Winfield Scott, Aug. 8, 1861, ALPLC; Cooling, *Symbol, Sword, and Shield*, 146.

3. *CW*, V 9–10; Winfield Scott to Simon Cameron, Aug. 9, 12, Oct. 4, 1861, ALPLC; Peskin, *Winfield Scott and the Profession of Arms*, 259, 261; McPherson, *Ordeal by Fire*, 213–14; Waugh, *Lincoln and McClellan*, 54–56; Cooling, *Symbol, Sword, and Shield*, 146.

4. *OR*, Ser. III, I, 698–708; Waugh, *Lincoln and McClellan*, 65–66, 71–72; McPherson, *Ordeal by Fire*, 216.

5. *CW*, V, 111–12, 149–50; Waugh, *Lincoln and McClellan*, 73–74; Wayne Mahood, *General Wadsworth: The Life and Times of Brevet Major General James S. Wadsworth* (Cambridge: Da Capo Press, 2003), 75–76, 81.

6. Mahood, *General Wadsworth*, 4, 46, 58–59, 61–62, 67, 69; Lewis F. Allen, *Memorial of the Late Gen. James S. Wadsworth* (Buffalo: Franklin Steam Printing House, 1864), 18, 20; *Proceedings of the Century Association in Honor of the Memory of Brig.-Gen. James S. Wadsworth and Colonel Peter A. Porter* (New York: D. Van Nostrand, 1865), 19; Doster, *Lincoln and Episodes of the Civil War*, 41–42, 52; Waugh, *Lincoln and McClellan*, 67, 75; Johnston, *Surviving Freedom*, 121.

7. Mahood, *General Wadsworth*, 83, 85–87, 102; Doster, *Lincoln and Episodes of the Civil War*, 48, 49; Waugh, *Lincoln and McClellan*, 76.

8. *OR*, Ser. I, V, 100–101; *WNR*, Jan. 7, May 14, June 26, Aug. 18, 27, Oct. 16, Nov. 1, 1862; *WDC*, April 27, 1864; Adams, *Doctors in Blue*, 151–52, 161; Brooks, *Washington, D.C., in Lincoln's Time*, 17, 155, 160.

9. Amanda Akin Stearns, *The Lady Nurse of Ward E* (New York: Baker & Taylor, 1909), 14, 16, 42; *WDC*, April 27, 1864; *WNR*, Aug. 18, 27, 1862.

10. *Armory Square Hospital Gazette*, Jan. 20, Sept. 24, 1864; *WDC*, June 9, 1863; Stearns, *Lady Nurse of Ward E*, 7–8, 20–21; Willard Oliver and Nancy Marion, *Killing the President* (Santa Barbara, CA: Praeger, 2010), 46–48.

11. Perry, *Mrs. Robert E. Lee*, 245–51; *WNR*, June 4, 1862; Giesberg, *Civil War Sisterhood*, 120–22.

12. *WNR*, June 4, 13, 1862; Giesberg, *Civil War Sisterhood*, 13, 115–16, 120; Stephen B. Oates, *A Woman of Valor: Clara Barton and the Civil War* (New York: Free Press, 1994), 45; Ashburn, *A History of the Medical Department*, 82; Perry, *Mrs. Robert E. Lee*, 254.

13. *WNR*, May 16, 1862; McPherson, *Ordeal by Fire*, 242–43; Giesberg, *Civil War Sisterhood*, 120; Drew Gilpin Faust, *This Republic of Suffering: Death and the American Civil War* (New York: Knopf, 2008), 59.

14. Whitman, *Memoranda*, 21–22; *WNR*, May 16, June 5, July 7, 1862, May 14, 16, 1864; *WDC*, June 7, 1864; Giesberg, *Civil War Sisterhood*, 120; Robert M. Poole, *On Hallowed Ground: The Story of Arlington National Cemetery* (New York: Walker, 2009), 44.

15. *WNR*, May 16, June 21, July 26, Sept. 11, 1862; *WES*, Sept. 14, 1861, May 4, 1862; Stearns, *Lady Nurse of Ward E*, 253; McPherson, *Ordeal by Fire*, 242–43; Oates, *Woman of Valor*, 45–46, 50.

16. *WNR*, June 18, 21, 23, 24, 25, 30, 1862; Mahood, *General Wadsworth*, 104.

17. George B. McClellan to Lincoln, Aug. 29, 1862, ALPLC; Hay, *Lincoln and the Civil War*, 45–46, 176; McPherson, *Ordeal by Fire*, 251, 254–55; Reardon, *With a Sword in One Hand*, 71–73.

18. *WDC*, Nov. 11, 1862; *WES*, Aug. 15, 1861.

19. Hay, *Lincoln and the Civil War*, 46; Mahood, *General Wadsworth*, 101, 104; Oates, *Woman of Valor*, 54, 76; Doster, *Lincoln and Episodes of the Civil War*, 154;

McPherson, *Tried by War*, 119; Poole, *On Hallowed Ground*, 44–45; *WNR*, Sept. 3, 4, 1862.

20. *WNR*, June 18, Aug. 5, Sept. 2, 3, 4, 9, 13, 23, 26, 1862; *WDC*, Jan. 10, 1863.

21. Special Orders, No. 218, *CMPP*, VI, 122; *WNR*, Sept. 2, 9, 11, 1862; McPherson, *Tried by War*, 119–20, 121; Waugh, *Lincoln and McClellan*, 132–33; Cooling, *Symbol, Sword, and Shield*, 134; Mahood, *General Wadsworth*, 102.

22. *WNR*, Sept. 1, 2, 1862; Hay, *Lincoln and the Civil War*, 47; Adams, *Doctors in Blue*, 190–92.

23. Corra Bacon-Foster, *Clara Barton, Humanitarian* (Washington: Columbia Historical Society, 1918), 6; Oates, *Woman of Valor*, 5–8, 10, 11–12.

24. *WNR*, June 18, 1862; Oates, *Woman of Valor*, 5–8, 12–13, 24.

25. *WNR*, June 9, 1862; Oates, *Woman of Valor*, 7, 49, 51–52; Bacon-Foster, *Clara Barton, Humanitarian*, 12.

26. Oates, *Woman of Valor*, 59, 63, 65, 104, 133; Schultz, *Women at the Front*, 38.

27. *OR*, Ser. III, I, 262; *U.S. Statutes at Large*, XIII, 38th Cong., 1st Sess., Chap. xxvii, 20–22; *WNR*, Sept. 30, 1862.

28. *WNR*, Aug. 11, Oct. 15, 31, 1862; *WDC*, March 2, 1863.

29. *WDC*, Nov. 27, Dec. 9, 1862; *WNR*, Sept. 15, 19, Nov. 1, 1862.

30. *WNR*, Sept. 5, 19, Oct. 4, 24, 1862, May 26, 1863; *WDC*, Jan. 6, 1863; Adams, *Doctors in Blue*, 157, 189, 190–92.

31. *U.S. Statutes at Large*, XII, 37th Cong., 2nd Sess., Chap. CCI, 597–600; *WNR*, Aug. 14, 1862; McPherson, *Ordeal by Fire*, 250–51; James W. Geary, *We Need Men: The Union Draft in the Civil War* (Dekalb: Northern Illinois University Press, 1991), 27–28, 33–34, 38; Eugene C. Murdock, *One Million Men: The Civil War Draft in the North* (Madison: State Historical Society of Wisconsin, 1971), 160–61.

32. *WNR*, Aug. 13, Sept. 15, 25, Oct. 25, 1862; *WDC*, Nov. 14, Dec. 16, 1863; Geary, *We Need Men*, 37, 47; Murdock, *One Million Men*, 202–3.

33. Proc. No. 1, *U.S. Statutes at Large*, XIII, 730; Neely, *Fate of Liberty*, 52–53, 55.

CHAPTER 16 "On the Soil Where They Were Born"

1. James S. Wadsworth to Ward H. Lamon, May 18, 1862, ALPLC; *WNR*, May 24, 1862; Lamon, *Recollections of Abraham Lincoln*, 255–57; Mahood, *General Wadsworth*, 77, 91–92; Henry Greenleaf Pearson, *James S. Wadsworth of Geneseo: Brevet Major-General of United States Volunteers* (New York: Charles Scribner's Sons, 1913), 135–36, 138, 140; John Alexander Kress, *Memoirs of Brigadier General John Alexander Kress, United States Army (Retired)* (Merion, PA: Privately Printed, 1928), 8.

2. Lamon, *Recollections of Abraham Lincoln*, 256–57; Mahood, *General Wadsworth*, 91–92.

3. *CW*, V, 224; *OR*, Ser. II, I, 817; *WNR*, May 24, 1862; Lamon, *Recollections of Abraham Lincoln*, 256–57; Mahood, *General Wadsworth*, 91–92; Johnston, *Surviving Freedom*, 125.

4. *WNR*, April 8, May 14, 17, 1862.

5. *WNR*, May 19, 22, 23, 24, 28, 31, June 7, 1862; Brooks, *Washington, D.C., in Lincoln's Time*, 179; Harris, "Lincoln and the Question of Slavery," 9.

6. *WNR*, May 14, 17, 23, June 7, Aug. 29, 1862.

7. *CW*, V, 329; *U.S. Statutes at Large*, XII, 37th Cong., 2nd Sess., Chap. CXCV, 589–92, Chap. CCI, 597–600; *WNR*, May 23, Aug. 22, 1862; Phillip Shaw Paludan, *The Presidency of Abraham Lincoln* (Lawrence: University Press of Kansas, 1994), 145–46; Geary, *We Need Men*, 29.

8. *CW*, V, 330, 338, VI, 356–57; *WNR*, May 23, July 17, Aug. 22, 29, 1862; Fleischner, *Mrs. Lincoln and Mrs. Keckly*, 222.

9. *WNR*, March 28, April 8, May 29, 1862; *WES*, March 26, 1862; *WDC*, Feb. 19, 1863; Doster, *Lincoln and Episodes of the Civil War*, 8, 10; Mahood, *General Wadsworth*, 118; Pearson, *James S. Wadsworth*, 133, 135; Johnston, *Surviving Freedom*, 121.

10. *WNR*, March 28, May 24, 1862; Doster, *Lincoln and Episodes of the Civil War*, 164–65; Mahood, *General Wadsworth*, 118; Everly, "Freedmen's Bureau in the National Capital," 33; Berlin et al., *Wartime Genesis of Free Labor*, 263.

11. *WNR*, April 8, March 28, May 29, 1862; Doster, *Lincoln and Episodes of the Civil War*, 163, 164–65, 244; Adams, *Letter from Washington*, 51.

12. *WNR*, May 8, Oct. 30, 1862; Johnston, *Surviving Freedom*, 158–59.

13. Harrold, *Subversives*, 57, 226–27; Everly, "Freedmen's Bureau in the National Capital," 6, 11, 34–35.

14. *WES*, March 22, April 10, 1862; *WDC*, Nov. 11, 1863; Harrold, *Subversives*, 57, 226–27; Everly, "Freedmen's Bureau in the National Capital," 34–35, 57; Felix James, "The Establishment of Freedman's Village in Arlington, Virginia," *Negro History Bulletin* 33 (April 1970), 90.

15. *WNR*, June 23, 1862, Feb. 26, July 27, Nov. 14, 1863; *WES*, Sept. 6, 1861, Jan. 11, March 10, 1862; *WDC*, March 3, 1863, Jan. 5, 1864; Margaret Humphreys, *Intensely Human: The Health of the Black Soldier in the American Civil War* (Baltimore: Johns Hopkins University Press, 2008), 84–85; Jim Downs, *Sick from Freedom: African-American Illness and Suffering during the Civil War and Reconstruction* (New York: Oxford University Press, 2012), 99–100; Everly, "Freedmen's Bureau in the National Capital," 35–37; Johnston, *Surviving Freedom*, 119, 121, 155.

16. *WES*, Jan. 18, March 4, April 25, 29, 1862; *WNR*, April 9, 12, 1862, March 16, Nov. 14, Dec. 18, 1863; *WDC*, Dec. 13, 1862, March 16, Oct. 24, 1863.

17. *WNR*, July 24, Aug. 11, 1862; Stoddard, *Inside the White House*, 122; Doster, *Episodes of Lincoln and the Civil War*, 64, 75, 165; Johnston, *Surviving Freedom*, 121; Thomas Holt, Cassandra Smith-Parker, and Rosalyn Terborg-Penn, *A Special Mission: The Story of Freedmen's Hospital, 1862–1962* (Washington: Howard University, 1975), 2; Lee, *Mr. Lincoln's City*, 26–27; Everly, "Freedmen's Bureau in the National Capital," 37; *Report of a Committee of the Representatives of New York Yearly Meeting of Friends upon the Condition and Wants of the Colored Refugees, 1862*, Friends Historical Library, Swarthmore College, 4.

18. D. B. Nichols, "From the Washington Contraband Depot," in Emancipation League, *Facts Concerning the Freedmen: Their Capacity and Their Destiny* (Boston: Press of Commercial Printing House, 1863), 10; *WNR*, Oct. 30, 1862; *WDC*, Feb. 4, 11, May 25, June 12, 1863.

19. Nichols, "Washington Contraband Depot," 10; *WNR*, July 24, Aug. 5, 11, 29, Oct. 30, Nov. 6, 1862; Johnston, *Surviving Freedom*, 138–39; Green, *Secret City*, 62; Berlin et al., *Wartime Genesis of Free Labor*, 289; *Second Report of a Committee of the Representatives of New York Yearly Meeting of Friends upon the Condition and Wants of the Colored Refugees, 1863*, Friends Historical Library, Swarthmore College, 8–9.

20. *WNR*, April 9, Aug. 11, 1862, Feb. 26, 1863; Humphreys, *Intensely Human*, 11; Doster, *Lincoln and Episodes of the Civil War*, 165; Johnston, *Surviving Freedom*, 121–22; Everly, "Freedmen's Bureau in the National Capital," 39; *Report of a Committee of Representatives*, 5.

21. *WDC*, Dec. 1, 1862, March 3, 17, 1863, Sept. 17, 1864; *WNR*, Feb. 4, 19, 1863, Jan. 16, 1864; Berlin et al., *Wartime Genesis of Free Labor*, 290–91.

22. *WES*, April 10, 1862; *WNR*, May 1, 8, 12, Aug. 1, 11, Oct. 30, 1862; *WDC*, Dec. 1, 1862, Nov. 26, 1863; Nichols, "From the Washington Contraband Depot," 10; Harrold, *Subversives*, 243; Everly, "Freedmen's Bureau in the National Capital," 37, 57; Johnston, "Surviving Freedom," 170; Gibbs, *Black, Copper, and Bright*, 115; Harrison, *Washington During Civil War and Reconstruction*, 39–40; Roberta Schildt, "Freedman's Village: Arlington, Virginia, 1863–1900," *Northern Virginia Heritage* 7 (Feb. 1985), 12.

23. *Second Report of a Committee of Representatives*, 8–9; *WDC*, Dec. 1, 1862; *WNR*, Nov. 6, 1862; Nichols, "From the Washington Contraband Depot," 10; Everly, "Freedmen's Bureau in the National Capital," 39; Berlin et al., *Wartime Genesis of Free Labor*, 252, 270, 288.

CHAPTER 17 "The Step Which, at Once, Shortens the War"

1. *CW*, V, 420; Paludan, *Presidency of Abraham Lincoln*, 145–46; McPherson, *Ordeal by Fire*, 250–53; McPherson, *Tried by War*, 129.

2. *CW*, V, 318, 389, 460–61; Berlin et al., *Wartime Genesis of Free Labor*, 19; Guelzo, *Lincoln's Emancipation Proclamation*, 114.

3. McPherson, *Tried by War*, 123, 125–26; McPherson, *Ordeal by Fire*, 287; Waugh, *Lincoln and McClellan*, 143, 167; Foner, *Fiery Trial*, 219–20; Guelzo, *Lincoln's Emancipation Proclamation*, 118–23.

4. *CW*, V, 388; *WNR*, Aug. 20, 1862; McPherson, *Tried by War*, 126, 134.

5. *CW*, V, 474, 484; Doster, *Lincoln and Episodes of the Civil War*, 182–83; McPherson, *Tried by War*, 133–34, 140, 141–42; McPherson, *Ordeal by Fire*, 259; Waugh, *Lincoln and McClellan*, 167, 174.

6. *WNR*, Sept. 23, Oct. 1, 1862; *WDC*, Nov. 28, 1862; *WDC*, Jan. 2, 1863; *WNI*, Sept. 23, 1862; Green, *Secret City*, 62; Masur, *Example for All the Land*, 31–32;

Nell Irvin Painter, *Sojourner Truth: A Life, a Symbol* (New York: W. W. Norton, 1996), 203.

7. *CW*, VI, 28–30; *WNR*, July 17, 1862; Guelzo, *Lincoln's Emancipation Proclamation*, 179–81.

8. *CW*, VI, 28–30, emphasis added; Guelzo, *Lincoln's Emancipation Proclamation*, 179–81; Magness and Page, *Colonization After Emancipation*, 7.

9. Guelzo, *Lincoln's Emancipation Proclamation*, 182–83, 186; Redkey, *Respect Black*, 3–4.

10. *U.S. Statutes at Large*, XIII, 38th Cong., 1st Sess., Chap. CLXVI, 200; *WDC*, Nov. 12, 1862; Doster, *Lincoln and Episodes of the Civil War*, 26–27, 52, 166–67; Allen, *Memorial*, 21, 26; Mahood, *General Wadsworth*, 121–22, 251.

11. McPherson, *Ordeal by Fire*, 302–3, 315–21.

12. *OR*, Ser. III, I, 107, 133; Gibbs, *Black, Copper, and Bright*, 4; Kennedy, *Population of the United States in 1860*, xvii; Ira Berlin, Barbara J. Fields, Steven F. Miller, Joseph P. Reidy, and Leslie S. Rowland, *Slaves No More: Three Essays on Emancipation and the Civil War* (New York: Cambridge University Press, 1992), 199, 203; Ira Berlin, Joseph Reidy, and Leslie Rowland, eds., *The Black Military Experience*, Ser. II, Vol. 1 of *Freedom: A Documentary History of Emancipation, 1861–1867* (New York: Cambridge University Press, 1982), 80; Fleischner, *Mrs. Lincoln and Mrs. Keckly*, 222–23. At that time, "military age" was eighteen to forty-five.

13. *CW*, VI, 154; *OR*, Ser. III, I, 626; Berlin et al., *Slaves No More*, 199–200.

14. *CW*, VI, 149–50, 342, VII, 449–50, 482; *OR*, Ser. III, III, 100; General Orders No. 143, *OR*, Ser. III, III, 215–16; Berlin et al., *Slaves No More*, 199–200.

15. American Freedmen's Inquiry Commission Records, 1863, NARA Microfilm Publication M619, Reel 200, File 1; J. D. Turner to Lincoln, April 25, 1863, William G. Raymond to Lincoln, April 25, 1863, John Landan, William Henry Channing, and William Y. Brown to Lincoln, April 26, 1863, ALPLC; *WDC*, Feb. 6, 1863; *WNR*, May 5, 1863; Berlin et al., *Slaves No More*, 203; Gibbs, *Black, Copper, and Bright*, 24–27, 28; Redkey, "Henry McNeal Turner," 338; *PCR*, Jan. 10, 1863.

16. *WNR*, May 2, 5, 1863; *WDC*, May 5, Sept. 2, 1863; Gibbs, *Black, Copper, and Bright*, 27, 30–31.

17. *CW*, VI, 212; *WDC*, May 8, 16, 1863; *WNR*, May 11, 28, 1863; Gibbs, *Black, Copper, and Bright*, 32–33, 34; *PCR*, July 4, 1863.

18. Berlin, *Black Military Experience*, 354–55; *WDC*, April 3, May 14, 1863; *WNR*, May 12, 1863; Gibbs, *Black, Copper, and Bright*, 34, 62.

19. *WNR*, May 23, 1863; *WDC*, June 3, July 9, 1863; Stoddard, *Inside the White House*, 174.

20. *WDC*, June 3, 6, 12, 1863; Gibbs, *Black, Copper, and Bright*, 37, 40–41, 243; Mary E. Curry, "Theodore Roosevelt Island: A Broken Link to Early Washington, D.C. History," *RCHS* 71/72 (1971–72), 19–21, 25; *PCR*, July 4, 1863.

21. *WDC*, June 3, 6, 19, July 9, 1863; *WNR*, June 6, 9, 17, 1863; Gibbs, *Black, Copper, and Bright*, 41; Ezra J. Warner, *Generals in Blue: Lives of the Union Commanders* (Baton Rouge: Louisiana State University Press, 1964), 35.

22. *WDC*, June 3, 6, 19, July 9, 1863; *WNR*, June 6, 9, 17, 1863; Stoddard, *Inside the White House*, 173; Masur, *Example for All the Land*, 43.

23. *CW*, VI, 495; Walt Whitman to Louisa Van Velsor Whitman, June 30, 1863, *Walt Whitman Archive*, http://www.whitmanarchive.org/; Gibbs, *Black, Copper, and Bright*, 49–50, 55.

24. *OR*, Ser. III, III, 470–71;*WDC*, Aug. 3, 1863; Redkey, "Henry McNeal Turner," 338–41; Gibbs, *Black, Copper, and Bright*, 2, 49–50; Berlin, ed., *Black Military Experience*, 356–58.

25. Redkey, "Henry McNeal Turner," 338–41; Berlin, ed., *Black Military Experience*, 359; Gibbs, *Black, Copper, and Bright*, 120, 122–23, 179, 198–200; Angell, *Bishop Henry McNeal Turner*, 53–54; Calder, "Recollections of Walt Whitman," 833.

26. McPherson, *Ordeal by Fire*, 349; Angell, *Bishop Henry McNeal Turner*, 56–57; Redkey, "Henry McNeal Turner," 345–46.

27. *CWS*, 198; *U.S. Statutes at Large*, XIII, 38th Cong., 1st Sess., Chap. CXXIV, 129; Frederick Douglass, *Life and Times of Frederick Douglass Written By Himself: His Early Life as a Slave, His Escape from Bondage, and His Complete History* (London: Collier, 1962), 347–50; James Oakes, *The Radical and the Republican: Frederick Douglass, Abraham Lincoln, and the Triumph of Antislavery Politics* (New York: W. W. Norton, 2007), 211, 214–16; Blight, *Frederick Douglass' Civil War*, 166–67, 169; Barbara A. White, *Visits with Lincoln: Abolitionists Meet the President at the White House* (Lanham, MD: Lexington Books, 2011), 69–70; McPherson, *Ordeal by Fire*, 349.

28. *CW*, VI, 357, VII, 302–3, 328–29; Douglass, *Life and Times*, 348–49; Berlin et al., *Slaves No More*, 214–16; McPherson, *Ordeal by Fire*, 349–50, 454–55; Oakes, *The Radical and the Republican*, 214–16; White, *Visits with Lincoln*, 69–70.

29. Gibbs, *Black, Copper, and Bright*, 173, 175, 182. Profile of the regiment's origins compiled from the official roster in Gibbs, *Black, Copper, and Bright*, 228–59.

30. *CW*, VII, 380; *U.S. Statutes at Large*, XII, 37th Cong., 3rd Sess., Chap. LXXV, 731–37, XIII, 38th Cong., 1st Sess., Chap. XIII, 6–11; Edward Bates, "Citizenship," *Official Opinions of the Attorneys General*, X, 382–413; James P. McClure, Leigh Johnsen, Kathleen Norman, and Michael Vanderlan, eds., "Circumventing the Dred Scott Decision: Edward Bates, Salmon P. Chase, and the Citizenship of African Americans," *Civil War History* 43 (Dec. 1997), 279–309; Oakes, "Natural Rights, Citizenship Rights, States' Rights, and Black Rights," 123–25; Foner, *Fiery Trial*, 235; Oakes, *Freedom National*, 357–59.

31. *WNR*, Nov. 21, 1863; *WDC*, Feb. 16, 1863, Dec. 24, 1864; Geary, *We Need Men*, 65–67, 73, 81, 84; Murdock, *One Million Men*, 178–80, 197; Berlin et al., *Slaves No More*, 198–200, 232; Angell, *Bishop Henry McNeal Turner*, 51–52.

CHAPTER 18 "Defend What Is Our Own"

1. *WNR*, May 27, 1863; *WDC*, May 30, 1863; Everly, "Freedmen's Bureau in the National Capital," 39–42; Joseph P. Reidy, " 'Coming from the Shadow of the

Past': The Transition from Slavery to Freedom at Freedmen's Village, 1863–1900," *Virginia Magazine of History and Biography* 95 (Oct. 1987), 415; Harrold, *Subversives*, 229–30; Holt et al., *A Special Mission*, 3; James, "Establishment of Freedmen's Village," 92; Berlin, ed., *Black Military Experience*, 355.

2. Brigadier General Daniel H. Rucker was chief quartermaster of the Department of Washington. Nichols, "From the Washington Contraband Depot," 11; *WNR*, May 27, June 20, Dec. 4, 1863; *WDC*, June 30, July 7, 17, 24, 1863; Berlin et al., *Wartime Genesis of Free Labor*, 298; Everly, "Freedmen's Bureau in the National Capital," 44–46; Schildt, "Freedman's Village," 12; Harrold, *Subversives*, 230.

3. *WNR*, June 20, Nov. 24, 1863, Jan. 4, 1864; Everly, "Freedmen's Bureau in the National Capital," 46–49; *WDC*, July 17, Aug. 3, Dec. 29, 1863, Jan. 4, 30, April 21, 1864.

4. *WNR*, June 3, 20, Dec. 18, 1863; *WDC*, June 5, 30, Aug. 3, Dec. 29, 1863; Holt et al., *A Special Mission*, 3; Schildt, "Freedman's Village," 11; Downs, *Sick from Freedom*, 31.

5. *WDC*, Feb. 19, April 13, Dec. 29, 1863, Jan. 4, 30, July 29, 1864; *WNR*, Nov. 24, Dec. 3, 4, 1863; Everly, "Freedmen's Bureau in the National Capital," 49–50; Reidy, "Coming from the Shadow of the Past," 410; James, "Establishment of Freedmen's Village," 92; Harrold, *Subversives*, 140.

6. *WNR*, Nov. 24, Dec. 4, 1863; *WDC*, July 29, 1864; Everly, "Freedmen's Bureau in the National Capital," 49–50; Schildt, "Freedman's Village," 12–13; Holt et al., *A Special Mission*, 7–9, 11, 13.

7. Nichols told the American Freedmen's Inquiry Commission that an army captain had practiced corporal punishment at Camp Barker, but "I have never seen it"; Berlin et al., *Wartime Genesis of Free Labor*, 290. Thomas J. Carlile, Capt. & A.Q.M. Head Quarters Defs. So. of P., Arlington, to Nichols, Nov. 21, 1862, Lt. Col. & Chief Quartermaster Charles M. Greene to Nichols, Feb. 19, 25, April 2, 19, May 6, 1864, DBNS; American Freedmen's Inquiry Commission Records, 1863, NARA Microfilm Publication M619, Reel 200, File 1; *WDC*, July 29, 1864; *WNR*, Dec. 3, 4, 1863; Everly, "Freedmen's Bureau in the National Capital," 49–50; Holt et al., *A Special Mission*, 7–9, 11, 13; Schildt, "Freedman's Village," 12–13; Berlin et al., *Wartime Genesis of Free Labor*, 256, 295, 328, 330; *PCR*, June 4, 1864.

8. *WDC*, Feb. 25, April 21, 1864; Berlin et al., *Wartime Genesis of Free Labor*, 255, 293, 320; Reidy, "Coming from the Shadow of the Past," 411, 413; James, "Establishment of Freedman's Village," 91; Schildt, "Freedman's Village," 12.

9. Charles M. Greene to Nichols, Feb. 19, March 4, April 28, 1864, E. A. Holman to Nichols, March 29, 1863, H. Diebitsch to Nichols, March 23, 1863, DBNS; *WDC*, Feb. 25, April 21, 1864; Berlin et al., *Wartime Genesis of Free Labor*, 255, 293, 320.

10. *WNR*, Feb. 4, Dec. 4, 1863.

11. Horatio C. King, Acting Chief Q. M. Dept of Wash, to Nichols, Aug. 31, 1863, Charles M. Greene to Nichols, Jan. 8, March 24, 26, April 11, 26, May 1, Aug.

15, 1864, DBNS; *WNR*, Feb. 4, Dec. 4, 1863; Reidy, "Coming from the Shadow of the Past," 409; Poole, *On Hallowed Ground*, 51.

12. M. R. Collins, Chief Clerk, Office of the Chief Quartermaster to Nichols, March 21, 1864, DBNS; *WDC*, April 21, 1864; James D. Lockett, "Abraham Lincoln and Colonization: An Episode That Ends in Tragedy at L'Île à Vache, Haiti, 1863–1864," *Journal of Black Studies* 21 (June 1991), 436–40; Vorenberg, "Abraham Lincoln and the Politics of Black Colonization," 38–39; Jason H. Silverman, " 'In Isles Beyond the Main': Abraham Lincoln's Philosophy on Black Colonization," *Lincoln Herald* 80 (Fall 1978), 120; Berlin et al., *Wartime Genesis of Free Labor*, 333.

13. *CW*, VI, 164; Charles M. Greene to Nichols, March 1, 4, 1864, DBNS; *WDC*, March 16, 21, 1864; Lockett, "Abraham Lincoln and Colonization," 439–42; Magness and Page, *Colonization After Emancipation*, 11–12, 94; Hay, *Lincoln and the Civil War*, 203; Vorenberg, "Abraham Lincoln and the Politics of Black Colonization," 41, 44; Silverman, "In Isles Beyond the Main," 120.

14. *CW*, IV, 415; Robert Dale Owen to Lincoln, Sept. 17, 1862, ALPLC; 38th Cong., 1st Sess., Senate Ex. Doc. No. 53; Berlin et al., *Wartime Genesis of Free Labor*, 19. Chase delivered Owen's letter to Lincoln on September 19, 1862; Miers, *Lincoln Day by Day*, III, 140.

15. 38th Cong., 1st Sess., Senate Ex. Doc. No. 53, 2–3, 10, 13; Gerteis, *From Contraband to Freedman*, 34–35; Richard William Leopold, *Robert Dale Owen: A Biography* (Cambridge: Harvard University Press, 1940), 361–62.

16. M. R. Collins to Nichols, March 30, 1864, Charles M. Greene to Nichols, April 1, May 12, Aug. 15, 1864, DBNS; *WDC*, March 21, June 29, July 29, 1864; Berlin et al., *Wartime Genesis of Free Labor*, 349; Everly, "Freedmen's Bureau in the National Capital," 21, 51–52, 77; Johnston, "Surviving Freedom," 123, 159; Holt et al., *A Special Mission*, 5; "Civil War Washington, D.C.," http://civilwarwashingtondc1861–1865.blogspot.com/2012/02/1st-us-colored-troops-at-roosevelt.html.

17. Reidy, "Coming from the Shadow of the Past," 414–15, 417, 419, 421–22, 424–25, 426–27.

CHAPTER 19 "Never Forget What They Did Here"

1. *MTL*, 96; Baker, *Mary Todd Lincoln*, 229.
2. *CW*, VI, 260, 474, VII, 34, 35; *MTL*, 139, 157–58, 159–60, 175.
3. Packard, *Lincolns in the White House*, 112–13; Fleischner, *Mrs. Lincoln and Mrs. Keckly*, 228–29.
4. *WNR*, March 26, 29, 1862; Washington, *They Knew Lincoln*, 85–87; Packard, *Lincolns in the White House*, 115–16, 119; Brownstein, *Lincoln's Other White House*, 133; Gerry, *Through Five Administrations*, 17.
5. *CW*, V, 326–27; *CWS*, 132; French, *Witness to the Young Republic*, 389; Noah Brooks, *Lincoln Observed*, 13; Keckley, *Behind the Scenes*, 36, 231; Baker, *Mary Todd Lincoln*, 211.

6. *WNR*, June 7, 1862; *WDC*, May 15, 1864; Gerry, *Through Five Administrations*, 21; Baker, *Mary Todd Lincoln*, 216; Fleischner, *Mrs. Lincoln and Mrs. Keckly*, 237; Rietveld, "Lincoln White House Community," 44.

7. *MTL*, 189; *WNR*, Jan. 2, 1864; Fehrenbacher and Fehrenbacher, *Recollected Words*, 428; Keckley, *Behind the Scenes*, 49; Rietveld, "Lincoln White House Community," 44; Packard, *Lincolns in the White House*, 171.

8. The peak occupancy of Washington's military hospitals was 18,267, which occurred on July 9, 1864. I am grateful to my colleague Susan C. Lawrence, coordinator of the Humanities in Medicine Program at the University of Nebraska–Lincoln, for providing this information from the database of military hospital capacity and occupancy that she is compiling from Record Group 94, NARA. The Washington press reported that during the seven-month period between December 3, 1863, and July 1, 1864, deaths of sick and wounded soldiers and contrabands in Washington totaled 3,632 and 1,062, respectively; *WDC*, Sept. 17, 1864. In 1860, the District of Columbia had six undertakers; Kennedy, *Population of the United States in 1860*, 590. *WES*, Dec. 31, 1860; *WDC*, July 1, 1864; Schantz, *Awaiting the Heavenly Country*, 14; Faust, *This Republic of Suffering*, 62–63.

9. Schantz, *Awaiting the Heavenly Country*, 70–71; Stanley French, "The Cemetery as Cultural Institution: The Establishment of Mount Auburn and the 'Rural Cemetery' Movement," *American Quarterly* 26 (March 1974), 37–59; Faust, *This Republic of Suffering*, 62–63, 89; Garry Wills, *Lincoln at Gettysburg: The Words That Remade America* (New York: Simon & Schuster, 1992), 64.

10. Brinton, *Personal Memoirs*, 245; Schantz, *Awaiting the Heavenly Country*, 13–14; Faust, *This Republic of Suffering*, 65–67, 71–73, 88; John R. Neff, *Honoring the Civil War Dead: Commemoration and the Problem of Reconciliation* (Lawrence: University Press of Kansas, 2005), 33.

11. Hay, *Lincoln and the Civil War*, 182; *WNR*, May 10, 1864; Faust, *This Republic of Suffering*, 72, 79; Mahood, *General Wadsworth*, 248–57.

12. *WES*, May 25, Oct. 18, 29, 1861; *WNI*, April 15, 1862; Faust, *This Republic of Suffering*, 91–92, 94–95, 98; Thomas J. Craughwell, *Stealing Lincoln's Body* (Cambridge: Harvard University Press, 2007), 7–8; Neff, *Honoring the Civil War Dead*, 45–47.

13. *WNI*, April 15, 1862; *WES*, Oct. 18, 1861, Dec. 14, 1861, Feb. 22, April 25, 1862; *WNR*, April 26, May 12, July 2, 1862; *WDC*, Nov. 20, 1862; Faust, *This Republic of Suffering*, 96–97; Craughwell, *Stealing Lincoln's Body*, 7–8; Lloyd Lewis, *Myths after Lincoln* (New York: Harcourt, Brace and Company, 1929), 121.

14. Adams, *Doctors in Blue*, 150; Pinsker, *Lincoln's Sanctuary*, 1, 3–4, 5, 25, 72; Packard, *Lincolns in the White House*, 136–37; Brownstein, *Lincoln's Other White House*, 13, 115–19.

15. *WNR*, March 24, 1862, Aug. 19, 1863, Feb. 23, 27, 1864; *WDC*, Dec. 29, 1862, Sept. 3, 1863, Oct. 17, 1864; Pinsker, *Lincoln's Sanctuary*, 32.

16. *WNR*, April 26, 1862; *WDC*, Nov. 13, 20, 21, 27, 1862, Jan. 1, June 19, 1864; Poole, *On Hallowed Ground*, 47.

17. *WDC*, Feb. 12, June 1, 3, 14, 15, 1864; *WNR*, June 22, 1864; Neff, *Honoring the Civil War Dead*, 46.

18. *WDC*, Jan. 2, 1863, April 28, June 1, 3, July 23, 1864; Faust, *This Republic of Suffering*, 98; Neff, *Honoring the Civil War Dead*, 46.

19. *CW*, VI, 257; McPherson, *Ordeal by Fire*, 323–24, 329–30.

20. *CW*, VI, 327–28; Hay, *Lincoln and the Civil War*, 67; Nicolay, *Oral History*, 88; Wills, *Lincoln at Gettysburg*, 19; *WNR*, July 13, 1863.

21. *WDC*, March 15, 1864; Boritt, *Gettysburg Gospel*, 9, 11, 14, 21, 31, 36–38, 43, 44; Neff, *Honoring the Civil War Dead*, 50, 109–12; Faust, *This Republic of Suffering*, 69, 81.

22. *CW*, VII, 22–23, emphasis added; Wills, *Lincoln at Gettysburg*, 25, 29, 32, 36; Neff, *Honoring the Civil War Dead*, 111; Faust, *This Republic of Suffering*, 99–100.

23. *U.S. Statutes at Large*, XII, 37th Cong., 2nd Sess., Chap. XCVIII, 422–26; Anthony J. Gaughan, *The Last Battle of the Civil War: United States Versus Lee, 1861–1883* (Baton Rouge: Louisiana State University Press, 2011), 3, 20–21, 26, 28, 33–35; Faust, *This Republic of Suffering*, 99; Perry, *Mrs. Robert E. Lee*, 275; Poole, *On Hallowed Ground*, 47, 56, 60–61.

24. Miller, *Second Only to Grant*, 260; Poole, *On Hallowed Ground*, 58–59, 62; John Perry, *Mrs. Robert E. Lee*, 276.

25. *U.S. Statutes at Large*, XIV, 39th Cong., 2nd Sess., Chap. LXI, 399–401; Poole, *On Hallowed Ground*, 70–71; Neff, *Honoring the Civil War Dead*, 243–46.

26. *WDC*, Dec. 27, 1862; Stearns, *Lady Nurse of Ward E*, 42; Brinton, *Personal Memoirs*, 245; Bayne, *Tad Lincoln's Father*, 72.

27. *MTL*, 179; *WNR*, June 6, Aug. 27, Dec. 10, 1862; *WDC*, Feb. 16, 1863.

28. The location of Johnson's burial is controversial. Possibilities include Arlington National Cemetery, the Congressional Cemetery, and Columbian Harmony Cemetery, where other African American smallpox victims were interred; Phillip W. Magness and Sebastian Page, "Mr. Lincoln and Mr. Johnson," *New York Times* Online Edition, Feb. 1, 2012; Allen C. Guelzo, "The Path to Proclamation," *Wall Street Journal* Online Edition, Oct. 7, 2010. In the absence of conclusive evidence to the contrary, I have retained the traditional location, Arlington National Cemetery. Stoddard, *Inside the White House*, 108; Washington, *They Knew Lincoln*, 129, 135–41; Burlingame, *Abraham Lincoln: A Life*, II, 578–79; Donald, *Lincoln*, 467; Cornelius, "William H. Johnson, Citizen."

29. *CW*, VII, 156–57, VIII, 354; Washington, *They Knew Lincoln*, 107–8; Harrold, *Subversives*, 234, 238.

30. During the late 1850s, the Slades moved to Cleveland, Ohio, but returned to Washington soon after the Civil War began. U.S. Manuscript Census, Free Population Schedule, Cleveland, Ohio, 1860; *WDC*, April 30, Dec. 24, 1863, Feb. 6, 1864; *WNR*, Dec. 24, 1863, Jan. 5, 1864, Jan. 20, 1865; Washington, *They Knew Lincoln*, 129; Harrold, *Subversives*, 234, 238; Catherine Clinton, *Mrs. Lincoln: A Life* (New York: Harper, 2009), 159–60; Masur, *Example for All the Land*, 34; Masur, "African American Delegation," 125; Fleischner, *Mrs. Lincoln and*

Mrs. Keckly, 207–8; Seale, *President's House*, 437; Berlin et al., *Wartime Genesis of Free Labor*, 356–57; PCR, Nov. 29, 1862.

31. Adams was the first president to occupy the White House, beginning in 1800. His slaveowning successors were Jefferson, Madison, Monroe, Jackson, Tyler, Polk, and Taylor. In addition to the five regular White House employees, the Interior Department hired William Johnson as a fireman in 1861 at Lincoln's request. *CWS*, 64; U.S. Manuscript Census, Free Population Schedule, Washington, DC, 1860; *Register of Officers and Agents, Civil, Military, and Naval, in the Service of the United States on the Thirtieth September, 1861* (Washington: Government Printing Office, 1861), 95; *Register of Officers and Agents, Civil, Military, and Naval, in the Service of the United States on the Thirtieth September, 1863* (Washington: Government Printing Office, 1864), 118; Seale, *President's House*, 99, 101, 122, 181; Clarence Lusane, *The Black History of the White House* (San Francisco: City Lights Books, 2011), 145; Paul Jennings, *A Colored Man's Reminiscences of James Madison* (Brooklyn: George C. Beadle, 1865); Elizabeth Dowling Taylor and Annette Gordon-Reed, *A Slave in the White House: Paul Jennings and the Madisons* (New York: Palgrave Macmillan, 2012); Ricks, *Escape on the Pearl*, 40, 42–43; Pacheco, *The Pearl*, 70.

32. *MTL*, 61; *WDC*, Aug. 14, Dec. 24, 1863; *WES*, July 5, 1864; Washington, *They Knew Lincoln*, 84; Keckley, *Behind the Scenes*, 48.

33. *MTL*, 140–41; Keckley, *Behind the Scenes*, 40; Fleischner, *Mrs. Lincoln and Mrs. Keckly*, 252; Brian Dirck, "Mary Lincoln, Race, and Slavery," in Frank J. Williams and Michael Burkhimer, eds., *The Mary Lincoln Enigma: Historians on America's Most Controversial First Lady* (Carbondale: Southern Illinois University Press, 2012), 49–50; Baker, *Mary Todd Lincoln*, 231.

34. *CW*, VI, 380; U.S. Manuscript Census, Free Population Schedule, Cleveland, Ohio, 1860; Keckley, *Behind the Scenes*, 68, 277; Washington, *They Knew Lincoln*, 105, 109–10; Fleischner, *Mrs. Lincoln and Mrs. Keckly*, 207–8, 291–92; Clinton, *Mrs. Lincoln*, 159–60; Pinsker, *Lincoln's Sanctuary*, 113.

CHAPTER 20 "Worth More than a Victory in the Field"

1. Winfield Scott held the brevet rank of lieutenant general; *CW*, V, 10. *CW*, VII, 236, 239–40; Ulysses S. Grant to Lincoln, Aug. 23, 1863, ALPLC; McPherson, *Ordeal by Fire*, 233, 359, 411–12; *WNR*, March 9.

2. *WNR*, March 9, May 25, 26, 1864; *WDC*, April 3, 1863, June 8, 1864; Eaton, *Grant, Lincoln and the Freedmen*, 186–87.

3. *OR*, Ser. III, III, 470, IV, 94, 125, 463; *WNR*, July 16, 23, Aug. 8, Nov. 19, Dec. 18, 1863, Jan. 5, 1865; *WDC*, Sept. 23, 1863, April 13, Sept. 10, 1864; Doster, *Lincoln and Episodes of the Civil War*, 56; Miers, *Lincoln Day by Day*, III, 252.

4. *WNR*, Oct. 30, 1863, Feb. 2, 19, March 8, 11, 23, May 23, 1864; *WDC*, July 28, 30, Aug. 17, Sept. 23, Nov. 11, 14, Dec. 16, 1863, Jan. 18, March 26, July 22, Sept.

20, 1864; Hay, *Lincoln and the Civil War*, 75; Doster, *Lincoln and Episodes of the Civil War*, 12.

5. Hay, *Lincoln and the Civil War*, 75; *WDC*, July 30, Dec. 12, 19, 1863, Sept. 20, Oct. 6, 1864; *WES*, July 4, 1864; *WNR*, Aug. 3, Sept. 30, Dec. 18, 1863.

6. *CW*, 7, 380; *WNR*, Aug. 3, 28, 29, 1863, May 24, 1864, Feb. 20, 1865; *WDC*, Aug. 10, 12, 15, 25, 1863, July 23, 24, 28, Sept. 12, 29, 1864; *WES*, July 1, 1864; Geary, *We Need Men*, 137.

7. Hay, *Lincoln and the Civil War*, 68; *WDC*, Feb. 2, July 31, Aug. 25, 1863, March 31, 1864; *WES*, Dec. 14, 16, 1861; *WNR*, July 31, 1862, Feb. 12, 1863, April 4, 1864; Stoddard, *Inside the White House*, 187; Ramold, *Baring the Iron Hand*, 237–38.

8. McPherson, *Ordeal by Fire*, 345, 357–58; Chandra Manning, *What This Cruel War Was Over: Soldiers, Slavery, and the Civil War* (New York: Vintage, 2007), 90; Ramold, *Baring the Iron Hand*, 231.

9. *WNR*, Oct. 24, 1862, May 23, 27, 29, Aug. 27, Nov. 21, 1863, March 10, April 27, 1864; *WDC*, March 6, April 7, Nov. 9, 1863, May 7, 18, Oct. 29, 1864.

10. *CW*, VI, 132–33; Welles, *Diary of Gideon Welles*, 232; *WDC*, Aug. 25, 1863, Nov. 17, 1864; Ramold, *Baring the Iron Hand*, 219.

11. *CW*, VI, 414–15, VII, 208, VIII, 349–50; Proc. No. 26, *U.S. Statutes at Large*, XIII, 752–53; *WNR*, Aug. 28, 1863.

12. *OR*, Ser. III, IV, 159; *WNR*, Dec. 31, 1863, Jan. 16, 1864.

13. *U.S. Statutes at Large*, XIII, 38th Cong., 1st Sess., Chap. CCXXXVII, 379–80; *WDC*, July 31, 1863, Jan. 16, Feb. 18, May 7, July 28, Aug. 19, 25, Sept. 9, 1864; *WNR*, Jan. 16, 1864; Brooks, *Lincoln Observed*, 72; Geary, *We Need Men*, 131, 135–36; Berlin et al., *Slaves No More*, 203, 205.

14. *CW*, VI, 226–27; General Orders No. 105, *OR*, Ser. III, III, 170; *Armory Square Hospital Gazette*, Jan. 20, 1864; *WDC*, May 9, June 13, July 21, Oct. 13, 20, 26, Nov. 18, 19, 1863, March 4, 14, 17, 1864; *WNR*, Sept. 10, Oct. 10, 1863, March 18, 19, 1864; Brooks, *Lincoln Observed*, 92; Morris, *Better Angel*, 113–14.

15. Cooling, *Symbol, Sword, and Shield*, 187, 192, 194; John Henry Cramer, *Lincoln Under Enemy Fire: The Complete Account of His Experiences During Early's Attack on Washington* (Baton Rouge: Louisiana State University Press, 1948), 4, 6–9.

16. *CW*, VII, 438; *OR*, Ser. III, IV, 532; *WDC*, July 9, 11, 1864; Cooling, *Symbol, Sword, and Shield*, 197, 202, 205; Cramer, *Lincoln Under Enemy Fire*, 9–10.

17. Hay, *Lincoln and the Civil War*, 208–10; *WDC*, July 11, 12, 14, 16, 1864; Cooling, *Symbol, Sword, and Shield*, 197; Cramer, *Lincoln Under Enemy Fire*, 9, 14–18, 20–21, 54; William V. Cox, "The Defenses of Washington—General Early's Advance on the Capital and the Battle of Fort Stevens, July 11 and 12, 1864," *RCHS*, 4 (1900), 137.

18. *WDC*, March 10, May 14, 1863, Feb. 22, June 3, 1864; *PCR*, Dec. 14, 1861.

19. U.S. Manuscript Census, Free Population Schedule, Washington, DC, 1860; *WES*, July 10, 1861; *WNR*, Jan. 13, Oct. 31, 1862, Aug. 7, 10, Oct. 24, 1863; *WDC*, Aug. 28, Oct. 26, 1863, Feb. 18, April 20, 1864; William Tindall, "Beginnings of Street Railways in the National Capital," *RCHS*, 21 (1918), 25–26;

McShane and Tarr, *Horse in the City*, 55, 59; Howard P. Chudacoff, *The Evolution of American Urban Society* (Englewood Cliffs, NJ: Prentice-Hall, 1975), 67–70. Cabs, one-horse two-wheeled vehicles, came into use after the Civil War.

20. *WNR*, May 14, 16, July 28, Oct. 1, 1862; *WDC*, July 30, 1864; Tindall, "Beginnings of Street Railways," 26–27, 35, 50, 57, 64, 76–77; McShane and Tarr, *Horse in the City*, 63–67; Chudacoff, *Evolution of American Urban Society*, 70–71.

21. *WNR*, July 7, 1862, Sept. 12, Oct. 29, 31, Nov. 20, 28, 1863; *WDC*, June 4, Aug. 25, 28, Oct. 29, 1863, Dec. 12, 1864; Masur, *Example for All the Land*, 45.

22. *CG*, 38th Cong., 1st Sess., 553–55; *WNR*, Feb. 10, 12, 1864.

23. *U.S. Statutes at Large*, XIII, 37th Cong., 1st Sess., Chap. CXC, 326–31, 38th Cong., 2nd Sess., Chap. CXIX, 536–37; *CG*, 38th Cong., 1st Sess., 553–55, 815–16; *WNR*, Feb. 12, March 30, June 22, 27, 1864; Tindall, "Beginnings of Street Railways," 35–36, 64; Masur, *Example For All the Land*, 101–2, 107.

24. *WDC*, June 12, Dec. 24, 1863; Eric Foner, *Freedom's Lawmakers: A Directory of Black Officeholders During Reconstruction* (New York: Oxford University Press, 1993), xx–xxii, xxv; Berlin et al., *Wartime Genesis of Free Labor*, 247; Painter, *Sojourner Truth*, 121–31, 200.

25. Nell Irvin Painter, ed., *Narrative of Sojourner Truth* (New York: Penguin, 1998), 119–21; Painter, *Sojourner Truth*, 204–7; White, *Visits with Lincoln*, 121–22.

26. Painter, *Sojourner Truth*, 210–11, 212–14; Masur, *Example for All the Land*, 107–8.

27. *CW*, VII, 500, 507; Painter, *Sojourner Truth*, 200; White, *Visits with Lincoln*, 119–20.

28. *CW*, VII, 514–15; *WDC*, Aug. 27, Oct. 22, 1864; McPherson, *Ordeal by Fire*, 438–40, 441, 442–43, 446.

29. *WDC*, Oct. 5, 11, Nov. 7, 8, 1864; French, *Witness to the Young Republic*, 466; McPherson, *Ordeal by Fire*, 456–58; Josiah Henry Benton, *Voting in the Field: A Forgotten Chapter of the Civil War* (Boston: Privately Printed, 1915), 4.

EPILOGUE "The Country Was Ready to Say Amen"

1. Stoddard did not date his recollection, but Michael Burlingame cites a contemporary article in the *Boston Recorder* to situate the episode on January 1, 1865; Stoddard, *Inside the White House*, 214–15. Douglass, *Life and Times*, 365–66; Stoddard, *Inside the White House*, 172; Oakes, *The Radical and the Republican*, 141–43; Painter, *Sojourner Truth*, 203; Ronald C. White Jr., *Lincoln's Greatest Speech: The Second Inaugural* (New York: Simon & Schuster, 2002), 29–30.

2. White, *Lincoln's Greatest Speech*, 33; Foner, *Fiery Trial*, 312–13; Guelzo, *Lincoln's Emancipation Proclamation*, 231–32.

3. White, *Lincoln's Greatest Speech*, 33.

4. McPherson, *Ordeal by Fire*, 184; Grimsley, *The Hard Hand of War*, 3–4; White, *Lincoln's Greatest Speech*, 43.

5. *CW*, VIII, 332–33.

6. *WDC,* Jan. 12, 14, 1864; Oakes, *The Radical and the Republican,* 216.

7. *CW,* VI, 226.

8. *CW,* V, 115, 149, 151; Hay, *Lincoln and the Civil War,* 46; *WDC,* Dec. 29, 1863; McPherson, *Tried by War,* 73, 92, 179.

9. Washington's provost marshal estimated that the civilian population of the District of Columbia increased from 75,000 in 1860 to 200,000 by March 1862; Doster, *Lincoln and Episodes of the Civil War,* 57. The Metropolitan Police Department's estimate was 140,000 in 1864; 38th Cong., 1st Sess., H. Exec. Doc. 1, Pt. 3, 720. Masur, *Example for All the Land,* 1, 126; Harrison, *Washington During Civil War and Reconstruction,* 13.

10. Lamon, *Recollections of Abraham Lincoln,* 265; Michael W. Kauffman, *American Brutus: John Wilkes Booth and the Lincoln Conspiracies* (New York: Random House, 2004), 158; Pinsker, *Lincoln's Sanctuary,* 50, 72, 179–80.

11. Henry W. Fisher, *Abroad with Mark Twain and Eugene Field: Tales They Told to a Fellow Correspondent* (New York: Nicholas L. Brown, 1922), 148–49; Lamon, *Recollections of Abraham Lincoln,* 265–68; Stimmel, *Personal Reminiscences of Abraham Lincoln,* 28; Pinsker, *Lincoln's Sanctuary,* 50.

12. Whitman, *Memoranda,* 39–41; Lamon, *Recollections of Abraham Lincoln,* 269; Pinsker, *Lincoln's Sanctuary,* 60–61.

13. *CWS,* 194; *WNR,* Feb. 11, 12, 1864; *WDC,* July 3, 1863, Feb. 11, 12, 1864; *WNI,* April 21, 1862; Nicolay, *With Lincoln in the White House,* 126; Stimmel, *Personal Reminiscences of Abraham Lincoln,* 15, 17–18, 38–40; Boyden, *Echoes from Hospital and White House,* 143–44; Thomas Chamberlin, *History of the One Hundred and Fiftieth Regiment Pennsylvania Volunteers* (Philadelphia: J. B. Lippincott, 1893), 32–33; Donald, *Lincoln,* 579; Pinsker, *Lincoln's Sanctuary,* 102–6.

14. *WNR,* Jan. 2, 1864; Hay, *Lincoln and the Civil War,* 236; Gerry, *Through Five Administrations,* 1–2, 4–6, 8; Pinsker, *Lincoln's Sanctuary,* 14–15; Hamand, "Lincoln's Particular Friend," 30–31.

15. Ward H. Lamon to John G. Nicolay, Dec. 15, 1864; Stoddard, *Inside the White House,* 108; Pinsker, *Lincoln's Sanctuary,* 50; Hamand, "Lincoln's Particular Friend," 32.

16. *CW,* VIII, 403; *WDC,* Jan. 14, 1864; Burlingame, *Lincoln: A Life,* II, 801–3.

17. *MTL,* 284–85; William Hanchett, *The Lincoln Murder Conspiracies* (Urbana: University of Illinois Press, 1998), 37; Donald, *Lincoln,* 588, 593; Burlingame, *Lincoln: A Life,* II, 801–3.

INDEX